FIRST EDITION 2001

FIRST EDITION 2001

A Very Remote Period Indeed

*Papers on the Palaeolithic
Presented to Derek Roe*

Edited by
Sarah Milliken and Jill Cook

Oxbow Books

Published by
Oxbow Books, Park End Place, Oxford OX1 1HN

ISBN 1 84217 056 2

This book is available direct from

Oxbow Books, Park End Place, Oxford OX1 1HN
(Phone: 01865–241249; Fax: 01865–794449)

and

The David Brown Book Company
PO Box 511, Oakville, CT 06779, USA
(Phone: 860–945–9329; Fax: 860–945–9468)

or from our website

www.oxbowbooks.com

Front Cover: Derek Roe in Swaziland, 1977.

Printed in Great Britain at
The Short Run Press
Exeter

Table of contents

Contributors v
Editorial vii
The authors xii

1. Variability in primary and secondary technologies of the Later Acheulian in Africa.. 1
   J. Desmond Clark

2. The shape of handaxes, the structure of the Acheulian world 19
   Clive Gamble & Gilbert Marshall

3. An Acheulian settlement pattern in the Upper Karoo region of South Africa...................................... 28
   C. Garth Sampson

4. The shape of things to come. A speculative essay on the role of the Victoria West phenomenon 37
   at Canteen Koppie, during the South African Earlier Stone Age
   John McNabb

5. Diamonds, alluvials and artefacts. The Stone Age in Sierra Leone and the Cotton Tree Museum 47
   Phillip Allsworth-Jones

6. Some notes on fish and fishing in Africa 63
   Ray Inskeep

7. Europe and Africa during the Palaeolithic 74
   Marcel Otte

8. The initial peopling of Eurasia and the early occupation of Europe in its Afro-Asian context:
   major issues and current perspectives 78
   Nicholas Rolland

9. In the quest for Palaeolithic human behaviour 95
   Ofer Bar-Yosef

10. Cleavers: their distribution, chronology and typology 105
    Vadim A. Ranov

11. Ex Africa aliquid semper novi: the view from Pontnewydd 114
    Stephen Aldhouse-Green

12. A newly identified Acheulian handaxe type at Tabun Cave: the Faustkeilblätter 120
    Zinovy Matskevitch, Naama Goren-Inbar & Sabine Gaudzinski

13. The Palaeolithic industries in Korea: chronology and related new find-spots 133
   Hyeong Woo Lee

14. Lower and Middle Palaeolithic occupation in Central Kazakhstan: the Batpak Valley and environs 138
   Norah Moloney, Sandra L. Olsen & Valery Voloshin

15. Venta Micena, Barranco León-5 and Fuentenueva-3: three archaeological sites
   in the Early Pleistocene deposits of Orce, south-east Spain 144
   Josep Gibert, Lluís Gibert, Carlos Ferràndez-Canyadell, Alfredo Iglesias & Fernando González

16. Excavations at Cueva Negra del Estrecho del Río Quípar and Sima de las Palomas del Cabezo Gordo:
   two sites in Murcia (south-east Spain) with Neanderthal skeletal remains,
   Mousterian assemblages and late Middle to early Upper Pleistocene fauna 153
   Michael J. Walker

17. Acheulian handaxe variability in Middle Pleistocene Italy: a case study 160
   Sarah Milliken

18. Palaeoliths in a lost pre-Anglian landscape 174
   John Wymer

19. New Lower Palaeolithic finds from the Upper Thames 180
   Terry Hardaker

20. One step beyond. Flint shortage above the Goring Gap: the example of Wolvercote 199
   Nick Ashton

21. A river runs through it: a decade of research at Stanton Harcourt 207
   Katherine Scott & Christine M. Buckingham

22. Recent investigations at Dickett's Field, Yarnhams Farm, Holybourne, Hants. 214
   Julie E. Scott-Jackson & Vicky Winton

23. The _Sackung_ Hypothesis: a challenge for Palaeolithic prospection 223
   Simon Collcutt

24. A Lyngby point from Mildenhall, Suffolk, and its implications for the British Late Upper Palaeolithic 234
   Alison J. Roberts & R. Nick E. Barton

25. Out of Abbeville: Sir John Evans, Palaeolithic patriarch and handaxe pioneer 242
   Mark J. White

26. Old collections – a new resource? The history of some English Palaeolithic collections in Cardiff 249
   Elizabeth A. Walker

27. A burnt Mesolithic hunting camp on the Mendips:
   a preliminary report on structural traces excavated on Lower Pitts Farm, Priddy, Somerset 260
   Joan J. Taylor

28. Derek Roe, A Bibliography 271

Site Index 273

Contributors

Stephen Aldhouse-Green, Department of Humanities & Science, University of Wales College Newport, Caerleon Campus, PO Box 179, Newport NP6 1YG, UK

Phillip Allsworth-Jones, Department of History, University of the West Indies, Mona Campus, Kingston 7, Jamaica

Nick Ashton, Quaternary Section, Department of Prehistory and Early Europe, The British Museum, Franks House II, 38–46 Orsman Road, London N1 5QJ, UK

Nick Barton, Department of Anthropology, Oxford Brookes University, Oxford OX3 0BP, UK

Ofer Bar-Yosef, Department of Anthropology, Peabody Museum, Harvard University, Cambridge MA 02138, USA

Christine Buckingham, Baden-Powell Quaternary Research Centre, University of Oxford, 60 Banbury Road, Oxford, OX2 6PN, UK

J. Desmond Clark, 1941 Yosemite Road, Berkeley, California 94707, USA

Simon Collcutt, Oxford Archaeological Associates Ltd, 2 Polstead Road, Oxford, OX2 6TN, UK

Jill Cook, Department of Prehistory and Early Europe, The British Museum, Great Russell Street, London, WC1B 3DG, UK

Carlos Ferràndez-Canyadell, Departamento de Estratigrafia y Paleontologia, Universidade de Barcelona, Martí Franquès s/n, 08028 Barcelona, Spain

Clive Gamble, Centre for the Archaeology of Human Origins, Department of Archaeology, University of Southampton, Southampton, SO17 1BJ, UK

Sabine Gaudzinski, Römisch-Germanisches Zentralmuseum Mainz, Forschungsbereich Altsteinzeit, Schloss Monrepos, 56567 Neuwied, Germany

Josep Gibert, Institut de Paleontologia M. Crusafont, Escola Industrial 23, 08201 Sabadell, Spain

Lluís Gibert, Institut de Paleontologia M. Crusafont, Escola Industrial 23, 08201 Sabadell, Spain

Fernando González, Institut de Paleontologia M. Crusafont, Escola Industrial 23, 08201 Sabadell, Spain

Naama Goren-Inbar, Institute of Archaeology, Hebrew University, Mount Scopus, Jerusalem 91905, Israel

Terry Hardaker, Oxford Cartographers, Oasis Park, Eynsham, Oxford, OX8 1TP, UK

Alfredo Iglesias, Departamento de Prehistoria, Universidade de Santiago, Plaza Universidade s/n, 15701 Santiago de Compostela, Spain

Ray Inskeep, 75 Walton Street, Oxford, OX2 6EA, UK

Hyeong Woo Lee, Department of Anthropology, Chonnam National University, 300 Yougbong-Dong, Puk-Ku, Kwangju 500–757, South Korea

Gilbert Marshall, Centre for the Archaeology of Human Origins, Department of Archaeology, University of Southampton, Southampton, SO17 1BJ, UK

Zinovy Matskevich, Institute of Archaeology, Hebrew University, Mount Scopus, Jerusalem 91905, Israel

John McNabb, Centre for the Archaeology of Human Origins, Department of Archaeology, University of Southampton, Southampton, SO17 1BJ, UK

Sarah Milliken, Department of Archaeology, University College Cork, Republic of Ireland

Norah Moloney, Institute of Archaeology, University College London, 31–34 Gordon Square, London WC1H 0PY, UK

Sandra Olsen, Carnegie Museum of Natural History, O'Neill Research Center, 5800 Baum Boulevard, Pittsburgh, PA 152906, USA

Marcel Otte, Université de Liège, Préhistoire, Place du XX Août (A1), 4000 Liège, Belgium

Vadim Ranov, Department of Archaeology, Institute of History, Rudaki Ave 33, Dushanbe 734025, Tadjikistan

Alison Roberts, Department of Antiquities, Ashmolean Museum, Beaumont Street, Oxford, OX1 2PH, UK

Nicholas Rolland, Department of Anthropology, University of Victoria, British Colombia, P.O. Box 3050, Victoria, V8W 3P5, Canada

C. Garth Sampson, Department of Anthropology, Southern Methodist University, Dallas, TX 75275–0336, USA

Katherine Scott, Baden-Powell Quaternary Research Centre, University of Oxford, 60 Banbury Road, Oxford, OX2 6PN, UK

Julie Scott-Jackson, Baden-Powell Quaternary Research Centre, University of Oxford, 60 Banbury Road, Oxford, OX2 6PN, UK

Joan Taylor, Department of Archaeology, University of Liverpool, Hartley Building, Liverpool L69 3BX, UK

Valery Voloshin, Microregion H-5, Building 21, Apt. 89, Astana, Kazakhstan

Elizabeth Walker, Department of Archaeology and Numismatics, National Museum and Galleries of Wales, Cathays Park, Cardiff CF1 3NP, UK

Mark White, Department of Archaeology, University of Durham, South Road, Durham, DH1 3LE, UK

Vicky Winton, Baden-Powell Quaternary Research Centre, University of Oxford, 60 Banbury Road, Oxford, OX2 6PN, UK

John Wymer, 17 Duke Street, Bildeston, Ipswich, IP7 7EW, UK

Editorial

Unlike many Festschrifts, this volume has not been organised to coincide with the retirement of the honoree who, in this case, is still very active as Professor of Palaeolithic Archaeology at Oxford University. However, it was felt that a special honorary volume was long overdue to acknowledge Derek Roe's positive influence on Palaeolithic studies over nearly four decades. This book therefore unites papers written in tribute by his students, colleagues and associates.

Derek Roe was educated at St Edward's School in Oxford, and he continues to maintain close ties with his Alma Mater by serving as a member of the Governing Body. After fulfilling his national service with the Royal Sussex Regiment and the Intelligence Corps in Berlin, he went on to study Archaeology and Anthropology at Cambridge University, where he was a member of Peterhouse, graduating with a First Class Honours degree in 1961. Before he had completed his postgraduate studies, he was appointed University Lecturer at Oxford University in 1965, which delayed the submission of his PhD thesis until 1967.

At Oxford he conceived the idea of setting up a Quaternary research facility. He raised the funding by approaching Francis Baden-Powell for a generous benefaction in memory of his father, Donald Baden-Powell, and the Donald Baden-Powell Quaternary Research Centre was officially opened in 1975. Since then Derek Roe has served as its Honorary Director.

He was a founding Fellow of St Cross College, where he continues to play an active role, and served as Vice-Master of the College for three years (1988–1990).

'Derek joined St Cross as a Fellow at the beginning of 1970, and in his thirty-plus years in the College he has been the most devoted member of the community. Well-known for his ready wit, which has enlivened many a social gathering and Governing Body meeting, having also, in the latter case, served on occasion to defuse difficult situations as well, he has always been more than willing to take on the responsibilities of College office, notably as Treasurer and Vice Master. In the former capacity, and indeed throughout his time in the College, Derek has shown a particular interest in, and

gift for, friend and fund raising. The Barclays Visiting Fellowship programme, which for some fifteen years brought interesting people to the College, was established on his initiative, and his efforts were critical in bringing to the College a major benefaction enabling the construction of the first purpose-built College building, now a focal point of College life. Derek's considerable knowledge of antiques and fine art has also regularly been called upon, to the great benefit of the College. Especially knowledgeable about glass and silver, he has had the care of the College's collections of both, and has himself generously contributed pieces to them. He has also had the care of an extremely generous benefaction of fine watercolours, supervising the hanging of them and their restoration and preservation. The attractive display of these and other objects, which regularly excite admiring comments from visitors to the College, owe a great deal to Derek's expertise, imagination and hard work. I am very pleased to add this collegiate dimension to the more general testimony to Derek's many achievements throughout his long career. St Cross has certainly benefited enormously from his presence' (*Dick Repp*, Master of St Cross College, Oxford University).

Apart from his teaching and research activities, and the supervision of numerous doctoral and Master's degree students, Derek Roe has also served various terms of office as Director of Graduate Studies in Archaeology at Oxford University. He was a member of the Archaeology Committee of the National Museum of Wales from 1982 to 1999, and is currently a member of the National Museum of Wales Collections and Education Committee. He also serves on the Scientific Advisory Panel of the Irene Levi-Sala CARE Foundation for Prehistoric Research in or related to Israel, as well as the editorial advisory boards of *Proceedings of the Prehistoric Society*, *World Archaeology*, *L'Anthropologie*, *Geoarchaeology* and *The Review of Archaeology*.

Derek Roe was awarded a DLitt from Oxford University in 1983, and other honours include his election as a Fellow of the Society of Antiquaries of London in 1978, and the award of the Henry Stopes Medal by the Geologists' Association of London in 1985. In 1997 he was conferred the title of Professor of Palaeolithic Archaeology at Oxford University.

As many readers of this volume will have recognized, the title is taken from John Frere's publication of the Hoxne handaxes, and is appropriate for a volume written for Derek Roe, whose research has been devoted to this category of artefact. His PhD thesis, *A study of handaxe groups of the British Lower and Middle Palaeolithic, using methods of metrical and statistical analysis, with a Gazetteer of British Lower and Middle Palaeolithic sites*, represents a milestone in Palaeolithic studies. The method for the morphometric description and analysis of handaxes which he devised is still widely used throughout the world, as many of the contributions to this volume clearly testify, while the Gazetteer represents an invaluable source of reference for scholars of the British Palaeolithic. After his exhaustive study of the British Lower Palaeolithic material, Roe went on to apply his methods to the assemblages of handaxes and cleavers from various sites in sub-Saharan Africa, including Olduvai Gorge and Kalambo Falls. He visited Olduvai several times, and his friendship with Mary Leakey led him to play a key role in the writing of her autobiography. Most recently Derek Roe has been instrumental in getting the third volume on Kalambo Falls finalised, proofed and published, when the eyesight of its editor, Professor Desmond Clark, started to fail.

The papers in this volume are testimony to the influence Derek Roe has had on scholars working throughout the world.

*

Bill Waldren was a former research student of Derek Roe and received his DPhil from Oxford University in 1979. He is now Director of DAMARC (Deia Archaeological Museum and Research Centre) and a Research Associate at the Baden-Powell Quaternary Research Centre. Waldren has spent many years researching the archaeology of the Balearic islands, and in particular that of Mallorca.

'It is a pleasure and an honour to have been asked to assist and contribute to this Festschrift dedicated to Derek Roe. Although I am not a Palaeolithic specialist, I am an archaeologist involved in prehistoric archaeology and culture and one of Derek's many graduate students, as well as a close colleague of his for the last 25 years. During this long and to me precious time, I feel that I have had the great fortune, as well as privilege, of having had a first-hand opportunity to observe and to have been on the receiving end of some of his truly extraordinary human qualities.

At the best of times it is difficult to express one's feelings concerning those whom we most admire, especially those who are larger than life. I feel certain that my personal experience and sentiments concerning Derek are not all

that different from those felt by others contributing here, when I say that I have personally known no finer human being or more dedicated scholar and teacher than Derek.

Regarding the present occasion, I sincerely believe that all the contributors to this collection of papers dedicated to Derek will agree that this concerted effort can be but a small contribution, honouring a friend and colleague for whom we all have the highest esteem and affection. We have, as colleagues and friends, a shared experience of his special qualities, generosity of spirit and, seemingly, endless knowledge of his field. Those who know him well and those who have, perhaps, only come to know him on an occasional basis, know of his willingness to share his knowledge openly and equally without regard to one's status or rank. To Derek, the amateur, student or professional alike, can equally benefit of his interest and time. I have seen this generosity and deep consideration repeated endlessly over the years and I have never ceased to marvel at his infinite patience in these respects towards his students and colleagues.

My first association with Derek was as a graduate student in 1975, the same year that the Donald Baden-Powell Quaternary Research Centre opened. Derek has served as its director and, along with Ray Inskeep and Donald Baden-Powell, was one of its founders. Since that time, the Centre has under Derek's guidance and direction become an international hub of Palaeolithic studies, as well as a home away from home for graduates, postgraduates, visiting fellows and a parade of eminent specialists.

For me, Derek has always been someone of enormous patience, kindness and thoughtfulness and as one of his former graduate students, I for one owe a great debt to him. I was not one of his particularly 'brilliant' examples and as a 'mature' student, I needed a lot of his particular kind of patience and understanding. With his special brand of these qualities and as my supervisor, a job he took on, after having worn out a few others during my long 'writing up', I finally made it through. I can truthfully say that he read every word I wrote and sometimes more than once. I was to realize years later and after a long association, that Derek did this for most of his students, but I still remain convinced he spent more time on mine. In any event, for this, I will be eternally grateful.

As for Derek's special form of thoughtfulness, this is best illustrated by a casual remark I made as a graduate student at one of the many functions at the Centre. It was one of the annual parties when I tasted and admired a plate of meringues which I later found out were one of Derek's many baking specialities. Since then on every occasion when he has whipped up a batch of meringues, the next morning I have found a metal tin full of these delicacies on my office desk, with as note to the fact that he knew I savoured them and had made extra, knowing how I might enjoy them. He is the only person I have ever met who could fashion icing to look exactly like any stone tool you wanted. These exacting reproductions adorned the cakes he made for the congenial parties he organized on special occasions when one of his students graduated or when the Queen of Denmark once visited. Such gestures speak volumes as to his very particular form of thoughtfulness, kindness and willingness to give of his time. I am sure that all of us who know Derek have their own special and unique examples of this side of his ever generous and congenial nature.

I have had many opportunities and the on-going privilege over the past two decades, as both a graduate student and research associate, to experience many congenial moments over tea and coffee around the library table at 60 Banbury Road. These include being introduced to such notables as Mary and Richard Leakey, Philip Tobias, Glynn Isaac and many other scholars of international repute, all of whom have been generously and casually made known to me and whoever had the good fortune to be present at the time. For this is something that Derek is equally skilled at, as he is with the identification, knowledge and analysis of Palaeolithic tools or the explanation of a specific level or chronological horizon of a cave or geological context half the world away. He does it with equal enthusiasm and sincerity. For with Derek there has never been social differentiation between student and expert, only the pleasure of getting people together on the most casual and down to earth basis. This in turn speaks for his special universal and human qualities and nature.

Personally, I feel that I can not say enough in this brief introduction to what is an appreciation of his unusual character and nature and that it may be too little in laud of the legacy of fine work and great knowledge of the field of Palaeolithic research for which he has gained world acclaim. I cannot hope to match achievement with the experts whose Palaeolithic contributions are found in this Festschrift. The ages of my concern follow well after the Palaeolithic, but it does not exclude my appreciation, respect and interest in it and most of all in the person for whom this effort is dedicated.

In all events, words always fail when they are necessary to describe the person behind the work and when they are used to describe such traits as greatness, devotion, dedication and appreciation, but we must try despite their inadequacy. And even more so when the person is very much living and still giving.

It is therefore with humility and gratitude that we salute Derek in this modest attempt to show our esteem and appreciation for all he has done, not only to clarify the Palaeolithic and prehistory in general, fields which in themselves are less ambiguous and fragmentary because of such scholars as Derek, but, also for enlightening us in other more human ways. Our thanks Derek'.

*

R.J. MacRae is an independent archaeologist who recalls here his long association with Derek Roe and the Baden-Powell Quaternary Research Centre.

'Tributes in this book to Derek Roe from friends and colleagues will exhibit a diversity of form and substance reflecting one way or another the influence of a distinguished prehistorian whose achievements are so outstanding. For my part, as an amateur archaeologist, I recall a few of the events in which Derek was involved during the thirty years I have been privileged to know him as a friend. Inevitably such recollections are personal, most of them inseparable from a house in Oxford's Banbury Road known affectionately as Number Sixty.

It was Derek Roe who, in 1969, persuaded me to let the Pitt Rivers Museum have custody of three thousand early Palaeolithic artefacts I had rescued from the Highlands Farm gravels laid down in the Caversham (or Ancient) Channel of the Thames at Henley, and since assigned to the Anglian stage or even earlier. John Wymer, whom I had known for some years and who had published in detail his excavation of this predominantly Clactonian site, had told me to go searching there. Though not in primary context, the finds comprise 'the earliest set of archaeological material in our Oxford region' (Roe 1994). In a recent reassessment Derek upheld the validity of the Clactonian as a tradition separate from the Acheulian ovates also found in the channel. Now the weight of the evidence in favour of a distinct core-and-flake tradition seems indisputable, and the flame of the controversy has dwindled to a small flicker.

Room had to be found for the Highlands Farm artefacts, so in 1970 a basement room in Norham Gardens in north Oxford was acquired. In addition to the Highlands Farm material, it housed quite a lot of handaxes, flakes and cores from locations in southern Britain and East Anglia which I had amassed from gravel pits during the previous five years. For business reasons as well as archaeological reasons I had moved in 1969 from Warwickshire to Cassington, and for a further five years was able to do more handaxe hunting with some success. Identifying sites became easier because of Derek's invaluable *Gazetteer of British Lower and Middle Palaeolithic Sites*. The search, sometimes profitable, sometimes not, goes on to this day, notwithstanding my 86 years.

Donald Baden-Powell had become a close friend, and for a long time we shared a room in Norham Gardens, where Derek was an occasional visitor. A lot of work went into that place, sorting, labelling, recording and bringing in new acquisitions. Among these was a large consignment of handaxes and flakes transferred from Ipswich Museum. These were valuable but poorly provenanced and gave us a tough time deciding which sites they belonged to. The aim at Norham Gardens was to form a corpus of British Palaeolithic material as a start to a more ambitious 'Study Centre'. Donald's untimely death occurred before the Quaternary Research Centre came into being in 1975, with Derek as Director.

The Norham Gardens tenancy had expired, and I had nowhere to go. The museum authorities vaguely promised 'some sort of accommodation'. Rooms in the beautiful mid-Victorian house in Banbury Road were being allocated or argued about even as internal renovations were being carried out, and competition for space was keen. With the help of the energetic young Peter Jones, later to be assistant to Mary Leakey at Olduvai, I jumped the gun, and in one hectic weekend we transferred all the shelving and flint-filled boxes into a small ground floor room, and re-erected the lot. Our authority to do this was questionable, as was the procurement of the key, but by Monday morning possession became nine points of the law. Protests from would-be occupants were brazened out. That room became 'Mac's room', and it still holds the greater part of the Pitt Rivers Museum's British Palaeolithic collection. The weighty mass of Highlands Farm material was soon afterwards stored in the cellar.

A little later hoards of handaxes which a former curator had stashed away in all sorts of odd places in Oxford, with little or no written record, twenty-five years before, were drawn back together at Number 60. With the connivance of Dr Schuyler Jones, then Curator-designate of the Pitt Rivers Museum, several car-loads of lithic treasure were liberated from the vaults under University College, the old Power Station at Osney, and even from the half-forgotten drawers on the top floor of the main Museum. Everything British went into Mac's room, was sorted out into new boxes and made safe, I hope, for posterity. Also recovered from dusty oblivion were assemblages of stone tools excavated by Dorothy Garrod in Palestine, as well as material collected in Uganda, South Africa, Egypt and India, which were placed in other rooms in Number Sixty to add to the now considerable lithic collections from many sources and periods housed for the use of students and visiting prehistorians.

As Number Sixty grew in scope and status into an institution held in international esteem, Derek was not only steering young people to their doctoral destinies so to speak, but was producing in book form the results of his own research. *The Lower and Middle Palaeolithic Periods in Britain* appeared in 1981, and remains of prime importance in understanding our remote prehistory. The copy Derek gave me is still the most valued occupant of my bookshelf. If it needs revision to take in new discoveries and embody new ideas, his subsequent work, published in various forms, is always abreast of current thought. In the Tom Hassall Lecture he gave in Oxford in 1994, he said that '... our whole perception of the Pleistocene sequence in Britain has altered, the time-scale has extended and a far more detailed succession of climatic changes has been recognised'.

My brief here is not to list Derek's scholarly achievements but to record a few of the ways in which he influences my own activities. I was fortunate in intervals of a busy working life in a craft not at all connected to archaeology to be able to be a frequent visitor to Number Sixty. In the course of about twenty years I enjoyed the company of many of the students who came, triumphed and went. It would be invidious to name names, but some are still valued friends. Derek was always welcoming when I came into the Common Room, ready with a chair, coffee and an introduction to a new visitor. Invariably good-humoured, prone at times to perpetrating preposterous puns, his gentle banter prevented table-talk from becoming too serious. This genial donishness, I thought, masks awesome erudition. My place was all the more unusual because I had been granted the use of all the facilities I needed in the department, although I was not a member of any University. I had never sought academic recognition, and all I could contribute were a few thousand Palaeolithic stones and some ideas on how to write about them.

What better model than Derek could anyone aspiring to write on archaeological matters have? Not many of the conference papers, lectures and books that have come my way achieve the fluency, the analytical insight and the clarity of good English shown in his work. In contrast one sometimes has to suffer effusions by people who are by no means incompetent, they are merely incoherent. Too commonly is good research translated into polysyllabic verbosity. Derek, I remember, once collected samples of obscurantism and sheer gobbledegook. I wish he would publish them!

From the late 1960s to the late 1990s my passion for the muddy delights of gravel pits was incurable. I brought my finds to Derek as they occurred and gained his pleased approval. In the years from 1982 until I left Oxford, frequent papers on matters Palaeolithic were published in the appropriate journals, all embodying Derek's suggestions and cautious emendations. The Palaeolithic is the most complex of lithic studies and is abidingly fascinating, and I have been grateful for Derek's guidance in trying to understand some of its intricacies.

Two prolific gravel pits, Berinsfield (near Wallingford) and Stanton Harcourt in the Upper Thames, meant about three hundred palaeoliths having to be packed into Mac's room. These finds have been published, putting into perspective the surprisingly high proportion of non-flint items among the more conventional handaxes. Recognition of quartzite as a tool-making material, particularly in the Oxford region, was endorsed by Derek and led to a very rewarding collaboration with Norah Moloney, resulting in 1988 in an edited monograph to which fifteen archaeologists and geologists contributed articles. This volume was the first comprehensive study of quartzite tools in the British Palaeolithic. Certainly for me it was a thoroughly enjoyable experience. We had asked Derek for a short preface to the volume, and left all the papers with him. In a very short time we got instead a two thousand word pre-publication review written in his inimitable style in which he summarised not only the contents of the book but expanded his comments into a wide-ranging survey of the state of Palaeolithic studies in Britain and beyond. This essay stands out as one of Derek's best, and it was a memorable instance of his generosity in giving time and support to what he regarded as a worthwhile project.

One of the landmarks in the continuing expansion of the Quaternary Research Centre was the opening in June 1986 of the splendid Hunter-Gatherer exhibition, conceived and arranged by Ray Inskeep, assistant curator of the Pitt Rivers Museum. In orderly sequence, the displays bring to life the story of Man's rise through technological advance from the crudely chipped stones at Olduvai to the lifestyles of modern peoples. This exhibition, as well as the adjoining gallery devoted to musical instruments, was made possible by extensive new building into the former gardens of the old house. One day, perhaps the new Pitt Rivers Museum, so long promised, will arise on the site.

Bones as well as stones belong to the Quaternary, and it was characteristic of Derek that when he saw the potentially great importance of a 200,000 year-old buried channel of the Upper Thames at Stanton Harcourt he gave his support in a number of ways to its controlled excavation by palaeontologist Dr Katherine Scott. For eight years the work went on, and I was frequently at the 'Mammoth Dig' and saw with wonder the riches that this recently discovered interglacial channel yielded in the way of faunal, molluscan, coleopteran and other diagnostic remains. Full publication is pending, and the facilities at Number Sixty are being used towards that end. Unhappily, the site now lies under layers of landfill rubbish, despite efforts to preserve it. Dr Scott, irrepressible as ever, looks to new worlds to conquer. She has been a valued friend from the time when together we fished out bison bones and reindeer antlers from the newly opened Cassington gravel pit in the Devensian floodplain. That was in 1989. Since then Terry Hardaker has untiringly amassed an astonishing number of palaeoliths, mainly of quartzite, from the Cassington pit.

Anecdotage, they say, is coupled with senescence, and must have a stop, though there could be much more to recount. For instance, Derek cannot fabricate handaxes in flint very well, but he can produce good replicas, in icing sugar, which went down well at some of the pleasant get-togethers celebrating something-or-other at Number Sixty. Cooking is one of his relaxations and another is fly fishing. He also collects watercolours, of the Norfolk school I think. He is a founder-member of St Cross College and is increasingly involved in administrative affairs within the University. His professorial status was granted belatedly. May he long defer retirement and remain at Number Sixty'.

ACKNOWLEDGEMENTS

The editors would like to acknowledge the help of Joan Taylor in surreptitiously procuring an up-to-date bibliography of Derek Roe's publications as well the photograph used on the cover. Sarah Milliken would like to thank Paul Pettitt and Ray Inskeep for the helpful suggestions which they made when she first decided to organise this Festschrift.

The authors

J. Desmond Clark is Professor Emeritus at the University of California, Berkeley. He received his PhD from the University of Cambridge, and then spent twenty-three years in Zambia as Director of the National Museum and founder of the National Monuments Commission, before moving to the University of California. Clark opens this Festschrift with a commentary essay on Acheulian technology based on his extensive knowledge acquired from more than sixty years of working in Africa and other parts of the Old World.

Clive Gamble is Professor of Archaeology at Southampton University, and Director of the Centre for the Archaeology of Human Origins. Gamble's contribution to this volume, which is co-authored by *Gilbert Marshall*, also of South-ampton University, presents the preliminary results of a research project on Acheulian handaxe variability in Africa and Europe, of which Derek Roe is one of the principal investigators.

C. Garth Sampson currently holds joint appointments at Southern Methodist University and the South African Museum. With degrees from the Universities of Cape Town, Cambridge and Oxford, he has taught at the Universities of Capetown, Berkeley, Oregon and Witwatersrand. Sampson has directed the Seacow Valley Archaeological Project since 1979, and his contribution to this volume discusses the results of that project and presents a reconstruction of Acheulian settlement patterns in the Upper Karoo region of South Africa.

John McNabb is Lecturer in Archaeology at Southampton University. Having worked for many years on the Clactonian in Britain, his attentions have shifted to South Africa where he has recently been co-directing the excavations at Canteen Koppie with Peter Beaumont. McNabb's contribution to this volume is a speculative essay on the role of the Victoria West phenomenon in the South African Earlier Stone Age.

Phillip Allsworth-Jones is Senior Lecturer at the University of the West Indies in Jamaica. He holds degrees from

Oxford and Cambridge, and worked at the University of Ibadan in Nigeria before moving to Jamaica. In his paper Allsworth-Jones discusses prehistoric artefacts which he collected during a visit to Sierra Leone in 1986, as well as those that were housed in the Cotton Tree Museum.

Ray Inskeep was Lecturer in African Archaeology at Oxford University and Assistant Curator at the Pitt Rivers Museum. He taught Derek Roe at Cambridge University, and subsequently worked in the same department as him in Oxford for nearly thirty years. In his paper Inskeep provides an account of the development of fishing in Africa.

Marcel Otte is Professor of Archaeology at the University of Liège. He has carried out fieldwork in many parts of the world, including Belgium, Turkey, the Crimea and Portugal. In his paper he provides a critical discussion of the evidence for contacts and cultural influences between Africa and Europe during the Palaeolithic.

Nicholas Rolland is Professor Emeritus at the University of Victoria, British Colombia. In his contribution to this volume Rolland discusses the anthropic, geochronological and palaeoenvironmental evidence for the earliest occupation of Europe from a biogeographical perspective.

Vadim Ranov is Professor of Archaeology at the Institute of History in Dushanbe, and a corresponding Member of the Academy of Sciences, Republic of Tadjikistan. His research is primarily concerned with the Palaeolithic of Central Asia. Ranov's paper reviews the distribution, chronology and typology of cleavers in the Lower Palaeo-lithic.

Ofer Bar-Yosef is Professor of Prehistoric Archaeology at Harvard University and Curator of Palaeolithic Archae-ology at the Peabody Museum. He moved to Harvard from the Hebrew University in Jerusalem, where he had been an undergraduate, postgraduate, and then Professor of Prehistoric Archaeology. Bar-Yosef's paper reviews pattern and purpose in twentieth century Palaeolithic research paradigms.

Stephen Aldhouse-Green is Professor of Archaeology at University of Wales College Newport. He has excavated some important British Palaeolithic sites, including Paviland and Pontnewydd caves. In his paper he addresses the evidence for the appearance of modern behaviour in Europe by early Neanderthals before the last interglacial, and suggests that there was broad synchroneity in the process of becoming human in the continents of Africa and Europe.

Naama Goren-Inbar is Associate Professor at the Hebrew University in Jerusalem. She has excavated at many important Palaeolithic sites in Israel, including 'Ubeidiya and Gesher Benot Ya'aqov. Goren-Inbar's contribution to this volume, which is co-authored by *Zinovy Matskevitch*, a colleague from the Hebrew University, and *Sabine Gaudzinski*, from the Römisch-Germanisches Zentralmuseum in Neuwied, introduces a previously unrecognised handaxe type in Israel and Europe.

Hyeong Woo Lee received his DPhil from Oxford University in 2000 under Derek Roe's supervision, with a thesis on the Palaeolithic archaeology of the Upper Thames Valley. He is currently Lecturer in Archaeology at Chonnam University in South Korea, and his contribution to this volume presents a timely overview of the Palaeolithic period in Korea, and discusses several new discoveries.

Norah Moloney is a College Teacher at London University. She received her PhD from London University with a thesis on Middle Pleistocene quartz assemblages from Iberia, and has subsequently collaborated in fieldwork projects in Turkey, Jordan and Kazakhstan. Her paper, which is co-authored by *Sandra L. Olsen* of the Carnegie Museum of Natural History, and *Valery Voloshin* of the Institute of History in Astana, discusses the preliminary results of a new research project in the Batpak Valley in Kazakhstan, where various Lower and Middle Palaeolithic sites have been found.

Josep Gibert is a Researcher at the Institut de Paleontologia M. Crusafont at Sabadell. His paper in this volume presents a synthesis of the results of twenty-five years of research in the region of Orce, a key area for studies of human and cultural evolution in the Lower Pleistocene. The sites discussed in this paper have been the subject of some contention, and an important contribution was made to the debate by Derek Roe, who was the first independent researcher to consider the lithic material as genuine. Gibert's paper is co-authored by *Lluís Gibert* and *Fernando González*, colleagues at the Institut de Paleontologia M. Crusafont at Sabadell, *Alfredo Iglesias* from the University of Santiago de Compostela, and *Carlos Ferràndez-Canyadell* from the University of Barcelona.

Michael Walker is Professor of Physical Anthropology at Murcia University. After reading Physiology and Medicine as an undergraduate, he took a Distinction in the Diploma of Archaeology at Oxford University as a student of Derek Roe and Dennis Britton. Derek Roe has collaborated with Michael Walker in a Spanish Major Research Project and two previous governmental Anglo-Spanish Joint Actions. Since 1994 Michael Walker has been principal investigator of the Earthwatch Institute's field research project on 'The Search for Neanderthals in S.E. Spain'. He is director of the excavations at Cueva Negra del Estrecho del Río Quípar, and co-director (with Josep Gibert) of the excavations at Sima de las Palomas. Michael Walker's contribution to this volume gives an account of the latest results from these field projects.

Sarah Milliken is Lecturer in Archaeology at University College Cork, Ireland. A former research student of Derek Roe, she received her DPhil from Oxford University in 1991. She has worked extensively on various aspects of the Italian Palaeolithic and Mesolithic, and is currently directing field projects on the Middle-Upper Palaeolithic and Mesolithic-Neolithic transitions in south-east Italy. In her contribution to this volume she presents the results of an Italian case study which explores the question of Acheulian handaxe variability.

John Wymer recently retired from a long career in archaeology which involved excavations at some of the most important Lower Palaeolithic sites in Britain, including Swanscombe, Barnfield Pit, Hoxne and Clacton-on-Sea. Most recently he spearheaded the Southern Rivers Palaeolithic Project and the English Rivers Palaeolithic Survey, sponsored by English Heritage, and the Welsh Lower Palaeolithic Project, sponsored by Cadw. In his paper he discusses a number of Lower Palaeolithic sites around Feltwell in East Anglia which could have profound implications for the chronology of the earliest occupation of Britain.

Terry Hardaker is an independent archaeologist. He has been collecting Palaeolithic artefacts from gravel pits in Oxfordshire for many years, and his paper in this volume discusses some of his recent finds from the Upper Thames gravels, which allow a reappraisal of the significance of quartzite as a raw material during the Lower Palaeolithic in this region.

Nick Ashton is a Curator in the Quaternary Section of the Department of Prehistory and Early Europe at The British Museum in London. Ashton's paper addresses the possible relationship between raw material shortage and the strikingly individual character of the handaxes from Wolvercote in Oxfordshire.

Katherine Scott is a Research Associate at the Baden-Powell Quaternary Research Centre at Oxford University.

Her contribution to this volume, which is co-authored by *Christine Buckingham*, a graduate student at Oxford Brookes University, discusses the lithic artefacts found during ten years of research at the late Middle Pleistocene site of Stanton Harcourt in Oxfordshire, a project with which Derek Roe has collaborated closely.

Julie Scott-Jackson received her DPhil from Oxford University in 1996 under Derek Roe's supervision, and subsequently founded the PADMAC Unit (Unit for the study of Palaeolithic Artefacts and associated Deposits Mapped as Clay-with-flints). Her contribution to this volume, on the recent investigations at the Lower and Middle Palaeolithic site of Dickett's Field in Hampshire, is co-authored by *Vicky Winton*, one of Derek Roe's current graduate students who is researching the lithic technology at this and other high-level sites.

Simon Collcutt received his DPhil from Oxford University in 1985 under Roe's supervision, and subsequently set up his own company, Oxford Archaeological Associates Ltd. Collcutt introduces the '*Sackung* Hypothesis', which suggests that Middle and Upper Palaeolithic sites will more commonly be found in association with relatively soft geologies, whereas Lower Palaeolithic sites are more likely to have survived on harder geologies.

Nick Barton was a research student of Derek Roe and received his DPhil from Oxford University in 1986. He is now Senior Lecturer in Biological Anthropology at Oxford Brookes University. Nick Barton has worked extensively on various aspects of the European Palaeolithic and Mesolithic, and he is currently involved in research projects studying the biogeography of human colonisations and extinctions in the Late Pleistocene of southern Iberia and northern Africa, and human-landscape relations in Late Glacial and Postglacial south-western Britain. Nick Barton's contribution is co-authored by *Alison Roberts*, also an ex-student of Oxford University, who worked for some years at The British Museum before taking up her present post as Registrar at the Ashmolean Museum in Oxford. Their paper adopts a typological approach for determining the likely provenance of a tanged point found at Mildenhall in Suffolk, and discusses the implications which arise concerning human activity in Britain during the Late Glacial interstadial.

Mark White is Lecturer in Archaeology at Durham University. White received his PhD from Cambridge University, with a thesis that re-examined the nature of Acheulian handaxe variability in southern Britain and in particular the ovate and pointed handaxe traditions that Derek Roe had highlighted thirty years earlier. In his contribution to this volume, White offers a retrospective on the life and work of Sir John Evans, whom he considers to be the original British Palaeolithic specialist.

Elizabeth Walker is Collections Manager at the National Museum and Galleries of Wales, an institution with which Derek Roe has had a long and close association. In her paper, Walker presents the little-known English Palaeolithic collections which are housed in Cardiff, and provides a history and inventory to encourage their use.

Joan Taylor is Reader in Archaeology at Liverpool University. As a newly arrived American in Cambridge in 1964, Derek Roe tutored her for the Certificate in Archaeology, a necessary prerequisite for going on to do PhD research. In so doing, Roe managed to instil in her an interest in stone tools, which was then fostered by John Coles who encouraged her to take part in the excavation and post-excavation of the Somerset Levels and Morton Farm. Subsequently, while Curator of Archaeology and History at the Bristol City Museum, she initiated the Priddy Plateau Project, which involved the excavation of flint scatters around the Lower Pitts Farm area in the Mendips. Her contribution to this volume presents a preliminary report on this Mesolithic site.

Jill Cook is a former research student of Derek Roe, and is now Deputy Keeper and Head of the Quaternary Section in the Department of Prehistory and Early Europe at The British Museum. She has worked on Palaeolithic collections from many parts of the world, including Britain, the Sudan and India.

1. Variability in primary and secondary technologies of the Later Acheulian in Africa

J. Desmond Clark

ABSTRACT

As their dating has improved, it has become possible to correlate African lithic assemblages across regions. A review of the evidence for the Later Acheulian shows that these industries first appear about 600 kyr ago but are best known between 300–200 kyr. Technological choices appear to be expedient and based on raw material availability. Variation seems to be driven by function, while environment and habitat do not seem to have had a significant influence.

INTRODUCTION

Variability in both primary flaking and secondary retouch has long been recognized in Africa, but it has not been easy to correlate these different kinds of variability across time and regions because we lacked any means of dating most of these archaeological assemblages and contexts in the Palaeolithic. Within the last two decades, however, a number of lithic assemblages have been dated radiometrically, and the faunal assemblages associated with others are now well placed in the Late Pliocene and Lower, Middle and Early Upper Pleistocene. As a result, we can now begin to correlate these assemblages across regions and can see that the variability recognized in the Acheulian Industrial Complex falls mostly within a range of 500–200 kyr BP, with the most apparent variation being concentrated between 300–200 kyr BP. It can now be seen that most of the Acheulian assemblages that are known on the continent of Africa fall within the later stages of this Industrial Complex.

ENVIRONMENT AND HABITAT

The broad variability of plants and animals in the environmental contexts associated with Acheulian assemblages clearly derived from a number of interacting ecological habitats. It was this range from grasslands to open woodlands, sometimes associated with gallery forest, swamps, springs and even the seashore, that in large part dictated some of the variability observable in the Later Acheulian assemblages. Given the new, more detailed research and experimentation undertaken in recent years, with particular regard to the primary knapping techniques and different raw materials with which these assemblages are associated, it has now become much more apparent that it is the nature of the raw material that was largely responsible for dictating the primary technique used to produce the bifaces characteristic of the Acheulian. It is my contention that raw material has been all important in producing the variability to be seen in the handaxes, cleavers, and picks in Acheulian assemblages. Lithic technologies in the Middle Pleistocene were limited by the intellectual abilities and horizons of the makers, and the same kinds of tool kits are found in all ecological zones, except primary evergreen forest, and though the plant and animal resources are often different, the tool kits used to deal with these were basically the same. This paper therefore reviews a number of sites with which the author is acquainted, or has personally excavated (Fig. 1.1).

Fig. 1.1. Map showing locations of the sites referred to in the text.

MODE I AND MODE II ASSEMBLAGES

It is clear that by the time of the Later Acheulian, from around 600–500 kyr ago, there were still two basic technologies in use. These are referred to as Modes. Mode II consists of the large bifacial tools that are so characteristic of the Acheulian, as well as flake and core/chopper tools. The latter are characteristic of Mode I. They appear earlier and then persist alongside the bifaces of Mode II up to the end of the Acheulian Industrial Complex around 200–100 kyr ago. Sometimes only the bifaces are found in conjunction with the debitage from their manufacture. Sometimes only Mode I flake and core/chopper tools and debitage are found. More often, however, the products of both these two Modes are mixed together. This variability in assemblage composition does not appear to be related to raw material, except with regard to the availability of source material. Research shows that such variation may be interpreted in several different ways. It seems apparent that it may be the result of functional needs, but what induced such differences is not so obvious. In the Middle Awash area, where we have worked since 1981, we have found Mode I assemblages not only in association with the sediments of the lakeshore and plains, but also with the stratigraphically later regimen of channel-cutting and deltaic sediments (Heinzelin *et al.* 2000). This would seem to suggest that it is not so much the habitat that is responsible for these changes, but rather a socio-economic reason such as the opportunistic need of small hominid groups ranging widely for food to use the raw material immediately available to them for making stone tools and manufacturing artefacts from materials other than stone (Rose and Marshall 1996). Mammalian bones are usually present and these suggest the expedient manufacture of a Mode I industry from immediately local materials adequate for processing the carcass. For different reasons, the same can perhaps be said for the Mode II Acheulian biface assemblages where these occur without the usually associated Mode I component. Thus, it is not so much environment or habitat but expediency that can better explain the assemblage variability seen in the Middle Awash area, a large part of East Africa and more generally in northern and southern Africa (Heinzelin *et al.* 2000).

Other possible reasons for assemblage variability may, perhaps, be associated with the composition of the hominid groups making use of these Mode I and II artefacts. Age, sex and skill levels, for example, must also be taken into account. These factors are not yet identifiable, but are clearly important. Juveniles are likely to be less skilled and lack the strength of adult males. Females are, perhaps, more likely to have been the makers of Mode I industries; these are commonly associated with carcass processing. The adult males would have had the necessary strength and skill to produce the primary flakes for the manufacture of bifaces. Opportunistic need is deemed to be perhaps the most important factor that produces the Mode I type of assemblages. These are indicative of small groups, and sometimes include poorly made small handaxes with the flakes and core/choppers within the Acheulian Industrial Complex (Leakey 1967). The assemblages that combine both Mode I and II artefacts and debitage usually contain many artefacts and suggest that larger groups of hominids were responsible, or that they may have returned seasonally for some period of time.

Although it is now some 150 years since bifaces were first found in Europe and almost the same time in Africa, little progress has been made in the attempt to determine their primary function. Some bifaces that have been examined for micro-wear and polish show use for butchering and/or working plant materials, as at Hoxne, Suffolk, England (Keeley 1980; Singer *et al.* 1993). Certainly, experiments show that they can be used successfully to dismember large carcasses (Jones 1980). However, as mentioned above, the artefact assemblages most often associated with butchery appear to be those of the flakes and core/choppers of Mode I (Clark and Haynes 1970). In general, however, whether these sites are in desert, grassland, woodland, or what are now forested areas, one consistent factor is their close proximity to water and, one may add, so far as the grassland and more wooded localities are concerned, the presence of gallery forest.

SITES AND CHRONOLOGY

The sites that can be included in the Later Acheulian complex mostly fall within a 300–200 kyr range, but sometimes the dates extend back to 600–500 kyr. Certain of these sites are radiometrically dated by potassium-argon in association with the palaeomagnetic reversal sequence and seem to fall within Oxygen Isotope Stages

7–6 and, perhaps, 5, which cover the climatic fluctuations of the anti-penultimate glaciation and the Last Interglacial. Within these zones, the industries are found within a range of regionally diverse habitats but tend to favour more open country. One of the earliest with which we are concerned is the site of Bodo, in the Middle Awash area of the Afar Rift in Ethiopia, where the context of the cranium is dated to around 600–500 kyr (Clark *et al.* 1984), the associated fauna to 500–300 kyr, and where contemporary assemblages of mixed Mode I and Mode II, as well as Mode I exclusively, are found in the same time horizon (Heinzelin *et al.* 2000). The associated hominid cranium is that of an archaic *Homo sapiens* (Conroy *et al.* 1978). Gadeb, in the highlands on the South-East Plateau of Ethiopia, is in the Webi Shebeli valley and has a broad range of dates between 2.3 myr and 0.8 myr or less for the Acheulian. The Later Acheulian here is found usually in secondary, but in two instances primary, contexts within the sediments of the late Middle Pleistocene (Clark and Kurashina 1979; Williams *et al.* 1979). In North Africa, the site of Ternifine (Tighennif) now has a date between 300–200 kyr and is no longer considered to be of earlier Acheulian age (Geraads *et al.* 1986; Szabo 1982). The associated hominid in this case is described as *Homo erectus* (Arambourg 1954). At Bir Sahara, late Acheulian sites in a lake basin and spring date to 448 kyr (lakes) and 542 kyr (spring) (Wendorf *et al.* 1993). Other sites in the eastern Sahara associated with wetter climatic episodes, when water was reasonably available, date from more than 300 kyr to less than 100 kyr (Miller *et al.* 1991; Szabo *et al.* 1989, 1995). The above are some of the earliest dated Acheulian sites that can be seen to show Later Acheulian technology. Other sites, such as Elandsfontein, have similar dates based on fauna. Other late Acheulian industries fall within the later time range of 300–200 kyr.

South of the desert, in Kenya, the site of Kapthurin in the Baringo basin shows interesting variability within close time horizons. These are late Acheulian assemblages, Mode I industry, identified as Middle Stone Age and Sangoan assemblages with dates around 280–260 kyr (McBrearty *et al.* 1996). At Olorgesailie in the Rift south of Nairobi, the latest Acheulian is dated to approximately 400 kyr by U-series and K/Ar (Potts 1989). Kariandusi, in the Naivasha/Nakuru lake basin section of the Rift, has much the same radiometric age estimate and has many handaxes in obsidian (Gowlett and Crompton 1994). At Isimila in Tanzania, the late Acheulian is dated to around 260 kyr with many handaxes and cleavers in mylonite (Howell *et al.* 1972). At Nsongezi in western Uganda, the M–N Horizon dates between 300–200 kyr (Cole 1967; Van Riet Lowe 1952). In Southern Africa, the site of Rooidam in the Orange Free State is clearly late Acheulian and falls within the 300–200 kyr age (Fock 1968; Szabo and Butzer 1979). Duinefontein, also in the western Cape, dates to around 290–260 kyr (Klein *et al.* 1999), and the fine Acheulian from Kathu Pan in the southern Kalahari in the northern Cape also dates to about 500 kyr and perhaps later (Beaumont *et al.* 1984).

Certain of these sites, and a number of others, are now well dated by associated faunal assemblages, and fall within the later part of the Middle Pleistocene and the beginning of the Last Interglacial. In Morocco, the STIC Quarry at Sidi Abderrahman, Casablanca, yielded a fauna contemporaneous with that at Ternifine, Algeria (Biberson 1961; Geraads *et al.* 1986), and at Sidi Zin in Tunisia, the final Middle Pleistocene late Acheulian is also dated by the associated fauna (Gobert 1950). In the eastern Sahara, the dates for the fauna at Gilf Kebir, as well as U-series estimates, suggest an age between 300–200 kyr (McHugh *et al.* 1988; Szabo 1993). In northern Tanzania, the site at Lake Ndutu, with a partial hominid cranium, is perhaps earlier, if an amino-acid racimization date of 600–500 kyr is acceptable, but an age of approximately 400 kyr is more likely (Mturi 1976). South of the Sahara, Elandsfontein, as mentioned above, in the western Cape, is perhaps one of the earliest to be associated with an archaic *Homo sapiens* partial cranium and an industry described as Fauresmith (Deacon and Geleijnse 1985; Klein and Cruz-Uribe 1991). At the site of Cornelia (Butzer *et al.* 1974), the Acheulian is dated by its associated fauna, and the same can be said for the cave site of Wonderwerk in the southern Kalahari/northern Cape. This is again the case with the three levels of the Acheulian in the Cave of Hearths in the Makapan Valley in the northern Transvaal, here associated with fragmentary hominid remains and fire where a thick deposit of bat guano was burned (Mason 1962). Broken Hill (Kabwe) in central Zambia has two horizons, one with Mode II bifaces overlying a horizon with a Mode I assemblage, with little or no time interval between them. These are dated by the fauna associated with the cranium and post-cranial bones of an archaic *Homo sapiens* (Clark 1959; Klein 1973). Various other late Acheulian sites on the watershed between the Zambezi and Limpopo drainages in western Zimbabwe, such as Lochard, are associated with good faunal assemblages (Bond 1967). In South Africa the mound spring site of Amanzi in the Cape, with fauna and plant remains, is associated with a Mode II industry, in quartzite.

These sites, and many more, show much variability in biface technology and form, but some require further special notice for the significant difference manifest in major components which go beyond technique and form. A site of special importance in this respect is Kapthurin, where assemblages characteristically Acheulian with Modes I and II, another assemblage exclusively Mode I, and Sangoan assemblages where the core-axe or pick becomes the most significant type of tool, are all closely contemporary. The Mode I industry comprising small tools and debitage has also been described as Middle Stone Age (McBrearty *et al.* 1996). At Redcliff, a sealed brecciated old cave site near Que Que in central Zimbabwe, the earliest lithic assemblages appear to belong to a Sangoan aggregate, dated by the

fauna to more than 300 kyr, and overlain by a series of Middle Stone Age horizons (Cooke 1978; Klein 1978). A Sangoan is present again at Simbi, in western Kenya, where the dates are within the 200 kyr range and the fauna is late Middle Pleistocene (McBrearty 1988). Kilombe (beginning perhaps at 100 kyr) is another important site with this kind of variability in both biface size, the combination of assemblages of Acheulian Modes I and II, as well as Sangoan material within late Middle Pleistocene faunal contexts (Crompton and Gowlett 1993). Bouri, on the west side of the Middle Awash study area, has yielded several late Middle Pleistocene faunal assemblages and late Acheulian industries with dates within the 300–200 kyr range which are also associated here with hippo butchery sites (Heinzelin *et al.* 2000). In the latest assemblages, bifaces are both large and small and the Levallois technique makes its appearance in the latest Acheulian dated between 300–200 kyr.

LEVALLOIS TECHNOLOGY AND THE FINAL ACHEULIAN

The Levallois method adds a new dimension to Acheulian technology, but it is not easy to be sure of the time when it is first found in Africa. The long known sites at Victoria West in the South African Karoo and the Tabalbala/Tachengit sites in the Ahmar Mountains in the north-west Sahara are still, so far as I am aware, undated. At Kathu Pan, the Levallois method is dated before 260 kyr, and this now seems the most likely age of the sites referred to above. In northern Africa, the Levallois technique is present at the Kharga Oasis at the Bulug and Refuf Passes where the 'Lower Levalloisian' with 'Acheuleo-Levallois' is dated between 300–200 kyr (Kleindienst *et al.* 1997). However, at Kalambo Falls on the plateau at the south-east corner of Lake Tanganyika, the late Acheulian has a Uranium-series age estimate of about 200–150 kyr on a sample of wood. The late Acheulian is here sealed in sediments at water-level and below, where it is found in association with rich plant remains and evidence of fire. It is overlain by the Sangoan industry in fine-grained sediments, dating to about 80–100 kyr. These dates are probably too young, as the Acheulian almost certainly dates to 300 kyr. Where Sangoan industries are found in East Africa, it can be suggested that the environment may have been a more important factor in favouring the heavy duty tools. Pollen cores and macro plant remains suggest Sangoan sites are associated with woodlands and open grassland, having woodland within close vicinity. The Levallois technique does not appear at Kalambo Falls before the early Lupemban industry, which might date to approximately 100 kyr. Elsewhere, within East Africa and the Sahara, in more open country, the Levallois method certainly appears earlier than it seems to in the woodland areas of south-central Africa. At some late Acheulian sites, the Mode I artefacts look for all intents and purposes to be the same as those of the early Middle Stone Age (finely retouched scrapers and points), and might well be so called. At Kapthurin, as stated above, they occur only as a Mode I assemblage, whereas at Kalambo Falls they form part of the Acheulian assemblage, as well as the Sangoan industry that follows it. In the Middle Awash, it is the latest assemblages only that contain evidence for the Levallois technique. It is clear that a major technological and functional change was taking place at the time of these Final Acheulian industries. This transition can be seen to have its roots within the Later Acheulian and to be present in both North Africa and the sub-continent south of the Sahara. The reason for the development of the proto-Levallois technique would now seem to be associated with the need for obtaining large flakes and pieces of rock that were relatively thin in section from which to make bifaces. This technique was sometimes adapted if the nature of the raw material used to obtain them favoured one or other method for the primary working technology. So far as the Mode I component of an Acheulian assemblage is concerned, it shows little change except for the degree of refinement in some cases present with the late Acheulian, but, in general, is much the same from beginning to end. The Levallois method undergoes change in the latest Acheulian assemblages and the proto-Levallois flakes are replaced by smaller, lighter and thinner Levallois flakes and blades.

PRIMARY TECHNOLOGY

It is the primary technology related to the production of bifaces that shows the greatest degree of variability in the selection of raw material for production. This is not only on account of the texture and degree of hardness of the raw material, but also the form and context in which it occurs. In some instances the raw material is in the form of nodules and small blocks, in others large boulders, and in yet others it is found in outcrops and large fallen blocks, all of which were utilized for the production of bifaces. Where the raw material is primarily in the form of nodules and cobbles within gravels, the bifaces are made directly from these, which control size and form, the great majority being retouched into handaxes, often with the butts retaining the original cortex. This was the primary form of the raw material in Europe, and this was perhaps the reason why cleavers are rare except in such places as the Valley of the Garonne in southern France, where quartzite was used, and where the bifaces were made from large flakes, and cleavers occur in association with the handaxes. This is also the case at many of the sites in Spain. It also occurs at one or two of the sites in the Middle Awash in Ethiopia, in the Sahara and at Kharga (Caton-Thompson 1952) and Dakhla Oases (Schild and Wendorf 1977) in the Egyptian Western Desert, where nodules and flat blocks were used. Cleavers are not common at these sites, but they do occur. It may be that some social factor determines the extent to

which the cleaver is present when the raw material is in the form of nodules, but the cleaver may represent the partial reduction of the primary flake which needed no further reduction, the two lateral edges and cutting bit being adequate.

Perhaps the simplest way of reducing a large boulder was to throw one at another of more or less equal size, until one or both broke and a large flake could be obtained. Further core reduction could yield a number of flakes of large size that could be trimmed into bifaces of different size. This was the technique that was used at Kalambo Falls. The assemblages show that the primary flakes so produced were sometimes carried into the activity areas where they were worked into handaxes and cleavers (Toth 2001). At Ternifine and the STIC Quarry at Casablanca (Fig. 1.3), which are of similar faunal age, large triangular flakes were removed from boulder-like cores which were trimmed into trihedrals with equal success. At Bodo, a number of 'giant cores' were found. These may have been carried onto the site as it is just possible to pick them up, and they are too large and heavy to have been geologically transported in the sediment. At Gadeb (Fig. 1.5), interesting variability was found. Most of the artefacts were made from head-sized boulders of basalt, but others were made from a welded tuff obtained from outcrops some distance away from the activity sites. The flakes obtained from the basalt boulders were more often flaked on both faces to produce standard types of handaxe, lanceolate to elongated ovate in form. Every so often, a primary flake with cortex on the dorsal surface was retouched along the lateral edges of the ventral face so as to form a unifacial handaxe, the reverse face being formed by cortex. The handaxes and cleavers made from the outcrops of welded tuff were again different in that the handaxes were more elongated and sometimes pointed at both ends. Cleavers were commonly found in both lava and tuff. The tuff was softer than the basalt, and had to be more regularly retouched on both faces to produce stronger, more resistant, chopping and cutting edges. This variability was entirely due to the ways in which the raw material could best be handled by the hominids.

It is clear that by the time of the late Acheulian, there was considerable skill in both the primary and secondary techniques employed and, through time, biface dimensions seem to have become generally smaller and thinner. This is particularly noticeable in the latest or Final Acheulian, in which bifaces are quite small and ovate to sub-triangular in form. Such was the case with the beautiful silicified, banded ironstone at Kathu Pan and other spring sites in the northern Cape and southern Kalahari. It was also the case in the Middle Awash at Bouri, where in late Acheulian times silicified limestone and fine-grained volcanic rocks, including obsidian, were also used in producing similar small and ovate to sub-triangular bifaces (Gowlett and Crompton 1994). At Gadeb, four smallish ovate handaxes made from obsidian were found. There is only one known source of obsidian on the South-East Plateau, on the edge of the Rift escarpment some 150 km or more to the west, and it is clear that these bifaces were carried in from a considerable distance away. This use of fine-grained raw material produces the stereotype biface of the late Acheulian and, more particularly, the light duty flake tool component of the Acheulian. Primary technique in association with the context of the raw material is best seen at Olduvai Gorge, where sites apart from those in the Masek Beds all belong with the earlier Acheulian but the evidence from the sourcing and experimental work by Jones (1980) is equally applicable to the Later Acheulian. It is here that the various ways of working the different materials, including quartzite, quartz, ignimbrite, basalt and other rocks, are clearly demonstrated (*ibid.*). At Melka Kunturé in the headwaters of the Awash River, cobbles were also commonly used, as were much larger flakes from boulders and outcrops. An increasing use of obsidian through time, to the exclusion, in the Final Acheulian, of other materials, can also be seen here (Chavaillon *et al.* 1979). At the Tunisian site of Sidi Zin, a waning spring site where three horizons of Acheulian are stratified, the lowest and uppermost consist of typical lanceolate forms of handaxe, while the middle horizon is composed predominantly of ovates and cleavers, as well as more unifacial handaxes like those from Gadeb. The raw material in each horizon was the same, namely silicified limestone. There is no indication that the time interval between the levels was anything but geologically brief and it is possible that, since the material is the same, two different hominid groups are involved. A fourth horizon within tufa sealing the site shows the first appearance of the Levallois technique.

At other sites where boulders were used, the method was different and there is evidence for the Kombewa technique. When a boulder is split, it will produce one half with a negative scar and the other half with a positive scar. If the latter is struck again, a flake with two positive bulbs of percussion, one on each face, will result. Kombewa flakes are a common form in the Middle Awash on both the east and west sides of the river, as they are also in the Jordan valley at Jisr Banat Yacub (Gesher Benot Ya'aqov). They are also common at the Nsongezi sites in the M–N Horizon where they were first recognized and described (Van Riet Lowe 1952). Some raw materials were sometimes carried in from considerable distances. Perhaps one of the most impressive examples is that at Gadeb, mentioned above, where the evidence suggests that Middle Pleistocene hominids ranged widely over their territories. Similarly, the nearest sources of a welded vitric tuff found at Adrar Bous are some 80 and 240 km distant to the north-east and east. It is, however, rare, and the small handaxes made from this material suggest it must have been carried in. The silicified limestone used for the bifaces at Bouri-A8 is not local and neither is the silicified lava breccia cobble used to produce flakes and the missing core found with the Bouri-A8 butchered hippo carcass. Again, the obsidian used at Kariandusi is not local and must also have been carried in, as was the obsidian at the

Bouri-A10 hippo site. Distances comparable and greater than Jones' sources at Olduvai can be expected (Jones 1980).

In the Middle Awash (Fig. 1.6), the greatest changes in the technology of the Acheulian assemblages are most marked on the east and west sides of the major fault across the Bouri Peninsula. Here the earlier Acheulian on the west side is well dated at 1.1 myr. The earliest assemblages east of the fault are undated, but are most unlikely to be any older than 500 kyr, and are perhaps younger. The technological change is highly significant. In the earlier Acheulian on the west side, the technique used for making bifaces is that of hard hammer which produces large, rather deep flake scars and wavy, sinusoidal profiles on the raw material, which is lava. In the Later Acheulian on the east side of the Middle Awash, silicified limestone as well as lavas were used to produce bifaces by soft hammer retouch. These handaxes and cleavers have a symmetrical plan form and straight profile which are in marked contrast to those of the earlier stages of the Acheulian. Indeed, the Acheulian sequence which begins around 1.8 myr as seen at Konso-Gardula in southern Ethiopia, shows that these earliest Acheulian bifaces, as well as others of comparable age from East Africa, are relatively crudely made except for the fine points of the handaxes, and they often retain some of the original cortex over the lower part of the tool. Such fine pointed bifaces are rare with the earlier Acheulian from the west side of the Awash River at Bouri but, here also, large and more elongated handaxes and cleavers do occur. The technique is essentially that of hard hammer, with minimal or no evidence of more refined secondary retouch by soft hammer. The Levallois method is not present.

The proto-Levallois technique is present in East and South Africa and again in north-western Africa and the Sahara, where it is clearly designed to produce a single large flake that could be trimmed into one or other form of biface. This technique was first recognized in the Karoo in South Africa at Victoria West (Fig. 1.2). The flakes were obtained in two main ways. The dolerite and andesite boulders were trimmed radially to flatten one of the faces. A striking platform was worked at right angles to this on the lower face, and the boulder was then struck, presumably on an anvil or by a hand-held stone hammer, to remove a single large flake: either a single broad side flake, if the platform and blow was on one longer edge of the core, or a more rounded Levallois flake, if the core was struck at one end. Both forms show evidence of radial preparation and a multi-facetted striking platform. Many cores of these two types known as Victoria West I and II were found together with some of the primary flakes and handaxes, the rest having been removed to the activity areas. Victoria West appears essentially to have been a factory and workshop site and few of the cores are prepared for a further flake removal after re-preparation. Another site where the proto-Levallois technique is well in evidence is Kapthurin, where Mary Leakey excavated a hominid

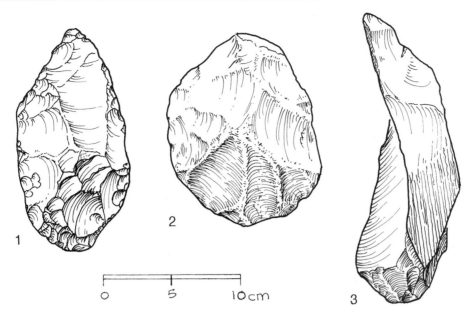

Fig. 1.2. Proto-Levallois cores and handaxe from Victoria West, Cape Province, South Africa: handaxe (1); Victoria West I (horsehoof) core (2); Victoria West II (henbeak) core, profile view (3) (illustration by Peggy Burkitt in Burkitt 1928).

associated site perhaps dating to around 260 kyr. Here the raw material was a fine-grained chert or, perhaps, ignimbrite or rhyolite, from which large soup-plate size, oval shaped cores were found with the flakes removed from them for making bifaces. The proto-Levallois technique is also well known in the north-western Sahara at Tabalbala and Tachengit (Fig. 1.4.2) on the west side of the Saoura drainage and the Ahmar mountains. Here, both side and end struck cores and many Levallois flakes have been collected (Alimen 1957). Even more skillful is the way that a pre-formed cleaver was produced by what is known as the Tachengit technique (Fig. 1.11). This involved radial preparation of the upper face and preparation of a striking platform on one of the long sides. When struck, a flake was obtained which required little additional trimming to produce a usable cleaver. The proto-Levallois technique is also said to be present in the Grotte des Ours in the Sidi Abderrahman Quarry at Casablanca (Biberson 1961). Another interesting proto-Levallois site is that of Arba (Fig. 1.9) at the south end of the Afar Rift, west of the Awash National Park. Here we found both handaxes and cleavers in a lag gravel associated with Levallois flakes and the cores from which they were obtained. The proto-Levallois cores and flakes are made of rhyolite and come from outcrops in the next valley to the west, found a year or two later by my colleague T.D. White. These were outcrops with many large and small blocks in the talus that were trimmed into Levallois cores, both struck and un-struck. The lag gravel overlies a Pliocene locality with fauna. The Arba gravel is at present undated though it must be closely contemporary with the Middle Awash Later Acheulian sites, but without the Levallois artefacts that we

have studied on both the east and the west banks of the river. Arba is late in the Acheulian complex, as is another site to the north of Lake Langano (Chavaillon *et al.* 1979) and also the site of Gademotta (Wendorf and Schild 1974) on the west side of Lake Zwai, both in the Ethiopian Lakes Rift. At these latter sites, the raw material used is obsidian, obtained at Gademotta from nearby outcrops, and at Langano imported in larger blocks obtained from more distant outcrops.

In summary, it is clear from studies of primary flaking methods in use in Later Acheulian assemblages that the makers were equally skilled at working both soft and hard rocks, as well as the different forms and contexts in which they occur: large boulders, big and small cobbles, and outcrops. Archaic *Homo sapiens* toolmakers appear to have been intellectually equipped and technically skilled to cope with all kinds of lithic raw materials, whatever the form in which they occurred. Bifaces made from the hardest textured rocks are as well made as those from softer textured raw materials at this primary stage (Fig. 1.10). This is demonstrated at many sites, for example in South Africa in the Later Acheulian assemblages from the Vaal River terraces around Barkly West and again at Cape Hangklip on the south-west coast of South Africa where hard quartzite was used. At Kalambo Falls (Fig. 1.7), handaxes and cleavers made from hard quartzite boulders are as finely finished as those made from the softer felspathic quartzite, which is much easier to work. Silicified mudstone, which occurred in the form of small blocks in narrow veins, was sometimes used for handaxes at Kalambo Falls, although more often this material was used for making smaller flake tools. Silicified mudstone bifaces were smaller due to size

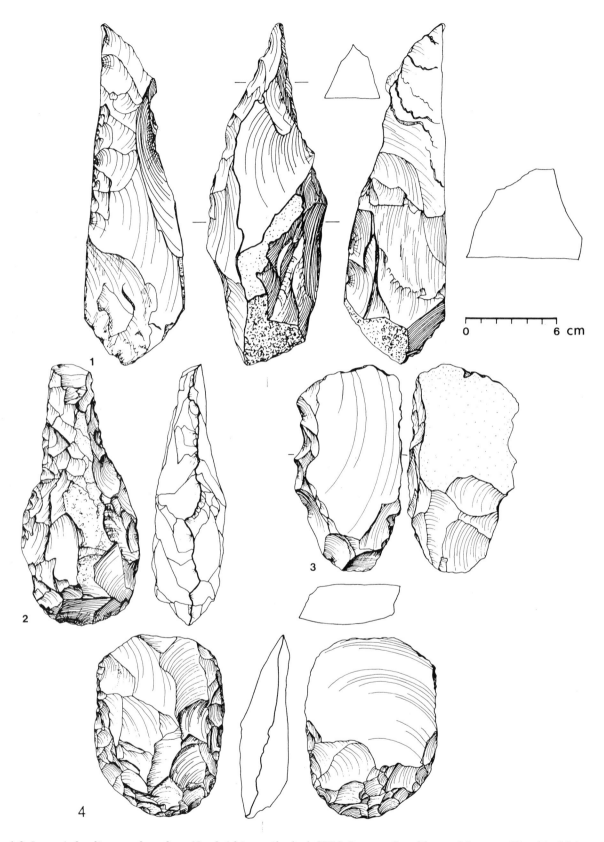

Fig. 1.3. Later Acheulian artefacts from North Africa: trihedral, STIC Quarry, Casablanca, Morocco (1); chisel (biseau) ended handaxe, Ternifine, Algeria (2); cleaver, Ternifine, Algeria (3); cleaver (from Levallois flake?), Tachengit, Algerian Sahara (4) (after Clark 1992).

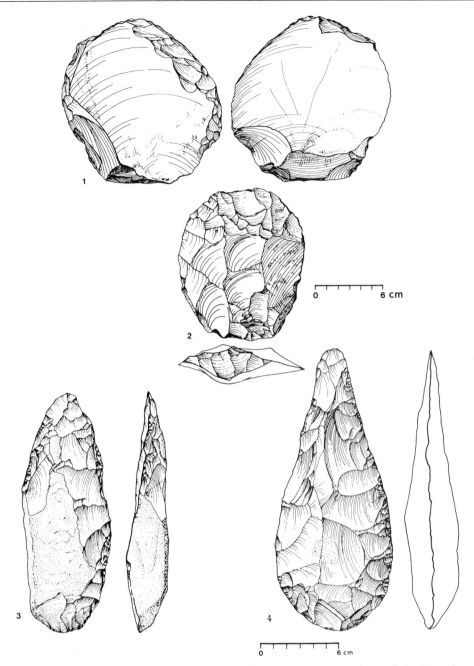

Fig. 1.4. Late Acheulian artefacts from North Africa: large side scraper on a Kombewa flake, Ternifine, Algeria (1); proto-Levallois flake, Tachengit, Algerian Sahara (2); prondnik-type handaxe/knife, Mound spring KO-10, Kharga Oasis (3); ovate-acuminate handaxe, Mound spring KO-10, Kharga Oasis, Egypt (4) (after Clark 1992).

limitations and a tendency for 'bladiness' that resulted from the right angle fracture within the blocks themselves. Quartzite also has a tendency to produce flake-blades from platform cores rather than irregular flakes. One can generally say that, with regard to both the earlier and Later Acheulian, the flakes from the manufacture of bifaces were in no way controlled at the primary stages, and that the irregular nature of the flakes removed in the course of biface manufacture is preserved throughout the time of the Acheulian Industrial Complex, through the final stages and also the Sangoan.

There was an increasing preference through time for these much more homogeneous, fine-grained rocks, such as ignimbrite, rhyolite, chert, silcrete and obsidian, and the increased emphasis on blade production is something that is clearly present in the latest Acheulian assemblages in the Middle Awash and localities in East Africa. This is probably a general tendency in the continent at the end of the Acheulian. Why the proto-Levallois technique should have been employed from time to time is unclear. The main reason seems to have been the need for large flakes, as well as the production of flakes that were relatively thinner than

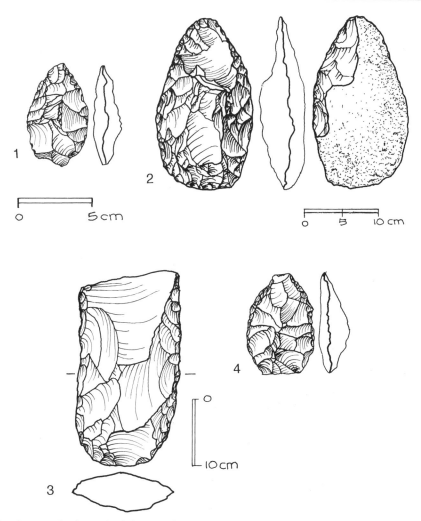

Fig. 1.5. Later Acheulian tools from Gadeb, Locality 8E, South-East Plateau, Ethiopia: small handaxe with some denticulation (1); unifacial handaxe (2); parallel-sided cleaver (3); diminutive elongate ovate handaxe (4).

those which could be obtained by other methods available at the time. The thinness of the Levallois flakes obtained from the fine-grained siliceous rocks is clearly a preferred form in the latest stages of the Acheulian in Africa. When these thinner blanks were retouched around the edges and ends, much finer end products could be produced than was possible with the thicker flakes obtained by the Kombewa method. Some rocks appear to be sufficiently malleable that the Levallois technique was not necessary, as with the *grés polymorph* (polymorphic sandstone) in many of the central and southern parts of the Congo River basin. The well documented site of Kamoa in the southern province of Shaba (formerly called the Katanga Province of the Belgian Congo), excavated by Cahen (1968), also shows that use of the Levallois technique came later. The fine-grained quartzite used there produced some finely finished bifaces. It also favoured a tendency to blade production. The primary source of the quartzite used for the late Acheulian assemblages are angular blocks naturally broken in the scree talus found below the outcrops some distance from

the activity sites (*ibid.*). The same tendency to produce blades is seen in the quartzite (mostly cobbles) used on the Moroccan coast at Casablanca and Rabat in the final stages of the Acheulian. The Levallois technique in its refined form first makes its appearance in Stage 8. At Adrar Bous, in the central Sahara, the raw materials used for Acheulian bifaces were mostly metamorphic rocks from the massif itself, fine-grained granite, quartzite, hornblende and also, rarely, a welded tuff, which was sufficiently fine-grained to produce thin, elegant bifaces in the final stages of the Acheulian, and which became the main material imported by the makers of the Aterian Industrial Complex. This preference for fine-grained materials is understandable, but the Levallois method at Victoria West using dolerite, a hard textured tough rock, is surprising. Presumably, this was all that was immediately available, and the technical skill of the hominids was fully competent for the radial preparation of the upper face of the core and the flake removal, showing that even the hardest rocks could be used when necessary. Whichever method was used, it shows

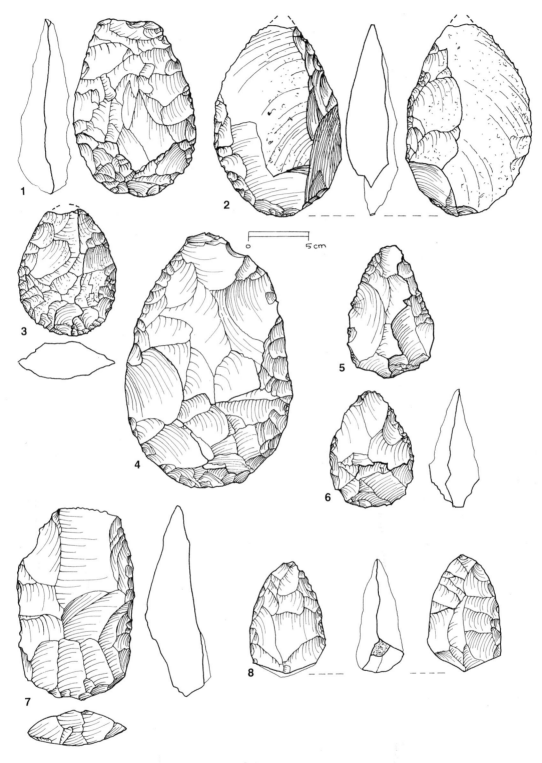

Fig. 1.6. Later Acheulian tools from the Middle Awash study area, Afar Rift, Ethiopia: elongate ovate handaxe in limestone from Bouri-A8 (1); cleaver on a Kombewa flake from Dawatoli-A6 (2); fine ovate handaxe with tranchet removal of distal end from Hargulia-A4 (3); elongate ovate from Maka-A2 (4); small sub-triangular handaxe with some cortex at butt from Maka-A2 (5); small cordiform handaxe in proximity to Bouri-A10 hippo butchery site (6); double-sided scraper or parallel-sided cleaver on a Levallois flake. Bouri-A10 hippo butchery site (7) (after Heinzelin et al. 2000).

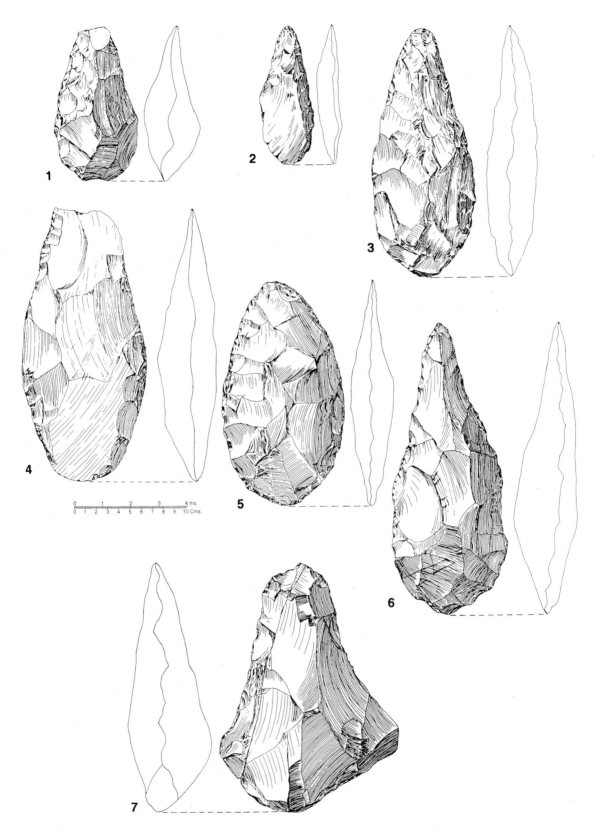

Fig. 1.7. Late Acheulian artefacts (1–6) and a Sangoan Industry core-axe from Kalambo Falls, B Site: small ovate handaxe (1); lanceolate handaxe on a side struck flake (2); lanceolate handaxe with convex point (3); convergent cleaver with straight bit (4); finely made elongate ovate in the standard form (5); lanceolate handaxe trimmed over greater part of both faces by hard and soft hammer technique (6); Sangoan core-axe (7).

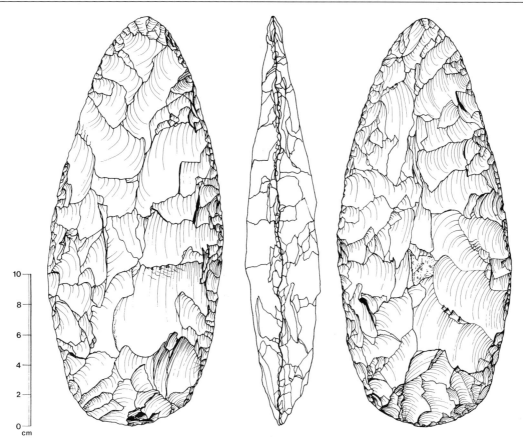

Fig. 1.8. A fine elongate handaxe from late Acheulian Horizon V at Kalambo Falls, B Site, shows squamous parallel flaking, marginal retouch or resharpening, straight profile and lenticular cross-section.

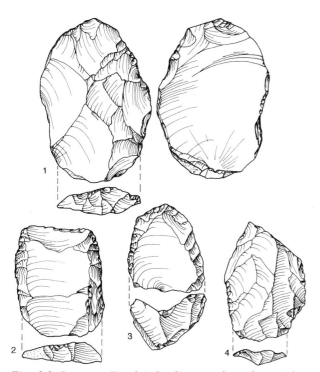

Fig. 1.9. Later or Final Acheulian artefacts from Arba, south end of the Afar Rift: Levallois flake (1); parallel-sided cleaver on a Levallois flake (2); struck Levallois core (3); small thin Levallois flake (4) (after Kurashina 1978).

the extent of experience with the material. Whether the method used was a hand-held cobble, block-on-block (*enclume*), Kombewa, or Levallois, the finished retouched bifaces were equally well made, irrespective of the material used, although the fine-grained rocks can be reduced to give thinner, more lenticular cross-sections.

RETOUCH

A considerable amount of variability in the nature of the end product can be seen among artefacts modified by retouch. Firstly, there are essential differences between handaxes and cleavers. It is quite clear that the cleaver is initially a halfway stage of the primary flaking to produce a large thick flake that can be retouched and refined into cleavers and handaxes. In many instances, cleavers become dominant to the exclusion of handaxes. A cleaver with a sharp bit formed by intersecting flake scars produces, if the raw material is of a hard enough texture, a sharp cutting edge without any further need for retouching. The lateral edges and more often the butts are retouched, unifacially or bifacially trimmed, and the platform reduced to produce an efficient tool distinct from the handaxe and presumably equally efficient. Functionally, the retouched lateral edges give tougher edges suitable for scraping or heavier work,

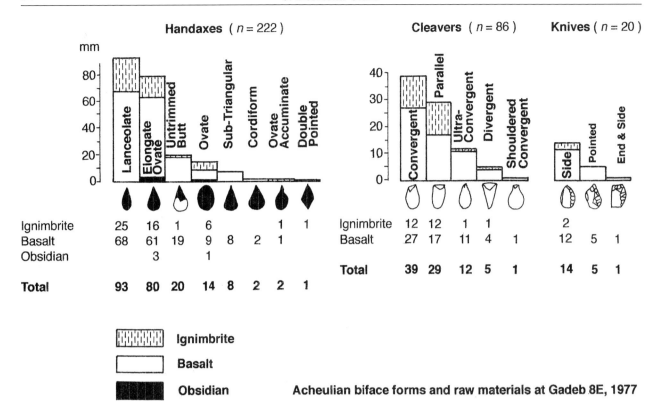

Acheulian biface forms and raw materials at Gadeb 8E, 1977

Fig. 1.10. Plan forms of handaxes and cleaver from Gadeb excavations and raw materials used showing preferred plan forms and equal skills with hard and soft material.

as are comparable edges on handaxes. It appears that the cleaver form produced a functionally competent tool that required no further reduction. The handaxes, on the other hand, are mostly bifacially retouched to reduce the thickness of the original primary flake and this provides resistant edges for various functions. The handaxe, particularly in the earlier part of the Later Acheulian, is more elongated and lanceolate in form. The distal end, often finely re-touched, shows that this, besides the lateral edges, was an important functional part of the tool. Butt ends are also consistently retouched to form a bifacially worked cutting or chopping edge. The cleaver bit is much more rarely found damaged by irregular retouch or use, at some Later Acheulian sites in sub-Saharan Africa. In Europe, however, where the material is often flint, cleavers are both rare and usually show retouch scars on the bit. Whether this is due to resharpening or the need for a more resistant edge is unclear, but in Africa the harder textured rocks used required no such modification of the bit.

This sharp bit was undoubtedly a significant feature of cleavers, since a sharp but strong bit is also a feature of some late Acheulian handaxes, namely those with *biseau* distal ends (Fig. 1.3.2). These are common at Ternifine and the Moroccan sites, at Kalambo Falls and in the Middle Awash, where they are classified as ultra-convergent cleavers (Fig. 1.7.4). These *biseau* bits are formed by striking a *tranchet* blow on one edge near the distal end to remove the terminal point. There is no indication that this

was a mistake, or that the *biseau* was re-sharpened. *Biseau* bitted handaxes are found throughout the Acheulian world, and clearly the fine chisel end was an important functional feature, as was the cleaver bit.

The inference that the biface was indeed a multi-purpose tool is probably a correct one. Until the latest Acheulian stages, it is likely to have been hand-held rather than mounted in some kind of haft, as can be perhaps deduced from some of the latest Acheulian small handaxes and, of course, those of the Middle Stone Age, where small bifaces are sometimes still present, perhaps for use as adzes.

The fine, soft hammer retouch found on bifaces is likely, as stated above, to have appeared somewhere around 600–500 kyr and produced a much more refined tool than those in the earlier Acheulian assemblages, which in the Middle Awash are dated to about 1 myr. The secondary trimming flakes were removed by using a hammer of bone, horn, or hard wood, or again by striking the artefact on a circular anvil, or with a softer hand-held spheroidal hammerstone, the essential feature being that the material being trimmed is harder than the material of the hammer. Experiments show that all of these materials and methods will produce much the same results, depending upon the angle of the striking platform, the amount of force behind the blow and the size of the edge area (platform) struck. The resulting flakes are all thin, wavy and long, often splitting as they come off the artefact. This results in a series of interlocking

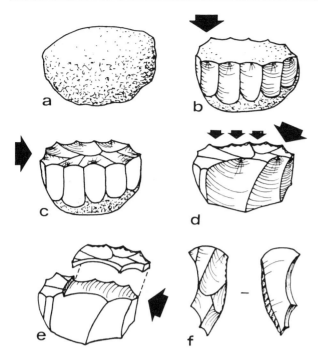

Fig. 1.11. Stages in the production of a preformed cleaver by the Tabalbala/Tachengit technique (after Clark 1992).

scars which may be marginal, semi- or fully invasive, and cover both faces of the tool. This yields a refined and relatively thin biconvex to lenticular cross-section. The long lanceolate and ficron forms still continue to the end of the Acheulian Industrial Complex, but there is a tendency in the later stages for the handaxes to become broader and more elongate to ovate in their plan form. In some instances, particularly at Kalambo Falls, the refined retouch takes the form of parallel or near parallel flaking down the lateral edges and at both ends, producing relatively long, thin, blade-like flakes (Fig. 1.8). The whole of both faces is, again, often completely retouched in this way. Such flaking clearly shows a masterly control of the flaking tool, and the minimal breadth or point form of the platform on the edge of the tool. It is also apparent that these handaxes have been resharpened or further reduced by more marginal, fine flaking around all or part of the circumference. Some of this reduction might be due to use, but it can in many instances be seen as a product of the resharpening of part or all of an edge. Such marginal scars frequently show feather edges (scalar), as well as step flaking. In the latest Acheulian in the Middle Awash, there is evidence for fairly extensive reduction and resharpening of bifaces (Fig. 1.6). The same can be seen at Kalambo Falls where, every so often, an *outre passé* flake removes part of the under face of the tool opposite the platform. Biface trimming flakes are highly characteristic, and show steeply inclined plat-forms with a small nipple-like bulb and facetted or plain restricted platform. The flake is thin, concavo-convex in profile, and on the dorsal face are the remains of intersecting

retouch scars. Such biface trimming flakes are found in association with bifaces at Olorgesailie and in many other Later Acheulian assemblages in eastern Africa. In the Middle Awash, we found these biface trimming flakes in clear association with the processed bones of hippo carcasses: the handaxes from which they were struck were found nearby and often show a considerable amount of reduction, indicating that one or more of these tools may have been used over the carcass processing time, perhaps to provide new sharp flakes. While, therefore, it is the raw material that dictates the choice of method used to obtain the large flakes for biface manufacture, the texture, shape and context of the raw material are also important factors in influencing the form of the final plan shape of the tool. This possibly ensures the best use of the material and so the choice. Both probably produce the general standard form in an assemblage in all materials used.

Raw material can also dictate the degree of refinement needed for both handaxes and cleavers, the harder rocks sometimes requiring less refined, squamous flaking, and the confinement to marginal and semi-invasive flaking and deeper flake scars with broader platforms. The softer rocks, however, required much more retouching. With the develop-ment of the first hafted stone tools at the beginning of the Middle Stone Age or, possibly, at the end of the Acheulian, the biface literally disappears in Africa. Rare examples occur with the Aterian industries in the Sahara and, again, rarely, in the Ethiopian Lakes region, where obsidian is the dominant raw material. Some of the best evidence for hafted tools are the Levallois points found in the Mousterian in the Near East and in Europe, and in the Middle Stone Age in eastern Africa and the Sahara, in particular in the Nile valley. The trapeziums and large lunates associated with the Howieson's Poort variation of the Middle Stone Age in South Africa, and those of the later Lupemban/Tshitolian in the Congo and an equivalent but as yet unnamed assemblage from Mumba Cave in the Lake Eyassi Rift of East Africa, may be mentioned as evidence of hafting (Mehlman 1987). There is also some evidence in the Middle Stone Age at Kalambo Falls for the presence of small, refined, Levallois cores and the flakes derived from them, and of blades that have been broken and retouched at both ends and down one side to produce trapeziums. Both blades and thin Levallois flakes are clearly necessary to the hafting of Middle Stone Age artefacts. As yet, I have seen no clear evidence within the latest Acheulian that any of these artefacts were hafted. The scraper forms in the late Acheulian, which closely resemble those of the Mousterian of the Near East and Europe, are generally thick and often steeply and repeatedly retouched until being discarded when the edge angle is too steep. It is quite likely that these scrapers were still hand-held or mounted in a mastic holder for the various purposes for which they were used. It is in the plan form of the bifaces that the element of preference is perhaps best seen and appears to be unrelated to the raw material. An industry will have a dominant plan form for the bifaces. At Kalambo Falls the preferred cleaver form is convergent, but parallel-sided and divergent edged forms are also present. The predominant handaxe form is an elongate ovate, but other forms are also present. In the Middle Awash, the lanceolate or ficron elongate ovate forms are more usual, but there are always some other forms present and where the raw material is not that from the usual source, it may be evidence for the presence of visiting individuals from other groups using different sources. At Gadeb the dominant handaxe form is lanceolate, but with many elongate ovates irrespective of the raw material (Fig. 1.10).

Subjective classification of this kind obscures the overall pattern in an industry, and by far the best visual presentation of this is to be seen in the dimensional plots developed by Derek Roe, initially for the British Lower Palaeolithic (Roe 1968), and adapted for use in Africa at Olduvai Gorge (Roe 1994) and Kalambo Falls (Roe 2001). These bring out all the dominant forms, degrees of variability and the 'odd-balls'. It can be conjectured that by the late Acheulian there were enough skilled individuals in a group that they could have been the means whereby a group tradition emerged that might change as new individuals introduced their own preferences for form. Where aggregates include bifaces of different form and source material, this may relate to changing group composition and a new identity may be suspected.

In East African terminology the Later Acheulian knife (handaxe with a blunted back) is a regularly occurring form. Another feature of the Acheulian in East Africa and at Kalambo Falls is intentional asymmetry at the distal end of a handaxe, so that in plan form this end is concavo-convex. It is not a common feature, but it occurs sufficiently often to show that it was designed and had functional significance. Another such trait in the late Acheulian in the Western Desert of Egypt, is the *prondnik* type of backed knife found at Kharga and Dakhla Oases (Fig. 1.4.3), as well as in central Europe. The above, and other variations, are indications of transition and new functional needs and preferences. Denticulation of natural edges is also a feature sometimes seen which is clearly intentional and can best be seen in the profile views of handaxes. Denticulation can best be seen in the Lupemban industry in Angola where long lanceolates are carefully denticulated.

SUMMARY AND DISCUSSION

In summary, the later African Acheulian industries make their appearance about 600 kyr, but are best known from a number of sites dating between 300–200 kyr. In these, variability is most clearly demonstrated. Component differences between assemblages with mixed Mode I and II artefact forms and others comprising only those of Mode I or of Mode II may be more functionally and opportunistically dictated or may be connected with group composition. Environment and habitat do not appear to have been dominant factors influencing component differences, and

the same tool kits are found throughout the continent, whatever the biome.

The evidence presented here identifies the raw materials used for biface manufacture as the most important influence on the blanks, or pre-forms, for retouching into bifaces and the various methods that were adopted to obtain these. The method selected was that best suited to the material and the form in which it occurs. Hard textured rocks were more often used for the bifaces, but the small light duty flake tools were more often made in fine-grained rocks.

The secondary retouch is that which demonstrates best the variability in form, since this is the product of soft hammer flaking producing symmetric plan forms, straight profiles and thinner biconvex cross-sections. By the Final Acheulian, the more homogeneous materials were sought out and there is preference for particular sources. At the same time, bifaces became smaller and more finely re-touched, though larger forms are also a regular component.

The cleaver and handaxe are the main kinds of large cutting tools and considerable variability in both has been examined. Some of this is material related and some appears to be the local preference of the makers. By the final stages of the Acheulian, new tool forms make their appearance, the most significant of which is the Sangoan core-axe in higher rainfall areas and the refinement of the Levallois technology from large proto-Levallois flakes to the smaller thin flakes and blades seen in the Final Acheulian, in particular in the drier and more arid ecozones.

Where the biface is absent from some assemblages, the industry is no different from that type of a typical Middle Stone Age aggregate, and it is the disappearance of the biface that marks the end of the Acheulian and the lithic industries that follow are the immediate successors of the regional Final Acheulian.

The hominid associated with the late Acheulian is an archaic *H. sapiens* that, through time, shows an increasing number of modern traits. The crania from Jebel Irhoud in Morocco are not far removed from being modern and are dated to about 90 kyr. The jaw fragments from Haua Fteah are also now seen to show modern features and they were found associated with a Mousterian industry. The crania and other remains associated with the Aterian Industrial Complex are robust but anatomically modern humans and may be 60–70 kyr old (Cremaschi *et al.* 1998). Some time around 100 kyr, the first anatomically modern humans emerged in sub-Saharan Africa in or out of the Final Acheulian, and the small migrating groups began the population replacement of Eurasian archaic forms of hominid. New and increasing field studies and new fossils in context can be expected to provide convincing proof to confirm this scenario.

EPILOGUE

This paper is by way of a commentary essay on Acheulian technology acquired from some sixty or more years working in Africa, in the field and in the laboratory, as well as in some other parts of the Old World where the Acheulian is present. It is essentially a commentary on what this author has concluded about the skills and ability of the later Middle Pleistocene hominids responsible for the later stages of the Acheulian Industrial Complex. The sites and assemblages used here are those with which the author has experience or has personally excavated and made more understandable by experimentation in stone technology. The evidence is most advantageously improved by the research and experimentation of numerous scholars and the great advances in understanding the technologies and methods used at this time. Behavioural interpretations are purposely minimal, but some supposition has been necessary, indeed welcome, in an essay of this kind, especially when supported by data, but the precision of a research paper is missing since with diminished eyesight, and no longer having the use of my library, I have been unable to comb the literature and check the references carefully. This is a paper dictated from memory onto tape and drafted and re-drafted by supporting assistants to whom my deep appreciation is acknowledged here. In particular I thank Elizabeth Agrilla, Sabrina Minter, Aimee Ellis, Kyle Brown and my daughter Elizabeth Winterbottom; without their help this paper could not have been completed. I am especially grateful to Richard Klein for reading through this paper and checking and providing dates, spellings, and suggestions for improvement. My thanks also to Kathy D. Schick for providing the map (Fig. 1.1). It has been a pleasure to have participated in this Festschrift, in particular because of the deep respect we all have for Derek Roe, for his great contribution to understanding the abilities, mind and world of the Acheulian. I am glad to contribute to this volume in his honour.

REFERENCES

Alimen, H. 1957. *The Prehistory of Africa*. Hutchinson Scientific and Technical, London.

Arambourg, C. 1954. L'hominien fossile de Ternifine (Algérie). *Comptes Rendus de l'Académie des Sciences de Paris* D 239, 893–895.

Beaumont, P.B., van Zinderen Bakker, E.M. and Vogel, J.C. 1984. Environmental changes since 32 kyrs B.P. at Kathu Pan, Northern Cape, South Africa. In J.C. Vogel (ed.) *Late Cenozoic Palaeoclimates of the Southern Hemisphere*, 324–338. A.A. Balkema, Rotterdam.

Biberson, P. 1961. *Le Paléolithique Inférieur du Maroc Atlantique*. Publications du Service des Antiquités du Maroc 17, Rabat.

Bond, G. 1967. River valley morphology, stratigraphy, and paleoclimatology in Southern Africa. In W.W. Bishop and J.D. Clark (eds.) *Background to Evolution in Africa*, 303–312. University of Chicago Press, Chicago.

Burkitt, M.C. 1928. *South Africa's Past in Stone and Paint*. Cambridge University Press, Cambridge.

Butzer, K.W., Clark, J.D. and Cooke, H.B.S. 1974. *The Geology, Archaeology and Fossil Mammals of the Cornelia Beds, OFS*. Memoirs of the National Museum 9, Bloemfontein.

Caton-Thompson, G. 1952. *Kharga Oasis in Prehistory*. The Athlone Press, London.

Cahen, D. 1968. Chronologie intern de la station Acheuléen de la Kamoa, Katanga. *Africa-Tervuren* 14, 103–110.

Chavaillon, J., Chavaillon, N., Hours, F. and Piperno, M. 1979. From the Oldowan to the Middle Stone Age at Melka Kunturé (Ethiopia): understanding cultural changes. *Quaternaria* 21, 87–114.

Clark, J.D. 1959. Further excavations at Broken Hill, Northern Rhodesia. *Journal of the Royal Anthropological Institute* 89, 201–232.

Clark, J.D. 1992. The Earlier Stone Age/Lower Paleolithic in North Africa and the Sahara. In F. Klees and R. Kuper (eds.) *New Light on the Northeast African Past*, 17–39. Heinrich Barth Institut, Köln.

Clark, J.D. and Haynes, C.V. 1970. Elephant butchery site at Mwangandas village, Karonga, Malawi, and its relevance for paleolithic archaeology. *World Archaeology* 1, 390–411.

Clark, J.D. and Kurashina, H. 1979. Hominid occupation of the East-Central Highlands of Ethiopia in the Plio-Pleistocene. *Nature* 282, 33–39.

Clark, J.D., Asfaw, B., Assefa, G., Harris, J.W.K., Kurashina, H., Walter, R.C., White, T.D. and Williams, M.A.J. 1984. Paleoanthropological discoveries in the Middle Awash Valley, Ethiopia. *Nature* 307, 423–428.

Cole, G.H. 1967. The later Acheulian and Sangoan of southern Uganda. In W.W. Bishop and J.D. Clark (eds.) *Background to Evolution in Africa*, 481–528. University of Chicago Press, Chicago.

Conroy, G.C., Jolly, C.J., Cramer, D. and Kalb, J.E. 1978. Newly discovered fossil hominid skull from the Afar Depression, Ethiopia. *Nature* 275, 67–70.

Cooke, H.B.S. 1978. Africa: the physical setting. In V.J. Maglio and H.B.S. Cooke (eds.) *Evolution of African Mammals*, 17–45. Harvard University Press, Cambridge, Massachusetts.

Cremaschi, M., Di Lernia, S. and Garcea, E. 1998. Some insights on the Aterian in the Libyan Sahara: chronology, environment, and archaeology. *African Archaeological Review* 15, 261–287.

Crompton, R.H. and Gowlett, J.A.J. 1993. Allometry and multidimensional form in Acheulean bifaces from Kilombe, Kenya. *Journal of Human Evolution* 25, 175–199.

Deacon, H.J. and Geleijnse, V. 1985. The prehistory of South Africa – a survey. *L'Anthropologie* 89, 285–305.

Fock, G.J. 1968. Rooidam, a sealed site of the First Intermediate. *South African Journal of Science* 64, 153–159.

Geraads, D., Hublin, J.-J., Jaeger, J.-J., Tong, H., Sen, S. and Toubeau, P. 1986. The Pleistocene hominid site of Ternifine, Algeria: new results on the environment, age, and human industries. *Quaternary Research* 25, 380–386.

Gobert, E.G. 1950. Le gisement paléolithique de Sidi Zin. *Karthago* 1, 1–51.

Gowlett, J.A.J. and Crompton, R.H. 1994. Kariandusi: Acheulean morphology and the question of allometry. *African Archaeological Review* 12, 3–42.

Heinzelin, J. de, Clark, J.D., Schick, K.D. and Gilbert, W.H. 2000. *The Acheulean and the Plio-Pleistocene Deposits of the Middle Awash Valley, Ethiopia*. Department of Geology and Mineralogy, Annales des Sciences Géologiques 104. Royal Museum of Central Africa, Tervuren.

Howell, F.C., Szabo, B.J., Oakley, K.P., Cole, G.H. and Kleindienst, M.R. 1972. Uranium series dating of bone from the Isimila prehistoric site, Tanzania. *Nature* 237, 51–52.

Jones, P.R. 1980. Experimental butchery with modern stone tools and its relevance for Palaeolithic archaeology. *World Archaeology* 12, 153–175.

Keeley, L.H. 1980. *Experimental Determination of Stone Tool Uses: A Microwear Analysis*. University of Chicago Press, Chicago.

Klein, R.G. 1973. Geological antiquity of Rhodesian Man. *Nature* 244, 311–312.

Klein, R.G. 1978. Preliminary analysis of the mammalian fauna from the Redcliff Stone Age cave site, Rhodesia. *Occasional Papers of the National Museum of Southern Rhodesia* 4, 343–374.

Klein, R.G. and Cruz-Uribe, K. 1991. The bovids from Elandsfontein, South Africa, and their implications for the age, palaeoenvironment, and origins of the site. *African Archaeological Review* 9, 21–79.

Klein, R.G., Avery, G., Cruz-Uribe, K., Halkett, D., Hart, T., Milo, R.G. and Volman, T.P. 1999. Duinefontein 2: an Acheulian site in the Western Cape Province of South Africa. *Journal of Human Evolution* 37, 153–190.

Kleindienst, M.R., Schwarcz, H.P., Nicoll, K., Churcher, C.S., Frizano, J., Giegengack, R.W. and Wiseman, M.F. 1997. Water in the desert: Uranium-series dating of Caton-Thompson's and Gardner's 'Classic' Pleistocene sequence at Refuf Pass, Kharga Oasis. *The Second Dakhleh Oasis Project Research Seminar*, 16–20 June 1997. University of Toronto, Toronto.

Kurashina, H. 1978. *An Examination of Prehistoric Lithic Technology in East-Central Ethiopia.* Unpublished PhD thesis, University of California, Berkeley.

Leakey, M.D. 1967. Preliminary survey of the cultural material from Beds I and II, Olduvai Gorge, Tanzania. In W.W. Bishop and J.D. Clark (eds.) *Background to Evolution in Africa*, 417–446. University of Chicago Press, Chicago.

Mason, R.J. 1962. *Prehistory of the Transvaal.* University of the Witwatersrand Press, Johannesburg.

McBrearty, S. 1988. The Sangoan-Lupemban and Middle Stone Age sequence at the Muguruk Site, western Kenya. *World Archaeology* 19, 388–420.

McBrearty, S., Bishop, L. and Kingston, J. 1996. Variability in traces of Middle Pleistocene hominid behavior in the Kapthurin Formation, Baringo, Kenya. *Journal of Human Evolution* 30, 563–580.

McHugh, P., Breed, C.S., Schaber, G.G., McCauley, J.F. and Szabo, B.J. 1988. Acheulian sites along the Radar rivers, southern Egyptian Sahara. *Journal of Field Archaeology* 15, 361–379.

Mehlman, M.J. 1987. Provenience, age, and associations of archaic *Homo sapiens* crania from Lake Eyasi, Tanzania. *Journal of Archaeological Science* 14, 133–162.

Miller, G.H., Wendorf, F., Ernst, R., Schild, R., Close, A.E., Friedman, I. and Schwarcz, H.P. 1991. Dating lacustrine episodes in the Eastern Sahara by the epimerization of Isoleucine in ostrich eggshells. *Palaeogeography, Palaeoclimatology, Palaeoecology* 84, 175–189.

Mturi, A.A. 1976. New hominid from Lake Ndutu, Tanzania. *Nature* 262, 484–485.

Potts, R.B. 1989. Olorgesailie: new excavations and findings in Early and Middle Pleistocene contexts, Southern Kenya Rift Valley. *Journal of Human Evolution* 18, 477–484.

Roe, D.A. 1968. British Lower and Middle Palaeolithic handaxe groups. *Proceedings of the Prehistoric Society* 34, 1–82.

Roe, D.A. 1994. A metrical analysis of selected sets of handaxes and cleavers from Olduvai Gorge. In M.D. Leakey and D.A. Roe (eds.) *Olduvai Gorge Volume 5: Excavations in Beds III, IV and the Masek Beds, 1968–1971*, 146–234. Cambridge University Press, Cambridge.

Roe, D.A. 2001. The Kalambo Falls large cutting tools: a comparative metrical and statistical analysis. In J.D. Clark (ed.) *Kalambo Falls Prehistoric Site, III: The Earlier Cultures: Middle and Earlier Stone Age*, 429–599. Cambridge University Press, Cambridge.

Rose, L. and Marshall, F. 1996. Meat eating, hominid sociality, and home bases revisited. *Current Anthropology* 37, 307–338 .

Schild, R. and Wendorf, F. 1977. *The Prehistory of Dakhla Oasis and Adjacent Desert.* Polish Academy of Sciences, Warsaw.

Singer, R., Gladfelter, B.G. and Wymer, J.J. 1993. *The Lower Palaeolithic Site at Hoxne, England.* University of Chicago Press, Chicago.

Szabo, B.J. 1982. Uranium-series disequilibrium date from tooth fragments from the fossil hominid site at Ternifine, Algeria. *South African Journal of Science* 78, 205.

Szabo, B.J. and Butzer, K.W. 1979. Uranium-series dating of lacustrine limestones from pan deposits with final Acheulian assemblage at Rooidam, Kimberley District, South Africa. *Quaternary Research* 11, 257–260.

Szabo, B.J., McHugh, W.P., Schaber, G.G., Haynes, C.V. and Breed, C.S. 1989. Uranium-series dated uthigenic carbonates and Acheulian sites in southern Egypt. *Science* 243, 1053–1056.

Szabo, B.J., Haynes, C.V. and Maxwell, T.A. 1995. Ages of Quaternary pluvial episodes determined by uranium-series and radiocarbon dating of lacustrine deposits of the Eastern Sahara. *Palaeogeography, Palaeoclimatology, Palaeoecology* 113, 227–242.

Toth, N. 2001. Experiments in quarrying large flake blanks at Kalambo Falls. In J.D. Clark (ed.) *Kalambo Falls Prehistoric Site, III: The Earlier Cultures: Middle and Earlier Stone* Age, 600–604. Cambridge University Press, Cambridge.

Van Riet Lowe, C. 1952. *The Pleistocene Geology and Prehistory of Uganda. Part II: Prehistory.* Uganda Geological Survey Memoir 6. Benham and Company, Colchester.

Wendorf, F. and Schild, R. 1974. *A Middle Stone Age Sequence from the Central Rift Valley, Ethiopia.* Polish Academy of Sciences, Warsaw.

Wendorf, F., Schild, R. and Close, A. 1993. *Egypt During the Last Interglacial: The Middle Palaeolithic of Bir Tarfawi and Bir Sahara East.* Plenum Press, New York.

Williams, M.A.J., Williams F.M., Gasse, F., Curtis, G.H. and Adamson, D.A. 1979. Plio-Pleistocene environments at Gadeb prehistoric site. *Nature* 282, 29–33.

2. The shape of handaxes, the structure of the Acheulian world

Clive Gamble and Gilbert Marshall

ABSTRACT

Derek Roe's metric description of handaxe form has endured for almost four decades, and its resilience is witnessed by the relative lack of any alternative methods of analysis. With shape successfully described, however, we remain in the dark as to what this variability really means. Function remains largely speculative while the striking spatial and temporal spread of the Acheulian is difficult to explain in the context of our understanding of early hominid behaviour. Recent work on the English Acheulian by Ashton, McNabb and White, has suggested that the divisions proposed by Roe, namely ovate and pointed, can be explained to a large extent by raw material differences, and in particular shape and size. Moreover, they argue that ovates represent the preferred form, contingent of course on suitably shaped raw materials being available. This paper outlines some results from a recent study of handaxe collections from South Africa, in which Roe's descriptive methods have been applied. Like the English examples, bifaces from South Africa suggest that final shape was indeed associated with that of the blank, in turn strongly influenced by the shape of the nodules, boulders or outcrops themselves. However, irrespective of the shape of the original raw material being exploited, flake blanks were the preferred form even in collections where exclusive use was being made of rolled nodules. The evidence from the debitage component of the South African collections indicates that broad flakes were the preferred blank form, and that subsequently the intractable nature of much of the raw material available would have encouraged the principle of least effort in the making of bifaces. The suggestion, therefore, that ovates represent the preferred form is supported by the South African evidence, though the reason for this is more likely to be that the path of least resistance was being followed. Whether or not this indicates deliberate choice is unclear, but it does suggest that in the South African context, the more interesting groups of bifaces are going to be elongate ones, simply because they run counter to this model of least resistance.

INTRODUCTION

The handaxe is a rock on which Palaeolithic explanations have often foundered. Although it is two hundred years since John Frere penned their existence to the Society of Antiquaries, they still remain the key artefact for charting most of our earliest prehistory, yet are notoriously difficult when it comes to navigating their interpretation. Fortunately, during the past 40 years, we have had a pilot on the bridge who has made the navigation easier and sent out the lifeboat when yet another grand theory ran aground. Derek Roe not only pioneered the systematic, quantified and computer based study of these remarkable objects, but also undertook the most comprehensive sample of their geographical distribution. No one else has developed a system of descriptive analysis, the Roe method, and then applied it to a full survey of the British Palaeolithic (Roe 1964, 1968a, 1968b), as well as to the Olduvai bifaces (Roe 1994) and the series from Kalambo Falls in Zambia, Southern Africa (Roe 2001).

Here we will concentrate on a sample of 1500 bifaces from South Africa studied in 1999 as part of a wider project on Lower Palaeolithic technology, in which Roe is a principal investigator. Our goal is to document biface variation over at least half a million years and 10,000 km of the Acheulian world in Africa and Europe. Our strategy has been to create a public archive of digitally photographed bifaces which can then be studied using automatic tracing software which we have developed. In addition, we have recorded technological attributes and raw material data. The purpose in creating a standardised sample is to address the question of variability and, indeed, the apparent lack of it, across the Acheulian world. This is a question which many have commented upon (Clark 1976; Clark 1969; Gamble 1997; Gowlett 1988; Klein 1999; Wymer 1982), but with little agreement as to the appropriate interpretation.

PREFERRED SHAPES

Roe's morphometrical study of the British handaxes revealed three major traditions: pointed, ovate and intermediate. As this Festschrift volume so richly demonstrates, the significance of this patterning in biface assemblages has been much debated. It is sufficient for this contribution to note that chronological and functional differences still do not adequately explain the variation which Roe documented. However, as White's (1998) recent British based study shows, the shape, size and quality of flint raw material still holds out some prospects for a general understanding of the Acheulian. In this contribution we set out to widen White's raw material hypothesis by looking at a geologically different region from the other end of the Acheulian world, South Africa. In particular, we are asking three questions concerning the shape of handaxes:

- are raw materials and blank form largely responsible for the different proportions of ovate and pointed types?
- did reworking result in ovates being reduced to pointed forms?
- is it possible through inter-regional comparison to recognise a 'default' handaxe shape and, if so, what are the implications?

THE SOUTH AFRICAN EARLY STONE AGE (ESA)

The rich archaeological record of the South African ESA is at once both similar to and different from the British Lower Palaeolithic. Points of similarity:

- The ESA in South Africa has a long history of artefact collection during the twentieth century, and a comparatively small number of controlled excavations (Deacon and Deacon 1999). The historic parallels with the British Palaeolithic (Roe 1981; Wymer 1999) are therefore close, much more so than with the East African ESA where the record has been built up by systematic survey and excavation (Isaac 1989; Leakey 1971).

- The South African ESA has potentially greater time depth, as revealed at Sterkfontein (Kuman 1998). Dating for most sites, however, is not good (Klein 1999). Where it does exist it points to a later Lower Pleistocene/Middle Pleistocene age, comparable to parts of Europe. The likelihood is that many of the collections in both regions can be grouped in the time frame from about 300 kyr–1 myr years ago (Carbonell *et al.* 1999). Within Europe, the British Acheulian is currently dated after 600 kyr (Roberts *et al.* 1995).

Points of contrast:

- In terms of raw materials South Africa is a non-flint area. Within the sub-continent a variety of knappable stone resources are found. These differ in hardness, fracture properties, nodule size and hence tractability for working. Such variety is not found among the British flints except in terms of nodule size and quality (White 1998). Quartzite is the one significant raw material found in both regions (MacRae and Moloney 1988).

- The South African Acheulian is well known for its bifaces, a descriptive category which includes both cleavers, handaxes and picks. Britain, by contrast, is dominated by handaxes. Cleavers are always rare.

- The Pleistocene history of Southern Africa is different from that of north-west Europe and the British Isles. However, precise palaeoecological data are not required to make the case that these two regions at either end of the Acheulian world were different in terms of resources, seasonality and, during the Middle Pleistocene, the recurrent effects of climatic cycles.

THE BIFACE SAMPLE

The sample consists of eight assemblages (Table 2.1). Six of these are from open localities, while Montagu Cave contains two stratified levels. The Fauresmith assemblage consists of four smaller collections marked by strong typological similarities and an exclusive use of hornfels. The eight assemblages are believed to date between 250 kyr and one million years. The digitally photographed sample comprises 1537 complete bifaces as defined by Kleindienst (1962). In this paper we examine the handaxes using Roe's (1968a) metrical analysis of shape.

RAW MATERIAL AND BLANK FORM

Preferred raw material

In order to assess whether there was a preference for certain raw materials because of their influence on the shape (pointed or ovate) of handaxes, our sampling strategy aimed to select localities which offered a variety of raw materials.

Collection	Site location	Location of collection sampled	Cleavers (n=524)	Handaxes (n=958)	Picks (n=55)	Total (n=1537)	Key references
Cape Hangklip	Open coastal site on south-eastern tip of False Bay below the cliffs of Groot Hangklip	South African Museum, Cape Town	88	168	2	258	Goodwin and Van Riet Lowe (1929, 22), Sampson (1962), Sampson (1972, 40)
Montagu layer 5	Cave located in small gully within north facing foothills of Langeberg Mountains east of Montagu village to the north-east of Cape Town	South African Museum, Cape Town	111	98	3	212	Goodwin and Van Riet Lowe (1929, 22), Keller (1973), Sampson (1972, 45)
Montagu layer 3	As above	As above	62	48	2	112	As above
Elandsfontein	Shifting dunes east of Saldahna Bay to the north of Cape Town	South African Museum, Cape Town	28	238	5	271	Klein and Cruz-Uribe (1991), Malan (1962), Singer and Crawford (1957), Singer and Wymer (1968)
Amanzi Springs	Open hilltop site with Acheulian artefacts within now largely defunct sulphurous spring eyes located north of Port Elizabeth	Albany Museum, Grahamstown	46	148	25	219	Deacon (1970), Inskeep (1965)
Pniel 6	Material derived through diamond dredging and coffer dam construction along the banks of the Vaal River near Kimberley	McGregor Museum, Kimberley	120	109	0	229	Deacon and Deacon (1999, 81), Goodwin and Van Riet Lowe (1929, 35)
Doornlaagte	Open seasonal lake edge lag deposit between Kimberley and Schmidtsdrift	McGregor Museum, Kimberley	54	47	17	118	Butzer (1974), Mason (1966, 1967)
Fauresmith (Kimberley Townlands, DeBeers Floors, Samaria Road, Susannahkop)	Four small collated collections derived from open sites in the Kimberley area	McGregor Museum, Kimberley	15	102	1	118	

Table 2.1. The South African sample of digitally photographed bifaces

The sample contains ten different raw materials of which silcrete, quartzite, andesite and hornfels (Table 2.2) are the major types. These are normally found in abundance at or very near the localities. For example, the localities at which quartzite and andesite were used, were either directly on the raw material source or, in the case of Montagu Cave, actually within it. The longest transfers in our sample are found at Elandsfontein. Here quartz porphyry and milky quartz respectively came from 20 km and probably 30 km distant. However, despite the variety of raw materials

Raw material	Amanzi Springs	Cape Hangklip	Montagu layer 5	Montagu layer 3	Elandsfontein	Pniel 6	Fauresmith	Doornlaagte	Totals
Andesite	0	0	0	0	0	206	23	118	347
Chert	0	0	0	0	0	1	0	0	1
Ferricrete	0	0	0	0	1	0	0	0	1
Hornfels	0	0	0	0	0	19	91	0	110
Sandstone	0	0	0	0	23	0	0	0	23
Quartz	0	5	0	0	2	0	0	0	7
Quartzite	218	247	212	112	34	3	4	0	830
Quartz porphyry	0	0	0	0	32	0	0	0	32
Silcrete	0	6	0	0	176	0	0	0	182
Mudstone	1	0	0	0	0	0	0	0	1
Unclear	0	0	0	0	3	0	0	0	3

Table 2.2. Raw materials in the South African assemblages

available to hominids in South Africa, no preference can be observed between a dominant raw material type and overall shape preference for handaxes (Fig. 2.1). Only among the minority raw materials in an assemblage was there a suggestion of shape preference. For example, at the coastal site of Elandsfontein no stone occurs in the dunes. The seven raw materials which were brought in to the site came from between 10 to 30 km distant (Deacon and Deacon 1999, 85) and are dominated by silcrete. When compared by handaxe shape (Table 2.3) no preferred raw material emerges apart from the higher proportion of quartz porphyry ovates compared to quartzite pointed handaxes (Fig. 2.2): this is the only pattern which is significant ($\chi^2 = 9.74$). Similarly, at the Vaal River site of Pniel 6, 22 percent of pointed handaxes were made on hornfels compared to 15 percent of the ovates. Since the assemblage is dominated by ovates it might be possible to argue that a slight preference existed in the use of hornfels nodules, a minority raw material (Table 2.2), to make pointed forms.

Raw material size and blank form

We also investigated the size of raw materials. Andesite (Pniel 6 and Doornlaagte), quartzite (Cape Hangklip and Montagu Cave) and probably silcrete (Elandsfontein) occur as outcrops and large boulders. This contrasts with Amanzi Springs where rolled quartzite nodules were probably being collected from the floodplain below the site (Deacon 1970, 99). At Pniel 6, where local andesite dominated (Table 2.2), small to medium sized rolled nodules of hornfels were also being used. Similarly, the few white quartz bifaces used at Cape Hangklip were probably collected either directly or as eroded nodules from geological veins which are generally less than 10 cm in width. It has been noted before that these differences in raw material size, and therefore potential blank form, can play a role in determining

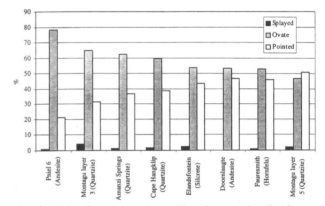

Fig. 2.1. The shape groupings of handaxes in South African assemblages.

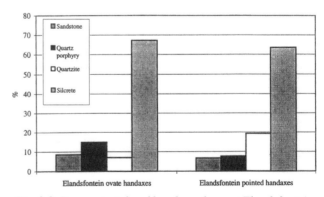

Fig. 2.2. Raw material and handaxe shape at Elandsfontein.

handaxe shape (Goodwin and Van Riet Lowe 1929, 36; Sampson 1962, 29–30). We found that the production of handaxes in all the assemblages (Fig. 2.3; Table 2.4) was dominated by the use of flake blanks (*débitage*) rather than nodules (*façonnage*). This was even the case at Amanzi Springs where rolled nodules formed the raw material.

However, it can be seen that Amanzi contains a higher proportion of handaxes made by *façonnage* than any of the other assemblages (Fig. 2.3). When we compared ovates with pointed forms at Amanzi (Fig. 2.4), we found that pointed shapes, while poorly represented in the assemblage, were twice as commonly made on nodules than ovates. Similarly, pointed handaxes made on rolled hornfels nodules at Pniel 6 were almost twice as common as ovates made on the same raw material.

Summary

In our South African sample, handaxe shape does not correlate with the dominant raw material in any of the eight assemblages. Instead the influence of raw materials on technology is seen in their size and shape, rather than their geological composition. This affected the decision to work nodules (*façonnage*) rather than make handaxes on large flake blanks (*débitage*). In our sample, the use of nodules as raw materials was very much the exception. Even at Amanzi Springs, where the most *façonnage* was found (Fig. 2.3), the majority of handaxes were still made on flake blanks. However, as Fig. 2.1 shows, the proportion of pointed forms is considerable in several of the assemblages, and will be discussed further below.

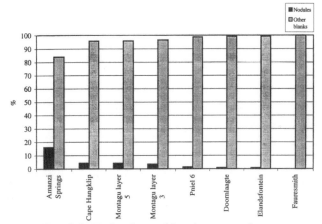

Fig. 2.3. Technology of handaxe manufacture.

Raw material	Elandsfontein pointed handaxes	Elandsfontein ovate handaxes
Sandstone	7	11
Quartz porphyry	8	19
Quartzite	20	9
Silcrete	66	86
Ferricrete	1	0
Quartz	1	1
Unclear	1	2
Total	104	128

Table 2.3. Raw material and handaxe shape at Elandsfontein

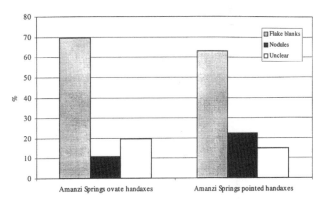

Fig. 2.4. Technology of handaxe manufacture at Amnzi Springs.

Collection	Predominant raw material	Number of handaxes made on nodules	Number of handaxes made on flake blanks
Pniel 6	Large andesite boulders and outcrops	3	226
Doornlaagte	Large andesite boulders and outcrops	1	117
Amanzi Springs	Rolled quartzite nodules (less than 300 mm long)	35	184
Montagu layer 3	Large quartzite boulders and outcrops with frequent exfoliation slabs, rolled quartzite boulders and pebbles	4	108
Montagu layer 5	Large quartzite boulders and outcrops with frequent exfoliation slabs, rolled quartzite boulders and pebbles	9	203
Cape Hangklip	Large quartzite boulders and outcrops with frequent exfoliation slabs, rolled quartzite nodules (less than 350 mm long)	11	247
Elandsfontein	Probably large boulders and outcrops of silcrete, quartz porphyry and quartzite	2	269
Fauresmith	Unclear	0	118

Table 2.4. Raw material characteristics and technology of handaxe production

THE REDUCTION MODEL APPLIED TO SHAPE

The reduction model is best known from the work of Dibble (1987, 1988, 1991) on the Middle Palaeolithic and Mc-Pherron on the Lower Palaeolithic (1994, 1995). It is based on the premise of efficiency, measured by the currency of energy, in the production and use of technology. Time and distance provide values for the currency, and the results are described by such well-known concepts in lithic studies as artefact maintenance, curation and recycling. Such dynamic processes lead to changes in dimensions with the eventual artefact shape representing a final stage in its 'biography'. When applied to handaxes, the cumulative working of the upper edges results in the migration of the widest point towards the butt, so transforming an ovate into a point according to Roe's (1968a) classification.

We tested the reduction model by asking the following questions:

- does it work dimensionally? In other words, are ovates larger than pointed handaxes?
- does it work in terms of symmetry? Are pointed handaxes more symmetrical than ovates?
- does it work in terms of edge shaping? Is more of the circumference worked amongst pointed handaxes than ovates?

Size

The reduction model was not strongly supported by length, breadth or thickness measurements in any of the eight South African assemblages. To illustrate the underlying similarity we examined, using cumulative frequency graphs, the dimensions of handaxes from Elandsfontein. Since all lithics had to be carried into the locale, efficiency, operating according to the reduction model, should be apparent. Pointed handaxes were slightly smaller but the results were not statistically significant.

Symmetry

The tendency towards equal bifacial working of both edges of handaxes is apparent in most of the assemblages. As predicted by the reduction model, such continuous working should result in greater symmetry amongst pointed forms since they generally have longer worked edges than ovates. We measured symmetry with our automatic trace software using the Continuous Symmetry Measure (CSM) as applied by Saragusti *et al.* (1998). In the Elandsfontein assemblage the differences were small but typical of the majority of the other assemblages where ovates, rather than pointed forms, were marginally more symmetrical. None of these differences are significant at the 0.05 level using a two sample test.

Edge working

The reduction model is based on the maintenance of edges through retouch. Under this process the broadest point not only migrates towards the butt, but at the same time more of the circumference becomes a worked edge. Therefore, we should expect that pointed handaxes are more extensively retouched than ovates. Once again, no statistically significant differences at the 0.05 level using a two sample test were noted in the proportion of circumference working in any of the assemblages. Visually, however, in three of the assemblages ovates were identified as more extensively worked, while only Cape Hangklip followed the prediction with pointed handaxes slightly more extensively worked.

Summary

The reduction model was not strongly supported by these non-flint handaxe assemblages. Pointed types were slightly smaller but this was not statistically significant. The lack of increased symmetry and circumference working amongst pointed handaxes suggests that the regular reduction of ovates into pointed forms did not occur. Convergence to a specific dimension rather than reduction to a type is a more parsimonious explanation. However, we note in passing that another biface form, cleavers, were significantly larger than handaxes in all assemblages and, not unexpectedly, both less symmetrical and with less edge-working. We do not have space here to explore further this aspect of the reduction model, but we note that cleavers can become handaxes and, if this happens, they are possibly more likely to be ovates.

DEFAULT SETTINGS AND THE ACHEULIAN WORLD

Our final question asks if either of these major handaxe shapes, pointed and ovate, can be considered as a default setting? By 'default' we mean that, for whatever reason, ovates rather than pointed handaxes, or vice versa, were the shape which would habitually result from an ESA/LP hominid's close involvement with stone. Roe again provides the framework for addressing such a question. In his primary sort of the 38 handaxe assemblages from England, he applied a threshold of 60 percent to indicate automatic membership into either the pointed or ovate tradition (Roe 1968a, table IV). Those assemblages which failed this threshold were reserved as uncommitted for further analysis. Among his 12 uncommitted examples, only three sites showed a near 50:50 split (*ibid.*). White, in his study (1998), confirms this basic finding that the British assemblages are generally clearly dominated by either one shape or the other (Fig. 2.5). There are few uncommitted assemblages just as there are less than 3 percent cleavers in White's sample.

The South African handaxe data reveal a different pattern (Fig. 2.1). In our sample, only one assemblage, Montagu 5, has more pointed than ovate forms. However, the percentage difference is never as marked as it is among the British data. Judged by Roe's 60 percent threshold, five of the eight South African assemblages would fall in the strongly uncommitted category. So, while ovate handaxes are more common than pointed ones, neither shape dominates assemblages in the manner that Roe, and subsequently White, have shown with the British data. This pattern, however, only considers handaxes. In his study of bifaces at Kilombe, in Kenya, Gowlett (1988) statistically demonstrated two modes in the material:

- a main group consisting of larger handaxes and cleavers
- a minor group consisting of small handaxes, without cleavers, and with other types of handaxes such as those associated with the Developed Oldowan.

Following Gowlett, a combined shape diagram for our South African sample, where cleavers make up 34 percent of all bifaces, results in six of the eight assemblages now qualifying for ovate membership. The only uncommitted assemblages are those from Fauresmith (59.3%) and Elandsfontein where 59% of the bifaces are either ovate or splayed. Roe's (1994) data from Olduvai support this pattern. Again, using the L1/L ratio (1994, table 8.23), seventeen of the eighteen handaxe assemblages qualify for automatic membership in the ovate tradition. The one uncommitted assemblage, HEB West 3, has 50 percent pointed and 50 percent ovates, the latter being a combined figure of ovate (48%) and splayed (2%) shapes. Cleavers are not common at Olduvai, comprising only 13 percent of all bifaces.

Discussion

What might account for this geographical patterning, and is it significant in terms of describing an aspect of hominid variability in the Acheulian world? When we started our project, Roe predicted that blank technology would distinguish Africa from Europe and he was of course right.

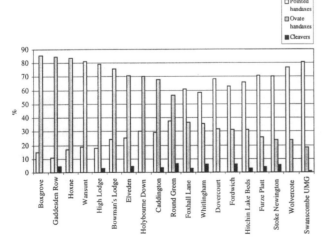

Fig. 2.5. The shape groupings of handaxes in British assemblages (after White 1998).

Our systematic sample confirms earlier work that the trademark of the African Acheulian is the production of bifaces from large flake blanks (Callow 1994, 253; Goodwin and Van Riet Lowe 1929, 36; Jones 1994, table 10.10; Ludwig and Harris 1998, 99–102; Sampson 1962, 29–30). The Acheulian is essentially a *débitage* based technology, not only in much of Africa but also in India (Korisettar and Rajaguru 1998; Petraglia 1998) and south-west Asia (Goren-Inbar 1995). Viewed against this widespread pattern it is perhaps ironic that those first handaxes, so beautifully illustrated by Frere in 1800 from Hoxne in eastern England, should be pointed examples made by *façonnage*. Two hundred years later we are able to account for these shapes because we now know that Acheulian hominids did not move stone very far, and habitually responded to nodule size and shape. Our study shows, however, that across much of the Acheulian world their involvement with stone produced flake blanks and from that engagement flowed the higher frequency of ovate shapes.

CONCLUSION: THE ROE LINE

Having demonstrated a default setting, which Jones (1994, 271) also regards as the natural outcome of manufacture and use, what accounts for it? White (1998, 22–23) argues for ovates as more efficient butchery tools. Wynn and Tierson (1990, 81) prefer instead a cultural difference in the learned standards of acceptable shapes. For others the handaxe is a non-negotiable mental template (Wenban-Smith 2000) while its symmetry is explained by sexual selection (Kohn and Mithen 1999). Finally, it is common, following Clark (1969), to find the entire Acheulian lumped as an undifferentiated Mode 2 technology.

The Acheulian, and particularly the handaxe, attracts universal explanations of this sort. The problem is that such interpretations smooth out the very variation which they should be looking to explain. To reintroduce the prospect of variation into the Acheulian, and in recognition of Roe's seminal contribution to this entity, we propose drawing a line across the Acheulian world that will structure future discussion. This Roe Line supersedes the famous division of handaxe and pebble tools drawn by Movius (1948) which, with the discovery of classic handaxes in the Bose Basin, south China (Hou *et al.* 2000), can no longer be sustained. The Roe Line separates the Acheulian into a flake (*débitage*) and nodule/core (*façonnage*) distribution. The line runs through Israel and across to West Africa. To the north is a world of *façonnage*, a tendency to more pointed forms and a greater control over shape set by the initial size and form of the raw material. To the south, and eastwards to India, are bifaces, including cleavers, made on flake blanks by *débitage*. Of course, flake blanks are found north of the Roe Line just as nodule/core reduction is found to the south, but these will be islands and isolates rather than continuous distributions over large territories.

Now, what becomes interesting about this new division

of the Acheulian world is the potential it affords to ask more interesting questions about shape. What it immediately highlights are those pointed forms. To what extent are these another 'default setting' where north of the Roe Line raw material size and shape conditioned the application of *façonnage* rather than *débitage*? What proportions of pointed forms might we expect to occur 'naturally' within a technological practice south of the Roe Line where ovates were the default because of large flake production? Beyond these techniques can we demonstrate, as Field (pers. comm.) suggests, that these pointed forms are 'thought about', representative perhaps of a discursive rather than a practical consciousness? Using a related vocabulary (Gamble 1999), are these pointed bifaces examples of specific skills employed by individuals at a place, rather than the generic skills of a social technology which yields ovates across regions? Finally, if we accept that technological skills are at the same time social skills, then Roe's analysis of shape, which brought order to an apparently random world, will have delivered promises we can still only guess at.

ACKNOWLEDGEMENTS

The research was supported by the Arts and Humanities Research Board (Grant No. AN5347/APN8525 'Lower Palaeolithic technology, raw material and population ecology') and the digital photography was assisted by Vicky Elefanti. We would like to express our sincere thanks to our South African colleagues. In particular Graham Avery of the South African Museum in Cape Town for access to collections and the opportunity to experience first hand the site of Elandsfontein. To Johann Binneman at the Albany Museum in Grahamstown for access to the Amanzi Springs collection, and to Peter Beaumont at the McGregor Museum in Kimberley for use of collections, numerous enthusiastic discussions and visits to the spectacular Vaal River sites. Also to Ray Inskeep for advice, suggestions and infectious enthusiasm. Mr J. Kriel for permission to visit Montagu Cave and to Mr P. Niven for permission to visit Amanzi Springs. John McNabb, Annabel Field and Dmitra Papagianni provided many helpful suggestions on earlier drafts.

REFERENCES

Butzer, K.W. 1974. Geo-archaeological interpretation of Acheulian calc-pan sites at Doornlaagte and Rooidam (Kimberley, South Africa). *Journal of Archeological Science* 1, 1–27.

Callow, P. 1994. The Olduvai bifaces: technology and raw materials. In M.D. Leakey and D.A. Roe (eds.) *Olduvai Gorge Volume 5: Excavations in Beds III, IV and the Masek Beds, 1968–1971*, 235–253. Cambridge University Press, Cambridge.

Carbonell, E., Mosquera, M. and Rodríguez, X.P. 1999. Out of Africa: the dispersal of the earliest technical systems reconsidered. *Journal of Anthropological Archaeology* 18, 119–136.

Clark, J.D. 1976. *The Prehistory of Africa*. Thames and Hudson, London.

Clark, J.G.D. 1969. *World Prehistory: A New Outline*. Cambridge University Press, Cambridge.

Deacon, H.J. 1970. The Acheulian occupation at Amanzi Springs, Uitenhage District, Cape Province. *Annals of the Cape Provincial Museums (Natural History)* 8, 89–189.

Deacon, H.J. and Deacon, J. 1999. *Human Beginnings in South Africa: Uncovering the Secrets of the Stone Age*. Altamira Press, Walnut Creek CA.

Dibble, H.L. 1987. The interpretation of Middle Palaeolithic scraper morphology. *American Antiquity* 52, 109–117.

Dibble, H.L. 1988. Typological aspects of reduction and intensity of utilization of lithic resources in the French Mousterian. In H.L. Dibble and A. Montet-White (eds.) *Upper Pleistocene Prehistory of Western Eurasia*, 181–198. The University Museum, University of Pennsylvania, Philadelphia.

Dibble, H.L. 1991. Local raw material exploitation and its effects on Lower and Middle Palaeolithic assemblage variability. In A. Montet-White and S. Holen (eds.) *Raw Material Economies among Prehistoric Hunter-Gatherers*, 33–46. University of Kansas Publications in Anthropology 19, Kansas City.

Gamble, C.S. 1997. The skills of the Lower Palaeolithic world. *Proceedings of the Prehistoric Society* 63, 407–410.

Gamble, C.S. 1999. *The Palaeolithic Societies of Europe*. Cambridge University Press, Cambridge.

Goodwin, A.J.H. and Van Riet Lowe, C. 1929. The Stone Age cultures of South Africa. *Annals of the South African Museum* 27, 1–289.

Goren-Inbar, N. 1995. The Lower Palaeolithic of Israel. In T.E. Levy (ed.) *The Archaeology of Society in the Holy Land*, 93–109. Leicester University Press, London.

Gowlett, J.A.J. 1988. A case of developed Oldowan in the Acheulean? *World Archaeology* 20, 13–26.

Hou, Y.M., Potts, R., Yuan, B.Y., Guo, Z.T., Deino, A., Wang, W., Clark, J., Xie, G.M. and Huang, W.W. 2000. Mid-Pleistocene Acheulean-like stone technology of the Bose Basin, South China. *Science* 287, 1622–1626.

Inskeep, R.R. 1965. Earlier Stone Age occupation at Amanzi, a preliminary investigation. *South African Journal of Science* 62, 229–242.

Isaac, G. 1989. *The Archaeology of Human Origins: Papers by Glynn Isaac edited by Barbara Isaac*. Cambridge University Press, Cambridge.

Jones, P.R. 1994. Results of experimental work in relation to the stone industries of Olduvai Gorge. In M.D. Leakey and D.A. Roe (eds.) *Olduvai Gorge Volume 5: Excavations in Beds III, IV and the Masek Beds, 1968–1971*, 254–298. Cambridge University Press, Cambridge.

Keller, C.M. 1973. *Montagu Cave in Prehistory: A Descriptive Analysis*. University of California Press Anthropological Records 28, Berkeley.

Klein, R.G. 1999. *The Human Career: Human Biological and Cultural Origins*. University of Chicago Press, Chicago.

Klein, R.G. and Cruz-Uribe, K. 1991. The bovids from Elandsfontein, South Africa, and their implications for the age, palaeoenvironment, and the origins of the site. *African Archaeological Review* 9, 21–79.

Kleindienst, M.R. 1962. Components of the East African assemblage, analytical approach. *Actes du IVe Congrès Panafricain de Préhistoire et de l'Etude du Quaternaire*. Léopoldville 1959, 81–111.

Kohn, M. and Mithen, S. 1999. Handaxes: products of sexual selection? *Antiquity* 73, 518–526.

Korisettar, R. and Rajaguru, S.N. 1998. Quaternary stratigraphy, palaeoclimate and the Lower Palaeolithic of India. In M.D. Petraglia and R. Korisettar (eds.) *Early Human Behaviour in Global Context: The Rise and Diversity of the Lower Palaeolithic World*, 304–342. Routledge, London.

Kuman, K. 1998. The earliest South African industries. In M.D. Petraglia and R. Korisettar (eds.) *Early Human Behaviour in Global Gontext: The Rise and Diversity of the Lower Palaeolithic World*, 151–186. Routledge, London.

Leakey, M.D. 1971. *Olduvai Gorge: Excavations in Beds I and II, 1960–1963*. Cambridge University Press, Cambridge.

Ludwig, B.V. and Harris, J.W.K. 1998. Towards a technological reassessment of East African Plio-Pleistocene lithic assemblages. In M.D. Petraglia and R. Korisettar (eds.) *Early Human Behaviour in Global Context: The Rise and Diversity of the Lower Palaeolithic World*, 84–107. Routledge, London

MacRae, R.J. and Moloney, N. (eds.) 1988. *Non-Flint Stone Tools and the Palaeolithic Occupation of Britain*. British Archaeological Reports British Series 189, Oxford.

Malan, B.D. 1962. The stone industry of the site at Elandsfontein, Hopefield, South Africa. *Actes du IVe Congrès Panafricain de Préhistoire et de l'Etude du Quaternaire*. Léopoldville 1959, Section 3, 225–232.

Mason, R.J. 1966. The excavation of Doornlaagte Earlier Stone Age camp, Kimberley district. *Actas del V Congreso Panafricano de Prehistoria y de Estudio del Cuaternario*. Tenerife 1963, Section 2, 187–188.

Mason, R.J. 1967. Analytical procedures in the Earlier and Middle Stone Age cultures in Southern Africa. In W.W. Bishop and J.D. Clark (eds.) *Background to Evolution in Africa*, 737–764. University of Chicago Press, Chicago.

McPherron, S.P. 1994. *A Reduction Model for Variability in Acheulian Biface Morphology*. Unpublished PhD dissertation, University of Pennsylvania.

McPherron, S.P. 1995. A re-examination of the British biface data. *Lithics* 16, 47–63.

Movius, H. 1948. The Lower Palaeolithic cultures of southern and eastern Asia. *Transactions of the American Philosophical Society* 38, 239–420.

Petraglia, M.D. 1998. The Lower Palaeolithic of India and its bearing on the Asian record. In M.D. Petraglia and R. Korisettar (eds.) *Early Human Behaviour in Global Context: The Rise and Diversity of the Lower Palaeolithic World*, 343–390. Routledge, London.

Roberts, M.B., Gamble, C.S. and Bridgland, D.R. 1995. The earliest occupation of Europe: the British Isles. In W. Roebroeks and T. van Kolfschoten (eds.) *The Earliest Occupation of Europe*, 165–191. University of Leiden Press, Leiden.

Roe, D.A. 1964. The British Lower and Middle Palaeolithic: some problems, methods of study and preliminary results. *Proceedings of the Prehistoric Society* 30, 245–267.

Roe, D.A. 1968a. British Lower and Middle Palaeolithic handaxe groups. *Proceedings of the Prehistoric Society* 34, 1–82.

Roe, D.A. 1968b. *A Gazetteer of British Lower and Middle Palaeolithic Sites*. Council for British Archaeology Research Report 8, London.

Roe, D.A. 1981. *The Lower and Middle Palaeolithic Periods in Britain*. Routledge and Kegan Paul, London.

Roe, D.A. 1994. A metrical analysis of selected sets of handaxes and cleavers from Olduvai Gorge. In M.D. Leakey and D.A. Roe (eds.) *Olduvai Gorge Volume 5: Excavations in Beds III, IV and the Masek Beds, 1968–1971*, 146–234. Cambridge University Press, Cambridge.

Roe, D.A. 2001. The Kalambo Falls large cutting tools: a comparative metrical and statistical analysis. In J.D. Clark (ed.) *Kalambo Falls Prehistoric Site, III: The Earlier Cultures: Middle and Earlier Stone Age*, 429–599. Cambridge University Press, Cambridge.

Sampson, C.G. 1962. The Cape Hangklip main site. *Journal of the University of Cape Town Science Society* 5, 15–24.

Sampson, C.G. 1972. *The Stone Age Industries of the Orange River Scheme and South Africa*. Memoirs of the National Museum 6, Bloemfontein.

Saragusti, I., Sharon, I., Katzenelson, O. and Avnir, D. 1998. Quantitative analysis of the symmetry of artifacts: Lower Palaeolithic handaxes. *Journal of Archaeological Science* 25, 817–825.

Singer, R. and Crawford, J.R. 1957. The significance of the archaeological discoveries at Hopefield, South Africa. *Journal of the Royal Anthropological Institute* 88, 11–19.

Singer, R. and Wymer, J.J. 1968. Archaeological investigations at the Saldanha skull site in South Africa. *South African Archaeological Bulletin* 25, 63–74.

Wenban-Smith, F.F. 2000. Technology and typology. In F.F. Wenban-Smith, C.S. Gamble and A.M. ApSimon (eds.) The Palaeolithic site at Red Barns, Portchester, Hampshire. *Proceedings of the Prehistoric Society* 66, 209–255.

White, M.J. 1998. On the significance of Acheulean biface variability in southern Britain. *Proceedings of the Prehistoric Society* 64, 15–44.

Wymer, J.J. 1982. *The Palaeolithic Age*. Croom Helm, London.

Wymer, J.J. 1999. *The Lower Palaeolithic Occupation of Britain*. Trust for Wessex Archaeology and English Heritage, Salisbury.

Wynn, T. and Tierson, F. 1990. Regional comparison of the shapes of later Acheulean handaxes. *American Anthropologist* 92, 73–84.

3. An Acheulian settlement pattern in the Upper Karoo region of South Africa

C. Garth Sampson

ABSTRACT

The Karoo is semi-desert plateau with sparse plant cover, thin soils and extensive surface erosion. Consequently, Acheulian lithic assemblages are almost all at the surface and are highly visible, so that reasonably complete site distribution maps can be compiled. One such map covering 5000 sq km is analyzed here. It contains over 400 Acheulian sites and some 600 Acheulian quarries at major hornfels outcrops. There are no adequate chronological controls for dividing this sample into phases. Acheulian sites are organized in three large concentrations on the landscape, with almost empty ground between them. These swarms of sites do not correlate with thinner sediment cover nor are they found in areas which were more intensively searched. The only general correlation is with areas where larger bodies of hornfels are more abundant and concentrated, although individual sites are not themselves close to such outcrops. More remarkably, hominids appear to have systematically avoided spring eyes and riverbanks, in fact all places with surface water. This contrasts sharply with the Holocene settlement pattern in which most sites are clustered tightly around the water points. Isolated handaxes bespeak mobility between Acheulian sites and perhaps between site concentrations, but their distribution provides no strong support for the notion that the site clusters reflect territories.

INTRODUCTION

The research potential of systematically compiled maps of Acheulian find-spots at a regional scale was first demonstrated by Derek Roe in his classic paper *The British Lower and Middle Palaeolithic: some problems, methods of study and preliminary results* (Roe 1964). His comprehensive map provides the inspiration for this modest essay in spatial analysis of some Acheulian site location choices in a very different environment, namely the Karoo scrub desert of central South Africa. Unlike the collections randomly accumulated over the course of a century which Roe so carefully documented and plotted (Roe 1968), this essay is based on a single, systematic survey (Sampson 1985, 30–37) conducted between 1979–81 in the upper and middle reaches of the Seacow (also written Seekoei or Zeekoe) River valley, an area of some 5000 square kilometers (Fig. 3.1). Museum collections were not consulted, and almost everything that will be mentioned here is still lying in the veldt where we found it.

SITE NUMBERS AND DISTRIBUTION

An Acheulian presence at the southern end of the African continent was recognized at about the same time as the initial discoveries in France (Cohen 1999), and subsequent surface collecting has demonstrated a quite astonishing density of sites in those places where knowing eyes have searched (Clark 1967). However, professional interest in Acheulian studies has lagged far behind those of later periods, and the map of excavated Acheulian sites (Fig. 3.1) would have looked much the same in 1970 (Butzer 1974; Deacon 1970; Fock 1968; Humphreys 1969; Keller

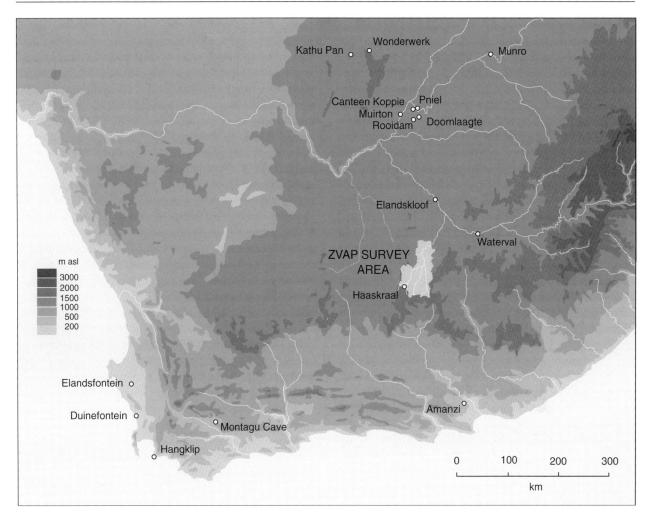

Fig. 3.1. Location of the Zeekoe Valley Archaeological Project (ZVAP) in the upper Karoo, South Africa, showing relief, main drainage patterns and excavated Acheulian sites.

1973; Klein 1978; Mason 1966, 1969; Sampson 1962, 1972; Singer and Wymer 1968), with only three new excavations reported in the last 30 years (Beaumont 1990a, 1990b; Beaumont *et al.* 1984; Binneman and Beaumont 1992; Klein *et al.* 1999; Partridge and Dalbey 1986), plus a few others still under investigation (P. Beaumont pers. comm.).

Most of the artefact assemblages recovered from these buried sites turned out to be derived, and without datable associations. Even the rare finds with potentially intact spatial patterning are not easily interpreted in terms of modern human behaviour (Klein in press). Like most other regions in Africa (the Rift Valley spectacularly excepted), datable Acheulian sites with fauna in trustworthy contexts are hard to find. Until some novel approaches to the study of the abundant surface material can be developed, professional indifference to Lower Palaeolithic (colloq. 'Early Stone Age') problems in Africa's southernmost region is likely to persist. This is a pity. The superabundant, ubiquitous surface record plus the astounding riverine occurrences like those exposed

in the Vaal gravels (Power 1955) point squarely to the intriguing possibility that the south was, for much of the Middle Pleistocene, the most densely populated region on earth. Cases like Montagu Cave layer 3, where almost a quarter of a million artefacts accumulated (Schick 1992, 21) reinforce this view.

An easily tested model to explain such a build-up would run something like this: demographic pressure on a southward-dispersing hominid population, undergoing a successful adaptation that allows it to break free from its parent habitat in the tropical savannah belt, encounters a continental cul-de-sac. Unlike the northward expansion of *Homo erectus* (*sensu lato*) into entire new continents, the southerners have nowhere to go and the landscape simply fills up. While this is an intuitively reasonable scenario, it remains to be systematically tested. Once established, we will be in a better position to judge whether higher population density in the south can be linked to subsequent evolutionary events, particularly the emergence of anatomically and behaviourally modern humans.

DEFINING HIGHER POPULATION DENSITIES

How are we to establish that Middle Pleistocene population densities were indeed higher in this part of Southern Africa? The only possible avenue by which the proposition can be tested is to map and count sites on a massive scale (Paddaya 1991, 115) and in several regions. A good place to start is the Karoo, as demonstrated by the results presented here. Our fieldwork yielded some 1100 Acheulian occurrences, more than doubling the known inventory of all Acheulian sites in South Africa. Of these, only the site of Haaskraal Pan was sealed, potentially datable and associated with a few scraps of fauna (Partridge and Dalbey 1986). Although it remains stubbornly intractable to dating in spite of the full array of modern geoarchaeological techniques applied to it (Dalbey in prep.), Haaskraal Pan at least demonstrates an Acheulian presence in Isotope Stage 9 or earlier. The rest of the sites are all surface occurrences traditionally regarded as lacking in any potential, their organic associations long gone, and their spatial patterning wrecked. For age estimates we are obliged to fall back on shaky typological comparisons with the East African Acheulian record, and can only surmise that there is no evidence of an 'Early' stage of technology, a few with 'Middle' stage biface reduction, while most, including Haaskraal Pan, have specimens with 'Later' stage attributes, following the classic definitions of Isaac (1975). There are also many with associated Levallois technology and traditionally ascribed to the 'Fauresmith' Industry (Goodwin and Van Riet Lowe 1929, 71–94). This subjective impression has yet to be tested by measuring patination thicknesses on typical bifaces.

So much for chronological controls, or rather the lack of them. However, the survey covers a large enough area, and is complete and systematic enough, that fresh opportunities emerge for studying patterns of site distribution in ways not possible with Lower Palaeolithic data bases from other parts of the world. In most places where Acheulian artefacts are found, the overriding problem with this approach is that false blanks may occur on the assembled distribution map due to patches where many sites remain buried and out of sight. In the Seacow valley, however, matters are greatly helped by the notoriously rapid rate of Karoo surface erosion. Here, the sediment mantle is seldom more than ten centimetres thick and any deeper alluvial strips are all post-Acheulian in age. Indeed, most of the Acheulian occurrences we found had probably never been buried, and all the artefacts are heavily patinated. Thus it is reasonably certain that the distribution patterns which emerge from this study do not result from differential site burial and/or exposure histories, but really do reflect the locational choices by the hominids who formed those sites. If there are blank spots on the map it is because there are no sites there: we have evidence of absence rather than absence of evidence.

HABITAT AND OCCUPATION

The sheer number of occurrences is itself remarkable when we consider the challenging habitat in which they occur. There are only three recurring landforms dominated by vast plains made up of typical Karoo flats (Fig. 3.2), all above 1200 m elevation, interspersed with low dolerite hills and ridges. The mountains rise to 2000 m and are restricted to the south and south-east flank of the study area. Today, this is a treeless scrub desert with unreliable summer rainfall which supports a thin, seasonal grass cover. The grass disappears entirely in the winter, when severe night frosts occur for 3–4 months and snow falls once or twice during the season. Although the valley is now subdivided into large sheep farms, in the nineteenth century it still supported huge herds of game thanks both to the small fleshy leaves of the Karoo scrub bushes, most of which have very high nutritional values, as well as to the many dependable waterholes. In late Holocene and historical times a wide variety of grazing ungulates lived here, plus all the usual carnivores and scavengers in attendance. Lions were particularly common, and hippos were present in the long, deep pool chains found along the middle and lower reaches of the river, hence its name, derived from the Dutch 'Zeekoe' (Neville 1996; Plug and Sampson 1996).

Two decades of research here suggests that human occupation of the valley was restricted to the interglacial episodes attributed to Isotope Stages 1, 3, 5 and 7. More by implication than by any direct evidence (see above), Acheulian occupation was probably restricted to Stage 9 and to an unknown number of preceding interglacials. During the major glacial episodes, populations dwindled to below the level of archaeological visibility, and it can be assumed that cold desertic conditions prevailed (Tyson 1999, 340). Traces of mid-Holocene occupation are also elusive (Bousman 1991), which suggests there may have been brief and/or minor population crashes during earlier interglacials as well. Even during the warmest intervals, the vegetation must have been sparse, possibly grassier than today, with a thin scatter of acacias in the lower reaches. Otherwise it would have been treeless as it is today, a marginal habitat by any definition.

Whenever the Acheulian pioneers first arrived here, they focused their tool-making activities at several specific swarms of low ridges and hills and in the immediately adjacent flats. The south-west headwaters were clearly more attractive. Mountains were generally avoided, as were the huge open plains (Fig. 3.2). However, handaxes were carried out on to those plains, and occasionally up into the mountains, where they were abandoned several kilometers or more from the nearest site (Fig. 3.3). This map provides the most compelling evidence yet that handaxes were carried from place to place. While more recent handaxe carriers cannot be ruled out, the hominids themselves must be responsible for the bulk of such isolates.

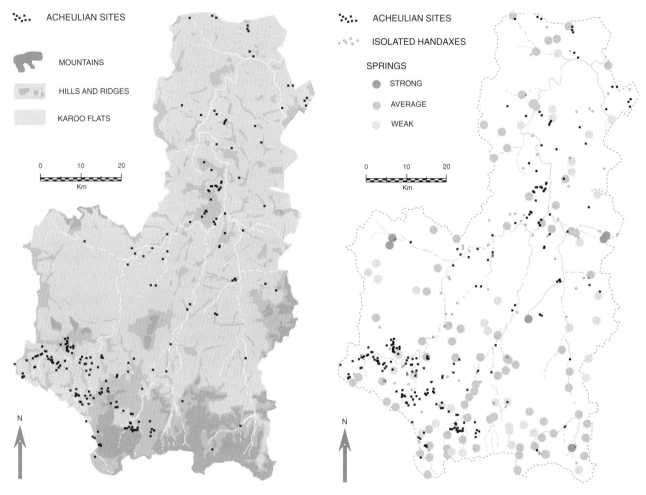

Fig. 3.2. Distribution of some 400 Acheulian sites in the upper and central reaches of the Seacow (also Seekoei, Zeekoe) River, with main relief features.

Fig. 3.3. Almost all Acheulian sites and isolated handaxes are found more than 1 km distant from spring eyes, the only reliable waterpoints. Although few springs flow at the surface today (windpumps have lowered the watertable), nineteenth century farm survey diagrams describe their relative strengths (Neville 1996).

Those same hominids were at special pains not to linger within a half-hour's walk (1 km radius) of any spring eye, even the larger and more reliable ones. Note, however, that a few sites in the headwaters were located nearer to, but never at, spring eyes. This map makes a vivid contrast with that of the late Holocene and historical traces of Bushman campsites in those same areas. Literally thousands of these 'Smithfield' sites, many of them large, dense lithic scatters with elliptical stone windbreak anchors, form tight clusters near the centres of the 1 km spring eye radii (Sampson 1984, 1985, 92). Evidently the Bushmen were better able to counter the threat from large nocturnal predators, particularly lions, than were the *Homo erectus* (*sensu lato*) groups who caused the Acheulian sites to accumulate. Bushmen bands warded off attack by locating on boulder-strewn dolerite ridge tops overlooking the spring, and by the judicious use of bonfires. Acheulian groups handled the threat by simply staying out of the danger area.

Any doubts that the Middle Pleistocene locations of these spring eyes may have differed from today can be swiftly dispelled. Springs erupt at intersections between dolerite dykes and prevailing drainage basins, and are thus dictated by bedrock geology. Under these constraints it is impossible for a spring eye to 'migrate' over time.

The other doubt which can be quickly disposed of is that spring activity has buried nearby Acheulian occurrences in sediment. Local springs run remarkably clear and do not carry heavy sediment loads leading to spring mounds. Every eye in question has been massively trenched and widened by Dutch trekboer settlers, and the heavily calcified sediment was usually scraped up into a catchment dam immediately upstream of the eye (Neville 1996). While such dam walls are littered with Later Stone Age lithics, we have never found Acheulian material in any of them.

There are also many less reliable seeps and minor, seasonal water holes, but these were also off-limits to

Acheulian settlement, with one notable exception in the central headwaters where several contiguous seeps occur (Fig. 3.4).

Some deep pools in the river channels, fed by minor springs in the streambed, once doubled as hippo wallows in historical times (*ibid.*). These too were avoided, except for one chain of pools in the south-west corner of the study area (Fig. 3.5). Apart from these pools, most of the river channel beds remain dry for much of the year, particularly the upstream stretches, but they do flow episodically in summer when they could serve as ephemeral water points.

Although some stretches of riverbank appear to be the focus of settlement, they do not exercise a convincing 'pull' on the settlement pattern, in fact more than half of all Acheulian sites are over a kilometer from the nearest modern riverbank (Fig. 3.6). Since all channels are incised into dolerite 'poorts' (gaps) they are locked into position

and unable to migrate laterally. Although they must have flowed in much the same pattern in Middle Pleistocene times, the possibility that they have been scoured out up to a kilometer on either side in post-Acheulian times has yet to be investigated.

This would be worth doing, because it is generally assumed that the Acheulian reflects a riverbank and lakeshore adaptation, an impression heavily reinforced by the British Acheulian mapping project which inspired this study. Indeed, so strong is this impression that it is in danger of becoming elevated to a formal proposition (Deacon 1998, 27; Deacon and Deacon 1991, 81). Alas, our results do not confirm that impression. Evidently handaxe-making hominids kept their distance from the isolated water points so typical of a Karoo landscape, going some distance from their workstations to drink along with the rest of the game, and exercising the same due caution as other animals while at the water's edge. The

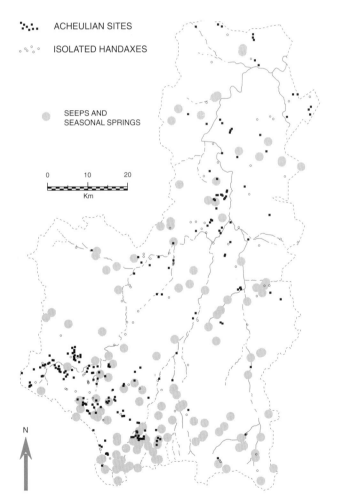

Fig. 3.4. With one exception in the central headwaters, Acheulian sites and isolated handaxes are found more than 1 km distant from seeps and minor seasonal springs that flow only after rains.

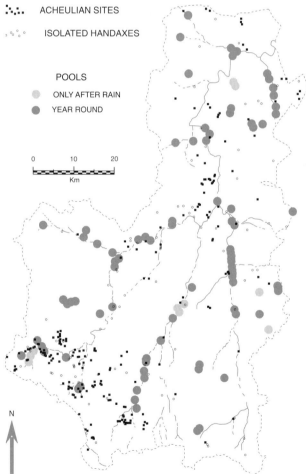

Fig. 3.5. With two exceptions in the headwaters, Acheulian sites and isolated handaxes are found more than 1 km distant from the pools shown on nineteenth century farm survey diagrams (Neville 1996). Many of these have been altered by modern dams and weirs.

evidence suggests that loitering at waterholes to hunt or scavenge was not encouraged.

This raises the intriguing possibility that on English rivers it may have been the flint gravels rather than the water itself which was the main attraction. Large, continually flowing rivers would have been less likely to concentrate the game at specific places at particular times of day, so the risk of carnivore attack would have been more diffuse. It would follow that many places with large, high quality flint gravel exposures near water would be that much less hazardous.

WATER SOURCES VERSUS RAW MATERIALS

In the Seacow valley, the shales and soft sandstones found in the gravels are unsuitable for knapping. Hornfels, a thermally indurated shale/sandstone, is the only stone available which is suitable for making tools. It outcrops at

some 1600 point sources in the study area. All of these were quarried in the past, including a huge Late Tertiary gravel fan which has masked a major set of hornfels outcrops (Fig. 3.7). Not all outcrops were quarried by Acheulian toolmakers, only those exposures yielding large and unflawed blocks of stone. Acheulian quarry debris is easily distinguished from later debris by its larger size, distinctive technology, and highly characteristic patination, the colour, texture and thickness of which matches that on artefacts on the Acheulian sites. Not surprisingly, more high-quality hornfels quarries occur in and around areas with large numbers of hornfels outcrops (Fig. 3.7). However, only two of the several clusters of Acheulian sites are within one kilometer of a quarry (Fig. 3.8). Evidently the Acheulian population in this valley was not uniformly 'tethered' by the whereabouts of the best quality stone. At many sites, all the rock used there had to be carried from over a kilometer away. The hornfels quarries could not have been particularly dangerous places at which to loiter, since they would not

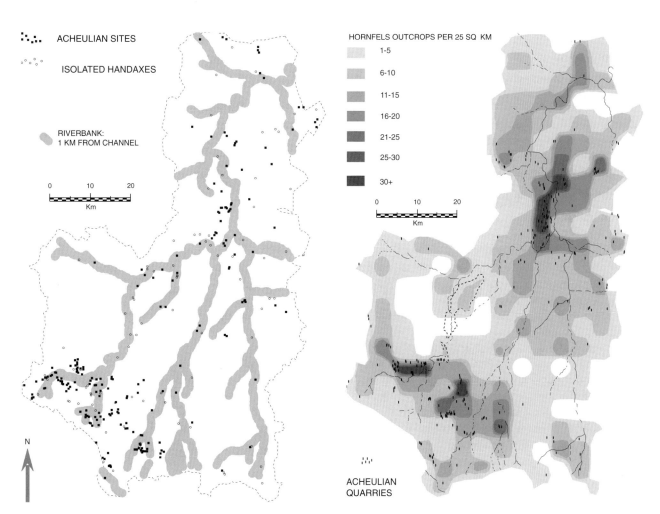

Fig. 3.6. More than half the Acheulian occurrences are located over 1 km from the modern stream bank.

Fig. 3.7. Hornfels outcrops are seldom much larger than an office desk, but they are very densely distributed on this landscape. About 600 of the largest and least flawed outcrops were quarried by Acheulian toolmakers.

attract other prey and hence large carnivores. While the odd predator may have learned to lie in wait for those foraging for stone, there is no reason to suspect that this became a widespread predatory tactic.

So why did Acheulian people go to the trouble of carrying rock such distances? Common sense dictates that they would try to locate the main foci of their activities at places equidistant from both water and hornfels. Preliminary attempts to hand-fit Thiessen polygons to our mapped data show some potential for this line of enquiry, in that several Acheulian sites do fall at or near polygon intersections, but this is by no means a universal pattern and the few 'hits' thus far observed could be due to random chance. Further investigation has been postponed until all the data are erected on a GIS platform and locations have been aligned with the original air photos used in the field. GIS will permit a more rapid and accurate completion of the search.

However, some clear patterns do emerge from this first phase of investigation. The distribution pattern of Acheulian sites is different from that of Seacow River Bushmen. The Bushman mobility pattern must reflect a rational approach operating within particular territories, which can be understood by comparison with the Kalahari Bushman. In the most simplistic model, the Bushman camp rotated periodically from one spring eye to another. With each new halt, band members radiated out daily from camp to the surrounding minor water points for hunting, gathering, and collecting firewood. Of course, the reality of their movements was much less orderly than this, and there was a lot of seasonal aggregation when circumstances allowed, giving rise to camp sizes far greater than those encountered in the Kalahari (Neville 1996). All of this must have contributed to those dense clusters of 'Smithfield' sites at spring eyes, with the halos of different kinds of small chipping station in the countryside between springs.

The Acheulian pattern certainly cannot be interpreted in such terms. Even if we do not have a living analogue for it, it is neither random nor chaotic. There are two loose groups of contiguous sites focused on quarries (Fig. 3.9), two contiguous groups focused on springs, one on pools, another on seeps and yet another on seeps and pools.

The largest cluster of Acheulian sites relates to hornfels quarries along the left bank of the main Seacow drainage channel, downstream from the junction of all the major tributaries. Today, this stretch of channel contains standing water at several points during all times of year. The latter are probably fed by seeps in the river bed, and it is tempting to suppose that they were also present during the Acheulian. If so, then there was no need to locate their group activities (sites) too far from the quarries, because more extensive surface water with a lower risk of predator attack was near to hand. The same applies to that smaller 'quarry focus' group in the south-west corner of the study area. Not only is there a reliable spring close to the quarries, but there is standing water in the bend of the river to its south. In the higher headwaters, the channels seldom carry standing water

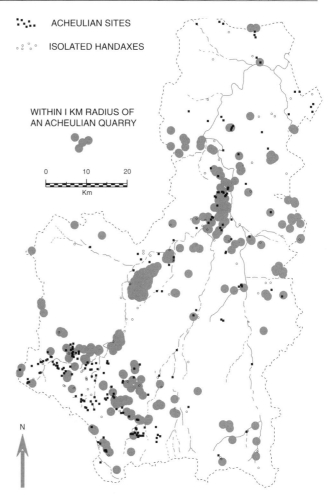

ACHEULIAN SITES

ISOLATED HANDAXES

WITHIN I KM RADIUS OF
AN ACHEULIAN QUARRY

0   10   20
Km

N

Fig. 3.8. While many Acheulian sites are within 1 km of a quarry, the pattern is patchy and there are as many which are farther afield.

for more than a few days, hence the need to locate closer to even quite ephemeral water points, and the willingness to carry stone farther away from the quarries.

The test implications of this model are clear. If we extended the survey further downstream, we should expect to find Acheulian site clusters entirely focused on quarries because even more standing water would have been available. At the same time we should find no further clusters of Acheulian sites focused on springs, seeps, and pools.

None of this helps to explain the locations of those few Acheulian sites which are some distance, in some cases far, from both hornfels and water. Assuming that we have not missed something in our survey, one possibility is that these are places where hominids were able to get early control of some large mammal carcass and to retain possession of it while it was completely consumed. Without faunal preservation we are in no position to test such models, but we could at least test the null hypothesis by a repeat search to make sure we have not missed a not-too-distant hornfels outcrop or a minor seep. However, it is unlikely

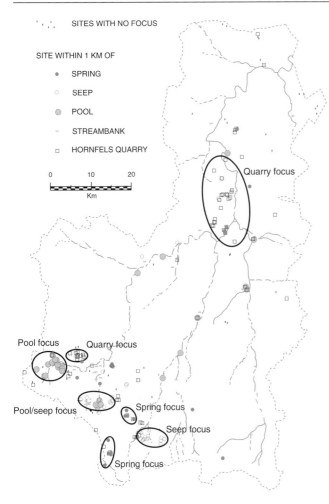

Fig. 3.9. Clusters of Acheulian sites with a common focus. i.e. all within 1 km of either a quarry, spring eye, pool or seep. Note also the rare sites far from any water point or stone source.

that any amount of re-survey will alter the overall pattern which has emerged, namely dense swarms of occurrences, one in the south-western headwaters, one in the south-central headwaters and another just downstream from the convergence of the major tributaries (Fig. 3.9). Are these the residues of individual groups each tethered to a territory and habituated to circulating among the outcrops and water points within those territories? Alternatively, are the clusters just the smeared signal of a larger, perhaps random circulation of personnel habituated to camping near a particular set of resources each time they passed through that way on some infinitely larger pattern of drift across the Karoo landscape?

Such questions can only be addressed when the potential of hornfels for chemical and mineralogical source tracking is better understood. If handaxes can be elementally fingerprinted to their parent rock outcrops, the way becomes open to investigating the distances and directions they were carried. Current pilot studies by XRD, XRF, and microscopy, indicate pronounced chemical variability between

outcrops. However, a carefully designed and tightly controlled study of 37 outcrops near Haaskraal Pan by INAA suggests that within-outcrop variability is so wide (Jarvis 2000) that this rather costly method may not be feasible. The advent of more sensitive, and quicker methods, such as laser ablation ICP-MS, may improve the odds.

CONCLUSION

Difficulties notwithstanding, our map provides unique insights into Acheulian spatial organization not obtainable from other sources. There are over 400 sites and 600 quarries which can be correlated to the Acheulian on the basis of similar patination and technology. The site distribution is markedly unlike those of the terminal Pleistocene and Holocene industries in the same area, which are sharply concentrated around the many available water points. Acheulian sites are organized into three large concentrations on the landscape, with relatively empty ground between them. These site swarms cannot be explained as spurious or random, nor do they equate with areas of thinner sediment cover, nor do they occur in more intensively searched areas. The only loose correlation seems to be with the abundance of hornfels outcrops, although individual sites are seldom closely tethered to the outcrops. With two small exceptions in the drier, upper headwaters, spring eyes were consistently avoided. Isolated handaxes indicate that these objects were carried from one site to another. One possible interpretation is that the concentrations represent group ranges. Another is that they were way-stations within even larger mobility patterns or within some larger pattern of group movement. Whichever pattern future source-tracking studies may support, the sheer abundance of material in this marginal habitat hints strongly that mounting population pressure was encouraging dispersal into such treeless, poorly watered niches at the very limit of their adaptive capabilities. Only when comparable semi-desert habitats in North Africa, Spain, the Near East and India have been sampled on this scale, will we know for certain if the South African landscape was the most heavily populated.

ACKNOWLEDGEMENTS

The foot survey and mapping of this huge area was accomplished by David Arter, Britt Bousman, Tim Dalbey, Emily Lovick, Steve Lovick, Les Peters, Joe Saunders and the author. All logistics were directed by Beatrix Sampson. Funding for the survey was provided by the National Science Foundation, Washington, D.C.

REFERENCES

Beaumont, P.B. 1990a. Wonderwerk Cave. In P. Beaumont and D. Morris (eds.) *Guide to Archaeological Sites in the Northern Cape*, 101–134. McGregor Museum, Kimberley
Beaumont, P.B. 1990b. Kathu Pan. In P. Beaumont and D. Morris

(eds.) *Guide to Archaeological Sites in the Northern Cape*, 75–100. McGregor Museum, Kimberley.

Beaumont, P.B., van Zinderen Bakker, E.M. and Vogel, J.C. 1984. Environmental changes since 32 kyrs B.P. at Kathu Pan, Northern Cape, South Africa. In J.C. Vogel (ed.) *Late Cenozoic Palaeoclimates of the Southern Hemisphere*, 324–338. A.A. Balkema, Rotterdam.

Binneman, J. and Beaumont, P.B. 1992. Use-wear analysis of two Acheulian handaxes from Wonderwerk Cave, northern Cape. *Southern African Field Archaeology* 1, 92–97.

Bousman, C.B. 1991. *Holocene Paleoecology and Later Stone Age Hunter-Gatherer Adaptations in the South African Interior Plateau.* Unpublished PhD dissertation, Southern Methodist University, Dallas.

Butzer, K.W. 1974. Geo-archaeological interpretation of Acheulian calc-pan sites at Doornlaagte and Rooidam (Kimberley, South Africa). *Journal of Archaeological Science* 1, 1–27.

Clark, J.D. 1967. *Atlas of African Prehistory.* University of Chicago Press, Chicago.

Cohen, A. 1999. Mary Elizabeth Barber, the Bowkers and South African prehistory. *South African Archaeological Bulletin* 54, 120–127.

Deacon, H.J. 1970. The Acheulian occupation at Amanzi Springs, Uitenhage District, Cape Province. *Annals of the Cape Provincial Museums (Natural History)* 8, 89–189.

Deacon, H.J. 1998. Elandsfontein and Klasies River revisited. In N. Ashton, F. Healy and P. Pettitt (eds.) *Stone Age Archaeology: Essays in Honour of John Wymer*, 23–28. Lithics Studies Society Occasional Paper 6, Oxbow Monograph 102. Oxbow Books, Oxford.

Deacon, H.J. and Deacon, J. 1999. *Human Beginnings in South Africa: Uncovering the Secrets of the Stone Age.* Altamira Press, Walnut Creek CA.

Fock, G.J. 1968. A sealed site of the First Intermediate. *South African Journal of Science* 64, 153–159.

Goodwin, A.J.H. and Van Riet Lowe, C. 1929. The Stone Age Cultures of South Africa. *Annals of the South African Museum* 27, 1–289.

Humphreys, A.J.B. 1969. Later Acheulian or Fauresmith? A contribution. *Annals of the Cape Provincial Museums (Natural History)* 6, 87–101.

Isaac, G.Ll. 1975. Stratigraphy and cultural patterns in East Africa during the middle ranges of Pleistocene time. In K.W. Butzer and G.Ll. Isaac (eds.) *After the Australopithecines: Stratigraphy, Ecology and Culture Change in the Middle Pleistocene*, 543–569. Mouton, The Hague.

Jarvis, H.W. 2000. *Lithic Sourcing and the Detection of Territoriality among Later Stone Age Hunter-Gatherers in South Africa.* Unpublished PhD dissertation, State University of New York at Buffalo.

Keller, C.M. 1973. *Montagu Cave in Prehistory: A Descriptive Analysis.* University of California Press Anthropological Records 28, Berkeley.

Klein, R.G. 1978. The fauna and overall interpretation of the 'Cutting 10' Acheulean site at Elandsfontein (Hopefield), southwestern Cape Province, South Africa. *Quaternary Research* 10, 69–83.

Klein, R.G. in press. The Early Stone Age of southern Africa. *South African Archaeological Bulletin.*

Klein, R.G., Avery, G., Cruz-Uribe, K., Halkett, D., Hart, T., Milo, R.G. and Volman, T.P. 1999. Duinefontein 2: an Acheulian site in the Western Cape Province of South Africa. *Journal of Human Evolution* 37, 153–190.

Mason, R.J. 1966. The excavation of Doornlaagte Earlier Stone Age camp, Kimberley district. *Actas del V Congresso Panafricano de Preistoria y de Estudio del Cuaternario.* Tenerife 1963, Section 2, 187–188.

Mason, R.J. 1969. The Oppermansdrif Dam project – Vaal basin. *South African Archaeological Bulletin* 24, 182–192.

Neville, D.E. 1996. *European Impacts on the Seacow River Valley and its Hunter-Gatherer Inhabitants.* Unpublished PhD dissertation, University of Cape Town.

Paddaya, K. 1991. The Acheulian culture of the Hungsi-Baichbal valleys, peninsular India: a processual study. *Quatär* 41–42, 111–138.

Partridge, T.C. and Dalbey, T.S. 1986. Geoarchaeology of the Haaskraal Pan: a preliminary palaeoenvironmental model. *Palaeoecology of Africa* 17, 69–78.

Plug, I. and Sampson, C.G. 1996. European and Bushman impacts on Karoo fauna in the nineteenth century: an archaeological perspective. *South African Archaeological Bulletin* 51, 26–31.

Power, J.H. 1955. Power's Site, Vaal River. *South African Archaeological Bulletin* 10, 96–101.

Roe, D.A. 1964. The British Lower and Middle Palaeolithic: some problems, methods of study and preliminary results. *Proceedings of the Prehistoric Society* 30, 245–267.

Roe, D.A. 1968. *A Gazetteer of British Lower and Middle Palaeolithic Sites.* Council for British Archaeology Research Report 8, London.

Sampson, C.G. 1962. The Cape Hangklip main site. *Journal of the University of Cape Town Science Society* 5, 15–24.

Sampson, C.G. 1972. *The Stone Age Industries of the Orange River Scheme and South Africa.* Memoirs of the National Museum 6, Bloemfontein.

Sampson, C.G. 1984. Site clusters in the Smithfield settlement pattern. *South African Archaeological Bulletin* 39, 5–23.

Sampson, C.G. 1985. *Atlas of Stone Age Settlement in the Central and Upper Seacow Valley.* Memoirs of the National Museum 20, Bloemfontein.

Schick, K. 1992. Geoarchaeological analysis of an Acheulian site at Kalambo Falls, Zambia. *Geoarchaeology* 7, 1–26.

Singer, R. and Wymer, J.J. 1968. Archaeological investigations at the Saldanha skull site in South Africa. *South African Archaeological Bulletin* 25, 63–74.

Tyson, P.D. 1999. Late Quaternary and Holocene paleoclimates of southern Africa: a synthesis. *South African Journal of Geology* 102, 348–390.

4. The shape of things to come. A speculative essay on the role of the Victoria West phenomenon at Canteen Koppie, during the South African Earlier Stone Age

John McNabb

ABSTRACT

The Victoria West is a much discussed component of the broader Prepared Core Technology phenomenon. Yet its origins and relationship with the MSA in Africa remain poorly understood. This paper offers some observations on Victoria West technology, and speculates on what they may mean.

INTRODUCTION

Derek Roe's name is synonymous with bifaces. I would like to pay tribute to him by focusing on one aspect of biface studies, that of the manufacture of blanks for bifaces and cleavers in Southern Africa. In particular, I wish to concentrate on the site of Canteen Koppie, near Kimberley in the Northern Cape, South Africa. This was a site much beloved of archaeological practitioners during the first great era of Palaeolithic research, and many myths have grown up around it. This is at heart an artefact paper, and I hope Derek will enjoy the spirit in which it is offered.

THE VICTORIA WEST DISCOVERED AND DEFINED

What is the Victoria West phenomenon? The label is applied to the African form of prepared core technology and so refers to cores and flakes of a particular visual character, made by the application of specific patterns of flaking. Artefacts of this kind were first discovered in the vicinity of Victoria West in the Karoo region by a local magistrate who published a short note on his discoveries (Jansen 1926). Originally he believed these artefacts to be tools rather than cores. In his seminal 1929 synthesis, A.J.H. Goodwin described the three variants noted by Jansen (Fig. 4.1). The visually distinctive side struck

variant was known as *hoenderbek*, or hen's beak, because of its shape when looked at in cross-section. These were originally labelled uncinate. The second distinctive form was the horse hoof variety, *pêrdehoef*, which today we would label as end struck. Not quite as visually striking were the high backed cores which were a variation on the side struck form. It was clear from the beginning that the visual distinctiveness of these artefacts guaranteed them the status of type fossils and, consequently, they acquired cultural significance. Using the type fossil/culture historical approach, Goodwin (*ibid.*) identified an Earlier, Middle and Later Stone Age. The Earlier Stone Age was further subdivided as shown in Table 4.1.

Goodwin (1934) later modified these variants, by which time a combination of sufficient examples, and the influence

Subdivision	Character
Stellenbosch	Bifaces and cleavers. Now termed Acheulian
Victoria West	Distinctively shaped cores and flakes
Fauresmith	Industry based on hornfels with bifaces and flake tools

Table 4.1. Subdivisions of the Earlier Stone Age of Southern Africa

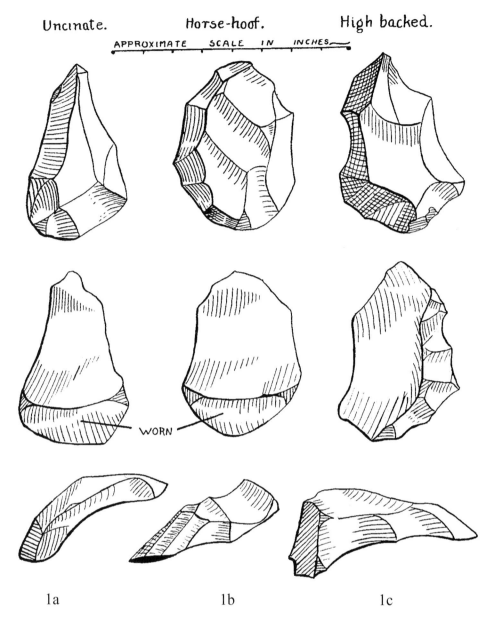

Uncinate.   Horse-hoof.   High backed.

APPROXIMATE   SCALE   IN   INCHES

WORN

1a   1b   1c

Fig. 4.1. The three variants of Victoria West technology as originally conceived by Jansen (after Goodwin 1929, Plate VI).

of the Abbé Breuil, had led to the three forms being placed in a temporal succession. Here Canteen Koppie played an important part in the interpretation of the Victoria West. Based on observations at the site during a ground breaking field trip in 1929 by the British Association, Breuil (in Goodwin 1934), and then Goodwin (*ibid.*) were both able to place the variants in a single evolving succession. The side struck *hoenderbek* were the earliest examples, followed by the high backed, and then the *pêrdehoef* end struck form.

Space does not permit a detailed discussion of the history of the Victoria West phenomenon or of Canteen Koppie. Fuller treatments are given in Kuman (in press) and Beaumont 1990.

CURRENT WORK AT CANTEEN KOPPIE

Beaumont (Beaumont 1999; Beaumont and McNabb 2000) has established the basic stratigraphic succession for the site. A plan and section are presented in Figs. 4.2a and 4.2b and the nature of the deposits is summarised in Table 4.2.

The only systematic archaeological fieldwork conducted at Canteen Koppie is that by Beaumont (1990, 1999; Beaumont and McNabb 2000). Four important observations have arisen out of this ongoing programme:

1.   Fauresmith is present at the site, but confined to the

Strata	Description
Stratum 1	The uppermost deposit is a sand unit, known locally as the Hutton Sands. Helgren (1979) considers them to be the result of a number of colluvial episodes. Beaumont has recognised at least four phases of development. The sands contain MSA and Fauresmith material.
Stratum 2a	A matrix supported gravel. Clasts are predominantly andesite and range from pebble to boulder grade in size. Large boulder sized clasts are very common. This is either an alluvial terrace gravel (Younger Gravels II of Söhnge *et al.* 1937), an alluvial gravel with some colluvial input (Rietputs A of Helgren 1979), or a predominantly colluvial gravel with some alluvial input (Beaumont 1999 and pers. comm.).
Stratum 2b Upper unit	A matrix supported sandy gravel. This is not seen in every section of the pit and it is not yet clear whether it is localised in pockets, or a more extensive feature confined to part of the pit. Clasts are smaller and more infrequent, and can be seen to form horizontal and sub-horizontal lines of trail, possibly representing ephemeral open surfaces resulting from pauses in the deposition of the 2b Upper unit. In Area 1 where this deposit has been excavated and studied in detail, Stratum 2b Upper unit dips to the south-east, but the lines of trail dip to the west (pers. observ.). It is provisionally interpreted as a series of distinct washes of colluvial sandy infill.
Sratum 2b Lower unit	Matrix supported sandy gravel similar to Stratum 2a resting on andesite bedrock.

Table 4.2. Description of the deposits observed at Canteen Koppie.

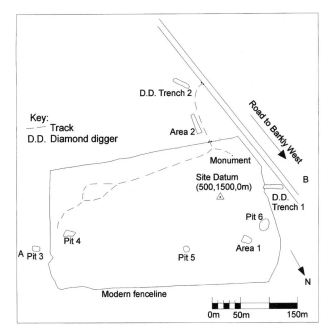

Fig. 4.2a. Plan of Canteen Koppie, South Africa, showing main archaeological areas and sections cut in old and modern diamond digger workings (marked D.D.).

Hutton Sands, and the topmost 30–40 cm of Stratum 2a.

2. The Acheulian is present in Stratum 2a, below about 30–40 cm, and in both sub-units of Stratum 2b.
3. Below 30–40 cm, *pêrdehoef* and *hoenderbek* cores are distributed evenly throughout the remainder of Stratum 2a (see below). This is the traditional gravel described by Söhnge *et al.* (1937) and Helgren (1979). They are however entirely confined to this unit (Beaumont 1999; Beaumont and McNabb 2000).
4. Sporadic Levallois material is present in Stratum 2a and Stratum 2b Upper unit. This does not include *pêrdehoef* and *hoenderbek* cores (for definition see

below). The artefacts from Stratum 2b Lower unit remain to be analysed.

The overall interpretation of the site is as follows: Acheulian hominids used Canteen Koppie as a factory site for making blanks for bifaces and cleavers (Van Riet Lowe in Söhnge *et al.* 1937). However, *contra* Van Riet Lowe, hominids exploited the colluvial gravels in order to obtain andesite boulders which were the source for flake blanks. They did not make bifaces and cleavers out of the specific type of Victoria West flakes found at Canteen Koppie (Beaumont and McNabb 2000).

Dating the site is difficult. On the basis of typological parallels and faunal comparisons, Beaumont (1999) has suggested that the lower part of Stratum 2a pre-dates the Middle Pleistocene, thus making it greater than 787 kyr. This remains to be tested, and a Middle Pleistocene age would be equally possible as suggested by Mason (1962).

As the Victoria West only occurs in Stratum 2a, the remainder of this paper will focus on data from this unit at Canteen Koppie.

THE TERMINOLOGY OF THE VICTORIA WEST

Even a cursory examination of the literature on Victoria West and Levallois technology in the South African Earlier Stone Age reveals how complicated this enigmatic phenomenon really is. Little standardisation exists in either the use of terminology or its application (compare Kuman in press; Sampson 1974; Volman 1984). Conceptually, an end struck Victoria West core is no different from an MSA radial Levallois core, or the Baker's Hole type radial/tortoise core common in the European later Lower Palaeolithic. However, in terms of physical appearance, differences do exist. In the African Earlier Stone Age, prepared core technology (PCT) tends to be large and 'chunky', whereas in the South African MSA it is smaller, and on a

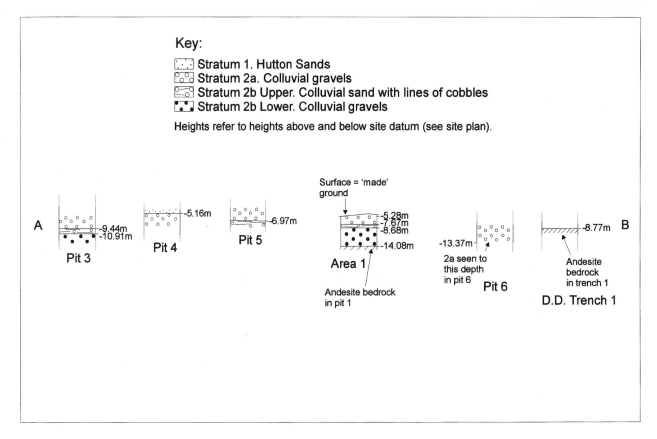

Fig. 4.2b. Section at Canteen Koppie illustrating the relationship of various sedimentary units to the undulating bedrock.

subjective basis appears better made. Choices of raw material are different too. Many MSA examples are in finer grained raw materials and these undoubtedly influence final form.

Victoria West side and end struck cores are variants of the radial Levallois pattern. In the Earlier Stone Age, radial technology provides large blanks for large tools. In the MSA, radial technology provides smaller blanks for different tools. So this similarity in appearance reflects the persistence of a specific pattern of manufacture, but one that is put to different uses in different archaeological periods. However, the conceptual approach is not that different. Both involve the fashioning of a domed surface, the configuration of which will influence the shape of the preferential flake. For the purposes of this paper, I will follow Goodwin's 1934 lead. The label Victoria West is restricted to the side and end struck variants of radial Levallois technology, and confined to the Earlier Stone Age as defined by its occurrence on sites with bifaces, cleavers, or other evidence of their manufacture. In other words, the Victoria West phenomenon is the radial Levallois of the Acheulian in South Africa. The remaining variants of PCT in the Earlier Stone Age, the convergent and parallel techniques, are sufficiently visually homogenised for the label Levallois to be applied to them in this context. They continue into the earliest MSA and continue to be visually

similar; so the term Levallois is still appropriate for these pieces.

VARIABILITY WITHIN THE VICTORIA WEST

Extending a cursory glance from the literature on Victoria West artefacts to the figures which illustrate them, another feature becomes quickly apparent. Within the Victoria West, as defined here, there is morphological variability. In my opinion, this variability is deliberate and polarises around two distinctive concepts of the side struck radial pattern (see below).

Boëda (1995) has refined the understanding of the Levallois in Europe considerably. He recognises a series of approaches to making PCT cores and flakes:

* Cores which produce single preferential flakes and then need to be re-prepared in order to take off another preferential flake are described as linear. These would be radial Levallois and convergent Levallois/point technologies.
* Those cores from which a number of flakes can be removed without re-preparing the flaking face are termed recurrent. These would include unipolar and bipolar Levallois blades, and flake blades. More

difficult to identify are the flakes knapped off the domed surface of a radial PCT core, which manifest no standardisation in outline shape. They are detached from the domed Levallois flaking face and as such are to be classified as Levallois flakes, but the knapper does not position the removal as with a linear approach, he or she simply takes flakes off the domed surface from the margin. So these pieces never exhibit any similarity in outline shape. They are recognised, in the first instance, by their complex multidirectional flake scar patterns, and are termed recurrent radial Levallois flakes. That they are deliberate and preconceived as such is shown by the core reconstructions from Maastricht-Belvédère (Schlanger 1996).

In terms of the nomenclature preferred here, the Victoria West side and end struck pieces are the product of linear preferential prepared core technology. Boëda's system highlights an important point, one that is picked out by the variability seen in illustrations of Victoria West technique in South Africa: outline plan form of the Levallois flaking face plays a significant part in the shape of the flake removed. This is because of the domed character of the face from which the Victoria West flake will be detached. A radial Victoria West core which is longer than it is wide, will usually produce a linear preferential flake of more or less the same shape. The same applies to a radial core that is wider than it is long. Subjectively, the impression given is that the side and end preference is achieved quickly through the primary flaking of the core and is not usually accompanied by much elaborate secondary shaping. Fig. 4.3a is an example. We may call these ordinary Victoria West side and end struck cores and flakes. On the other hand, many large non-PCT cores are equally capable of producing clear side and end struck flakes. In these cases, the final form the flake takes, reflects a fortuitous configuration of the flaking face on the core. The cores are not difficult to spot; non-PCT but with a big side or end struck flake scar. If worked into a biface, these flakes are more difficult to spot. When possible, we may call these generalised side and end struck cores and flakes.

What is equally apparent from looking at illustrated examples, is the visual distinctiveness of the *hoenderbek* morphology at Canteen Koppie and at other sites. Compare the generalised Victoria West side struck core in Fig. 4.3a with that of the *hoenderbek* in Fig. 4.3b. The asymmetrical almond shaped outline of the *hoenderbek* is markedly different and distinctive. At Canteen Koppie the Victoria West side struck cores are exclusively *hoenderbek*, and show considerable visual similarity. The striking platform is always on the straight edge at the 'top' of the core, and is often in the upper third nearer the 'tip' of that edge. What gives the *hoenderbek* its distinctive shape is the careful flaking of the tapering edge. This produces the asymmetric/almond shape in plan form. These pieces are clearly a product of careful outline

shaping. The degree of shaping that goes into the *hoenderbek* form means that its outline shape is particularly difficult to reproduce accidentally. This implies to me that the specificity of shape was a desired end product. I would like to suggest that the *hoenderbek* is a deliberately conceptualised sub-variant of the Victoria West side struck core. We may call these specific Victoria West side struck cores and flakes.

SPECIFIC SIDE STRUCK VICTORIA WEST TECHNOLOGY USED FOR BIFACES AT CANTEEN KOPPIE

If the traditional interpretation of Canteen Koppie as a factory site for the manufacture of bifaces from specific Victoria West side struck cores were true, then we could confidently expect that the majority of artefacts at the site, excluding flake debitage, would be either bifaces, partially finished examples, roughouts and Victoria West cores and flakes. Certainly, the impression from museum collections and received wisdom would support this.

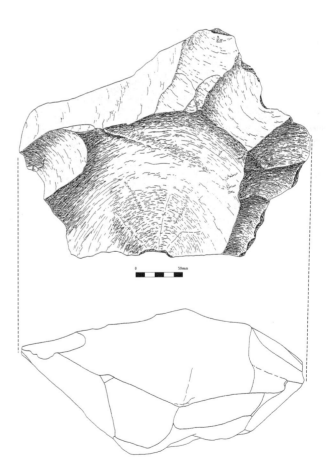

Fig. 4.3a. A generalised side struck Victoria West core from the Vaal-Harts river, site DB3 (after Kuman in press. Illustration by D. Voorvelt).

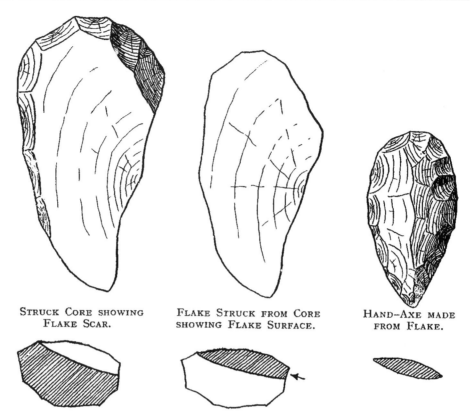

Struck Core showing   Flake Struck from Core   Hand–Axe made
Flake Scar.   showing Flake Surface.   from Flake.

Fig. 4.3b. Sidestruck hoenderbek *Victoria West core, and the ventral face of the resulting flake (after Van Riet Lowe 1937, Fig. 15).*

However, Beaumont's excavations have revealed a different picture. The relevant data are presented in Tables 4.3 and 4.5, and the implications are summarised in the text table below:

Observed pattern in Beaumont's data sample
Bifaces do not occur as frequently as might be expected (Table 4.5)
Biface thinning flakes, broken bifaces in the early stages of manufacture, and roughouts are infrequent
Victoria West cores do not occur as frequently as expected (Table 4.3)
There are other core working techniques which produce more suitable blanks for making bifaces (Table 4.3)
Bifaces do not show the tell-tale signs of Victoria West flakes

The first three points in the text table are relevant to the numbers of artefacts we could reasonably expect, given the inferred function of the site, and the nature of the deposits present. It is important to remember that the frequencies given in Tables 4.3 and 4.5 represent artefacts from a time averaged assemblage. Stratum 2a is a colluvial lobe (Beaumont 1999) which was built up over many thousands of years. Here time averaging works in our favour since the artefact content represents the sum of activity accumulated over the total time that the unit was aggrading. In this case, the numbers of bifaces and Victoria

Core type	Andesite	Other raw materials
Victoria West side struck	42	–
Victoria West end struck	14	–
Victoria West general	1	–
Victoria West roughout	5	–
Other PCT cores	18	2
Boulder cores	144	1
Chopper cores	14	16
Discoids	10	9
Discoidally worked	24	7
Edge cores/Core scrapers	4	2
Irregular polyhedrons	46	16
Polyhedrons	20	5
Small single/multiple platform cores	1	37

Table 4.3. Frequency of core types tabulated by raw material type in Stratum 2a, Canteen Koppie. Other PCT cores refer to point, blade, flake blade, and non-diagnostic PCT cores. Discoidally worked cores are those with more than 40% but less than 60% of their circumference worked by alternate flaking (as opposed to discoids which have more than 60%). Irregular polyhedrons are all 'shapeless' cores with more than 2 scars that do not fit into any other group. Small single/multiple platform cores are usually less than 5 cm maximum length.

West cores appear low if they were the principal focus of activities at the site during this time span. What about other explanations? Perhaps, they were removed from the site. If so, where are the huge numbers of Victoria West cores that were their blanks? Where are the by-products of manufacture? If frequency is equated with importance, then in terms of absolute numbers I suggest that the data imply that biface manufacture was not the central focus of activity here, nor was the manufacture of Victoria West flakes and cores.

Is it possible that flakes from *hoenderbek* cores were used as blanks for cleavers rather than bifaces? No, the low core frequency argument would still hold. Also, there are technical grounds for disputing this. The widest end of the side struck Victoria West flake is the convex, lateral edge formed by the careful convex preparation of this edge on the core (Fig. 4.3b). This wide portion would represent the cleaver blade. However, the cleavers from the site, and elsewhere in Southern Africa, follow a different pattern. The cleaver blade is almost always a single flake scar or flat natural surface with the cutting edge of the blade, in cross-section a tapering (i.e. feathered) and, usually, unretouched termination. Markedly convex blades with truncated centripetal preparatory flake scars are not noted. Although the end struck variant would be more suitable for cleavers, the convex distal end would still show the centripetal scar pattern. Clearly, *hoenderbek* flakes were not the blanks for cleavers either.

The data in Table 4.3 identify two other reasons for disbelieving that *hoenderbek* flakes are the blanks for bifaces. The first is a technological one. With regard to shaping and thinning, it is evident from Fig. 4.3b that the *hoenderbek* flake is almost a pointed biface when the flake is detached. It would only require the re-shaping via bifacial thinning of the narrow end of the flake. This would remove the former butt of the flake, shape the tip, and produce a symmetrical point. The remainder of the blank already possesses the desired shape. It would be reasonable, therefore, to expect bifaces to show a degree of standardisation in outline, more bifacial thinning and shaping at the tip, and truncated centripetal flake scars on the butt (i.e. the dorsal of the flake blank). However,

personal observation indicates that a wide variety of outline shapes is present in the biface sample and no standardisation is apparent. Only a single andesite biface possesses the outline shape that could be a result of further working a *hoenderbek* flake. None of the bifaces possess the combination of a tip heavily worked on one edge, a minimum of other thinning elsewhere, and truncated centripetal flaking on one face of the biface's butt.

The second reason for believing that *hoenderbek* flakes were not the blanks for bifaces and cleavers focuses on the presence of other core forms which would make far more suitable blanks. Table 4.3 shows that the most frequent core type is the one provisionally described as the boulder core. These represent 32.88% of all core morphologies in any raw material. These cores are defined on a particular approach to knapping the large angular clasts which make up the colluvial gravels. These boulder cores are characterised by wide flat faces with the angles between them rounded off during colluvial movement downslope. Some common shapes noted in cross-section are presented in Table 4.4 to illustrate this point, and show how the knappers exploited the angles between these natural striking platforms and flaking faces. They vary in size between cobble grade (64–256 mm in length) and boulder grade (>256 mm). Fifty percent (n=72)

Type	Andesite	Other raw materials
Biface	10	24
Cleaver	19	4
Bifacial point	1	1
Uniface	3	–
Roughout	7	–
Indeterminate	6	3
Pick	–	–
Total	46	32

Table 4.5. Frequency of large cutting tools in Stratum 2a, Canteen Koppie.

	Flaking directions					
	No other	1 other	2 other	3 other	4 other	5 other
No corners worked by alternate flaking	–	8	8	2	3	2
1 corner worked by alternate flaking	52	17	9	–	1	–
2 corners worked by alternate flaking	25	4	5	–	–	–
3 corners worked by alternate flaking	3	1	–	–	–	–
4 corners worked by alternate flaking	1	–	–	–	–	–

Table 4.4. Provisional data showing the variety of patterns seen in the flaking of boulder cores at Canteen Koppie, for those artefacts where this kind of data could be recorded. For example, there are nine boulder cores which have had one corner flaked by alternate flaking, and have also had flakes removed from two other directions.

of the andesite boulder cores (n=144) have a length between 203 and 261.5 mm (median length is 230 mm), and the median flake scar length for the largest scar on each core is 150 mm. The median length of flake scars on all Victoria West side struck cores is 139 mm, while the median length for andesite bifaces, unifaces and roughouts is 135 mm, only four mm less. This leaves little scope for shaping and thinning the tips of specific side struck flakes into bifaces. From the point of view of size, the flakes from boulder cores would be far better as blanks. On average boulder cores have six flakes removed indicating that working was not extensive on these pieces. Personal observation of their flake scars indicates that many of these produce generalised side and end struck flakes.

In conclusion, there are strong grounds for believing that a one-to-one correlation between the *hoenderbek* flake and biface blank production at Canteen Koppie does not exist. Given this, I think it is possible to support the traditional interpretation of the site as a factory location at least during Stratum 2a times, but one dedicated to making big flakes from boulder cores and then removing them for modification into bifaces and cleavers elsewhere.

SO WHAT WERE THE *HOENDERBEK* FLAKES FOR? A SPECULATIVE SUGGESTION

If the premise that *hoenderbek* flakes are not blanks is accepted, then what are they? A key to this may be found in the standardisation already alluded to. There is a significant investment by the knapper in consistently striving to achieve a morphology that is so conservative. In other words, the shape of the *hoenderbek* core and its resultant flake is a matter of choice and that choice is deliberate.

Another clue may lie in the shape of the final flake itself. As the outline in Fig. 4.3b indicates, one of the main features of the Victoria West side struck flake is that it possesses a naturally sharp and long convex cutting edge, with a sharp tip. The butt of the flake provides a convenient finger rest. In fact, the whole flake makes an ideal knife, and as such would require little to no further shaping or thinning. I would like to suggest that the *hoenderbek* flake is a knife, and one that is deliberately made as such. But why a knife of that particular shape? Other big flakes at the site have edges that would cut just as effectively, and many of the big flakes from boulder cores could be trimmed down to serve as knives just as well. Why go to the time and trouble of making a knife with such a specific shape? I suggest the shape of the *hoenderbek* knife is not conditioned by its function in whatever activity it was a part of, rather that this activity involved a tradition of having knives of this shape and made in this way. The activity empowered and validated the knife's shape. Here, an item of material culture had a specifically symbolic visual form, whose distinctiveness would have meaning for those who saw it. While

not denying any functional qualities of these artefacts, I believe the true function of the *hoenderbek* flake was as a visual trigger to initiate particular chains of meaning in particular social contexts.

I hesitate to take the final step and suggest just what was the activity or social institution that required and conditioned the use of such items of material culture. Their infrequency suggests that the activity was not a common one, but the investment in time and effort suggests that it was nonetheless an important one to the Acheulian people who made and used these knives.

EXTENDING THE SPECULATION

Recently archaeologists of the Stone Age have begun to explore a new and potentially fruitful approach to the analysis of material culture (Dobres 2000; Dobres and Hoffman 1999). This follows the rediscovery of the study of technology and the social context of manufacture as fruitful areas of research in anthropology. What is emphasised here is the act of manufacture, and the recognition of that act as a socially situated practice. The process of manufacture then becomes a route to explore the social patterns that generated, conditioned, and required the production of finished objects by people.

In a recent article, Pfaffenberger (1999) has reanimated an old idea of Bronislaw Malinowski. He argues that the manufacture of material culture triggers a pre-energised social template with a multiplicity of meanings, all or some of which will be understood by those who participate in the act of manufacture, or consume its end product. He implies that not only finished items, but the very act of manufacture itself, as well as where and how it occurs, are the stitches that bind the maker to the social fabric. Now in matters of detail, archaeologists may never recover the wealth that Pfaffenberger describes for the socially situated acts of manufacture that he uses as his examples (yam houses in Melanesia and the Cornish tin mining trade). This is unfortunate because it is these details of symbol and metaphor (sign and signifier?) that allow the anthropologist to make use of a notion like a pre-energised social template. Does this mean we should not explore the possibilities it offers? No. If archaeology cannot provide all of the pieces of the puzzle it can certainly provide some of the most important ones. For example, through technological analysis and replication, the much maligned processualist approach can reconstruct the practices of manufacture. In addition, archaeology is ideally suited to reconstruct the physical context of manufacture, as well as provide the physical context in which material culture is consumed. In one aspect we can even score over the anthropologist, we can track the diachronic character of the making and using of material culture.

Pfaffenberger elaborates on Malinowski's original concept. The act of manufacture validates the individual in terms of his or her acceptability to the collective. This operates on at least two levels. In making an object that the collective recognise as valuable (on any level), the maker demonstrates to the collective that he or she is capable of producing items that the collective deem worthy. Through making something, people show themselves to be 'good and useful' contributors. The act of making is a validating process. Who knows, perhaps we can speculate that the often incomprehensible quantity of bifaces found at many Acheulian sites reflects a consistent need for members of the collective to be recognised as useful and viable members of the group? In such a speculative scenario, each biface would be a continual reminder to the group that someone could pull their weight. Manufacture then becomes not only action and validation, but a transforming process as well. Secondly, the act of making itself, and the various stages of manufacture, as much as the thing being made, are enveloped in meaningful social associations. These set up a resonance between the collective and the maker who is consciously or unconsciously appealing to a social template whose meanings the collective can identify with. Here there are important possibilities for the archaeologist interested in how things are made and what they might mean. Even if we cannot specify exactly what the act of making a biface or *hoenderbek* flake meant to each group in every temporal and geographical location where they were made, this kind of approach does offer the possibilities of exploring the social meaning behind Palaeolithic material culture.

What, then, might we infer for the *hoenderbek* flakes at Canteen Koppie? The visual distinctiveness of the *hoenderbek* is designed to speak to the collective as a whole. It triggers a pre-energised social template that invests the maker or possessor with a social identity, possibly one that associates him or her with a smaller portion of the collective. So we may argue that within the larger social pattern of the hominids who came to Canteen Koppie there existed specific sub-groups with a sense of their own identity and traditions involving particular items of material culture. Moreover, the act of successfully making *hoenderbek* flakes and cores suggests the right of the individual to be a part of that sub-group, and serves to reassure that the maker is fit to belong. At the very least it implies that within Acheulian societies there existed sub-divisions which did not relate exclusively to subsistence activities, and people could perhaps express their existence through the transforming action of making a particular item of material culture for all the world to see.

CONCLUSION

Derek Roe's early work offered the possibility that biface outline was deliberate, and that variations in outline reflected choices. It began a dialogue yet to be concluded. In this, admittedly speculative paper, I have tried to show that in other items of Acheulian material culture the possibility of recognising choice and message is also present. Like Derek Roe, I am at heart an artefact lover, and I hope that he will agree with me that the study of material culture in context still has a significant part to play in our construction of the past.

ACKNOWLEDGEMENTS

I am very grateful to Peter Beaumont and the staff of the McGregor Museum at Kimberley for the opportunity of working at Canteen Koppie and publishing part of our results ahead of our site report. Also to Kathy Kuman and Ron Clarke for introducing me to Peter and helping me in every way possible. The staff and students of the Archaeology Department at the University of the Witwatersrand as ever made me feel a part of the family. I am grateful for the comments and suggestions made by Annabel Field and Erica Gittins who read early drafts of this paper. I am particularly grateful to the surveyors from de Beers who gave so cheerfully of their time and expertise, and the de Beers managers at Kimberley who set it all up for us. Also to Dr Rob Hosfield and Bryn 'Chewie' Jones who completed the Canteen Koppie Surveying.

REFERENCES

Beaumont, P. 1990. Canteen Koppie. In P. Beaumont and D. Morris (eds.) *Guide to the Archaeological Sites in the Northern Cape*, 14–16. McGregor Museum, Kimberley.

Beaumont, P. 1999. Canteen Koppie, Barkly West. In P. Beaumont (ed.) *Northern Cape. INQUA XV International Conference Field Guide*, 1–41.

Beaumont, P. and McNabb, J. 2000. *Report for the National Monuments Council of South Africa on Excavations by Peter Beaumont at Canteen Koppie, Barkly West, Northern Cape Province, South Africa.*

Boëda, E. 1995. Levallois: a volumetric construction, methods, a technique. In H.L Dibble and O. Bar-Yosef (eds.) *The Definition and Interpretation of Levallois Technology*, 41–68. Prehistory Press, Madison.

Dobres, M.A. 2000. *Technology and Social Agency: Outlining a Practice Framework for Archaeology*. Blackwell, Oxford.

Dobres, M.A. and Hoffman, C.R. (eds.) 1999. *The Social Dynamics of Technology: Practice, Politics and World Views*. Smithsonian Institution Press, Washington.

Goodwin, A.J.H. 1929. Part III. The Victoria West Industry. In A.J.H. Goodwin and C. Van Riet Lowe (eds.) The Stone Age Cultures of South Africa. *Annals of the South African Museum* 27, 1–289.

Goodwin, A.J.H. 1934. Some developments in technique during the Earlier Stone Age. *Transactions of the Royal Society of South Africa* 21, 109–123.

Helgren, D.M. 1979. *River of Diamonds: An Alluvial History of the Lower Vaal Basin, South Africa*. Department of Geography Research Paper 185, University of Chicago, Chicago.

Jansen, F.J. 1926. A new type of stone implement from Victoria West. *South African Journal of Science* 23, 818–825.

Kuman, K. in press. An Acheulean factory site with prepared core technology near Taung, South Africa. *Journal of Archaeological Science*.

Mason, R. 1962. *Prehistory of the Transvaal.* University of the Witwatersrand Press, Johannesburg.

Pfaffenberger, B. 1999. Worlds in the making: technological activities and the construction of intersubjective meaning. In M.A. Dobres and C.R. Hoffman (eds.) *The Social Dynamics of Technology: Practice, Politics and World Views*, 147–164. Smithsonian Institution Press, Washington.

Sampson, C.G. 1974. *The Stone Age Archaeology of Southern Africa.* Academic Press, London.

Schlanger, N. 1996. Understanding Levallois: lithic technology and cognitive archaeology. *Cambridge Archaeological Journal* 6, 231–254.

Söhnge, P.G., Visser D.J.L. and Van Riet Lowe, C. 1937. *The Geology and Archaeology of the Vaal River Basin.* Memoirs of the Geological Survey of the Union of South Africa 35, Pretoria.

Volman, T.P. 1984. Early prehistory of southern Africa. In R.G. Klein (ed.) *South African Prehistory and Palaeoenvironments*, 169–220. A.A. Balkema, Rotterdam.

5. Diamonds, alluvials, and artefacts.
The Stone Age in Sierra Leone and the Cotton Tree Museum

Phillip Allsworth-Jones

ABSTRACT

The potential significance of the Quaternary sequence in Sierra Leone and its possible relevance for the earlier Stone Age prehistory of West Africa became clear with the publication in 1980 by Thomas and Thorp of thirty-eight radiocarbon dates from alluvial contexts in the east central part of the country. The majority of the dates related to the period after 12,430 years ago, but there were six between 35,900 and 20,500 BP. In the more northerly of the two areas which they investigated, Carleton Coon's excavations at Yengema Cave had previously revealed an upper occupation with ground stone axes and pottery TL dated to between 4150 and 3450 BP. Beneath this occupation was one characterised by bifacially flaked implements called by Coon 'Lupembo-Tshitolian' and regarded by him as early Holocene in date. In the light of the new discoveries it was thought worthwhile to re-examine the situation, and a visit to Sierra Leone was accordingly made in October 1986. Apart from obtaining information and collecting artefacts derived from the alluvial deposits at Yengema (thanks to the courtesy of the National Diamond Mining Company of Sierra Leone), the opportunity was also granted to study the collections at the Sierra Leone National Museum in Freetown, many of which also came from the alluvial deposits. It appears that the majority of this material does belong to the later part of the Stone Age sequence, but there are occasional indications of an earlier presence. It seems opportune to publish these results at this time, when conditions in Sierra Leone have deteriorated so drastically. A scientific visit to the diamond fields today would be out of the question, and it is not clear how far the collections at the Cotton Tree Museum have survived the ravages of the civil war. The 'international community' should awake to its responsibilities in this regard.

INTRODUCTION

Diamonds were first discovered in Sierra Leone in 1930 by J.D. Pollett in the gravels of the Gbobora river near the village of Fotingaia in the east central part of the country (Pollett 1937). Soon afterwards, commercial operations were commenced by the Sierra Leone Selection Trust (SLST). Originally, they were given rights covering the whole country, but subsequently they were confined to the two main areas of Yengema and Tongo, while 'tributors' operated outside these areas (Hall 1973). Ownership of the leases was later transferred to the National Diamond Mining Company of Sierra Leone (NDMC), and at the time of my visit in 1986 'tributors' were active along the Gbobora river not far from where the original diamond find was made (Plate 5.1). The Yengema and Tongo leases are situated on tributaries of the Sewa and Moa river systems (Fig. 5.1) and the diamonds are released by weathering into these systems from kimberlite dykes in the region (Clarke 1969; Morel 1976). In the course of alluvial mining operations over the years, many artefacts were found and some were presented to the Sierra Leone National Museum (SLNM), popularly known as the Cotton Tree Museum from its position at a cross roads in the centre of Freetown (State House 1980). Regular donors included H.H. Jackson,

Plate 5.1. Gbobora river east of Fotingaia, 17 October 1986

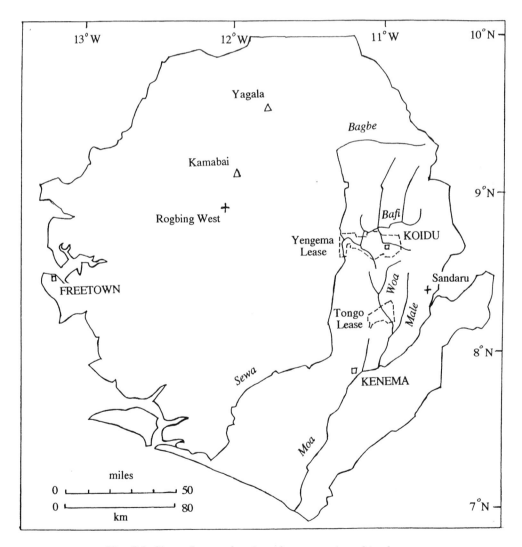

Fig. 5.1. Sierra Leone showing places mentioned in the text

Area Superintendent of the Mines Division based in Koidu, and J.D. Pollett, of the Geological Survey Division, as well as various employees of the SLST. At the Museum, the finds were catalogued, but so far as I am aware the only overall appraisal carried out was by P.A. Cole-King on behalf of Unesco (Cole-King 1976). He commented that although this was a large collection, 'unfortunately there is in most cases little precise indication of locality for each find', nor was there an adequate description of the circumstances in which they had been found.

DATED DEPOSITS IN THE MINING AREAS

The significance of the alluvial deposits which were being mined for diamonds from the point of view of Quaternary climatic reconstruction, and also potentially in regard to the archaeological material, was made clear when M.F. Thomas and M.B. Thorp visited the country and made a detailed study of several sections along the rivers in the mining areas (Thomas 1983; Thomas and Thorp 1980). They obtained thirty-eight radiocarbon dates from nine locations (fifteen individual sites) of which four locations

(five sites) were in the Tongo lease and five locations (ten sites) were in the Yengema lease. Relatively speaking, therefore, the bulk of the evidence has come from Yengema, which produced thirty-two out of the thirty-eight dates, and all the most important sections with multiple dates. In the Yengema lease, four sites were located on the Upper and Middle Gbobora river, five on the Upper and Lower Moinde, and one at the mouth of the Boyi river (Fig. 5.2). The most important sections with multiple dates are MG10 (Thomas and Thorp 1980, fig. 8) UM8 and LM7 (Thomas and Thorp 1980, figs. 7b and 9) on the Gbobora and Moinde rivers respectively. Together these three sites produced eighteen of the radiocarbon dates. Six of the thirty-eight dates relate to the period between 35,900 and 20,500 BP whereas the remainder run from 12,430 BP up to the present. It is suggested that the gap between 20,500 and 12,430 BP corresponds to the Ogolian arid phase recognised elsewhere in West Africa. There is a further less complete gap between 7030 and 3240 BP, occupied by only two radiocarbon dates of 6010±130 and 4290±55 BP, and the suggestion is that this corresponds to a further period of relative but not uniform dessication. The period from 12,430 to 7030 BP is characterised as an early Holocene 'pluvial', whereas

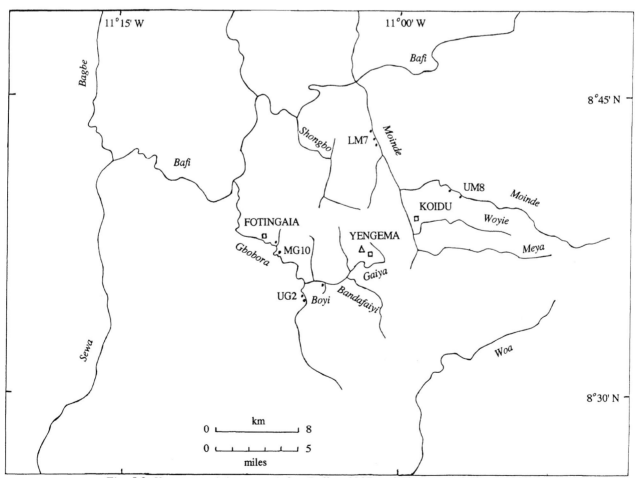

Fig. 5.2. Yengema mining area (after Pollett 1937 and Thomas and Thorp 1980)

from 3240 BP onwards it is believed that 'forest clearance for agriculture in these catchments' had already begun (Thomas and Thorp 1980, fig. 6). According to M.B. Thorp (in litt. 29 August 1979) dolerite artefacts, unweathered and unrolled, were found at the mining sites where the recorded sections were established, but they were not *in situ* and could not be linked with any given horizon.

YENGEMA CAVE

In situ material in the area was found by Carleton Coon in 1965 as a result of his excavations in Yengema Cave, not far from the headquarters of the mining company (Plate 5.2). He excavated a trench 2.5 by 5 metres in size to a maximum depth of 2 metres in the southern part of the cave, but its dimensions decreased as he neared the base of the deposits (Coon 1968, figs. 1 and 2). He divided the material into an Upper, Middle, and Lower Yengeman corresponding to grouped levels within the cave, and in terms of raw material, as follows (Table 5.1).

As can be seen, the Lower Yengeman (excavated over a very restricted area) practically consisted of quartz alone. Coon emphasised that it was not a microlithic industry, but by this he meant that it did not contain geometric microliths. It was still small sized, since the quartz tools in the cave as a whole weighed on average no more than

24 grams each (Coon 1968, 28). The boundary between the Upper and Middle Yengeman was established somewhat arbitrarily, since as Coon himself recognised (partly because of the different degrees of lateritization of the dolerite tools), the floor of the upper unit was likely to have dipped down below 60 cm in places. In that case, it is reasonable to regard the pottery (which Lamberg-Karlovsky characterised as rather homogeneous and indicative of a single occupation over a relatively short period of time) as having belonged exclusively to the Upper Yengeman. Partly on these grounds Coon described this occupation as Early Neolithic. A little pottery of a different kind was found by Janet Stone in an intrusive pit in 1964, and this was described as Late Neolithic, although it might possibly be Iron Age in character (Coon 1968, plate 29; Hill 1971). Celts and celt blanks, mainly of dolerite, also formed an 'essential part' of this complex (Coon 1968, plates 25c, 26–28). In view of their small size, Coon commented that it was difficult to understand exactly what these celts were used for, and he surmised that they may even have had a votive significance. TL dates were obtained on two potsherds at depths of 0–30 and 40–60 cm respectively; they were expressed in years BC, but for the sake of comparability with the radiocarbon dates quoted here we may regard them as equivalent to 3450±350 and 4150±470 BP.

The Middle Yengeman was characterised above all by

Yengeman Level	Quartz	Dolerite	Haematite	Schist	Other	Pottery	Total
Upper 0–60 cm	4450	659	68	48	8	262	5495
Middle 60–160 cm	8364	1765	326	341	8	15	10,819
Lower 160 cm-base	649	3	0	0	0	0	652
Total	13,463	2427	394	389	16	277	16,966

Table 5.1. Stratigraphic distribution of raw materials recovered in Yengema Cave.

Plate 5.2. Yengema Cave from the east, 16 October 1986

the presence of bifacially worked dolerite tools, which Coon divided into two main classes, convergent (Coon 1968, plates 10–12, 13a) and parallel-sided (Coon 1968, plates 13b–d, 14a–b). Coon expressed the view that the convergent pieces were 'introduced into the Yengeman industry fairly late in the pre-ceramic period and were abandoned when celts came into common use'. Many of the parallel-sided pieces were snapped off, which Coon thought may have been intentional, and he regarded them as having been used for chopping before they too were 'replaced by celts'. He characterised the industry as a whole as 'Lupembo-Tshitolian', by comparison with Central Africa, and he regarded it as probably early Holocene in date.

Elsewhere in Sierra Leone, two further rock shelters were excavated by Atherton at Yagala and Kamabai (Atherton 1984). A date of 4510±115 BP from level 10 at Kamabai according to Atherton immediately pre-dates the appearance there of an Early Neolithic occupation not unlike that at Yengema, except that in this case there are some geometric microliths in quartz. As at Yengema, there was an accompanying use of dolerite, which was favoured for the production of celts (Atherton 1984, fig. 5). There was no equivalent to the Middle Yengeman. Summarising the Late Stone Age of West Africa as a whole, Shaw suggested that it might be divided into two chronological phases and four facies which appeared to correlate with either forested or savannah conditions (Shaw 1985, 71). The Middle Yengeman was included in aceramic phase I facies B (non-microlithic), whereas Yagala and Kamabai were placed in

ceramic phase II facies B (with microliths and implied savannah conditions). The Upper Yengeman also formed part of phase II but was placed in facies C as without microliths in a forested environment. This is an interesting scheme, but so far as Yengema is concerned it must be remembered that quartz was a constant component of all the industries at the site, and that this component is only 'non-microlithic' in the sense that geometric microliths are absent.

THE ALLUVIAL SEQUENCE IN THE MINING AREAS

The geology of the alluvial diamond mining fields was described in detail by Hall (1973) and the validity of his basic framework was confirmed by Thomas (1983) and Thomas and Thorp (1980). Hall's description in turn reflected abundant experience and observation by local mining engineers and geologists, as summarised in Figs. 5.3 and 5.4, redrawn from originals kindly given to me by the management of the NDMC in Yengema. Fig. 5.3, a 'cross-section of a typical valley in the West African humid zone', was prepared by H.J.E. Haggard in 1958 and is based on 'actual examples in Sierra Leone'. The key and the scale are as given by him; by 'lateritic gravel' is meant chiefly fragments of old laterite, plus laterite concretions 'in situ', and vein quartz. Fig. 5.4, 'typical profiles of Sierra Leone diamond deposits', was drawn by C. Brown in 1979 and illustrates in particular various localities of the general type shown in Fig. 5.3. Descriptions of the deposits

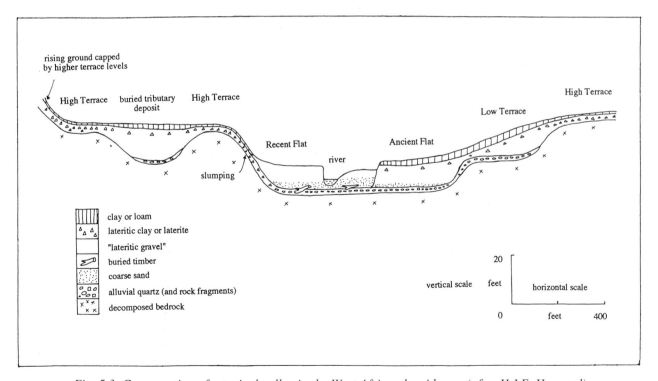

Fig. 5.3. Cross-section of a typical valley in the West African humid zone (after H.J.E. Haggard)

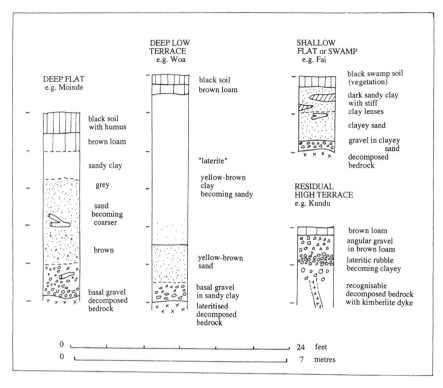

Fig. 5.4. Typical profiles of Sierra Leone diamond deposits (after C. Brown)

again follow those given in the original. Both drawings provide a useful reference point for comparison with the published accounts of the authors mentioned above.

Broadly speaking, the deposits can be divided into two series, the 'Recent Flat' or floodplain gravels, and the flanking terraces which lie at a higher elevation, and which are presumably older than them. Hall recognised three high terraces, of which the second and third were considered to be late Pliocene in age. Much of the first high terrace had been removed by erosion but recognisable alluvial gravels or gravel residues remained, particularly where it had been cut by 'swamps' containing 'abundant reconcentrated terrace material'. These are presumably the 'buried tributary deposits' illustrated by Haggard. Low terrace gravels, under a deep overburden, represent according to Hall earlier floodplains recently incised, and were regarded as being of Quaternary age. Two or three low terraces of slightly differing elevations could sometimes be recognised in one section of a valley. 'The lowest and youngest' of the low terraces was classified as 'Ancient Flat' (as shown by Haggard) and was by definition almost at the same level as the floodplain; but the validity of this subdivision according to Hall was 'questionable'. The morphology of the lower slopes, as remarked by Thomas and Thorp, suggests 'broad shallow valleys with an original sedimentary volume some 30–50% greater than the more recent floodplains and swamps; they are the equivalent of the *graviers sous berge* of French speaking miners in West Africa' (Thomas and Thorp 1980, 147). These underbank gravels, as defined by Vogt (1959) and Tricart (1972), and

taken by them to have been formed in a semi-arid climate different from that of the present, are of considerable importance elsewhere in West Africa from the archaeological point of view, particularly at Mayo Louti where they contained a characteristic Middle Stone Age industry (Allsworth-Jones 1986, 158–159).

Hall described a typical soil profile in the 'Recent Flat' deposits as consisting of four elements: (1) black mud with a high content of organic debris, (2) grey clay silt or sand, and (3) bleached angular quartz gravel sometimes in a clay matrix, above (4) decomposed bedrock. The deposits frequently took the form of long narrow 'swamps', which actually constituted about 80% of the drainage network in the mining areas (Hall 1973, 27). 'This description has been checked against many field sections and it is clear that the sequence is common, but the thickness of individual layers is highly variable' (Thomas 1983, 205). All the radiocarbon samples came from these deposits. Organic material, most commonly in the form of large buried tree trunks and branch wood, was said to occur throughout the sections (as already indicated by Haggard and Brown) and samples of this material were collected from freshly exposed mining faces (Thomas and Thorp 1980, 148). At the base of the sequence, in the larger rivers at least, there was some deposition of gravel around large rock cores, in a manner which indicates a period of fluvial scour when these valleys were carved out (Thomas 1983, fig. 92, Moinde valley). Sometimes timbers were jammed beneath these boulders. Such sub-boulder timbers at UM8 were dated to 12,430±155 and (the odd man out in normally stratigraphically consistent results) 900±45 BP (Thomas and Thorp 1980, fig. 7b). At MG10 a date of 10,500±95 BP was obtained on similar sub-boulder timbers (Thomas and Thorp 1980, fig. 8).

The oldest dates in the Yengema area however come from 'buried swamp' deposits at LM7 where 'sticky black clays' dated to 35,900+1750/–2240 BP underlay 'pale white clays' dated to 25,090+880/–1000 BP in a 'cut and fill' relationship (Thomas and Thorp 1980, fig. 9). These early dates are supported by two others from UG2 (27,750+960/ –1100 BP) and LM6 (20,500±500 BP) as well as two further ones from the Tongo lease (25,969+1240/–1075 and 20,590±350 BP: Thomas and Thorp 1980, fig. 7a). Clearly, therefore, if there was a scouring episode at about 12,000 or 10,000 BP these deposits escaped it. The mechanism whereby they did so is well illustrated at LM7, where due to meander migration the oldest dated swamp 'at the edge of the main floodplain' was cut off by an 'abandoned channel'. 'Other sites display similar cutoff hiatuses'. Hence 'similar sedimentary sequences have been formed at different times, and several cut-and-fill episodes have occurred' throughout the history of these valleys (Thomas 1983, 206). It would be interesting to know what relationship, if any, these earliest dated deposits bear to the underbank gravels, but so far we are none the wiser on that point.

According to Thomas, the general conclusion is clear, that 'in this part of West Africa all stream activity has been profoundly influenced by fluctuations in discharge arising from climatic changes' and that 'the chronology of the sedimentary events' closely matches 'inferred climato-environmental' changes elsewhere during the Quaternary, both in the Sahel to the north and in the forested zone where Yengema is presently situated (Thomas 1983, 208; Thomas and Thorp 1980, 156). It is only regrettable that so far the archaeological material from this area cannot be more firmly tied in to this established sequence.

THE MUSEUM COLLECTION
AND THE MATERIAL RECOVERED IN 1986

Quite a large proportion of the material stored at the Sierra Leone National Museum could be classified as broadly speaking Neolithic or even Iron Age in nature. Characteristic of the latter are a number of clay crucibles which were presumably connected to the practice of metallurgy. Two of them (nos. 64.47.11 and 12) were recorded as having been found in gravels at depths of 6 and 8 feet near Kombaya and Sukudu respectively. There are some potsherds, including relatively complete vessels, for example four pieces said to have been found at depths of 14–18 feet in gravels of the Bafi river (nos. 64.47.1–4). Potsherds were also encountered during my visit to the Yengema lease in 1986. Mr George Dunbar, a mining engineer with the NDMC, showed me the operations then under way in a low terrace of the Woyie river, with lateritised sandy

clay above diamondiferous gravel in deposits up to 11 metres deep. Following our visit, some sherds were found there in hard black clay above the gravel at a depth of about 2.5 metres, and one of these pieces with a clear design pattern is illustrated in Plate 5.3. In the museum collection, there are many perforated round stones, commonly regarded as digging weights and frequently mentioned in accounts of Sierra Leone's prehistory (e.g. Atherton 1984, fig. 9); they were regarded by Coon as specifically Late Neolithic (Coon 1968, 4). Ten (catalogued together as no. 62.6.9) were said to have been found 'in or near the Moinde and Bafi rivers lying on, in, or under diamondiferous gravel at about 20 feet deep'. They are not to be confused with lighter and smaller spinning weights. These still continued in use up to the present and one (no. 64.80.22) was purchased by Mr H.H. Jackson from its owner for the museum. Nonetheless they also occurred in gravels up to 10 or even 30 feet deep at Jopowahun and Bakidu respectively (nos. 64.47.7 and 8). Presumably such small objects could easily sink to great depths, but they provide a warning, if one were needed, that in this context recorded depth is no criterion of antiquity. Other stone objects include steatite stamps or pestles and pieces with transverse grooves said to have been used for smoothing roughly worked bone or stone beads, strung on a leather thong and rubbed across their surface (no. 64.80.9). The best known steatite objects are of course small statuettes known as 'nomoli', and these have also been found in alluvial diamond mining deposits (Atherton 1984, figs. 7 and 8). Of potentially great interest is the presence of artefacts made of perishable materials, such as the '17 inch long wooden spoon' (no. 62.7.14) discovered by Mr T.R. Yamba in the Kono district 'during alluvial diamond mining operations' (Plate 5.4), but at

Plate 5.3. Pottery from the Woyie river, 22 October 1986

Plate 5.4. Wooden spoon, found by Mr T.R. Yamba during alluvial mining operations in the Kono district.

present there is no means of knowing how old such finds may be.

One of the most common categories of artefacts stored in the museum comes under the general heading of 'stone implements' or sometimes more specifically 'celts'. Thus, forty-five 'stone implements' were presented by Mr Jackson in 1962 and are described as having been found 'in or near the Moinde and Bafi rivers lying in or on diamondiferous gravel, which itself covers bedrock, sometimes under as much as 20 feet of overburden' (nos. 62.21.1–45). Similar quantities were presented by him on different occasions and were described in more or less the same way. 'All have been discovered in river valleys'. Occasionally those presented by other persons were more specifically linked to a certain locality. Thus, Mr A. Nabby gave the museum a 'large flat axe blade 20 cm long' (Plate 5.5) which he had found beside the Kenyie stream near Reyima 'in gravel at 12 feet' (no. 64.80.16), and Alhaji B. Kallon presented them with a 'hard black axe blade 13 cm long' which he had found in the Sewa river near Nyandehun also 'in gravel at 12 feet' (no. 64.80.18). Unusually, neither of these artefacts is of dolerite, and both are unequivocally ground stone axes. Among the dolerite artefacts there are also definite examples of this type, either whole or broken, but the majority of the 'stone implements' can be described only as bifacially worked pieces which may have been the equivalent either of Coon's celt blanks (Upper Yengeman) or of his 'Lupembo-Tshitolian' tools (Middle Yengeman). As Coon commented, it was precisely the merit of his excavations to have separated out stratigraphically these two units, which elsewhere had been 'found together, either scrambled in surface finds, or excavated without reference to stratigraphy' (Coon 1968, 2). Clearly the museum collection represents a mixture of these two elements, and it is impossible to sort them out on any kind of objective basis, although subjectively my impression was that the majority resembled celt blanks.

There are two artefacts in the collection which fall outside these parameters, both remarked upon by Cole-King (1976) who in fact found one of them on a trip out of

Plate 5.5. Ground stone axe, found by Mr A. Nabby beside the Kenyie stream.

Freetown in April–May of that year. In the Bombali district, centred on Makeni, he discovered 'a fine dolerite side flake, of MSA type, in a shallow rain gully' at Rogbing West. 'It shows no signs of abrasion and is only lightly laterite stained. Nothing else could be found in spite of careful search among the pebble and angular chunks in the gully'. He concluded therefore that the flake was out of context, but it is certainly interesting, and no doubt provides the main foundation for his remark, that 'occasional artefacts of MSA type have been found in the northern areas'. This artefact is illustrated in Fig. 5.5.3. It measures 60×51×14 mm, and in my opinion can better be classified as a worked out disc core than a side flake. The fact that it is so fresh suggests that it cannot have come from far, and it certainly has an MSA appearance to it. The second artefact is illustrated in Plate 5.6. This was described by Cole-King as 'a magnificent Acheulian handaxe, in lightly abraded

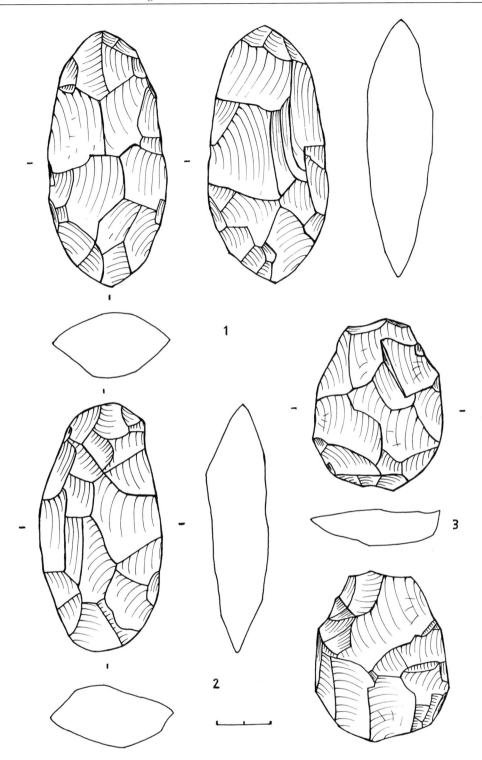

Fig. 5.5. Yengema lease: bifacial implements (1–2); Rogbing West: disc core (3)

white quartz'. It measures 270×133×80 mm and is inventoried among the 45 artefacts presented by Mr Jackson in 1962 as coming from a depth of 20 feet in or near the Moinde and Bafi rivers (no. 62.21.17). It again substantiates Cole-King's remark that although 'no early sites have so far been found' in Sierra Leone, 'a few of the artefacts in the large unprovenanced collections in the Cotton Tree Museum suggest that they may exist'. Mr Robert Ashton, a geologist with the NDMC, showed me another unabraded quartz artefact very similar to this which he had found near Sandaru on the border with Guinea. It had come from a 1 metre section in 30 cm thick gravels at the base. These hints suggest therefore that both ESA and MSA sites do exist in Sierra Leone and that one day they may be found.

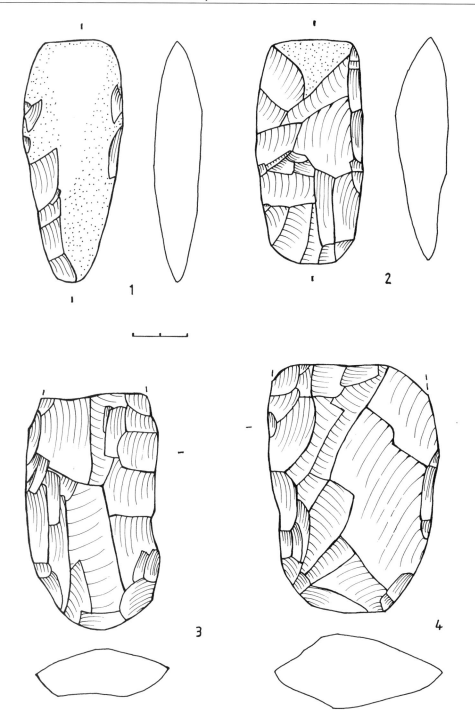

Fig. 5.6. Yengema lease: ground stone axes and preforms

During my visit to the Yengema lease, I was able to make a collection of dolerite artefacts from the mining tailings, and in addition I was presented with some which had been obtained by Mr Aliu Mahdi, Assistant General Manager of the NDMC, over a period of time. Both collections are similar, and consisted of sixty-six artefacts all told. There were fifteen flakes and one blade, thirty-three more or less complete bifaces and nine which were quite seriously broken, as well as eight ground stone axes. The flakes and blades are very similar to those illustrated by Coon (1968, plates 15a and 19b) and there is also a general similarity between the various bifacial artefacts and those classified by Coon as celts or celt blanks and convergent or parallel-sided tools from the Upper and Middle Yengeman respectively. Although therefore the collection made or received in 1986 cannot in any sense be regarded as homogeneous, it was felt that it would be worthwhile to try to compare it metrically as well as morphologically with Coon's collection from the cave site. This task was made easier by the fact that Coon

Plate 5.6. Quartz handaxe, among artefacts found by Mr H.H. Jackson in or near the Moinde and Bafi rivers.

himself provided meticulous measurements for the artefacts recovered in 1965.

In his table 12 Coon listed the full dimensions of thirteen dolerite celt blanks, and eighteen celts of dolerite or schist, thirty-one in all. In his table 5 he listed the full dimensions of nineteen dolerite convergent bifaces, to which may be added one of schist, and six dolerite parallel-sided bifaces, twenty-six in all. Statistics for these two sets of artefacts taken as a whole, representing the Upper and Middle Yengeman respectively, have been recalculated and are shown (in mm) in Figs. 5.8 and 5.9. The figures for the Middle Yengeman use the actual lengths of the implements, not the 'restored' lengths which Coon estimated for some of them. In terms of all parameters the Upper Yengeman bifacial implements are noticeably smaller than the Middle Yengeman. There are interesting distinctions within the two data sets. Thus, the means for the lengths, breadths, and thicknesses of the Upper Yengeman celts and celt blanks taken separately are as follows:

Artefact	Length	Breadth	Thickness
Celts	54.06	29.22	13.78
Celt blanks	59.00	32.31	19.62

These differences are evident in the scattergrams, which also show that Coon had reason on morphological grounds to separate out the two 'flat celts' as he did. The corresponding figures for the Middle Yengeman convergent and parallel-sided bifaces are as follows:

Shape	Length	Breadth	Thickness
Convergent	65.20	39.75	20.20
Parallel	65.17	46.67	25.67

In this case, there is practically no difference in length, but there are quite considerable differences in breadth and thickness, as can be seen in the scattergrams. In all cases there is a positive correlation between breadth and thickness and length and breadth for these artefacts, the highest figure being 0.71 for breadth vs. thickness of the Middle Yengeman pieces taken as a whole.

The collection recovered in 1986 contained seven ground stone axes and thirty-two other bifacial tools for which complete dimensions could be reliably obtained. Two of the ground stone axes (both from the Mahdi collection) are illustrated in Figs. 5.6.1 and 5.6.2. The first example has a little chipping on one side, whereas the second has quite extensive chipping all over. It is, however, regular in shape, and the top has been carefully ground on both sides. The remaining artefacts were divided at the time into ground stone axe preforms and those which could be considered comparable to Coon's 'Lupembo-Tshitolian' implements. This was an admittedly subjective decision. Twenty-four of the complete pieces were classified as ground stone axe preforms and eight as other bifacials. Preforms are illustrated in Figs. 5.6.3 and 5.6.4, and other bifacials at Figs. 5.5.1 and 5.5.2. Both the preforms were broken (not recently) at one end and (despite their initial classification) they do of course also look quite similar to Coon's parallel-sided Middle Yengeman artefacts. As can be seen, the two 'Lupembo-Tshitolian' artefacts are rather oval in shape with lenticular cross-sections and neither was much abraded. Statistics for the collection as a whole are given (in mm) in Fig. 5.7. There are some distinctions within these artefacts when measured separately, as follows, but they are nowhere near as consistent or pronounced as in the case of the different categories from Yengema Cave:

Artefact	Length	Breadth	Thickness
Axes	78.29	40.43	18.14
Preforms	85.33	43.37	21.54
Bifacials	82.87	42.00	23.25

The way in which the categories merge into one another is shown in the scattergram, the correlation for breadth vs. thickness in this case being 0.46. Obviously in terms of mean length these pieces as a whole are much bigger than any of those from Yengema Cave, but in terms of mean breadth and thickness (42.56 and 21.28 mm respectively) this collection is far closer to the Middle Yengeman than to the Upper Yengeman. The ground stone axes clearly represent a Neolithic element but, my initial impression notwithstanding, I conclude from this that the bulk of the bifacial artefacts derived from alluvial contexts in 1986 are indeed, in Coon's terminology, more 'Lupembo-Tshitolian' than anything else. The distinction between

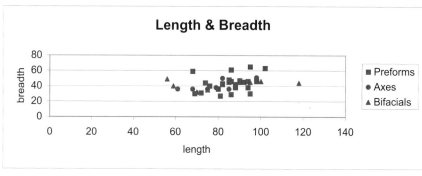

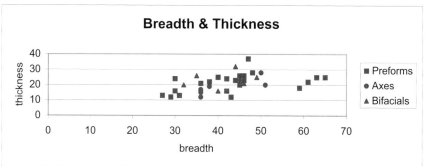

Length	
Class	Frequency
50 - 59	2
60 - 69	4
70 - 79	7
80 - 89	13
90 - 99	10
100 - 109	2
110 - 119	1

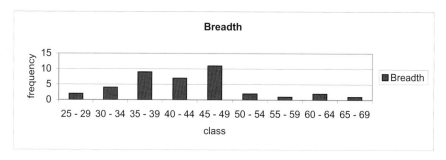

Breadth	
Class	Frequency
25 - 29	2
30 - 34	4
35 - 39	9
40 - 44	7
45 - 49	11
50 - 54	2
55 - 59	1
60 - 64	2
65 - 69	1

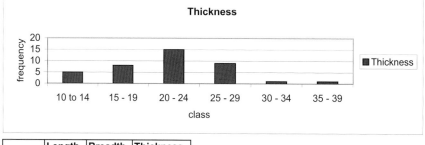

Thickness	
Class	Frequency
10 to 14	5
15 - 19	8
20 - 24	15
25 - 29	9
30 - 34	1
35 - 39	1

	Length	Breadth	Thickness
Mean	83.57	42.56	21.28
SD	12.84	9.12	5.61

Fig. 5.7. Dimensions of ground stone axes, preforms, and other bifacial implements: Yengema lease 1986

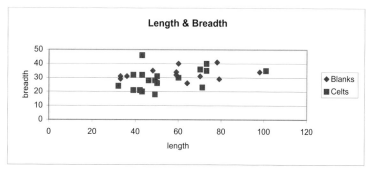

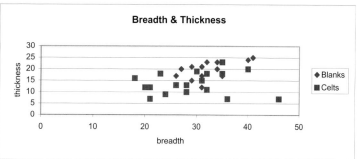

Length	
Class	Frequency
30 - 39	6
40 - 49	8
50 - 59	5
60 - 69	3
70 - 79	7
80 - 89	0
90 - 109	2

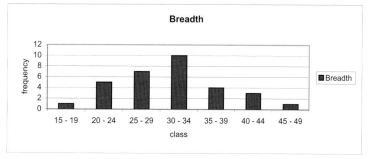

Breadth	
Class	Frequency
15 - 19	1
20 - 24	5
25 - 29	7
30 - 34	10
35 - 39	4
40 - 44	3
45 - 49	1

Thickness	
Class	Frequency
5 to 9	4
10 to 14	7
15 - 19	10
20 - 24	9
25 - 29	1

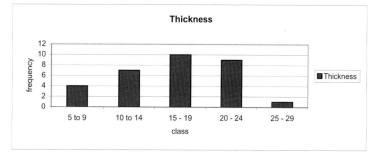

	Length	Breadth	Thickness
Mean	56.13	30.52	16.23
SD	18.07	6.51	5.27

Fig. 5.8. Dimensions of celts and celt blanks: Yengema Cave 1965

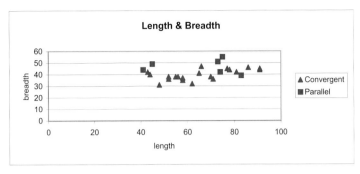

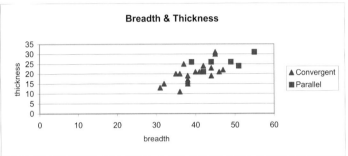

Length	
Class	Frequency
40 - 49	5
50 - 59	6
60 - 69	3
70 - 79	7
80 - 89	3
90 - 99	2

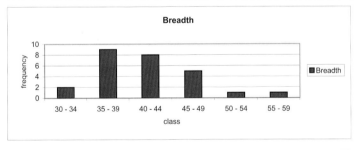

Breadth	
Class	Frequency
30 - 34	2
35 - 39	9
40 - 44	8
45 - 49	5
50 - 54	1
55 - 59	1

Thickness	
Class	Frequency
10 to 14	2
15 - 19	6
20 - 24	11
25 - 29	4
30 - 34	3

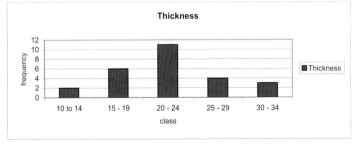

	Length	Breadth	Thickness
Mean	65.19	41.35	21.46
SD	15.24	5.67	5.2

Fig. 5.9. Dimensions of convergent and parallel-sided bifacial implements: Yengema Cave 1965

celt blanks and parallel-sided bifacial implements (as Coon demonstrated) requires stratigraphy to support it, nor would one want to rely on measurements alone, but morphologically, as well as metrically, there is nothing in the collection which would contradict this revised assessment.

DISCUSSION AND CONCLUSION

The thirty-eight radiocarbon dates obtained by Thomas and Thorp from alluvial deposits in east central Sierra Leone provide a useful indicator of climatic change which may be correlated with other sequences in West Africa (Thomas and Thorp 1980, fig. 6). Unfortunately, it is still true that the dated deposits cannot be positively linked with known archaeological finds. Large numbers of such finds have been recovered from the deposits as a result of the mining operations which commenced in the 1930s. The majority of these finds can be regarded as broadly Neolithic in nature, including pottery and ground stone axes, but the attribution of the bifacially flaked stone artefacts is somewhat more uncertain. As a result of his excavations at Yengema Cave, Coon distinguished an Upper Yengeman and a Middle Yengeman, the first of which had both celts and celt blanks, and the second of which had exclusively flaked convergent and parallel-sided bifaces. He called the second industry 'Lupembo-Tshitolian', regarding it as 'forest-linked' and part of a larger complex extending all the way from Central Africa to Dakar (Coon 1968, 'Yengema cave and pertinent other sites', map with Foreword). Metrically and morphologically, the majority of the bifacially flaked artefacts recovered from the alluvial deposits in 1986, as well as certain of the finds in the Sierra Leone National Museum, appear to correspond more or less to the Middle Yengeman. It is tempting to assume that they do belong to the period after 12,000–10,000 BP when, as we know from the investigations of Thomas and Thorp, the valleys were scoured out in a new phase of erosion. If so, broadly speaking Coon was right, and the Middle Yengeman can be regarded as essentially early Holocene in age.

Whether it can properly be called 'Lupembo-Tshitolian' is another matter. As is now known, there are a number of other early Holocene industries with a macrolithic component in West Africa (MacDonald and Allsworth-Jones 1994, fig. 13). Some of them, such as Manianbougou in Mali, are factory sites; but others, such as Blandè in Guinea as well as Yengema itself, are habitation sites. There is a tendency in such sites for polished stone axes not to be associated with the macrolithic industries at their first occurrence, and initially the goal of production may have been simple flaked instruments which could have been 'useful for chopping wood and digging'. We suggested, rather as Coon did himself, that 'polished stone axes, which appear to be rare in comparison to these unpolished implements, may have been more important as status or ceremonial objects than as items of everyday utility' (MacDonald and Allsworth-Jones 1994, 98). As for the

ESA and the MSA, they are, of course, sparsely represented in Sierra Leone at the moment, but one day reconnaissance may be able to tell us more about them.

One day. There lies the rub. At the time of my visit in 1986, the country may have been somewhat run down, but it was safe enough. The minefields were accessible, the university functioned, and the collections in the Cotton Tree Museum were available for study. As from 1991, all this changed with the commencement of the civil war. To a large extent, diamonds have been at the root of it. Their malign influence was already chronicled by Graham Greene in 'The Heart of the Matter' (1948) and they determined the fate of Major Scobie and his Syrian friend the diamond dealer Yusef. Later, Hall was altogether too optimistic in thinking that smuggling had been reduced to negligible proportions and that the picture was now one of 'stability' (Hall 1973, 6–7). On the contrary, as Robert Kaplan put it in his persuasive study of the 'coming anarchy' (1994), Sierra Leone became a 'microcosm of what is occurring in West Africa and much of the underdeveloped world: the withering away of central governments, the rise of tribal and regional domains, the unchecked spread of disease, and the growing pervasiveness of war'. According to Else *et al.* (1999) the Cotton Tree Museum 'suffered' during the *coup* of 1997, and as for the eastern part of the country, it was at that time 'a centre of rebel activity and off limits to travellers'. No doubt cultural and educational matters take a back seat in situations like this; but it is time that the 'international community' recognised its responsibilities in this domain also.

ACKNOWLEDGEMENTS

My visit to Sierra Leone would have been impossible without the financial support of the British Prehistoric Society and the Cambridge Philosophical Society, who together made available the sum of £350. At the time when I was severely strapped for foreign exchange this made all the difference. Formally speaking I was invited by the University of Sierra Leone, and my thanks go to the then Director of the Institute of African Studies, Professor C. Magbaily Fyle, for his help in this regard. My visit to the diamond mines would likewise have been impossible without the willing assistance of all the staff of the NDMC, particularly Professor Victor Strasser-King, the then Chairman and Head of the Geology Department at the University, Mr Abu Koroma, the Managing Director, and Mr Keith Mantell, the General Manager at Yengema. In the mining areas I was greatly assisted by Mr Aliu Mahdi, Mr Ahmed Kamara, Mr George Dunbar, and Mr Robert Ashton. For permission to work at the museum in Freetown and for granting me free access to the collections I am most grateful to Mrs Dorothy Cummings and the other members of staff. Mr Joseph Opala provided me with a great deal of useful information, and the artefacts collected at Yengema were left in his care on behalf of the Institute of African Studies. For assistance in preparing Figs. 5.7–5.9 I am grateful to Ms Esther Rodriques, at the University of the West Indies. I am very pleased to include this article in the volume presented to Professor Derek Roe, who has taken a consistent interest in African pre-history and also quantitative studies, as well as helping me on the various occasions when I have been resident in Oxford, particularly as a visiting scholar at Wolfson College.

REFERENCES

Allsworth-Jones, P. 1986. Middle Stone Age and Middle Palaeolithic: the evidence from Nigeria and Cameroun. In G.N. Bailey and P. Callow (eds.) *Stone Age Prehistory: Studies in Memory of Charles McBurney*, 153–168. Cambridge University Press, Cambridge.

Atherton, J.H. 1984. La préhistoire de la Sierra Leone. *L'Anthropologie* 88, 245–261.

Clarke, J.I. 1969. *Sierra Leone in Maps*. Hodder and Stoughton, London.

Cole-King, P.A. 1976. *Development of the New National Museum and Preservation of Antiquities*. Restricted Technical Report. Unesco, Paris.

Coon, C.S., in collaboration with H.M. Bricker, F. Johnson and C.C. Lamberg-Karlovsky, 1968. *Yengema Cave Report*. The University Museum, Philadelphia.

Else, D., Newton, A., Williams, J., Fitzpatrick, M. and Roddis, M. 1999. *West Africa*. Lonely Planet Publications, Melbourne.

Greene, G. 1948. *The Heart of the Matter*. Heinemann, London.

Hall, P.K. 1973. *The Diamond Fields of Sierra Leone*. Geological Survey of Sierra Leone, Bulletin Number 5. Geological Survey Division, Freetown.

Hill, M.H. 1971. Towards a culture sequence for southern Sierra Leone. *Africana Research Bulletin* 1 (2), 3–12. Institute of African Studies, Fourah Bay College.

Kaplan, R.D. 1994. The coming anarchy. *The Atlantic Monthly* 273 (2), 44–76.

MacDonald, K.C. and Allsworth-Jones, P. 1994. A reconsideration of the West African macrolithic conundrum: new factory sites and an associated settlement in the Vallée du Serpent, Mali. *African Archaeological Review* 12, 73–104.

Morel, S.W. 1976. *The Geology and Minerals of Sierra Leone*. Fourah Bay College Bookshop Limited, Freetown.

Pollett, J.D. 1937. The diamond deposits of Sierra Leone. *Bulletin of the Imperial Institute* 35, 333–348.

Shaw, T. 1985. The prehistory of West Africa. In J.F.A. Ajayi and M. Crowder (eds.) *History of West Africa*, Volume 1, 48–86. Longman, Harlow.

State House 1980. *Background to Sierra Leone*. Office of the President, Freetown.

Thomas, M.F. 1983. Contemporary denudation systems and the effects of climatic change in the humid tropics – some problems from Sierra Leone. In D.J. Briggs and R.S. Waters (eds.) *Studies in Quaternary Geomorphology*, 195–214. GeoBooks, Norwich.

Thomas, M.F. and Thorp, M.B. 1980. Some aspects of the geomorphological interpretation of Quaternary alluvial sediments in Sierra Leone. *Zeitschrift für Geomorphologie, Supplementband* 33, 140–161.

Tricart, J. 1972. *The Landforms of the Humid Tropics, Forests and Savannas*. Longman, Harlow.

Vogt, J. 1959. Aspects de l'évolution morphologique récente de l'ouest africain. *Annales de Géographie* 68, 193–206.

6. Some notes on fish and fishing in Africa

Ray Inskeep

ABSTRACT

Fish are abundant in many of Africa's inland and coastal waters, and as such must have constituted an important resource in the past which tends to be overlooked in modern considerations of subsistence. This paper reviews the distribution of fish around the continent, and the various fishing techniques that have been documented in the recent past. These data are then used to consider the evidence for fishing in antiquity.

INTRODUCTION

When Juliet Clutton-Brock edited a collection of papers on patterns of domestication, pastoralism and predation in Africa (1989) she entitled the volume *The Walking Larder*, and this is probably the way most people think of the protein resources of Africa. We are so used to seeing pictures of the massed migrations of wildebeest in East Africa, or we think of the mountains of meat in such animals as elephants, hippos, rhinos, and some of the larger ungulates, or even of the teeming micro-mammals that seem to be everywhere, that it is easy to forget that there is also in Africa, in its inland and coastal waters, a mass of most excellent protein less dangerous, and often less difficult to secure. Despite Lee's (1968) demonstration that among at least some African peoples plant foods may provide as much as eighty percent of the dietary intake, animal foods are still highly important as sources of protein, as well as being preferred foods, and may also play important roles in magico-religious contexts. But whilst animal protein is usually seen as 'meat on the hoof', until recently little attention seems to have been given to 'flesh on the fin' which is odd, given the abundance of fish in some of Africa's inland and coastal waters.

Just as terrestrial beasts are not uniformly abundant across the African landscape, so fish are not uniformly abundant in African waters. Of course, streams, rivers, pools and lakes do not occur everywhere in Africa, any more than do grasslands, bush savannah or tropical forest, but it is interesting to consider what may have been available, and to see to what extent, and how, fish may have been exploited in prehistoric times. It may not be possible to produce for fish the same kind of quantification that Bourliére (1963) did for some large mammals in parts of tropical Africa, but some information is available that can give us a feel for the abundance of this rich source of protein. The figures quoted in modern geographies are not unreservedly helpful as they tend to include fish trawled in waters which would always have been beyond the reach of pre-contact Africans, and for inland waters these figures often now include farmed fish, for the most part in tropical Africa. Nonetheless, there are some interesting facts to be garnered.

FISH AS A RESOURCE

Cold water currents rich in nutrients flow from north and south along the west coast of Africa and these, combined with a favourably wide continental shelf, have resulted in immensely rich fishing grounds both inshore and offshore, along parts of the west coast. In 1981, annual landings of marine and fresh water fish in Africa were in the order of five percent of the world output, up to two thirds of which were of marine origin. The west coast waters accounted for ninety percent of the latter, with South African, Namibian and Moroccan waters being the most prolific. However, the richness of these west coast marine fisheries is said to be equalled or even surpassed by inland waters: the rivers, lagoons and lakes of the hinterland (Oliver and Crowder 1981, 303).

The west coast

This abundance of fish in Africa's coastal and inland waters is every bit as variable as that of the creatures that inhabit its plains and forests. Just as the terrestrial fauna are influenced in their distribution and abundance by social and dietary habits, whether grazer, browser, mixed feeder or carnivore, gregarious or solitary, so, too, are the fish. There are areas where they occur in superabundance and others where they are relatively scarce. The richest marine fishing grounds occur where the west coast of Africa is washed by cold currents rich in nutrients, and, even in those places untouched by the currents, the inshore waters are rich in fish and have a long history of exploitation by local fishermen. The lagoons of the Gulf of Guinea teem with small fish which are taken both with cast-nets and elaborate wickerwork mazes, providing a trading surplus of around 8000 tons a year (Church 1963, 139). At the beginning of the seventeenth century, the natives of the Gold Coast (now Ghana) fished daily throughout the year, adapting their gear to the kinds of fish available according to the seasons of the year (Van Dantzig and Jones 1987, 121). Barbot (Hair *et al.* 1992 volume 2, 519, 533) writing of the same area later in the same century, describes fleets of several hundred canoes moving slowly out in the morning to a distance of 'one and a half or two leagues' (evidently six to ten kilometres), before returning with the sea breeze at about noon. Their gear, which included hooks and lines, harpoons, plunge-baskets (for the shallow beaches), and large-mesh nets up to 'twenty fathoms long', bespeaks a long and well-established tradition of fishing. For small fish they used baited hooks on a hand-held line. At other times, and for other species (presumably shoal fish), they used a long line loaded with hooks and weighted at the end, which they used to foul-hook what they could from the shoal. After a morning's fishing the men '... sit together on the beach knitting their nets in the afternoon ...', a description that evokes a not unfamiliar image from nearer to home.

The east coast

Compared with the west coast, that bordering the Indian Ocean is far less productive (Bell 1972, 245), and hugely less productive than the inland waters of east Africa (Morgan 1973, 125). MacLaren (1958, 35) observed that 'the east coast Bantu ... do not appear to have important fisheries'. But remarks on abundance are, of necessity, culled mainly from modern geographies and have limited relevance in the context of even the most recent prehistoric communities other, perhaps, than to indicate localities of such abundance as to explain why the archaeological record of fish and fishing in some parts of Africa is so much richer than in others, and why some communities sought their protein primarily in the water while others preferred land, and four-footed prey. Despite real differences in productivity between the west African and Somaliland coastal waters, Chinese records of the fifteenth century report that the inhabitants of Barawa, in southern Somalia, subsisted entirely on fish (Duyvendak 1939 quoted in Horton and Mudida 1993, 675) and that, at Mogadishu, horses, sheep, and camels were actually fed on dried fish (*ibid.*). Further down the coast, at Shanga, fishing was an important activity throughout the life of the site, from around 800 AD to 1400 AD. Tens of thousand of bones, representing more than 6000 fish belonging to fifty-four species, were taken from the shallow inshore waters, mostly by spear and trap, with little to indicate that nets or watercraft were necessary or employed.

Inland waters

Clearly, the warm, coastal waters of the Indian Ocean, whilst they lag behind the cold west coast, are capable of supplying the subsistence needs of sizable populations, though the people known to have been exploiting the resource in historical times were also pastoralists and/or hunters of wild game. But whilst it is the cold waters of the Atlantic that have engendered native fishing on a really large scale on the west coast, it is the warm waters of lakes and rivers in the tropical interior that support large fish populations. Lake Chad, and the Chari and Logone rivers flowing into the south of the lake, between them, were yielding, in the 1960s, from 60,000 to 80,000 tons of fish a year to some 10,000 Chadian fishermen, while the same two rivers yielded an additional 40,000 to 80,000 tons to Cameroonian fishermen, much of it taken by primitive methods (Hance 1964, 296). Further east, such shallow lakes as Naivasha and Lake George '... may yield 20 tonnes of fish annually per km^2 of surface area' (Grove 1978, 81). Lake Rukwa and the Bangweulu swamps are equally productive. The key to the richness of these shallow lakes and swamps lies in a combination of warmth, sunshine, the right amount of aquatic vegetation, and a favourable substrate conducive to the growth of abundant phytoplankton, and a zooplankton fauna, to support the pyramid of increasingly large creatures preying on them and on each other. Warm, shallow, well-oxygenated waters are the ideal. Equally important is the plant detritus, particularly that derived from *Phragmites australis* and the root fragments and rhizomes of such plants as papyrus and waterlilies and, one may add, hippo dung. Too much decaying vegetation, however, and the water may be deprived of its essential oxygen: a through-flow from rivers and streams, and by seepage, is essential. However, exceptions do occur. The Malagarasi swamps, in Tanzania, on account of their unusually clear waters, support only a sparse plankton population, but contain 'great numbers of fish'. These are apparently supported by two species of small fish which subsist on waterlilies and their seeds, as well as other plant materials, which they helpfully process and excrete to provide the main food for other species, especially *Tilapia* (Grove 1978, 82).

Generalisations about the fertility of lakes and rivers are only part of the story. Habitats within a lake, or along the length of a river, may vary as between open water, shore zones, reed or papyrus swamps, and so on, each with its own suite of species, and each demanding its own particular fishing techniques. Lake Chad is highly productive throughout, but the archipelagoes of low, sand islands to the north and east, with their organic-rich waters, and reeds for shelter, literally teem with fish to such an extent that, at times of lowered lake level, the densities become so great as to cause serious degenerative conditions in the fish (Sikes 1972, 120).

Warm, shallow lakes may be highly favourable to an abundant fish fauna but, by nature, they occur in broad, shallow basins and are subject to problems of instability. Bangweulu experiences a definite, if modest, seasonal rise and fall in its waters, in both the lake and its adjacent swamps, of around 1.2 m which, because of the shallowness of the basin, affects a wide area with consequent effects on the lives of the inhabitants and the methods they can employ in fishing. Rising and falling waters are conducive to the use of weirs and basket-traps. Falling waters also have the effect of concentrating the fish in the more permanent pools and channels, and the late dry season is considered the best of times for fishing (Brelsford 1946, 20) and, for the Batwa, with only fish, lechwe and aquatic plants for food, this is obviously a good time.

Superimposed on the annual rise and fall at Bangweulu are poorly understood cyclical episodes which have profound ecological and social consequences. Fish may be concentrated at times of low water but, at the same time, breeding grounds may be lost, leading to an overall reduction in numbers, whilst negotiation of the swamps by canoe and on foot is made immensely more difficult. The original inhabitants of the swamps, the Batwa, were exclusively hunter-fisher-gatherers. At an unknown date, thought to be in the early nineteenth century, the Batwa became subject to a group of Bemba-speaking people who settled with them in the swamps, introducing agriculture to some of the larger sand islands, and so enjoyed all the natural products of the swamps, with the added benefit of cultivated crops. With a vicarious rise in the water level their gardens vanished, the game was driven away, and their idyllic life-style suddenly collapsed (Hughes 1932, paraphrased in Brelsford 1946). Even their island homes became flooded and they were driven to build huts on floating platforms of reeds, a device probably adopted

from their Batwa neighbours, and not uncommon among lake fisherfolk.

Sikes (1972, 83–84) describes similar periodic fluctuations in Lake Chad: not to be confused with those major climate-based fluctuations in the late Pleistocene and Holocene (see, for example, Grove 1993, and summary in Stewart 1989, 12–17). From 1905 to 1906 and again in 1916 the lake was reduced to a vast swamp, with small areas of water surrounded by forests of ambatch trees. The creeks of the eastern archipelagoes became stagnant pools of brackish water and the north pool, normally one of the major open-water areas, became so dessicated that fish died in large numbers and lay rotting on the sand or decomposing in stagnant pools. If the Bangweulians had suffered setbacks, for the denizens of Chad it must have been a near disaster. No doubt such events could be recounted for other lakes and swamps across tropical Africa, though few have been so intensely studied as Chad and Bangweulu and, whilst primarily of interest in the context of local or regional human affairs historically, and for future management, they also serve to alert us to the problems that quite certainly affected those early fishing communities associated with the shallow lake basins and rivers of the Sahara in antiquity. At various times and places in the past fishing has been a secure and relatively undemanding source of sustenance, but there must have been many occasions on which populations found their livelihood seriously threatened.

FISHING TECHNIQUES

The task of reconstructing how this wealth of fish was exploited in antiquity is complicated and fraught with difficulties. Fishing devices are rather sparsely represented in the archaeological record. Equipment and methods reflect in part the nature of the quarry, in part the habitat in which the quarry is at home, and in part the level of technological sophistication at the disposal of the fisherman. If one is lucky enough to find well-preserved fish bones they may be informative but, depending on the parts preserved and the species involved, identification is seldom possible beyond the level of genus, and sometimes only to family; yet identification is needed to determine the behaviour of the fish and its preferred habitat and, consequently, the possible means by which it may have been taken. Reviewing recent traditional practices is one way in, and is a subject of no little interest in itself.

Scavenging and grabbing by hand

Scavenging is clearly the most primitive of methods, surely the oldest, and never really abandoned. Dapper, writing of the Cape Hottentots in the seventeenth century, says 'they look along the shore for dead fish' (Schapera and Farrington 1970, 57) and Livingstone, on his various trips on the Zambezi, found the Barotse keen enough to 'race across the river' to recover the remains of a fish dropped from its perch by a fish-eagle and, on the same stretch of river, dead fish were picked up and eaten 'however far gone', boiled, and the liquor used as soup (Livingstone 1857, 240; Livingstone and Livingstone 1865, 305). Such simple means of capture are still practised when opportunity and knowledge combine. Elster (1959, quoted in Gautier and van Neer 1989, 145) describes modern Egyptian fishermen locating the spawning holes of *Tilapia*, often clustered in water less than 50 cm deep, with their feet, and grabbing the adult fish by hand as they stand guard over the nest. Similarly, David and Charles Livingstone (1865, 431) mention 'a curious fish in holes in the claybank taken by hand whilst wading in the water'. This was probably *Protopterus*, the African lungfish, which aestivates in burrows for as much as seven or eight months when pools or streams dry up. *Protopterus* is one of the largest of African freshwater fishes, and a much favoured food.

Active involvement in fish procurement is most likely to have occurred in low-lying plains adjacent to lakes or rivers subject to seasonal flooding. At times of flooding various species may spread into the shallow waters, but the principal species to do so are members of the genus *Clarias*. *Clarias* breed at the onset of flooding, often within a few hours of the waters rising and, 'after a heavy rain adult fishes in breeding condition can be found in flooded areas struggling through grass in water that barely covers their bodies' (Jubb 1961, 110), in order to deposit their eggs on the submerged vegetation, which provides the young with both shelter and food. At such times they are vulnerable to a variety of predators, including humans. The opportunities are repeated toward the end of the flood season when the pools are drying up and the water is muddy and deoxygenated. Most other fish will have returned to the main body of water or will have died of asphyxiation, but *Clarias*, equipped with special breathing organs, can tolerate such conditions and, remaining too long in the pools, again fall easy prey. Nothing more complex than clubbing or hand-grabbing is needed to secure them, though spears and plunge-baskets may ease the task.

Spearing and harpooning

In the absence of watercraft facilitating the use of spears or nets in more open water, the bulk of fishing would, of necessity, be concentrated in the littoral waters of lakes or rivers, or in the streams and pools of swamp lands. No man-made weapon has a known history as long as that of the spear: Schöningen, Lehringen, Clacton, and Kalambo take its roots well back into the Acheulian, and it is most likely that, of all devices, it was the spear that was first employed as a fishing device. As an aid to hunting or fighting it is known the length and breadth of Africa, and its potential for stabbing fish probably goes back a long way once the desire to reach fish other than in the shallow water of floodplains arose. *Tilapia*, already mentioned,

spawn throughout the year, making their nests in clusters often in water less than 50 cm deep (Gautier and van Neer 1989, 142); the adult guarding the nest would be a tempting target.

On the Nile, the spearing of fish by the Kytch [*sic*] tribe, a few miles downstream of Bor, was 'a mere hazard, as they cast the harpoon at random among the reeds ... out of three or four hundred casts, they may, by luck, strike a fish'. Their harpoon was 'neatly made ... attached to a pliable reed about twenty feet [6 m] long, secured by a long line' (Baker 1962 volume 1, 50–51). Further on in his travels Baker (*ibid.*, 38–39) noted that the harpoons of the Nuer, fishing from canoes, were made with a single barb, though of what material he does not say. And harpoons are mentioned again in a fishing village on Lake Albert 'leaning against the huts' (*ibid.* volume 2, 360–361). More recently, Jackson (1923, 139) says the Nuer used neither net nor lines, only the spear, harpoon and 'baskets not unlike lobster-pots' which must have been plunge-baskets. The head of the harpoon was of iron, about 10 cm long, with a single barb, attached to a 'stout but smallish rod about eight feet [c. 2.5 m] long, by some 9.0 m of stout cord wrapped around a stick about 2 feet [0.6 m] long, held in the left hand'. The head being detachable, it is not clear what happened to the shaft when a strike was made. In the late winter, when the pools and streams were low, organised fishing parties of a hundred or more men, armed with spears, took place, some striking their spears into the reeds by the shore, in order to drive the fish into open water where others would 'transfix them with harpoons' (Jackson *ibid.*, 140). As the water became cloudy, the women came behind with plunge-baskets to boost the catch.

Such observations could be repeated *ad nauseam* throughout tropical Africa, and the universality of such practices inclines one to suppose them ancient. To the south, however, there is less talk of fish and fishing. Most of the southern Bantu refuse to eat fish (Schapera and Goodwin 1962, 133), or regard it as 'a food of last resort' (Boxer 1959, 208 n.2). Despite the abundance of fish in Lake Ngami and its rivers 'none of the Bechuanas take the trouble to catch them' (Andersson 1856, 473), and Ashton (1939, 161) remarks that the 'Basutoland rivers are poorly stocked with fish ... [and] few people take the trouble to catch them'. Stow (1964, 72) in his researches into the native races of South Africa in the mid nineteenth century, records that the Bushmen of the Vaal and Orange Rivers and their tributaries 'made very ingenious harpoons' for taking fish, the heads of which were armed with 'long, sharp points of bone' which they employed with 'dexterity and unerring aim ... [and] landed fish of a considerable size'. Nor was this the only method by which they secured fish.

Despite the Kalahari rivers being generally dry in winter, some retain a series of pools which may contain 'great numbers of fish' which were trapped by Bushmen in funnel-shaped baskets placed in openings in stone-built weirs when the rivers were flowing again (Dornan 1925, 106). Sometimes they spread grass on the surface of small pools, which the men then pushed before them, driving the fish into the shallows 'where they can easily be caught' (*ibid.*, 107), although by what means he does not say. At Walvis Bay, on the Namibian coast, Andersson (1856, 15) saw natives, presumably Khoi pastoralists, fish with spears 'tipped with a gemsbok's horn, affixed to a slender stick'. This was at low tide when fish became stranded in the *vlei* (or lagoon) that extended inland for about a mile. The Cape 'Hottentots', too, were adept with the spear: Tavernier, in the 1660s, says those without an iron-tipped spear would 'take instead a stick as thick as a thumb and as long as their throwing-spears, of a very hard wood ... they go with these to the seashore, and as soon as a fish comes a little above the water they never fail to hit it' (Raven-Hart 1971 volume 1, 71). The same observation was made in 1698 by Lequat (*ibid.* volume 2, 436) and in 1694 Langhansz remarked that spearing with a stick was their only manner of fishing (*ibid.*, 409).

Baskets

If the spear was the oldest artefact for capturing fish, then the plunge-basket was probably the second. Its use in Africa in recent times has been dealt with in detail by Leth and Lindblom (1933). Basically, it is a 'bottomless, conical basket with an opening at the top', which is used in shallow waters (preferably not more than knee deep), whether in lakes, rivers, backwaters or floodplains. The fisherman, or more usually woman, simply wades about in the shallow water ready to plunge the basket down over any un-suspecting fish, which is then removed through the hole in the apex. There is much local variation in minor details: whether the spines are bound to a hoop at the bottom or allowed to project, whether the retrieval opening is at the apex or below it to one side, whether the overall proportion was broad and shallow or tall and more narrowly conical, and so on. Whatever the design, the function and mode of employment remain the same. The device may be used by a solitary operator moving slowly forward in the water, jabbing the basket indiscriminately into the mud on the off chance of trapping a fish, or doing so when a fish has been spotted. On other occasions, generally in residual pools late in the dry season, the hunt may be more systematic, when a line of fishers moves slowly through the water, driving the fish before them whilst wielding their baskets. Fish removed are threaded through the eyes or gills onto a cord attached to a wooden or metal (or bone?) pin, carried at the waist.

There are no examples of plunge-baskets from archaeo-logical contexts in Africa, though there are two excellent representations in Fifth Dynasty (c. 4450–4300 BP) tombs at Saqqara (Brewer and Friedman 1989, figs. 2.26, 2.27 and plates IV, V). Well-preserved fragments of basketry and cordage from Uan Afuda, in the Libyan Sahara, dated to 8790 BP (Di Lernia 1998), show that the technology for fabricating such baskets was well established at the time of high Holocene lake levels in the Sahara. Leth and Lindblom (1933, 3) suggest that the specially made plunge-basket may have arisen 'from a secondary employment of ordinary baskets incidentally used as entrapping implements by women attending the fishing-ground for the purpose of carrying home the men's catch'. This may well be so, in which case the men must be supposed to have been securing their fish in some other way. Unless this was simply the clubbing or hand-grabbing of *Clarias* during spawning, or when stranded in drying pools, we must suppose they were fishing with spears of some kind, as suggested above.

Fishing from watercraft

Without the use of watercraft, fishing with spears or harpoons, of necessity, would be limited to the margins of lakes or rivers and, at an early stage, it must have become apparent that watercraft of some sort could extend, con-siderably, the scope for fishing. The oldest known boat in Africa is the 8.5 m long dugout found under 5 m of mud at Dafuna, in the upper Yobe valley, west of Lake Chad (Holl 1997, 36). The tree from which it was fashioned is 'usually found in closed forest and forest fringing the moister savannah regions' (*ibid.*), and its age, at 8000 BP, places it early in the local Later Stone Age. It lay on what would, at the time, have been the western shore of Mega-Lake Chad. At that age, it is unlikely to have been fashioned for trade or communication, and fishing on the great lake seems the most likely reason for its existence. Dugout canoes are so much a part of the recent ethnography of the great river basins of tropical Africa that it seems something of a surprise to encounter one in the Stone Age, yet other evidence suggests that Dafuna need not be viewed as an isolated example. Quite recently Later Stone Age occupation, associated with fish remains and barbed bone points, has been discovered in Zanzibar (Chami and Wafula 1999) which would have involved a sea crossing of at least 30 km. In south-east Lesotho, rock paintings at three locations (Goodwin 1949; Vinnicombe 1960) depict people spearing fish from watercraft resembling neither a dugout nor reed-built platforms. Clark (1960), commenting on the paintings, observes that there are no historical references to the use of boats by Bantu south of the Limpopo. He includes a photograph of Batla (Zambia) spearing fish from boats of shallow, canoe-like form, made by raising grass-bundle washstrakes on a platform of millet stalks. The postures of the Batla are strikingly like those of the figures depicted in the Tsoelike paintings. Of interest too, are the extremely long hafts of the spears used by the Batla fishermen and those depicted in the Tsoelike paintings. Both are remi-niscent of the 6 m long, pliable reed shafts seen by Baker on the Nile (see above), and of the 'fish-spear elongated by means of a reed [which] sliding through the hand' gives the Ila spear men better control of the weapon (Smith and Dale 1920 volume 1, 161). It seems likely that these very long spears, and harpoons, are designed to target particular fish rather than for random stabbing, for which they may be too unwieldy.

In those areas where trees suitable for dugout canoes were not available, various kinds of craft are made from reed or papyrus bundles, or from the stems of the cork-like ambatch trees: for example, Chad (Sikes 1972, 178–180), Baringo (Worthington 1932, 283), Lake Tana (Cheesman 1936, 90 ff.), Lake Turkana (Worthington and Worthington 1933, 30–31) and, of course, the Egyptian Nile (Vinson 1994, 11–12). All these craft are designed, primarily, to liberate the fisherman from the restrictions of shore fishing, to extend the range of what can be achieved with lines, spears and hand-nets, and to make possible the use of nets of a much larger size. But perhaps the strangest of these devices is the gourd-boat used by the Yedina on Lake Chad. This consists of 'an enormous gourd, or calabash, with an opening of between 15 cm and 25 cm diameter at the top ... the fisherman lies on top of the gourd with his stomach over the opening, and his fishing spear over his shoulder (held in the fold between his neck and shoulder). Then, using his hands and feet, he paddles along looking like some kind of enormous spider. In this way he lays his lines and nets (carried to the site inside the gourd), and then returns later to inspect them'. Any fish caught on the line or in the net are removed and, lifting his stomach to one side, are slipped into the gourd: large fish may be speared first (Sikes 1972, 186). It is, however, a device obviously limited to calm waters.

Line fishing

The survey of fish-hooks, including gorges, by Lagercrantz (1934) and the tackle with which they were used could probably not be improved on other than to extend the distribution to the north and the south, primarily on the basis of archaeological specimens from the Sahara, the Nile Valley, and from south of the Limpopo River, and a précis would not be helpful in the present context. However, a few examples of unusual forms of angling may deserve notice. On Lake Baringo, the Worthingtons noted fishermen using a natural fly, lashed with a hair to a barbless hook, not to fish in the open water, but to bait *Tilapia* guarding their nests in shallow water. The fish are said, at such times, to be edgy and inclined to strike at anything that attracts them. They are, however, timid and the angler must play his game carefully (Worthington and Worthington 1933, 180–181). On Lake Victoria, a particular species of *Tilapia* 'often chew at tufts of green water-moss, or filamentous algae, which grow attached to rocks and stones near the water's edge; the fish do not eat these algae, but suck off the microscopic plants which adhere to the filaments ... The angler fixes a tuft of algae on his hook and, by dangling it among the rocks in likely places, may often kill several pounders in the course of half an hour' (*ibid.*, 181).

The same two writers (*ibid.*, 133) have given us a rare example of indigenous knowledge of fish behaviour and the food chain on Lake Albert. Bundles of grass or brushwood are weighted with stones and lowered from canoes six to nine metres to the sandy bottom of the lake, the cord being marked at the surface with a float of ambatch wood. These are left overnight, during which time tiny *Haplochromis* fish worm their way into the bundles to escape from tiger-fish. In the morning, the bundles are retrieved and the tiny fish removed for bait. A small rod and barbless hook are used on which one of the tiny fish is impaled and dangled over the side of the canoe until it is taken by a tiger-fish which, hauled into the canoe, is in turn impaled on an 'enormous' barbed hook attached to a stout rope and turned loose with the object of attracting the attention of a large Nile perch. Should the bait be taken by a fish too large to land, the rope is tied to the canoe which the fish is then allowed to tow around until it is exhausted and can be landed.

Baker (1962 volume 2, 368) describes an intriguing version of line-fishing intended for very large fish. Rows of bamboo poles are stuck firmly in the mud in some 2 m of water, and 4.5 m to 9 m apart. 'On top of each was a lump of ambatch wood about ten inches [25 cm] in diameter. Around this was wound a powerful line and, a small hole being made in the [ambatch] float, it was lightly fixed on the point of the bamboo ... The line was securely fixed to the bamboo ... [and] the hook, baited with a live fish, was thrown some distance beyond'. Rows of these devices were set every morning from canoes, and watched throughout the day. At night they were left to themselves. If a large fish took the bait, the ambatch float would be dislodged and, revolving on the water, paid out the line. When entirely run out, the float served to check and wear out the fish.

Traps

Knowledge of fish behaviour is evident in the widespread recognition of the habit of some small fish to seek safety in places of shelter. On the upper Zambezi, in areas where small mormyrid fishes occur, piles of stones are placed in the water, in which the fish then take shelter. When the fish have become accustomed to using the stones they are surrounded by unvalved baskets, the stones are removed for use at another site, and the fish are taken up in the baskets (MacLaren 1958, 11). MacLaren (*ibid.*), who had worked as a fisheries officer in both Nigeria and Northern Rhodesia (Zambia), lists at least twenty-four methods used for taking fish in central and southern Africa and, whilst there are regional variations, and occasional gaps, and some devices (such as large nets) may not be appropriate in all waters, the principles involved are virtually universal in Africa, suggesting a substantial, though elusive, antiquity for most of them. The idea of damming up draining streams or pools at the end of the dry season to prevent the escape of fish is so simple that one supposes it must have been practised at an early date. If, as Leth and Lindblom suggest, baskets used by women to collect fish caught by their menfolk in shallow, floodplain pools, gave rise at an early date to plunge-baskets, then it is likely that they were also adapted at an early date for scooping fish from pools, and for dragging through pools. Dams and weirs are effective ways of retaining fish for spearing in flowing water and, as such, can be made even more effective by inserting baskets in gaps to collect the fish swept into them. Like the plunge-basket, the conical, probably unvalved basket-traps used in such barriers are depicted in Fifth Dynasty tombs in Egypt (Brewer and Friedman 1989, 32 ff.) and, at the opposite end of the continent, were in use by Bushmen in the nineteenth century (Lichtenstein 1930, 55). Such baskets may be of quite small proportions and be deployed in relatively gently flowing water, with the weir made of nothing more robust than a row of upright reed stems (Brelsford 1946, 60). At the other extreme, Stanley (1878 volume 2, 252) describes how, on the River Congo, the Wenya constructed not weirs but massive structures in the raging water of a cataract. 'Enormous' baskets were secured by rattan cane cables to structures of heavy poles, wedged between the rocks of the cataract for up to 100 m on each side of the river, with a 300 m gap unattainable in the middle. He reckoned some sixty or seventy baskets were set in the torrent on each side of the river. The catch was variable, but from half a dozen baskets brought up for Stanley, twenty-eight large fish were collected, one of them weighing 7.7 kg. The Wenya were noted fishermen and it is probable that much of their industry was used in trading with their neighbours. The Bushongo of the lower reaches of the Kasai River invested their labour in a different way, but again in the cause of basket-trapping. At low water, during the dry season, channels were excavated 1.2 m to 1.8 m deep and up to several hundred metres long, from the river bank inland. At high water the entrances were closed with weirs and basket-traps and the enclosed fish captured as the waters receded (Torday 1925, 200).

Nets

Nets come in many shapes and sizes, from hand-held nets of various designs for scooping small fish from pools, to giant, communal efforts where nets may be linked to form a barrier 360 m to 450 m long, into which the fish are driven from canoes (Brelsford 1946, 59). These and smaller, but still impressive, nets are for use in the open waters of lakes and large moderately-flowing rivers, and require canoes for their deployment. On occasion, they may be used with platforms of reeds trailing from the upper edge of the net to catch any fish that jump the nets: a fine example belonging to the Barotse king, and deployed on a branch of the Zambezi, is illustrated by Gluckman (1951, plate II.3). As with basketry, so with nets, evidence for their early history is bedevilled by their fragility. Brewer and Friedman (1989, 38) mention a Neolithic net from El Omari, and Stewart (1989, 161) mentions netting from the Fayum, though without stating its age. Fragments of netting have been found in several Later Stone Age

contexts in the southern Cape Province of South Africa, both inland and coastal, with a time-depth of at least 5000 years, and nets used in hunting are depicted in the rock paintings of the south-western Cape (Manhire *et al.* 1985). At Melkhoutboom the netting, of a fine two-strand cord of fibres of *Cyperus textilis*, was made with a 10 mm mesh, using the common fisherman's netting knot (Deacon 1976, 42). Elsewhere in Africa, fine-meshed nets are widely used for scooping tiny fish, often at night from canoes and with the aid of torches to attract the fish.

Tidal fish traps

Because it was the nature of explorers, traders, hunters, and missionaries to head inland after making landfall on the shores of Africa, nearly all surviving references to fishing relate to inland waters, and the bulk of these are from the tropics. Whilst these cover just about every conceivable approach to fishing (including several omitted from these notes), they do not embrace an intriguing set of devices used for taking marine fish, so far only reported from the southern shores of Africa. These are the stone-built, tidal fish-traps first reported by Goodwin (1946) and examined in greater detail by Avery in 1975. They occur intermittently along a thousand-mile stretch of South Africa's coast, from St. Helena Bay in the west to Kosi Bay in the east. They are made where there are gently shelving beaches with sufficient quantity of boulders small enough to be man-handled but big enough to withstand wave attack. They consist of walling which may be built across a convenient gully or, more usually, looping out in deep arcs from the shore. Pools are created as the boulders are cleared to construct the walls, and may occur singly or in groups along a stretch of shoreline, often extending as much as 180 m into the sea, and with outer walls springing from those closer to the shore. They are constructed with the outer wall battered both to withstand wave attack and to make for calmer water so as not to alarm approaching fish. The inner wall is more vertical the better to trap the fish as the tide recedes. Avery (*ibid.*) has established that they are most effective for a few days either side of a spring high tide, when the wall should be covered by 0.5 m to 1 m of water, and on the basis of this and what is known of Holocene sea levels, has suggested they may date to between 3000 and 1700 BP 'or earlier', which raises interesting questions as to the authorship of the traps: whether San, or Khoi pastoralists. Some of the traps have been kept in order by local indigenous fishermen who, at Avery's request, kept records of fish caught at several spring tides, and it is known that, whilst variable, catches may amount to several thousand fish at a time, with *Mugil*, a shoaling, inshore fish being the most common. The fish traps and shell middens occupy differing shore localities partly, no doubt, because the best shellfish gathering places are not those best suited for construction of the traps, and there is much still to learn as to how the two resources were built into the local economy.

FISHING IN ANTIQUITY

Apart from scavenging, hand-grabbing and, perhaps, the clubbing of fish floundering in shallow or muddy water, the basic techniques of deliberate fishing are few: spearing, trapping, angling, netting, and poisoning, and these are all found pretty well throughout the length and breadth of Africa, suggesting a considerable antiquity for all of them. Measuring that antiquity is more problematic.

The Nile Valley

It looks as if freshwater fish were exploited, not necessarily in a sophisticated way, earlier than were marine fish. Marine fish do not offer themselves up as easy prey in the way that spawning *Clarias* do, or even *Tilapia* guarding their nests in shallow water. Thus it is no surprise to find Late Middle Palaeolithic and Upper Palaeolithic sites in the Upper Egyptian and Nubian Nile Valley, mostly with no evidence of fishing equipment, in which fish remains are abundant and dominated by *Clarias* (Gautier and van Neer 1989; Greenwood 1968). Among the numerous Kubbaniyan sites, however, there are three in which bone gorges occur. They are similar to those from two South African coastal sites mentioned below. The sites are three of only four in which eels are present (two other sites each yielded a single bone), and it is suggested that the gorges were used to catch eels. The evidence is suggestive, but it is curious that, if the technique of line fishing with gorges was known, evidence of its use is not found in the numerous other Kubbaniyan sites, either as artefacts or in the evidence of fish remains. There is no sign of fishing equipment in either of the Late Middle Palaeolithic (Khormusan) sites numbered 1017 and 440 on the Nubian Nile. Site 1017 is dated to greater than 36,750 BP, and site 440 is thought to be still older (Wendorf 1989, 780). Whilst the former has only *Clarias* present, the latter, surprisingly, contains remains of no less than five genera. Apart from those of *Clarias*, the numbers of individual bones (or bone fragments) are low, and for *Bagrus*, *Synodontis*, and *Lates* they amount to only 73, most of which are fin spines or vertebrae. Two other Khormusan sites, ANW-3 and 2004, together with 440, have led Wendorf (1989, 789) to suggest 'a well developed fishing technology in the Nile Valley during the Middle Palaeolithic'. But in both cases the number of individual specimens is small (Gautier and van Neer 1989, table 6.16, and Greenwood 1968 for details). The one site not dominated by *Clarias* is 2004, with 94.5% Cyprinidae, mostly *Barbus*. But only 36 bones are present, and nine of these probably come from a single pectoral fin. The data really seem too meagre to support the claim of 'developed fishing technology'. The fish remains from Olduvai Gorge (Greenwood and Todd 1970), with one exception, belong to two families, Clariidae and Cichlidae; most probably *Clarias* and *Tilapia*, both of which we know to be obtainable without sophisticated technology. Unless we are to suppose that these were merely geological fossils, which seems un-

necessary, they most probably reflect the exploitation of spawning runs and shallow water capture. With small numbers of bones, the picture can be severely distorted by the presence of a scavenged wash-up, or a fish dropped by a fish eagle and collected by a scavenger. Olduvai is in the heart of fish-eagle country, and whilst the Nubian sites lie at the present northern limit of the species (Mackworth-Praed and Grant 1952, 190) a specimen was collected as recently as 1947 south of Aswan (Houlihan and Godman 1988, 148). Thus, in situations where plains are seasonally flooded by lakes or rivers, spawning *Clarias* and, occasionally, other species caught in the shallow water, are likely to have been taken, opportunistically, by human populations from the earliest times, and the occasional unexpected species does not have to imply advanced fishing technology.

Inland sites

The earlier Nile record is blank because sites with faunal remains older than the Khormusan have not been found. The earliest evidence for fishing with dedicated equipment comes from the site of Ishango (Heinzelin 1957) where barbed bone points, some harpoon heads and others, probably leister points, are now known to be of late Pleistocene age, probably between 20,000 BP and 30,000 BP (Brooks and Smith 1987). At present Ishango remains curiously isolated at such an early date, and it is not until nine or ten thousand years ago that barbed bone points begin to appear at other sites, such as FxJj12 at Koobi Fora (Stewart 1989, 42), Early Khartoum (Arkell 1949, 75), Lowasera (Phillipson 1977) and subsequently in a broad swathe across the Sahara during the time of the early and later Holocene wet phases (Stewart 1989, 31–34; Sutton 1974). The switch to specialist fishing gear is clearly reflected in the increased quantities and wider range of species taken: eight genera at Early Khartoum and the later assemblages at Atbara, and the pattern is repeated as far afield as the Fayum B sites. It is commonly supposed that barbed bone points are a translation into a different raw material of spearheads set with small stone insets, similar to the Australian 'death spears', and the device need not have had a single point of origin. They survive until between 2375 BP and 1260 BP in the vicinity of Lake Chad (Holl 1993), to later than 2660 BP in Zanzibar (Chami and Wafula 1999), and in Botswana they persist from the mid-Holocene to the beginning of the local Iron Age (Robbins *et al.* 1994).

Coastal sites

At the coastal sites of Elands Bay Cave (Parkington 1976, 924) and Nelson Bay Cave (Klein 1972), on the southwest and south coasts of South Africa, shellfish and fish begin to appear in the deposits soon after 11,000 BP and, with the exception of an hiatus of 4000 years at EBC, fish at both sites continue to be an important element in the fauna, though with subtle and not clearly understood shifts in species frequencies at NBC and sizes (maturity) at EBC. The methods by which the fish were taken can only be guessed at, though there are some clues. At both sites capture by tidal fish traps is ruled out, not only by the absence of any physical evidence for such traps anywhere near the caves, but also by the species composition of the faunas.

Interestingly, double-pointed slivers of bone, interpreted as fish gorges, make an early appearance at both sites. At Nelson Bay Cave, there are fifteen in three units dating to around 11,000 to 10,000 BP (Deacon 1984, fig. 108) whereas in the later levels, including those excavated by Inskeep (1987, 157, fig. 54b) which continues the sequence without a break to 500 years ago, there are only two specimens. Much the same is true at Elands Bay Cave, where Parkington (1976, 101) records almost 500 (seventy in a patch 2 cm by 6 cm, as if having lain in a pouch) from two units spanning a period, approximately, from 10,000 to 7500 years ago. In the later levels, 3500 BP to the present, there are just five. The species caught are the same throughout the deposit, but there is a marked change in the sizes of fish coinciding with the gorges, to those caught subsequently. Data available for white steenbras, the most abundant fish, show that fish from the gorges levels fall well within the size-range of fish commonly found in estuaries, whilst those of the later levels are larger and match very closely the sizes of fish found along open shores: the cave is situated on the south side of an estuary and overlooking the sea. The whole situation is rather strange, since one might have expected spears to have been the weapon of choice in the shallow waters of the estuary, and angling more appropriate to the open sea (Parkington 1976, 101 ff.). For five and a half thousand years after the group of gorges at Nelson Bay Cave, there is nothing to indicate how fish may have been caught, but from 4500 BP small, grooved pellets of shale occur with regularity, and are taken to be line sinkers. Similar sinkers have been reported from two other sites on the same stretch of coast (Deacon 1970; Louw 1960, fig. 53.5). Those reported in Louw's report were interpreted as beads, but seem more likely to have been sinkers (Inskeep 1987, 142). Some of the smaller fish at Nelson Bay Cave favour intertidal rock pools, and may have been taken by hand or with small nets. However, eleven of the fourteen species most commonly taken are unlikely to have been caught by means other than angling, and the absence of anything other than small shale sinkers is a salutary lesson in the problems of 'invisible' material culture, and one possibility is that gorges, or hooks, of wood were employed and have not survived.

The two caves just reviewed, with their long sequences and well-preserved fauna, are currently our best evidence on the early history of sea fishing in Africa. But the fact that, in both cases, fish make their appearance around 11,000 BP does not mean that this was when sea fishing first began. It rather marks the moment when, after the low sea-level of the Last Glacial Maximum, the caves ceased to be 'inland' sites and fell within reach of the encroaching sea. Whether there was systematic fishing before then, when it started, and what form it took are questions for which answers are still needed. In the long Middle Stone Age succession with well preserved fauna at Klasies River Mouth, fish are poorly represented throughout (Singer and Wymer 1982, 208) and Klein (1989, 539) is convinced that MSA people did not actively fish. This conclusion has recently been challenged on the basis of fish remains from Blombos Cave, midway between Elands Bay and Nelson Bay caves, where 'large fish' of three species are present in Middle Stone Age deposits dated to around 50,000 to 60,000 years ago. The reports give no details of the numbers of fish represented though they do say 'fish bones are infrequent in the MSA' (Henshilwood and Sealy 1997, 1998). Given that *Cymatoceps nasutus* is one of the three species listed, and that this has been described as a wary biter and tenacious fighter, one is inclined to have reservations: if such a fish could be caught, more evidence of success would be expected. More detail is needed before we can say with confidence that fishing was practised in the Middle Stone Age.

CONCLUSION

Much of interest and importance has, of necessity, been omitted from these notes. Fish hooks have been recorded from several inland Later Stone Age sites in South Africa, and nothing has been said of hooks from Holocene sites in the Sahara and Nile Valley, nor has mention been made of fishing among Iron Age communities, or of fish in art or belief systems. But enough has been said to indicate what a rich and abundant source of protein and fats is to be had from African waters. The ethnographic evidence leaves us in no doubt that this resource was being exploited the length and breadth of Africa before the advent of Arab and European influences, and exploited with a great deal of knowledge and ingenuity. It not only fed people but, in many cases, fostered trade and stimulated the development of appropriate technologies. The archaeology of fish and fishing in Africa has only recently begun to emerge as a serious study in its own right, but it will surely grow in importance.

REFERENCES

Andersson, C.J. 1856. *Lake Ngami*. Hurst and Blackett, London.

Arkell, A.J. 1949. *Early Khartoum*. Oxford University Press, Oxford.

Ashton, E.H. 1939. A sociological sketch of Sotho diet. *Transactions of the Royal Society of South Africa* 27, 147–214.

Avery, G. 1975. Discussion on the age and use of tidal fish-traps (visvywers). *South African Archaeological Bulletin* 30, 105–113.

Baker, S.W. 1962. *The Albert Nyanza: Great Basin of the Nile and Exploration of the Nile Sources*. Sidgwick and Jackson, London.

Bell, B.E. 1972. Marine fisheries. In W.T.W. Morgan (ed.) *East*

Africa: Its Peoples and Resources, 243–253. Oxford University Press, London.

Bourliére, F. 1963. Observations on some large African mammals. In F.C. Howell and F. Bourliére (eds.) _African Ecology and Human Evolution,_ 43–54. Viking Fund Publications in Anthropology 36. Wenner Gren Foundation for Anthropological Research, New York.

Boxer, C.R. 1959. _The Tragic History of the Sea, 1589–1622._ Hakluyt Society Second Series 112. Cambridge University Press, Cambridge.

Brelsford, W.V. 1946. _Fishermen of the Bangweulu Swamps._ The Rhodes-Livingstone Institute, Livingstone.

Brewer, D.J. and Friedman, F.R. 1989. _Fish and Fishing in Ancient Egypt._ Aris and Phillips, Warminster.

Brooks, S.S. and Smith, C.C. 1987. Ishango revisited: new age determinations and cultural interpretations. _African Archaeological Review_ 5, 65–78.

Chami, F. and Wafula, G. 1999. Zanzibar in the Aqualithic and early Roman periods: evidence from a limestone underground cave. _Mvita. Bulletin of the Regional Centre for the Study of Archaeology in Eastern and Southern Africa_ 8, 1–14. National Museums of Nairobi, Nairobi.

Cheesman, R.E. 1936. _Lake Tana and the Blue Nile: An Abbysinian Quest._ Macmillan and Co., London.

Church, A.J.H. 1963. _West Africa: A Study of the Environment and Man's Use of It._ Longmans, Green and Co., London.

Clark, J.D. 1960. A note on early river-craft and fishing practices in south-east Africa. _South African Archaeological Bulletin_ 15, 77–79.

Clutton-Brock, J. (ed.) 1989. _The Walking Larder: Patterns of Domestication, Pastoralism and Predation._ Unwin Hyman, London.

Deacon, H.J. 1970. Two shell midden occurrences in the Tsitsikana National Park, Cape Province: a contribution to the study of the ecology of the Strandloopers. _Koedoe_ 13, 37–49.

Deacon, H.J. 1976. _Where Hunters Gathered: A Study of Holocene Stone Age People in the Eastern Cape._ South African Archaeological Society Monograph Series 1. Claremont, Cape.

Deacon, J. 1984. _The Later Stone Age of Southernmost Africa._ British Archaeological Reports International Series 213, Oxford.

Di Lernia, S. 1998. Early Holocene pre-pastoral cultures in the Uan Afuda cave, wadi Kessan, Tadrart Acacus (Libyan Sahara). In M. Cremaschi and S. Di Lernia (eds.) _Wadi Teshuinat: Palaeoenvironment and Prehistory in South-Western Fezzan (Libyan Sahara),_ 123–154. CNR Quaderni di Geodinamica Alpina e Quaternaria 7. Edizione All'Insequa del Giglio, Firenze.

Dornan, S.S. 1925. _Pygmies and Bushmen of the Kalahari._ Seeley, Service and Co. Ltd., London.

Gautier, A. and van Neer, W. 1989. Animal remains from the late Palaeolithic sequence at Wadi Kubbaniya. In A.E. Close (ed.) _The Prehistory of Wadi Kubbaniya,_ Volume 2, 119–158. Southern Methodist University Press, Dallas.

Gluckman, M. 1951. The Lozi of Barotseland in north-western Rhodesia. In E. Colson and M. Gluckman (eds.) _Seven Tribes of British Central Africa,_ 1–93. Oxford University Press for the Rhodes-Livingstone Institute, London.

Goodwin, A.J.H. 1946. Prehistoric fishing methods in South Africa. _Antiquity_ 20, 134–141.

Goodwin, A.J.H. 1949. A fishing scene from East Griqualand. _South African Archaeological Bulletin_ 6, 51–53.

Greenwood, P.H. 1968. Fish remains. In F. Wendorf (ed.) _The Prehistory of Nubia,_ Volume 1, 100–109. Southern Methodist University Press, Dallas.

Greenwood, P.H. and Todd, E.J. 1970. Fish remains from Olduvai. In L.S.B. Leakey and R.J.G. Savage (eds.) _Fossil Vertebrates of Africa,_ Volume 3, 225–241. Academic Press, London.

Grove, A.T. 1978. _Africa._ Oxford University Press, Oxford.

Grove, A.T. 1993. Africa's climate in the Holocene. In T. Shaw, P. Sinclair, B. Andah and A. Okpoko (eds.) _The Archaeology of Africa: Food, Metals and Towns,_ 32–42. Routledge, London and New York.

Hair, P.E.H., Jones, A. and Law, R. (eds.) 1992. _Barbot on Guinea: The Writings of Jean Barbot on West Africa._ Hakluyt Society, London.

Hance, W.A. 1964. _The Geography of Modern Africa._ Columbia University Press, New York.

Heinzelin, J. de, 1957. _Les Fouilles d'Ishango._ Institut des Parcs Nationaux du Congo Belge, Bruxelles.

Henshilwood, C. and Sealy, J. 1997. Bone artefacts from the Middle Stone Age at Blombos Cave, southern Cape, South Africa. _Current Anthropology_ 38, 890–895.

Henshilwood, C. and Sealy, J. 1998. Blombos Cave: exciting new finds from the Middle Stone Age. _The Digging Stick_ 15, 1–14.

Holl, A. 1993. Transition from Later Stone Age to Iron Age in the Sudano-Sahelian zone: a case study from the perichadian plain. In T. Shaw, P. Sinclair, B. Andah and A. Okpoko (eds.) _The Archaeology of Africa: Food, Metals and Towns,_ 330–343. Routledge, London and New York.

Holl, A.F.C. 1997. Holocene settlement and expansion in the Chadian Plain. In B.E. Barich and M.C. Gatto (eds.) _Dynamics of Populations: Movements and Responses to Climatic Change in Africa,_ 28–41. Bonsignori Editori, Rome.

Horton, M. and Mudida, N. 1993. Exploitation of marine resources: evidence for the origin of the Swahili communities of east Africa. In T. Shaw, P. Sinclair, B. Andah and A. Okpoko (eds.) _The Archaeology of Africa: Food, Metals and Towns,_ 673–693. Routledge, London and New York.

Houlihan, P.F. and Godman, S.M. 1988. _The Birds of Ancient Egypt._ American University in Cairo Press, Cairo.

Inskeep, R.R. 1987. _Nelson Bay Cave, Cape Province, South Africa: The Holocene Levels._ British Archaeological Reports International Series 357, Oxford.

Jackson, H.W. 1923. The Nuer of the Upper Nile Province. _Sudan Notes and Records_ 6, 123–189.

Jubb, R.A. 1961. _An Illustrated Guide to the Freshwater Fishes of the Zambezi River, Lake Kariba, Pungwe, Sabi, Lundi and Limpopo Rivers._ Stuart Manning, Bulawayo.

Klein, R.G. 1972. Preliminary report on the July through September excavations at Nelson Bay Cave, Plettenberg Bay (Cape Province, South Africa). In E.M. van Zinderen Bakker (ed.) _Palaeoecology of Africa 6, 1969–1971,_ 177–208. Balkema, Cape Town.

Klein, R.G. 1989. Biological and behavioural perspectives on modern human origins in southern Africa. In P. Mellars and C.B. Stringer (eds.) _The Human Revolution: Behavioural and Biological Perspectives on the Origins of Modern Humans,_ 177–208. Edinburgh University Press, Edinburgh.

Lagercrantz, S. 1934. _Fish-Hooks in Africa._ Riksmuseets Etnografiska Avdeling. Smärre Meddelanden, Stockholm.

Lee, R.B. 1968. What hunters do for a living. In R.B. Lee and I. de Vore (eds.) _Man the Hunter,_ 30–48. Aldine Publishing Co., Chicago.

Leth, T. and Lindblom, G. 1933. _Two Kinds of Fishing Implements._ Riksmuseets Etnografiska Avdeling. Smärre Meddelanden, Stockholm.

Lichtenstein, H. 1930. _Travels in Southern Africa in the Years 1803, 1804, 1805 and 1806._ The Van Riebeek Society, Cape Town.

Livingstone, D. 1857. _Missionary Travels and Researches in South Africa._ John Murray, London.

Livingstone, D. and Livingstone, C. 1865. _Narrative of an Expedition to the Zambesi and its Tributaries 1858–64._ John Murray, London.

Louw, J.T. 1960. Prehistory of the Matjes River shelter. _Memoirs of the National Museum (Blomfontein)_ 1, 1–43.

Mackworth-Praed, C.W. and Grant, C.H.B. 1952. *Birds of Eastern and North Africa*. Longmans, Green and Co., London.

MacLaren, P.L.R. 1958. *The Fishing Devices of Central and Southern Africa*. Occasional Papers of the Rhodes-Livingstone Museum 12. Rhodes-Livingstone Museum, Livingstone.

Manhire, T., Parkington, J. and Yates, R. 1985. Nets and fully recurved bows: rock paintings and hunting methods in the western Cape, South Africa. *World Archaeology* 17, 161–174.

Morgan, W.T.W. 1973. *East Africa*. Longman, London.

Oliver, R. and Crowder, M. 1981. *The Cambridge Encyclopedia of Africa*. Cambridge University Press, Cambridge.

Parkington, J. 1976. *Follow the San: An Analysis of Seasonality in the Prehistory of the Southwestern Cape, South Africa*. Unpublished PhD thesis, University of Cambridge.

Phillipson, D.W. 1977. Lowasera. *Azania* 12, 1–32.

Raven-Hart, R. 1971. *Cape of Good Hope 1652–1702: The First Fifty Years of Dutch Colonisation as Seen by Callers*. Balkema, Cape Town.

Robbins, L.H., Murphy, M.L., Stewart, K.M., Campbell, A.C. and Brook, G.A. 1994. Barbed bone points, palaeoenvironment and the antiquity of fish exploitation in the Kalahari Desert, Botswana. *Journal of Field Archaeology* 21, 257–264.

Schapera, I. and Farrington, E. 1970 *The Early Cape Hottentots* (seventh impression). First published 1933 by The Van Riebeek Society. Negro University Press, Westport, Connecticut.

Schapera, I. and Goodwin, A.J.H. 1962. Work and wealth. In I. Schapera (ed.) *The Bantu-Speaking Tribes of South Africa*, 131–172. Maskew Miller, Cape Town.

Sikes, S.K. 1972. *Lake Chad*. Eyre Methuen, London.

Singer, R. and Wymer, J.J. 1982. *The Middle Stone Age at Klasies River Mouth in South Africa*. University of Chicago Press, Chicago and London.

Smith, E.W. and Dale, A.M. 1920. *The Ila-Speaking Peoples of Northern Rhodesia*. Macmillan and Co., London.

Stanley, H.M. 1878. *Through the Dark Continent*. Sampson Low, Marston, Searle and Rivington, London.

Stewart, K.M. 1989. *Fishing Sites of North and East Africa in the Late Pleistocene and Holocene: Environmental Change and Human Adaptation*. British Archaeological Reports International Series 521, Oxford.

Stow, G.M. 1964. *The Native Races of South Africa*. Facsimile reproduction of the first (1905) edition. Struik, Cape Town.

Sutton, J.E.S. 1974. The aquatic civilisation of middle Africa. *Journal of African History* 15, 527–546.

Torday, E. 1925. *On the Trail of the Bushongo*. Seeley, Service and Co. Ltd., London.

Van Dantzig, A. and Jones, A. (eds.) 1987. *Pieter dee Marees: Description and Historical Account of the Gold Kingdom of Guinea*. Oxford University Press for The British Academy, Oxford.

Vinnicombe, P. 1960. A fishing scene from the Tsoelike River, south-eastern Basutoland. *South African Archaeological Bulletin* 15, 15–19.

Vinson, S. 1994. *Egyptian Boats and Ships*. Shire Publications Ltd., Princes Risborough.

Wendorf, F. 1989. Summary and synthesis. In A.E. Close (ed.) *The Prehistory of Wadi Kubbaniya*, Volume 2, 768–824. Southern Methodist University Press, Dallas.

Worthington, E.B. 1932. The lakes of Kenya and Uganda. *The Geographical Journal* 79, 275–297.

Worthington, S. and Worthington, E.B. 1933. *Inland Waters of Africa*. Macmillan and Co., London.

7. Europe and Africa during the Palaeolithic

Marcel Otte

ABSTRACT

In recent years, the interpretation of the European Palaeolithic has been dominated by the 'Out of Africa' theory and archaeological frameworks developed in France. This paper argues that both approaches have introduced bias. It suggests that the non biface industries of Europe may have an Asian origin, and that the Solutrean may originate in Spain as a result of North African, Aterian, connections.

INTRODUCTION

As the geographic expansion of human groups advanced, so restrictive marine boundaries were encountered and overcome. The settlement of the Pacific Islands is, for example, most remarkable in its progress (Garanger 1986) with communities adapting to an entirely different marine environment, overcoming constraints to exploit available resources and create a new way of life. In the northern Pacific successive passages, initially in a mainly southerly direction, through the coastal islands towards America must have been extremely rapid (Dixon 1999). Early voyages between New Guinea and Australia were probably of a different nature. The seafaring traditions of the navigators would have been unnecessary on the vast Australian continent, and were gradually lost. The technological experience which was crucial for a certain period could be lost from the collective memory, just as knowledge of traditional crafts and skills are gradually forgotten today.

Seas do not seem to have prevented prehistoric human expansion from Africa, but they influenced the manner in which migrations took place. For example, during the Mesolithic, the presence of the same traditions on the coasts of Tunisia and southern Italy suggests that the islands in between formed a sort of linking marine territory (Otte 1997). Such a situation is reminiscent of that in the Marquises and Society Islands of the Polynesian archipelago, where family clans maintained their connections. Certain areas of the Mediterranean can thus be considered as hunting territories just like those of inland nomadic hunters or even the circuits of peripatetic merchants. Conversely, cultural distinctions may exist between opposite coastlines despite seafaring capabilities. In such cases, ethnic and cultural cohesion can be a more powerful influence than the possible technological difficulties, as in the example of the Christians and Arabs during the Middle Ages (Braudel 1977–78).

Sea crossings must also be of value to those making them, and in this respect the example of Cyprus is informative. Always separated by an arm of the sea, the island was nevertheless episodically exploited by hunters with technological capabilities identical to those observed in Anatolia (Otte *et al.* 1995; Simmons 1998). The island seems to have been used for its game resources until its indigenous species were brought to extinction and there was nothing left to exploit. Occupation did not resume until the introduction of cereal cultivation made settlement worthwhile once again. Sardinia presents a similar case (Martini and Palma di Cesnola 1993) where the sea presented no barrier to Palaeolithic (Levallois) expansion, but where occupation seems to have ended as faunal resources dwindled.

OUT OF AFRICA

It is clear that sea crossings over considerable distances were possible during the Palaeolithic and could have occurred as and when the need arose. The dangers and difficulties of such crossings do not seem to have deterred people if they had sufficient cause and motivation. The Straits of Gibraltar provide an example of this. Lowering of sea levels during the Pleistocene narrowed the Straits, but a land bridge never formed. However, despite the fact that the opposite coasts were in sight of one another, there is no archaeological evidence for contact during the Middle Palaeolithic. This is corroborated by the palae-ontological data which show clearly differentiated human remains on each shore (Hublin 1992).

In the light of this, the often proposed hypothesis of an African origin for *Homo antecessor*, discovered at Ata-puerca in Spain, has always seemed to me to be fragile and requires better justification than mere proximity. Indeed, the technology of the stone tools from Gran Dolina, dated to about 800 kyr, does not reflect any of the contemporary traditions in North Africa (Bermúdez de Castro *et al.* 1999). Instead, it has much more in common with the small tools probably used for making elaborate wooden equipment, which were being produced in the temperate forest environ-ments of Eurasia at this time. Moreover, the wide geographic corridor formed naturally by the steppes of eastern Europe entirely justifies such a relationship along a fixed latitudinal axis. Movements across land could have taken place spontaneously, following the movement of the sun and avoiding the seas, as has been demonstrated to be the case in more recent historical migrations (Otte and Keeley 1990). This idea has also been argued and clearly illustrated by Rolland (1992) for the continental fauna of the Early Pleistocene. In a more general manner, and to draw this part of the discussion to a close, all of the industries of eastern Europe, as well as the hominid remains, present infinitely more similarities with central and eastern Asia than with contemporaneous African forms (Davis 1987; Movius 1948; Ranov 1976). For more than a million years, movements of populations were clearly and logically Asian in origin, not African. This also applies to anatomically modern humans, but that is another story. Support for this view may be found in the pioneering work of Roe (1981) and, using a different approach, of J.K. Koslowski (Kos-lowski and Koslowski 1979, 44), as well as in the publi-cations of certain Spanish researchers (Jordá Cerdá and Fortea Pérez 1976; Perricot 1955). Unfortunately, the opinions of certain French schools adopted in the United States have overshadowed such evidence, and we must return to seek the aid of other arguments.

AFRICAN INFLUENCES ON THE EUROPEAN LOWER PALAEOLITHIC

The European continent was populated by human groups using a limited tool kit lacking bifaces and primarily designed for the manufacture of wooden equipment. Microscopic traces clearly demonstrate this at Hoxne (Keeley 1993), and the tools themselves have occasionally been spectacularly preserved as at Schöningen (Thieme 1996). Such traditions, typically Asian, can be found as far as southern Spain, for example at Orce (Gibert this volume) and Atapuerca (Bermúdez de Castro *et al.* 1999), between one million and 500 kyr ago. They link sites as far apart as Bilzingsleben, Thuringia, Germany (Mania 1995), La Micoque, Dordogne, France, in the Tayacian (Rolland 1986), High Lodge, England (Ashton *et al.* 1992) and Isernia, Italy (Peretto 1991; Peretto *et al.* 1983). The European tradition is thus technologically, if not anthropo-logically, clearly indigenous, whereas those elements which relate to African and Levantine traditions are intrusive.

The situation changes abruptly about 500 kyr ago. Evidence of massive migrations appears. These must come either via Gibraltar or Sicily. The biface is the technological evidence of a diffusion of ideas and human migration. The earliest evidence for bifaces seems to be at the site of Notarchirico at Venosa (Piperno 1999), estimated to be 600 kyr old. In the Iberian Peninsula, the influence may be seen in assemblages associating massive choppers with equally large bifaces, such as at Ambrona (Butzer 1965), and a similar picture may be found at Latamne in Syria (Clark 1968). In the west, this migratory wave overcame the challenge of the Straits of Gibraltar and there was rapid, deliberate, systematic and continuous expansion to the north, causing a mixing of populations with entirely different origins and values. This spread can be followed to the Somme Valley in northern France (cf. Tuffreau 1996), Belgium (Cahen 1984; Ulrix-Closset 1975) and England (Roberts and Parfitt 1999). In this north-western extremity, the two traditions are superimposed, sometimes on the same site, giving rise to controversies as ridiculous as they are fruitless, as in the case of the debate about the Clactonian and the Acheulian (Ohel 1979). At Boxgrove, Roberts (Roberts and Parfitt 1999) was able to demonstrate that the artefacts dispersed across an immense excavated area were in fact contemporaneous although *sensu stricto* typo-logically distinct. Variations in artefact forms which would have been chronologically significant for Bordes (1968) could be seen to follow the stages in the *chaîne opératoire* from a single block. The European Acheulian is quite recent by comparison with that in Africa. At about 500 kyr, it is seen in an evolved phase which arrived late. The variability observed requires other explanations, such as function, ethnicity, or just pure speculation.

The strong African influence on the European Lower Palaeolithic was intense but brief. Its effects were disparate and, moreover, limited to western Europe. The Rhine axis and other large rivers seem to have limited its expansion to the east with the exception of rare sites such as Mark-kleeberg (Mania 1983). For the rest, European traditions resumed quickly. Earlier traditions were abandoned and tool kits were made on prepared flakes.

AFRICAN INFLUENCES ON THE EUROPEAN UPPER PALAEOLITHIC

The second Palaeolithic contact with Africa was again abrupt, clear and limited, although it was more complex as a result of the subtle interactions between populations over the course of the Upper Palaeolithic. Terminal Aterian traditions, limited to the west of the Maghreb, modified their technologies in different, characteristic ways (Debénath 1992; Debénath *et al.* 1986). In effect, after 30 kyr ago, blade blanks were progressively introduced while flat bifacial retouch became flatter and more invasive. The tool kit was reduced in size and Levallois blanks were abandoned in favour of light, standardised blades. A great variety of forms appeared among the points including foliate, tanged and triangular types. This range of tools largely predates the appearance of similar forms in the European Solutrean, the structure of which is anything but clear. The Solutrean in France seems to have appeared without technological links to earlier or later industries. Spanish colleagues have tried to justify an early Solutrean on the Mediterranean coast by comparisons with France, but this essentially nationalistic reflex has proved in vain (Otte and Keeley 1990). In reality, the early Spanish dating is supported on the basis of the internal structure of the Solutrean rather than for its origins. This makes any controversy difficult as it allows each protagonist an apparently legitimate opinion.

An archaic facies of the Soutrean appears in Spain from Late Aterian roots. It is said to correspond to the French Middle Solutrean because that is believed to have evolved from a purported Proto-Solutrean. However, the latter is nothing more than a classic evolved Gravettian with point blades (Bosselin and Djindjian 1997). Regarding the Solutrean as Gravettian in origin creates an entirely artificial French sequence for the Solutrean, and denies the possibility of a Spanish and, ultimately, African origin from the Aterian. The Solutrean sequence thus changes meaning, status and form according to the way it is considered: in France it is a mixture of two traditions, one local, one external; eastern Spain has a middle phase Solutrean by comparison with France, or an evolved Aterian; in Morocco, it is the early and late phases of the Aterian. There seems to be a phobia against a southern Spanish and, ultimately, African origin for the Solutrean which has prevented the observation of actual cultural movements in the French region where groups could only converge. This mental block prevents proper comparison of the striking similarities between the French Middle Solutrean, early outside France, and assemblages such as that from Mugharet El'Aliya, Tangier, Morocco, just fifteen kilometres from the Spanish coast (Howe and Movius 1947).

CONCLUSION

Speculation sometimes invades prehistoric research. Although some have the courage to denounce it, their efforts are not guaranteed success. Alternative views such as those supported by Roe (1981), Rolland (1992, 1995), J.K. Koslowski (Koslowski and Koslowski 1979) and myself (Otte 1997) are obscured by dominant French views which often have no more support or direction than a kite.

REFERENCES

Ashton, N.M., Cook, J., Lewis, S.G. and Rose, J. 1992. *High Lodge: Excavations by G. de Sieveking, 1962–68, and J. Cook, 1988.* British Museum Press, London.

Bermúdez de Castro, J.M., Arsuaga, J.L., Carbonell, E. and Rodríguez, J. (eds.) 1999. *Atapuerca: Nuestros Antecesores.* Fundacíon del Patrimonio Histórico de Castilla y León, León.

Bosselin, B. and Djindjian, F. 1997. L'Aurignacien tardif: un faciès de transition du Gravettien au Solutréen. *Préhistoire Européenne* 10, 107–125.

Bordes, F. 1968. *The Old Stone Age.* McGraw Hill, New York.

Braudel, F. 1977–78. *La Méditerranée: l'Espace et l'Histoire.* Arts et Métiers Graphiques, Paris.

Butzer, K.W. 1965. Acheulian occupation sites at Torralba and Ambrona: their geology. *Science* 150, 1718–1722.

Cahen, D. 1984. Le Paléolithique inférieur et moyen en Belgique. In D. Cahen and P. Haesaerts (eds.) *Peuples Chasseurs de la Belgique dans leur Cadre Naturel*, 133–155. Institut Royal des Sciences Naturelles de Belgique, Bruxelles.

Clark, J.D. 1968. The Middle Acheulian site of Latamne, North Syria. *Quaternaria* 10, 1–60.

Davis, R.S. 1987. The implications of improved chronological determination for the Soviet Central Asian Palaeolithic. In H.L. Dibble and A. Montet-White (eds.) *Upper Pleistocene Prehistory of Western Eurasia*, 297–301. The University Museum, University of Pennsylvania, Philadelphia.

Debénath, A. 1992. Hommes et cultures matérielles de l'Atérien marocain. *L'Anthropologie* 96, 711–720.

Debénath, A., Raynal, J.-P., Roche, J., Texier, J.-P. and Ferembach, D. 1986. Stratigraphie, habitat, typologie et devenir de l'Atérien marocain: données récentes. *L'Anthropologie* 90, 233–246.

Dixon, E.J. 1999. *Bones, Boats and Bison: Archaeology and the First Colonization of Western North America.* University of New Mexico Press, Albuquerque.

Garanger, J. 1986. À la recherche des anciens Polynésiens. In C. Gleizal (ed.) *Encyclopédie de la Polynésie.* Multipress, Tahiti.

Howe, B. and Movius, H.L. 1947. *A Stone Age Cave Site in Tangier: Preliminary Report on the Excavations at the Mugharet el 'Aliya or High Cave in Tangier.* Papers of the Peabody Museum of American Archaeology and Ethnology 28 (1). Harvard University, Cambridge, Massachussetts.

Hublin, J.-J. 1992. Recent human evolution in northwestern Africa. *Philosophical Transactions of the Royal Society of London* 337, 185–191.

Jordá Cerdá, F. and Fortea Pérez, J. 1976. El Paleolitico superior y Epipaleolitico mediterraneo español en el cuadro del Mediterraneo occidental. In G. Camps (ed.) *Chronologie et Synchronisme dans la Préhistoire Circum-Méditerranéenne*, 99–127. Preprints of the IXth UISPP Congress, Nice.

Keeley, L.H. 1993. The utilization of lithic artifacts 1: microwear analysis of lithics. In R. Singer, B.G. Gladfelter and J.J. Wymer (eds.) *The Lower Palaeolithic Site at Hoxne, England*, 129–138. University of Chicago Press, Chicago.

Kozlowski, J.K., and Kozlowski, S.K. 1979. *Upper Palaeolithic and Mesolithic in Europe.* Prace Komisji Archaeologicznej 18, Warsaw-Cracow.

Mania, D. 1983. Altsteinzeitliche Funde von Markkleeberg bei Leipzig. *Archäologisches Korrespondenzblatt* 13, 137–156.

Mania, D. 1995. The Elbe Saale region. In W. Roebroeks and T. van Kolfschoten (eds.) *The Earliest Occupation of Europe*, 85–101. University of Leiden Press, Leiden.

Martini, F. and Palma di Cesnola, A. 1993. L'industria paleolitica de Riu Altana (Sassari): il complesso clactoniano arcaico. *Rivista di Scienze Preistoriche* 45, 3–11.

Movius, H.L. 1948. The Lower Palaeolithic cultures of Southern and Eastern Asia. *Transactions of the American Philosophical Society* 38, 329–420.

Ohel, M. 1979. The Clactonian: an independent complex or an integral part of the Acheulean? *Current Anthropology* 20, 685–726.

Otte, M. 1997. Contacts trans-méditerranéens au Paléolithique. In J.M. Fullola and N. Soler (eds.) *El Món Mediterrani Deprés del Pleniglacial (18,000–12,000 BP)*, 29–39. Museum of Catalunya, Serie Monographica 17, Girona.

Otte, M. and Keeley, L.H. 1990. The impact of regionalism on palaeolithic studies. *Current Anthropology* 31, 577–582.

Otte, M., Yalçinkaya, I., Léotard, J.-M., Kartal, M., Bar-Yosef, O., Kozlowski, J.K., López Bayón, I. and Marshack, A. 1995. The Epi-Palaeolithic of Ökuzini cave (SW Anatolia) and its mobilary art. *Antiquity* 69, 931–944.

Peretto, C. (ed.) 1991. *Isernia La Pineta: Nuovi Contributi Scientifici*. Istituto Regionale per gli Studi Storici del Molise V. Cuoco, Isernia.

Peretto, C., Terzani, C. and Cremaschi, M. (eds.) 1983. *Isernia la Pineta: Un Accampamento più Antico di 700.000 Anni*. Calderini, Bologna.

Perricot, L. 1955. Sur les connexions européennes de l'Atérian: état actuel du problème. *Actes du IIeme Congrès Panafricain de Préhistoire (Algiers)*, 375. Arts et Métiers Graphiques, Paris.

Piperno, M. (ed.) 1999. *Notarchirico: Un sito del Pleistocene Medio Iniziale nel Bacino di Venosa*. Edizione Osanna, Venosa.

Ranov, V.A. 1976. The Palaeolithic of the Central Asia: a revision. In A. Ghosh (ed.) *Le Paléolithique Inférieur et Moyen en Inde, en Asia Centrale et dans le Sud-Est Asiatique*, 91–129. Preprints of the IXth UISPP Congress, Nice.

Roberts, M.B. and Parfitt, S.A. 1999. *Boxgrove: A Middle Pleistocene Hominid Site at Eartham Quarry, Boxgrove, West Sussex*. English Heritage, London.

Roe, D.A. 1981. *The Lower and Middle Palaeolithic Periods in Britain*. Routledge and Kegan Paul, London.

Rolland, N. 1986. Recent findings from La Micoque and other sites in southwestern and Mediterranean France: their bearing on the 'Tayacian' problem and Middle Palaeolithic emergence. In G.N. Bailey and P. Callow (eds.) *Stone Age Prehistory: Studies in Memory of Charles McBurney*, 121–151. Cambridge University Press, Cambridge.

Rolland, N. 1992. The Palaeolithic colonization of Europe: an archaeological and biogeographic perspective. *Trabajos de Prehistoria* 49, 69–111.

Rolland, N. 1995. Biogéographie et préhistoire: le cas du peuplement Paléolithique inférieur de l'Europe. In M. Otte (ed.) *Nature et Culture*, 11–61. ERAUL 68, Liège.

Simmons, A.H. 1998. Of tiny hippos, large cows and early colonists in Cyprus. *Journal of Mediterranean Archaeology* 11, 232–241.

Thieme, H. 1996. Altpaläolithische Wurfspeere aus Schöningen, Niedersachsen: ein Vorbericht. *Archäologisches Korrespondenzblat* 26, 377–393.

Tuffreau, A. 1996. *L'Acheuléen dans l'Ouest de l'Europe*. CREP, Lille.

Ulrix-Closset, M. 1975. *Le Paléolithique Moyen dans le Bassin Mosan en Belgique*. Universa, Wettern.

8. The initial peopling of Eurasia and the early occupation of Europe in its Afro-Asian context: major issues and current perspectives

Nicholas Rolland

ABSTRACT

This paper reviews issues, the anthropic record, geochronological and Quaternary palaeoenvironmental evidence concerning the first settling of Europe from the perspective of biogeography, including concepts of dispersal probabilities, palaeoecology, and anthropological theory. Since the colonization of Europe post-dated that of Asia, this event can be discussed meaningfully only by considering antecedent biocultural hominization in sub-Saharan Africa, and initial phases of hominid dispersals into Asia. Direct evidence is surveyed from Western Asia, the Indian sub-continent, South-East Asia, East Asia and Central Asia, outlining the relevant palaeoenvironmental characteristics and discussing the issues raised by these earlier dispersals. The record seems to indicate that hominid occupation of Western Asia and perhaps the Indian sub-continent preceded that of the Far East by a significant amount of time. This may have been because of the palaeogeographic conditions prevailing in Western Asia prior to the Middle Pleistocene, and the distinctive biogeographical and ecological patterns of monsoon Asia. The hypothesis of migratory drift would see the tropical and subtropical biomes of Asia then being settled first, followed by movements circumventing the major orogenic physical barriers of inland Asia towards Central Asia. It appears that hominids did not occupy habitats north of the 40–43° parallels until much later, owing in part to difficulties in coping with the short duration of winter daylight. Major aspects are discussed relating to the first colonization of Europe, such as the anthropic evidence, chronology, adaptive trends, and alternative dispersal paths. While no firm conclusions can yet be reached, the available evidence suggests two phases in the initial occupation of Europe, documented perhaps as early as 900–780 kyr in the Iberian peninsula and originating in the Maghreb, thereby illustrating a 'sweepstake' dispersal movement, followed by movements covering most of the Mediterranean and temperate Europe by 600 kyr. The latter may indicate that hominids began to overcome the 43° climatic boundary by that time.

INTRODUCTION

Research on the antiquity of the human species during the twentieth century led to the conclusion that its genesis was a natural historical event by evolution, which took place outside Europe, implying a colonization by immigration, with a stratified rather linear anthropic record. Issues and empirical evidence from the fossil and Palaeolithic anthropic record, as well as Quaternary research relating to this theme, are reviewed here within a conceptual framework of alternative models, considering anthropological theory, biogeography and ecology. The initial peopling of Europe was a special aspect of a larger, momentous event:

the gradual expansion of hominids from their African cradle into Eurasia. Meaningful discussions of its colonization must therefore consider antecedent African hominization, and earlier hominid dispersals into Asia.

FORMATIVE BIOCULTURAL STAGES IN AFRICA PRIOR TO HOMINID EXPANSION INTO EURASIA

Many lines of evidence testify that anthropogenesis happened exclusively in sub-Saharan Africa. Humans were an endemic element of the Ethiopian faunal region which was a perennial mammalian evolutionary and dispersal centre. Hominids emerged from the same hominoid ancestors as living chimpanzees and gorillas. A body of palaeoanthropological discoveries in mesic woodlands of East and South Africa of Pliocene times testifies to anthropogenesis back to six million years ago. Sub-Saharan Africa also provides evidence for several stages of somatic and behavioural evolution, as well as episodes of early hominid adaptive radiations into several genera (*Australopithecus, Paranthropus, Homo*) although little consensus exists about their taxonomy and phylogeny (Wood and Collard 1999). Basic biocultural formative developments providing necessary conditions for dispersals beyond sub-Saharan Africa are outlined in Table 8.1.

CAUSES OF HOMINID DISPERSAL OUT OF AFRICA

Hominid population movements beyond their original cradle probably resulted from converging causes, leading to extensive home range displacements. These include evolutionary traits acquired through long-term processes: bipedalism; a broader omnivorous diet with a significant meat-eating component and a capacity for cultural behaviour including regular toolmaking, correlated with an expanded brain cortex surface (Santangelo 1998). Major arid shifts taking place around 2.8, 1.7 and 1.0 myr, favoured the spread of open savannah/woodland habitats (Menocal 1999). These environmental changes coincide with the appearance of the robust australopithecine *Paranthropus* and early *Homo*. They probably influenced biocultural evolution by intensifying seasonal stresses while opening new adaptive opportunities, including a more omnivorous diet involving regular ungulate exploitation, improved early human survival during lengthy dry seasons in grassland habitats, and reduced exposure to woodlands where sleeping sickness was endemic. Hominid expansion entailed new structural constraints essential to a carnivorous subsistence pattern, which required more extensive home ranges to maintain low predator/prey ratios, while retaining sufficiently large local groups to ensure safety from other large carnivores living in the same landscapes (Shipman and Walker 1989). It has been hypothesized that a long-term hominid/carnivore co-evolution is related to this dispersal event (Turner 1982). Other factors could include extinctions caused by the overexploitation of large herbivores (>1000 kg) such as *Deinotherium, Sivatherium, Ancylotherium* and *Anancas*, whose size and lack of fear and the instinct to escape when faced by predators, made them vulnerable to humans armed with simple thrusting weapons (Schüle and Schuster 1999). Prolonged arid shift phases also induced repeated home range displacements which eventually spread beyond Africa.

THE INITIAL COLONIZATION OF ASIA

A conceptual framework for large-scale, long-range prehistoric colonization events is unavailable. The factors referred to above relate to the causes of migrations beyond the African cradle, but not to the processes involved in exploring and settling unoccupied, unfamiliar zones and habitats. Dispersals can be described as stochastic, rather than linear, space/time movements, involving repeated expansions into new regions, as well as episodic localized extinctions of overstretched founder populations, often leaving suitable habitats as empty quarters. By shifting perspectives to encompass biogeography and time depth, hominid dispersals appear as multi-directional, unless

Development	Period
Initial bipedalism e.g. 'Millennium Man', Tugen Hills, Kenya	by 6 myr
Australopithecine evolutionary grades	from 6.0 to 2.5 myr
Expansion of australopithecines into Central and Southern Africa	between 4.0 and 3.0 myr
Radiation of australopithecines into *Paranthropus* subspecies. Appearance of *Homo* grades from *H. habilis/rudolfensis* to *H. erectus*	between 2.5 and 1.8 myr
Intensified bipedalism and improved thermoregulation	
Emergence of cultural behaviour with regular toolmaking, systematic lithic raw material procurement with prehensile hands and handedness. Bone tool use or modification limited	by 2.5 myr
Omnivorous diet including increased meat consumption, based on organized predation or scavenging of ungulates	by 2.5 myr
Expansion of Plio-Pleistocene hominids into ecologically varied home-ranges	
Accelerating encephalization and brain cortex expansion trends from *Homo habilis* to *Homo erectus*	
Elaboration of the Oldowan or Mode 1 toolmaking complex, with specialized facies (Karari variant)	
Progressive technological developments from Oldowan to Acheulian Mode 2	

Table 8.1. Major biocultural developments in sub-Saharan Africa prior to the first hominid dispersals.

impeded, confined or favoured by obstacles such as topography, climate, ecology, latitudes, altitudes or bio-climatic fluctuations which cause dispersal probabilities to vary (Table 8.2). Techno-ecological repertoires and land use strategies could also be efficacious factors.

in the first dispersals; discovering whether they branched out into separate lineages across Eurasia; assessing which Lower Palaeolithic toolmaking repertoire can be identified within assemblage variability; identifying migratory drift paths; determining whether successive Quaternary bio-climatic and tectonic changes altered dispersal paths; and

WESTERN ASIA

Table 8.3 summarises major anthropic localities in Asia. The gradual Pleistocene settlement of Eurasia more than doubled the realm of hominid occupation, but there are several important points at issue when considering this diaspora. These include: establishing a datum for the earliest anthropic remains, whether fossil or archaeo-logical; determining which *Homo* biotype was involved

Type	Dispersal probability	Example
Corridor	High for most animals	Eurasian Palearctic corridor
Filter	Limited to some species	Central American filter
Sweepstake	Restricted by major obstacles. Rare migrations	Australasian sweepstake routes

Table 8.2. Concepts of dispersal probabilities (after Simpson 1962).

Location	Human evidence		Fauna	Chronology	
	Archaeological	Fossil		Era	Radiometric age estimate
Bizat Ruhama, Israel	Atypical Acheulian		X	Late Matuyama	>780 kyr
'Ubeidiya, Israel	Acheulian & Atypical Acheulian		X	Lower Pleistocene	1.25–1.40 myr
Evron, Israel	Acheulian		X	Lower Pleistocene	1.0 myr
Gesher Benot Ya'aqov, Israel	Acheulian			Lower Pleistocene	>780 kyr
Dauqara Formation, S. Jordan	Atypical Acheulian		X	Lower Pleistocene	0.9–1.0 myr
Dmanisi, Georgia	Atypical Acheulian	X	X	Lower Pleistocene	1.6–1.7 myr
Achalkalaki, Georgia	Atypical Acheulian		X	Middle Pleistocene	?
Azykh 7–10, Azerbaidjan	Atypical Acheulian		X?	Lower Pleistocene	>780 kyr
Dursunlu, Turkey	Atypical Acheulian		X	Late Matuyama	>780 kyr
Amar Merdeg, Iran	Atypical Acheulian		X	Middle Pleistocene	?
Pabbi Hills, Pakistan	Atypical Acheulian		X	Plio-Pleistocene	1.9 myr?
Bori loc.1, India	Acheulian			Middle Pleistocene	680–700 kyr
Bori loc.4, India	Atypical Acheulian			Lower Pleistocene	1.4 myr?
Irrawaddy Terraces, Burma	Non-Acheulian			Middle Pleistocene	?
Ban Don Mun, Thailand	Non-Acheulian			Late Matuyama	>780 kyr
Mae Tha South, Thailand	Non-Acheulian			Late Matuyama	>780 kyr
Sambungmachan, Java	Non-Acheulian			Middle Pleistocene?	600–700 kyr
Ngebung, Java	Non-Acheulian			Lower Pleistocene?	900 kyr
Modjokerto, Java		X	X	Lower Pleistocene	1.2–1.0 myr
Sangiran, Java		X	X	Lower Pleistocene	900 kyr
Bose, S. China	Acheulian	X	X	Middle Pleistocene	800 kyr?
Gongwangling, N. China	Non-Acheulian	X	X	Lower Pleistocene	1.0 myr
Donggutuo, N. China	Non-Acheulian		X	Lower Pleistocene	1.0–0.8 myr
Xiaochangliang, N. China	Non-Acheulian		X	Lower Pleistocene	1.0–0.8 myr
Huojiadi, N. China	Non-Acheulian		X	Lower Pleistocene	1.0–0.8 myr
Banshan, N. China	Non-Acheulian		X	Lower Pleistocene	1.0–0.8 myr
Maliang, N. China	Non-Acheulian		X	Lower Pleistocene	1.0–0.8 myr
Manjungou, N. China	Non-Acheulian		X	Lower Pleistocene	1.0–0.8 myr
Takamori, Japan	Non-Acheulian			Middle Pleistocene	570 kyr
Kamitakamori, Japan	Non-Acheulian			Middle Pleistocene	570 kyr
Kamitakamori (base), Japan	Non-Acheulian			Middle Pleistocene	>600 kyr
Ogasaka, Japan	Non-Acheulian			Middle Pleistocene	480–500 kyr
Ittouchi Matsuba-yama, Japan	Non-Acheulian			Middle Pleistocene	720 kyr
Kul'dara, Tadzhikistan	Non-Acheulian		X	Lower Pleistocene	800 kyr
Khonako, Tadzhikistan	Non-Acheulian			Middle Pleistocene	720 kyr
Kashaf Rud, Iran	Non-Acheulian			Lower Pleistocene	?

* Although virtually all the localities from the Far East and Central Asia have Non-Acheulian repertoires, this should not imply that bifaces are absent from the former region. Bifaces are well represented in Java, Vietnam, China, Korea and Japan, but they are not Acheulian handaxe types, with the exception of a few implements from Bose.

*Table 8.3. Major Lower and earlier Middle Pleistocene anthropic localities in Asia.**

establishing what biogeographic and ecological conditions prevailed during initial colonization events.

Correlating the earliest anthropic presence in Asia with the major arid shift events in sub-Saharan Africa and identifying these as push factors calls for precise evidence. Similarly, the question of whether ancient hominids occupied North Africa before Western Asia calls for the identification of dispersal routes. The Maghreb remained an Ethiopian biogeographic island throughout the Pleistocene, implying intermittent connections with sub-Saharan Africa, but the Nile Valley followed its modern course after 1.0 myr. The earliest securely identified and dated human presence is represented by Acheulian sites in the Maghreb including Sidi Abderrahman, STIC, Tighennif, and Aïn Hanech, which are not older than the early Middle Pleistocene (Debénath 2000; Geraads *et al.* 1986). This dating refutes the notion of a Pre-Acheulian horizon in the Maghreb and points to a time lag between the oldest known occupation of this region by comparison with the first human presence in Western Asia. Since the peopling of North Africa required Saharan oasis pathways during wetter episodes, the 1.0 myr arid shift may be ruled out as a cause for this initial presence in the Maghreb. Movements across the Bab Al Mandib Strait from the African Horn directly into Western Asia, feasible under certain palaeogeographic conditions in the Afar Depression (Cachel and Harris 1999, 134), suggests this more likely human dispersal path from the African Horn directly into Western Asia.

The most reliable datum line in Western Asia is represented by the deeply stratified site of 'Ubeidiya, dated to between 1.4–1.25 myr, with alternating typical and atypical (handaxe free) Acheulian layers, and Evron Quarry (1.0 myr), Bizat Ruhama and Gesher Benot Ya'aqov III-2 (both >780 kyr) in Israel, and the Dauqara Formation in south Jordan, 0.9–1.0 myr (Parenti *et al.* 1997). Sites such as Sitt Markho and Sheikh Muhamad in Syria may also belong to this horizon. Discoveries at Dmanisi, in Georgia, could imply an earlier date for hominids settling western Eurasia. An argon-dated basalt horizon of 1.8 myr underlies redeposited sediments containing a Plio-Pleistocene fauna, cranial remains of three hominids, and artefacts without handaxes. One mandible belongs within an evolved *Homo erectus* grade (Henke *et al.* 1999), but two recently discovered skulls indicate archaic *Homo* biotypes. Their morphology and relative dating could testify to earlier hominid incursions deep into Eurasia (Balter and Gibbons 2000), synchronous with the 1.7 myr African arid shift which was possibly a decisive factor in the earliest extra-African dispersals. No *a priori* reasons exist for ruling out population movements out of Africa as early as 1.7–1.6 myr. The main issue relates to how the migrating hominids overcame major biogeographic and ecological barriers.

The mild humid climate, lush Colchian vegetation and varied fauna of the Transcaucasus offer favourable settings for human life, but areas lying across presumed migratory paths between the Levant and Transcaucasus, as known today, would confront technologically simple incoming *Homo* groups with major obstacles. Eastern Anatolia has an extreme, harsh climate in difficult Alpine terrain (Fisher 1963, 327), while the Anatolian plateau is an enclosed, high altitude, arid landscape, with impoverished plant and animal life (*ibid.*, 325). The southern coastline and adjacent foothills of Anatolia have adequate habitats and migratory conditions, as indicated by the Late Matuyama Dursunlu Palaeolithic site (Güleç *et al.* 1999), but the Taurus and north-west Zagros form an intricate array of arcs of irregular folds difficult for migrations which would also have been obstructed by the West Taurus wall, where the protracted faunal endemism goes back to 1.0 myr. Eastern Anatolia is part of the European, rather than the Near Eastern, Pleistocene faunal province (H.-P. Uerpmann pers. comm.), indicating a complex biogeographic history.

Dmanisi thus presents a paradox when considering the initial peopling of Western Asia. Resolution will remain elusive until a detailed Pleistocene geomorphological history of Western Asia, marked, like Central Asia and the Far East, by tectonic instability, becomes available. The folded physiography of Eastern Anatolia suggests a complex history of multidirectional orogenic uplift and subsidence, unlike the densely packed alignment of the mainly Jurassic Central Zagros ridges (Fisher 1963, 20–21, 280). Intensified tectonic events and deteriorating climatic conditions since the Lower Pleistocene could have made previous dispersal paths from the Levant to the Transcaucasus less accessible by 850 kyr. Before Middle Pleistocene uplifts and faults created the Levant Rift and adjacent hills (Horowitz 1979), rolling plains and drainage systems formed much of the Levant landscapes, wedging perhaps as far north as the Transcaucasus through humid and less rugged landscapes with more widespread Colchian rainforests. These presented fewer physical and bioclimatic barriers for an early human penetration this far north.

The most likely population movements further into Asia followed ecologically familiar sub-tropical zones in Western Asia, along the Fertile Crescent, as suggested by the Amar Merdeg sites (Biglari *et al.* 2000), and south of the Iranian Plateau (Howell 1960, 225). The latter was inaccessible across most of the Zagros range as far as Baluchistan, while the south Iranian Plateau remained desolate, inhospitable and hazardous (Fisher 1963, 288; Spooner 1972, 248). Lack of research in regions between the Levant and India means that there are no relevant data for this area.

THE INDIAN SUB-CONTINENT

This vast region combines the environmental characteristics of Africa, Western and South-East Asia. Besides being the likely route to the Far East, it had optimally rich habitats for omnivorous foragers (Paddaya 1994). Evidence of extensive grasslands back to the Miocene in the north, is much earlier than in Africa. Many areas supported animal food biomasses comparable to East and Central Africa

(Schaller 1967), with riverine gallery forests (Korisettar and Rajaguru 1998, 334–335). Human occupation became dense during semi-arid grassland episodes (Petraglia 1998, 375–379). Monsoon fluctuations induced episodic shifts of tropical evergreen forest and savannah ecosystems. Pleistocene mammals were mostly endemic with Palearctic elements (Kretzoi 1961–64), instead of being part of the Oriental region. This suggests ecological filters such as dense forests in Assam and Bengal, separating the sub-continent from South-East Asia, which may explain the greater similarities between the Palaeolithic of India, Western Asia, Africa and Europe, than between India and the Far East (Petraglia 1998, 366–372). Schüle and Schuster hypothesize significant anthropic impact on Plio-Pleistocene megafaunas and extinctions in South Asia (1999, 232).

An outstanding issue is to establish a datum for early hominid occupation of the sub-continent. Later Acheulian horizons are better known than early ones. The oldest datable occurrences come from the sub-Himalayan Pabbi Hills, Pakistan (Hurcombe and Dennell 1992), and the Bori area, Central India (Mishra *et al.* 1995), dating around 650–700 kyr. A tephra bed in Central India (Korisettar *et al.* 1989) and finds from Pakistan, the dating of which remains at issue, offer long-term prospects for better chronological resolution (Mishra and Rajaguru 1998). Ongoing fieldwork in localities containing *in situ* sites and preserved palaeoenvironmental evidence (Korisettar 1994), frequent use of radiometric and lithostratigraphic methods, awareness of recent Plio-Pleistocene finds from Western Asia and of the fact that early hominid occupation in the Far East is estimated to be at least 1.1–1.2 myr, make an initial settling of the sub-continent during the Lower Pleistocene, around 1.6 myr, seem more plausible (Mishra 1999; Petraglia 1998). Evidence for Mode 1 Oldowan has not been found.

SOUTH-EAST ASIA

This part of the Indo-Pacific region and monsoon Asia has a markedly oceanic geography whose continental and numerous insular habitats display varying degrees of faunal endemism. Large islands such as Sumatra, Java and Borneo were linked with the mainland by land bridges during sea-level regressions. The region is dominated by a tropical forest complex ranging through evergreen rainforest, monsoon, dry and moist teak and thorny woodland forests. Pleistocene fluctuations induced some cooling, animal size increases, and patches of localized grassy biomes as for example in eastern Java, but the absence of drought-adapted equids, giraffids and camelids, rules out large-scale arid shifts as in India or sub-Saharan Africa (Pope 1985). The scarcity of carbohydrate rich plant food staples, especially in evergreen forests where seasonally available edible tubers on drought adapted plants and seeds were lacking, as well as the difficulty of hunting or scavenging

the solitary game animals of forest environments (Hutterer 1983), probably inhibited populations from coming into tropical woodlands. However, abundant edible rainforest invertebrates would have offered valuable food sources (Paoletti *et al.* 2000) while the extensive uplands and river valley regions of Burma, Thailand, Vietnam and South China presented bioclimatically stable habitats rich in food and with convenient dispersal paths (Schepartz *et al.* 2000).

Dispersals into South-East Asia required significant adaptive shifts by omnivorous hominids surviving hitherto in open landscapes. Pre-adaptive episodes could have happened when wet fluctuations favoured the spread of evergreen forests in regions of South India, or when cooler and drier phases in South-East Asia created enclaves of open habitat. Monsoon and teak forest biomes were more suitable for early humans. This may imply that India, as part of a widespread semi-arid grassland culture area covering Western Asia and Africa (Dennell 1998), was settled much earlier than South-East Asia, where human expansion was more dependent on modified adaptive strategies.

Apart from the finds of *Homo erectus* concentrated in Java, anthropic remains are rare in South-East Asia. Except for the poorly dated and provenanced artefact horizons in the Irrawaddy terraces in Burma, the only early Palaeolithic mainland finds come from the Lampang and Phrae region of northern Thailand, at Ban Don Mun and Mae Tha South, calibrated to 800 kyr or the final Lower Pleistocene (Keates in press; Sørensen 1998). Major taphonomic difficulties in tracing a Lower Palaeolithic are due to the intense mechanical erosion which has disturbed sites and their contents. The technically correct 1.8 myr argon dating of the first hominids in Java overlooks their uncertain provenance. The zoogeographic history of Java precludes a human presence prior to 1.2 myr (Bergh *et al.* 1996; Pope and Keates 1994), while artefacts from Sambungmachan and Ngebung, and the Pacitanian, may be more recent. Since an initial presence in Java was contingent on low sea levels, it post-dated that of the mainland. The geological contexts of early Middle Pleistocene Palaeolithic sites in Sulawesi and Flores, implying an early mastery of navigation across some 19 km of water, require confirmation, and may be Upper Pleistocene in date (Keates 1998).

Overall, two characteristics characterise the early hominid record in South-East Asia: sites are relatively scarce by comparison with India, and classic Acheulian implements seem to be absent. The first reflects sporadic research, and/or the sparseness of foraging populations in tropical forests. The second has been ascribed to the Far East being an impoverished Palaeolithic evolutionary and cultural backwater where the *Homo erectus* population survived in isolation for a long time using a technology attributed to the Chopper-Chopping Tool Complex (Movius 1948). This version of the Movius Line notion is now untenable. Assemblages of choppers and large flakes found in South-East Asia and South China are now considered to represent adaptations to tropical and subtropical bamboo/karst forest settings (Pope 1988; Watanabe 1985) or a modified, non-Acheulian variant (Rolland 1996).

EAST ASIA

Intensive research in the vast area of the Far East has yielded a large body of evidence which has made the classic Movius Line model redundant. The latter now needs a broader, revised definition, and a comprehensive reinterpretation which gives function a key role. It is essential to stress some basic natural factors relating to this emerging record. Most of monsoon East Asia, influenced by oceanic conditions without intervening arid zones, has summer precipitation and reduced winter rainfall. The consequence of this climatic pattern is that coastal and insular areas, from South China to Korea and Japan, are dominated by varied successions of luxuriant forest biomes, varying from tropical, subtropical, temperate, boreal to taiga and including bamboo. These features, as well as unmatched primary production and biodiversity, offered optimal scope for exploiting various plant food staples and lignic raw material (timber, vines, bark) for toolmaking and shelter, in addition to solitary game. Movements into the Far East have been constrained by ongoing tectonic uplifts of the Asian core since mid-Tertiary times, with progressively isolating physical barriers, except through the South-East Asian ecological filter and, later on, Siberia.

China contains a rich Palaeolithic, fossil human, and Quaternary record. Anthropic finds dated to 1.8 myr at Longgupo need confirming. The oldest established human presence, primarily in woodland temperate settings, includes, among others, the Gongwangling Palaeolithic and *Homo erectus* finds, and the numerous Palaeolithic sites in the Nihewan Basin at Donggutuo, Xiaochangliang, Huojiadi, Banshan, Maliang and Manjungou (Hou 1998; Pope and Keates 1994; Schick and Dong 1993; Wei and Hou 1999). The Nihewan sites lie near continental steppes but their fluviolacustrine contexts indicate milder Early Pleistocene climatic phases, while establishing that ancient humans could live as far north as the 40–42° latitudes, 1.0 myr ago. Bose, in South China, dated to 800 kyr or later (Hou *et al.* 2000; Koeberl *et al.* 2000) contains a few typical handaxes. The occupation of northern China made possible further dispersals into the Korean Peninsula and the Japanese archipelago.

An early Palaeolithic occupation of lands around the Yellow Sea and the Sea of Japan is now certain. Investigations in Korea began recently and have brought to light occurrences such as those at Kulpori, Kampari and Chongokni (Bae 1999; Choi 1987; Lee this volume) which have thick bifacial implements. These are probably late Middle Pleistocene in age and must post-date the initial occupation of the Peninsula. To date, most of the Palaeolithic occurrences come from hydraulically disturbed or redeposited sediments (Yi pers. comm. 2000), probably in

dense humid temperate forest settings. Early discoveries from Japan, where a calibrated sequence of tephras in Honshu (Machida 1999; Soda and Sugiyama 1999) confirms a human presence perhaps as early as 720 kyr, imply a colonization across the Korean Strait at low sea levels during isotopic Stages 18 or 20. The lower horizons at Ittouchi Matsuba-yama (Ono *et al.* 1999; Kajiwara pers. comm. 2000), lack bifaces and provide further evidence of this initial hominid presence in Japan. Anthropic structures include: claims, now in doubt, of cache pits with bifaces and hut postholes in Kami-takamori layer 16, dated to >570 or 539 kyr by tephra, geomagnetism and TL; post-holes and ground plans of two huts, underlain by artificial mounds at Ogasaka, dated to 450–500 kyr, and several pits at Nagaone, dated to around 400 kyr. These remarkable features of worldwide significance are currently unique for this time period and, if confirmed, may suggest that the behavioural capabilities of *Homo erectus* need to be reassessed.

Apart from the broad geographic demarcations, most of the original criteria determining the Movius Line, such as cultural uniformity, stagnation and marginality, or the evolutionary isolation of *Homo erectus*, have been empirically refuted. Bifacial flaking recurs at different times during the Pleistocene in South-East Asia, China, Korea, and especially Japan, although genuine Acheulian handaxes remain scarce. More comprehensive future investigations should consider functional evidence, by means of use wear analysis, investigation of lithic raw material selection, experimentation, and further research on collateral organic remains, sites and regional settings, as well as the morphological attributes and flaking techniques (Pope and Keates 1994), all this relating specifically to monsoon environments of Asia. While animal food biomasses would be lower, the primary production of temperate forests exceeds that of the predominantly grassland biomes of regions to the west. A broad covariance between these environmental features and modified cultural repertoires fits with the anthropological principle that cultures are more subject to change when entering new environments, but change slows down as people begin to fit into unfamiliar settings (Kroeber 1963, 6). In the process of adapting to the environments of South-East Asia, technology changed. The character of basic reduction sequences and simple large cutting tools were retained, but some products, such as handaxes, were phased out, or were modified, as in the case of thick bifacial artefacts, or, like choppers and flake tools, became a more consistent component of the toolkit.

Retaining some major distinctions between technological and ecological traditions of the Old World Palaeolithic remains legitimate. In the Far East, physically isolating factors such as the high altitude orogenic rise and forbidding climate of the Qinghai-Xizang (Tibet) Plateau and Himalayan system (Liu *et al.* 1996), and dense tropical forest ecological filters between India and South-East Asia, played a decisive role. On the other hand, the Palaeolithic record of the Far East varies through time and space, with original developments and specializing trends (Ono *et al.* 1999; Wang 1998), while sharing broad toolmaking traits with the West. It may be timely to rename the Movius Line which overstressed boundaries to the detriment of the archaeology, and tentatively apply the Co-tradition concept, devised for Precolombian archaeology, to the Palaeolithic of the Far East. This would emphasize correlations in natural history and distinctions between culture historical developments within a vast and internally variable culture area through time.

CENTRAL ASIA

Since the Middle Pleistocene, the accelerating uplift of the Qinghai-Xizang Plateau has increasingly isolated Xinjiang and other inland regions from East Asian monsoon circulations, making the arid zones of Takla Makan, Ala Shan and the Qaidam Basin more continental and forbidding than previously for human settlement (Kukla and Čilek 1996; Liu and Ding 1984; Wang 1984; Zhang 1988). With the exception of the long, calibrated Tadzhik-Afghan Depression loess sequences, reliably dated, *in situ* Lower Palaeolithic occurrences remain scarce throughout Central Asia. The Obi-Mazar area contains several Lower Palaeolithic horizons, with artefact assemblages reminiscent of Nihewan industries, from the 11th and 12th palaeosols at Kul'dara which have a Late Matuyama reversed polarity age of 800 kyr (Davis and Ranov 1999; Ranov *et al.* 1987, figs. 5–7). These horizons correlate stratigraphically with the nearby Lower Pleistocene Lakhuti faunal horizon. Lower Palaeolithic horizons in the same area at Khonako date to 720 kyr (Schäfer *et al.* 1998). Lower Pleistocene occurrences further west come from the playas of the Kashaf Rud Basin, north-east Khorassan, in Iran (Ariai and Thibault 1975–77). The northern and western inland arc of lower slopes, Pleistocene playas, and alluvial areas surrounding the Iranian Plateau, connected with Central Asia by a string of oasis habitats and the episodically expanding, luxuriant temperate Hyrcanian rainforest, offered viable habitats. In the Transcaucasus, anthropic finds include Lower Palaeolithic occurrences at Achalkalaki (0.8 to 1.0 myr), and Kudaro and Azykh caves (0.5–0.6 myr) (Lordkipanidze 1999), as well as the evolved *Homo erectus* mandible from Dmanisi. The former may perhaps have originated separately in the East before moving into this lush Colchian rain forest region.

Alternative models may account for an early and probably intermittent hominid occupation of Central Asia. The first supposes multidirectional dispersals from the Near East by populations with Mode 1 assemblages (Gladilin and Ranov 1986), and is plausible because of the location of Dmanisi beyond the Taurus and Armenian Knot ranges. As an alternative, Rolland (1992) proposed protracted latitudinal movements across the heart of Eurasia, from Western Asia through South Asia, bypassing the Zagros to Qinghai-Tibet Plateau barriers, spreading into the Far East and north into China, Korea and Japan, then filtering west through Central Asia, during wetter, milder Lower Pleistocene conditions, along the main Palearctic migration axis. This argument rests largely on biogeographic circumstances. The Lower Palaeolithic of Central Asia may have phyletic links with the Non-Acheulian of East Asia, rather than with Mode 1, but anthropic find densities throughout Central Asia remain insufficient to make this argument compelling. The record may reflect scattered, low density populations, and brief, discontinuous occupations between lengthy, severe stadials, as suggested by the massive loess deposits (Kukla and Čilek 1996).

OVERVIEW: ASIA

Ancient hominids had settled vast portions of Eurasia by 800 kyr. This implies that these Ethiopian primates could adjust to unfamiliar Palearctic and Oriental biomes (Fig. 8.1). However, anthropic finds have not been recovered beyond latitudes 40–43°. This is probably due to shorter winter daylight, as well as more severe winter temperatures (Dennell 1983, 37). Given the apparent lack of domestic fire making before 400 kyr, such conditions would have made survival problematic.

Hominids began exploiting rich animal food resources from the Palearctic Eutrophic Zone (Schüle and Schuster 1999, 232–233), during the Galerian Dispersal Event (Azzaroli 1983; Guthrie 1984). Large-scale extinctions of Plio-Pleistocene species occurred at this time. These mammals were replaced by the rapid evolution of Pleistocene species over temperate Eurasia, as shown by horizons 1 and 2 at Lakhuti. Whether this event was punctuated everywhere during the Jaramillo, or was protracted, is debatable (Roebroeks and van Kolfschoten 1994, 495–496; Sher 1992, 130). The origin of the Galerian fauna appears to be in continental Asia by 1.4–1.2 myr, during the Siberian Olyor Land Mammal Age (Sher 1992). Galerian cervids and bovids show striking characteristics, including gigantism and neotenous traits such as large antlers or horns, which are diagnostic of pioneer populations (Geist 1971). This might suggest, or have induced, hominid home range displacements in similar directions.

THE FIRST PEOPLING OF EUROPE

Europe, like South-East Asia, South Africa and North Africa, was a cul-de-sac for mammal migrants and, consequently, fostered endemic tendencies, rather than being a corridor, like the Near East, a filter, like Central Asia, or an evolution centre and supplier of emigrants, like most of Africa and Siberia. As with the Transcaucasus and Siwaliks, population movements could come from several directions. A prevailing view is that Europe was colonized later than most of Asia, although by how long is debated by the proponents of opposing long and short chronologies

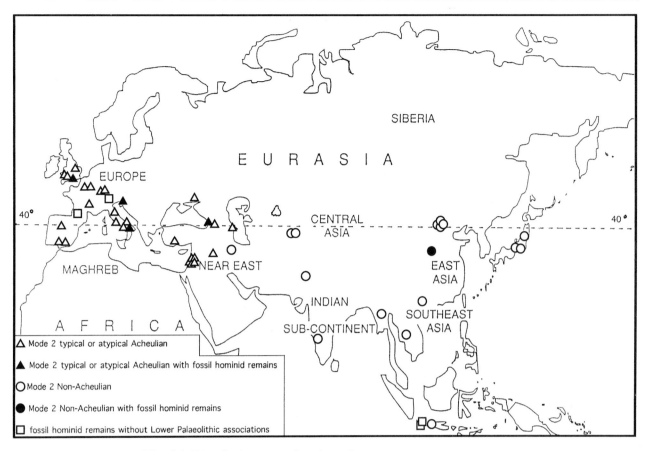

Fig. 8.1. Distribution map of early anthropic occurrences in Eurasia

(Arribas and Palmqvist 1999; Bonifay and Vandermeersch 1991; Bosinski 1996; Carbonell *et al.* 1995; Roebroeks 1994).

Table 8.4 sets out possible reasons for this dichotomy. It suggests that physical barriers such as the Mediterranean and, perhaps, the Balkans and Anatolia, but mainly latitude and bioclimatic obstacles, were key factors delaying colonization. Dmanisi, although quite close to Europe, suggests a much earlier Pleistocene colonization excluding Europe, over a realm encompassing Western Asia, stretching perhaps as far as India and representing precocious dispersals out of Africa under palaeogeographic conditions which ceased to exist after 850 kyr. This means that Europe, north of the Mediterranean, was colonized after a substantial time lapse, perhaps not before 500–600 kyr (Dennell and Roebroeks 1996). The reasons for this remain basic questions of prehistoric research and transcend chronological problems.

ANTHROPIC EVIDENCE

Evidence for the earliest peopling of Europe depends on archaeological data as fossil human remains are relatively scarce. Much discussion revolves around establishing secure criteria for identifying the residues of past human

Obstacle	Example
Physical	Mediterranean and Turkish Straits
Bioclimatic	Temperate latitudes, winter temperatures, dense temperate or boreal forests
Competition	Hominids outmatched by Plio-Pleistocene carnivore guild in Europe <500–600 kyr
Adaptation	Unable to adapt to severe winters and reduced winter daylight above 40–43° latitude

Table 8.4. Possible causes for a lag in the initial Lower Palaeolithic peopling of Europe.

activities, particularly modified lithic objects (Baales *et al.* 2000; Roebroeks and van Kolfschoten 1995), as well as primary context, provenance and chronology. Artificial structures and bone artefacts, rare before final Lower Palaeolithic stages, as well as unequivocal traces of hominid processing of animal carcasses, may give independent testimonies (Bonifay 1988), although remains of exploited animals associated meaningfully with artefacts are infrequent for the early European Palaeolithic (Gaudzinski and Turner 1996). Detailed discussions of these aspects exceed the scope of this paper. Table 8.5 gives the more reliable and informative summary of the anthropic record up to 450 kyr. Table 8.6 lists find-spots for which dating is less precise, leaving out controversial finds. Two

Location	Human evidence		Fauna	Chronology	
	Archaeological	Fossil		Era	Radiometric age estimate
Fuentenueva-3, S. Spain	Atypical Acheulian		X	Lower Pleistocene	900 kyr
Cúllar de Baza, S. Spain	Atypical Acheulian		X	Middle Pleistocene	700 kyr?
Atapuerca-TD6, N. Spain	Atypical Acheulian	X	X	Lower Pleistocene	>780 kyr
Atapuerca-TD4, N. Spain	Atypical Acheulian		X	Lower Pleistocene	>780 kyr
Soleihac, C. France	Atypical Acheulian		X	Middle Pleistocene	600 kyr
La Rafette, SW. France	Acheulian	X	?	Middle Pleistocene	600 kyr
Abbeville, Carrière Carpentier, N. France	Acheulian		X	Middle Pleistocene	>600 kyr
Abbeville, Champ de Mars, N. France	Acheulian		X	Middle Pleistocene	550 kyr
Saint-Acheul, M. Berthelot, N. France	Acheulian		?	Middle Pleistocene	550 kyr
Boxgrove, S. England	Acheulian	X	X	Middle Pleistocene	500 kyr
Westbury-sub-Mendip, S. England	Atypical Acheulian		X	Middle Pleistocene	500 kyr
High Lodge, S. England	Atypical Acheulian		X	Middle Pleistocene	500 kyr
Kent's Cavern, SW. England	Acheulian		X	Middle Pleistocene	500 kyr
Kärlich G, W. Germany	Atypical Acheulian		X	Middle Pleistocene	600 kyr
Miesenheim 1, W. Germany	Atypical Acheulian		X	Middle Pleistocene	600 kyr
Mauer, W. Germany	Atypical Acheulian?	X	X	Middle Pleistocene	550 kyr
Ca' Belvedere, N. Italy	Atypical Acheulian			Lower Pleistocene?	900 kyr?
Visogliano, N. Italy	Atypical Acheulian & Acheulian	X	X	Middle Pleistocene	500 kyr?
Castro dei Volsci, C. Italy	Atypical Acheulian			Middle Pleistocene	600 kyr?
Ceprano, C. Italy		X		Middle Pleistocene	700 kyr?
Fontana Ranuccio, C. Italy	Acheulian		X	Middle Pleistocene	458 kyr
Isernia La Pineta, S. Italy	Atypical Acheulian		X	Middle Pleistocene	620 kyr
Venosa-Notarchirico, S. Italy	Atypical Acheulian & Acheulian	X	X	Middle Pleistocene	640 kyr
Venosa-Loreto, S. Italy	Atypical Acheulian		X	Middle Pleistocene	640 kyr?
Gerasimovka, S. Russia	Atypical Acheulian		X	Middle Pleistocene	600–700 kyr?

* Although many occurrences contain few or no handaxes, their synchronous or post-dating presence with others containing typical Acheulian assemblages, as well as instances e.g. Venosa-Notarchirico showing interstratifications of layers with or without handaxes, suggest strongly that they are atypical facies, due to sampling or activity facies, as part of an Acheulian Mode 2 polythetic technocomplex, rather than with a residual Mode 1 or 'Pre-Acheulian' horizon. This would apply as well to the earlier sites from Iberia because their ultimate region of origin already contain *bona fide* Acheulian repertoires.

Table 8.5. Major anthropic localities in Europe of late Lower or earlier Middle Pleistocene age.*

Region	Palaeolithic sites without handaxes	Palaeolithic sites with handaxes
Iberia	El Aculadero, Monfarracinos, El Espinar, Talaveira de la Reina, Molino del Imperador, Puente Morena, Middle-Upper Douro Terraces, Guadalquivir Upper Terrace	Pinedo
France, Mediterranean	Fabron, Saint-Thibéry, Vallonet Cave, Vidauban	
France, Massif Central	Chilhac III	
France, South-west	Les Pierres, Camp de Peyre, Les Vergnes, Maleret, Saint-Selve, Verdier, Sept-Fronts, La Nauterie Cave 14, Les Graves, Barbas 7, Caillevat-Beuret	
France, Northern	Pont de la Hulauderie, Pointe de Saint-Colomban 5	Pointes aux Oies
France, Eastern	Côte Bar, Vergranne, Hangenbieten, Achenheim	
England		Caversham Channel, Burnham, Warren Hill, Knowle Farm
Italy	Montauto, Collinaia, Colle Marino, Fontana Liri, Arce, Casella di Maida, Costa del Forgione	
Central Europe	Červeny kopec PK-X, Bečov 1, Stránská skála? Svédské šance? Starě město?	
Eastern Europe	Trzebnica, Korolevo VII, VIII, Néa Skala I, II (Kephalinia Island, Greece)	

Table 8.6. Palaeolithic localities in Europe of possible late Lower or earlier Middle Pleistocene age.

patterns stand out: sites are concentrated in the western Mediterranean and western Europe, and are scarce or absent until later in more continental zones (Fig. 8.1). This may reflect selective occupation of favourable, milder habitats. Archaeological assemblages vary in artefact numbers, but several rich ones, like Isernia La Pineta, Ca' Belvedere di Monte Poggiolo and Venosa-Loreto, have few or no handaxes, implying that they represent either atypical Acheulian facies, parallel phyla, or an older Pre-Acheulian horizon. Interassemblage variability, prominent within the Acheulian technocomplex of Africa, Western Eurasia or India, has several causes (Rolland 1996, fig.1 and table 2).

CHRONOLOGY

As the resolution of age estimates provided by bio-chronology, lithostratigraphy, tephrochronology, geo-magnetism and radiometric techniques improves, useful chronological markers are being discerned but ambiguities and inconsistent biozone criteria persist (Kolfschoten 1990, 56–63). This makes correlations between localities and regions tentative. Table 8.7 gives a summary based on the standard Pleistocene subdivisions for north-west Europe, revised biozones, and the Central European loess sequence, correlated with magnetostratigraphy and marine isotopic stages.

Throughout Europe north of the Pyrenees and the Alps, reliably identified or dated anthropic evidence is not older than the late Cromerian complex, or Mauer Temperate Time Span, correlated with Stages 13 or 14, or 550 or 600 kyr (Baales *et al.* 2000, fig. 1). The appearance of *Arvicola terrestris cantiana* in the microtine faunal record provides a chronological nexus with the earliest confirmed anthropic occurrences. This biozone, although not chronometrically dated, correlates with Cromer IV (Roe-broeks and van Kolfschoten 1995). South of the Alps and the Pyrenees, dating is less straightforward: Isernia La Pineta, Italy, dates back to the Late Matuyama, according to tentative geomagnetic dating and K/Ar determinations of non-redeposited ashes, but the associated microfauna with *Arvicola*, if not accidentally mixed with the Galerian macrofauna as a result of rodent burrowing, implies a Late Cromerian or Stage 13 horizon (Mussi 1995). The more archaic Galerian macrofauna of Venosa (Loreto and Notarchirico), dates to 640 kyr at the earliest (Piperno *et al.* 1998, 123), placing the Isernia fauna slightly before 600 kyr. Geomagnetism dates Ca' Belvedere di Monte Poggiolo to 0.9 myr, but considering this locality as a datum for the initial occupation of Italy or of Europe would be premature, given the lack of biozonal evidence and the tentative lithostratigraphy. Iberia contains evidence implying a human presence before the Cromerian or Mauer Span. The Atapuerca Gran Dolina Aurora Horizon TD6 layer (Bermúdez de Castro *et al.* 1999; Carbonell *et al.* 1995) contains homi-

nid remains, artefacts, and mammals, indicating a Late Matuyama age or >780 kyr, on the strength of an intensive geomagnetic reversal, as well as the presence of the older *Mimomys savini* microfauna. The Orce Basin findings, rich in Plio-Pleistocene and early Galerian faunas, suggest provisionally an even earlier human presence in Iberia. Fuentenueva-3a contains artefacts within a geomagnetic series, datable to the Jaramillo subchron or earlier (Martínez Navarro *et al.* 1997; Roe 1995; Tixier *et al.* 1995). Discoveries in Iberia, adding artefacts from the Guadalquivir and Douro terraces (Raposo and Santonja 1995, 21), therefore suggest a pre-Middle Pleistocene hominid settlement of Europe.

Chronological resolution, although not an end in itself, is essential in palaeoanthropology. Without a handle on time co-ordinates, discussing hominid activities and developments is both tentative and provisional, although nonetheless a task which remains incumbent on prehistorians. Dealing with gaps in the record relating to the dating of the initial settlement of Europe requires continuing research, especially in the peninsular regions. Iberia constitutes in fact a small, more isolated sub-continent of Europe (Arribas and Palmqvist 1999, 579), with an endemic fauna including some African elements. Its record may imply a human presence earlier than elsewhere, perhaps by 800–900 kyr. Italy, with closer biogeographic connections to the rest of Europe, has sites not much older than the 500–600 kyr datum. The southern Balkans remain a blank.

ADAPTATION

Some hypotheses link hominid dispersals with immigrant Galerian carnivores, adding African species such as lion, panther, cheetah and spotted hyaena (Turner 1982), or even Pliocene ones such as the short-nosed hyaena and sabre-toothed cats (Arribas and Palmqvist 1999). One causal explanation for the short chronology is suggested by Turner (1992), who argues that hominids may have relied mainly on scavenging and could not compete successfully with members of the European carnivore guild until the 500 kyr faunal turnover. Meat procurement probably included planned scavenging in favourable situations. Hominids may have become aware that the episodic drowning of large numbers of bison, as in the Isernia area, often created scavenging opportunities but this alone could not supply many essential nutrients. Carcass appropriation by scavenging entailed as many confrontational risks with competitors such as hyaenas, as predation would. Furthermore, ancient humans did co-exist with these same archaic carnivore species in China.

Occupying Europe permitted the exploitation of the Palearctic Eutrophic Zone ungulate biomass (Schüle and Schuster 1999, 232–233). Pleistocene climatic shifts allowed higher latitude settlement during temperate episodes only, until around 400 kyr, when occurrences such as Schöningen coincide with more open habitats. Later

kyr	Standard NW Europe	Loess	Biozone	Major localities			Isotopic stages	Magneto-stratigraphy
				Mediterranean	Western	Central/ Eastern		
	Holsteinian						11	
500	Elsterian	E		Fontana Ranuccio			12	
		F	TORINGIAN (*Arvicola*)		La Rafette, Boxgrove, Westbury-sub-Mendip		13	
				Visogliano			14	
600								*BRUNHES* (normal)
		H		Cúllar de Baza, Castro dei Volsci, Venosa (Loreto & Notarchirico), Isernia, Ceprano	Soleihac, Abbeville Carrière Carpentier	Kärlich G, Gerasimovka	15	
							16	
700	Cromerian Complex	I					17	
				Ca'Belvedere (?)			18	
							19	
800			BIHARIAN (*Mimomys*)					
		J		Atapuerca TD6, TD4			20	*LATE MATUYAMA* (reversed)
							21	
900				Fuenteneva-3			22	*Jaramillo* (normal)
	Bavelian Complex							
		K						*MATYUAMA* (reversed)

Table 8.7. Schematic chronology of major early hominid locations in Europe during the late Lower Pleistocene and early Middle Pleistocene (after Baales et al. 2000, Kukla and Čilek 1996 and Roebroeks and van Kolfschoten 1995).

Saalian sites are found during Stage 6 stadial conditions, such as La Cotte de St-Brelade, but temperate phases offered a more diverse range of plant food staples.

Surviving beyond latitudes 40–43° by 500–600 kyr in north-west and central Europe, under short winter daylight and possibly without the domestic use of fire before 400 kyr, required a major adaptive shift for coping with such unfamiliar winter conditions, but the archaeological record remains silent about this. By contrast the colonization of Mediterranean peninsulas mainly involved overcoming physical barriers, as had been the case before for the rest of Eurasia. Penecontemporaneous hut and pit structures found in Japan may provide new clues about the organisation and development of settlements.

FOSSIL EVIDENCE

With the exception of Atapuerca, the fossil hominid record is sparse, fragmentary and has limited taxonomic scope. One leading phylogenetic scheme views European hominids as an endemic branch of the genus *Homo*, *H. heidelbergensis* or *H. antecessor* (Bermúdez de Castro *et al.* 1999), implying a long-lasting reproductive isolation, compatible with the notion of Europe as a biogeographic cul-de-sac. This raises palaeobiological problems mentioned here in passing because of their implications. These include the identification of palaeo-species and the question of whether pre-modern hominids throughout Eurasia diverged into several species (Tattersall 1986) or remained a single one, with total morphological pattern clusters of isolated, low density, autapomorphic mating networks (Zeitoun 2000), by anagenesis through random genetic drift and intermittent gene flow (Templeton 1993; Wolpoff 1998). The first alternative relies exclusively on biological criteria. The latter includes culture, *sensu lato,* as a defining criterion and unifying factor in maintaining *H. erectus* as a single polymorphic group. Culture may consequently be considered as having been part of the long-term process of hominization since early *Homo*, with continuous co-evolutionary feedbacks between encephalization (brain volume growth and cortical tissue expansion), and emerging symbolic behaviour (Deacon 1997; Santangelo 1998).

DISPERSAL PATHS INTO EUROPE

Europe could have been settled from different directions, simultaneously or separately, and given the apparently sparse population densities, discontinuously or episodically. Possible paths are: South-West Asia, from the Levant through Anatolia; the Straits of Gibraltar; the Sicilian-Tunisian Strait; and Eastern Europe north of the Caucasus (Alimen 1975; Bordes 1968, 89). All these routes involve crossing physical barriers, such as the Mediterranean, the Turkish Straits, the Taurus range, and the ecologically impoverished Anatolian Plateau, or the climatic and latitudinal barriers of Eastern Europe. This means that dispersals into Europe could take place only by overcoming water barriers, reduced or eliminated by glacio-eustatic low sea levels. Furthermore, most lands adjacent to Europe, from the Maghreb to the Transcaucasus, had been settled by 1.0 myr, increasing the likelihood of immigrations from several directions. However, anthropic evidence approximating to this datum is only found in Iberia between 0.90 to 0.78 myr, while north of Iberia and Italy, only by 500–600 kyr.

Figs. 8.2A–8.2D summarise alternative models of dispersal. These are referred to as Old Europe, >2.0–1.5myr, Mature Europe, 0.9 myr, and Young Europe, 0.5–0.6 myr, with Lower Palaeolithic repertoires linked to the initial peopling of Europe from African and/or Asian antecedents (Carbonell *et al.* 1995). The Old Europe model could result from basic biocultural changes caused simultaneously by the emergence of the genus *Homo* and the post-2.8 myr arid shift, but empirical support is controversial. By 1.7–1.6 myr, Western Asia and possibly India could represent an extension of the African hominid biogeographic realm with a Mode 1 repertoire diffusing with hominid dispersals around 2.0 myr, which still fits only with the Old Europe model. The Young Europe alternative sees a rapid hominid spread by 500–600 kyr. The severe isotopic Stage 16 glacio-eustatic marine regression, correlated with the severe loess cycle H climate of Central Europe (Kukla and Čilek 1996; Shackleton *et al.* 1984), could have created conditions for crossing the dry Turkish Straits, or negotiating the much narrower Straits of Gibraltar. In the first case, population movements could have circumvented the Anatolian physical barriers along narrow continental shelf strips up to the Straits, then through the southern Balkans, across the dry Adriatic continental shelf into Italy, and into the rest of Europe. Crossing the Straits of Gibraltar may have been less problematic as low sea levels narrowed the crossing but never resulted in a landbridge, allowing for a sweepstake dispersal of humans and a few African carnivores (Martínez Navarro and Palmqvist 1995).

The Mature Europe model considers new evidence from Iberia which suggests that settlement was earlier here than in the rest of Europe. The severe isotopic Stage 22 (0.9 myr) would have improved opportunities for migrating across the Straits of Gibraltar, following the initial occupation of the Maghreb. This idea is compatible with the anthropic evidence clustered in Western Europe, as well as with the notion of a long-lasting pre-modern human endemism in Europe. Most early occurrences without handaxes represent small samples or facies within a polythetic technocomplex, and are insufficient to constitute a Pre-Acheulian horizon. This, and dates for the Young and Mature models, not to mention a widespread Acheulian presence in regions neighbouring Europe, rule out a Mode 1 diagnosis. The only valid criteria for establishing a Pre-Acheulian horizon in Europe require an unequivocal, robust chronological, mammalian, and archaeological database documenting the spread of the Non-Acheulian repertoire from the Far East and Central Asia into Europe (Rolland 1992), linked perhaps with the Galerian Dispersal Event (Turner 1991). However, evidence suggesting this so-called Long Journey does not reach west beyond Iran or the Transcaucasus.

OVERVIEW

This survey has attempted to synthesise and update knowledge about evidence and issues for the peopling of Eurasia,

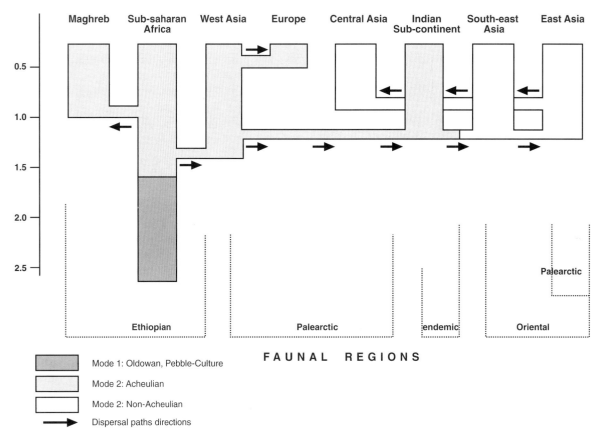

Fig. 8.2A. The 'long chronology' and the 'Old Europe' dispersal model. The first dispersal out of Africa took place shortly after the appearance of the genus Homo, *with its more advanced biocultural characteristics and the first major arid shift in sub-Saharan Africa both being possible causal factors.*

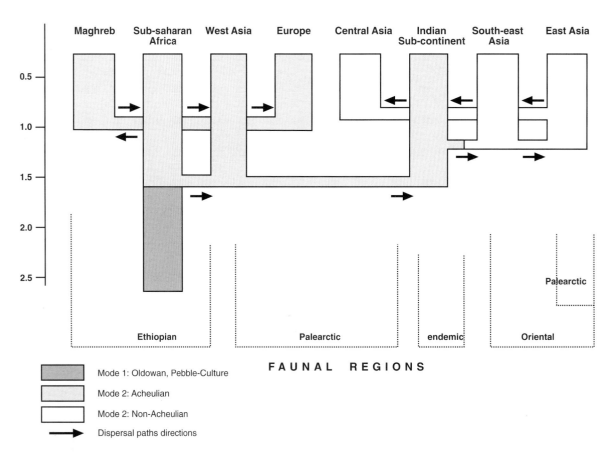

Fig. 8.2B. The 'short chronology' and the 'Young Europe' dispersal model. The first dispersal event out of Africa took place with Homo erectus *and its Mode 2 Acheulian repertoire, first into Western Asia by 1.4 myr, then towards the Indian sub-continent by 1.2 myr, and into the Far East between 1.2 and 1.0 myr.*

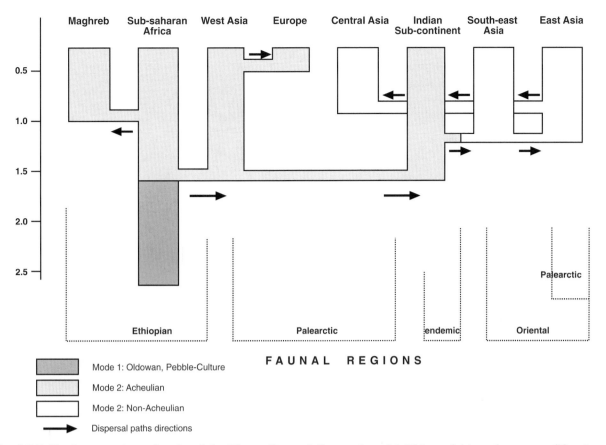

Fig. 8.2C. The 'mature chronology' and the 'Young Europe' dispersal model. This model introduces a modification of the chronology and possible ancient hominid adaptive patterns with respect to Western Asia and the Indian sub-continent.

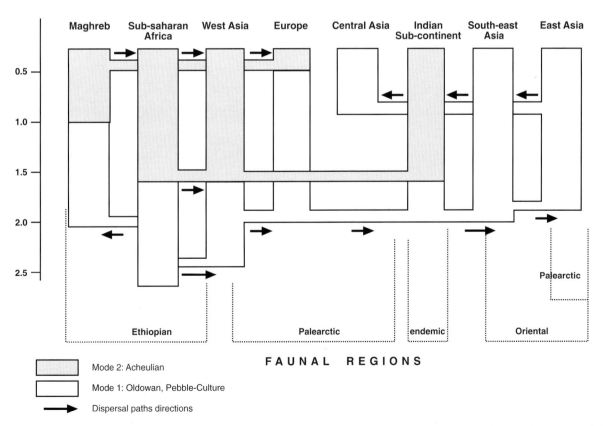

Fig. 8.2D. The 'mature chronology' and the 'Mature Europe' dispersal model. This model builds on that of Fig. 8.2C and concerns only the peopling of Europe. In this case, new evidence from Iberia suggests a colonization directly out of Africa from the Maghreb at 1.0 myr or less.

by connecting direct and indirect evidence from different regions. The record underscores how provisional and coarse resolution remains, with much to be done in geochronology and taphonomy. Despite impressive progress in refining and widening dating methods, many retain flaws, while few sites offer scope for simultaneous applications. To construct a coherent conceptual framework beyond descriptive levels requires the integration of different types of evidence and analyses, from individual sites, locational and regional settings, to the biogeographic and chronological dimensions. The preserved primary situation of many localities in East Africa, along with sophisticated research designs, has yielded informative findings about early hominid behavioural ecology (Oliver et al. 1994), but comparatively few sites in Eurasia, other than Atapuerca, Boxgrove, Soleihac, Fontana Ranuccio, Isernia, Venosa, Xiaochangliang and Ogasaka, offer similar opportunities.

Serious difficulties in reconstructing behaviour from earlier biocultural hominization stages stem from the lack of living analogues, and our inability to detect meaningful patterns from the fragmentary record of the past. Actualist parallels are limited to observations from recent foraging societies, or from primate and social carnivore behavioural ecology. Ancient humans were intimately tied to their ecosystems, but early cultural stages already show a trajectory witnessing the emergence, through symbolic behaviour, of repertoires involving a progressively wider techno-ecological margin for mediating human/habitat interactions, and of a new, complex environment made of social relation networks, both becoming a hominid specialization.

REFERENCES

Alimen, H. 1975. Les 'isthmes' hispano-marocains et siculo-tunisiens aux temps Acheuléens. L'Anthropologie 79, 399–436.

Ariai, A. and Thibault, C. 1975–77. Nouvelles précisions à propos de l'outillage paléolithique ancien sur galets du Khorassan (Iran). Paléorient 3, 101–108.

Arribas, A. and Palmqvist, P. 1999. On the ecological connection between sabre-tooths and hominids: faunal dispersal events in the Lower Pleistocene and a review of the evidence for the first human arrival in Europe. Journal of Archaeological Science 26, 571–585.

Azzaroli, A. 1983. Quaternary mammals and the 'end-Villafranchian' dispersal event: a turning point in the history of Eurasia. Palaeogeography, Palaeoclimatology, Palaeoecology 44, 117–139.

Baales, M., Joris, O., Justus, A. and Roebroeks, W. 2000. Natur oder Kultur? Zur Frage ältester paläolithischer Artefaktenensembles aus Hauptterrassenschottern in Deutschland. Germania 78, 1–20.

Bae, K. 1999. Handaxe industries of the Hantan Imjin river basin, Korea, and its implications. Abstracts of From Sozudai to Kamitakamori. World View on the Early and Middle Palaeolithic in Japan. Symposium to Commemorate the 80th Birthday Celebrations of Professor Chosuke Serizawa, October 29–31st, Tohoku Fukushi University.

Balter, M. and Gibbons, A. 2000. A glimpse of humans' first journey out of Africa. Science 288, 948–950.

Bergh, G.D. van den, Mubroto, B., Aziz, F., Sondaar, P.Y. and de Vos, J. 1996. Pleistocene zoogeographic evolution of Java (Indonesia) and glacio-eustatic sea-level fluctuations. The Chiang Mai Papers 1. Bulletin of the Indo-Pacific Prehistory Association 14, 7–21.

Bermúdez de Castro, J.M., Carbonell, E. and Arsuaga, J.L. (eds.) 1999. Gran Dolina Site: TD6 Aurora Stratum (Burgos, Spain). Journal of Human Evolution 37, 309–700.

Biglari, F., Norkandeh, G. and Heydari, S. 2000. A recent find of a possible Lower Palaeolithic assemblage from the foothills of the Zagros Mountains. Antiquity 74, 749–750.

Bonifay, M.-F. 1988. L'autre préhistoire. Remarques sur les faunes contemporaines du très vieux Paléolithique français. Archaeozoologia 2, 181–188.

Bonifay, E. and Vandermeersch, B. (eds.) 1991. Les Premiers Européens. CTHS, Paris.

Bordes, F. 1968. The Old Stone Age. McGraw Hill, New York.

Bosinski, G. 1996. Les Origines de l'Homme en Europe et en Asie: Atlas des Sites du Paléolithique Inférieur. Errance, Paris.

Cachel, S. and Harris, J.W.K. 1999. The adaptive zone of Homo erectus from an African perspective. In H. Ullrich (ed.) Hominid Evolution: Lifestyles and Survival Strategies, 128–137. Archaea, Schwelm.

Carbonell, E., Mosquera, M., Rodriquez, X.P. and Sala, R. 1995. The first human settlement of Europe. Journal of Anthropological Research 51, 107–114.

Choi, M.C. 1987. Le Paléolithique de Corée. L'Anthropologie 91, 755–786.

Davis, R.S. and Ranov, V. 1999. Recent work on the Paleolithic of Central Asia. Evolutionary Anthropology 8, 186–193.

Deacon, T.W. 1997. The Symbolic Species: The Co-evolution of Language and the Brain. Norton, New York.

Debénath, A. 2000. Le peuplement préhistorique du Maroc: données récentes et problèmes. L'Anthropologie 104, 131–145.

Dennell, R.W. 1983. European Economic Prehistory: A New Approach. Academic Press, London.

Dennell, R.W. 1998. Grasslands, tool making and the hominid colonization of southern Asia: a reconsideration. In M.D. Petraglia and R. Korisettar (eds.) Early Human Behaviour in Global Context: The Rise and Diversity of the Lower Palaeolithic Record, 280–303. Routledge, London.

Dennell, R.W. and Roebroeks, W. 1996. The earliest colonization of Europe: the short chronology revisited. Antiquity 70, 535–542.

Fisher, W.B. 1963. The Middle East: A Physical, Social and Regional Geography. Methuen, London.

Gaudzinski, S. and Turner, E. 1996. The role of early humans in the accumulation of European Lower and Middle Palaeolithic bone assemblages. Current Anthropology 37, 153–156.

Geist, V. 1971. The relation of social evolution and dispersal in ungulates during the Pleistocene, with an emphasis on the Old World Deer and the genus Bison. Quaternary Research 1, 283–315.

Geraads, D., Hublin, J.-J., Jaeger, J.-J., Tong, H., Sen, S. and Toubeau, P. 1986. The Pleistocene hominid site of Ternifine, Algeria: new results on the environment, age, and human industries. Quaternary Research 25, 380–386.

Gladilin, V. and Ranov, V. 1986. Ot Pamira do Karpat. Znanie Sila 2, 29–31.

Güleç, E., Howell, F.C. and White, T.D. 1999. Dursunlu: a new Lower Pleistocene faunal and artifact-bearing locality in southern Anatolia. In H. Ullrich (ed.) Hominid Evolution: Lifestyles and Survival Strategies, 349–364. Archaea, Schwelm.

Guthrie, D. 1984. The Galerian Dispersal Event and the origin of the modern megafauna: its implications for Early Man in the Northern Hemisphere. *The Quarterly Review of Archaeology* 5, 15–16.

Henke, W., Rothe, H. and Alt, K.W. 1999. Dmanisi and the early Eurasian dispersal of the genus *Homo*. In H. Ullrich (ed.) *Hominid Evolution: Lifestyles and Survival Strategies*, 138–155. Archaea, Schwelm.

Horowitz, A. 1979. *The Quaternary of Israel*. Academic Press, New York.

Hou, Y. 1998. New observations on the Paleolithic in China reflected by three sites. *Documenta Praehistorica* 25, 1–15.

Hou, Y., Potts, R., Yuan, B., Guo, Z., Deino, A., Wang, W., Clark, J., Xie, G. and Huang, W. 2000. Mid-Pleistocene Acheulian-like stone technology of the Bose Basin, South China. *Science* 287, 1622–1626.

Howell, F.C. 1960. European and northwest African Middle Pleistocene hominids. *Current Anthropology* 1, 195–232.

Hurcombe, L. and Dennell, R.W. 1992. A Pre-Acheulian Lower Pleistocene industry in the Pabbi Hills, Northern Pakistan? In C. Jarrige, J.P. Gerry and R.H. Meadow (eds.) *South Asian Archaeology 1989*, 133–136. Prehistory Press, Madison.

Hutterer, K. 1983. The natural and cultural history of Southeast Asian agriculture: ecological and evolutionary considerations. *Anthropos* 78, 169–212.

Keates, S.G. 1998. A discussion of the evidence for early hominids on Java and Flores. *Modern Quaternary Research in Southeast Asia* 15, 179–191.

Keates, S.G. in press. The Lower Palaeolithic of Thailand: the evidence from Lampang. In C. Falguères, D. Grimaud-Hervé and F. Sémah (eds.) *Origines des Peuplements et Chronologie des Cultures Paléolithiques dans le Sud-Asiatique*. Institut de Paléontologie Humaine, Paris.

Koeberl, C., Glass, B.P. and Keates, S. 2000. Tektites and the age paradox in Mid-Pleistocene China. *Science* 287, 507.

Kolfschoten, T. van. 1990. The evolution of the mammal fauna in the Netherlands and the Middle Rhine area (Western Germany) during the Late Middle Pleistocene. *Mededelingen Rijks Geologische Dienst* 43 (3), 1–69.

Korisettar, R. 1994. Quaternary alluvial stratigraphy and sedimentation in the Upland Deccan Region, Western India. *Man and Environment* 29, 29–41.

Korisettar, R. and Rajaguru, S.N. 1998. Quaternary stratigraphy, palaeoclimate and the Lower Palaeolithic of India. In M.D. Petraglia and R. Korisettar (eds.) *Early Human Behaviour in Global Context: The Rise and Diversity of the Lower Palaeolithic Record*, 304–342. Routledge, London.

Korisettar, R., Venkatesan, T.R., Mishra, S., Rajaguru, S.N., Somayajulu, B.L.K., Tandon, S.K., Gogte, V.D., Ganjoo, R.K. and Kale, V.S. 1989. Discovery of a tephra bed in the Quaternary alluvial sediments of Pune district (Maharashtra), Peninsular India. *Current Science* 58, 564–566.

Kretzoi, M. 1961–64. Mammal faunae and the continental geology of India. *Acta Geologica Academiae Scientiarum Hungarica* 7–8, 301–312.

Kroeber, A.L. 1963. *Cultural and Natural Areas of Native North America*. University of California Press, Berkeley.

Kukla, G. and Čilek, V. 1996. Plio-Pleistocene megacycles: record of climate and tectonics. *Palaeogeography, Palaeoclimatology, Palaeoecology* 120, 171–194.

Liu, T. and Ding, M. 1984. The characteristics and evolution of the palaeoenvironment of China since the late Tertiary. In R.O. Whyte (ed.) *The Evolution of the East Asian Environment*, 11–40. Centre of Asian Studies, Hong Kong.

Liu, T., Ding, M. and Derbyshire, E. 1996. Gravel deposits on the margins of the Qinghai-Xizang Plateau and their environmental significance. *Palaeogeography, Palaeoclimatology, Palaeoecology* 120, 159–170.

Lordkipanidze, D. 1999. Early humans at the gates of Europe. *Evolutionary Anthropology* 8, 4.

Machida, H. 1999. Quaternary widespread tephra catalog in and around Japan: recent progress. *Quaternary Research* 38, 194–201.

Martínez Navarro, B. and Palmqvist, P. 1995. Presence of the African machairodont *Megantereon whitei* (Broom, 1937) (Felidae, Carnivora, Mammalia) in the Lower Pleistocene site of Venta Micena (Orce, Granada, Spain), with some considerations on the origin, evolution and dispersal of the genus. *Journal of Archaeological Science* 22, 569–582.

Martínez Navarro, B., Turq, A., Agusti Ballester, J. and Oms, O. 1997. Fuente Nueva-3 (Orce, Granada, Spain) and the first human occupation of Europe. *Journal of Human Evolution* 33, 611–620.

Menocal, P.B. de, 1999. Plio-Pleistocene African climate. *Science* 270, 53–59.

Mishra, S. 1999. Developing an Indian Stone Age chronology. In T. Murray (ed.) *Time and Archaeology*, 80–88. Routledge, London.

Mishra, S. and Rajaguru, S.N. 1998. Progress in chronology of Stone Age cultures in Western India: a geoarchaeological perspective. In T.P. Verma and R. Kumar (eds.) *Dating in Indian Archaeology: Problems and Perspectives*, 1–12. Bharat Itihas Sankalan Samiti, Mysore.

Mishra, S., Venkatesan, T.R., Rajaguru, S.N. and Somayajulu, B.L.K. 1995. Earliest Acheulian industry from Peninsular India. *Current Anthropology* 36, 847–851.

Movius, H.L. 1948. The Lower Palaeolithic cultures of Southern and Eastern Asia. *Transactions of the American Philosophical Society* 38, 329–420.

Mussi, M. 1995. The earliest occupation of Europe: Italy. In W. Roebroeks and T. van Kolfschoten (eds.) *The Earliest Occupation of Europe*, 27–49. Leiden University Press, Leiden.

Oliver, J.S., Sikes, N.E. and Stewart, K.M. (eds.) 1994. *Early Hominid Behavioural Ecology*. Academic Press, London.

Ono, A., Oda, S. and Matsu'ura, S. 1999. Palaeolithic cultures and Pleistocene hominids in the Japanese Islands: an overview. *Quaternary Research* 38, 177–183.

Paddaya, K. 1994. Investigations of man-environment relationships in Indian archaeology: some theoretical considerations. *Man and Environment* 29, 1–28.

Paoletti, M.G., Dufour, D.L., Cerda, H., Torres, F., Pizzoferrato, L. and Pimentel, D. 2000. The importance of leaf and litter feeding invertebrates as sources of animal protein for the Amazonian Amerindians. *Proceedings of the Royal Society of London* B 267, 2247–2252.

Parenti, F., Al-Shiyab, A.H., Santucci, E., Kadafi, Z., Palumbo, G. and Guerin, C. 1997. Studies in early Near Eastern production, subsistence and environment. In H.G.K. Gebel, Z. Kadafi and G.O. Rollefson (eds.) *The Prehistory of Jordan II: Perspectives from 1997*, 7–22. Ex Oriente, Berlin.

Petraglia, M.D. 1998. The Lower Palaeolithic of India and its bearing on the Asian record. In M.D. Petraglia and R. Korisettar (eds.) *Early Human Behaviour in Global Context: The Rise and Diversity of the Lower Palaeolithic Record*, 343–390. Routledge, London.

Piperno, M., Lefèvre, D., Raynal, J.-P., Tagliacozzo, A. and Vernet, G. 1998. Préhistoire du bassin de Venosa au Pléistocène moyen. Une révision d'après les recherches récentes à Notarchirico (Basilicata, Italie). *Proceedings of the XIII Congress. U.I.S.P.P.*, Volume 2, 121–125. ABACO, Forlì.

Pope, G. 1985. Taxonomy, dating and paleoenvironment: the paleoecology of the early Far Eastern hominids. *Modern Quaternary Research in Southeast Asia* 9, 65–80.

Pope, G. 1988. Current issues in Far Eastern palaeoanthropology. In P. Whyte (ed.) *The Palaeoenvironment of East Asia from the*

Mid-Tertiary, 1097–1123. Centre of Asian Studies, Hong Kong.

Pope, G. and Keates, S.G. 1994. The evolution of human cognition and cultural capacity: a view from the Far East. In R.S. Corrucini and R.L. Ciochon (eds.) *Integrative Paths to the Past: Paleoanthropological Advances in Honor of F. Clark Howell*, 531–567. Prentice Hall, Englewood Cliffs.

Ranov, V.A., Dodonov, A.E., Lomov, S.P., Pakhomov, M.M. and Penkov, A.V. 1987. Kul'daranovyi nizhnepaleoliticheskii pamiatnik iuzhnovo Tadzhikistana. *Buletin Komissii po i Zucheniu Chetvertichnaia Perioda* 56, 65–75.

Raposo, L. and Santonja, M. 1995. The earliest occupation of Europe: the Iberian peninsula. In W. Roebroeks and T. van Kolfschoten (eds.) *The Earliest Occupation of Europe*, 7–25. Leiden University Press, Leiden.

Roe, D.A. 1995. The Orce Basin (Andalucia, Spain) and the initial Palaeolithic of Europe. *Oxford Journal of Archaeology* 14, 1–12.

Roebroeks, W. 1994. Updating the earliest occupation of Europe. *Current Anthropology* 35, 301–305.

Roebroeks, W. and van Kolfschoten, T. 1994. The earliest occupation of Europe. *Antiquity* 68, 489–503.

Roebroeks, W. and van Kolfschoten, T. (eds.) 1995. *The Earliest Occupation of Europe*. Leiden University Press, Leiden.

Rolland, N. 1992. The Palaeolithic colonization of Europe: an archaeological and biogeographic perspective. *Trabajos de Prehistoria* 49, 69–111.

Rolland, N. 1996. Biogéographie et préhistoire: le cas du peuplement Paléolithique inférieur de l'Europe. In M. Otte (ed.) *Nature et Culture*, 11–61. ERAUL 68, Liège.

Santangelo, A. 1998. *Culture. Growing Brain Size and Cerebral Cortical Surface: Genus Homo*. Sabaini, Milan.

Schäfer, J., Ranov, V.A. and Sõsin, P.M. 1998. The 'cultural evolution' of man and the chronostratigraphical background of changing environments in the loess palaeosoil sequences of Obi-Mazar and Khonako (Tadzhikistan). *Anthropologie* (Brno) 36, 121–135.

Schaller, G.B. 1967. *The Deer and the Tiger*. University of Chicago Press, Chicago.

Schepartz, L.A., Miller-Antonio, S. and Bakken, D.A. 2000. Upland resources and the early Palaeolithic occupation of Southern China, Vietnam, Laos, Thailand and Burma. *World Archaeology* 32, 1–13.

Schick, K.D. and Dong, Z. 1993. Early Palaeolithic of China and eastern Asia. *Evolutionary Anthropology* 2, 22–35.

Schüle, W. and Schuster, S. 1999. Ethology and population dynamics: keystones for anthropogenic extinctions and hominid expansion. The Eutrophic Zone, its genesis and implications. In H. Ullrich (ed.) *Hominid Evolution: Lifestyles and Survival Strategies*, 224–239. Archaea, Schwelm.

Shackleton, N.J., van Andel, T.H. and Runnels, C.N. 1984. Coastal palaeogeography of the central and western Mediterranean during the last 125,000 years and its archaeological implications. *Journal of Field Archaeology* 11, 307–314.

Sher, A. 1992. Beringian fauna and early Quaternary mammalian dispersal in Eurasia: ecological aspects. *Courier Forschungsinstitut Senckenberg* 153, 125–133.

Shipman, P. and Walker, A. 1989. The cost of becoming a predator. *Journal of Human Evolution* 18, 373–392.

Simpson, G.G. 1962. *Evolution and Geography*. Oregon State System of Higher Education, Eugene.

Soda, T. and Sugiyama, S. 1999. Tephrochronological study of the Lower Palaeolithic culture of Takamori and Kamitakamori sites, northeast Japan. Abstracts of the *International Symposium on Palaeoanthropology, 12–16 October, Beijing, China, in Commemoration of the 70th Anniversary of Discovery of the First Skull of Peking Man at Zhoukoudian*.

Sørensen, P. 1998. A reconsideration for the chronology of the Early Palaeolithic Lannathian culture, North Thailand. *Indo-Pacific Prehistory: the Melaka Papers III, Volume 1. Bulletin of the Indo-Pacific Prehistory Association* 17, 70.

Spooner, B. 1972. The Iranian deserts. In B. Spooner (ed.) *Population Growth: Anthropological Implications*, 245–268. MIT Press, Cambridge.

Tattersall, I. 1986. Species recognition in human paleontology. *Journal of Human Evolution* 15, 165–175.

Templeton, A.R. 1993. The 'Eve' hypotheses: a genetic critique and re-analysis. *American Anthropologist* 95, 51–72.

Tixier, J., Roe, D., Turq, A., Gibert, J., Martínez, B., Arribas, A., Gibert, L., Gaete, R., Maillo, A. and Iglesias, A. 1995. Présence d'industries lithiques dans le Pléistocène inférieur de la région d'Orce (Grenade, Espagne): quel est l'état de la question? *Comptes Rendus de l'Académie des Sciences de Paris* Series 2, 321, 71–78.

Turner, A. 1982. Hominids and fellow travellers. *South African Journal of Science* 78, 231–237.

Turner, A. 1991. Origine des grands mammifères Plio-Pléistocènes d'Europe et migrations humaines. In E. Bonifay and B. Vandermeersch (eds.) *Les Premiers Européens*, 267–271. CTHS, Paris.

Turner, A. 1992. Large carnivores and earliest European hominids: changing determinants of resource availability during the Lower and Middle Pleistocene. *Journal of Human Evolution* 22, 109–126.

Wang, P. 1984. Progress in late Cenozoic palaeoclimatology of China: a brief review. In R.O. Whyte (ed.) *The Evolution of the East Asian Environment*, 165–187. Centre of Asian Studies, Hong Kong.

Wang, Y. 1998. Human adaptations and Pleistocene environments in South China. *Anthropologie* (Brno) 36, 165–175.

Watanabe, H. 1985. The Chopper-Chopping Tool Complex of Eastern Asia: an ethnoarchaeological-ecological reexamination. *Journal of Anthropological Archaeology* 4, 1–18.

Wei, Q. and Hou, Y. 1999. Major Paleolithic archaeological sites in Nihewan Basin (October 8–11, 1999). *Excursion Guide, 1999 Beijing International Symposium on Palaeoanthropology*.

Wolpoff, M. 1998. Concocting a divisive theory. *Evolutionary Anthropology* 7, 1–3.

Wood, B. and Collard, M. 1999. The changing face of genus *Homo*. *Evolutionary Anthropology* 8, 195–207.

Zeitoun, V. 2000. Révision de l'espèce *Homo erectus* (Dubois, 1893). *Bulletins et Mémoires de la Société d'Anthropologie de Paris* 12, 1–200.

Zhang, K. 1988. The trend towards dryness in north and western China since the Mid-Pleistocene. In P. Whyte (ed.) *The Palaeoenvironment of East Asia from the Mid-Tertiary*, 445–452. Centre of Asian Studies, Hong Kong.

9. In the quest for Palaeolithic human behaviour

Ofer Bar-Yosef

ABSTRACT

As popular interest in our prehistoric past increases, it can often seem frustrating that archaeological research generates such dim images of early societies from huge quantities of data. In the quest to sharpen our view, this paper reviews the pattern and purpose of twentieth century research paradigms. In considering the successes and failures, it seeks an enlightening way forward.

AN OPENING STATEMENT

Investigating Lower Palaeolithic sites can be a frustrating experience. Imagine that in the course of excavating such a site we visit our colleagues who are digging an historical locality. The houses, streets, silos, sculptures, and other material elements in their site provide a sound basis for telling an interesting story. Returning to our trenches where the geological deposits are not easily decipherable, the animal bones require both detailed palaeontological and zooarchaeological analyses, and the often crude stone artefacts are not always in mint condition, we face the apparently insurmountable difficulties of translating our evidence into a 'good story'. However, there is always hope. Our site could become a media item when a human bone is discovered, and the more the better. As we all know from the history of the profession, human fossils are the best fund raisers. Even if our story turns out to be 'wrong', at least with funds available we can keep on digging. In rare cases we can hope to convey even a dim image of a prehistoric society. Identifying the individual members is a rare option, available only when skeletal remains are reasonably well-preserved. The reconstruction of faces of one or two early hominids is attractive, but it is more so when an entire group is uncovered like at Atapuerca (Bermúdez de Castro *et al.* 1999).

Hence, as anthropologists we are indefatigably launching enquiries into the most remote past of humankind. We are energized by the wish to discover how humans evolved and how they behaved as individuals and as groups. We search the material elements for any detectable changes in their behaviour, social organisation, and their capacity for culture as we understand it, from 2.5 myr ago to a time when archaeological remains produce a clearer image of daily life. At that point we tend to conclude that our recent ancestors behaved like modern foragers.

In pursuing this great endeavour, we are continually encouraged by brain scientists, evolutionary psychologists, linguists, and of course journalists who are constantly fascinated by the evolution of the human mind and its potential implications for understanding modern behaviour. Sometimes, when obtaining funds for field research, a permit for an excavation, or while struggling with day-to-day activities in the field in an often inhospitable environment, we wish that all those well-wishing colleagues would join us and witness the efforts needed to attain the desired noble goal. We know all too well that it is a difficult and energy consuming task to get the hard data and produce a reasonable interpretation. In spite of our tedious systematic analyses, almost every aspect of our interpretations is open to criticism. The future of our interpretations is even worse.

Not only do we sometimes revise our own original views, but often others are quick to do it for us. Nevertheless, as archaeologists we are an optimistic breed, and at time of misgivings we look back to the days of John Frere and console ourselves with the progress that has been made. Indeed, it is in the same spirit of cautious conviction, that these pages are written.

ON BEING CAUTIOUS IN OUR INTERPRETATIONS

The question of how human behaviour evolved assumes that once early hominids began making stone tools, physical evolution, as reflected in the skeletal record, was related to the advantages provided by the sharp cutting edges of the flakes. In other words, employing stone tools was the major force in changing patterns of individual and group behaviour, and this in turn had an impact on human morphology. However, the preliminary assumption needs to be re-examined. Perhaps a starting point would be to provide a persuasive answer to the question: what were the behavioural differences between the earliest tool-making hominids and other contemporary primates? The subsequent question would then be: did the stone tools provide the competitive edge for hominids over sympatric primates? Presumably other behavioural features evolved, so the next question is: what behavioural and morphological changes, if any, facilitated the expansion of the early hominids into the new environments of North Africa and Eurasia? In other words, can we as archaeologists find evidence of the mental capacities, motor habits of making stone tools, or changes in social organisation, which facilitated the success of the first migrations 'out of Africa'?

None of the above questions can be answered to the satisfaction of all parties. Moreover, proposed interpretations are often criticised according to current fashionable ideologies. For example, it is solely in contemporary affluent societies, where biological survival is secured by supportive socio-political systems, that archaeologists can afford to dismiss the long-held notion that Palaeolithic ways of life were determined by the struggle for biological survival as depicted by some archaeologists, artists, and museum dioramas (Dobres 2000; Otte 1999). While there is no doubt that many of the visual presentations derived their artistic concepts from the ethnographic records collected over five centuries of European colonial expansion, other sources of information are available. For example, Egyptian wall reliefs, and the works of Greek and Roman artists and historians, played a major role in documenting human technical actions. The same may be said about gender roles in manufacturing tools, objects, or performing various activities. It is the cautious attitude of current scholars, having no assurance of the identity of the knappers of the Palaeolithic stone tools, that resulted in producing drawings of the hands of stone tool makers without identifying their gender, and not, as claimed by Moore (1994, 49–50), the wish to cover 'over what we do

not wish to have revealed' (cited by Dobres 2000, 29).

There is, therefore, no need to advocate caution during model building, collection of primary data, and the simplifications of our scientific explanations when pressed by various media agencies. The Palaeolithic story as uncovered by the archaeological investigations, including 'photo opportunities', begins with the field work at particular localities. These do not always lend themselves to straightforward, simple interpretations.

IN THE BEGINNING IS THE SITE

In the course of digging open-air sites and caves, the techniques for providing detailed stratigraphic and contextual information were adopted from Quaternary geology (Bordes 1954; Hay 1976; Laville et al. 1980; Leakey 1971 inter alia). As caves and rockshelters were the first to produce early Palaeolithic sequences, I will make a few relevant comments on this point, although I have dealt with this subject elsewhere (Bar-Yosef 1993, 1998, 2001).

Numerous caves and rockshelters were excavated over the course of the last two centuries. Over time and through the efforts of various schools, field techniques changed and improved the quality of the data recovered. For example, grid systems were not commonly used before the Second World War. The surface of the cave or rockshelter was subdivided into sections and each section was dug to bedrock. Thus early prehistorians were able to see the entire stratigraphy and, while conducting the subsequent excavation, their stratigraphic control was better than in the first section. This of course assumes that the layers identified in the original trench, often on the basis of colour and the nature of the sediments, were continuous through the following sectors.

In spite of the good intentions of the excavators, numerous questions remained unanswered. Cultural continuity was often ultimately an illusion. In most sites there is no depositional continuity, let alone constant human occupation. Examine, for instance, Tabun cave on Mount Carmel with 23 meter thick deposits, located in a prime area with high carrying capacity, and flint resources for fabricating stone tools. Unfortunately, the digging techniques as practiced by Dorothy Garrod and her associates in the 1930s left a lot to be desired. Stratigraphic gaps became more apparent during the new excavations (Jelinek 1982) and the TL datings (Mercier et al. 1995). The earlier 'coarse-grain' method of excavation used by Garrod may explain her difficulties in attributing the Tabun I woman's skeleton to a particular layer. The ambiguous nature of her records resulted in debates on the geochronological position of this individual which still rage (Bar-Yosef and Callander 1999; Grün and Stringer 2000).

On the whole, from the 1950s onward, archaeologists did better. Sedimentological techniques were introduced to site studies, but in many of the previously excavated caves and rockshelters only limited portions of the original deposits were preserved. Consequently, current digs of these sites are less likely to respond to a frequently posited query: how did humans use the entire space? Archaeological sites are finite, and every excavation is a process of destruction.

The development of taphonomy as the study of how bone accumulations formed in the past resulted, among others, in the recognition that caves could have been used intermittently by both humans and hyaenas. Studies in South African, European and Chinese caves demonstrated the complexity of interpreting the excavated contexts (Binford and Ho 1985; Brain 1981, 1993; Stiner 1994). There is thus a constant need to improve field observations, and more so to integrate the testing of findings in the field with the appropriate laboratory techniques.

Among the new techniques, micromorphology seems to be the best for examining the micro-structure of the archaeological layers, identifying the extent of post-depositional alterations and detecting the presence of charcoal not visible to the naked eye (Courty *et al.* 1989; Goldberg and Bar-Yosef 1998; Goldberg *et al.* 2001). Originally borrowed from soil scientists and now coupled with mineralogical analysis, it provides a powerful tool to inform us of the integrity of the excavated prehistoric contexts (Karkanas *et al.* 2000; Weiner *et al.* 1995).

The combination of these techniques is not limited only to cave sites and rockshelters but has also proved useful on open-air sites (Courty *et al.* 2001; Macphail and Cruise 2001). One may wonder why these techniques are not being used on Lower Palaeolithic sites in East Africa. The general sequences of palaeoenvironments where early hominids thrived and became extinct are well recorded by the traditional geological methods (Feibel 1997; Hay 1990 *inter alia*) and isotopic techniques (Cerling and Hay 1986; Cerling *et al.* 1993, 1997; Kingston *et al.* 1994). However, if we are to maximize the amount of information from contexts of particular archaeological layers, whether at Olduvai, East Turkana or other localities, the use of micromorphology and mineralogy is required. It is only with an accumulation of detailed contextual information that we can test the inferences we make concerning human behaviour and their habitats.

ON FIRE AND COOKING

Much more can be done to resolve other questions. Recent concern about the use of fire by early hominids (James 1989) has led to the adoption of techniques that uncover the mineralogical residues of ash (Schiegl *et al.* 1994). In revisiting Zhoukoudian, a site renowned for early control of fire by humans, we obtained results that differ from past interpretations (Weiner *et al.* 1998). Although our work was limited to the remaining western section of the site, the supposed accumulation of 4–6 meters of ash of Layer 4 turned out to be redeposited loess with organic inclusions. The indirect evidence for the probable use of fire by humans are the burnt bones found in every archaeological horizon from layer 10 upwards. This means that the earliest date for the use of fire is about 500 kyr.

The claims for the earlier presence of hearths in East Turkana sites (Bellomo 1993; Rowllet in Wrangham *et al.* 1999) need to be substantiated by additional evidence. The lack of burnt bones and thermally scarred lithics in site FxJj20 is definitely a warning sign. Even finding thermally altered Palaeolithic stone objects on the surface of other African landscapes would not constitute definite proof that early hominids were responsible for this type of damage through the systematic use of fire. This specific type of shattering could have been the result of salt weathering, as well as of bush fires, or over-heating followed by sudden rain. Hence, while most scholars agree that the use of fire by humans modified environments, and caused substantial changes in plant associations, its origin requires better dating. Those who argue for a long timescale would see *Homo ergaster* and *Homo erectus*, as old as 1.7 myr ago or more, as hominids armed with fire, while others would rely on the direct evidence which is hardly older than 500,000 years.

Despite the importance attributed to cooking for the evolution of male–female bonding (Wrangham *et al.* 1999), evidence from the field does not yet support the proposition that the consumption of any part of the omnivorous diet required the use of fire at this early stage. No one would deny the crucial role of cooking in human societies, so perhaps we should seek not only well founded documentation for prehistoric hearths, but concurring evidence from human biology: testing the alternative hypotheses of early versus late use of fire may require genetic data. Eating cooked foods, especially meat, means that certain enzymes are no longer needed by humans, but others are essential because of nutritional deficiencies and/or advantages caused by the cooking process. The presence or absence of digestion-related enzymes and its correlation to culture is well documented, for example, in the case of lactose malabsorption (Durham 1991).

One cannot argue with success. The evolution of early hominids, prior to about 1 myr, was as hunters and efficient scavengers who consumed animal meat, seeds, nuts, fruits, insects, and perhaps tubers. They fed themselves as they went about their day (Isaac 1984) and could have shared portions of their diet, in particular the meat, with their own kin or with other group members.

Meat eating has received considerable attention and has been subject to numerous debates. The rival interpretations attributed to the accumulations of fractured bones as reflecting hunting versus scavenging, or both, are well-known (Binford 1981; Blumenschine 1991; Blumenschine and Cavallo 1992; Bunn 1991; Bunn *et al.* 1991; Fernández-Jalvo *et al.* 1998; Speth 1991; Tappen and Wrangham 2000). The pendulum keeps swinging, and the current balance tends more toward hunting than scavenging.

Was it paternal in addition to maternal caring that

promoted pair and group bonding, or were groups simply fluid agglomerations of males around females and their infants? It appears that whatever is the correct interpretation, and whether using fire or not, the social structure commonly defined as 'simple hunter-gatherers' began to evolve during this period.

LANDSCAPE ARCHAEOLOGY: A BUZZ WORD OR ACHIEVABLE GOAL?

A relatively new aspect of Palaeolithic research is known as landscape archaeology. It was first conceived by Glynn Isaac who phrased it as 'the scatter between the patches' (Isaac 1984, 1986; Stern 1993). Landscape archaeology is currently practiced at Olorgeisailie (Potts 1989), and through the OLAPP project at Olduvai (Blumenschine and Peters 1998). This type of investigation attempts to associate the low density, but widely dispersed, scatters of artefacts with the known sites containing dense accumulations of lithics and bones, to generate a palaeoecological context where inferences concerning human activities across the entire landscape can be reconstructed. The idea was derived from what is known about recent foragers and their use of the environment. Unfortunately, what can be recorded for historical hunter-gatherers or those of Holocene age, and perhaps for Terminal Pleistocene foragers, can hardly be achieved for the Plio-Pleistocene situations. In the latter case the chronological resolution for a given layer or 'bed' is rarely less than 100,000 years (Stern 1993).

Justifiably, landscape archaeology of Lower Palaeolithic sites searches the wide spectrum of today's African habitats for analogies to past ecological niches (Blumenschine and Peters 1998). The difficulty lies not in finding comparable localities, but in deriving adequate inferences from the prehistoric deposits. As recently demonstrated by Tappen (2001 and references therein), the traditional use of the Serengeti savannah as the proto-type for the Plio-Pleistocene environment is probably exaggerated. Tappen demonstrates that no less important analogies can be drawn from the more wooded savannah of the Virunga National Park. There, for example, the search for carcasses produced different results from the surveys conducted in the Serengeti, and raised doubts about riparian habitats being the optimal locations for scavenging by early hominids. In addition, one must doubt the existing assumptions concerning the degree of seasonality of these habitats and its impact on the behaviour of various mammals. The well defined seasonal differences which characterised the Serengeti during the last century are not necessarily the same as the Plio-Pleistocene (2.5–1 myr) conditions. Adaptation to a seasonal regime particularly by antelopes, and the ensuing repercussions for carnivores, served as a basis for modelling early hominid behaviour. Hence, Tappen (2001) wisely raises the issue of behavioural changes by certain species that are often present in early Palaeolithic East African sites. This issue, hardly ever mentioned in the context of palaeoanthropological interpretations, makes one wonder why we so easily accept the behavioural shifts among early hominids and exclude, for example, the mammalian world from similar treatment.

Studies of isotopes of soil carbonates have already demonstrated that the palaeoecological conditions in the area where early hominids evolved were different from the simplified scenarios of forests versus savannah. It is high time to get the details from the palaeobotanical remains that seem to be present in various layers of well known East African sites. While pollen is not always well preserved (Bonnefille 1995), phytoliths and microscopic fossil wood elements should be pursued as critical data for the contextual record. This type of information could provide a more precise picture of plant associations which may explain why chimpanzee fossils are never found in human occupational sites. It seems that chimpanzee ancestors and early *Homo* sp. were allopatric species, whereas the various australopithecine species and the latter were sympatric and shared the same environments. This is supported by the dietary analysis of hominids of both *Homo* cf. *ergaster* and *Australopithecus robustus* in South Africa, which demonstrated that both were omnivorous (Lee-Thorpe *et al.* 2000; Sponheimer and Lee-Thorpe 1999).

In sum, the future success of landscape archaeology of Lower Palaeolithic African sites, and perhaps others in Eurasia, may satisfy the curiosity of our colleagues in evolutionary psychology and cognitive studies. If images of their living terrains were embedded in human cognition and visual memory forever after, then the studies of the palaeoenvironments may elucidate certain of today's perceptual biases concerning the extent to which habitats were open or closed (Orians and Heerwagen 1992). Hence, landscape archaeology has a future once the microscopic view is incorporated into the suite of techniques employed in reconstructing past environments. Until now this scene has been painted with a broad brush on a rough canvas.

THE TERMINOLOGICAL MAZE

Classification is a process generated by the human mind. We constantly define, scale, and categorise daily activities, objects, plants, forces of nature, and the like. This is practiced at least, but not exclusively, by all genetically identified modern humans. Classifications are employed by hunter-gatherers to monitor their environments (Ichikawa and Terashima 1996; Meehan 1982 *inter alia*). Hence, categorisation and ordering is an elementary component of scientific recording, and is reflected in the archaeological literature by a series of definitions of stone artefacts and clusters of assemblages often known as industries. We use these descriptive categories to communicate our observations. The most rudimentary categories refer to the products of intentionally fractured rocks: nodule, core, flake and so on. Additional attributes are often metrical, including measurements in millimetres, angles of striking platforms, and sometimes size ratios to distinguish flakes and blades, for example. They may also be descriptive, recording the attributes of butts, cortical flakes, overall shapes, and so on. Sometimes we disagree about which words should be used, such as naming the two faces of a flake as ventral and dorsal, as opposed to interior and exterior (Dibble 1995; Inizan *et al.* 1999), but we do agree that the flakes are the product of fracture mechanics. We have difficulties created by translations from one language into another, but in essence we have a common understanding of most knapping techniques practised during the Lower and Middle Pleistocene.

Interpretations diverge in the course of the second level of description of the acquired data. In summarizing the humanly modified stone objects recorded from an excavated level or layer, scholars employ a series of categories. A basic category is the term assemblage, which in its most simplified sense means the total of the excavated sample. However, we often face unsettling questions about the degree of contemporaneity among the pieces recovered. This may lead to the discussion of what constitutes living floors (Dibble *et al.* 1997; Villa 1976). A high degree of affirmation concerning the contemporaneity of objects within an assemblage is reached through refitting, when items such as blanks and retouched pieces are put back together in order to form the original nodule. If this goal is not achievable, we may learn something about the movement of pieces within the site and the possible transportation of artefacts across the landscape.

From the early nineteenth century, archaeologists created classifications in order to arrange the artefacts in museum collections, exhibits, and books. Without repeating a well known story, the basic terms started with the Stone Age, Bronze Age and Iron Age, followed by the subdivision of the Stone Age into Lower, Middle and Upper Palaeolithic. When these terms were translated into phases in social evolution, it seemed that early hominids evolved both physically and culturally from 'Savagery to Civilization', in which the Lower Palaeolithic was labelled as 'Lower Savagery' (Clark 1953).

Entities, defined by clustering several similar lithic assemblages, were labelled following the palaeontological-geological rule which specifies that newly defined artefacts or assemblages should be named after the site where they were first discovered. A partial list of some of the labels coined in Europe includes the Abbevillian, Acheulian, Clactonian, Tayacian, Mousterian and, later, as the African finds were reported, the Pebble culture, Oldowan, Sangoan, and the like. Some of these designations of supposed prehistoric cultures were later abandoned.

African researchers did not approve of the Greek-based term Palaeolithic, and re-named these phases as Early, Middle and Late Stone Age. The first half of the twentieth century continued to be the age of discovery and building of the general prehistoric sequences. Communication among the small number of prehistorians operating within the Western world was good, in spite of the necessity of relying on mailed correspondence. Cables were exchanged in cases of significant discoveries. Newly coined archaeological terms were often respected.

With the rapidly increasing number of field archaeologists in the second half of the twentieth century and the greater involvement of the sciences, changes were inevitable. Investigators were requested to make their research goals and their methods and techniques of recording data explicit. Paradigms demanded that scholars free themselves from implicit evaluation of the evolutionary status of a given prehistoric culture, and thus new terms were offered. Grahame Clark (1953) replaced his early spectrum of 'Savagery to Civilization' by another one, this time labelling categories Modes 1–6 (Clark 1969, 1970). These numbered units reflect the basic knapping techniques according to their time of appearance and persistence, and are thus presented as objective categories (Foley and Lahr 1997; Schick 1994). Mode 1 was to replace what others would call core-chopper or core and flake industries such as the Oldowan and Clactonian. Mode 2 referred to the manufacture of bifacial tools and replaced the term Acheulian. Clark (1970, 72) noted that 'there is evidence in some areas for progressive refinement in the technique during the course of time, and there was obviously scope for wide variation in relation to local ecological circumstances'. However, his generalised view of the geographic distribution of the Acheulian industries was in part incomplete, as eastern Asia, and central and eastern Europe, were beyond the Movius line (Klein 1999, fig. 5.2). As a result he thought that 'bifacial techniques failed to spread as far east as China and southeast Asia ...' (Clark 1969, 72), whereas not all Palaeo-Europeans were endowed with the technical knowledge to make bifaces.

Mode 3 was supposed to represent the Levallois technique or, as Clark phrased it, 'production of flakes from well prepared cores' (Clark 1970, 74), as well as other flake industries with disc cores. By employing European examples, he also envisioned the possibility that bifaces and foliates continued to be made, as for example in the Micoquian, Mousterian and Szeletian.

Mode 4, as even those who never read the original text may guess, represented the Upper Palaeolithic blade industries. Mode 5 characterised the Mesolithic, or the production of microliths, and in Mode 6 axes and adzes made a showing, thereby marking the Neolithic.

World prehistory as summarised by Clark (1969) does not differ in its description of the lithic industries from Bordes' (1968) brief summary in which the old terms were used. However, Clark stressed the socio-economic aspects of prehistoric societies, and the need to decouple the cultural entities as classified by the archaeologists from the biological evolution as represented by the skeletal remains.

It is time, as recently advocated by Gamble (2001), to move beyond the schematic periodisation, whether the old or the relatively new one. Palaeolithic entities can be conceived as units delineated by time and space. The procedure of clustering Lower Palaeolithic sites or assemblages is not different from the way it is done for Late Palaeolithic (Late Stone Age) industries. The difference lies, for example, in how we interpret the meaning of persistence or slow change in core reduction strategies during the Lower and Middle Pleistocene, which contrasts with the relatively rapid changes within the millennia of the Upper Palaeolithic. In addition, the regrettably rare preservation of organics other than bones is not only an obstacle to learning about ways of life some 2.5 to 0.25 myr ago, it also hampers similar efforts in studying Terminal Pleistocene sites.

THE ATTRACTION OF STONE TOOLS
AND THE AMBIGUITY OF THE INTERPRETATIONS

Studies of primate behaviour in the last three decades demonstrate that humans are not only genetically closely related, but also behaviourally similar, to chimpanzees (Boesch and Boesch 1990; Boesch *et al.* 1994; McGrew 1992, 1994; Wrangham *et al.* 1994). This led to the use of primate studies as building blocks for models that strive to explain the early phases of hominid behaviour. It also provided reasons for heated debates.

Direct comparisons between tools generated by chimpanzees and artefacts left by early hominids demonstrated that the early humans did better. First, experiments with Kanzi (Toth *et al.* 1993), an intelligent bonobo, indicated that even in nature Kanzi most likely would not have left behind the kind of accumulation that characterises the Plio-Pleistocene archaeological contexts (Mithen 1996). In addition, the behavioural variability of chimpanzees in their habitats in Mahale, Gombe, and Taï, although complex, did not incorporate any of the variable stone tool making methods which characterise early Lower Palaeolithic sites in Africa (Roche and Texier 1995; Schick and Toth 1993; Toth 1985, 1987, 1991; as compared to Boesch and Boesch 1990). True, the nutcracking stone tools of west African chimpanzees are impressive (Joulian 1996), and the motions as shown by that author could be the same as the percussion gestures for producing flakes. In certain archaeological contexts, such as Olduvai, pitted anvils could have served for the same purpose as the nutcracking rocks (Leakey 1971; Leakey and Roe 1994). However, there is no record that chimpanzees at any time produced flakes in order to obtain sharp, usable edges. Their hands, as reported in a comprehensive review, do not demonstrate the same effective grip as human hands, which are better suited for producing stone tools (Marzke and Marzke 2000).

Moreover, what makes the difference between chimpanzees and early hominids is not the repeated occupation of the same locality, but the constant need for objects with sharp cutting edges and the ability to make them. Without entering a debate on scavenging versus hunting, the benefits of freshly detached flakes in getting the meat from carcasses larger than colobus monkeys, and the use of hammerstones for cracking the bones for marrow, provided the early hominids with an adaptive edge not shared by other primates.

Contemporary primates of early *Homo* sp. were the late australopithecines, whose evolutionary origins are deeper in time than those of the earliest members of the genus *Homo* (Klein 1999; Leakey *et al.* 2001; Lieberman 2001; Pilbeam 1996; White *et al.* 1994). During the long period from probably more than 5.0 myr to about 2.5 myr, from the first appearance of *Homo rudolfensis*, several australopithecine species coexisted in what, by a coarse environmental resolution, seem to have been similar conditions. Interestingly, certain australopithecines continued to survive to a late date of about 1 myr.

Uncovering the fossil remains of the australopithecines in archaeological sites in South Africa indicated that they were hunted by various predators, including humans (Brain 1981). Indeed, in several contexts they were also associated with stone and bone artefacts (Backwell and d'Errico 2001; Brain 1993). This concurrence raised the hypothesis that at least one species (*Paranthropus robustus*) had a hand grip that allowed the manufacturing of stone tools (Susman 1998). The archaeological evidence does not allow us to reject or support this proposition, as having the right grip is meaningless because knapping stone artefacts lies in the realm of teaching by imitation as well as with the aid of language (Gowlett 1990, 1996). We can imagine, by looking into the late Lower Pleistocene, that the ancestors of *Homo ergaster* were the first tool makers, and by transmission through numerous generations their descendants continued to do so.

Another issue is related to the use of bone fragments which morphologically resemble bone tools of later prehistory. Recent macroscopic and microscopic analyses of both archaeological specimens and replicas demonstrated that these objects most likely were utilised for digging into termite mounds (Backwell and d'Errico 2001). This line of evidence may suggest that humans, who are known to consume insects (Menzel and D'Aluisio 1998), chimpanzees, and the australopithecines all shared a taste for the same food resources.

My conclusion, which is not a novel one, is that only those species that fall within the genus *Homo* sp. systematically produced stone tools by fracturing cobbles and pebbles, either unifacially, bifacially or by continuing to detach flakes from various planes of a nodule. They also shaped spheroids through intensive use, creating what is known as the Oldowan Industrial Complex.

However, if the fossil record will not support this contention, it means that there was more than one species that fabricated and used stone tools, and that similar objects are not species or population specific. In addition there is a lesson, learned already from the Middle Palaeolithic industries, that forms of stone tools do not reflect environmental adaptations, neither in Africa nor in Eurasia. What could be more telling than the evidence that the early colonisers of Eurasia, apparently *Homo eragaster* at Dmanisi, in the foothills of the Lesser Caucasus (Georgia), employed the same types of stone tools as their sub-Saharan ancestors (Gabunia *et al.* 2000), and the contemporary *Homo erectus*.

CONCLUDING REMARKS

In a comprehensive approach to reconstructing the evolutionary history of humans, Laland *et al.* (2000) propose to incorporate not only the selective pressures of the natural environments but also what they call niche construction. Niche construction combines the 'population genetic processes, information-acquiring ontogenetic processes, and cultural processes' that together 'can influence both biological and cultural change' (Laland *et al.* 2000, 139). In other words, cultural innovation within one population, when spread by learning, will have feedback effects on the biological evolution of humans, and may in due course cause a change in the environment. The increase in brain size of humans is seen as one example of a change related to cultural actions such as cooking (Aiello and Wheeler 1995). However, given the similarity in brain size of the newly discovered hominids at Dmanisi (Gabunia *et al.* 2000), at what may even be body size with the African habilines, it would be presumptuous to assume that it was the knowledge of cooking that facilitated the spread of *Homo* cf. *ergaster* into Eurasia.

In the context of the Lower Palaeolithic, it would be appropriate to view the systematic production and use of stone tools as a major component of niche construction. It was one of the significant elements in cultural transmission which generated, according to Wilson (1985), the behavioural drive and led to accelerated morphological changes. However, Laland *et al.* (2000) correctly warn that cultural processes could accelerate or decelerate evolution (Feldman and Cavalli-Sforza 1976) and, as a result, we may expect periods of stasis.

It is in Oldowania, to use a term suggested by Gamble (2001) for the original homeland of the first stone tool producers, that one can witness a long interval of continuity, which lasted from about 2.5 myr until the accepted date for the first Acheulian migration 'out of Africa' at about 1.7–1.6 myr. During the first million years we find the early hominids only in their 'homeland' in sub-Saharan Africa, and as far as we know at the time of writing, nowhere else. If this scenario holds, and our archaeological interpretations are confirmed by new discoveries, then the migration 'Out of Oldowania' was a major step in human evolution. Was this migration facilitated by new technology, or a new social structure, and by new methods of communication not visible in the preserved record? This is a question that is easily asked but difficult to answer. Was this migration instigated by the impact of the climate change on the population of Oldowania around the time of the Olduvai event, or was it simply a coincidence? The expansion and colonisation considerably increased the territory and types of habitats exploited by early hominids. North Africa, the Mediterranean and temperate belts of Eurasia were ephemerally occupied during the next half million years, namely from about 1.7–1.6 to about 1.2–1.1 myr (Bar-Yosef 1998; Klein 1999; Petraglia and Korisettar 1998; Raynal *et al.* 2001; Sahnouni and de Heinzelin 1998; Schick 1994). There is no doubt, I believe, that in the course of this process numerous populations became extinct. But the success of *Homo* sp. was established.

Hence, at the close of a field season with a view of the glowing red sunset, or after viewing a slide of the same image at the end of a public lecture, we are left with some old questions as well as new ones. The efforts to tell a good story about our African ancestors based on an incomplete puzzle of field and laboratory investigations, the probing minds of students and colleagues, and sometimes a smart journalist who joins for photo opportunities, force us to rethink what we said or wrote. It often feels that the intricate relationships between habitats, hominid activities and morphological changes still need a more satisfactory explanation. We are going to try to produce one because, as I said, we are an optimistic breed.

ACKNOWLEDGEMENTS

This paper, like the others in this volume, is dedicated to Derek Roe, with whom I share an interest in the Lower Palaeolithic. I still remember how before we met, while studying the first handaxe assemblages from 'Ubeidiya with the late David Gilead, we employed Derek Roe's metrical attributes for recording the newly discovered artefacts. In addition, I have benefited from many discussions on similar issues with others who do not necessarily share my current views. They are gratefully acknowledged for their endless patience: Anna Belfer-Cohen, Naama Goren-Inbar, Paul Goldberg, David Pilbeam, and Martha Tappen. For the comments on nutrition and digestion, I thank Larry Schulman (Technion, Haifa), and Yosef Dror (Faculty of Agriculture, Hebrew University). Thanks go to Wren Fournier who skillfully edited this manuscript.

REFERENCES

Aiello, L.C. and Wheeler, P. 1995. The expensive-tissue hypothesis: the brain and digestive system in human and primate evolution. *Current Anthropology* 36, 199–221.

Backwell, L.R. and d'Errico, F. 2001. Evidence of termite foraging by Swartkrans early hominids. *Proceedings of the National Academy of Sciences* 98, 1358–1363.

Bar-Yosef, O. 1993. Site formation processes from a Levantine viewpoint. In P. Goldberg, D.T. Nash and M.D. Petraglia (eds.) *Formation Processes in Archaeological Context*, 11–32. Monographs in World Archaeology 17. Prehistory Press, Madison.

Bar-Yosef, O. 1998. Early colonizations and cultural continuities in the Lower Palaeolithic of Western Asia. In M.D. Petraglia and R. Korisettar (eds.) *Early Human Behaviour in Global*

Context: The Rise and Diversity of the Lower Palaeolithic Record, 221–279. Routledge, London.

Bar-Yosef, O. 2001. A personal view of earth sciences' contribution to archaeology. In P. Goldberg, V.T. Holliday and C.R. Ferring (eds.) *Earth Sciences and Archaeology*, 473–488. Kluwer Academic/Plenum, New York.

Bar-Yosef, O. and Callander, J. 1999. The woman from Tabun: Garrod's doubts in historical perspective. *Journal of Human Evolution* 37, 879–885.

Bellomo, R.V. 1993. A methodological approach for identifying archaeological evidence of fire resulting from human activities. *Journal of Archaeological Science* 20, 525–553.

Bermúdez de Castro, J.M., Arsuaga, J.L., Carbonell, E. and Rodríguez, J. (eds.) 1999. *Atapuerca: Nuestras Antecesores*. Fundación del Patrimonio Histórico de Castilla y León, León.

Binford, L.R. 1981. *Bones: Ancient Men and Modern Myths*. Academic Press, New York.

Binford, L.R. and Ho, C.K. 1985. Taphonomy at a distance: Zhoukoudian, "the cave home of Beijing man"? *Current Anthropology* 26, 413–442.

Blumenschine, R.J. 1991. Hominid carnivory and foraging strategies, and the socio-economic function of early archaeological sites. *Philosophical Transactions of the Royal Society of London* B 334, 211–221.

Blumenschine, R.J. and Cavallo, J.A. 1992. Scavenging and human evolution. *Scientific American* 267 (4), 90–96.

Blumenschine, R.J. and Peters, C.R. 1998. Archaeological predictions for hominid land use in the paleo-Olduvai Basin, Tanzania, during lowermost Bed II times. *Journal of Human Evolution* 34, 565–607.

Boesch, C. and Boesch, H. 1990. Tool use and tool making in wild chimpanzees. *Folia Primatologica* 54, 86–99.

Boesch, C., Marchesi, P., Marchesi, N., Fruth, B. and Joulian, F. 1994. Is nutcracking in wild chimpanzees a cultural behavior? *Journal of Human Evolution* 26, 325–338.

Bonnefille, R. 1995. A reassessment of the Plio-Pleistocene pollen record of East Africa. In E. Vrba, G. Denton, T. Partridge and L. Burckle (eds.) *Paleoclimate and Evolution, with Emphasis on Human Origins*, 299–310. Yale University Press, New Haven.

Bordes, F. 1954. *Les Limons Quaternaires du Bassin de la Seine: Stratigraphie et Archéologie Paléolithique*. Archives de l'Institut de Paléontologie Humaine, Memoire 26, Paris.

Bordes, F. 1968. *The Old Stone Age*. McGraw Hill, New York.

Brain C.K. 1981. *The Hunters or the Hunted? An Introduction to African Cave Taphonomy*. University of Chicago Press, Chicago.

Brain, C.K. 1993. *Swartkrans: A Cave's Chronicle of Early Man*. Transvaal Museum Monograph 8, Pretoria.

Bunn, H.T. 1991. A taphonomic perspective on the archaeology of human origins. *Annual Review of Anthropology* 20, 433–467.

Bunn, H.T., Kroll, E.M. and Bartram, L.E. 1991. Bone distribution on a modern East African landscape and its archaeological implications. In J.D. Clark (ed.) *Cultural Beginnings: Approaches to Understanding Early Hominid Life-ways in the African Savanna*, 33–54. Rudolf Habelt, Bonn.

Cerling, T.E. and Hay, R.L. 1986. An isotopic study of paleosol carbonates from Olduvai Gorge. *Quaternary Research* 25, 63–78.

Cerling, T.E., Wang, Y. and Quade, J. 1993. Expansion of C4 ecosystems as an indicator of global ecological change in the late Miocene. *Nature* 361, 344–345.

Cerling, T.E., Harris, J.M., Ambrose, S.H., Leakey, M.G. and Solounias, N. 1997. Dietary and environmental reconstruction with stable isotope analyses of herbivore tooth enamel from the Miocene locality of Fort Ternan, Kenya. *Journal of Human Evolution* 33, 635–650.

Clark, J.G.D. 1953. *From Savagery to Civilization*. Henry Schuman, New York.

Clark, J.G.D. 1969. *World Prehistory: A New Outline*. Cambridge University Press, London.

Clark, J.G.D. 1970. *Aspects of Prehistory*. University of California Press, Berkeley.

Courty, M.A., Goldberg, P. and Macphail, R. 1989. *Soils and Micromorphology in Archaeology*. Cambridge University Press, Cambridge.

Courty, M.A., Goldberg, P. and Macphail, R. 2001. Microfacies analysis assisting archaeological stratigraphy. In P. Goldberg, V.T. Holliday and C.R. Ferring (eds.) *Earth Sciences and Archaeology*, 205–239. Kluwer Academic/Plenum, New York.

Dibble, H.L. 1995. Middle Paleolithic scraper reduction: background, clarification, and review of the evidence to date. *Journal of Archaeological Method and Theory* 2, 299–368.

Dibble, H.L., Chase, P.G., McPherron, S.P. and Tuffreau, A. 1997. Testing the reality of a "living floor" with archaeological data. *American Antiquity* 62, 629–651.

Dobres, M.A. 2000. *Technology and Social Agency: Outlining a Practice Framework for Archaeology*. Blackwell, Oxford.

Durham, W.H. 1991. *Coevolution: Genes, Culture, and Human Diversity*. Stanford University Press, Palo Alto.

Feibel, C.S. 1997. Debating the environmental factors in hominid evolution. *GSA Today* 7 (3), 1–7.

Feldman, M.W. and Cavalli-Sforza, L.L. 1976. Cultural and biological evolutionary processes: selection for a trait under complex transmission. *Theoretical Population Biology* 9, 238–259.

Fernández-Jalvo, Y., Denys, C., Andrews, P., Williams, T., Dauphin, Y. and Humphrey, L. 1998. Taphonomy and palaeoeoecology of Olduvai Bed-I (Pleistocene, Tanzania). *Journal of Human Evolution* 34, 137–172.

Foley, R. and Lahr, M.M. 1997. Mode 3 technologies and the evolution of modern humans. *Cambridge Archaeological Journal* 7, 3–36.

Gabunia, L., Vekua, A., Lordkipanidze, D., Swisher, C.C., Ferring, R., Justus, A., Nioradze, M., Tvalchrelidze, M., Antón, S.C., Bosinski, G., Jöris, O., de Lumley, M.-A., Majsuradze, G. and Mouskhelishvili, A. 2000. Earliest Pleistocene hominid cranial remains from Dmanisi, Republic of Georgia: taxonomy, geological setting, and age. *Science* 288, 1019–1025.

Gamble, C. 2001. Modes, movement and moderns. *Quaternary International* 75, 5–10.

Goldberg, P. and Bar-Yosef, O. 1998. Site formation processes in Kebara and Hayonim Caves and their significance in Levantine prehistoric caves. In T. Akazawa, K. Aoki and O. Bar-Yosef (eds.) *Neandertals and Modern Humans in Western Asia*, 107–125. Plenum Press, New York.

Goldberg, P., Holliday, V.T. and Ferring, C.R. (eds.) 2001. *Earth Sciences and Archaeology*. Kluwer Academic/Plenum, New York.

Gowlett, J.A.J. 1990. Technology, skill and the psychosocial sector in the long term of human evolution. *Cambridge Archaeological Review* 9, 82–103.

Gowlett, J.A.J. 1996. Mental abilities of early *Homo*: elements of constraint and choice in rule systems. In P. Mellars and K. Gibson (eds.) *Modelling the Early Human Mind*, 191–215. McDonald Institute for Archaeological Research, Cambridge.

Grün, R. and Stringer, C. 2000. Tabun revisited: revised ESR chronology and new ESR and U-series analyses of dental material from Tabun C1. *Journal of Human Evolution* 39, 601–612.

Hay, R.L. 1976. *Geology of the Olduvai Gorge: A Study of Sedimentation in a Semiarid Basin*. University of California Press, Berkeley.

Hay, R.L. 1990. Olduvai Gorge: a case history in the interpretation of hominid paleoenvironments in East Africa. In L.F. Laporte (ed.) *Establishment of a Geologic Framework for Paleo-*

anthropology, 23–37. Geological Society of America Special Paper 242, Boulder.

Ichikawa, M. and Terashima, H. 1996. Cultural diversity in the use of plants by Mbuti hunter-gatherers in northeastern Zaire: an ethnobotanical approach. In S. Kent (ed.) *Cultural Diversity Among Twentieth-Century Foragers: An African Perspective*, 276–293. Cambridge University Press, Cambridge.

Inizan, M.-L., Reduron-Ballinger, M., Roche, H. and Tixier, J. 1999. *Technology and Terminology of Knapped Stone*. CREP, Nanterre.

Isaac, G. 1984. The archaeology of human origins: studies of the Lower Pleistocene in East Africa 1971–1981. In F. Wendorf and A. Close (eds.) *Advances in World Archaeology* Volume 3, 1–87. Academic Press, New York.

Isaac, G. 1986. Foundation stones: early artefacts as indicators of activities and abilities. In G.N. Bailey and P. Callow (eds.) *Stone Age Prehistory: Studies in Memory of Charles McBurney*, 221–241. Cambridge University Press, Cambridge.

James, S.R. 1989. Hominid use of fire in the Lower and Middle Pleistocene: a review of the evidence. *Current Anthropology* 30, 1–26.

Jelinek, A.J. 1982. The Tabun Cave and Paleolithic Man in the Levant. *Science* 216, 1369–1375.

Joulian, F. 1996. Comparing chimpanzee and early hominid techniques: some contributions to cultural and cognitive questions. In P. Mellars and K. Gibson (eds.) *Modelling the Early Human Mind*, 173–189. McDonald Institute for Archaeological Research, Cambridge.

Karkanas, P., Bar-Yosef, O., Goldberg, P. and Weiner, S. 2000. Diagenesis in prehistoric caves: the use of minerals that form *in situ* to assess the completeness of the archaeological record. *Journal of Archaeological Science* 27, 915–929.

Kingston, J.D., Marino, B.D. and Hill, A. 1994. Isotopic evidence for neogene hominid paleoenvironments in the Kenya rift valley. *Science* 264, 955–959.

Klein, R.G. 1999. *The Human Career: Human Biological and Cultural Origins*. University of Chicago Press, Chicago.

Laland, K.N., Odling-Smee, F.J. and Feldman, M.W. 2000. Niche construction, biological evolution, and cultural change. *Behavioral and Brain Sciences* 23, 131–175.

Laville, H., Rigaud, J.-P. and Sackett, J. 1980. *Rock Shelters of the Perigord*. Academic Press, New York.

Leakey, M.D. 1971. *Olduvai Gorge: Excavations in Beds I and II, 1960–1963*. Cambridge University Press, Cambridge.

Leakey, M. and Roe, D.A. (eds.) 1994. *Olduvai Gorge Volume 5: Excavations in Beds III, IV and the Masek Beds, 1968–1971*. Cambridge University Press, Cambridge.

Leakey, M.G., Spoor, F., Brown, F.H., Gathogo, P.N., Kiarie, C., Leakey, L.N. and McDougall, I. 2001. New hominin genus from eastern Africa shows diverse middle Pliocene lineages. *Nature* 410, 433–440.

Lee-Thorp, J., Thackeray, J.F. and van der Merwe, N. 2000. The hunters and the hunted revisited. *Journal of Human Evolution* 39, 565–576.

Lieberman, D.E. 2001. Another face in our family tree. *Nature* 410, 419–420.

Macphail, R. and Cruise, J. 2001. The soil micromorphologist as team player: a multianalytical approach to the study of European microstratigraphy. In P. Goldberg, V.T. Holliday and C.R. Ferring (eds.) *Earth Sciences and Archaeology*, 241–267. Kluwer Academic/Plenum, New York.

Marzke, M.W. and Marzke, R.F. 2000. Evolution of the human hand: approaches to acquiring, analysing and interpreting the anatomical evidence. *Journal of Anatomy* 197, 121–140.

McGrew, W.C. 1992. *Chimpanzee Material Culture: Implications for Human Evolution*. Cambridge University Press, Cambridge.

McGrew, W.C. 1994. Tools compared: the material of culture. In R.W. Wrangham, W.C. McGrew, F.B.M. de Waal and P.G. Heltne (eds.) *Chimpanzee Cultures*, 25–40. Harvard University Press, Cambridge.

Meehan, B. 1982. *Shell Bed to Shell Midden*. Australian Institute of Aboriginal Studies, Canberra.

Menzel, P. and D'Aluisio, F. 1998. *Man Eating Bugs: The Art and Science of Eating Insects*. Ten Speed Press, Berkeley.

Mercier, N., Valladas, H., Valladas, G., Reyss, J.-L., Jelinek, A., Meignen L. and Joron, J.-L. 1995. TL dates of burnt flints from Jelinek's excavations at Tabun and their implications. *Journal of Archaeological Science* 22, 495–509.

Mithen, S. 1996. *The Prehistory of the Mind: The Cognitive Origins of Art, Religion and Science*. Thames and Hudson, London.

Moore, H.L. 1994. *A Passion for Difference*. Polity Press, Oxford.

Orians, G.H. and Heerwagen, J.H. 1992. Evolved responses to landscapes. In J.H. Barkow, L. Cosmides and J. Tooby (eds.) *The Adapted Mind: Evolutionary Psychology and the Generation of Culture*, 555–579. Oxford University Press, Oxford.

Otte, M. 1999. Modes of life in the Palaeolithic: not survival but well-being. In H. Ullrich (ed.) *Hominid Evolution: Lifestyles and Survival Strategies*, 248–251. Archaea, Schwelm.

Petraglia, M.D. and Korisettar, R. (eds.) 1998. *Early Human Behaviour in Global Context: The Rise and Diversity of the Lower Palaeolithic Record*. Routledge, London.

Pilbeam, D. 1996. Genetic and morphological records of the Hominoidea and hominid origins: a synthesis. *Molecular Phylogenetics and Evolution* 5, 155–168.

Potts, R. 1989. Ecological context and explanations of hominid evolution. *Ossa* 14, 99–112.

Raynal, J.P., Sbihi Alaoui, F.Z., Geraads, D., Magoga, L. and Mohi, A. 2001. The earliest occupation of North Africa: the Moroccan perspective. *Quaternary International* 75, 65–75.

Roche, H. and Texier, P.-J. 1995. Evaluation of technical competence of *Homo erectus* in East Africa during the Middle Pleistocene. In J.R.F. Bower and S. Sartono (eds.) *Evolution and Ecology of Homo erectus*, 153–167. Pithecanthropus Centennial Foundation, Leiden University, Leiden.

Sahnouni, M. and de Heinzelin, J. 1998. The Site of Aïn Hanech revisited: new investigations at this Lower Pleistocene site in Northern Algeria. *Journal of Archaeological Science* 25, 1083–1101.

Schick, K. 1994. The Movius Line reconsidered: perspectives on the earlier Paleolithic of eastern Asia. In R.S. Corruccini and R.L. Ciochon (eds.) *Integrative Paths to the Past: Paleoanthropological Advances in Honor of F. Clark Howell*, 569–596. Prentice Hall, Englewood Cliffs.

Schick, K. and Toth, N. 1993. *Making Silent Stones Speak: Human Evolution and the Dawn of Technology*. Simon and Schuster, New York.

Schiegl, S., Lev-Yadun, S., Bar-Yosef, O., El Goresy, A. and Weiner, S. 1994. Siliceous aggregates from prehistoric wood ash: a major component of sediments in Kebara and Hayonim caves (Israel). *Israel Journal of Earth Sciences* 43, 267–278.

Speth, J.D. 1991. Taphonomy and early hominid behavior: problems in distinguishing cultural and non-cultural agents. In M.C. Stiner (ed.) *Human Predators and Mortality*, 31–40. Westview Press, Boulder.

Sponheimer, M. and Lee-Thorpe, J.A. 1999. Isotopic evidence for the diet of an early hominid, *Australopithecus africanus*. *Science* 283, 368–370.

Stern, N. 1993. The structure of the Lower Pleistocene archaeological record. *Current Anthropology* 34, 201–225.

Stiner, M.C. 1994. *Honor Among Thieves: A Zooarchaeological Study of Neandertal Ecology*. Princeton University Press, Princeton.

Susman, R.L. 1998. Hand function and tool behavior in early hominids. *Journal of Human Evolution* 35, 23–46.

Tappen, M. 2001. Deconstructing the Serengeti. In C. Stanford and H. Bunn (eds.) *Meat-eating and Human Evolution*, 13–32. Oxford University Press, Oxford.

Tappen, M. and Wrangham, R. 2000. Recognizing hominoid-modified bones: the taphonomy of colobus bones partially digested by free-ranging chimpanzees in the Kibale Forest, Uganda. *American Journal of Physical Anthropology* 113, 217–234.

Toth, N. 1985. The Oldowan reassessed: a close look at early stone artifacts. *Journal of Archaeological Science* 12, 101–120.

Toth, N. 1987. Behavioral inferences from early stone artifact assemblages: an experimental model. *Journal of Human Evolution* 16, 763–787.

Toth, N. 1991. The importance of experimental replicative and functional studies in Paleolithic archaeology. In J.D. Clark (ed.) *Cultural Beginnings: Approaches to Understanding Early Hominid Life-ways in the African Savanna*, 109–124. Rudolf Habelt, Bonn.

Toth, N., Schick, K.P., Savage-Rumbaugh, E.S., Sevcik, R.A. and Rumbaugh, D.M. 1993. Pan the tool-maker: investigations into the stone tool-making and tool-using capabilities of a bonobo (*Pan paniscus*). *Journal of Archaeological Science* 20, 81–92.

Villa, P. 1976. Sols et niveaux d'habitat du Paléolithique inférieur en Europe et au Proche Orient. *Quaternaria* 19, 107–134.

Weiner, S., Schiegl, S., Goldberg, P. and Bar-Yosef, O. 1995. Mineral assemblages in Kebara and Hayonim caves, Israel: excavation strategies, bone preservation and wood ash remnants. *Israel Journal of Chemistry* 35, 143–154.

Weiner, S., Goldberg, P., Xu, Q., Liu, L. and Bar-Yosef, O. 1998. Evidence for use of fire at Zhoukoudian, China. *Science* 281, 251–253.

White, T.D., Suwa, G. and Asfaw, B. 1994. *Australopithecus ramidus*, a new species of early hominid from Aramis, Ethiopia. *Nature* 371, 306–333.

Wilson, A.C. 1985. The molecular basis of evolution. *Scientific American* 253 (4), 148–157.

Wrangham, R.W., McGrew, W.C., de Waal, F.B.M. and Heltne, P.G. (eds.) 1994. *Chimpanzee Cultures*. Harvard University Press, Cambridge.

Wrangham, R.W., Jones, J.H., Laden, G., Pilbeam, D. and Conklin-Brittain, N.L. 1999. The raw and the stolen: cooking and the ecology of human origins. *Current Anthropology* 40, 567–594.

10. Cleavers: their distribution, chronology and typology

Vadim A. Ranov

ABSTRACT

In reviewing the distribution, chronology and typology of cleavers throughout the Lower Palaeolithic of the Old World, this paper offers a strict definition which may help to specify the significance of these implements and the assemblages in which they occur.

INTRODUCTION

The publication of Roe's work on handaxes and, subsequently, his synthesis on the Lower and Middle Palaeolithic in Britain (1981) highlighted cleavers as a particular type of biface worthy of further investigation in their own right. Although true cleavers are not found where I work in Tadjikistan, I have been able to pursue my interest in them during visits to western Europe, Israel, India and the United States. As a result of the research discussed here, it can be suggested that cleavers have a specific chronological and geographical spread and might be regarded as a *fossile directeur*.

DISTRIBUTION AND CHRONOLOGY

Africa

Cleavers occur alongside handaxes from the Developed Oldowan right through the Acheulian in Africa and in all the environmental zones proposed by Clark (1970). This suggests an age range of between 1.75 myr based on K/Ar and thermomagnetic results for the Developed Oldowan in Bed II at Olduvai, extending to 1.35 myr for the beginning of the Acheulian given by the K/Ar determinations for Peninj, and continuing to between 300 and 200

kyr elsewhere in East Africa (Isaac 1967; Leakey 1971; Leakey and Roe 1994).

Needless to say, the density of Acheulian sites varies from region to region. In Southern Africa, the greatest concentrations of Acheulian localities occur on the southern coast, along the Vaal river and in Namibia, Mozambique and Zimbabwe (Sampson 1974, fig. 40). By contrast, no Earlier Stone Age sites are known in the central area covering Botswana and the Kalahari Desert. This distribution may represent a real pattern from the past reflecting resource availability and palaeoecological conditions or, particularly in more isolated areas, it could simply be the result of a research deficit. South Africa, as well as parts of the Maghreb, the Mediterranean and East Africa, have been quite well surveyed whereas equatorial Africa, the Kalahari and much of the east coast remain, archaeologically, largely unexplored. Such variability in the record inevitably affects how well assemblages with cleavers can be interpreted.

In South Africa, sites with cleavers such as Klippaadrif, Amanzi and the lower layer of the Cave of Hearths, seem to date to various stages of the Acheulian and, in general, it can be said that cleavers seem to be present at most sites (Mason 1962). Recent excavations at Sterkfontein have yielded cleavers in the early Acheulian of Member 5 dated by its fauna to between 2.0 and 1.5 myr (Kuman

1998). At Swartkrans a single cleaver found in member 3 extends this date range to 1.0 myr (*ibid.*, 154). Other sites have mostly been dated on the basis of their geological context and fall within the same time range.

Sites with cleavers are better known and investigated in East Africa (Clark 1970, fig. 18). At the early Acheulian site of Peninj handaxes and cleavers equally constitute 16% of all the finds. Handaxes and cleavers are also found in association at the Middle–Upper Acheulian sites of Kalambo Falls, Isimila and Olorgesailie. At the latter, dated to between 500 and 400 kyr by the K/Ar method, cleavers represent 23% of the artefacts analysed (Isaac 1977) whereas at Isimila they amount to 50% of the twelve categories of artefact found in layer 3 (Howell *et al.* 1962). A U/Th date of 300 kyr for Isimila suggests it is older than the 200 kyr suggested by Ar/Ar for Kalambo Falls (Isaac 1977, 214). Cleavers also occur at Nsongezi on the Kangera river, particularly in layer 8, at Kariandusi, Kenya, and in the Acheulian levels at Melka Kunturé, Ethiopia (Chavaillon and Chavaillon 1980).

By comparison, little is known about the Acheulian of central tropical and western coastal Africa. This may be due to lack of investigation or to low population densities in Palaeolithic times (Isaac 1982). Nevertheless, Isaac (*ibid.*) notes the presence of cleavers in collections from Maiidon Toro, Pingell and Nok on the Jos Plateau in Nigeria. At Maiidon Toro, cleavers are numerically predominant.

Many of the cleavers in collections from the Sahara come from redeposited accumulations, but assemblages with good contexts are known from the sites of Erg Tihodaïne between Hoggar and Tassili, and two sites to the west of Saoura in the Adrar Bous lake basin in the northern part of the Tenere Desert. Alimen (1960) notes that during the Late Acheulian of the Sahara, bifaces, including cleavers, were thin and well made, such as those from Tabalbala near Beni Abbes. Clark (1980, 530) has observed that the proportion of cleavers varies within each of his four Acheulian facies. Out of 126 bifaces found at Ternifine, 107 were cleavers, whereas at Kharga Oasis cleavers are few in number. Biberson (1961) records cleavers at the early Acheulian site at Sidi Abderrahman and Tixier (1956) reports 650 of these artefacts from seventeen localities in the Maghreb and Sahara. These sites are thought to date from >700 kyr to about 360 kyr on the basis of their biostratigraphy (Clark 1992 and this volume).

Spain

It is evident from the collections curated by the museums in Cadiz, Jerez de la Frontera and Seville that there are similarities between early Acheulian assemblages in Andalucia and those of Morocco. The older literature (Alimen 1975; Bordes 1968) attributes these similarities to migrations from south to north across the Straits of Gibraltar at periods of low sea level during the Riss cold period. New evidence (Aguirre and Carbonell 2001; Carbonell *et al.* 1999) indicates that the Spanish sites are much older than the Riss. In this case, *Homo erectus* must have crossed the Straits at an earlier period, but until the chronological framework is better understood (Raposo and Santonja 1995), it will not be possible to discuss the geographical distribution of sites with cleavers satisfactorily.

Cleavers are found all over Spain. In the south, at Janda near Cadiz and Laguna de Medina near Jerez de la Frontera, cleavers constitute 7.23% of all the stone artefacts and 19.29% of all the bifacial forms, whereas at Palmar de Conde they represent 29.16% of all the bifacial pieces (Giles Pacheco *et al.* 1990). Cleavers are also known from the terraces of the Guadalquivir, as well as Malaga and Valencia.

A number of Acheulian sites are known in the area between Madrid and Toledo on the terrraces of the Tagus and Manzanares rivers. These include the large Middle Acheulian site of Pinedo which is situated on a terrace on the right bank of the Tagus and dated to about 500 kyr. Bifaces here form 1.9% of the total number of artefacts and include seventy-four handaxes and thirty-eight cleavers. The latter are all made on flakes (Querol and Santonja 1980). In the same area, cleavers are known from Aridos and San Isidro on the outskirts of Madrid. The former site has been known for over one hundred years and the first object found there was a flake cleaver (Freeman 1975). The site of Acacia near Mejorada del Campo yielded typologically developed cleavers whilst at Sartolejo in the valley of the river Alagón more cleavers than handaxes were recovered.

The sites of Torralba and Ambrona near Soria, northeast of Madrid, have long provided a basis for comparing the Acheulian of Spain and North Africa. They are dated to about 400 kyr (Howell 1966, 116). At Torralba, Alimen (1975) noted that the forty-three cleavers and fifty-seven handaxes represented 7.9 and 10.5% of the total of 544 artefacts respectively. At Ambrona, ten cleavers and fourteen handaxes represented 1.5 and 2.0% of the total of 682 artefacts. A similar ratio of cleavers to handaxes occurs in the Saharan collections (Alimen 1975, 401; Howell 1966, 137). Only a few cleavers are present at Atapuerca although they are well represented in the northern part of the Meseta and the Iberian cordillera. Cleavers have also been collected from about fifty localities such as Burganes, Belver and Galisancho in the Maya district on the river Tormes, where they have been recovered both as surface finds and stratified in the colluvial and alluvial deposits of the 8 and 56 metre terraces. They are attributed to the Early, Middle and Late Acheulian (Santonja and Pérez González 1984). The site of La Maya III on the 56 m terrace is considered to be of similar age, c. 400 kyr, to Pinedo, while La Maya I, on the 8 m terrace, with its Late Acheulian, is Late Pleistocene (*ibid.*, 336).

In the north of Spain, a small number of cleavers have been recorded from Catalonia. The analysis of the finds from the site of Puig d'Esclats indicates that cleavers form only 1.72% of the total artefact assemblage whereas handaxes constitute 8.6%. In the district of La Selva this percentage drops to a meagre 0.2% (Canal and Carbonell 1989). By contrast, in the Mousterian level of the well-known cave of Castillo near Santander, cleavers form a significant part of the industry. Overall, it may be said that cleavers are known in varying quantities at almost all Acheulian sites in Spain. According to Alimen (1975), they are also present in the Acheulian and Mousterian collections made by Breuil and Zbyszewski in Portugal.

France

Defining cleavers as implements made on flakes and excluding bifaces with transverse edges, Alimen (1975, 400) has identified only ten assemblages with this type of tool in France. Almost all of these are found in the south, in the Pyrénées Atlantiques, Haute Pyrénées and Dordogne, where they occur as sporadic surface finds or, occasionally, in cave sites. Cleavers are only found as a significant part of a Mousterian assemblage similar to that from Castillo, Spain (*infra*), at the cave of Ola near Cambo de Ben, where they are dated to the last interglacial.

Among the many artefacts illustrated from Provence by de Lumley (1969), there are few cleavers and these artefacts constitute only 2.2% of the assemblage from Terra Amata where the biostratigraphy of level Cla suggests an age of 450–380 kyr with TL age estimates on burnt flint of 380 kyr (Lumley 1976, 823). By contrast, the valleys of the Tarn and Garonne have yielded many examples made on flakes and cobbles. Around Montauban, for example, cleavers represent 11.5% of the total number of finds (Tavoso 1975, 15). On the terraces of the Tarn, Acheulian and Mousterian surface sites include cleavers. In the former, cleavers made on flakes may be as numerous as handaxes. Lumley (1976) notes cleavers in small numbers from other parts of the country. At the junction of the Rhône and Isère, the open-air site of Cantalouette has cleavers on flakes, bifacial cleavers and cleavers made on debitage (Guichard 1976). Tuffreau (1976) notes bifacial cleavers at the Middle Acheulian site of Bondeville, as well as Cagny-la-Garenne in the Somme Valley. The Garenne formation is dated to OIS 12 to 11 and has an ESR age estimate of 400±101 kyr (Tuffreau and Antoine 1995). Bordes (1954) recorded cleavers from loess deposits at Chaudon, Abbeville Carpentier, Saint-Pierre les Elbeuf and other sites which he associated with the Late Acheulian. He also noted the occasional occurrence of cleavers in the Middle Palaeolithic in assemblages designated as Mousterian of Acheulian Tradition, which extend the age range into the last interglacial.

Belgium, Holland and Germany

Cleavers do not seem to have been recorded from Belgium (Cahen 1984) and there seem to be only two from Holland (Peeters *et al.* 1988). Bosinski and Luttropp (1971) record almost equal numbers of cleavers and handaxes from Reutersruh in Germany with totals of 130 and 129 respectively. The former are classified into three types (*ibid.*, 67–69), only one of which coincides with the definition set by Tixier (1956). Bosinski (1995) notes cleavers from Münzenberg, Kärlich-Seeufer, Hohdale and Markkleeberg. Kärlich-Seeufer is dated to OIS 11, or about 400 kyr (*ibid.*, 117).

England

Cleavers form an integral part of the British Lower Palaeolithic and are particularly well-known from the Thames Valley (Roe 1981; Wymer 1968). As in Europe, they seem to occur within a period from about 500 to 200 kyr. Cleavers on flakes are rare (Cranshaw 1983, 68). Roe (1968, 31) considers cleavers as one of the three handaxe types defined by his metrical analysis. In general, the cleaver form does not exceed 1–3% of an assemblage, only exceptionally rising to 8.9% and no higher.

Central Europe

With some rare exceptions, cleavers are known only from the Czech Republic and the Ukraine. These differ from the classic cleaver forms known in western Europe and Africa. For the Czech Republic, Fridrich (1997) notes that cleavers occur mainly in Lower Palaeolithic assemblages and only rarely in the Middle Palaeolithic. Table 10.1 summarises the proportions in which they are present at three sites.

Chulachula (1992) records cleavers made on limestone in the Middle Palaeolithic in central Moravia. At Korolevo in the western Ukraine, cleavers constitute between 2.9 and 13.5% of the Acheulian units 6, 5a and 5 (Gladilin and Sitlivy 1990). These levels are dated to the middle to late Middle Pleistocene or, using the old Alpine scheme, from a Mindel interglacial in level 6, through the Riss glacial in level 5a to the Riss 2/3 interstadial in level 5 (*ibid.*, 12).

Site	% cleavers	Artefact total
Beroun 2	2.17	92
Bečov 2 - 175	12.54	1396
Prezletiče 60	8.19	733

Table 10.1. Proportion of cleavers to other artefact types in sites in the Czech Republic. The oldest of these sites may be Beroun A-III on the surface of a terrace of the river Vraj. It is attributed to the Olduvai Event, 1.96–1.78 myr, but there is considerable doubt about this dating (Valoch 1995, 67). Bečov and Prezletiče are considered to be early Middle Acheulian, dating between 590–660 kyr, although an older dating of 750–840 kyr has also been suggested (Fridrich 1997, 30).

Italy

The Acheulian of Italy is distinct from that of continental Europe because the majority of the sites do not have handaxes or cleavers. Cleavers have been found in two sites in south-west Sicily on the maritime terraces at Pergole and Contrada Maddaluso. According to Alimen (1975, 417) pebble cleavers fall outside her definition of cleavers which, *sensu stricto*, are made on flakes, but she considers these finds might confirm the possibility of connections with North Africa at periods of low sea level. Conversely, Villa (2001) considers that the Lower Palaeolithic of Italy indicates that the peninsula was occupied from the north rather than from Africa. Piperno (1974) illustrates four cleavers from peninsular Italy found at Rosaneto in Calabria.

Near East, Caucasus and Central Asia

Cleavers are present in assemblages in varying proportions throughout the Acheulian in the Near East (Table 10.2). The rough bifacial cleaver forms from the Early Acheulian site of 'Ubeidiya in the Jordan Valley (Stekelis 1966) are among the oldest known, if the formerly disputed dating of c. 1.4 myr is accepted. By contrast, the cleavers from the Middle Acheulian site of Gesher Benot Ya'aqov, at the headwaters of the river Jordan, are well made on Kombewa or Levallois flakes, and the ratio of handaxes to cleavers is similar to that found in African sites of this period (Gilead 1973, 76). They are dated to about 700 kyr (Goren-Inbar and Saragusti 1996; Goren-Inbar *et al.* 1991, 2000). The dating of cleavers from various levels

Site	Proportion of cleavers
Gesher Benot Ya'aqov Stratum 4, Israel	ratio of handaxes to cleavers 2.3 (95:40)
'Ubeidiya, Israel	2% of all large implements
Evron Quarry, Israel	3% or 5 out of 160 bifaces
Ma'ayan Barukh, Israel	2.2% or 7 out of 300 bifaces
Berzine, Syria	1.42% out of 248
Latamne, Syria	2% out of 289
Joubb Jannine, Lebanon	3.9% out of 944
Azraq, Jordan	25%

Table 10.2. Proportion of cleavers present in Acheulian assemblages from sites in the Near East. The Syrian site of Latamne on the Oront river was attributed to the early Middle Pleistocene by its excavator (Clark 1966) and recent RSL age estimates have given results between about 300 and 600 kyr (Dodonov et al. 1993, 191). Similarly, Joubb Jannine in the Bekaa valley is considered to be mid Middle Pleistocene/Mindel in age (Hours 1981,169) whereas Azraq C-Spring has been attributed to a more recent OIS 8, 242–301 kyr, age (Clark 1966; Copeland 1991; Copeland and Hours 1979).

in the Evron Quarry spreads across the middle to late Middle Pleistocene (Gilead and Ronen 1977, 82). The cleavers selected by Gilead (*ibid.*) from Umm Qatafa and Tabun seem doubtful. Neither Garrod (Garrod and Bate 1937) nor Neuville (1951) mention cleavers from these sites.

There has been relatively little investigation of Lower Palaeolithic sites in the Caucasus and Central Asia. However, cleavers have been noted by Lubin (1968) at the caves of Kudaro 1, Zona and Azykh, as well as the open-air sites of Laše-Balta, Jaštuch and some others in the Caucasus. At Zona the ratio of cleavers to handaxes is 1:5 (*ibid.*). Level 5a at this site has RSL age estimates of 360±70 kyr for the bottom and 350±90 for the top. Islamov and Krakhmal (1995) record cleavers from ancient strata in Sel'ungar Cave in Kirghizia (Central Asia) where they constitute 4.2% or thirteen out of 306 artefacts. These authors (*ibid.*) date these deposits between 1.0 myr and 600 kyr, but a younger, late Middle Pleistocene age, can also be argued (Ranov 1995).

Despite the existence of many sites with bifaces in Kazakhstan, only one on the Mangishlak Peninsula is said to have cleavers. These occur in a Middle Acheulian facies with Levallois technique and some of the pieces described as cleavers are unmodified Kombewa flakes (Medoev 1982, 15). There is only one reference to cleavers from Mongolia. These occur in a depression called 'Bottom of Gobi' in the district of Mandal-Gobi (Okladnikov and Abramova 1994).

India, Pakistan and Nepal

Cleavers are numerous and recorded throughout the subcontinent (Allchin 1963; Sankalia 1974; Terra and Paterson 1939). By comparison with sites from the regions mentioned so far, the proportion of cleavers to handaxes tends to be higher. For example, in Pakistan cleavers may constitute as much as 38% of an assemblage (Paterson and Drummond 1962; Salim 1997) whilst at Morgah the seventeen cleavers recovered represent 50% of the biface total (Graziosi 1964, 27–29) and in the Kangra Valley cleavers exceed handaxes in number (Joshi 1979). Jayaswal (1978) presents data on cleavers from fifteen other sites in India. At three of these, Lalitpur, Nagarjunkonda and Chirkinala, cleavers exceed handaxes, while cleavers made on flakes exceed bifacial cleavers at all sites. Table 10.3 summarises the data from Jayaswal (1978), Misra and Rajaguru (1986), Sankalia (1952), Paddaya (1982) and Blumenschine *et al.* (1983), to show the significance of cleavers in assemblages from several regions. The work of Korisettar and Rajaguru (1998), Joshi *et al.* (1978) and Petraglia (1998, 361) suggests that most of these sites date to the Middle Pleistocene, between about 400 and 160 kyr. A U/Th age estimate on a sample from a site in the Didvana district of the Thar Desert in Rajastan has given a date of 390±50 kyr (Misra and Rajaguru 1986, 419)

Overall, it may be said that outside Africa, cleavers are

most significant within the Lower Palaeolithic assemblages of the Indian sub-continent. In Nepal, Corvinus (1987) notes cleavers at Patu in the east but the assemblage is possibly post-Palaeolithic, whereas at the site of Gadari in the Dang Valley in the west of the country, three Palaeolithic handaxes, a cleaver and other artefacts were recovered (Corvinus 1998).

China

Although China is rich in Palaeolithic sites, cleavers are few in number and unlike those found elsewhere. Noting the particular features of the Chinese types which occur in both the Lower and Middle Palaeolithic, Li (1992) records these implements from Shuigou in Henan province, Dingcun in Shanxi province, Miaohoushan in Liaoning province, and Zhoukoudian locality 1. These sites are dated from the Middle to the Upper Pleistocene. Dingcun is more recent with a date of 100 kyr whereas Shuigou is dated to the mid Middle Pleistocene, which is also the age of the Lower Palaeolithic in Miaohoushan cave which has uranium series age estimates of 400–142±13–11 kyr (Chen and Huang 1998; Ho and Jiang 1993). However, an artefact which might be a cleaver from locality 15 at Zhoukoudian may be the oldest in China, possibly dating from the beginning of the Brunhes, OIS 14–16 (Larichev 1977, 26).

Korea

To date, cleavers are known only from Chongokni in Kyung-gi province in the north of South Korea. There are eighty-six cleavers and thirty-seven handaxes from this site (Chung 1984). These artefacts have been dated to between 600 and 300 kyr (*ibid.*, 901) although a new, younger date of about 45 kyr has also been published (Yi 1992, 195).

Japan

A recent review by Astrakhov (1999) indicates that cleavers are present in both the Early and Middle Palaeolithic of Japan, notably at Kamitakamori, Sodekhara 3 and Nakajdimajama. At Kamitakamori, the artefacts were retrieved from immediately below tefra KS-1 dated to 560 kyr whereas at Sodekhara they are about 300 kyr old. Astrakhov (*ibid.*, 19) considers that their dating probably covers a longer period, between 130–45 kyr.

Vietnam

Boriskovsky (1966, 17–18) records axe-like implements from Mount Do but it is uncertain whether they are cleavers or not. It is possible that they are Neolithic in date (Matjukhin 1990).

Summary

From the above review, it may be seen that cleavers are known throughout the Acheulian from 33° south to 51° north. Their distribution is the same as that for the Acheulian (Isaac 1982, fig. 3.8). In Africa and the Near East, cleavers appear at the beginning of the Acheulian about 1.5 myr ago. In Europe, they first seem to appear about 500 kyr ago and in India, where they are particularly abundant, about 300 kyr ago. They seem to disappear from the archaeological record about 70–60 kyr ago.

Site	Number of handaxes	Number of cleavers
Lalitpur	93	138
Nagarjunkonda	111	157
Chirkinala	194	244
Adamgarh	55	18
Vadamadura-2	81	10
Gudian-2	76	12
Anagwadi	104	49
Rajastan (9 sites)	45	15
Singi Talar (Thar Desert)	16%	2.5%
Orissa	58	12
Godavari river (3 localities)	6	9
Hungsi Valley locality 5	18	28
Hungsi Valley locality 6	10	9
Patpara, Son Valley	12	11

Table 10.3. Proportion of cleavers to handaxes at selected sites from the Indian sub-continent.

TYPOLOGY

As the preceding review of their chronology and distribution has shown, there are several definitions of cleavers in use around the world and it is important to consider these so that comparisons and contrasts can be properly drawn. Clark (1959, 57) suggests that the term cleaver was in use at the turn of the twentieth century, and it certainly appears in the works of both Breuil and Cammiade and Burkitt dated to 1930. In everyday English usage, the word is used for a metal tool used as an axe for wood, or a chopper knife with a large rectangular blade used for chopping meat. Its archaeological meaning is necessarily less specific because the exact functions of the tools referred to as cleavers are not known. Movius (1944, 41) regarded them as choppers and this seems to be supported by experimental work which suggests they could be used for cutting, splitting and trimming wood, removing animal hide or separating joints of meat (Leakey 1960; Matjukhin 1983). However, as Roe (1994, 149) notes, no use wear studies have been carried out on them.

As a result, it is their similarity to modern axes rather than archaeological evidence that has governed their interpretation, and this may be a barrier to proper classification (*ibid.*).

In the absence of evidence which might provide a functional classification of these tools, it is their shape and technological features which have been used as defining characteristics. The technological characteristics defined by Tixier (1956) for cleavers found in North Africa is the basis used by many others (Bordes 1961, 63–66; Bray and Trump 1979, 61; Brézillon 1968, 249–251; Heinzelin 1962, 44 *inter alia*). Tixier states: '*le principe dominant qui a dirigé la fabrication d'un hachereau est, on le sait, l'obtention d'un tranchant transversal terminal ... Le tranchant, qui est toujours naturel, c'est- à- dire exempt de retouches intentionelles, est obtenu, cela va de soi, par la rencontre de deux plans: plan de la face d'éclatement et un des plans de la face supérieure, ce que impose immuablement un outil sur éclat*' (the main aim in making a cleaver is to produce a transverse cutting edge at one end. The cutting edge which is always natural, that is to say unmodified by intentional retouch, is usually produced by the convergence of two surfaces: the ventral surface and the modified dorsal face, this means that it is invariably a flake tool) (1956, 916). This definition may be strictly applied (Alimen 1975) so that bifacial cleavers and those made on cobbles are excluded. However, more often the essential feature of the transverse cutting edge is taken as the defining characteristic, whether or not the cleaver is made on a flake (Gilead 1973, 73; Lubin and Guede 2000, 27; Roe 1994, 151–152). This working edge may be perpendicular to the main axis of the tool, or slightly oblique on tools which may have an overall U or V shaped outline (Gilead 1973; Paddaya 1982). In general retouch is absent from the transverse or oblique edge, which on bifacial cleavers and those made on cobbles may be formed by a tranchet blow on one or both faces (Roe 1994, 151) but examples of such edges formed by several removals have been illustrated (Guichard 1976, fig. 4; Stekelis and Gilead 1967, plate XXIV; Tavoso 1975, fig. 10.1). In a study of the cleavers made on cobbles found around Montauban, France, Tavoso (1975) has defined variations in edge form. He shows that the straight working edge is most common (44.1% of finds) with some slightly convex (16.1%), markedly convex (5.9%), angular (2.6%) and concave (1.5%) forms. The presence of retouch on the sides of cleavers may relate to the nature of the blank or the function of the tool. Kombewa or Victoria West flakes (Pant and Jayaswal 1991, fig. 44) may provide suitable blanks without the need for further modification (Medoev 1982). However, Van Riet Lowe (1952, 41) noted that modification of the edges produced forms closer to the modern metal axe, and suggested that it might have been deliberate to improve function, although this would have been hand-held rather than hafted (Semenov 1957, 151).

Following from his basic definition, Tixier (1956) subdivided cleavers into five groups based on the nature of the blank on which they were made and, for type V, the presence of invasive retouch on both faces. This sub-division has been followed by other authors, such as Santonja and Pérez González (1984) in Spain. Other classifications, such as those of Chavaillon (1964) and Cranshaw (1983), have been based on the character of the working edge or overall shape, as in the scheme used by Clark and Kleindienst for the Gadeb material (Clark 1994) and also applied in India (Misra 1967; Mohapatra 1962). Roe (1964, 1968, 1994) offers a metrical approach to form which makes no distinction between bifacial or handaxe cleavers and cleavers made on flakes. Within the Olduvai report, this allows Callow (1994, 253) to show that cleavers and handaxes found in the Developed Oldowan differ in both size and technology from those in the Acheulian. This observation suggests questions for further lines of enquiry.

CONCLUSION

On the basis of this review, I would suggest that the most important characteristic of a cleaver is the transverse working edge. Both the nature of the blank and secondary working are relevant to this edge. These features suggest a predetermined concept of manufacture deliberately aimed at producing a form with the required transverse edge. This strict definition would exclude the cleaver-like artefacts described from sites in Central Asia, China and the Far East. I would also suggest, like Mortillet and Mortillet (1903) and Obermaier (1913) before me, that it is necessary to equate bifaces with transverse edges with handaxes, rather than cleavers, and consider their typology separately.

REFERENCES

Aguirre, E. and Carbonell, E. 2001. Early human expansions in Eurasia: the Atapuerca evidence. *Quaternary International* 75, 11–18.

Alimen, H. 1960. *Préhistoire de l'Afrique*. Foreign Language Edition, Moscow.

Alimen, H. 1975. Les 'isthmes' hispano-marocains et siculo-tunisiens aux temps Acheuléens. *L'Anthropologie* 79, 399–436.

Allchin, B. 1963. The Indian Stone Age sequence. *Journal of the Royal Anthropological Institute* 93, 210–234.

Astrakhov, S.N. 1999. *Early Palaeolithic in Japan*. Institute for the History of Material Culture, St Petersburg.

Biberson, P. 1961. *Le Paléolithique Inférieur du Maroc Atlantique*. Publications du Service des Antiquités du Maroc 17, Rabat.

Blumenschine, R.J., Brandt, S.A. and Clark, J.D. 1983. Excavations and analysis of Middle Palaeolithic artefacts from Patpara, Madhya Pradesh. In G.R. Sharma and J.D. Clark (eds.) *Palaeoenvironments and Prehistory in the Middle Son Valley, Madhya Pradesh, North-Central India*, 39–100. Abinash Prakashan, Allahabad.

Bordes, F. 1954. *Les Limons Quaternaires du Bassin de la Seine: Stratigraphie et Archéologie Paléolithique*. Archives de l'Institut de Paléontologie Humaine Mémoire 26, Paris.

Bordes, F. 1961. *Typologie du Paléolithique Ancien et Moyen*. Delmas, Bordeaux.

Bordes, F. 1968. *The Old Stone Age*. McGraw Hill, New York.

Boriskovsky, P.I. 1966. *Prehistoric History of Vietnam*. Nauka, Moscow.

Bosinski, G. 1995. Western Central Europe. In W. Roebroeks and T. van Kolfschoten (eds.) *The Earliest Occupation of Europe*, 103–128. University of Leiden Press, Leiden.

Bosinski, G. and Luttropp, A. 1971. *Reutersruh*. Bohlau Verlag, Köln.

Bray, W. and Trump, D. 1979. *The Penguin Dictionary of Archaeology*. Penguin Books, Aylesbury.

Breuil, H. 1930. Premières impressions de voyage sur la préhistoire sud-africaine. *L'Anthropologie* 40, 209–223.

Brézillon, M.N. 1968. *La Dénomination des Objets de Pierre Taillée*. CNRS, Paris.

Cahen, D. 1984. Paléolithique inférieur et moyen en Belgique. In D. Cahen and P. Haesarts (eds.) *Peuples Chasseurs de la Belgique Préhistorique dans leur Cadre Naturel*, 133–155. Institut Royal des Sciences Naturelles, Bruxelles.

Callow, P. 1994. The Olduvai bifaces: technology and raw materials. In M.D. Leakey and D.A. Roe (eds.) *Olduvai Gorge Volume 5: Excavations in Beds III, IV and the Masek Beds, 1968–1971*, 235–253. Cambridge University Press, Cambridge.

Cammiade, L.A. and Burkitt, M.C. 1930. Fresh light on the Stone Age in southeast India. *Antiquity* 4, 327–339.

Canal, J. and Carbonell, E. 1989. *Catalunya Paleolítica*. Patronat Eiximenis, Girona.

Carbonell, E., Mosquera, M., Rodriquez, X.P. and Sala, R. 1999. Out of Africa: the dispersal of the earliest technical systems reconsidered. *Journal of Anthropological Archaeology* 18, 119–136.

Chavaillon, J. 1964. *Classification des Pièces Présentant un Biseau Terminal*. Laboratoire de Géologie du Quaternaire. CNRS, Bellevue.

Chavaillon, J. and Chavaillon, N. 1980. Evolution de l'acheuléen à Melka Kunturé (Ethiopia). *Anthropologie* (Brno) 18, 153–159.

Chen, T. and Huang, Y. 1998. Chronological study of Chinese Palaeolithic archaeology and palaeoanthropology. *Jahrbuch des Römisch-Germanischen Zentralmuseums Mainz* 35, 97–109.

Chulachula, J. 1992. Une industrie calcaire du paléolithique en Moravie (République Tchéque). *Anthropologie* (Brno) 30, 241–267.

Chung Y.-W. 1984. Acheulian handaxe culture of Chongok-ni in Korea. In R.O. Whyte (ed.) *The Evolution of the East Asian Environment*, 895–914. Centre of Asian Studies, Hong Kong.

Clark, J.D. 1959. *The Prehistory of Southern Africa*. Penguin Books, London.

Clark, J.D. 1966. Acheulian occupation sites in the Middle East and Africa: a study in cultural variability. *American Anthropologist* 68, 202–229.

Clark, J.D. 1970. *The Prehistory of Africa*. Praeger, New York.

Clark, J.D. 1980. Human populations and cultural adaptations in the Sahara and Nile during prehistoric times. In M.A.J. Williams and H. Faure (eds.) *The Sahara and the Nile: Quaternary Environments and Prehistoric Occupations in North Africa*, 527–582. Balkema, Rotterdam.

Clark, J.D. 1992. The Earlier Stone Age/Lower Palaeolithic in North Africa and the Sahara. In F. Klees and R. Kuper (eds.) *New Light on the Northeast African Past*, 17–39. Heinrich Barth Institut, Köln.

Clark, J.D. 1994. The Acheulian industrial complex in Africa and elsewhere. In R.S. Corruccini and R.L. Ciochon (eds.) *Integrative Paths to the Past: Paleoanthropological Advances in Honor of F. Clark Howell*, 451–469. Prentice Hall, Englewood Cliffs.

Copeland, L. 1991. The Late Acheulian knapping floor at C-Spring, Azraq Oasis, Jordan. *Levant* 23, 1–6.

Copeland, L. and Hours, F. 1979. Le paléolithique du Nahr el-Kebir. In P. Sanlaville (ed.) *Quaternaire et Préhistoire du Nahr el-Kebir Septentrional*, 31–119. CNRS, Paris.

Corvinus, G. 1987. Patu, a new Stone Age site of a jungle habitat in Nepal. *Quartär* 37–38, 135–187.

Corvinus, G. 1998. Lower Palaeolithic occupations in Nepal in relation to South Asia. In M. Petraglia and R. Korisettar (eds.) *Early Human Behaviour in the Global Context: The Rise and Diversity of the Lower Palaeolithic Record*, 391–417. Routledge, London.

Cranshaw, S. 1983. *Handaxes and Cleavers in Selected English Acheulian Industries*. British Archaeological Reports British Series 113, Oxford.

Dodonov, A.E., Deviatkin, E.V., Ranov, V.A., Khatib, K. and Nseir, H. 1993. The Latamne Formation in the Orontes river valley. In P. Sanlaville, J. Besançon, L. Copeland and L. Muhesen (eds.) *Le Paléolithique de la Vallée Moyenne de l'Oronte (Syrie)*, 189–194. British Archaeological Reports International Series 587, Oxford.

Freeman, L.G. 1975. Acheulian sites and stratigraphy in Iberia and the Maghreb. In K.W. Butzer and G.Ll. Isaac (eds.) *After the Australopithecines: Stratigraphy, Ecology and Culture Change in the Middle Pleistocene*, 661–743. Mouton, The Hague.

Fridrich, J. 1997. *Staropaleolitickè Osídlení Čech*. Památky Archeologické Supplementum 10. Institute of Archaeology, Prague.

Garrod, D.A.E. and Bate, D.M. 1937. *The Stone Age of Mount Carmel*. Oxford University Press, Oxford.

Gilead, D. 1973. Cleavers in early Palaeolithic industries in Israel. *Paleorient* 1, 73–86.

Gilead, D. and Ronen, A. 1977. Acheulian industries from Evron on the western Galilee coastal plain. *Eretz Israel* 13, 56–86.

Giles Pacheco, F., Santiago Pérez, A., Gutiérrez López, J.M. and Aguilera Rodríquez, L. 1990. Un technocomplejo del pleistoceno medio en la desembocadura del rio Guadalete. El yacimiento achelense del Palmar del Conde. *Revista de Historia de el Puerto* 5, 11–30.

Gladilin, V.N. and Sitlivy, V.I. 1990. *Acheulian of Central Europe*. Naukova Dumka, Kiev (in Russian).

Goren-Inbar, N. and Saragusti, I. 1996. An Acheulian biface assemblage from Gesher Benot Ya'aqov, Israel: indications of African affinities. *Journal of Field Archaeology* 23, 15–30.

Goren-Inbar, N., Zohar, I. and Den-Ami, D. 1991. A new look at old cleavers. Gesher Benot Ya'aqov. *Mitekufat Haeven* 24, 7–33.

Goren-Inbar, N., Fiebel, C.S., Versoub, K.L., Melamed, Y., Kislev, M., Tchernov, E. and Saragusti, I. 2000. Pleistocene milestones on the out of Africa corridor at Gesher Benot Ya'aqov, Israel. *Science* 289, 944–947.

Graziosi, P. 1964. Prehistoric research in northwestern Punjab. *Scientific Reports of the Italian Expedition to Karakorum (K2) and Hindu Kush* 1, 55–74. E.J. Brill, Leiden.

Guichard, G. 1976. Les civilisations du Paléolithique inférieur en Perigord. In H. de Lumley (ed.) *La Préhistoire Française*, 908–928. CNRS, Paris.

Heinzelin de Braucourt, J. de, 1962. *Manuel de Typologie des Industries Lithiques*. Institut Royal des Sciences Naturelles, Bruxelles.

Ho, C.K. and Jiang, P. 1993. Adaptations au pleistocène moyen et au pleistocène supérieur dans le nord-est de la Chine. *L'Anthropologie* 97, 355–398.

Hours, F. 1981. Le paléolithique inférieur de la Syrie et du Liban. Le point du question en 1980. In M.-C. Cauvin and P. Sanlaville (eds.) *Préhistoire du Levant: Chronologie et Organisation de l'Espace depuis les Origines jusqu'au 6e Millénaire*, 165–183. CNRS, Paris.

Howell, F.C. 1966. Observations on the earlier phases of the European Lower Palaeolithic. *American Anthropologist* 68, 88–201.

Howell, F.C., Cole, G.H. and Kleindienst, M.R. 1962. Isimila, an Acheulian occupation site in the Iringa Highlands Province, Tanganyika. *Actes du IVe Congrès Panafricain de Préhistoire et de l'Etude du Quaternaire*. Leopoldville 1959, 43–80.

Isaac, G. 1967. The stratigraphy of the Peninj group – early Middle Pleistocene formations west of Lake Natron, Tanzania. In W.W. Bishop and J.D. Clark (eds.) *Background to Evolution in Africa*, 229–257. University of Chicago Press, Chicago.

Isaac, G. 1977. *Olorgesailie*. University of Chicago Press, Chicago.

Isaac, G. 1982. The earliest archaeological traces. In J.D. Clark (ed.) *The Cambridge History of Africa, Volume 1: From the Earliest Times to c. 500 BC*, 157–247. Cambridge University Press, Cambridge.

Islamov, U.I. and Krakhmal, K.A. 1995. *Palaeoecology and Traces of Earliest Man in Central Asia*. Fan, Tashkent (in Russian).

Jayaswal, V. 1978. *Palaeohistory of India*. Agam Kala Prakashan, New Delhi.

Joshi, R.V. 1979. Stone Age environment and cultural sequence in Kangra Valley. In V.C. Ohri (ed.) *Prehistory of Himachal Pradesh: Some Latest Findings*, 1–42. Caxton Press, New Delhi.

Joshi, R.V., Rajaguru, S.N., Badam, G.L. and Khanna, P.C. 1978. Environment and culture of early Man in northwest India – a reappraisal. *Journal of the Geological Society of India* 19, 83–86.

Korisettar, R. and Rajaguru, S.N. 1998. Quaternary stratigraphy, paleoclimate and the Lower Palaeolithic of India. In M. Petraglia and R. Korisettar (eds.) *Early Human Behaviour in the Global Context: The Rise and Diversity of the Lower Palaeolithic Record*, 304–342. Routledge, London.

Kuman, K. 1998. The earliest South African Industries. In M. Petraglia and R. Korisettar (eds.) *Early Human Behaviour in the Global Context: The Rise and Diversity of the Lower Palaeolithic Record*, 151–186. Routledge, London.

Larichev, V.E. 1977. The discovery of handaxes in the territory of East Asia and the problem of local cultures in the Lower Palaeolithic. In N.L. Chlenova (ed.) *Problems in the Archaeology of Eurasia and North America*, 22–34. Nauka, Moscow (in Russian).

Leakey, L.S.B. 1960. *Adam's Ancestors*. Harper Torchbooks, New York.

Leakey, M.D. 1971. *Olduvai Gorge: Excavations in Beds I and II, 1960–1963*. Cambridge University Press, Cambridge.

Leakey, M.D. and Roe, D.A. (eds.) 1994. *Olduvai Gorge Volume 5: Excavations in Beds III, IV and the Masek Beds, 1968–1971*. Cambridge University Press, Cambridge.

Li, S. 1992. Cleavers in China. *Acta Anthropologica Sinica* 11, 193–201 (in Chinese).

Lubin, V.P. 1968. *The Acheulian Epoch in the Caucasus*. Petersburg Orientalist, St Petersburg (in Russian).

Lubin, V.P. and Guede, F.Y. 2000. *The Palaeolithic of the Republic of the Ivory Coast (West Africa)*. Petersburg Orientalist, St Petersburg (in Russian).

Lumley, H. de, 1969. *La Paléolithique Inférieur et Moyen du Midi Méditerranéen dans son Cadre Géologique*. CNRS, Paris.

Lumley, H. de, 1976. *La Préhistoire Française*. CNRS, Paris.

Mason, R. 1962. *Prehistory of the Transvaal*. University of the Witwatersrand Press, Johannesburg.

Matjukhin, A.E. 1983. The tools of the Early Palaeolithic. In *The Technology of Production in the Palaeolithic*, 134–187. Nauka, Leningrad.

Matjukhin, A.E. 1990. About the questionable date of the Palaeolithic (?) site of Mount Do, Vietnam. *Soviet Archaeology* 2, 92–98 (in Russian).

Medoev, A.G. 1982. *Geochronology of the Palaeolithic of Khazakhstan*. Nauka, Alma-Ata (in Russian).

Misra, V.N. 1967. The Acheulian industry of rockshelter IIIF-23 at Bhimbetka, Central India. *Australian Archaeology* 8, 63–106.

Misra, V.N. and Rajaguru, S.N. 1986. Environment et culture de l'homme préhistorique dans le désert du Thar, Rajastan, Inde. *L'Anthropologie* 90, 407–437.

Mohapatra, G.C. 1962. *The Stone Age Cultures of Orissa*. Deccan College, Poona.

Mortillet, G. de and Mortillet, A. de, 1903. *Le Préhistorique*. Edition du XX Siècle, St Petersburg (in Russian).

Movius, H. 1944. Early Man and Pleistocene stratigraphy in Southern and Eastern Asia. *Papers of the Peabody Museum of American Archaeology and Ethnography* 19, 1–125.

Neuville, R. 1951. *Le Paléolithique et le Mésolithique du Désert de Judée*. Masson, Paris.

Obermaier, G. 1913. *L'Homme Préhistorique*. Brokaus-Efron, St Petersburg (in Russian).

Okladnikov, A.P. and Abramova, Z.A. 1994. The Palaeolithic of Inner Asia-Mongolia. In *The Palaeolithic of Central and East Asia*. Nauka, St Petersburg (in Russian).

Paddaya, K. 1982. *The Acheulian Culture of the Hungsi Valley*. Deccan College, Poona.

Pant, P.C. and Jayaswal, V. 1991. *Paisra: The Stone Age Settlement of Bihar*. Agam Kala Prakashan, New Delhi.

Paterson, T.T. and Drummond, H.J.H. 1962. *Soan: The Palaeolithic of Pakistan*. Department of Archaeology in Pakistan, Karachi.

Peeters, H., Mush, J. and Wouters, A. 1988. Les industries acheuléenes des Pays-Bas. *L'Anthropologie* 92, 1093–1136.

Petraglia, M. 1998. The Lower Palaeolithic of India and its bearing on the Asian record. In M. Petraglia and R. Korisettar (eds.) *Early Human Behaviour in Global Context: The Rise and Diversity of the Lower Palaeolithic Record*, 343–390. Routledge, London.

Piperno, M. 1974. Presenza di hachereaux nel paleolitico inferiore italiano. *Memorie dell'Istituto Italiano di Paleontologia Umana* 2, 43–50.

Querol, M.A. and Santonja, M. 1980. L'industrie lithique du gisement acheuléen de Pinedo (Tolède, Espagne). *Bulletin de la Société Préhistorique Française* 77, 291–305.

Ranov, V.A. 1995. The Palaeolithic of the Middle Pleistocene in Central Asia. In J.M. Bermúdez, J.L. Arsuaga and E. Carbonell (eds.) *Human Evolution in Europe and the Atapuerca Evidence*, 367–386. Junta de Castilla y Léon, Valladolid.

Raposo, L. and Santonja, M. 1995. The Iberian Peninsula. In W. Roebroeks and T. van Kolfschoten (eds.) *The Earliest Occupation of Europe*, 7–25. University of Leiden Press, Leiden.

Roe, D.A. 1964. The British Lower and Middle Palaeolithic: some problems, methods of study and preliminary results. *Proceedings of the Prehistoric Society* 30, 245–267.

Roe, D.A. 1968. British Lower and Middle Palaeolithic handaxe groups. *Proceedings of the Prehistoric Society* 34, 1–82.

Roe, D.A. 1981. *The Lower and Middle Palaeolithic Periods in Britain*. Routledge and Kegan Paul, London.

Roe, D.A. 1994. A metrical study of selected sets of handaxes and cleavers from Olduvai Gorge. In M.D. Leakey and D.A. Roe (eds.) *Olduvai Gorge Volume 5: Excavations in Beds III, IV and the Masek Beds, 1968–1971*, 146–234. Cambridge University Press, Cambridge.

Salim, M. 1997. *The Palaeolithic Cultures of Potwar with Special Reference to the Lower Palaeolithic*. Sohail Altaf, Rawalpindi.

Sampson, C.G. 1974. *The Stone Age Archaeology of Southern Africa*. Academic Press, London.

Sankalia, H.D. 1952. *The Godavari Palaeolithic Industry*. Deccan College, Poona.

Sankalia, H.D. 1974. *The Prehistory and Protohistory of India and Pakistan*. Deccan College, Poona.

Santonja, M. and Pérez González, A. 1984. *Las Industrias Paleoliticas de La Maya I en su Ambito Regional*. Ministerio de Cultura, Madrid.

Semenov, S.A. 1957. *Prehistoric Technology*. Soviet Academy of Science, Moscow.

Stekelis, M. 1966. *Archaeological Excavations at 'Ubeidiya, 1960–1963*. The Israel Academy of Sciences and Humanities, Jerusalem.

Stekelis, M. and Gilead, D. 1967. *Ma'ayan Barukh: A Lower Paleolithic Site in Upper Galilee*. Mitekufat Haeven 8. Academon, Jerusalem.

Tavoso, A. 1975. Les hachereaux sur éclat de l'Acheuléen Montalbanais. *Quartär* 26, 13–31.

Terra, H. de and Paterson, T.T. 1939. *Studies on the Ice Age in India and Associated Human Cultures*. Carnegie Institution of Washington, Washington.

Tixier, J. 1956. Le hachereau dans l'Acheuléen nord-africain. Notes typologiques. *Congrès Préhistorique de France. Comptes Rendus de la XVe Session, Poitiers-Angoulème*, 914–923.

Tuffreau, A. 1976. Les civilisations du paléolithique inférieur dans la région Parisienne et en Normandie. In H. de Lumley (ed.) *La Préhistoire Française*, 945–955. CNRS, Paris.

Tuffreau, A. and Antoine, P. 1995. Continental Northwestern Europe. In W. Roebroeks and T. van Kolfschoten (eds.) *The Earliest Occupation of Europe*, 147–163. University of Leiden Press, Leiden.

Valoch, K. 1995. Eastern, Central and Southeastern Europe. In W. Roebroeks and T. van Kolfschoten (eds.) *The Earliest Occupation of Europe*, 67–84. University of Leiden Press, Leiden.

Van Riet Lowe, C. 1952. *The Pleistocene Geology and Prehistory of Uganda. Part II: Prehistory*. Uganda Geological Survey Memoir 6. Benham and Company, Colchester.

Villa, P. 2001. Early Italy and colonization of western Europe. *Quaternary International* 75, 113–130.

Wymer, J. 1968. *Lower Palaeolithic Archaeology in Britain as Represented by the Thames Valley*. John Baker, London.

Yi, S. 1992. Towards an explanation of the Northeast Asian Palaeolithic. In *Chronostratigraphy of the Palaeolithic in North, Central, East Asia and America*, 193–201. Nauka, Novosibirsk.

11. Ex Africa aliquid semper novi: the view from Pontnewydd

Stephen Aldhouse-Green

ABSTRACT

Recent studies have shown a deepening focus both on the progressive development of modern behaviours in Africa, from the inception of the Middle Stone Age, and on the issue of modern behaviours by last glaciation Neanderthals in Europe. Those same studies have generally either not dealt with, or have actually dismissed, evidence for the appearance of modern behaviour in Europe by early Neanderthals before the last interglacial. This paper seeks to redress that balance and suggests that a focus on fossils, and a consequential search for species, has diverted attention away from engagement with the evidence for broad synchroneity in the process of becoming human in the continents of Africa and Europe.

Ex Africa aliquid semper novi
There is always something new from Africa
(the Elder Pliny *Natural History* VIII, 17)

INTRODUCTION

Just as 'we are what we eat', so we are also formed by the lands where we live our lives. Accordingly, I would have to acknowledge myself as English, Sudanese and Welsh. As a Sudanese, and so an African, I was delighted by the celebration of Africa's past that was the core of the Bristol 'Human Roots' conference of Spring 2000 (Barham and Robson-Brown in press). We know, of course, that our very early ancestors, the australopithecine bipedal apes, were African. Bristol's message, however, was striking for we were confidently told that even later Middle Pleistocene Europe, with its early Neanderthals, was no more than a cul-de-sac or backwater. In terms of the key development in human evolution on which the conference focused, namely the appearance of modern human behaviour, Africa led the way. It was at this point that my Welshness kicked in and I began to wonder whether the rightly much heralded florescence of human culture in Africa was really unique. May it not have been happening in Europe at much the same time? Africa's supremacy in the development of

Australopithecus, of earliest *Homo*, and of anatomically modern humans seems unlikely to be seriously challenged. We, ourselves, are likewise descended from the people of African descent who seem to have colonised Europe under the name of Cro-Magnons. Even so, to diminish our very own Neanderthals to a footnote of history seemed to smack of colonialism in reverse. I decided to use Pontnewydd Cave (Green 1984) as a sounding board to examine a few key issues surrounding the developments of Middle Palaeolithic Europe. My focus in this paper lies with the later Middle Pleistocene, broadly Oxygen Isotope Stages 7 and 6 (c. 250–130 kyr).

READING THE BUMPS

During 1999, I had the pleasure of meeting over dinner an old friend, who is also one of the world's leading prehistoric archaeologists. The conversation touched on Lagar Velho, a then recently found ceremonial Gravettian burial in Portugal, where there were suggestions that a hybrid Neanderthal/Modern Human child had been interred. 'Do not believe a word of it' my friend said. 'Physical anthropology is just like phrenology: they read the bumps'. Of course there was more than an element of hyperbole in this, but it gave me occasion to reflect upon the limitations as well as the strengths of the physical anthropological approach. Interestingly, when Lagar Velho came up in discussion at Bristol, it was to suggest that the notion that the skeleton was a hybrid was possibly ill-founded. For the purpose of this paper, I propose to confine myself to the palaeo-behavioural data presented by the archaeological evidence. I shall not worry, in this context, whether the species of hominids involved are *Homo neanderthalensis, heidelbergensis, helmei* or *sapiens*. I shall, however, return to the issue in my conclusion.

Just such an archaeology-led approach was followed by Foley and Lahr (1997), when these authors made archaeological data the basis of their inferences concerning the phylogeny of human evolution in the Middle and Late Pleistocene. The main thrust of their research paper was to establish that the strongest evidence for the appearance of modern human behaviour, as represented by archaeological evidence, lay not with the Upper Palaeolithic but, rather, with the appearance of Middle Stone Age/Middle Palaeolithic (Mode 3) industries in the later Middle Pleistocene. Foley and Lahr saw the development of Levallois industries in Africa about 250 kyr ago as being chronologically coincident with molecular dates for the origins of anatomically modern humans. They viewed this technology as reflecting a cognitive leap which marked the inception of diversities in material equipment which themselves formed the basis for the increasing cultural complexity seen in the Middle Stone Age. Their paper made sense of many of the problems associated with the evident discrepancy between the appearance of modern humans on the one hand and of the Upper Palaeolithic on the other. They freed archaeologists from the tyranny of the formula 'blades=brains'. What they saw as important was the evolution of the brain rather than the evolution of the skeleton, for their focus was on cognition rather than on biomechanical functions. Thus, they note that development of the brain's neocortex reached a threshold about 300 kyr after which larger social groups and linkages may only have been sustained through the use of language (Aiello and Dunbar 1993). In one respect only did their reappraisal seem to occasion some potential grief, namely their requirement for the appearance in Africa of a common human population, namely *Homo helmei*, ancestral to both *Homo neanderthalensis* and *Homo sapiens*. This would link the spread of Mode 3 technologies with the expansion of *Homo helmei* out of Africa. Unfortunately, this seems unsupported not only by the molecular evidence for Neanderthal evolution but also by the wide acceptance of a dating of about 400 kyr for the Swanscombe skull which has incipient Neanderthal features (Stringer 1999, 37, 43–44; Wymer 1999, 77). This issue becomes even more complicated in the light of the views of the Atapuerca research team who see *Homo heidelbergensis* as a wholly European species that had evolved *in situ* from *Homo antecessor* (Bermúdez de Castro *et al.* 1997). McBrearty and Brooks (2000, 480) would differentiate the African 'heidelbergs' as *Homo rhodesiensis* and would be happier to see the European holotype and related specimens subsumed within *Homo neanderthalensis*. Klein, likewise, regards *heidelbergensis* as 'difficult to date, in large part because it is difficult to define', and raises thereby a question as to the phylogenetic status of this species (Klein 1999, 279–280). Similar problems of definition affect *Homo helmei*, a taxon which Stringer (pers. comm. December 2000) no longer finds useful.

PONTNEWYDD AND MODE 3 TECHNOLOGIES

The Middle Palaeolithic and, in Africa, the Middle Stone Age, or Mode 3 industries in Grahame Clark's terminology (1977), are generally characterised by the appearance of a range of flake tools. The Levallois technique was frequently used in their production. In Africa, an origin for the technique in the later Acheulian, at or after 300 kyr, is generally proposed (Barham 1997, 114) and the most reliable dating for the currency of Levallois technique comes from the Kapthurin formation of Kenya (McBrearty and Brooks 2000, 495–496), where centripetal flakes and blades are attested at an age of about 280 kyr on the basis of Argon/Argon dating. This is broadly coeval with the earliest date for the inception of the Middle Stone Age, which may be set at 279±47 kyr on the basis of ESR determinations from Florisbad, South Africa (Grün *et al.* 1996; Kuman *et al.* 1999). Levallois technology was likewise fully current in the Middle East by OIS 7, with its first appearance dated to about 240 kyr at Hayonim and to a similar age at Kharga Oasis in Egypt (Schwarcz and Rink 1998, 62, 65). Dates of the order of 270–250 kyr have been proposed using TL determinations on burnt flint from Tabun (Mercier *et al.* 1995, 506–507). The first appearance of the classic form of the Levallois technique in Britain and, more widely in Europe, was from OIS 8 onwards, interestingly at much the same time as in Africa (Barham 1997, 114; Gamble and Roebroeks 1999, 5). The Levallois technique is claimed from the site of Cagny-la-Garenne in France where it is dated to older than 400 kyr, probably early OIS 12, c. 470 kyr. The site, located on a river bank adjacent to a chalk cliff with exposed flint, produced an industry with handaxes and cores, including a few examples both of Levallois cores and of so-called *éclats préférentiels*, resembling Levallois flakes but produced from handaxes (Tuffreau and Antoine 1995, 147). In Britain, proto-Levallois technique is seen at Greenlands Pit, Purfleet, in Essex (Palmer 1975; Wymer 1999, 67), a gravel site dated to OIS 9 by Bridgland (1994) although Amino Acid Racemization (AAR) determinations would suggest an earlier date (Bowen *et al.* 1995).

The early development of the Levallois technique has been widely held to mark a significant leap in quality control, through the ability of the knapper to produce a series of blanks using secant plane technology (White and Pettitt 1995). Pontnewydd at about 225 kyr certainly has such Levallois products with flakes, blades and points all in production, apparently as part of the same assemblage (Green 1984, 114). Flake tools, whether or not on Levallois supports, include a range of side and transverse scrapers and a 'Mousterian point'. Also present are numerous handaxes, choppers, chopping tools and a flake cleaver. Pontnewydd undoubtedly is a Middle Palaeolithic industry but handaxes are present as a component of the Main Cave assemblage dated to 225 kyr. In the New Entrance, however, there is evidence for a later group of material at about 175 kyr of similar character but with handaxes rare or even absent (Aldhouse-Green 1998, 140–141; Aldhouse-Green *et al.* in press).

GRAVES

It is intriguing that at least five, and perhaps as many as fifteen dead Neanderthals found a last resting place at Pontnewydd Cave (Stringer and Compton in litt. October 2000). They seem to have been mostly male and mostly less than twenty years old. Hominid remains are distinctly rare in Britain, in spite of a profusion of caves with abundant evidence of accumulation of bones by hyaenas and other carnivores. It would seem perverse, then, to argue that carnivores played a special role at Pontnewydd in the introduction of remains of so many individuals to the site. I am more inclined, therefore, to see these remains at Pontnewydd as arising from a conscious deposition of the dead in the dark recesses of the cave (Aldhouse-Green 2000, 18). The remains may represent a single accumulation, later dispersed by debris flow action, for they were found, close to the base of the Lower Breccia debris flow, within a restricted locality of the cave, and interstratified with a fauna, including remains of hibernating bears, which had accumulated within a cave (Andrew Currant pers. comm.). This act of disposal may be paralleled in a slightly earlier context at the site of Atapuerca in northern Spain, where remains of over 30 individuals have been found at the base of the deep shaft known as the Sima de los Huesos (Bermúdez de Castro *et al.* 1997). Burial of the dead is one of the distinctive markers of human behaviour and conscious disposals, if correctly identified as such at Pontnewydd and Atapuerca, clearly reflect a different attitude to the dead from that seen over the preceding several million years of the existence of *Homo*. Such behaviour is not attested in Africa at this early date and does not appear there until the Upper Pleistocene at Border Cave, although taphonomic reasons may be responsible for this lacuna (Grün and Stringer 1991; Grün *et al.* 1990; Klein 1999, 395, 399; Sillen and Morris 1996).

CAVES

Kolen's paper (1999) on Middle Palaeolithic habitation presents a challenge to much established thinking. It would seem that 'all people that on earth do dwell', in the words of the famous hymn, had no dwellings unless, of course, they were cognitively advanced modern humans. Indeed, even the living structures of the most advanced archaic humans, appealingly named 'centrifugal living structures', were only a stage up from chimpanzee nests. In the same volume, however, Mussi (1999) recognised an increased use of caves in Italy by Neanderthals. Interestingly, a parallel development seems to have been taking place in Africa where cave occupation seemingly 'became more routine for Middle Stone Age populations' (McBrearty 1997, 274). This reflected a move, both in Africa and Europe, from riverine settlement to a wider use of the landscape (Deacon 1997, 521; Gamble 1997). To use the terminology of Deacon's Human Roots lecture, landscape use changed from stenotopic to eurytopic. In this context, it is becoming increasingly important to undertake a large-scale synthesis of secular data on cave availability and cave use in order to determine how far changing diachronic patterns in cave occupancy can be supported by in-depth analysis. The increased use of natural shelters would, however, appear to be a feature of the later Pleistocene both in Africa and Europe.

OCHRES

If Pontnewydd were in Africa, one might expect evidence of routine use of pigments. Thus, at Barham's site of Twin Rivers in Zambia yellow, red and black pigments, all clearly used by humans, can be dated between 350,000–200,000 years ago (Barham 2000, 241–242). In Kenya, sites with pigments near Lake Baringo underlie a volcanic ash layer dated to 240 kyr. Barham (1999) has summarised the evidence from Europe to the effect that 'pigments (mainly black) have been found in about half a dozen Neanderthal sites, but none is much earlier than 50,000–40,000 years ago'. This view is perhaps a shade Afro-centric, however, for it overlooks occurrences from sites broadly dated to 250–150 kyr including Maastricht-Belvédère in Holland (Roebroeks 1988, 38–40) (OIS 7); the Acheulian rock shelter of Bečov in the Czech Republic which yielded a rubbing stone, a striated piece of ochre and fragments of red ochre (Marshack 1981; Roebroeks 1988, 40) (OIS 6); Terra Amata in southern France (Lumley 1966) where ochre crayons of shades of yellow and red have been claimed, but now challenged by Wreschner (1982) (OIS 7); and, with context and dating less clear, from Ambrona in northern Spain (Marshack 1981, 1990; Wreschner 1975, 1980, 1982). The Maastricht-Belvédère finds consist of fourteen 'small dots' of ochre but the concentration of finds at Site C only, combined with the extreme rarity of ochre as a component of the local gravels, means that this material must either have been brought from *in situ* sources at a distance of 70 km or else have been the product of sustained and laborious collection from derived contexts. Accordingly, an anthropogenic origin seems established beyond reasonable doubt at Maastricht-Belvédère which, together with Bečov and Ambrona, present evidence of the use of red ochre during OIS 7. That is not to say, of course, that the use of pigments at sites in Africa or Europe necessarily arises from the use of colour as symbol, and so reflective of modern human behaviour. Something as prosaic as hide-preparation may have been involved (Keeley 1980, 170–172), although even here the ochre may have been applied more as a colorant than as a preservative. It would be going far beyond the available evidence, however, to argue for discrepant cognitions in the two continents with the use of colour in one region being 'sacred' and, in the other, 'profane'.

Pigments were not noted from Pontnewydd when the 1984 report was published (Green 1984). However, Tim Young has recently conducted a pilot study and has identified no fewer than four different types of ochre from the Lower Breccia, Silt beds and Upper Breccia (Aldhouse-Green *et al.* in press). All the ochres occurred as water-worn pebbles of small size, generally less than 10 grams in weight. The pilot study tells us that pigments were present but there is, as yet, no evidence that they were introduced by humans. This is, however, a point of the greatest importance and further study will be needed which will involve a review of all the exotics from these contexts. It will also involve, as a control, a study of the exotics from the underlying layers of the Intermediate complex and, especially, the Upper and Lower Sands & Gravels, for hominids were probably absent when these layers were formed. Research by Helen Livingston has shown that the local drift deposits are almost certainly of Devensian age and, so, are younger than the cave deposits. Even so, study of their content would offer a further control in respect of whether such ochres were locally available for incorporation in drift deposits. If such control samples were to lack haematite ores, an anthropogenic origin would become more likely for the Pontnewydd ochres.

REGIONAL VARIATION

A key area of evidence for the development of modern behaviours lies in the identification of regional diversification, pointing to enhanced self-awareness. In Africa, this phenomenon may be identified through regional styles in lithic technology, for example the distinctive OIS 7 Lupemban assemblages of Central Africa. Also seen in Africa, at the MSA site of Twin Rivers in Zambia, is inferential evidence for enhanced planning depth, in the form of small trapezes for hafting, at a date in excess of 200 kyr (Barham and Robson-Brown 2001). Precisely

similar technology is not known at this date from Europe but, on the basis of microwear evidence from Biache in northern France, it is reasonable to infer the mounting of convergent side-scrapers onto handles before 150 kyr (Beyries 1988, 220). The geography of Africa is, of course, vast compared with that of Europe which is less than a third of the area of Africa. Moreover, Europe lacks the huge desert areas of the Sahara and the Kalahari which expanded in the drier climates of glacial periods and, thereby, served to isolate human populations and to foster regional developments. Even so, regional variations can be detected in lithic industries in Europe. To some extent these industries are composed of the application of a suite of technologies to raw materials of widely differing size and properties. This view may, however, be too dismissive. It is clear, for example, at Pontnewydd that assemblage composition there was not so much responding to as *pace* the possibilities of the raw materials (Newcomer 1984). Accordingly, it would be interesting to look at such entities as the Micoquian (Bosinski 1967), the Taubachian (Schäfer 1981) or the Middle Palaeolithic Blade Group (Conard 1992, 88) from the standpoint of whether they may denote self-aware regional traditions.

THE ISSUE OF MODERN BEHAVIOUR

Should we then, to use my own words, see the world of the early Neanderthals at Pontnewydd as primarily 'resource-driven with the needs of food, water, raw materials, shelter and landmarks all being important factors' (Aldhouse-Green 1998) or is there any suggestion that we may detect there a few germs of explicitly modern human behaviour? The context is difficult: a world of debris flows, glaciation and secondary contexts. The evidence for the possible curation of fine silicic tuff gives a hint of planning depth (Green 1988) but sources may have been local and, indeed, all of the raw materials may have been present, through glacial action, in the vicinity of the cave. Second, there is the issue of corpse disposal. The events that may have taken place at Atapuerca and Pontnewydd are a long way from the Gravettian ceremonial burials of Paviland and Sunghir, but they may foreshadow in certain respects the burials of last glaciation Neanderthals. Third, there is the issue of the expansion of geographic range to new types of territory (McBrearty and Brooks 2000, 493) of which Pontnewydd is a clear example. Fourth, there seems to have been an enhanced use of natural shelters. Finally, the Pontnewydd ochres tell us *either* that they were available locally but not in use *or* that such pigments were in use by Neanderthals in North Wales quite as early as elsewhere in Europe or Africa. It is hoped that further research on the Pontnewydd raw materials, of which there was near total retention on site, may resolve this issue, for it clearly has huge implications for the roots of human behaviour.

DISCUSSION

The issue of the evolution of modern behaviour has been the subject of a major review by two of the contributors to the Human Roots conference (McBrearty and Brooks 2000). They argue that modern human behaviour did not appear as a package throughout the world 50–30,000 years ago but actually appeared progressively and cumulatively over a period of perhaps a quarter of a million years, since the inception of the MSA in Africa. As examples of such modern behaviours they instance 'blade and microlithic technology, bone tools, increased geographic range, specialized hunting, the use of aquatic resources, long distance trade, systematic processing and use of pigment, and art and decoration'. Most of these behaviours are of Upper Pleistocene age but the authors (*ibid.,* 530) identify pigment use and processing, blades and points, as having appeared before 150 kyr. The authors would link their appearance and development with the appearance of *Homo helmei,* the immediate precursor of *Homo sapiens,* at the beginning of the MSA. From my perspective, their broad thesis seems sound and, if widely accepted, will signal the death of the OIS 3 'creative explosion' associated with the expansion of anatomically modern humans.

I have sought in this paper to suggest that parallel behavioural developments were taking place in Europe at the same time by a species, *Homo neanderthalensis,* which cannot be closely related to the African *helmei/sapiens.* McBrearty and Brooks note the European evidence but regard it as too slight, by comparison with Africa, to be significant (2000, 531). Gamble (1996, 69) perceived the 'heidelbergs' as having introduced a 'fully formed behavioural package' which was inherited by the Neanderthals and only supplanted by the arrival of 'the dynamism of modern looking and behaving people'. This is to suppose a world in which innovations, whether in technology (Levallois and hafting), residence (caves), range expansion or symbolic behaviour (ochre), seemingly took place in both Africa and Europe but without contact between the two regions. These changes, in other words this process of sapientisation by accretion, more plausibly took place in the context of wide networks of communication. The ideas were probably not acquired directly but they were simple ideas and, once received, became socially embedded. What is clear, in the midst of all this muddle, is that those European and African hominids, who were the agents of later Middle Pleistocene innovations, were derived from the same Middle Pleistocene ancestral stock. Thus, the Neanderthals were different from their African contemporaries but their ancestry was the same. The implication is that the capacity for these behaviours was genetically embedded in the deep past of the Middle Pleistocene. Just because we are living examples of *Homo sapiens* we expect that our most direct ancestors will have had a monopoly of human behaviour. It is no surprise, therefore, to find such evidence in Africa where modern humans evolved. However, the European evidence, with such developments taking place *pari passu* with Africa, may cause us to reflect upon the likelihood that the capacity of the Neanderthal and *sapiens* brains may have been remarkably similar. Perhaps it is time for us to stop 'reading the bumps'.

EPILOGUE

It is a pleasure to offer these thoughts on developments in Wales, Europe and Africa to Derek Roe. I have known Derek since the later 1960s when he was influential in the structure of the lithic analyses I was then preparing for my PhD thesis. During my days in Milton Keynes he provided a welcome in Oxford at all times. Later he served on the Archaeology Committee of the National Museum of Wales for virtually all my years there. He was a constant source of support and advice, refereed all my papers and visited all my excavations. I owe him more than I can say. To Derek, both as an archaeologist equally at home in Africa and Europe and as keeper of the sacred flame of Quaternary archaeology at Oxford, I offer this paper as a tribute.

ACKNOWLEDGEMENTS

I am indebted to John McNabb for help and advice and for reading this text through in draft, to its great improvement. Also to Chris Stringer for his guidance on the issue of *Homo helmei.*

REFERENCES

Aiello, L.C. and Dunbar, R.I.M. 1993. Neocortex size, group size and the evolution of language. *Current Anthropology* 34, 184–192.

Aldhouse-Green, S.H.R. 1998. The archaeology of distance: perspectives from the Welsh Palaeolithic. In N. Ashton, F. Healy and P. Pettitt (eds.) *Stone Age Archaeology: Essays in Honour of John Wymer,* 137–145. Lithic Studies Society Occasional Paper 6, Oxbow Monograph 102. Oxbow Books, Oxford.

Aldhouse-Green, S.H.R. 2000. Palaeolithic and Mesolithic Wales. In F. Lynch, S.H.R. Aldhouse-Green and J.L. Davies (eds.) *Prehistoric Wales,* 1–41. Alan Sutton, Stroud.

Aldhouse-Green, S., Jackson, H. and Young, T. in press. Lithics, raw materials and ochre: interrogation of data from the Middle Pleistocene hominid site of Pontnewydd Cave, Wales, Europe. In E. Walker, F. Wenban-Smith and F. Healy (eds.) *Lithic Studies in the Year 2000.* Lithic Studies Society, London.

Barham, L. 1997. Stoneworking technology: its evolution. In J.O. Vogel (ed.) *Encyclopedia of Precolonial Africa,* 109–115. Altamira Press, London.

Barham, L. 1999. From art and tools came human origins. *British Archaeology* 42 (March 1999), 8–9.

Barham, L. 2000. *The Middle Stone Age of Zambia, South Central Africa.* Western Academic and Specialist Press Ltd., Bristol.

Barham, L. and Robson-Brown, K. (eds.) 2001. *Human Roots: Africa and Asia in the Middle Pleistocene.* Western Academic and Specialist Press Ltd., Bristol.

Bermúdez de Castro, J.M., Arsuaga, J.L., Carbonell, E., Rosas, A.,

Martínez, I. and Mosquera, M. 1997. A hominid from the Lower Pleistocene of Atapuerca, Spain: possible ancestor to Neanderthals and Modern Humans. *Science* 276, 1392–1395.

Beyries, S. 1988. Functional variability of lithic sets in the Middle Paleolithic. In H.L. Dibble and A. Montet-White (eds.) *Upper Pleistocene Prehistory of Western Eurasia*, 213–224. The University Museum, University of Pennsylvania, Philadelphia.

Bosinski, G. 1967. *Die Mittelpaläolithischen Funde im Westlichen Mitteleuropa.* Böhlau Verlag, Köln.

Bowen, D.Q., Sykes, G.A., Maddy, D., Bridgland, D.R. and Lewis, S.G. 1995. Aminostratigraphy and amino-acid geochronology of English lowland valleys: the Lower Thames in context. In D.R. Bridgland, P. Allen and B.A. Haggart (eds.) *The Quaternary of the Lower Reaches of the Thames: Field Guide*, 61–69. Quaternary Research Association, Durham.

Bridgland, D.R. 1994. *Quaternary of the Thames.* Chapman and Hall, London.

Clark, J.G.D. 1977. *World Prehistory: A New Perspective.* Cambridge University Press, Cambridge.

Conard, N.J. 1992. *Tönchesberg and its Position in the Palaeolithic Prehistory of Northern Europe.* Habelt, Römisch-Germanisches Zentralmuseum Mainz, Bonn.

Deacon, H.D. 1997. African cultures in transition and adaptation. In J.O. Vogel (ed.) *Encyclopedia of Precolonial Africa*, 320–324. Altamira Press, London.

Foley, R. and Lahr, M.M. 1997. Mode 3 technologies and the evolution of modern humans. *Cambridge Archaeological Journal* 7, 3–36.

Gamble, C. 1996. Hominid behaviour in the Middle Pleistocene: an English perspective. In C. Gamble and A.J. Lawson (eds.) *The English Palaeolithic Reviewed*, 63–71. Trust for Wessex Archaeology, Salisbury.

Gamble, C. 1997. The skills of the Lower Palaeolithic world. *Proceedings of the Prehistoric Society* 63, 407–410.

Gamble, C. and Roebroeks, W. 1999. The Middle Palaeolithic: a point of inflection. In W. Roebroeks and C. Gamble (eds.) *The Middle Palaeolithic Occupation of Europe*, 3–21. University of Leiden Press, Leiden.

Green, H.S. (ed.) 1984. *Pontnewydd Cave: A Lower Palaeolithic Hominid Site in Wales.* National Museum of Wales, Cardiff.

Green, H.S. 1988. Pontnewydd Cave: the selection of raw materials for artefact-manufacture and the question of natural damage. In R.J. MacRae and N. Moloney (eds.) *Non-Flint Stone Tools and the Palaeolithic Occupation of Britain*, 223–232. British Archaeological Reports British Series 189, Oxford.

Grün, R. and Stringer, C.B. 1991. Electron Spin Resonance dating and the evolution of modern humans. *Archaeometry* 33, 153–199.

Grün, R., Beaumont, P.B. and Stringer, C.B. 1990. ESR dating evidence for early modern humans at Border Cave in South Africa. *Nature* 344, 537–540.

Grün, R., Brink, J.S., Spooner, N.A., Taylor, L., Stringer, C.B., Franciscus, R.G. and Murray, A.S. 1996. Direct dating of the Florisbad hominid. *Nature* 382, 500–501.

Keeley, L.H. 1980. *Experimental Determination of Stone Tool Uses: A Microwear Analysis.* University of Chicago Press, Chicago.

Klein, R. 1999. *The Human Career: Human Biological and Cultural Origins.* University of Chicago Press, Chicago.

Kolen, J. 1999. Hominids without homes: on the nature of Middle Palaeolithic settlement in Europe. In W. Roebroeks and C. Gamble (eds.) *The Middle Palaeolithic Occupation of Europe*, 139–175. University of Leiden Press, Leiden.

Kuman, K., Inbar, M. and Clarke, R.J. 1999. Palaeoenvironments and cultural sequence of the Florisbad Middle Stone Age hominid site, South Africa. *Journal of Archaeological Science* 26, 1409–1425.

Lumley, H. de, 1966. *Les Fouilles de Terra Amata à Nice.* Bulletin de la Musée d'Anthropologie de Monaco 13.

Marshack, A. 1981. On palaeolithic ochre and the early uses of color and symbol. *Current Anthropology* 22, 188–191.

Marshack, A. 1990. Early hominid symbol and the evolution of the human capacity. In P. Mellars (ed.) *The Emergence of Modern Humans*, 457–498. Edinburgh University Press, Edinburgh.

McBrearty, S. 1997. Early African hominids: behavior and environments. In J.O. Vogel (ed.) *Encyclopedia of Precolonial Africa*, 269–275. Altamira Press, London.

McBrearty, S. and Brooks, A.S. 2000. The revolution that wasn't: a new interpretation of the origin of modern human behavior. *Journal of Human Evolution* 39, 453–563.

Mercier, N., Valladas, H., Valladas, G., Reyss, J.-L., Jelinek, A., Meignen, L. and Joron, J.-L. 1995. TL dates of burnt flints from Jelinek's excavations at Tabun and their implications. *Journal of Archaeological Science* 22, 495–509.

Mussi, M. 1999. The Neanderthals in Italy: a tale of many caves. In W. Roebroeks and C. Gamble (eds.) *The Middle Palaeolithic Occupation of Europe*, 49–80. University of Leiden Press, Leiden.

Newcomer, M.H. 1984. Flaking experiments with Pontnewydd raw materials. In S. Green (ed.) *Pontnewydd Cave: A Lower Palaeolithic Hominid Site in Wales*, 153–158. National Museum of Wales, Cardiff.

Palmer, S. 1975. A palaeolithic site at North Road, Purfleet, Essex. *Essex Archaeology and History* 7, 1–13.

Roebroeks, W. 1988. *From Find Scatters to Early Hominid Behaviour: A Study of Middle Palaeolithic Riverside Settlements at Maastricht-Belvédère (The Netherlands).* Analecta Praehistorica Leidensia 21, Leiden.

Schäfer, D. 1981. Taubach. *Ethnographisch-Archäologische Zeitschrift* 22, 369–396.

Schwarcz, H.P. and Rink, W.J. 1998. Progress in ESR and U-series dating of the Levantine Palaeolithic. In T. Akazawa, K. Aoki and O. Bar-Yosef (eds.) *Neandertals and Modern Humans in Western Asia*, 57–67. Plenum Press, London.

Sillen, A. and Morris, A. 1996. Diagenesis of bone from Border Cave: implications for the age of the Border Cave hominids. *Journal of Human Evolution* 31, 499–506.

Stringer, C. 1999. The fossil record of the evolution of *Homo sapiens* in Europe and Australasia. In B. Sykes (ed.) *The Human Inheritance: Genes, Language and Evolution*, 33–44. Oxford University Press, Oxford.

Tuffreau, A. and Antoine, P. 1995. The earliest occupation of Europe: continental northwest Europe. In W. Roebroeks and C. Gamble (eds.) *The Middle Palaeolithic Occupation of Europe*, 147–163. University of Leiden Press, Leiden.

White, M.J. and Pettitt, P.B. 1995. Technology of early palaeolithic western Europe: innovation, variability and a unified framework. *Lithics* 16, 27–40.

Wreschner, E. 1975. Ochre in prehistoric contexts: remarks on its implications to the understanding of human behaviour. *Mitekufat Haeven* 13, 5–11.

Wreschner, E. 1980. Red ochre and human evolution: a case for discussion. *Current Anthropology* 21, 631–644.

Wreschner, E. 1982. *Homo erectus* and pre-Neanderthals and the question of early red colour symbolism. Abstracts of the *Congrès International de Paléontologie Humaine*, Nice, 89.

Wymer, J.J. 1999. *The Lower Palaeolithic Occupation of Britain.* Trust for Wessex Archaeology and English Heritage, Salisbury.

12. A newly identified Acheulian handaxe type at Tabun Cave: the Faustkeilblätter

Zinovy Matskevich, Naama Goren-Inbar and Sabine Gaudzinski

ABSTRACT

This article identifies a previously unrecognized handaxe type in the assemblage of layer E of the Tabun Cave in Israel. An attempt to define, describe and analyse this type and its significance is combined with an overview of the chronostratigraphic position of European Micoquian assemblages in which similar tool types are present.

INTRODUCTION

Acheulian handaxes are regarded as the most characteristic tool type of the Levantine Lower Palaeolithic cultural sequence (Bar-Yosef 1994; Gilead 1970a, 1970b; Goren-Inbar 1995 *inter alia*). Their morphotechnological characteristics are used in prehistoric studies to describe a broad range of issues, such as refinement of the chronological sequence (Gilead 1970a, 1970b), cultural affinities of the assemblages (Goren-Inbar and Saragusti 1996) and the mental abilities of hominids (Belfer-Cohen and Goren-Inbar 1994), to name but a few.

The typological classification of handaxes has been considered a fundamental approach to Lower Palaeolithic research. With regard to the Levantine Acheulian, it is widely used and at times considered the primary method for chronological and cultural assignment of assemblages within the Lower Palaeolithic (Gilead 1970a, 1970b). The heavy reliance on typological analysis stems, among other reasons, from the abundance of surface Acheulian assemblages that lack any means of dating (Bar-Yosef 1994; Goren-Inbar 1995 and references therein).

Typological analysis is clearly not the only research tool at the disposal of modern prehistoric research, and is usually accompanied by various other methods. However, in certain cases, such as the one presented here, it retains its importance due to the specific circumstances. At Tabun, these stem from the complex history of the three major excavation expeditions carried out there during the last 70 years. In this case typological analysis contributes greatly to the identification of archaeological phenomena, as it integrates a diversity of morphological, technological and stylistic attributes.

Tabun Cave is known to have the longest stratigraphic record of its kind in the Levant. Much of this impressive sequence is assigned to the Lower Palaeolithic. Two projects were carried out during the 1930s and 1960s, exposing thousands of items classified as bifaces and other flint artefacts (Garrod and Bate 1937; Jelinek 1975, 1981; Jelinek *et al.* 1973). Handaxes were discovered by Garrod in layers F and E. In Jelinek's excavations handaxes were discovered mainly in the beds equivalent to layer E, and also in bed 90 which is equivalent to Garrod's layer G (Jelinek 1981, 1982; Rollefson 1978).

The industry (or industries) of layer E, the main focus of the present study, was defined by different researchers as Acheulo-Micoquian (Garrod and Bate 1937), Acheulo-Yabrudian and Amudian (or Pre-Aurignacian) (Garrod 1956), Late Acheulian of Yabrudian facies (Gilead 1970a, 1970b), Acheulo-Yabrudian (Copeland 1975) and Mugharan Tradition (Jelinek 1981, 1982, 1990). A rich repertoire of side-scrapers (including Quina, semi-Quina and *déjeté* types) and variable quantities of bifaces are generally regarded as its main characteristics (Copeland 1975; Garrod 1956; Garrod and Bate 1937; Gilead 1970a, 1970b; Jelinek 1975, 1981, 1990; Jelinek *et al.* 1973; Wright 1966).

The cultural assignment of the lithic assemblages was based on typological criteria and the degree of typological similarity to European and, to a lesser degree, Levantine tool types (due to the small number of excavated sites), with an emphasis on handaxes and flake tools. The early typological classification was elementary and, as Gilead has observed, did not enable detailed classification:

'Ninety-eight percent of the 1200 Tabun layer F hand-axes were classified as Pear-shaped; no handaxe types at all were recognized at Jabrud ... A meaningful analysis of the Umm Qatafa layer D2 handaxes could not be attempted as close to forty percent of them were classified as *divers*' (Gilead 1970a, 26–27).

After its publication in 1961, Bordes' type list was applied extensively to the Levantine material and served as an almost exclusive method for handaxe analysis by all those who studied the Tabun assemblages after Garrod's publication (Gilead 1970a; Jelinek 1981; Rollefson 1978; Wright 1966).

The aim of this study is to describe a small number of unique handaxes characterised by distinct features and a special reduction sequence. These traits constitute a special and definable morphotype. An additional objective is to demonstrate that museum collections of lithic assemblages are of scientific value and may be useful in enlarging the current knowledge, despite their being inappropriately archaeologically and statistically sampled.

MATERIAL AND METHOD

The lithic assemblages originating from the early excavations of Garrod are selective ones. The aesthetic attractiveness of the bifaces led to their retention but also caused

their dispersal (Garrod and Bate 1937). The following quotation describes the present state of the Tabun collections:

'The artifacts recovered in the initial excavation (in excess of 50,000) were distributed among many institutions in Europe, North America and Palestine, which has to some degree inhibited further examination of this material' (Jelinek 1975, 297; see also the list of the institutions holding Tabun material in Garrod and Bate 1937, VI).

The more recent excavations (Jelinek 1975, 1982; Jelinek *et al.* 1973) used advanced and precise techniques and resulted in unselective excavated samples of lithic assemblages per stratigraphic unit. Despite their high scientific value, these assemblages are not available for detailed analysis, as they are currently under study and are divided between the storage facilities of the Israel Antiquities Authority (Jerusalem) and Tucson, Arizona (USA).

It was demonstrated by Wright (1966) that typological analysis by Bordes' method of small samples drawn from Garrod's assemblage yielded similar results to those of Garrod. Nevertheless, there is a high probability of distortion and biased conclusions. The dispersal and the selective character of the Tabun lithic assemblages necessitate a research approach which emphasises specific aspects, concentrating on qualitative characteristics rather than the quantitative statistical significance of a phenomenon.

The quantitative compositions of the different handaxe samples originating from the Garrod and Jelinek excavations and their stratigrapical position are illustrated in Table 12.1. This is based on the Garrod collection curated by the Rockefeller Museum, Jerusalem, and the Jelinek collection housed in the Israel Antiquities Authority's storage facilities at ha'Argaman St., Jerusalem. The number of handaxes excavated by Garrod and available in Israel amounts to less than five per cent of the original sample retrieved during her excavations.

Garrod's stratigraphy	Jelinek's stratigraphy	Garrod's excavations (N)*	Jelinek's excavations (N)**	Handaxes stored in Jerusalem				Total
				Garrod		Jelinek		
				N	%	N	%	
D	II–IX (27–69)	47 (+9 of C and B)	16 (+3 of C)	2	3.6	2	10.5	75
Ea	X–XI (70–77)	1003	648	6	0.6	55	8.4	1651
Eb	XII (78–80)	1866	684	14	0.7	0	0.0	2550
Ec	unidentified	616	–	42	6.8	–	–	616
Ed	XIII (81–85)	3813	322	295	7.7	0	0.0	4135
F	unidentified	1233	–	54	4.4	–	–	1233
G	XIV (90A–90J)	–	280	–	–	0	0.0	280

* Values are after Garrod and Bate (1937, 70–90).
** Values calculated after Rollefson (1978, 70). Rollefson's data are based on the initial stratigraphic division of Jelinek *et al.* (1973) rather than the updated one (Jelinek 1981) that appears in Table 12.1.

Table 12.1. Tabun Cave: Stratigraphy, frequency and availability of handaxes

Table 12.1 demonstrates that, of the handaxes stored in Jerusalem, only Garrod's collection from layer Ed and Jelinek's collection from layer Ea are suitable for detailed study, and that all the other samples are too small to enable meaningful analysis. The problematic correlation between some of Garrod's and Jelinek's stratigraphical units (Jelinek 1981, 1982) prevents detailed comparison of samples originating in these two excavations.

The present study is based on a morphotypological analysis of handaxes from layer E (Ea and Ed) originating from the excavations of Garrod (Garrod and Bate 1937) and Jelinek (Jelinek 1975, 1981, 1982; Jelinek *et al.* 1973) at Tabun. It concerns data retrieved from the analysis of three different samples. The first (A) originates from Jelinek's excavations and includes 57 items. This sample comprises the entire handaxe assemblage from these excavations available in Jerusalem. Of these, 55 handaxes are stratigraphically assigned to Jelinek's units X and XI, which correspond to Garrod's layer Ea. Two additional handaxes from Jelinek's units VI and IX, considered to correspond to Garrod's layer D (Garrod and Bate 1937, 77; Jelinek 1981, 268), are included in sample A. Both samples B and C comprise handaxes from Garrod's excavations of layer Ed. Sample B comprises 60 handaxes manufactured on pebbles; all retain remains of cortex on both faces. Sample C comprises 60 handaxes randomly selected from 235 additional handaxes of layer Ed that are stored in the Rockefeller Museum. It should be noted that the number of handaxes modified on pebbles in sample C is biased, due to the previous selection of 'pebbly' items that comprise sample B.

The study of the handaxes was carried out by attribute analysis. The set of attributes used is a modification of an existing one developed for the analysis of handaxes from Gesher Benot Ya'aqov (Goren-Inbar and Saragusti 1996) and includes, among others, morphometric variables that are based on the methods of Bordes (1961) and Roe (1964, 1968). It includes a typological definition, as well as recording such variables as blank type, amount of cortex, extent and location of retouch and the number of scars. Only a selection of the results of the detailed analysis will be discussed here.

THE DEFINITION OF THE TYPE

During the initial phases of the study, some handaxes with outstanding stylistic properties were noticed. These handaxes appear similar to European items which are found in Micoquian assemblages (Barta 1990; Bosinski 1967; Burdukiewicz 2000; Chmielewski 1969; Debénath and Dibble 1994; Desbrosse *et al.* 1976; Kozlowski 1989; Richter 1997; Veil *et al.* 1994) and are absent from Bordes' (1961) biface typology. All these types are present in the European assemblages and are termed *Keilmesser* (a bifacial backed knife with one well-retouched straight lateral edge opposite a blunt or backed edge); *Prondniks*

(a *Keilmesser* with a transverse blow from the distal extremity along a lateral edge); *Halbkeile* (a pointed handaxe with a convex-concave section and cortical base) and *Faustkeilblätter*. The latter is the subject of the present study. An additional type, that is not known in Micoquian assemblages, is a bifacial tool manufactured on an elongated pebble, intensively retouched only on the distal extremity so that the cortical proximal end resembles a tang. Although the presence of *Prondniks* (Jelinek 1982, 102) and other *Keilmesser* types (or *Faustkeilschaber*, according to Rollefson 1978, 105) at Tabun was already noted in previous studies, the additional Central European types, including the *Faustkeilblätter*, have never been recognised.

The definition of the classic European *Faustkeilblätter* (leaf-shaped handaxe) is as follows:

'... thin and markedly flat in section. The point is ... well made while the base is unworked. One of the faces is ... worked over the entire surface and is generally quite flat. Retouch on the opposite face is often confined to the distal point and the lateral edges' (Debénath and Dibble 1994, 156).

The distribution of this type beyond Central Europe is not clear, but similar specimens are known from assemblages in other parts of Europe, such as in England (Ashton and McNabb 1994, figs. 1a, 2a).

The *Faustkeilblätter* type was originally defined by H. Obermaier (Obermaier and Wernert 1914). According to Bosinski (1967) these items are typical of the early stages of the Micoquian industry in Central and Southern Germany (Bockstein and Klausennische phases). Several subtypes were also defined as 'broad', 'narrow', 'small', and 'miniature leaf-shaped' (*ibid.*, 28–29). The common features of all the variants are the thinness and flatness (low values of maximum thickness that are almost equal to the thickness of the tip) and a morphology which is dictated by the shape of the raw material (*ibid.*).

RESULTS

The definition of the *Faustkeilblätter* type by Bosinski (1967) was adopted here in order to classify the Tabun specimens. In sample A (layer Ea) three items of this type were identified (5%), in sample B (layer Ed, pebbles) eight (13%), thus amounting to eleven items. Similar artefacts were not found in sample C, probably due to the low number (only seven items) of handaxes modified on pebbles in this sample.

The *Faustkeilblätter* of Tabun are handaxes made on flat 'tabular' flint pebbles that are minimally flaked along the edges (Plates 12.1–12.5). The distal ends of the tools are pointed and the lateral edges, in most cases, are slightly concave. The trait common to these handaxes is their extreme thinness, extreme flatness and extensive cortex cover on the proximal part of both faces. These handaxes

Pl. 12.1

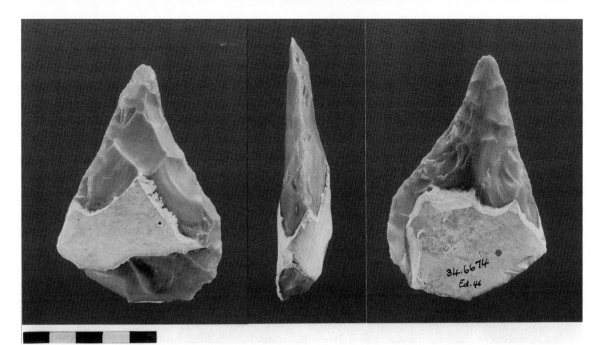

Pl. 12.2

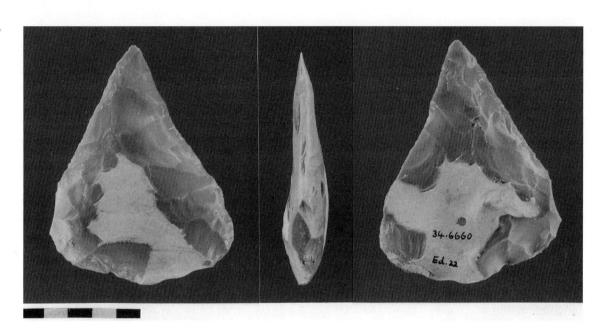

Pl. 12.3

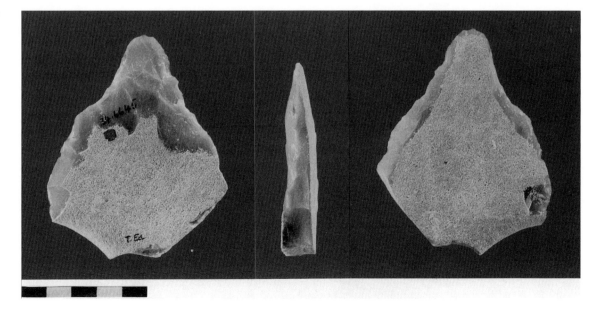

Plates 12.1–12.3. Faustkeilblätter

Pl. 12.4

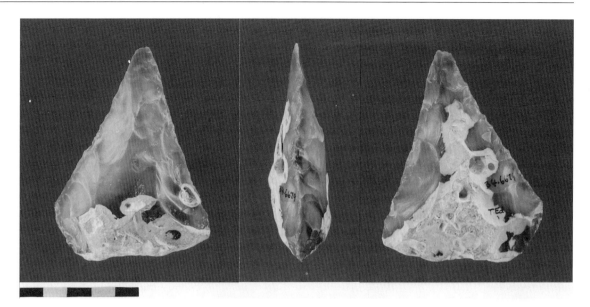

Pl. 12.5

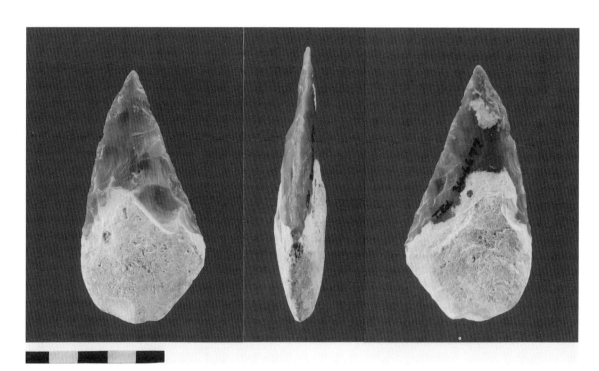

Plates 12.4 and 12.5. Faustkeilblätter

are of similar dimensions or slightly smaller than the rest of the analysed samples: the length ranges between 56 mm and 97 mm. Table 12.2 presents a comparison between metric data of *Faustkeilblätter* and handaxes of the other samples.

As demonstrated in Table 12.2, the *Faustkeilblätter* items are thinner and flatter than the other handaxes. Yet there is a considerable degree of variability in regard to the thickness and the ratio of maximum thickness/thickness of the upper fifth. This variability is expressed both within the *Faustkeilblätter* group and in all the other handaxe samples. Thus, some of the Tabun handaxes are thinner

and flatter than some of the *Faustkeilblätter*, as demonstrated in Fig. 12.1. This scattergram shows a certain clustering of the *Faustkeilblätter*. However, some of the other handaxe types do display the same metrical characteristics.

The traits that differentiate the *Faustkeilblätter* from the other handaxes are not restricted to their morphology, but include technological characteristics that predetermine the planform of the finished tool. These include selection of a particular raw material and utilisation of a specific reduction process, which is characterised by a minimal flaking surface.

Samples	N	Length (in mm)		Thickness (max)/thickness (on upper fifth)		Width (max)/thickness (max)	
		x	s.d.	x	s.d.	x	s.d.
Faustkeilblätter	11	81.55	12.75	2.12	0.55	3.48	1.24
A	54	83.78	19.48	2.15	0.61	2.04	0.47
B	52	91.40	14.52	2.48	0.76	2.13	0.46
C	60	93.08	20.78	2.33	0.71	2.01	0.45

Table 12.2. Metric parameters

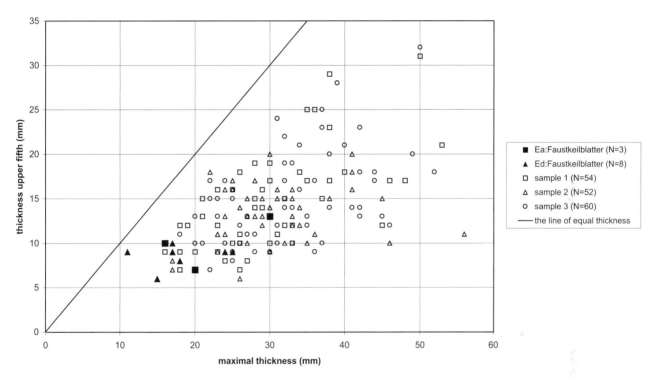

Fig. 12.1. Scattergram of upper fifth thickness and maximum thickness of the Tabun handaxes

A number of technological traits are common to all the *Faustkeilblätter* items. For the manufacture of particularly thin tools, tabular pebbles were selected (the maximum thickness between 11 and 30 mm). The flaking in most cases was restricted to a minimal retouch along the lateral edges and on the distal extremity. Such a reduction sequence resulted in items covered by a considerable amount of cortex on both faces (Table 12.3). Some are almost completely cortical (more than 75%).

The minimal amount of retouch on *both* faces of these tools distinguishes the Tabun *Faustkeilblätter* from their 'classic' European counterparts. In Europe, one face of this handaxe type is cortical while the other is often entirely flaked. Nevertheless, it has been noted that some of the 'classic' European examples have remains of cortex on both their faces (see Bosinski 1967, Taf. 25:3, 67:1–2, 68:2, 79:1, 80:6, 118:2.4.5; Debénath and Dibble 1994, fig. 11.56).

Three of the Tabun *Faustkeilblätter* bear less than 25%

Face 1	Face 2	N
0–25	25–50	3
25–50	25–50	2
25–50	50–75	2
50–75	50–75	2
50–75	75–100	2

Table 12.3. Amount of cortex on Faustkeilblätter *(in %)*

cortex on one face. On the other hand, none of these items bears less than 25% cortex on the entire surface of both faces. This trait distinguishes them as a group from the rest of the assemblage, in which most tools have less than 25% cortex (Fig. 12.2). As the proximal parts of the *Faustkeilblätter* tools are cortical, they retain the original shape of the selected pebble. In most cases (7), the cortex

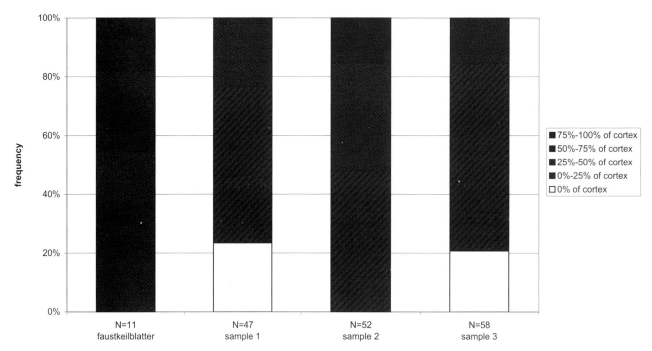

Fig. 12.2. Comparison of amount of cortex (on both faces) on handaxes of the different handaxe samples (excluding handaxes made on flakes)

residue on both faces is joined in the proximal part (butt) (Plates 12.2–12.5), and in some cases also in the proximal portion of the lateral (cortical) edge (Plate 12.1). On another item the cortex joins the two faces on both lateral edges, so that the width of the item is also dictated by the initial form of the pebble. In the rest of the cases the butts of the tools were only slightly retouched (or broken).

The average number of scars on the faces of the *Faustkeilblätter* is not significantly different from that of the rest of the handaxes in the assemblage (Table 12.4).

Nevertheless, it has to be taken into consideration that the same number of scars on the *Faustkeilblätter* is associated with a smaller retouched surface. In order to compare the ratio between the number of scars and the size of the surface covered by retouch, an index of 'retouch intensity' was constructed. The index is calculated as follows:

$$I = n / s, \text{ where: } s = (wuf + whl + wlf) / 3 \times mlen \times \% \text{ of the retouched surface}$$

In this equation 'n' is the absolute number of scars on a retouched surface, 'wuf', 'whl', 'wlf' and 'mlen' are the width in the upper fifth, in the middle and in the lower fifth of the length, and the maximum length of an item (in cm) respectively. The 's' is the area of retouched surface (in cm²). Table 12.5 presents the values of this calculated index; it shows that the retouch on the *Faustkeilblätter* differs from that of the other samples, and that it is more intensive than that characterizing the rest of the assemblages.

Only three *Faustkeilblätter* were defined as retouched

Samples	N	Face 1		Face 2	
		x	s.d.	x	s.d.
Faustkeilblätter	11	19.82	5.56	16.36	5.70
A	54	17.13	6.34	14.31	5.06
B	52	19.92	4.89	18.98	5.06
C	60	23.93	6.96	22.22	8.29

Table 12.4. Number of scars

Samples	N	Face 1, scars/cm²		Face 2, scars/cm²	
		x	s.d.	x	s.d.
Faustkeilblätter	11	0.83	0.32	0.90	0.40
A	54	0.50	0.22	0.51	0.24
B	52	0.55	0.21	0.67	0.29
C	60	0.55	0.18	0.56	0.19

Table 12.5. The intensity of retouch

by 'regular bifacial retouch' (large shallow scars covering the entire surface). The other eight items are retouched by 'scraper retouch' (steep intensive retouch along the edges) and by 'fine bifacial retouch' (shallow elongated small scars). In comparison, some 62% of the rest of the studied handaxes are retouched by 'regular bifacial retouch' and by 'thinning'. This observation indicates that the amount of effort invested in the production of the *Faustkeilblätter*, though they retain most of the cortex, was no less than that invested in order to manufacture entirely flaked handaxes.

The purpose of such a strategy seems to be to focus on the design of thin working edges and the formation of pointed distal ends, without investing effort in reducing the thickness and width of the proximal parts, which have remained in their natural form.

DISCUSSION

As demonstrated by the analysis in this study, the *Faust-keilblätter* handaxe type is a component of the Tabun E Mugharan sequence. Indeed, adoption of a different typological analysis, e.g. the application of Bordes' method (Bordes 1961), might have resulted in a different classification of the same handaxes. Two of the *Faustkeilblätter* could have been classified as lanceolate, six as triangular, one as elongated triangular, and two as cordiform. Furthermore, as all these items retain various amounts of cortex, they could have been classified as '*bifaces partielles*' (*ibid.*).

The presence of handaxes manufactured on very flat pebbles in Tabun E is determined by the availability and selection of suitable and specific raw material. Once it was procured, it was treated by a particular reduction sequence suitable for the production of a predetermined design. This phenomenon, which includes other rare handaxe types (*prondniks* and handaxes with a cortical 'handle': Plate 12.6), allows the presence of these particular handaxe types to be considered a significant cultural trait, though they are not common quantitatively.

When considering the *Faustkeilblätter* as a cultural phenomenon, its chronological and geographical distribution should be reviewed. Layer E, over 7 meters thick (Garrod and Bate 1937, 65), reflects a long process of sedimentation (Farrand 1979, 1994; Goldberg in Jelinek *et al.* 1973) as demonstrated by the results of diverse dating methods (for ESR dating see Grün *et al.* 1991; for TL dates see Mercier *et al.* 1995). The presence of the *Faustkeilblätter* (as well as *prondniks* and the handaxes with a cortical grip) in both Tabun Ea and Ed (the uppermost and the lowermost sub-layer respectively) may indicate the existence of a homogeneous and continuous cultural tradition throughout this entire sequence. At Tabun, layer E is dated between 350±33 kyr (unit XII) and 270±22 kyr (unit X), ranging from OIS 10 to OIS 8 (Mercier *et al.* 1995) and thus defining the age of the *Faustkeilblätter* in the Levant.

As the presence of *Faustkeilblätter* in the Levantine assemblages has not been previously recognized, the only means of comparing it with other Acheulian assemblages is through examination of the illustrated material of

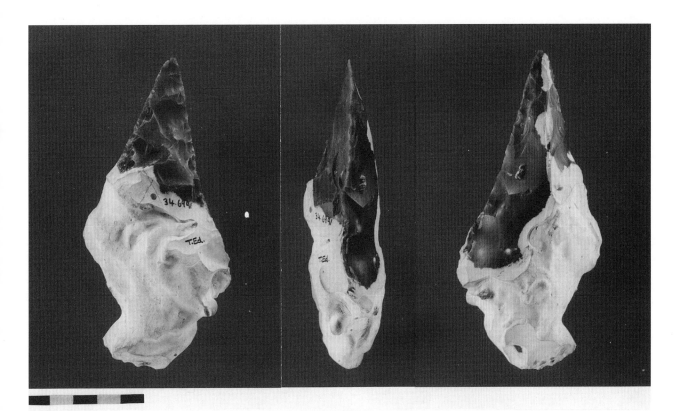

Plate 12.6. Handaxe with cortical 'handle'

published reports. Stekelis and Gilead (1967) mentioned the presence of handaxes manufactured on tabular pieces of flint in the surface assemblage of Ma'ayan Barukh. Nevertheless, preliminary examination of a substantial part of the assemblage (1435 bifaces) did not result in the identification of similar handaxes (pers. observ.). The handaxes of this assemblage that retained cortex on both faces are thick and bifacially flaked on almost their entire surface. This assemblage differs from that of Tabun both typologically (high frequency of ovaloid and discoid handaxes, rare Micoquian and triangular types) and technologically (flaking of the entire circumference of the handaxes).

An assemblage with items analogous to the Tabun *Faustkeilblätter* is the Late Acheulian of Evron Zinat in the Western Galilee (Gilead and Ronen 1977). There, some 4% of the handaxes have reserved cortical butts. The authors (*ibid.*, 59) observed that the form of these items is dictated by the form of the selected natural flint pebbles. Several of the illustrated implements are of special interest, as they closely resemble the Tabun *Faustkeilblätter*. These are manufactured on thin flat pebbles (*ibid.*, figs. 6:2, 10:2) or primary flakes (*ibid.*, fig. 8:2) and retouched only along the edges, while most of the surface remained unflaked. The retouch, though of minimal surface cover, is very intensive. In these cases, the form and thickness of the proximal part of the handaxe coincide with the form and thickness of the pebble.

Two additional items from the same assemblage (*ibid.*, figs. 8:1, 11:2) were classified as cordiform and triangular handaxes. One of their faces is almost entirely cortical and the other is entirely flaked, similar to the European variant of *Faustkeilblätter*. The handaxes are markedly flat and thin; their retouch is restricted to a small area along the lateral edges. The main difference between these examples and those from Tabun lies in the intensive flaking of one of their faces. Nevertheless, the outstanding flatness and thinness of these items, together with the lack of flaking on the other face, allow them to be considered variants of the same type.

A number of artefacts similar to the Tabun *Faustkeilblätter* were discovered in the Azraq Basin in Jordan. There, some handaxes of the Late Acheulian of Lion Spring (Copeland 1989a, figs. 1:1,3, 5:2) could be identified as *Faustkeilblätter*. Another specimen from the same locality (Copeland 1989b, fig. 6:1) is a typical *Prondnik* knife. Jelinek (1982, 72) suggested that the Azraq sites might be considered the closest analogue of the Mugharan tradition of Tabun.

All the assemblages reviewed above are assigned to the Late Acheulian. The appearance of the *Faustkeilblätter* type apparently has, among others, a chronological significance. It is absent from all Acheulian assemblages that pre-date the Late Acheulian ('Ubeidiya: Bar-Yosef and Goren-Inbar 1993; Evron Quarry: Gilead and Ronen 1977; Gesher Benot Ya'aqov: Goren-Inbar and Saragusti 1996). It is also absent from several Late Acheulian sites, such as

Ma'ayan Barukh (Stekelis and Gilead 1967), which is assigned to an earlier phase of the Late Acheulian (Gilead 1970a, 1970b).

Faustkeilblätter and other particular handaxe types at Tabun, as in other Levantine assemblages, comprise tool sets that are considered in Europe to characterise the late Middle Palaeolithic Micoquian (*sensu* Bosinski 1967; Günther 1964; Mania and Toepfer 1973; Valoch 1988) or are otherwise described as the *Keilmesser* group. In Europe, the appearance of this group is definitely of chronological significance. The term *Keilmesser* group refers to certain Weichselian, mainly Central European, Middle Palaeolithic assemblages (Veil *et al.* 1994). In addition to *Keilmesser*, these assemblages are characterised by highly standardised bifacially worked cutting-tools. These are retouched alternately along the edges; first one surface was retouched and then the opposite one ('*wechselseitig-gleichgerichtete Bearbeitung*', Bosinski 1967, or 'Kulna technique', Boëda 1995).

Lithic assemblages sharing these traits have been excavated in France, Germany, Poland, Moravia, Hungary and the Ukraine (Fig. 12.3). The majority of the important sites are either old excavations or newly discovered sites at a preliminary stage of analysis. This allows only typological and technological correlation of Western, Central and Eastern European assemblages.

Since the beginning of the 1950s the term 'Micoquian' has been used in order to differentiate these assemblages from the Mousterian of Western Europe (Bohmers 1951; Zotz 1951). Although 'Micoquian' is regularly used to refer to certain Middle European Weichselian bifacially worked inventories, this term is rarely used to describe the French Late Saalian Acheulian lithic assemblages (compare Bosinski 1968; Veil *et al.* 1994).

The classic subdivision of the Micoquian or *Keilmesser* group was defined by Bosinski in 1967 (Bosinski 1967, 1974) and was based on evidence from Central and Southern Germany. It comprised four chronological phases based on the quantitative presence of certain tool types (Bockstein phase, Klausennische phase, Schambach phase, Rörshain phase). The oldest Bockstein phase is characterised by Micoquian bifaces, elongated *Halbkeile, Fäustel*, some large *Faustkeilblätter* and leaf points, and many *Bocksteinmesser* and bifacially retouched scrapers. In the following Klausennische phase the frequencies of *Keilmesser* (Klausennische type) and large *Faustkeilblätter* increase. This phase was defined by few Micoquian bifaces and *Halbkeile*, many *Faustkeilblätter*, some *Bocksteinmesser*, and some leaf points, while *Prondniks* occur regularly. In the Schambach phase *Halbkeile* and small *Faustkeilblätter* occur only rarely and *Keilmesser* are more or less absent. Finally, in the Rörshain phase thick leaf points are a characteristic implement and occur frequently.

In 1967, when the subdivision of Central and Southern German Micoquian or *Keilmesser* group assemblages took place, it could be verified only partly by the stratigraphy

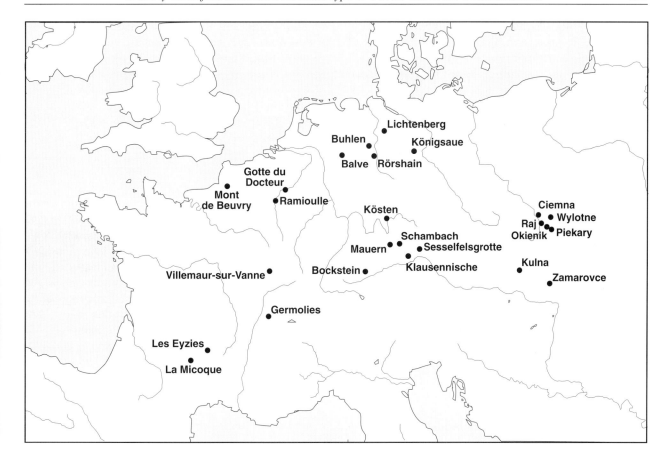

Fig. 12.3. Distribution map of European Micoquian or Keilmesser *group lithic assemblages (after Richter 1997)*

of Balver Cave in Germany (Günther 1964). Well-dated assemblages were rare.

Cave sediment stratigraphy, typology and a few absolute dates enabled a more precise chronology of the Micoquo-Prondnikian assemblages from Central Europe (Chmielewski 1969). Chmielewski distinguished between late Acheulian assemblages with Micoquian elements at the beginning of the Weichselian, before the Brörup Interstadial, Lower Micoquo-Prondnikian assemblages between the Brörup Interstadial and the first glacial maximum of the Weichselian, and an Upper Micoquo-Prondnikian during the first glacial maximum of the Weichselian.

New evidence (Boëda 1995; Richter 1997; Valoch 1988; Veil *et al.* 1994) and re-evaluation of sites and lithic assemblages (Jöris 1992, 1997; Pastoors 1996; Richter 1997; Rieder 1992; Uthmeier 1998) have contributed to a more detailed understanding of the discussed entities.

On the basis of an analysis of 13 lithic assemblages from the stratigraphical sequence of the Sesselfelsgrotte (Southern Germany), Richter (1997) suggests a modified chronology for the Micoquian or *Keilmesser* group horizon. According to his division, a first mode appears just after the end of the first glacial maximum within the Oerel/Glinde interstadial context (58–48 kyr BP, Behre

and van der Plicht 1992). Non-Levallois techniques are used and larger samples comprise bifacial tools that are attributed to the Bockstein phase of the classic subdivision.

A second phase is attributed to a late stage of the Oerel/Glinde interstadial complex. Exclusive use of the Levallois technique is considered to be characteristic and larger samples comprise tool types of the Klausennische phase of the classic subdivision (Richter 1997).

Within the Micoquian or *Keilmesser* group assemblages, certain variations in the typological composition are observed; for example, Königsaue A–C (Germany) contain *Faustkeilblätter* and *Keilmesser* but lack Micoquian bifaces (Mania and Toepfer 1973).

Whether the Micoquian or *Keilmesser* group horizon is restricted to the Interstadial complex after the end of the first glacial maximum as indicated by German sites such as Sesselfelsgrotte (Richter 1997) and Lichtenberg (Veil *et al.* 1994), or also occurs during the Early Weichselian Brörup (Oxygen Isotope Stage 5c)/Odderade (Oxygen Isotope Stage 5a) interstadial complex (Behre and Lade 1986), as indicated for example by the chronostratigraphic position of the German site of Königsaue (Mania and Toepfer 1973; Weismüller 1995) or the Czech site of Kulna (Rink *et al.* 1996), is a point of discussion (Richter 1997, 244–247;

Veil *et al.* 1994). Only rarely has a pre-Weichselian geochronological position been postulated for these assemblages (Foltyn *et al.* 2000).

In any case, the available evidence suggests that the Central European Micoquian or *Keilmesser* group horizon is restricted to the first half of the last glacial cycle and appears to represent the latest cultural heritage of Neanderthals in this region.

The Levantine data of Tabun differ drastically from the European data presented above. As demonstrated above, the radiometric date of Tabun layer E, between 350±33 kyr (unit XII) and 270±22 kyr (unit X), defines the age of the *Faustkeilblätter* in the Levant. Hence, it seems that over 200,000 years separate the Levantine *Faustkeilblätter* horizons from the Central European ones. On the other hand, it should be pointed out that the resemblance between the two complexes is not restricted to a single outstanding tool type, but is manifested by a whole series of specific phenomena, of great similarity in both cases. Is it possible that a striking similarity in handaxe typological composition appeared incidentally in entirely different times and places (spontaneous invention)? Or is it possible that the European Micoquian was at least partly an earlier phenomenon than is currently assumed? Finally, is cultural diffusion a satisfactory explanation for the observed similarities?

SUMMARY AND CONCLUSIONS

The presence of the *Faustkeilblätter* in the Levantine Acheulian has been established in the assemblage of Tabun Cave. The identification of this type is based on complex morphological, technological and stylistically distinct traits. The *Faustkeilblätter* are characterized by a particular reduction sequence, which comprises selection of a specific type of raw material and shaping of the tool in a characteristic manner. Thus, the *Faustkeilblätter* are the result of a system of unique technological choices throughout all stages of production (e.g. Karlin and Julien 1994). Therefore it is argued here that this is indeed a pre-planned entity and not a product resulting from raw material constraints, as suggested by some (Ashton and McNabb 1994; White 1998).

The presence of *Faustkeilblätter* in several Levantine Acheulian assemblages indicates that the type is restricted to the final stages of the Late Acheulian and does not appear in any of the earlier Lower Palaeolithic sites. The only radiometrically dated sequence is that of Tabun, where the *Faustkeilblätter* appear in the range of about 350–270 kyr (T/L dates by Mercier *et al.* 1995). The *Faustkeilblätter* disappear from the Levant, like all the other types of bifaces, with the beginning of the Mousterian period (Bar-Yosef 1975, 1994; Goren-Inbar 1995).

One of the intriguing questions concerning the presence of *Faustkeilblätter* in the Levantine assemblages is the presumably European affinity of the type. The series of

questions presented above cannot, unfortunately, be resolved at this stage of research. Further comparative analysis of the European and Levantine material, precise absolute dating and acquisition of new data, among other aspects, will contribute further to our knowledge. However, the outstanding similarity of these European and Levantine handaxe types requires closer scholarly scrutiny.

ACKNOWLEDGMENTS

The research was supported by the Israel Science Foundation funded by the Israel Academy of Sciences and Humanities. We owe thanks to Prof. Arthur Jelinek for his kind permission to study the unpublished Tabun handaxes from his excavations. Iris Yossefon, Alegre Savariego and Hava Katz of the Israel Antiquities Authority contributed much of their time to make the Tabun collection accessible and offered much help in carrying out this study. Anna Belfer-Cohen and Doron Dag read and commented on early drafts of this paper. We wish to thank Gabi Laron for the photographs, Regina Heckt for drawing Fig. 12.3 and Sue Gorodetsky for her invaluable editorial help. We are grateful to Sarah Milliken and Jill Cook for inviting us to participate in this volume.

REFERENCES

Ashton, N.M. and McNabb, J. 1994. Bifaces in perspective. In N.M. Ashton and A. David (eds.) *Stories in Stone*, 182–191. Lithic Studies Society Occasional Paper 4, London.

Barta, J. 1990. Mittelpaläolithische Funde im Gebiet der Slowakei. *Ethnographisch-Archäologische Zeitschrift* 31, 122–134.

Bar-Yosef, O. 1975. Archaeological occurrences in the Middle Pleistocene of Israel. In K.W. Butzer and G.Ll. Isaac (eds.) *After the Australopithecines: Stratigraphy, Ecology and Culture Change in the Middle Pleistocene*, 571–604. Mouton, The Hague.

Bar-Yosef, O. 1994. The Lower Paleolithic of the Near East. *Journal of World Prehistory* 8, 211–265.

Bar-Yosef, O. and Goren-Inbar, N. 1993. *The Lithic Assemblages of 'Ubeidiya: A Lower Paleolithic Site in the Jordan Valley*. Qedem 34. The Hebrew University, Jerusalem.

Behre, K.-E. and Lade, U. 1986. Eine Folge von Eem und 4 Weichsel-Interstadialen in Oerel/Niedersachsen und ihr Vegetationsablauf. *Eiszeitalter und Gegenwart* 36, 11–36.

Behre, K.-E. and van der Plicht, J. 1992. Towards an absolute chronology for the last glacial period in Europe: radiocarbon dates from Oerel, northern Germany. *Vegetation History and Archaeobotany* 1, 111–117.

Belfer-Cohen, A. and Goren-Inbar, N. 1994. Cognition and communication in the Levantine Lower Paleolithic. *World Archaeology* 26, 144–157.

Boëda, E. 1995. Steinartefakt-Produktionssequenzen im Micoquien der Kulna-Höhle. *Germania* 45–46, 75–98.

Bohmers, A. 1951. *Die Höhlen von Mauern, Teil 1: Kulturgeschichte der Altsteinzeitlichen Besiedlung*. J.B. Wolters, Groningen.

Bordes, F. 1961. *Typologie du Paléolithque Ancien et Moyen*. Delmas, Bordeaux.

Bosinski, G. 1967. *Die Mittelpaläolithischen Funde im Westlichen Mitteleuropa*. Böhlau Verlag, Köln.

Bosinski, G. 1968. Zum Verhältnis von Jungacheuleen und Micoquien in Mitteleuropa. In D. de Sonneville Bordes and F. Bordes (eds.) *La Préhistoire: Problèmes et Tendances,* 77–86. CNRS, Paris.

Bosinski, G. 1974. Der Mittelpaläolithische Fundplatz Buhlen, Kr. Waldeck (Hessen). *Archäologische Informationen* 2–3, 15–18.

Burdukiewicz, J.M. 2000. The backed biface assemblages of East Central Europe. In A. Ronen and M. Weinstein-Evron (eds.) *Toward Modern Humans: Yabrudian and Micoquian, 400–500 Years Ago,* 155–166. British Archaeological Reports International Series 850, Oxford.

Chmielewski, W. 1969. Ensembles Micoquo-Proundnikiens en Europe Centrale. *Geographia Polonica* 17, 371–386.

Copeland, L. 1975. The Middle and Upper Paleolithic of Lebanon and Syria in the light of recent research. In F. Wendorf and A.E. Marks (eds.) *Problems in Prehistory: North Africa and the Levant,* 317–350. Southern Methodist University Press, Dallas.

Copeland, L. 1989a. The Harding collection of Acheulian artifacts from Lion Spring, Azraq. In L. Copeland and F. Hours (eds.) *The Hammer on the Rock: Studies in the Early Palaeolithic of Azraq, Jordan,* 213–258. British Archaeological Reports International Series 540 (i), Oxford.

Copeland, L. 1989b. The artifacts from the sounding of D. Kirkbride at Lion Spring. In L. Copeland and F. Hours (eds.) *The Hammer on the Rock: Studies in the Early Palaeolithic of Azraq, Jordan,* 171–211. British Archaeological Reports International Series 540 (i), Oxford.

Debénath, A. and Dibble, H.L. 1994. *Handbook of Paleolithic Typology, Volume One: Lower and Middle Paleolithic of Europe.* University of Pennsylvania, Philadelphia.

Desbrosse, R., Kozlowski, J.K. and Zutate y Zuber, J. 1976. Prondniks de France et d'Europe Centrale. *L'Anthropologie* 80, 431–448.

Farrand, W.R. 1979. Chronology and paleoenvironment of Levantine prehistoric sites as seen from sediment studies. *Journal of Archaeological Science* 6, 369–392.

Farrand, W.R. 1994. Confrontation of geological stratigraphy and radiometric dates from Upper Pleistocene sites in the Levant. In O. Bar-Yosef and R. Kra (eds.) *Late Quaternary Chronology and Paleoclimates of the Eastern Mediterranean,* 33–53. Radiocarbon and Peabody Museum, Harvard.

Foltyn, E.M., Foltyn, E. and Kozlowski, J.K. 2000. Première évidence de l'âge pré-Eemien des industries à pièces bifaciales asymétriques en Europe Centrale. In A. Ronen and M. Weinstein-Evron (eds.) *Toward Modern Humans: Yabrudian and Micoquian, 400–500 Years Ago,* 167–172. British Archaeological Reports International Series 850, Oxford.

Garrod, D.A.E. 1956. Acheuléo-Jabrudien et 'Pré-Aurignacien' de la Grotte du Taboun (Mont Carmel). Etude stratigrafique et chronologique. *Quaternaria* 3, 39–59.

Garrod, D.A.E. and Bate, D.M. 1937. *The Stone Age of Mount Carmel.* Oxford University Press, Oxford.

Gilead, D. 1970a. *Early Paleolithic Cultures in Israel and the Near East.* Unpublished dissertation, Hebrew University of Jerusalem.

Gilead, D. 1970b. Handaxe industries in Israel and the Near East. *World Archaeology* 2, 1–11.

Gilead, D. and Ronen, A. 1977. Acheulian industries from Evron on the western Galilee coastal plain. *Eretz Israel* 13, 56–86.

Goren-Inbar, N. 1995. The Lower Paleolithic of Israel. In T.E. Levy (ed.) *The Archaeology of Society in the Holy Land,* 93–109. Leicester University Press, London.

Goren-Inbar, N. and Saragusti, I. 1996. An Acheulian biface assemblage from the site of Gesher Benot Ya'aqov, Israel: indication of African affinities. *Journal of Field Archaeology* 23, 15–30.

Grün, R., Stringer, C.B. and Schwarcz, H.R. 1991. ESR dating from Garrod's Tabun Cave collection. *Journal of Human Evolution* 20, 231–248.

Günther, K. 1964. *Die Altsteinzeitlichen Funde der Balver Höhle.* Bodenaltertümer Westfalens 8, Münster.

Jelinek, A.J. 1975. A preliminary report on some Lower and Middle Paleolithic industries from the Tabun Cave. In F. Wendorf and A.E. Marks (eds.) *Problems in Prehistory: North Africa and the Levant,* 297–315. Southern Methodist University Press, Dallas

Jelinek, A.J. 1981. The Middle Paleolithic in the Southern Levant from the perspective of Tabun Cave. In J. Cauvin and P. Sanlaville (eds.) *Préhistoire du Levant,* 265–280. CNRS, Paris.

Jelinek, A.J. 1982. The Middle Paleolithic in the southern Levant, with comments on the appearance of Modern *Homo sapiens.* In A. Ronen (ed.) *The Transition from Lower to Middle Palaeolithic and the Origin of Modern Man,* 57–104. British Archaeological Reports International Series 151, Oxford.

Jelinek, A.J. 1990. The Amudian in the context of the Mugharan tradition at the Tabun Cave (Mount Carmel), Israel. In P. Mellars (ed.) *The Emergence of Modern Humans,* 81–90. Cornell University Press, New York.

Jelinek, A.J., Farrand, W., Haas, G., Horowitz, A. and Goldberg, P. 1973. New excavations at the Tabun Cave, Mount Carmel, Israel, 1967–1972: a preliminary report. *Paléorient* 1, 151–183.

Jöris, O. 1992. Pradniktechnik im Micoquien der Balver Höhle. *Archäologisches Korrespondenzblatt* 22, 1–12.

Jöris, O. 1997. *Der Spätmittelpaläolithische Fundplatz Buhlen (Grabungen 1966–69): Stratigraphie, Steinartefakte und Fauna des oberen Fundplatzes.* Unpublished dissertation, University of Köln.

Karlin, C. and Julien, M. 1994. Prehistoric technology: a cognitive science? In C. Renfrew and E.B.W. Zubrow (eds.) *The Ancient Mind: Elements of Cognitive Archaeology,* 152–164. Cambridge University Press, Cambridge.

Kozlowski, J. 1989. La fin du Paléolithique moyen en Pologne. *L'Anthropologie* 27, 133–142.

Mania, D. and Toepfer, V. 1973. *Königsaue: Gliederung, Ökologie und Mittelpaläolithische Funde von der letzten Eiszeit.* Veröffentlichungen des Landesmuseums für Vorgeschichte Halle 26, Berlin.

Mercier, N., Valladas, H., Valladas, G., Reyss, J.-L., Jelinek, A., Meignen, L. and Joron, J.-L. 1995. TL dates of burnt flints from Jelinek's excavations at Tabun and their implications. *Journal of Archaeological Science* 22, 495–509.

Obermaier, H. and Wernert, P. 1914. Paläolithbeiträge aus Nordbayern. *Mitteilungen der Anthropologischen Gesellschaft in Wien* 44, 44–63.

Pastoors, A. 1996. *Die Steinartefakte von Salzgitter-Lebenstedt.* Unpublished dissertation, University of Köln.

Richter, J. 1997. *Sesselfelsgrotte III. Der G-Schichten-Komplex der Sesselfelsgrotte: Zum Verständnis des Micoquien.* Saarbrücker Druckerei und Verlag, Saarbrücken.

Rieder, K.-H. 1992. *Aspekte zur Geschichte der Höhlenverfüllung aus dem Hohlen Stein bei Schambach aus der Sicht der Profiluntersuchungen 1977–1992: Aspekte zur Geschichte der Höhlenverfüllung, ihrer Paläontologie und Archäologie.* Unpublished dissertation, University of Tübingen.

Rink, W.J., Schwarcz, H.P., Valoch, K., Seitl, L. and Stringer, C.B. 1996. ESR dating of Micoquian industry and Neandertal remains at Kulna Cave, Czech Republic. *Journal of Archaeological Science* 23, 889–901.

Roe, D.A. 1964. The British Lower and Middle Palaeolithic: some problems, methods of study and preliminary results. *Proceedings of the Prehistoric Society* 30, 245–267.

Roe, D.A. 1968. British Lower and Middle Palaeolithic handaxe groups. *Proceedings of the Prehistoric Society* 34, 1–82.

Rollefson, G.O. 1978. *A Quantitative and Qualitative Typological Analysis of Bifaces from the Tabun Excavations 1967–1972.* Unpublished PhD dissertation, University of Arizona.

Stekelis, M. and Gilead, D. 1967. *Ma'ayan Barukh: A Lower Paleolithic Site in Upper Galilee.* Mitekufat Haeven 8. Academon, Jerusalem.

Uthmeier, T. 1998. *Micoquien, Aurignacien und Gravettien in Bayern: Eine Regionale Studie zum Übergang vom Mittel-zum Jungpaläolithikum.* Unpublished dissertation, University of Köln.

Valoch, K. (ed.) 1988. *Die Erforschung der Kulna-Höhle 1961–1976.* Anthropos 24, Moravske Muzeum, Brno.

Veil, S., Breest, K., Höfle, H.-C., Meyer, H.-H., Plisson, H., Urban-Küttel, B., Wagner, G.A. and Zöller, L. 1994. Ein mittel-paläolithischer Fundplatz aus der Weichsel-Kaltzeit bei Lichtenberg, Lkr. Lüchow-Dannenberg. *Germania* 72, 1–66.

Weismüller, W. 1995. *Sesselfelsgrotte II: Die Silexartefakte der unteren Schichten der Sesselfelsgrotte. Ein Beitrag zum Problem des Moustérien.* Saarbrücker Druckerei und Verlag, Saarbrücken.

White, M.J. 1998. On the significance of Acheulean biface variability in southern Britain. *Proceedings of the Prehistoric Society* 64, 15–44.

Wright, G.A. 1966. The University of Michigan archaeological collections from et-Tabun, Palestine: levels F and E. *Papers of the Michigan Academy of Science, Arts, and Letters* 51, 407–423.

Zotz, L.F. 1951. *Altsteinzeitkunde Mitteleuropas.* Ferdinand Enke Verlag, Stuttgart.

13. The Palaeolithic industries in Korea: chronology and related new find-spots

Hyeong Woo Lee

ABSTRACT

The Palaeolithic in Korea is unique by comparison with the neighbouring regions of China and Siberia. Both the pattern of lithic variation and the chronological sequence are distinctive. Recent preliminary research in Junbuk Province offers an opportunity to gain new insights into the character of the Korean Palaeolithic, which divides simply into Earlier and Later phases.

INTRODUCTION

The number of Palaeolithic sites known in Korea has increased. In total, approximately 1000 Palaeolithic find-spots have been reported (Yi 2000, 1). Although there are still only a few systematically excavated sites (Fig. 13.1), recent discoveries are beginning to increase our understanding and provide a general framework.

GENERAL FRAMEWORK

Until the end of the 1970s, known and reported Earlier Palaeolithic finds consisted of choppers and chopping tools and various simply struck flake tools. The absence of handaxes seemed to support Movius' hypothesis that the Asian Palaeolithic was distinct from that of Africa and Europe (Movius 1944). Then, in the 1980s, Acheulian handaxes were recorded at the site of Chongokni (Kim 1989, figs. 1 and 2), as well as in China (Yi and Clark 1983). Since then, as research has increased, many bifaces of Acheulian type have been excavated and surface collected throughout Korea. Later Palaeolithic artefacts which have typical Upper Palaeolithic affinities have also been excavated, with micro-blade technology being found in many localities such as Suyanggae, Sokchangri and Sangmooryoungri (Fig. 13.1).

On the basis of such evidence, some archaeologists claim that there are three separate Palaeolithic periods in Korea: the Lower, Middle and Upper Palaeolithic periods. However, this western perspective has been challenged (Nelson 1993), and Yi (2000, 2) states that there is no actual archaeological evidence for making such cultural distinctions. Certainly, there are many artefacts which may be regarded as Lower and Upper Palaeolithic on the basis of typology, but Middle Palaeolithic forms and discrete assemblages are lacking, although there is some evidence for increasing technological complexity, typological variation, and improved raw material procurement within the stratified sequences. For example, at Sokchangri four different lithic assemblages were found in four separate successive geological levels. The lower deposit contains simply made core tools, while the upper layer yields typical microcores (Sohn 1993). At Sangmooryoungri there were two main tool kits. The lower layer produced crude core tools, mostly chopping tools and simple flake tools, whereas the upper layer contained microblades and cores (Hwang and Shin 1989). The core tools found in the lower layer are mostly made of locally available materials, while finely retouched and shaped microtools from the uppermost layer are all made of imported obsidian, the source of which is still being debated (Kiam and Yang 2000; Sohn 1989).

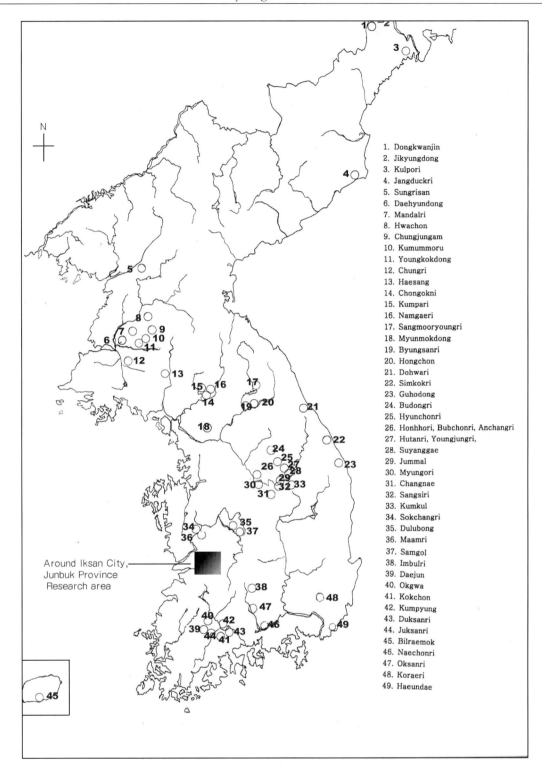

1. Dongkwanjin
2. Jikyungdong
3. Kulpori
4. Jangduckri
5. Sungrisan
6. Daehyundong
7. Mandalri
8. Hwachon
9. Chungjungam
10. Kumummoru
11. Youngkokdong
12. Chungri
13. Haesang
14. Chongokni
15. Kumpari
16. Namgaeri
17. Sangmooryoungri
18. Myunmokdong
19. Byungsanri
20. Hongchon
21. Dohwari
22. Simkokri
23. Guhodong
24. Budongri
25. Hyunchonri
26. Honhhori, Bubchonri, Anchangri
27. Hutanri, Youngjungri,
28. Suyanggae
29. Jummal
30. Myungori
31. Changnae
32. Sangsiri
33. Kumkul
34. Sokchangri
35. Dulubong
36. Maamri
37. Samgol
38. Imbulri
39. Daejun
40. Okgwa
41. Kokchon
42. Kumpyung
43. Duksanri
44. Juksanri
45. Bilraemok
46. Naechonri
47. Oksanri
48. Koraeri
49. Haeundae

Around Iksan City,
Junbuk Province
Research area

Fig. 13.1. Major Palaeolithic sites in Korea (all the illustrated ones are major excavated sites except for the present research area, Iksan City, Junbuk Province).

Artefacts of distinctive Middle Palaeolithic type have not been found. In the Young Dam Area, a couple of flake tools indicate the use of Levallois technology but, as the Levallois technique may also be found in the Lower and even the Upper Palaeolithic (Inizan *et al*. 1992, 48), these pieces are not necessarily indicative of a Middle Palaeolithic.

The Korean Palaeolithic seems more complicated than that of the adjacent regions of China and Siberia. According to Wu and Poirier (1995, 237), Middle Palaeolithic assemblages such as those known as Mousterian in Europe (Klein 1989, 291) are completely absent from China. The opposite is true in Siberia where Mousterian artefacts are prolific, especially in the Altai (Derev'anko 1990). For example, the Kara-Bom site has both Middle and Upper Palaeolithic industries (Derev'anko *et al.* 1998). The date obtained for Complex B, which consists of two Mousterian deposits, is roughly 60–45 kyr on the basis of C14 and ESR dating. The Mousterian is also found in Mongolia (Derev'anko 1990).

Similar regional variation may also be found in Early (or Lower) Palaeolithic assemblages. In China, the Early Palaeolithic includes not only choppers and chopping tools but also Acheulian bifaces. In Siberia the case is rather different. Derev'anko (1990, 5) identifies two chronological stages in the Early Palaeolithic of North Asia, the region extending from Siberia to the Russian Far East (Derev'anko 1992, 160). The first is the pebble tool culture (choppers and chopping tools) and the second is the stage which is characterised by a Levalloisian tool kit and large blades. This suggests that there are no Acheulian bifaces at any stage in Siberia. By contrast, Mongolia, located between China and Siberia, has yielded a large number of Acheulian handaxes and Levalloisian artefacts. The Korean Earlier Palaeolithic is similar in character to that of China and Mongolia because of the presence of handaxes, and distinct from that of Siberia. The Mousterian complex shows similar regional variation. No Mousterian artefacts are known in Korea and China but Siberia yields many. By contrast, Later (Upper) Palaeolithic sites in Asia are more widely distributed and have typological features in common. Microlithic techniques used in the production of prismatic and wedge-shaped microblades occur all over Mongolia, Siberia, China, Korea and even Japan (Derev'anko 1990, 1992). In Korea, approximately fourteen Later Palaeolithic sites have been discovered. Of these, absolute dating has been applied at Sokchangri and Suyanggae, giving age estimates of 20,830 BP and 18,630 and 16,400 BP respectively (Lee and Woo 1997). The assemblages are produced using microblade technique and the main raw materials, siliceous shale and obsidian, were imported over a long distance to the site.

In general it may be said that subdividing the Asian Palaeolithic on the basis of artefact typology produces a different framework from that known in Europe. Although Asian artefact types are not much different from those in Europe and Africa, their stratigraphic and geographic distribution suggests a rather different pattern of variation through time. No region in Asia has a site showing stratigraphic continuity from chopping tools to microliths. In Siberia, typical handaxes are unknown and the presence of the Lower Palaeolithic is not clear. In China and Korea, Middle Palaeolithic typological affinities are lacking and artefact types are not evenly distributed. In Korea, the number of handaxes per site is considerably smaller than any other type of tool. For instance, Chongokni, the most prolific handaxe site in Korea, has been excavated over

more than 20 years but only ten handaxes have been collected in total (Yi 2000). In the Bose Basin in China, more than one hundred Palaeolithic find-spots have been reported and several thousand artefacts found by excavation and surface collection. However, 90% of the tools are choppers, picks and hammer stones. Handaxes are relatively few in number (Huang 1992).

On the basis of such evidence, it may be suggested that the Palaeolithic of Asia is not only distinct from that of Europe and Africa but also varies regionally. In some respects the Chinese Palaeolithic presents the closest similarities to the Korean. However, although both have handaxes and similar microcores, the stratigraphic context of these forms are not the same. In China, a large number of hominid fossils have been excavated, while none are known from Korea. The earliest hominid known in China is *Homo erectus*. Although many hominid fossils have been excavated in North Korea, it is not quite clear whether there is evidence for pre-modern humans (Han 1990). Both the fossil remains and various scientific dating techniques give the earliest date for Chinese *Homo erectus* as more than 500 kyr ago (Barnes 1999). By contrast, the earliest occupation of Korea has been dated by geological information. The evidence is still being debated (Choi 1989). Bae (1989, 54) suggests that the geomorphological studies show that the oldest known sites were deposited after 200 kyr ago, whereas Yi (2000) claims that the earliest Palaeolithic assemblage, including the Acheulian type handaxes, date from Oxygen Isotope Stage 3 or 5a, less than 100 kyr ago. This is based on the presence of Aira-Tanzawa (AT) volcanic ash. Below the AT, large core tools dominate, while smaller artefacts and microliths are found above the AT. If the later dating is correct, all the early artefacts would be too young to be typical Lower Palaeolithic tools as perceived in the rest of Asia, Europe and Africa. Consequently, the Korean Palaeolithic chronology must be considered more carefully. It allows us to say that typologically the chopping tools and handaxes are assigned to the Lower Palaeolithic, although the actual chronology is not likely to make these contemporary with the Lower Palaeolithic as it is known elsewhere.

For these reasons, it is necessary to consider the Palaeolithic in Korea on its own terms. Using the terms Earlier and Later Palaeolithic might be considered more appropriate than applying western terminology. This dispenses with the term Middle Palaeolithic for which there is no evidence, and replaces the term 'Lower' which is inappropriate because the core tools from Korea are probably less than 100 kyr old. Replacing 'Lower' with 'Early' is not ideal because, in the opinion of the present author, it could be confused with the 'Early' Palaeolithic in China which it also seems to post-date. From this discussion of the chronological framework, it can be said that the Korean Palaeolithic sequence is unique by comparison with the Palaeolithic cultures of other regions. This view seems to be confirmed by new evidence from the recent field survey reported here.

REPORT ON PRELIMINARY FIELD SURVEYS IN JUNBUK PROVINCE

Last year, preliminary field research was initiated in Junbuk Province (Fig. 13.1). Several Palaeolithic localities were discovered, and significant Earlier and Later Palaeolithic assemblages were found. In total, twenty-three artefacts were recovered, mostly from surface collecting. Three of these sites are reported below.

Changpyungri

Four pieces were collected from this site. They include two chopping tools and two pyramidal core tools. The latter should not be confused with Upper Palaeolithic microblade cores (Inizan *et al*. 1992). They are simply made cores similar to those found in Clactonian assemblages. Wymer (1968, 38) classified them as choppers or chopper cores. All of the artefacts are made of local quartzite available from the site and exhibit the same abrasion pattern, suggesting that they were all subjected to the same post-depositional processes. Typologically, the chopping tools and pyramidal core tools are typical. The chopping tools have been made in a simple manner with locally available quartzite rocks. The working edges have a zigzag form lacking retouch. The side of the butt is covered with cortex which may have been left on for holding the tool. The pyramidal core tools have many angular facets, and do not retain much cortex.

The site is presumed to have had a single occupation because of the character of the stone artefacts. Technologically, the chopping tools and pyramidal core tools have the same technology: simple direct percussion. All of them were made by the so-called 'trial-and-error' mechanism (Wynn 1979, 377). There is no complicated manufacturing procedure on either type. Additionally, the abrasion pattern is so similar that they could have been made in a single period of time.

Sinmakri

Unlike Changpyungri, Sinmakri contained different types of tools. These include two pyramidal core tools, a handaxe and two microcores. As the field research is only at the reconnaissance stage, little is yet known of the geological context. However, two separate cultural layers were found partly exposed. The lower layer is formed by dark brown silt and clay, while the subsequent horizon, the upper layer, has pale brown silt and clay. Simple core tools and a handaxe were found in the lower layer, while the upper layer yielded the two microcores.

The two wedge-shaped microcores are made of siliceous shale which is not found in the region and must have been imported. Both are patinated and show the same yellow colouration. This suggests that they could be contemporary. They are small: one is 1.9 cm long, 2.4 cm wide and 0.9 cm thick, the other measures 1.9 cm in length, 2.5 cm in breadth and 1 cm in thickness. The arêtes of the flake scars have been examined and show that successive removals were made until the core was exhausted. The shape of the removal scars suggests that the cores belong to the Later Palaeolithic. They are remarkably regular in size and straight in shape, suggesting that they were produced by pressure flaking, a technique found only in the Upper (Later) Palaeolithic tradition. Such wedge-shaped microcores are common in East Asia (Barnes 1999, 59–60), including Korea.

A handaxe from the site has been classified as an ovate. Generally speaking, the ovate handaxe in Korea is uncommon. Most Korean handaxes are pointed forms, although there is an exception from Chongokni. In terms of raw material, the Korean core tools, including handaxes, were made of coarse-grain quartzite on which fine flaking was not easy and the overall shapes are inevitably crude because of the difficulty of knapping with this material (cf. MacRae 1986; Moloney 1988, 33; Roe 1981, 207). Since the handaxe from the site is also made of poor quality quartzite, greater refinement cannot be expected. In spite of this, several important characteristic features are found on it. The cross-section is plano-convex and the abrupt edge across the bottom is formed by numerous removals. Like other handaxes, most Korean handaxes retain some cortex on the butt and parts of the sides, but this ovate handaxe does not retain any cortex. To get rid of the sharpness on the butt, the bottom has been battered. Presumably, a toolmaker needed a blunt area by which to hold the tool, and such flaking was applied for that purpose.

Another core tool is a pyramidal form. Morphologically, it has a single pyramidal shape, not a bi-pyramidal one. The working edges have a zigzag form like those of the typical chopping tools. It is also made of coarse-grained quartzite and only primary flaking without further retouch was applied. There is no cortex left and direct blows were struck using adjacent scars as striking platforms.

Although few artefacts were recovered, the number of Palaeolithic occupations at the site could represent more than one period of time: the Earlier and Later Palaeolithic periods. This is suggested not only by the typological differences but also by the marked differences in the place of deposition, raw material procurement pattern and technology. The core tools are made of local quartzite, while the microcores are made of non-local siliceous shale. If the handaxe belongs to the Later Palaeolithic period, why was it not made from the imported obsidian or siliceous shale? In Korea, there is no evidence that handaxes were manufactured from these materials. Only the clearly Later Palaeolithic microlithics were made from such better quality rocks.

Yulchonri

At Yulchonri, four artefacts were recovered. These included a chopper, two pyramidal core tools and a steep-edged scraper. All of them result from surface collection.

Typologically, all the artefacts have an Earlier Palaeolithic affinity.

The chopper is unifacially worked and simply made. Only a few direct blows were applied to the pebble and no trimming scars are present. Deliberate human manufacture is not immediately evident but the angle of the working edge is much like that of other chopping tools and is regular. A flake tool and a pyramidal core tool were similarly made in a simple manner by direct percussion and without retouch.

A single debitage flake was found. It is made of siliceous shale which is the same material found at Sinmakri. At Sinmakri, this high quality material is only used for the typical Later Palaeolithic tools, but at Yulchonri this is not the case. The flake is deeply patinated. Both the colour and the texture are altered. The colour is yellow and the texture brittle due to deep patination. Despite this alteration, a hinge fracture at the distal end is visible suggesting a knapping error. The flake might also be regarded as relatively thick, 1.15 cm being greater than the mean thickness value of 0.61 cm for eleven handaxe trimming flakes measured in the Highlands Farm collection in England (Lee 2001). The fracture pattern and thickness suggest the flake is not a typical Later Palaeolithic artefact. It is unfortunate that the raw material source has not yet been found, so the distance between the source and site cannot be assessed.

CONCLUSION

It is unfortunate that only a few artefacts have so far been recovered during the current field research, which has concentrated on evaluation. However, the new localities will certainly make an important contribution to our understanding of the general character of the Korean Palaeolithic. As has been explained, there are two different sets of assemblages: simple core tool assemblages and microcore assemblages. By applying typological criteria, the simple core tools can be seen as quite close to the Earlier Palaeolithic and Sinmakri could have two different phases. Clearly, some lithic types, such as chopping tools, are common to more than one period. At the site of Sokchangri, typical chopping tools were found in the Later Palaeolithic deposit (Sohn 1993), but microcores were not made before the Later Palaeolithic. This distinction enables us to separate the Earlier and Later Palaeolithic.

REFERENCES

Bae, K.D. 1989. *Chongokni Site: Report of the Excavation of Chongokni Palaeolithic Site, 1986*. Seoul University Museum, Seoul (in Korean).

Barnes, G. 1999. *The Rise of Civilization in East Asia*. Thames and Hudson, London.

Choi, S.R. 1989. Chronology in Korean Archaeology. *Journal of the Korean Archaeological Society* 23, 5–20 (in Korean).

Derev'anko, A.P. 1990. *Palaeolithic of North Asia and the Problem of Ancient Migration*. Technical Report, Russian Academy of Sciences Siberian Division, Institute of Archaeology and Ethnography, Novosibirsk.

Derev'anko, A.P. 1992. In Y.J. Choi (ed.) *The Palaeolithic of East Asia*, 153–171. National Research Institute of Cultural Properties, Seoul.

Derev'anko, A.P., Petrin, V., Rybin, E. and Chevalkov, L. 1998. *Palaeolithic Complexes of the Stratified Part of the Kara-Bom Site*. Nauka, Novosibirsk.

Han, C.K. 1990. *The Prehistory of North Korea*. Baksan Culture, Seoul (in Korean).

Huang, W. 1992. The pebble-tool industry in Bose Basin. In Y.J. Choi (ed.) *The Palaeolithic of East Asia*, 47–63. National Research Institute of Cultural Properties, Seoul.

Hwang, Y.H. and Shin, B.S. 1989. Sangmooryoungri (an excavation report). In B.K. Choi (ed.) *Sangmooryoungri*, 481–660. Kangwon University Museum, Kangwon (in Korean).

Inizan, M.-L., Roche, H. and Tixier, J. 1992. *Technology of Knapped Stone*. CREP, Meudon.

Kim, J.Y. and Yang, D.Y. 2000. The Distribution and Origin of the Obsidian Material. Abstracts of the *First Conference of the Korean Palaeolithic Society* (in Korean).

Kim, W.Y. 1989. *Chongokni* (1st excavation report). National Research Institute of Cultural Properties, Seoul (in Korean).

Klein, R. 1989. *The Human Career: Human Biological and Cultural Origins*. Chicago University Press, Chicago.

Lee, H.W. 2001. *A Study of Lower Palaeolithic Stone Artefacts from Selected Sites in the Upper and Middle Thames Valley, with Particular Reference to the R.J. MacRae Collection*. British Archaeological Reports British Series 319, Oxford.

Lee, Y.J. and Woo, J.Y. 1997. Suyanggae, Cultural Complex and Prospects. In Y.J. Lee and J.K. Lee (eds.) *The 2nd International Symposium: Suyanggae and Her Neighbours*. Chungbuk University Museum, Chungbuk.

MacRae, R. 1986. Tool manufacture in quartzite and similar rocks in the British Palaeolithic. *Lithics* 7, 7–12.

Moloney, N. 1988. Experimental replication of bifacial implements using Bunter quartzite pebbles. In R.J. MacRae and N. Moloney (eds.) *Non-Flint Stone Tools and the Palaeolithic Occupation of Britain*, 25–47. British Archaeological Reports British Series 189, Oxford.

Movius, H.L. 1944. Early Man and Pleistocene stratigraphy in Southern and Eastern Asia. *Papers of the Peabody Museum of American Archaeology and Ethnology* 19, 1–125.

Nelson, S. 1993. *The Archaeology of Korea*. Cambridge University Press, Cambridge.

Roe, D.A. 1981. *The Lower and Middle Palaeolithic Periods in Britain*. Routledge and Kegan Paul, London.

Sohn, B.K. 1989. In search for the obsidian origin. In B.K. Choi (ed.) *Sangmooryoungri*, 781–796. Kangwon University Museum, Kangwon (in Korean).

Sohn, B.K. 1993. *Sokchangri Prehistoric Site*. Korean Institute of Prehistory, Seoul (in Korean).

Wu, X. and Poirier, F. 1995. *Human Evolution in China*. Oxford University Press, Oxford.

Wymer, J.J. 1968. *Lower Palaeolithic Archaeology in Britain As Represented by the Thames Valley*. John Baker, London.

Wynn, T. 1979. The intelligence of Later Acheulean hominids. *Man* 14, 371–391.

Yi, S.B. 2000. On the chronology and stratigraphy of the Korean Palaeolithic. *Journal of the Korean Archaeological Society* 42, 1–22 (in Korean).

Yi, S.B. and Clark, G.A. 1983. Observations on the Lower Palaeolithic of northeast Asia. *Current Anthropology* 24, 181–202.

14. Lower and Middle Palaeolithic occupation in Central Kazakhstan: the Batpak Valley and environs

Norah Moloney, Sandra L. Olsen and Valery Voloshin

ABSTRACT

This paper discusses the results which are emerging from a research project in the Batpak Valley in Central Kazakhstan. A number of Lower and Middle Palaeolithic sites have been found in the area, and the presence of long stratigraphic exposures facilitates an understanding of their chronology. Juxtaposed between Europe and the Far East, this region is of key importance to the question of early hominid movements between these two geographical areas.

INTRODUCTION

Major new findings and revisions increasingly indicate the early spread of humans into Asia and beyond. The site of Dmanisi, Georgia, has yielded *Homo erectus/ergaster*-like hominid remains and simple stone tools associated with Villafranchian fauna in secure deposits dated to between 1–1.7 myr (Gabunia and Vekua 1995; Gabunia *et al.* 2000). Recent revisions of dates for the Javanese hominid localities, if correct, would place the Modjokerto calvaria at 1.81 myr (Swisher *et al.* 1994), although the dating requires further clarification. No stone tools were associated with the calvaria. Although there are problems with many of the purported early sites in China, there is good evidence for hominid presence by 1 myr, if not before. Lithic assemblages in the Nihewan Basin of Northern China, and the *Homo erectus* cranium and stone tools from Lantian, are two examples (Schick and Dong 1993; Schick *et al.* 1991).

Sites with dates of about one million years have been claimed in Central Asia, but most are plagued with problems of dating and insecure contexts. However, it appears from those sites in good stratigraphic position, such as Korolevo and Kul'dara in Tadjikistan and Azykh in Azerbaijan (Ranov 1991), that hominids were in Central Asia between 0.8–1 myr. There is much more evidence for hominid

presence in Central Asia and Siberia after 500 kyr. For example, localities on the Lena River, Siberia, may well fall somewhere between 300–200 kyr (Waters *et al.* 1997). Sites such as Karatau and Lakhuti indicate that Central Asia was also part of the Neanderthal world (Stringer and Gamble 1993). Levallois technology and 'Mousterian' tools are well attested in the Altai region of Siberia (Otte and Derev'anko 2000), and in Uzbekistan at Kul'bulak which has a sequence spanning the Acheulian to Upper Palaeolithic (Kasymov and Grechkina 1994).

THE LOWER AND MIDDLE PALAEOLITHIC OF KAZAKHSTAN

The geographically central position of Kazakhstan, juxtaposed as it is between Europe and the Far East, makes it a possible gateway to regions beyond, such as Siberia, China, and Mongolia (Fig. 14.1). As evidence of the early occupation of Asia increases, the Lower Palaeolithic of Kazakhstan becomes important to our understanding of the distribution of hominids across Asia. Kazakhstan's low topographic relief and the absence of glacial sheets meant that it lacked serious geographic obstacles, although the climate was harsh at times during the Pleistocene. As home to a variety

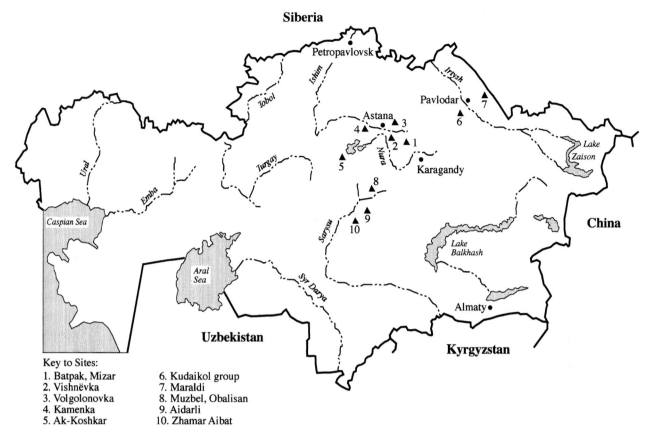

Fig. 14.1. Map of Kazakhstan with some of the sites mentioned in the text

Key to Sites:
1. Batpak, Mizar
2. Vishnëvka
3. Volgolonovka
4. Kamenka
5. Ak-Koshkar
6. Kudaikol group
7. Maraldi
8. Muzbel, Obalisan
9. Aidarli
10. Zhamar Aibat

of game species, including mammoth, the steppe and forest-steppe ecozones must have attracted hominids in their pursuit of food. The sparsely distributed river valleys were undoubtedly important for their rich flora and fauna, and as conduits to travel further north.

There are a number of Lower, Middle and Upper Palaeolithic sites in Kazakhstan that document hominid antiquity in the area, although the Lower Palaeolithic sites are less well known than the later period ones (Boriskovskii 1984; Derev'anko *et al.* 1997a, 1997b; Voloshin 1989, 1993, 1998). Choppers and chopping tools have been found at localities in the Karatau mountains of southern Kazakhstan (Boriskovskii 1984). Large flakes, denticulates, notches, chopper-like tools and pebble tools recovered from the travertine sites of Kochkurgan I and Shoktas in the south of the country have been dated by ESR to 500 kyr. Faunal evidence from the sites supports this date (Derev'anko *et al.* 1997a; Otte *et al.* 2000).

The steppe regions of Central and Northern Kazakhstan comprise large areas of loess covered interfluves with few deep stratigraphic exposures. Most of the lithic assemblages recovered in these regions are surface finds, often revealed through the effects of wind ablation on loess cover (Fig. 14.1). Ak-Koshkar, south-west of Lake Tengiz, and Kudaikol, on the west bank of the Irtysh river, just west of the city of Pavlodar, in north-east

Kazakhstan, are both open quarries on ancient terraces. The tools from these sites are highly eroded and include large choppers, picks or trihedrals, massive irregular flakes, pointed tools and biconical cores. The Upper Ishim and Sarysu regions are rich in Palaeolithic localities: Vishnëvka, Mizar, and Koktas have all produced Lower and Middle Palaeolithic material. Vishnëvka 4 and 6 are two adjacent quarries by the Ishim River that were exploited from the Lower Palaeolithic to Neolithic periods (Voloshin 1989, 1998).

THE BATPAK VALLEY

The Batpak Valley (Fig. 14.1) provides one of the few deep stratigraphic exposures in Kazakhstan. Located within the Nura-Ishim watershed, Batpak is in an area of low, rocky hills, known as the Aktastinsky Highlands, approximately 120 km south-east of the new Kazakh capital, Astana (previously known as Tselinograd and Aqmola).

For more than 30 years, Valery Voloshin has undertaken surveys and excavation in Central Kazakhstan and compiled ample evidence, particularly in the form of stone artefacts, of early hominid activity in the area. Twenty sites have been identified in the Batpak Valley, some tested and others excavated. At Voloshin's kind invitation, a team under the direction of Sandra Olsen visited the valley in July 2000 and had the opportunity of studying, albeit for a limited time, the geography of the valley, the sites currently undergoing excavation, and the lithic assemblages from the various Batpak localities.

The Batpak Valley is filled with Pleistocene alluvium and loess deposits totaling between 30 and 45 m in depth, in which a number of palaeomagnetic reversals have been distinguished. The composite stratigraphic profile (Fig. 14.2) provides a relatively complete sequence from Lower Palaeolithic at the base to Upper Palaeolithic at the top. Among the taxa of animals identified in the sequence are: *Mimomys, Marmota,* two types of *Equus, Elasmotherium, Mammuthus, Bison, Saiga, Cervus, Rangifer,* an un-designated carnivore, rhinoceros, and camel (Voloshin 1993).

The lowest purported archaeological deposits are in the Lower Aktasy Formation, which is 5–8 m thick and has primarily reversed polarity. It lies directly on top of red clays of the Pavlodar set of the Pliocene-Lower Pleistocene. The formation consists of heavy reddish-brown loam in the middle of which are cryogenic crevices. Pollen and spores indicate an herbaceous *Artemisia* steppe environ-ment, with fir forests and mosses along the rivers. The formation is topped with a thick pedocomplex of three

dark brown soils containing spores of green mosses, algae, and pollen of *Violae* (up to 75%), fir, pine, oak, elm and hornbeam, providing evidence for growing humidity and an expansion of forests to the detriment of the steppe (Voloshin 1993). The top of the Lower Aktasy Formation is marked by erosion above a level of sediments with normal polarity identified as belonging to the Jaramillo. A second erosional phase marking the base of the formation lies above a normal polarity level interpreted as the Olduvai interval. The Lower Aktasy Formation would appear to have an upper limit of 0.99 myr and a lower one of 1.77 myr (Berggren *et al.* 1995).

It was originally thought that stone pieces found in the Lower Aktasy Formation at Batpak had been humanly modified and were in fact artefacts. Based on reversals, an upper cryogenic level, and climatic fluctuations in the watershed loams, Voloshin (1993) dated the localities in which the putative artefacts were found to about 1.5 myr. Subsequent investigation of the stone pieces shows that they are more likely to be natural, according to two of the authors (N. Moloney and S. Olsen).

The Upper Aktasy Formation is 6 m thick and is separated from the Lower Aktasy Formation by an erosional phase. It consists of a uniformly medium and dark brown unlayered loam with reversed polarity through most of the column. It has a sequence of alternating reversed and normal polarity near the top of the formation that has been interpreted as the Matuyama-Brunhes transition. The temporal range of this formation would be approximately 1–0.78 myr. During the cryogenic phase, the upper surface of this pedocomplex was considerably damaged by soli-fluction.

The Batpak Formation series is up to 11 m thick and is composed of a yellow-gray loess-type loam, predominantly alluvial in its genesis. There are three soil horizons present in the formation, the upper two of which are black steppe soils. This formation has mostly a normal polarity, but at least six brief subchrons have been claimed. The climate, based on pollen diagrams, began as cold and humid, with a variety of grasses on the steppe, and fir trees contributing to 17% of the pollen. Gradually the area converted to forest-steppe, with up to 34.6% of the pollen derived from trees, including elms and oaks. By the end of the Batpak series, the climate was becoming semi-arid and grasses were replacing trees. The lithic assemblages found in the Batpak Formation are Mousterian (Voloshin 1993).

It is clear that the Batpak stratigraphy is not without its problems. Nowhere in the valley is the sequence complete. Rather it is a composite profile consisting of a series of sections from different areas, and it is possible that small local events might have affected and so distorted it. Furthermore, there are an alarming number of ice wedges in the sequence that can cause the mixing of sediments and their contents originating from different periods. The number of short duration subchrons needs to be verified, particularly with the presence of so many ice wedges. However, verification of the palaeomagnetic profile need

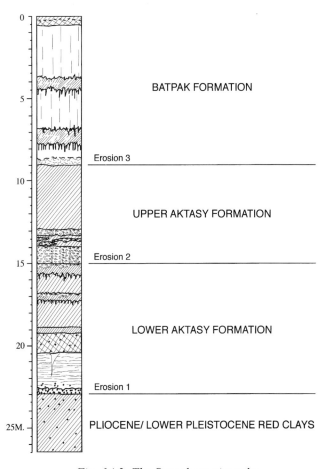

Fig. 14.2. The Batpak stratigraphy

not be a problem. Given the rarity of long sequences in Central Kazakhstan, and the possibility of finding sites in good context, it is clear that the deposits at Batpak deserve further attention.

The Lower and Middle Palaeolithic lithic collections that were examined by Moloney are comprised of pieces from both stratified and surface sites made from a range of raw materials. Some are homogeneous and appear easy to work, such as indurated sandstone and siltstone, but tough quartzite and poorer quality metamorphic rock and conglomerate were also exploited. It has become increasingly evident that the type of stone can affect the appearance of assemblages. Coarse material, for example, often gives an archaic cast to artefacts (Ashton and McNabb 1994; Moloney 1993, 1994; White 1998). However, there is evidence of Levallois working in nearly all materials including coarse-grained stone. It appears that hominids of the Lower and Middle Palaeolithic periods exploited primarily local sources of stone. However, Neolithic assemblages in the Batpak area are in a type of siliceous chert of unknown origin that may have been imported.

Vishnëvka 6

Vishnëvka 6, by the Ishim river, may be one of the rare open-air sites that has not suffered much postdepositional movement. It is a quarry site on a slightly raised outcrop of indurated siltstone. Materials recovered from excavation include unretouched and retouched flakes, cores, small ovate bifaces, biface thinning flakes and debris (Fig. 14.3). Similar pieces were seen on the surface during a visit to the area. The small, ovate bifaces and biface thinning

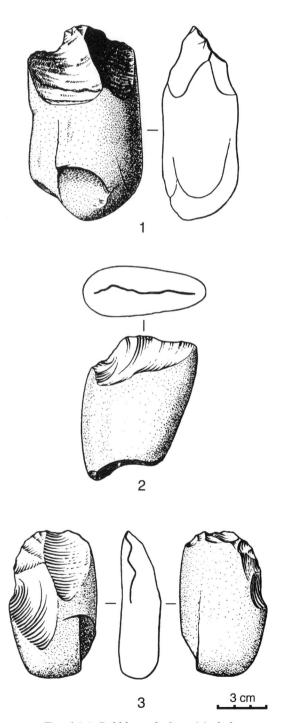

Fig. 14.3. Bifaces and flake tools from Vishnëvka 6

Fig. 14.4. Pebble tools from Muzbel

flakes show evidence of soft hammer use. Together, the retouched pieces and small bifaces are suggestive of a Middle Palaeolithic assemblage. However, the good raw material was in demand and exploited at other times as seen from the mixture of materials from different periods evident on the surface.

Muzbel I

The Muzbel artefacts were found on the surface of Late Pliocene pebble deposits in the Sarysu river (Voloshin 1989, 1998). The assemblage from Muzbel I is on quartzite pebbles (Figs. 14.4 and 14.5) and is often highly reminiscent of quartzite assemblages in Iberia (Moloney 1994). The quartzite is medium to fine grained and appears extremely tough to work. The artefacts studied include choppers, chopping tools, a few flake tools and unretouched flakes, a uniface, cleaver and a few cores with centripetal removals. The chopper/chopping tools could have been used as tools in themselves or as cores for the removal of flakes. In general appearance, the Muzbel artefacts appear 'crude', clearly resulting from the fact that the raw material consisted of well-rounded pebbles. Because of the nature of the lithic scatter, dating of the Muzbel pebble tools does not appear to be possible at this time.

DATING AND TYPOLOGY

Type and degree of weathering have often been used to assign a relative date to assemblages from Central Kazakhstan. It is often the only avenue available and can, at times, give a general date; for example, the presence of the Levallois technique indicates an undefined Middle Palaeolithic. However, it is much more dangerous to suggest an Early Lower Palaeolithic age on the basis of the presence of pebble tools and/or crudeness of manufacture, because, as mentioned above, this may be purely the result of raw material constraints. Furthermore, wind erosion of materials through exposure on the open steppes of Central Kazakhstan can cause pieces to appear older than they are. Relative dating based on surface erosion of artefacts can therefore be misleading.

CONCLUSION

Human penetration into Central Asia may well have occurred a million or more years ago. Voloshin's work has produced substantial evidence for the occupation in Central Kazakhstan during the Lower and Middle Palaeolithic, although at present, the dating of these occurrences is problematic due to the lack of long stratigraphic sequences. The Batpak Valley sequence is important in its potential to address questions of dating, and in facilitating a better understanding of the period of earliest occupation. It therefore merits renewed geological and geomorpho-

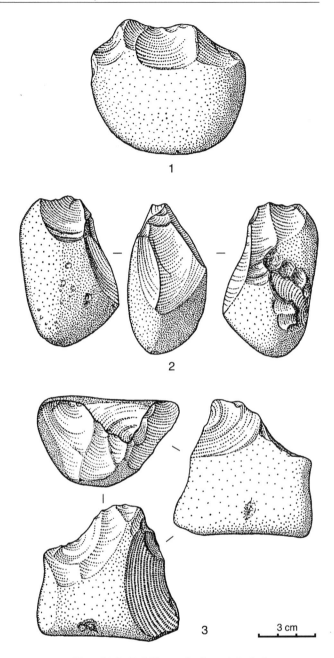

Fig. 14.5. Pebble tools from Muzbel

logical analyses to determine the taphonomic history of its sediments.

A second difficulty with the Kazakh sites is the predominance of surface materials, and the concomitant loss of information this implies. However, those of us who live outside the former Soviet Union and who do not read Russian have little access to information about the Palaeolithic of Kazakhstan. The surface materials deserve our attention as they can provide a significant contribution to our understanding of the Lower and Middle Palaeolithic, and allow us to place the occupation of Kazakhstan within the more immediate context of Central Asia, and the wider context of Eurasia.

ACKNOWLEDGEMENTS

The work undertaken in Kazakhstan was made possible by generous grants from the Foundation for Exploration and Research on Cultural Origins (FERCO) and the Ingall Foundation. Olsen and Moloney would like to thank the Presidential Cultural Center in Astana, Kazakhstan, and Valery Voloshin for the kind assistance and warm welcome extended to them. Dr Alan Walker was also an integral part of this project and obtained funding from the Ingall Foundation. We are very grateful for his participation and intellectual input.

REFERENCES

Ashton, N.M. and McNabb, J. 1994. Bifaces in perspective. In N.M. Ashton and A. David (eds.) *Stories in Stone*, 182–191. Lithic Studies Society Occasional Paper 4, London.

Berggren, W.A., Kent, D.V., Swisher, C.C. and Aubry, M.-P. 1995. A revised Cenozoic geochronology and chronostratigraphy. In W.A. Berggren, D.V. Kent, M.-P. Aubry and J. Hardenbol (eds.) *Geochronology, Time Scales, and Global Stratigraphic Correlation*, 129–212. Society for Economic Palaeontology and Mineralogy Special Publication 54, Tulsa, Oklahoma.

Boriskovskii, P.I. 1984. *The Paleolithic of the U.S.S.R.* Nauka, Moscow (in Russian).

Derev'anko, A.P., Petrin, V.T. and Taimagambetov, Z.K. 1997a. *Early Paleolithic Assemblages in Travertine, Southern Kazakhstan: A Variant of an Adaptive Model*. Technical Report, Russian Academy of Sciences Siberian Division, Institute of Archaeology and Ethnography, Novosibirsk.

Derev'anko, A.P., Petrin, V.T. and Taimagambetov, Z.K. 1997b. *Paleolithic Sites of Surficial Occurrence in the Arid Zone of Eurasia: Methods of Studying and Informative Potentialities*. Technical Report, Russian Academy of Sciences Siberian Division, Institute of Archaeology and Ethnography, Novosibirsk.

Gabunia, L., Vekua, A., Lordkipanidze, D., Swisher, C.C., Ferring, R., Justus, A., Nioradze, M., Tvalchrelidze, M., Antón, S.C., Bosinski, G., Jöris, O., de Lumley, M.-A., Majsuradze, G. and Mouskhelishvili, A. 2000. Earliest Pleistocene hominid cranial remains from Dmanisi, Republic of Georgia: taxonomy, geological setting, and age. *Science* 288, 1019–1025.

Gabunia, L. and Vekua, A. 1995. A Plio-Pleistocene hominid from Dmanisi, East Georgia, Caucasus. *Nature* 373, 509–512.

Kasymov, M.R. and Grechkina, T.Y. 1994. Kul'bulak (Uzbekistan) and its significance for the Paleolithic of Central Asia. In A.G. Kozintsev, V.M. Masson, N.F. Solovyova and V.Y. Zuyev (eds.) *New Archaeological Discoveries in Asiatic Russia and Central Asia*, 5–13. Institute of History of Material Culture, Russian Academy of Sciences, St Petersburg.

Moloney, N. 1993. Lithic production and raw material exploitation at the Middle Pleistocene site of El Sartalejo, Spain. *Papers from the Institute of Archaeology* 3, 11–22.

Moloney, N. 1994. *Lithic Assemblages from the Middle Pleistocene of Iberia: The Typology and Technology of Quartzite Artefacts in the Spanish Meseta and Portugal*. Unpublished PhD Thesis, University of London.

Otte, M. and Derev'anko, A.P. 2000. Transformations techniques au Paléolithique de l'Altai (Sibérie). In M. Otte (ed.) *Approches du Comportement au Moustérien*, 95–105. British Archaeological Reports International Series 833, Oxford.

Otte, M., Derev'anko, A.P., Petrin, V.T. and Taimagambetov, Z.K. 2000. Paléolithique au Kazakhstan. In M. Otte (ed.) *Approches du Comportement au Moustérien*, 106–114. British Archaeological Reports International Series 833, Oxford.

Ranov, V. 1991. Les sites très ancien de l'âge du pierre en U.R.S.S. In E. Bonifay and B. Vandermeersch (eds.) *Les Premiers Européens*, 209–216. CTHS, Paris

Schick, K.D. and Dong, Z. 1993. Early Paleolithic of China and Eastern Asia. *Evolutionary Anthropology* 2, 22–35.

Schick, K.D., Toth, N., Qi, W., Clark, J.D. and Etler, D. 1991. Archaeological perspectives in the Nihewan Basin, China. *Journal of Human Evolution* 21, 13–26.

Stringer, C. and Gamble, C. 1993. *In Search of the Neanderthals*. Thames and Hudson, London.

Swisher, C.C., Curtis, G.H., Jacob, T., Getty, A.G., Suprijo, A. and Widiasmoro 1994. Age of the earliest known hominids in Java, Indonesia. *Science* 263, 1118–1121.

Voloshin, V. 1989. The typological-stratigraphic scheme for the Paleolithic of Central Kazakhstan. *Margulana Archaeological Conference Proceedings*, 70–74 (in Russian).

Voloshin, V. 1993. Research at Batpak (Central Kazakhstan). *Siberian Anthropological Review*, 263–267 (in Russian).

Voloshin, V. 1998. New Paleolithic sites in the Sarysu Basin. In *The Stone Age of Kazakhstan*. Miras, Turkestan (in Russian).

Waters, M.R., Forman, S.L. and Pierson, J.M. 1997. Diring Yuriakh: a Lower Palaeolithic site in Central Siberia. *Science* 275, 1281–1284.

White, M.J. 1998. On the significance of Acheulean biface variability in Southern Britain. *Proceedings of the Prehistoric Society* 64, 15–45.

15. Venta Micena, Barranco León-5 and Fuentenueva-3: three archaeological sites in the Early Pleistocene deposits of Orce, south-east Spain

Josep Gibert, Lluís Gibert, Carlos Ferràndez-Canyadell,
Alfredo Iglesias and Fernando González

ABSTRACT

This contribution shows the results of twenty-five years of research in the region of Orce by a team led by one of the authors. During these years, more than twenty palaeontological localities have been discovered. Some of these are also archaeological sites but they have not all been excavated yet. After all these years of research, the Orce region has become a key area for understanding human biological and cultural evolution during the Lower Pleistocene. In this paper, we describe the three most important archaeological sites and their finds in the global context of the first dispersal of *Homo* out of Africa. In our opinion, this took place rapidly and followed different routes, one of them across the Straits of Gibraltar.

INTRODUCTION

Until 1976, the north-east sector of the Baza Basin (Orce region) was unknown from a palaeontological point of view. The site of Venta Micena was then discovered by a team from the Palaeontological Institute of Sabadell including N. Sànchez (now deceased), J. Agustí and J. Gibert who led the survey. Although no fossil remains had previously been reported from this area, its geological characteristics on the margin of a lake basin where shallow lacustrine, palustrine and alluvial sediments alternate, alerted the survey to the potential of new palaeontological sites. Thus, the first and most important site of Venta Micena was found. In subsequent surveys carried out in 1979 and 1981, further palaeontological localities were discovered. Then in 1982, the first excavation was carried out at Venta Micena. During this excavation a large collection of fossil material was recovered, and a human skull fragment was recognised amongst these fossils. Despite interruptions and difficulties, excavations led by J. Gibert have continued at various sites in the Orce region.

GENERAL SETTING

The archaeological sites of Venta Micena, Barranco León-5 and Fuentenueva-3 are situated in the north-east sector of the Guadix-Baza basin in south-east Spain (Fig. 15.1). This part of the basin exposes a continental sedimentary sequence more than one hundred metres thick. Sedimentation in this basin was almost continuous from the Late Miocene up to the Upper Pleistocene. The Plio-Pleistocene deposits which outcrop in this sector represent seven major depositional cycles. These began with fluviatile sedimentation and ended with lacustrine. The archaeological sites of Orce are located in the lacustrine deposits of the Lower Pleistocene or 'Venta Micena' cycle (L. Gibert *et al.* 1999).

Venta Micena

The Venta Micena deposits correspond to a calcareous mud plain located close to a palaeolake shoreline and affected by edaphic processes. The bed containing abundant fossil mammal remains is about 75 cm thick, and it can be traced for about two kilometres. The accumulation of mammal remains in these deposits can be attributed to the activities of carnivores close to the lake shore. During the last twenty years, the authorities have given permission for only six excavations at Venta Micena. Four of these were carried out in the 1980s and two in the 1990s. The last permit to excavate this site was granted in 1995. In the course of these excavations, 250 square metres were

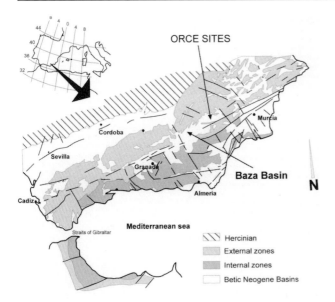

Fig. 15.1. Geological location of the Baza basin in south-east Spain

Class	Order	Species
Mammalia	Primates	*Homo* sp.
	Carnivora	*Homotherium latidens* *Megantereon* sp. *Lynx* sp. *Canis etruscus* *Canis falconeri* *Vulpes praeglacialis* *Pachycrocuta brevirostris* *Meles* sp. *Ursus etruscus*
	Perissodactyla	*Dicerorhinus etruscus brachycephalus* *Equus granatensis*
	Proboscidea	*Mammuthus meridionalis*
	Artiodactyla	*Hippopotamus amphibius antiquus* *Praemegaceros* sp. Cervidae indet. *Hemitragus alba* *Soergelia minor* *Bubalus* sp.
	Lagomorpha	*Apodemus* aff. *mystacinus* *Prolagus calpensis* *Oryctolagus* cf. *lacosti*
	Rodentia	*Allophaiomys pliocaenicus* *Eliomys intermedius* *Castillomys crusafonti* *Hystrix major*
	Insectivora	*Desmana* sp.
Amphibia	Anura	*Rana* sp.
Reptilia	Testudines	*Testudo* sp.
	Squamata	*Lacerta* sp.
Aves	Charadriiformes	indet.

Table 15.1. Fauna identified at Venta Micena.

partially excavated of three different surfaces of the same fossiliferous bed. The excavations have produced 10,335 bones representing at least 214 individual animals. This profusion of material is one reason for considering Venta Micena to be one of the most important Lower Pleistocene palaeontological sites in Europe. The fossils include three human fragments which show signs of carnivore scavenging. The species represented at the site are listed in Table 15.1.

Barranco León

Site BL-5 at Barranco León is located in a fine sand bed that corresponds to the distal part of a small and ephemeral alluvial system. The thickness of this bed varies between 10 and 25 cm (Gibert *et al.* 1992a). Systematic work on this site was carried out in the summer of 1995, and the area excavated was 20 square metres. The excavation revealed the mandible of *Hippopotamus amphibius antiquus* surrounded by more than a hundred stone artefacts and associated with *Castillomys* cf. *crusafonti*, *Mimomys* sp., *Allophaiomys* sp., *Equus granatensis* and a human molar fragment (Fig. 15.2) (Gibert *et al.* 1998b).

Fuentenueva-3

The Fn-3a site is located in a marginal zone of the basin. The sediments which outcrop there belong to a marginal lacustrine environment with different proportions of detrital material and organic matter in each level. The first stone artefacts were found on the surface together with fossil remains by J. Gibert and J. Serrallonga during a survey in 1990. In 1992, more artefacts turned up while an electricity company was at work nearby (Gibert *et al.* 1992a). This was followed by systematic excavations in

1995 when numerous stone artefacts were found in association with *Mimomys* sp., *Allophaiomys* sp., *Equus granatensis*, *Hippopotamus amphibius antiquus*, *Mammuthus meridionalis*, and indeterminate bovids. Most of the artefacts were closely associated with remains of large mammals (Gibert *et al.* 1998b).

CHRONOLOGY

Agustí *et al.* (1997) have reported a transition from reverse polarity to nine metres of normal polarity in the Barranco de Orce section. According to these authors, this normal polarity interval corresponds to the Olduvai event because of the presence of *Allophaiomys pliocaenicus* in the Orce-7 level. Stratigraphic correlations between the Orce-7 site and the archaeological site of Barranco León-5, show that both sites have a similar age (Gibert *et al.* 1998b).

New magnetostratigraphic data (Scott and Gibert 1999) revealed that the normal polarity reported by Agustí *et al.* (1997) from Barranco de Orce was in fact reversed. These new data, together with the stratigraphic framework (Gibert *et al.* 1998b) indicate that the site of Barranco León-5 is

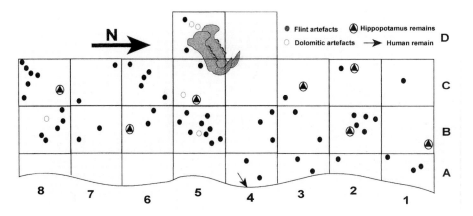

Fig. 15.2. Excavated surface at Barranco León

located in an epoch of reverse polarity. This was confirmed by new palaeomagnetic data from Barranco León (Oms *et al.* 2000). The new magnetic data show that up to now only reverse polarities have been found in the Orce area. The archaeological sites of Venta Micena, Barranco León-5 and Fuentenueva-3 are located in an epoch of reverse polarity between the Olduvai and Jaramillo events. The thickness of the lacustrine sediments of reversed polarity overlying these sites (12 metres at Fuentenueva-3; 15 metres at Barranco León-5) suggests that they are far from the Jaramillo epoch. This is confirmed by the presence of *A. pliocaenicus* at Venta Micena layers 1 and 2, and Barranco León layers 3 and 4, which indicates an early Lower Pleistocene age (Fig. 15.3) (Berggren *et al.* 1995).

The site of Dmanisi, Georgia, is also located in a reverse polarity interval close to the Olduvai event (Gabunia *et al.* 2000). Faunal comparisons between this site and Venta Micena indicate a similar age although the Spanish site is slightly younger. The chronological frameworks for the deposits containing human fossil remains and stone artefacts in the Orce region are therefore based on palaeomagnetic, palaeontological and stratigraphic data. These data do not allow the age of the sites to be exactly determined. However, both the faunal assemblages and the presence of thick sections with reverse polarity overlying the sites argue for a first human presence in this region at about 1.5 myr.

EVIDENCE OF HUMAN ACTIVITY

Venta Micena

Human activity is represented at Venta Micena by stone artefacts, as well as cut marks and percussion fractured bones. The cut marks are similar to those observed on bones from East African sites (Olduvai and East Lake Turkana). Cut marks are distinguishable from other surface marks on the bone cortex by their characteristic location and grouping, as well as features such as micro striations which can be observed using a scanning electron microscope (Fig. 15.4) (Gibert and Jiménez 1991). Study of the

fracture patterns on the bones from Venta Micena revealed percussion breaks attributable to human action (Gibert and Ferràndez 1989; Gibert *et al.* 1992b). The bones also show marks and fractures characteristic of carnivore activity, mainly that of hyaenids, thus suggesting competition between hominids and carnivores in obtaining proteins (Fig. 15.5).

Stone artefacts from Barranco León-5 and Fuentenueva-3

In 1995 excavations at Barranco León-5 (BL-5) yielded 116 stone artefacts and those at Fuentenueva-3a (Fn-3a) 100 artefacts. These are summarised by their raw materials in Table 15.2.

The flint from BL-5 is of good quality and mainly grey in colour. The cores are small (Fig. 15.6) with a mean length of 43 mm. Their surfaces show centripetal flake removals. Flakes are abundant and range between 20 and 61 mm long, with a mean length of 40.7 mm (Figs. 15.7–15.8). The butts are varied in their morphology and the dorsal surfaces usually lack cortex. Two chopper-cores, one of flint and the other of dolomite, have worked edges (Fig. 15.9). At Fn-3a, the flint is also of good quality but is uniformly white in colour. Some pieces have secondary iron oxide staining, and the cores exhibit centripetal flaking (Fig. 15.6). Their mean length is 65 mm. The flakes have plain butts, and their mean length is 59 mm with a range of 21–64 mm (Fig. 15.10). A chopper-core of quartzite (Fig. 15.9) is abraded on its cortical face and

Raw material	BL-5	Fn-3a
Flint	114	98
Quartzite	1	1
Jurassic dolomite	1	1
Dolomite manuports	4	20

Table 15.2. Artefacts from Barranco León-5 and Fuentenueva-3 by raw material.

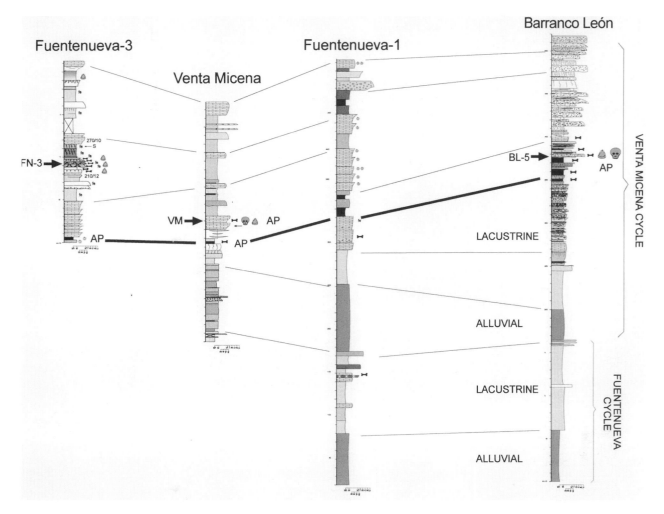

Fig. 15.3. Stratigraphic correlation between the sections at Venta Micena, Fuentenueva-3, Fuentenueva-1 and Barranco León. The correlation shows the relative position of the sites and the location of the beds with Allophaiomys pliocaenicus (AP).

Fig. 15.4. SEM photomicrograph of cut marks on a fossil bone from Venta Micena (VM-1270). The enlargement shows the microstriations typical of such marks.

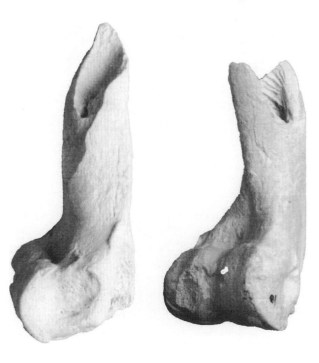

Fig. 15.5. Percussion (left) and carnivore (right) fractures of bone from Venta Micena.

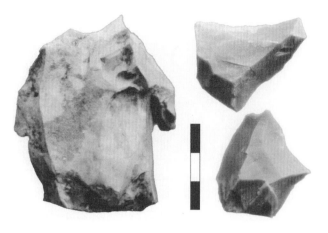

Fig. 15.6. Cores from Barranco León-5 (left) and Fuente-neuva-3 (right).

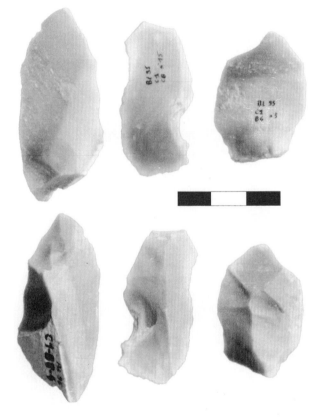

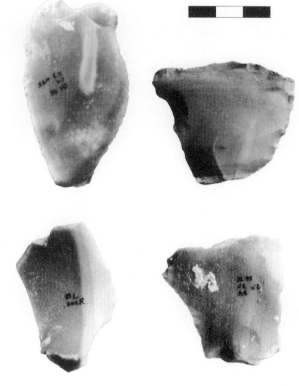

Fig. 15.7. Flakes from Barranco León-5.

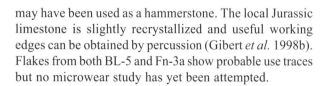

Fig. 15.8. Flakes from Barranco León-5.

Fig. 15.9. Flint chopper-core from Barranco León-5 and another in quartzite from Fuentenueva-3.

may have been used as a hammerstone. The local Jurassic limestone is slightly recrystallized and useful working edges can be obtained by percussion (Gibert *et al.* 1998b). Flakes from both BL-5 and Fn-3a show probable use traces but no microwear study has yet been attempted.

THE HUMAN REMAINS

Four human fossils have been described from the deposits in the Orce region, three of which are from Venta Micena and the fourth from Barranco León-5. The human remains from Venta Micena consist of a juvenile skull fragment (Fig. 15.11) referred to as VM-0 (Borja 1999; Borja *et al.* 1992, 1997; Campillo 1989, 1992; Campillo and Barcélo 1989; Campillo *et al.* in press; Gibert and Palmqvist 1995; Gibert *et al.* 1983, 1989a, 1989b, 1989c), a juvenile humeral shaft (Fig. 15.11), VM-1960 (Borja *et al.* 1997; Gibert *et al.* 1994a, 1999a; Sánchez *et al.* 1999), and an adult humeral shaft, VM-3691 (Gibert *et al.* 1994a; Sánchez *et al.* 1999). The only human fossil as yet identified at Barranco León is a molar fragment (Fig. 15.12), BL-0 (Gibert *et al.* 1999b).

Fig. 15.10. Flakes from Fuentenueva-3.

VM-0

The fragment of skull VM-0 consists of a small portion of the calvaria which includes the lambdoid region. The piece has some fracture lines, showing no signs of osseus regeneration but the deformation is of little importance. The maximum width is 76 mm and the maximum length is 80 mm. The borders of the occipital apex, which have been preserved, have a length of 17.5 mm at their right side and 10.5 mm at their left side, forming an angle of approximately 119°. The whole osseus surface is eroded forming a reticle with some considerably deep sulci which on occasion exceed one mm.

It is worth noting the presence of important fracture lines. The first is located in the most external part of the right parietal bone, rectilinear and parallel to the sagittal suture. A second, transverse fissure, somewhat oblique (16°), crosses the sagittal suture at 31 mm from the lambda point. Finally, a right posterior transverse fracture originates in the lambda point. There is no significant deformation.

The sutures are quite simple. The sagittal suture becomes simpler still 18 mm from the lambda, as it usually occurs in the obelic region. All the sutures are free, preserving no signs of synostosis. There is no posthumous erosion of the endocranial surface. The thickness of the bone is between 2 mm, or even less, at the depth of the digital impressions, and 4 mm approximately at the tips of the mammiliary protuberances. However, we must take into account the posthumous erosion of the exocranial surface. The whole of the surface appears quite dented due to the abundance of digital impressions which are more marked in the proximity of the lambdoid suture, and gradually fade as they move away from 35 mm of the lambda.

In the anterior part of the piece, the sagittal groove is practically imperceptible, becoming clearly visible from 32 mm of the lambda, where its width is approximately 7 mm and deepening along its trajectory. At 20 mm from the lambda, it has a width of 7.5 mm and depth of 1 mm, becoming separated from the middle line here and turning to the right. Just at the apex of the superior occipital angle, the groove is already at the right side in parasagittal position and its internal border (left side) has an osseus crest which originates in the middle line, rising rapidly and sticking out 5.5 mm with regards to the opening of the sagittal groove (7 mm including the thickness of the squama) at a distance of 15 mm from the apex. This crest is narrow, 1.8 mm in its higher point and 4 mm in its base, bending towards the right. The external border of the opening (the right one) is nearly imperceptible and it can only be perceived at 8 mm from the crest. In the same way as in the endocranium, sutures appear with no complications. The sagittal suture becomes irregularly dented from the lambda onwards, with no excessive complication, and at 18 mm its sinuosity diminishes, just as in the obelic region (Campillo 1989).

Some authors (Agustí and Moyà 1987; Moyà and Agustí 1989; Moyà and Kölher 1997) have questioned the identification of VM-0 as human and interpreted it as an equid. Their doubts are based mainly on the presence of a supposed coronal suture and have been rebutted. This supposed suture is actually a fracture, as has been demonstrated by radiological studies, as well as by comparative anatomical evidence (Campillo 1989, 1992; Campillo and Barcélo 1989; Campillo *et al.* in press; Gibert *et al.* 1989c, 1998a).

Humeral fragments

Two humeral fragments, VM-1960 and VM-3691, were excavated from the same faunal assemblage and stratigraphic level as the cranial fragment VM-0. The mor-

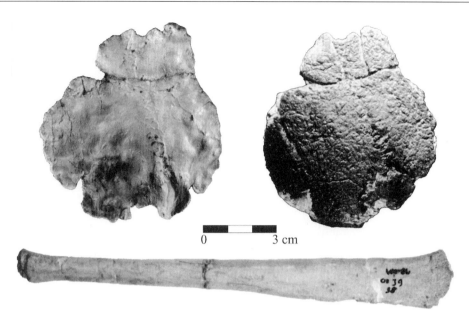

Fig. 15.11. Dorsal and ventral views of the human skull fragment VM-0 and humeral fragment VM-1960.

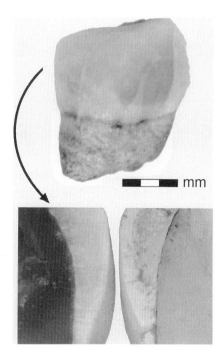

Fig. 15.12. Molar fragment from Barranco León-5 compared to a modern specimen to show the similarity in enamel thickness.

phology, morphometry and paleoimmunology of the two fragments were studied using several complementary methods. The results of these studies place the humeral fragments inside the range of variability for *Homo* and separates them from humeri of similarly sized carnivores and cercopithecoid species, both recent and fossil, occurring in the Lower Pliocene of south-eastern Spain (Gibert *et al*. 1994a, 1999a).

Molar fragment

The molar fragment from Barranco León, BL-0 (Fig. 15.12), was studied in detail using various methods (Gibert *et al*. 1999b). Several characters indicate that it should be assigned to *Homo*: the first stria of the imbricate portion of the enamel, the enamel prism pattern, the arrangement of the Hunter-Schreger bands, the enamel thickness, and the presence of perikimatas. All these data exclude this fossil from being a non-human mammal.

Immunological data

The fossils at Venta Micena are in a good state of preservation. They are found in almost pure, fine (micritic) carbonate sediments. This carbonate mud penetrated the trabecular bone and most probably helped to preserve the organic molecules found independently by two teams led by E. García-Olivares (University of Granada, Spain) and J.M. Lowenstein (University of California, USA). These immunological studies (Lowenstein 1995) detected human albumin and IGg in the skull fragment VM-0, as well as equid and bovid proteins in equid and bovid bones respectively, from the same site (Borja 1999; Borja *et al*. 1997).

THE STRAITS OF GIBRALTAR: A PLEISTOCENE BRIDGE TO EUROPE

The presence of human remains and Palaeolithic artefacts in the Lower Pleistocene of south-eastern Spain and Dmanisi, Georgia, suggests that the colonisation of Eurasia by *Homo* followed two routes, one via the Levant corridor, the other via the Straits of Gibraltar. At present, a distance of fourteen kilometres separates Europe from Africa across the Straits of Gibraltar. The possibility that *Homo* crossed such a wide marine barrier during the Lower Pleistocene is not one that is generally considered. However, when the evidence is analysed, the Straits become a probable alternative route for human dispersal out of Africa. Different kinds of data, palaeontological, geological, palaeogeographical, palaeoclimatic and oceanographic, all strengthen the hypothesis that *Homo* did cross the Straits of Gibraltar for the first time during the early Lower Pleistocene.

With regard to the palaeontological data, the presence of African mammal species in the Lower Pleistocene of the Iberian peninsula indicates the possibility of crossing the Straits during those times (see also Rolland this volume). The clearest evidence of faunal exchange between the two continents comes from the presence of *Theropithecus* cf. *oswaldi* in the Lower Pleistocene deposits of Cueva Victoria, Murcia, in south-east Spain. *Theropithecus* definitely has an African origin (Gibert *et al.* 1994b). Other species which might have an African origin and which are reported from Lower Pleistocene deposits in south-east Spain are *Hippopotamus amphibius antiquus* and *Equus granatensis*. At least one migration of a European species took place in the opposite direction to Africa. Geraads (1997) has reported *Ursus etruscus* from Upper Pliocene (2.4 myr) deposits in Morocco. This is a typical Plio-Pleistocene European species occurring in deposits dating between 3 myr (Etouaires, Villaroya) and 1.8–1.7 myr (Venta Micena, Olivola and Tasso). The available data do not allow the exact migration route of *U. etruscus* to Africa to be traced, although the Straits of Gibraltar cannot be excluded as a possibility. However, during the last three million years sea levels were lowered during various cold periods. Lowered sea levels considerably reduced the distance across water between Europe and Africa. This fact, together with the presence in the Iberian peninsula of African mammal species during the Lower Pleistocene, as well as the presence of at least one European species in north Africa during the Upper Pliocene, indicates that a faunal exchange took place between the continents.

A major Plio-Pleistocene fall of sea level of up to 130 m (Roberts 1992) reduced the distance between Europe and Africa through the Straits of Gibraltar to less than 5 km (Fig. 15.13), uncovering islands which might have acted as stepping stones for a selective crossing by land mammals. Such a distance probably did not represent a major barrier for organised groups of *Homo*. The penetration of *Homo* further north was probably constrained by colder climate.

CONCLUSION

Human remains, Palaeolithic artefacts and evidence of anthropic activity on bones occur in the Lower Pleistocene deposits of the Orce region. This evidence suggests a rapid dispersal of *Homo*, which probably reached the south-western part of Europe through the Straits of Gibraltar at the same time as migrating towards the east, to Georgia, China and Java.

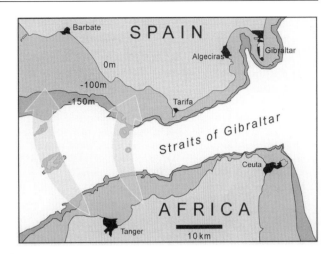

Fig. 15.13. Palaeogeographical reconstruction of the Straits of Gibraltar after a fall in sea level of 150 metres. The distance between Africa and Europe is reduced to 2– 5 kilometres and islands appear. Topographic sea floor data obtained from Sanz et al. *(1991).*

ACKNOWLEDGEMENTS

We are indebted to Professor Derek Roe. He was the first independent researcher to consider the lithic material from Orce as genuine artefacts during his first visit to the region in the summer of 1993. His support has helped us in our difficult research.

REFERENCES

Agustí, J. and Moyà, S. 1987. Sobre la identidad del fragmento craneal atribuido a *Homo* sp. de Venta Micena (Orce, Granada). *Estudios Geológicos* 42, 535–538.

Agustí, J., Oms, O. and Parès, J.M. 1997. Calibration of the Late Pliocene-Early Pleistocene transition in continental beds of the Guadix-Baza Basin (SE Spain). *Quaternary International* 40, 93–100.

Berggren, W.A., Kent, D.V., Swisher, C.C. and Aubry, M.-P. 1995. A revised Cenozoic geochronology and chronostratigraphy. In W.A. Berggren, D.V. Kent, M.-P. Aubry and J. Hardenbol (eds.) *Geochronology, Time Scales, and Global Stratigraphic Correlation*, 129–212. Society for Economic Palaeontology and Mineralogy Special Publication 54, Tulsa, Oklahoma.

Borja, C. 1999. Estudio de proteínas en fósiles. In J. Gibert, F. Sánchez, L. Gibert and F. Ribot (eds.) *The Hominids and their Environment during the Lower and Middle Pleistocene of Eurasia*, 49–64. Ayuntamiento de Orce, Museo de Prehistoria y Paleontología J. Gibert, Orce.

Borja, C., García-Pacheco, M., Ramírez-López, J.P. and García-Olivares, E. 1992. Cuantificación y caraterización de la albumina fósil del craneo de Orce. In J. Gibert (ed.) *Presencia Humana en el Pleistoceno Inferior de Granada y Murcia*, 415–424. Museo de Prehistoria y Paleontología J. Gibert, Orce.

Borja, C., García-Pacheco, M., García-Olivares, E., Scheuenstuhl, G. and Lowenstein, J. 1997. Immunospecifity of albumin detected in 1.6 million year old fossils from Venta Micena in Orce, Granada, Spain. *American Journal of Physical Anthropology* 103, 433–441.

Campillo, D. 1989. Study of the Orce man. In J. Gibert, D. Campillo and E. García-Olivares (eds.) *Los Restos Humanos de Orce y Cueva Victoria*, 187–220. Institut Paleontològic Dr M. Crusafont, Sabadell. Diputacío de Barcelona.

Campillo, D. 1992. Estudio del hombre de Orce. In J. Gibert (ed.) *Presencia Humana en el Pleistoceno Inferior de Granada y Murcia*, 341–371. Museo de Prehistoria y Paleontología J. Gibert, Orce.

Campillo, D. and Barceló, J.A. 1989. Morphometric study of the internal surface of the squama occipitalis. In J. Gibert, D. Campillo and E. García-Olivares (eds.) *Los Restos Humanos de Orce y Cueva Victoria, 109–186*. Institut Paleontològic Dr M. Crusafont, Sabadell. Diputacío de Barcelona.

Campillo, D., Rovira, M., Sánchez-Sánchez, J.A., Vila, S., Gibert, J. and Gibert, Ll. in press. The Orce skull (VM-0): X-ray study. *Human Evolution*.

Gabunia, L., Vekua, A., Lordkipanidze, D., Swisher, C.C., Ferring, R., Justus, A., Nioradze, M., Tvalchrelidze, M., Antón, S., Bosinski, G., Jöris, O., de Lumley, M.-A., Majsuradze, G. and Mouskhelishvili, A. 2000. Earliest Pleistocene hominid cranial remains from Dmanisi, Republic of Georgia: taxonomy, geological setting and age. *Science* 288, 1019–1025.

Geraads, D. 1997. Carnivores du Pliocène terminal de Ahl Al Oughlam (Casablanca, Maroc). *Geobios* 30, 127–164.

Gibert, J. and Ferràndez, C. 1989. Action anthropique sur les os à Venta Micena (Orce, Grenada, Espagne). In J. Gibert, D. Campillo and E. García-Olivares (eds.) *Los Restos Humanos de Orce y Cueva Victoria*, 295–327. Institut Paleontològic Dr M. Crusafont, Sabadell. Diputacío de Barcelona.

Gibert, J. and Jiménez, C. 1991. Investigations into cut-marks on fossil bones of Lower Pleistocene age from Venta Micena (Orce, Granada, Spain). *Human Evolution* 6, 117–128.

Gibert, J. and Palmqvist, P. 1995. Fractal analysis of the Orce skull sutures. *Journal of Human Evolution* 28, 561–575.

Gibert, J., Agustí, J. and Moyà, S. 1983. Presencia de *Homo* sp. en el yacimiento del Pleistoceno inferior de Venta Micena (Orce, Grenada). *Paleontologia i Evolució*, 1–9. Institut Paleontològic Dr M. Crusafont, Sabadell. Diputacío de Barcelona.

Gibert, J., Ribot, F., Ferràndez, C., Martínez, B. and Ruz, C. 1989a. Diagnosis diferencial del fragmento de cráneo de *Homo* sp. del yacimiento de Venta Micena (Orce, Granada). In J. Gibert, D. Campillo and E. García-Olivares (eds.) *Los Restos Humanos de Orce y Cueva Victoria*, 31–108. Institut Paleontològic Dr M. Crusafont, Sabadell. Diputacío de Barcelona.

Gibert, J., Ribot, F., Ferràndez, C., Martínez, B. and Caporicci, R. 1989b. Caracteristicas diferenciales entre el fragmento de cráneo de *Homo* sp. de Venta Micena (Orce, Granada) y los équidos. *Estudios Geologicos* 45, 121–138.

Gibert, J., Campillo, D., Caporicci, R., Ribot, F., Ferràndez, C. and Martínez, B. 1989c. Anatomical study: comparison of a hominid cranial fragment from Venta Micena (Orce, Spain) with fossil and extant mammals. *Human Evolution* 4, 283–305.

Gibert, J., Iglesias, A., Maillo, A. and Gibert, Ll. 1992a. Industrias líticas en el Pleistoceno inferior en la región de Orce. In J. Gibert (ed.) *Presencia Humana en el Pleistoceno Inferior de Granada y Murcia*, 219–283. Museo de Prehistoria y Paleontología J. Gibert, Orce.

Gibert, J., Ferràndez, C., Martínez, B., Caporicci, R. and Jiménez, C. 1992b. Roturas antrópicas en los huesos de Venta Micena y Olduvai. Estudio comparativo. In J. Gibert (ed.) *Presencia Humana en el Pleistoceno Inferior de Granada y Murcia*, 283–305. Museo de Prehistoria y Paleontología J. Gibert, Orce.

Gibert, J., Sánchez, F., Malgosa, A. and Martínez, B. 1994a.

Découvertes des restes humains dans les gisements d'Orce (Granada, Espagne). *Comptes Rendus de l'Académie des Sciences de Paris* Series 2, 319, 963–968.

Gibert, J., Leakey, M., Ribot, F., Gibert, Ll., Arribas, A. and Martínez, B. 1994b. Presence of the cercopithecid genus *Theropithecus* in Cueva Victoria (Murcia, Spain). *Journal of Human Evolution* 28, 487–493.

Gibert, J., Campillo, D., Arqués, J.M., García-Olivares, E., Borja, C. and Lowenstein, J. 1998a. Hominid status of the Orce cranial fragment reasserted. *Journal of Human Evolution* 34, 203–217.

Gibert, J., Gibert, Ll. and Iglesias, A. 1998b. Two 'Oldowan' assemblages in the Plio-Pleistocene deposits of the Orce region, southeast Spain. *Antiquity* 72, 17–25.

Gibert, J., Malgosa, A., Sánchez, F., Ribot, F. and Walker, M. 1999a. Humeral fragments attributable to *Homo* sp. from Lower Pleistocene sites at Venta Micena (Orce, Granada, Spain). In J. Gibert, F. Sánchez, L. Gibert and F. Ribot (eds.) *The Hominids and their Environment during the Lower and Middle Pleistocene of Eurasia*, 87–112. Ayuntamiento de Orce, Museo de Prehistoria y Paleontología J. Gibert, Orce.

Gibert, J., Albadalejo, S., Gibert, L., Sánchez, F., Ribot, F. and Gibert, J. 1999b. The oldest human remains of the Orce region. *Human Evolution* 14, 3–19.

Gibert, L., Maestro, E., Gibert, J. and Albadalejo, S. 1999. Plio-Pleistocene deposits of the Orce region (SE Spain): geology and age. In J. Gibert, F. Sánchez, L. Gibert and F. Ribot (eds.) *The Hominids and their Environment during the Lower and Middle Pleistocene of Eurasia*, 127–144. Ayuntamiento de Orce, Museo de Prehistoria y Paleontología J. Gibert, Orce.

Lowenstein, J.M. 1995. Immunological reactions on fossil bones from Orce. Abstracts of the *International Conference on Human Palaeontology (Orce, Granada)*, 27.

Moyà, S. and Agustí, J. 1989. Una reinterpretación del fragmento craneal de Orce: *Equus stenonis*. In J. Gibert, D. Campillo and E. García-Olivares (eds.) *Los Restos Humanos de Orce y Cueva Victoria*, 447–451. Institut Paleontològic Dr M. Crusafont, Sabadell. Diputacío de Barcelona.

Moyà, S. and Köhler, M. 1997. The Orce skull: anatomy of a mistake. *Journal of Human Evolution* 33, 91–97.

Oms, O., Parès, J.M., Martínez-Navarro, B., Agustí, J., Toro, I., Martínez-Fernández, G. and Turq, A. 2000. Early human occupation of western Europe: paleomagnetic dates for two Palaeolithic sites in Spain. *Proceedings of the National Academy of Sciences* 97, 10666–10670.

Roberts, N. 1992. Climatic change in the past. In S. Jones, R. Martin and D. Pilbeam (eds.) *The Cambridge Encyclopaedia of Human Evolution*, 174–178. Cambridge University Press, Cambridge.

Sánchez, F., Gibert, J., Malgosa, A., Ribot, F., Gibert, Ll. and Walker, M. 1999. Insights into the evolution of child growth from Lower Pleistocene humeri at Venta Micena (Spain). *Human Evolution* 14, 63–82.

Sanz, J., Acosta, J., Esteras, M., Herranz, P., Palomo, C. and Sandoval, N. 1991. *Prospección Geofisíca del Estrecho de Gibraltar*. Publicaciones Especiales 7, Institut Español de Oceanografia. Ministerio de Agricultura, Pesca y Alimentacíon, Madrid.

Scott, G. and Gibert, Ll. 1999. Evaluation of the Olduvai sub-chron in the Orce region. Abstracts of the EUROMAM workshop, *The Guadix-Baza Basin and the Chronostratigraphy of the Terrestrial Plio-Pleistocene in Europe (Orce, Spain)*, 11–12.

16. Excavations at Cueva Negra del Estrecho del Río Quípar and Sima de las Palomas del Cabezo Gordo: two sites in Murcia (south-east Spain) with Neanderthal skeletal remains, Mousterian assemblages and late Middle to early Upper Pleistocene fauna

Michael J. Walker

ABSTRACT

For the past decade field research has been conducted annually at Sima de las Palomas del Cabezo Gordo and Cueva Negra in Murcia province, south-east Spain. These sites incorporate numerous Neanderthal and pre-Neanderthal hominid remains, Mousterian assemblages, and abundant remains of both large fauna, as well as small mammals and birds. Sima de las Palomas del Cabezo Gordo is situated beside the coastal plain. Cueva Negra del Estrecho del Río Quípar lies ninety kilometres away in the north-western uplands. At both sites there are signs of the intentional use of fire. Brief summaries are offered of the salient points concerning hominid remains, Palaeolithic artefacts, faunal remains and environmental contrasts.

SIMA DE LAS PALOMAS

Sima de las Palomas ('Dove Hole') is an 18 metre deep natural karstic shaft, opening at 120 metres above sea-level on the 312 metre high Triassic limestone Cabezo Gordo hill which dominates the coastal plain beside the 'Mar Menor' Mediterranean salt water lagoon (Walker and Gibert 1999b). A century ago, iron miners removed most of its breccia fill apart from an 18 metre high column against its rear wall which spans 130,000–60,000 BP. Recent work has focused on these deposits.

Dating

Age estimates have been obtained from uranium-thorium (U/Th), optical sediment luminescence (OSL) and electron spin resonance (ESR) determinations. To assist in this work, Derek Roe and John Mitchell took sediment cores where background irradiation had been determined using a γ-ray spectrometer lent by Professor Michael Tite of Oxford University's Research Laboratory for Art and Archaeology, who, with Ed Rhodes, analyzed photon luminescence for OSL or optical sediment luminescence determination.

Unfortunately, all but one of the samples failed and even this was only partially saturated and not ideal. However, it did provide a maximum age of 157 kyr on a core taken half way down the Sima de las Palomas breccia column where background irradiation implies 1.25 Gray per millennium. This, in turn, suggests that ESR determinations obtained by Dr Peter Pomery and David Hunter of Queensland University can be corrected. Their results were obtained on three splinters of bone with breccia adhering to them which were found in the mine rubble before the excavations began. Assuming background irradiation of 1 or 2 Gray per millennium, age estimates of 83,000/42,000 and 146,000/73,000 were determined (Gibert *et al.* 1994). A third determination of 532,000/26,000 BP is anomalous (*ibid.*). Given the background irradiation calculated by Oxford, a correction to 66,000 and 117,000 BP may be in order for the first value of each of the alternative ESR determinations from Queensland.

These corrections are in line with the uranium-thorium determinations made by Dr Juan Antonio Sánchez-Cabeza and J. García-Orellana in the Department of Physics at the Autonomous University, Barcelona. An age of 56 kyr BP was achieved on an aragonite crystal found close to where the first hominid fossil was removed from the breccia column in 1991, near to the level now reached in our 'upper cutting'. An age of 124 kyr BP was obtained on another crystal removed from the foot of the column (Sánchez-Cabeza *et al.* 1999). As it gave only a maximum age, the OSL determination could fit with the two older U/ Th dates. A skull of the late Middle Pleistocene *Panthera pardus* cf. *lunellensis* was removed by spelaeologists from this low part of the breccia column. Charcoal samples submitted to Professor Robert Hedges of the Oxford laboratory contained insufficient carbon for radiocarbon dating.

Finds

Three six metre thick units of cemented lutite, silt, sand and angular stones are separated by calcretes that probably formed on partiallly eroded surfaces of pleniglacial aggradations. At the top of the breccia column, our 'upper cutting' measures two metres long but varies from 60 to 120 cm wide according to what was left by the miners. An eighteen metre high scaffolding tower built inside the shaft gives access to it. Excavation here from 1994 to 2000 has removed two metres of fill. Surprisingly for a karstic shaft, it shows a mainly horizontal stratigraphy only sporadically interrupted by intrusive scree from rock falls. Important finds here include an adult Neanderthal hemimandible, an infant mandible, teeth and postcranial bones of juveniles and adults, including a molar with grooving probably caused by tooth-picks, Mousterian artefacts and, in 1999 and 2000, a 20 cm thick 'hearth'. Near here, an adult Neanderthal mandible fused to the maxillae but now separated, was extracted from the breccia in 1991 by a spelaeologist, just outside the deepest part of our 'upper cutting'. U/Th suggests an age of 65 kyr–55 kyr BP. Significant finds also come from mine rubble on the hillside and at the bottom of the shaft which we have sieved. Sediments in the floor of the Main Chamber are being investigated in our two metre deep 'lower cutting'.

Artefacts

A total of 750 classifiable pieces, more than half of which are unretouched flakes, as well as 1650 fragments and spalls have been collected from the deposits. The material is considered to be Mousterian. The tools include Tayac, Levallois and pseudo-Levallois points, convergent scrapers ('stubby points'), side and endscrapers, as well as notched and denticulate pieces. There are also two thick retouched Levallois flakes which are carinated and have tiny awl-like noses and some hammerstones. The artefacts are made of flint, quartz, rock-crystal, limestone and quartzite. The source of the flint is unknown; no flint outcrops occur on Cabezo Gordo and the nearest known source of good quality flint is twenty kilometres away. A jasper core and flake must come from a known source twenty-five kilometres away.

Hominid remains

Over eighty fragmentary hominid bones and teeth have been recovered (Table 16.1; Walker and Gibert 1999a; Walker *et al.* 1998, 1999a, 1999b). Unstratified items include two right lateral parts of burnt frontal bones with supraorbital tori and lateral trigones which are compatible with a Neanderthal attribution, an infant's maxilla with tooth roots, a fragment of a juvenile mandible with an unerupted permanent canine from a child of about nine years old, two burnt adult hemimandibles (see below), and postcranial remains including long bones with typically narrow Neanderthal medullary cavities. Whilst these could come from high up in the breccia column (c. 55 kyr–65 kyr BP), it is more likely that the two unstratified burnt fragments with plesiomorphous pre-Neanderthal features came from burnt soil lenses low down in the breccia column where geophysical determinations imply an age of 130 kyr–115 kyr BP. Although gas chromatography did not indicate a high organic content within these lenses, X-ray diffraction analyses highlighted a preponderance of sand which indicates thermal effects, given the presence of carbonates, phosphates, as well as sand, in over- and under-lying sediments. Of the first two hominid fragments attributed to these lenses, one is a burnt left temporal squama with a salient, vertically thick, zygomatic process presenting a preglenoid planum rather than articular tubercle before an anteroposteriorly wide, vertically shallow, mandibular fossa (a planum and shallow fossa flatter than in children today). The second fragment is a burnt frontal central fragment of a robust left supraorbital torus (and postorbital sulcus) lacking nasofrontal sinus extension (cf. Saccopastore 2, Hexian PA-830) lateral to a vast frontal notch (cf. Steinheim, Zuttiyeh, Kabwe, Yunxian EV-9002, Zhoukoudian XII). These two fragments would certainly seem out of place among the 'upper cutting' Neanderthals.

Two burnt hemimandibles from the mine rubble show interesting differences. One, perhaps male, has a low, wide body and is chinless, albeit with a vertical symphyseal profile with a hint of a mental trigone though lacking mental eminences. It has a marked digastric fossa, a triangular submaxillary fossa and an oval mental foramen of great size due to burning at high temperature, and it resembles Middle Pleistocene specimens including those from Atapuerca Sima de los Huesos. The other, perhaps female, has a higher, narrower body containing crazed fragments of all the permanent teeth although only M_2 and M_3 are preserved above the neck. It has a chinless, vertical symphyseal profile (Sánchez *et al.* 1999).

Fauna

The faunal assemblage (Table 16.2) now exceeds 8000 classifiable skeletal elements, several of which are burnt. These occur in a rough ratio of five mammalian bones for every one tortoise and one avian bone. Twelve thousand indeterminate splinters have also been recovered. It should

Ident.	Bone or tooth type	Age	Found	Provenance at Sima de las Palomas
CG-1	mandible fused to maxilla	adult	1991	upper breccia
CG-2	right mandibular body	adult	1995	hillside, mine rubble
CG-3	occipital fragment	adult	1992	hillside, mine rubble
CG-4	parietal fragment	adult	1992	hillside, mine rubble
CG-5	parietal fragment	adult	1992	hillside, mine rubble
CG-6	left mandibular body	adult	1993	between main chamber scree slope and mine level
CG-7	mandibular body	child	1993	mine level
CG-8	axis vertebra	adult	1993	hillside, mine rubble
CG-9	axis vertebra	juvenile	1993	hillside, mine rubble
CG-10	intrasutural Wormian bone	adult	1993	mine level
CG-11	left temporal squama	young adult	1993	main chamber scree slope
CG-12	left temporal fragment	adult	1994	hillside, mine rubble
CG-13	parietal fragment	adult	1995	hillside, mine rubble
CG-14	left frontal fragment, supraorbital torus, trigone	adult	1994	hillside, mine rubble
CG-15	right frontal fragment, supraorbital torus	adult	1993	main chamber scree slope
CG-16	frontal fragment	adult	1992	hillside, mine rubble
CG-17	fibula fragment	adult	1994	hillside, mine rubble
CG-18	left ulna	baby/foetus	1994	upper cutting, layer (2b)
CG-19	right metacarpal III fragment	adult?	1994	main chamber scree slope
CG-20	left humeral fragment		1994	
CG-21	left epitrochlear humeral fragment		1994	hillside, mine rubble
CG-22	right maxillary canine	adult	1994	upper cutting, layer (2d)
CG-23	left mandibular medial incisor	adult	1994	upper cutting, layer (2)
CG-24	distal phalangeal bone of hand		1995	upper cutting, layer (2g)
CG-25	maxillary molar crown	child	1995	upper cutting, layer (Ia)
CG-26	left maxillary canine	adult	1995	upper cutting, layer (Ia)
CG-27	right maxillary medial incisor	adult	1995	hillside, mine rubble
CG-28	left mandibular deciduous molar	child	1995	upper cutting, layer (2f)
CG-29	left maxillary medial incisor	juvenile/adolescent	1995	upper cutting, layer (2k)
CG-30	right mandibular canine	adolescent	1995	upper cutting, layer (2f)
CG-31	right maxillary deciduous canine	child	1995	upper cutting, layer (2i)
CG-32	tooth germ	baby/foetus	1995	upper cutting, layer (2f)
CG-33	right mandibular molar	adult	1995	upper cutting, layer (2h)
CG-34	deciduous canine	child	1995	hillside, mine rubble
CG-35	left maxillary l deciduous medial incisor	infant	1995	upper cutting extension, layer (Ia)
CG-36	permanent molar crown	child	1995	upper cutting extension, layer (Ia)
CG-37	right maxillary lateral incisor	adult	1996	upper cutting extension, layer (Ib)
CG-38	molar fragment		1996	upper cutting extension, layer (Ib)
CG-39	left maxillary medial incisor	adolescent	1996	upper cutting extension, layer (Ia)
CG-40	right? mandibular medial incisor	adolescent	1996	upper cutting extension, layer (Ib)
CG-41	anterior right mandibular premolar	adolescent	1996	upper cutting extension, layer (Ib)
CG-42	germ of molar crown	infant	1996	upper cutting extension, layer (Ia)
CG-43	molar in maxillary fragment		1996	upper cutting extension, layer (I)
CG-44	worn single-root tooth	adult	1996	upper cutting extension, layer (Ib)
CG-45	root of single-root tooth		1996	upper cutting extension, layer (Ib)
CG-46	root of single-root tooth	adult	1995	upper cutting, layer (2i)
CG-47	right mandibular medial incisor	adolescent	1996	upper cutting extension, layer (Ib)B
	mandibular fragment	infant	1996	upper cutting extension, layer (2a)
	2 mandibular body fragments	infant	1996	upper cutting extension, layer (Ia)
	zygomatic fragment		1996	hillside, mine rubble
	distal phalangeal bone		1996	upper cutting extension, layer (Ib)
	humeral trochlea	infant	1996	hillside, mine rubble
	distal phalangeal bone		1996	upper cutting extension, layer (Ia)
	proximal humeral fragment	child	1995	upper cutting, layer (2i)
	mastoid process (tympanic bulla)		1996	hillside, mine rubble
	vertebral fragment		1996	hillside, mine rubble
	orbital fragment		1996	hillside, mine rubble
	vertebral fragment		1996	upper cutting extension, layer (Ib)
	head and neck of radius		1996	upper cutting extension, layer (2a)
	patella		1996	upper cutting extension, layer (Ia)
	patellar fragment		1996	hillside, mine rubble
	pubic bone fragment		1995	upper cutting, layer (2i)
	fragment of fibula shaft		1995	upper cutting, layer (2i)
	fragment of vertebral neural arch		1995	upper cutting, layer (2i)
	symphsyeal pubic fragment	adult/adolescent	1995	upper cutting extension, layer (Ia)
	left maxillary fragment	infant	1995	hillside, mine rubble
	proximal shaft of radius		1996	upper cutting extension, layer (Ia)
	tooth root in bone fragment		1996	upper cutting extension, layer (Ia)
	zygomatic/facial fragment		1996	hillside, mine rubble
	left maxillary fragment	adult	1997	hillside, mine rubble
	mandibular right anterior premolar	adult	1997	upper cutting extension, layer (2d)
	maxillary left posterior premolar	adult	1997	upper cutting extension, layer (2c)
	maxillary left lateral incisor	adult	1997	upper cutting extension, layer (2c)
	left mandibular body with dentition	adult	1998	upper cutting extension, layer (2f)
	molar*	adult	1998	upper cutting extension, layer (2d)
	premolar*	adult	1998	upper cutting extension, layer (2f)
	molar*	infant	1998	upper cutting extension, layer (2f)
	left frontal fragment with supraorbital torus	adult	1998	hillside, mine rubble
	middle phalangeal bone	adult	1999	found on scaffolding platform below top of tower
	middle phalangeal bone	adult	2000	hillside, mine rubble

Identification numbers CG-32 to CG-47 are provisional and subsequent items are awaiting assignation of numbers
* Still partly covered by breccia, in process of laboratory cleaning for identification

Table 16.1. Hominid remains from Sima de las Palomas

Class	Order	Species
Mammalia	Primates	*Homo sapiens* cf. subsp. *neanderthalensis* *Homo sapiens* cf. subsp. *heidelbergensis/ steinheimensis*
	Carnivora	*Panthera pardus* cf. subsp. *lunellensis* *Panthera (Leo)* sp. *Felis (Lynx)* cf. *spelaea* *Felis* cf. *sylvestris* *Crocuta crocuta* subsp. *spelaeus* Hyaenidae indet. *Ursus* sp. *Vulpes* sp. *Canis* sp. *Meles meles* subsp.
	Perissodactyla	*Equus caballus* subsp. *Equus (Asinus)* sp. *Stephanorhinus* sp.
	Proboscidea	Elephantidae indet.
	Artiodactyla	*Hippopotamus amphibius* *Bos/Bison* sp. *Capra* sp. *Cervus elaphus* *Dama* sp.
	Lagomorpha	*Oryctolagus cuniculus* subsp. Leporidae indet.
	Chiroptera	*Myotis* sp. Chiroptera indet.
	Insectivora	*Erinaceus* sp.
Reptilia	Testudines	*Testudo* cf. *graeca*
	Squamata	*Lacerta* cf. *lepida*
Aves	Falconiformes	*Falco tinnunculus* *Falco naumanni*
	Galliformes	*Alectoris rufa*
	Columbiformes	*Columba livia***
	Strigiformes	*Athene noctua*
	Passeriformes	*Galerida cristata/theklae* *Saxicola torquata* *Monticola solitarius* *Pyrrhocorax graculus** *Pyrrhocorax pyrrhocorax*** *Corvus corone* *Passer domesticus* *Emberiza* sp.*

Avian remains came mainly from our 'lower cutting' (heavily disturbed by mining), but asterisks indicate: * avian species *only* found in hillside mine rubble (mixed with modern bird species); ** avian remains found *also* in our upper cutting (undisturbed Pleistocene sediment).

Table 16.2. List of vertebrate fauna from Sima de las Palomas

be mentioned that although signs of burning are seen on several human remains found in the mine rubble, relatively few human remains from the 'upper cutting' show these, notwithstanding the presence of a hearth.

CUEVA NEGRA

Cueva Negra del Estrecho del Río Quípar ('Black Cave' of the river Quípar Gorge) lies ninety kilometres from Sima de las Palomas. Systematic excavation began in 1990. It is a north-facing rock-shelter in the north-western Murcian uplands lying 40 metres above the river, at 780 metres above sea-level in an Upper Miocene fossiliferous sandy limestone (biocalcarenite), where test-pits were dug in 1981 (Martínez Andreu *et al.* 1989). Neanderthal remains here comprise an ulnar shaft, part of a humeral shaft and six permanent teeth (Table 16.3). There are many Middle Palaeolithic stone tools made of flint, chert, quartzite and limestone, and three whittled-down antler pedicles, one retaining the dense skull bone of its insertion, which are probably soft hammer knapping billets. The scars were probably made artificially in order to cut away the rest of the antler. No distal antler fragments show such scars, nor do horns or bones, hence these objects are unlikely to be due to animal-gnawing. Furthermore no porcupine bones, teeth or quills have been found, an animal that often sharpens its teeth on the ends of broken horns or long bones (Brain 1981, 109–117).

Fauna

There is a rich fauna consisting of some 7000 mammalian, 2200 avian and 1300 tortoise remains, as well as 11,000 unclassifiable splinters and fragments (Table 16.4). A late Middle or earliest Upper Pleistocene chronology is suggested by *Prolagus*, *Macaca* (teeth and a maxillary fragment), and a skull fragment of *Megaceros* with attached massive crown-beam antlers which was excavated in unit 3. As stags bear antlers in the colder months of the year, this fossil might suggest that people frequented the Murcian uplands during that season when crown beams with cranial bone attached to the pedicle were available for whittling down into knapping billets, from cervids either killed by predators or hunted. Indeed, they may have been easier prey at this time of year because I have seen wild deer approach humans holding out forage when the Scottish Highlands are covered in deep snow, although in summer they avoid people. Cold conditions are implied by the 15% loess content of the soil and numerous retraction fissures. Faunal analysis suggests that different biotopes intersected at Cueva Negra: gallery woodland in the valley, perhaps with refuges of deciduous plants and trees (acorn-loving jays and wood-pigeons; monkeys); areas of swamps and even deep lakes (waterfowl including wading and even diving species, and migrants present only in the colder months of the year); grassland, scrub and stands of pine trees. The intersection of different biotopes occurs at other Mousterian sites (cf. Eastham 1989, 1999).

Rhinocerotid mandibles (*Stephanorhinus* (*Dicerorhinus*) cf. *hemitoechus*) have been found in unit 2. An adult hemimandible had its ascending ramus gnawed by a carnivore, a juvenile mandible lay beside its cranium within which were found a Neanderthal canine tooth and three chert pieces, and a Neanderthal ulnar shaft lay nearby. Other large herbivore remains include elephant, bison, aurochs, equids, cervids, boar and wild goat (ibex). Small

Ident.	Description	Metre square	Unit and spit
CN-1	left lateral lower permanent incisor (adult)	B1i	Disturbed surface soil
CN-2	left upper permanent canine (adult)	C3e	2c (excavated, closed find)
CN-3	left ulnar diaphysis	C3c	2c (excavated, closed find)
CN-4	right lower first permanent premolar (juvenile)	C2e	3ñ (excavated, closed find)
CN-5	right upper first permanent premolar (adult)	C1a	Disturbed surface soil
CN-6	left lateral upper permanent incisor (adult)	B2f	Disturbed surface soil
CN-7	anterior permanent tooth root	C4g	2c (excavated, closed find)
CN-8	proximal fragment of (right?) humeral diaphysis	C2i	2g (excavated, closed find)

Table 16.3. Hominid remains from Cueva Negra

game is plentiful, and some of the remains show signs of burning. These include fragments of bird bones and eggshell, tortoise, rabbit and hare, and may suggest intentional roasting. Hyaenas and bears were present, perhaps when humans were absent, and may have been responsible for introducing several of the cranial elements and teeth of the large herbivores excavated. However, detailed taphonomic and statistical analyses of the faunal assemblage are far from complete, and the chert fragments and Neanderthal tooth found touching a rhinocerotid skull might excite a different conjecture here.

Geochronology

Palaeopalynological (Carrión *et al.* 1999) and geophysical research has so far failed to provide geochronological information, but is continuing. The sediments inside the cave cannot be younger than the contiguous river terrace outside that stopped aggrading 40,000 years ago throughout the Segura drainage basin. Geological comparison with geophysical determinations from similar terraces elsewhere in Murcia and nearby Alicante implies an early Upper Pleistocene age for the fluviatile terrace which is apparently continuous with the sedimentary fill of Cueva Negra. Throughout the region, this '*glacis*-terrace B', the surface of which lies, here as elsewhere, at 35 to 40 metres above modern valley floors, aggraded during very cold conditions with low fluviatile activity, low rainfall, and low evapo-transpiration, capable only of permitting seasonal summer swamps on riverine floodplains (cf. Cuenca Payá and Walker 1985, 1986, 1995; Cuenca Payá *et al.* 1986; Walker *et al.* 1998). The absence of sorted gravels from our excavation implies cold conditions, low fluviatile activity, low rainfall and low evapo-transpiration. Rounded cobbles (>5 centimetres across) excavated from the deposits do not come from the Miocene biocalcarenite bedrock; these cobbles of flint, chert, quartzite, quartz and fine-grained siliceous metamorphosed Jurassic dolomite clasts were brought as manuports from a conglomerate outcrop exposed by Quaternary erosion some 800 metres away. In Upper Miocene Vindobonian (Tortonian) times this outcrop had been a pebble beach where the Tethys Sea lapped against Jurassic limestone cliffs. The use of this outcrop as a source of raw materials during the Middle Palaeolithic is confirmed

by the presence of discoidal cores both here and at the cave. Cobbles were also carried back to Cueva Negra for knapping and for use as hammerstones.

Artefacts

Twenty-five square metres of Cueva Negra are under excavation. To date this area has yielded 350 retouched artefacts and large unretouched flakes, as well as 4000 knapping spalls or fragments. Eighty percent of these are chert, while the remainder are limestone and quartzite. Amongst the tools, scrapers, denticulates and notched pieces predominate, with occasional burins and carinated pieces. Hammerstones have also been found. Two rock crystal fragments probably came from as far away as (or further than) Cabezo Gordo, which is the nearest source, although the rarity of exotic raw materials may imply little long-distance movement or exchange. The nature of the non-flint raw materials, and a tendency of the poor quality chert to break up into blocks along fracture planes, mean that even retouched pieces often lack distinct butts. Those that do exist are plain or facetted. Hints of spatio-temporal groupings of Palaeolithic artefacts in different layers and separate zones are being investigated with attention to conjoining analysis. The problem of comparing the relative abundance of artefacts in units 2 and 3 at Cueva Negra (Walker *et al.* 1998, 1999a) are gradually being overcome by extending the area under excavation. Although a one square metre test pit has reached a depth of 4 metres where in stratigraphical unit 4 a rhinoceros mandible, charcoal and chert artefacts were found, most of the twenty-five square metres in stratigraphical units 2 and 3 are still under excavation, in a series of steps leading down from the cave entrance where there are standing sections. Horizontal bedding predominates (Walker 1996, 1997, 1999).

CONCLUSIONS

Comparing Cueva Negra and Sima de las Palomas is still difficult because of the considerable difference in the areas excavated within them and the vast number of unstratified finds from mine rubble at the latter site (Walker and Gibert

Class	Order	Species
Mammalia	Primates	*Homo sapiens* cf. subsp. *neanderthalensis*
	Carnivora	*Crocuta crocuta* cf. subsp. *spelaeus* *Ursus* cf. *spelaeus* *Canis* cf. *lupus* Canidae indet.[a] Felidae indet.[b]
	Perissodactyla	*Stephanorhinus* (*Dicerorhinus*) cf. *hemitoechus* Rhinocerotidae indet. *Equus caballus* Equidae indet.
	Proboscidea	Elephantidae indet.
	Artiodactyla	Bovidae cf. *Bos primigenius*[c] *Capra ibex pyrenaica* *Megaceros* sp. *Cervus elaphus* Cervidae indet.[d]
	Lagomorpha	*Oryctolagus cuniculus* *Prolagus* sp. Leporidae indet.
	Rodentia	*Apodemus sylvaticus* *Arvicola* cf. *sapiolus* *Pitymys* sp. *Micromys* sp. *Microtus* sp.
	Chiroptera	Vespertilionidae indet.
	Insectivora	Soricidae indet.
Reptilia	Testudines	*Testudo* cf. *graeca*
Amphibia	Anura	indet.
Aves	Anseriformes	*Anser* sp.* *Tadorna* cf. *ferruginea* *Anas penelope* *Anas platyrhyncos* *Anas* cf. *strepera* *Anas crecca* *Anas* sp. *Netta rufina* *Aythya ferina* *Aythya nyroca*
	Falconiformes	*Milvus milvus* *Buteo buteo* *Buteo* cf. *rufinus* *Aquila* sp. *Falco tinnunculus* *Falco naumanni* *Falco peregrinus*
	Galliformes	*Gallus gallus** *Alectoris* cf. *barbara** *Alectoris rufa*
	Gruiformes	*Fulica atra*

Class	Order	Species
	Charadriiformes	*Pluvialis apricaria* *Vanellus vanellus* *Calidris minuta* *Gallinago gallinago* *Tringa hypoleucos*
	Columbiformes	*Columba palumbus** *Columba livia* *Strepopelia turtur*
	Strigiformes	*Tyto* cf. *alba* *Athene noctua**
	Caprimulgiformes	*Caprimulgus europaeus**
	Apodiformes	*Apus melba* *Apus apus*
	Coraciformes	*Merops apiaster*
	Piciformes	*Picus viridis**
	Passeriformes	*Alauda arvensis* *Lullula arborea* *Galerida cristata/theklae* *Ptyonprogne rupestris* *Riparia riparia* *Hirundo rustica* *Anthus spinoletta/campestris/novozeelandia* *Motacilla alba/cinerea* *Monticola saxatilis* *Monticola solitarius* *Turdus merula* *Turdus philomelos** *Acrocephalus arudinaceus** *Ficedula hypoleuca* *Parus major* *Garrulus glandarius* *Pica pica* *Pyrrhocorax graculus* *Pyrrhocorax pyrrhocorax* *Corvus corax* *Corvus corone* *Corvus* sp. *Fringilla coelebs* *Carduelis chloris* *Carduelis cannabina* *Pyrrhula pyrrhula* *Milaria calandra* *Emberiza citrinella* *Emberiza cirlus/cia*

[a]smaller than *Canis lupus*; [b]possibly *Felis* (*Lynx*) *lynx*; [c]a small *Bison*-like horn also occurs; [d]smaller than *C. elaphus*; *found in unstratified superficial soil only and possibly intrusive contaminants.

Table 16.4. List of vertebrate fauna from Cueva Negra

1999a; Walker *et al.* 1999b). Excavation is slow because at both sites excavated sediment is washed over nested geological sieves of 8, 6 and 2 mm mesh, so that microfaunal remains and tiny knapping spalls are collected. It would certainly be imprudent to propose site-catchment interpretations of plausible hominid behaviour until the role of non-human predators has been fully investigated. Likewise, despite the inhospitable winter climate at Cueva Negra even today, let alone in Ice Age times, our uncertainty as to whether there was any contemporaneity between the levels under excavation makes any speculation about possible seasonal palaeoeconomic complementarity between our two sites quite unwarranted. In any case, apart from having hominid skeletal remains, they do not otherwise stand alone in our region, because other undated Mousterian sites occur both upstream and downstream from Cueva Negra in the Quípar valley itself and several occur elsewhere throughout the Segura drainage basin, as well as near the Murcian coast, especially from Cartagena southwards.

ACKNOWLEDGEMENTS

We are most grateful to the Directorate-General for Scientific and Technological Research of the Spanish government for financial assistance during two three year-long major reseach projects (PB92–0971 and PB98–45) and for two Anglo-Spanish Joint Actions (HB1992–104, HB1995–0002), the Murcian Autonomous Community's Directorate-General for Culture for annual grants-in-aid from 1991 for excavation of either one or the other of our two sites and for providing gates and scaffolding at Sima de las Palomas, and The Earthwatch Institute for the support of its staff and members since 1994. The town councils of Caravaca de la Cruz and Torre Pacheco are thanked for greatly assisting us in many practical aspects of our annual field campaigns. I am also indebted to my co-directors: Dr José Gibert at Sima de las Palomas and Isaac Serrano and, formerly, Abel Gómez at Cueva Negra. Particular thanks are due to Anne Eastham for her analysis of the avifauna, and Alfonso Legaz for the micromammalian data. Many esteemed colleagues from several disciplines have and are continuing to make vital contributions to our research. I extend my gratititude to all of them.

REFERENCES

Brain, C.K. 1981. *The Hunters or the Hunted? An Introduction to African Cave Taphonomy.* University of Chicago Press, Chicago.

Carrión, J.S., Munuera, M., Navarro, C., Burjachs, F., Dupré, M. and Walker, M.J. 1999. Palaeoecological potential of pollen records in caves: the case of Mediterranean Spain. *Quaternary Science Reviews* 18, 67–78.

Cuenca Payá, A. and Walker, M.J. 1985. Comentarios sobre el Cuaternario continental en Alicante y Murcia. *Saitibi* 35, 207–218.

Cuenca Payá, A. and Walker, M.J. 1986. Palaeoclimatological oscillations in continental Upper Pleistocene and Holocene formations in Alicante and Murcia. In F. López-Vera (ed.) *Quaternary Climate in Western Mediterranean*, 365–376. Universidad Autónoma de Madrid, Madrid.

Cuenca Payá, A. and Walker, M.J. 1995. Terrazas fluviales en la zona bética de la Comunidad Valenciana. In V.M. Rosselló Verger (ed.) *El Cuaternario del País Valenciano*, 105–114. Asociación Española para el Estudio del Cuaternario y Universitat de València, Departament de Geografia, Valencia.

Cuenca Payá, A., Pomery, P.J. and Walker, M.J. 1986. Chronological aspects of the Middle Pleistocene in the coastal belt of southeastern Spain. In F. López-Vera (ed.) *Quaternary Climate in Western Mediterranean*, 353–363. Universidad Autónoma de Madrid, Madrid.

Eastham, A. 1989. Cova Negra and Gorham's Cave: evidence of the place of birds in Mousterian communities. In J. Clutton-Brock (ed.) *The Walking Larder: Patterns of Domestication, Pastoralism and Predation*, 350–357. Unwin Hyman, London.

Eastham, A. 1999. The role of birds in environmental reconstruction. In J. Gibert, F. Sánchez, L. Gibert and F. Ribot (eds.) *The Hominids and their Environment during the Lower and Middle Pleistocene of Eurasia*, 595–604. Ayuntamiento de Orce, Museo de Prehistoria y Paleontología J. Gibert, Orce.

Gibert, J., Walker, M.J., Malgosa, A., Sánchez, F., Pomery, P.J., Hunter, D., Arribas, A. and Maillo, A. 1994. Hominids in Spain: ice age Neanderthals from Cabezo Gordo. *Research and Exploration* 19, 120–123.

Martínez Andreu, M., Montes Bernárdez, R. and San Nicolás del Toro, N. 1989. Avance al estudio del yacimiento musteriense de la Cueva Negra de La Encarnación (Caravaca, Murcia). *Crónica. XIX Congreso Nacional de Arqueología, Castellón*

de la Plana 1987, Ponencias y Comunicaciones*, Volume 1, 973–983. Universidad de Zaragoza, Congresos Arqueológicos Nacionales, Zaragoza.

Sánchez, F., Gibert, J. and Walker, M.J. 1999. Descubrimiento de restos humanos del Pleistoceno medio en Murcia (Cabezo Gordo, España). In J. Gibert, F. Sánchez, L. Gibert and F. Ribot (eds.) *The Hominids and their Environment during the Lower and Middle Pleistocene of Eurasia*, 249–259. Ayuntamiento de Orce, Museo de Prehistoria y Paleontología J. Gibert, Orce.

Sánchez-Cabeza, J.-A., García-Orellana, J. and Gibert, L. 1999. Uranium-thorium dating of natural carbonates: application to the Cabezo-Gordo site (Murcia, Spain). In J. Gibert, F. Sánchez, L. Gibert and F. Ribot (eds.) *The Hominids and their Environment during the Lower and Middle Pleistocene of Eurasia*, 261–268. Ayuntamiento de Orce, Museo de Prehistoria y Paleontología J. Gibert, Orce.

Walker, M.J. 1996. El yacimiento del Pleistoceno Superior de la Cueva Negra del Estrecho de La Encarnación, Caravaca de la Cruz, Murcia: campaña 1990. *Memorias de Arqueología* 5, 11–19. Comunidad Autónoma de la Región de Murcia, Dirección General de Cultura, Instituto de Patrimonio Histórico, Murcia.

Walker, M.J. 1997. La Cueva Negra del Estrecho de La Encarnación, Caravaca de la Cruz, Murcia: campaña de 1991. *Memorias de Arqueología* 6, 11–16. Comunidad Autónoma de la Región de Murcia, Dirección General de Cultura, Instituto de Patrimonio Histórico, Murcia.

Walker, M.J. 1999. La Cueva Negra del Estrecho del Quípar de La Encarnación, Caravaca de la Cruz: campaña de 1993. *Memorias de Arqueología* 8, 43–49. Comunidad Autónoma de la Región de Murcia, Dirección General de Cultura, Instituto de Patrimonio Histórico, Murcia.

Walker, M.J. and Gibert, J. 1999a. Dos yacimientos murcianos con restos neandertalenses: La Sima de las Palomas del Cabezo Gordo y la Cueva Negra del Estrecho del Quípar de La Encarnación. *Actas del XXIX Congreso Nacional de Arqueología, Cartagena, 28–31 Octubre 1997*, Volume 1, 299–310. Comunidad Autónoma de la Región de Murcia, Dirección General de Cultura, Instituto de Patrimonio Histórico, Murcia.

Walker, M.J. and Gibert, J. 1999b. La Sima de las Palomas del Cabezo Gordo (Torre Pacheco, Murcia): investigaciones preliminares de 1993. *Memorias de Arqueología* 8, 33–41. Comunidad Autónoma de la Región de Murcia, Dirección General de Cultura, Instituto de Patrimonio Histórico, Murcia.

Walker, M.J., Gibert, J., Sánchez, F., Lombardi, A.V., Serrano, I., Eastham, A., Ribot, F., Arribas, A., Sánchez-Cabezas, J.-A., García-Orellana, J., Gibert, L., Albaladejo, S. and Andreu, J.A. 1998. Two SE Spanish middle palaeolithic sites: Sima de las Palomas del Cabezo Gordo and Cueva Negra del Estrecho del Río Quípar (Murcia province). *Internet Archaeology* 5 (autumn/winter 1998) http://intarch.ac.uk/journal/issue5/walker index.html

Walker, M.J., Gibert, J., Sánchez, F., Lombardi, A.V., Serrano, I., Gómez, A., Eastham, A., Ribot, F., Arribas, A., Cuenca, A., Gibert, L., Albaladejo, S. and Andreu, J.A. 1999a. Excavations at new sites of early man in Murcia: Sima de las Palomas del Cabezo Gordo and Cueva Negra del Estrecho del Río Quípar de la Encarnación. *Human Evolution* 14, 99–123.

Walker, M.J., Gibert, J., Sánchez, J., Lombardi, A.V., Serrano, I., Gómez, A., Ribot, F., Gibert, L., Cuenca, A., Albadalejo, S. and Andreu, J.A. 1999b. Sedimentologic study of Sima de las Palomas del Cabezo Gordo and Cueva Negra del Estrecho del Río Quípar de La Encarnación (Murcia, Spain): two hominid sites from the Middle and Upper Pleistocene. In J. Gibert, F. Sánchez, L. Gibert and F. Ribot. (eds.) *The Hominids and their Environment during the Lower and Middle Pleistocene of Eurasia*, 235–248. Ayuntamiento de Orce, Museo de Prehistoria y Paleontología J. Gibert, Orce.

17. Acheulian handaxe variability in Middle Pleistocene Italy: a case study

Sarah Milliken

ABSTRACT

This paper presents the results of a study of Acheulian handaxe variability in a series of assemblages from the Apennine foothills between Bologna and Imola in the region of Emilia-Romagna, north-east Italy. The assemblages derive from a number of Middle Pleistocene terrace units for which a detailed lithostratigraphic and geomorphological context has been established, and as a result the assemblages can be attributed with some confidence to four distinct Oxygen Isotope Stages. The aim of the study was to apply a modified version of the method for morphometric description and analysis of handaxes devised by Roe (1964, 1968), in order to examine whether any chronological patterns could be ascertained with regard to handaxe variability.

INTRODUCTION

The history of research on the morphological variability of handaxes mirrors changing theoretical paradigms over the course of the twentieth century. Culture-historical concerns with ideas such as a gradual evolution in handaxe morphology from crude and unsophisticated to more elaborate and refined forms, were replaced by a focus on reduction sequences and, in particular, the role played by lithic raw material type and blank form in conditioning handaxe shape (Ashton and McNabb 1994; Jones 1994; McPherron 1995, 2000; White 1998). Processual approaches such as these have recently been joined by attempts to apply a post-processual approach concerned with 'social technology', whereby the search for rules to explain handaxe variability is rejected as being unnecessary, and handaxes are simply treated as the material expressions of their makers (Gamble 1998; Kohn and Mithen 1999). Other ideas that have been rejected with the shift in theoretical paradigm away from culture-historical explanations include the possibility that different handaxe shapes may reflect mental templates in the minds of the makers, and that the predominance of certain handaxe shapes in assemblages may represent the inherited knapping traditions of different cultural groups (Ashton and McNabb 1994; Davidson and Noble 1993; White 1998).

In his discussion of the British Acheulian assemblages, Roe concluded that 'it is mainly the lack of clear dating for so many British sites that causes the picture to show bewildering variety rather than an orderly and predictable pattern of variation' (1981, 270). The question of what Roe termed 'vertical variation', which denotes differences between industries which occur in succession through a substantial period of time (*ibid.*, 131), has not been explored by later researchers working on the British material, despite the fact that revised dating of many of the sites, and in particular those in the Thames Valley (Bridgland 1994, 1998), would surely now permit such a line of enquiry. Likewise, outside of Britain, few studies have specifically explored the question of chronological trends in handaxe variability. In their study of more than 1100 handaxes from 17 sites in Africa, the Near East, India and Europe, Wynn and Tierson (1990) discovered regional patterns in the morphology of the handaxes but, given the absence of good dates for these sites, they were unable to determine whether chronological change may have been responsible for this. A specific attempt to search for chronological patterns was made by Saragusti *et al.* (1998), whose quantitative analysis of handaxe symmetry demonstrated a reduction in variability over time in small samples from three Acheulian sites in Israel, while an earlier study of Near Eastern handaxes by Gilead (1970) had demonstrated that these became smaller through time. However, once again the dating of these sites is tentative.

The assemblages discussed in this case study derive from a number of Middle Pleistocene terrace units for which a detailed lithostratigraphic and geomorphological context has been established, and as a result the assemblages can be attributed with some confidence to Oxygen Isotope Stages 13, 9, 7 and 6, thus covering the period from c. 500–130 kyr (Table 17.1). The aim of this study, which adopts an unashamedly processual stance, is to examine whether any chronological patterns can be ascertained with regard to handaxe variability over this time period, and to explore possible explanations for such variability. The handaxes were studied using a modified version of the method for morphometric description and analysis devised by Roe (1964, 1968), alongside analysis of the reduction sequence as discernible from raw material type, blank type and method of shaping. This case study does not pretend to resolve the apparent enigma of Acheulian handaxe variability, but merely aims to make a contribution to the debate by widening the geographic scope.

GEOMORPHOLOGY OF THE STUDY AREA

The region of Emila-Romagna is surrounded by the Apennines to the south-west, the Adriatic sea to the east and the river Po to the north. The region consists of five main geomorphological domains:

1. The Apennine mountain belt, where erosion strongly limits the possibilities of finding Palaeolithic sites.
2. The Apennine foothills, located between the outlet of the major river valleys and exposed to low sedimentation and erosion rates, where Palaeolithic artefacts are found both in secondary context and *in situ*.
3. Alluvial terrace units, deposited during humid-temperate periods and eroded during the cold-semiarid phases of the Pleistocene, where Palaeolithic artefacts are found both in secondary context and *in situ*.
4. The Po Plain, a flat surface consisting of Holocene alluvial, marsh and beach deposits, where artefacts of the Neolithic and later are found.
5. The flat coastal belt, which postdates the Flandrian transgression, where artefacts of the Bronze Age and later are found.

A detailed lithostratigraphic-geomorphological scheme of the continental Quaternary of the Apennine-Po Plain margin has recently been elaborated and the Middle Pleistocene is well documented with at least eleven units

in stratigraphic succession. The terraced deposits in the main valleys in this area are characterised by moderate thickness (2–6 metres), one or maybe two flooding events in quick succession, and only one pedogenized horizon at the upper boundary. These features are related on the one hand to the frequency and intensity of the tectonic uplift of the Apennines, and on the other hand to the flooding which occurred during the glacial-interglacial transition. The terraces mainly represent the glacial-interglacial transition periods and the warm interglacials, and are characterised by reddish or reddish-brown soils; the glacial periods are represented by only one yellow loess deposit

Terrace unit	OIS	Context of the assemblage	Sites
Bellaria	6	*in situ*	Bellaria Ca' Belvedere I Ca' San Carlo Collegio di Spagna Due Pozzi Fondo Vigna Fornace di San Lazzaro Il Borghetto Palazzina Palazzone-Ca' Roma Pescatore Piccolo Scornetta
San Biagio	7	*in situ*	Brusaida Ca' Rio La Cava Marascelle Pasotta Piangipane Poggio Domini Riniera Tombazza Villa Resta
Upper Molino	9	*in situ*	Ca' delle Donne Ca' Fontana Camponi Fontanaccio La Casaccia Peverella Podere Castello
Lower Molino	9	*in situ*	Ca' Rio Cava Fiorini Cava Valfiore Cave dall'Olio Cave S.A.F.R.A. Colombarina di Sopra Fornace di San Lazzaro Merlina Palazzina Poggio Domini Riniera
Oriolo	11	secondary context (redeposited from Stage 13 terrace)	Bellaria Cantiere Ca' delle Donne Ca' Fiume Casetta Tomba Dolina del Budriolo Passo della Portezza Podere Castello Torrente d'Idice

Table 17.1. Acheulian sites with handaxes in the study area

which is found in the Oxygen Isotope Stage 6 terrace unit (Farabegoli 1996; Farabegoli and Onorevoli 1996).

THE ACHEULIAN SEQUENCE IN THE STUDY AREA

Palaeolithic sites on the terraces of the rivers Sillaro, Savena, Zena, Idice and Quaderna, which lie along the 30 kilometre stretch between Bologna and Imola, first attracted the attention of antiquarians in the second half of the nineteenth century (Capellini 1870; Scarabelli 1850, 1890). Since then numerous surveys have been carried out by archaeologists and amateurs alike, in particular by Luigi Fantini in the 1950s (Fantini 1954, 1955, 1956). Fantini's collection, and the artefacts discovered in the second half of the twentieth century, are now housed at the Civic Museum in San Lazzaro di Savena, a suburb of the city of Bologna. To date there are 211 Acheulian find-spots from an area measuring approximately 100 square kilometres. These find-spots range from isolated artefacts to large assemblages numbering several thousand pieces (Lenzi and Nenzioni 1996).

The earliest Acheulian industries are found in secondary context in gravel deposits of the Oriolo terrace unit (OIS 11). These are thought to have derived from the Ca' Vallata unit (OIS 13) and are characterised by weathering. Younger Acheulian industries of a fresh condition are found *in situ* in four distinct geomorphological contexts: in red earth deposits in the lower part of the Molino terrace unit (OIS 9); in sandy silts at the top of the Molino terrace unit (OIS 9); in silts in the San Biagio terrace unit (OIS 7); and in loess deposits of the Bellaria terrace unit (OIS 6) (Table 17.1; Farabegoli and Onorevoli 1996).

Lithic assemblages from the Oriolo terrace unit and the lower part of the Molino terrace unit are characterised by macrolithic flakes with plain platforms, prominent bulbs and cortical dorsal surfaces, accompanied by flakes with centripetal flake scars struck from prepared cores. The assemblages are made up of variable quantities of un-retouched flakes, flake tools, handaxes, pebble tools/cores and platform cores. The typological composition of the assemblages appears to vary as a function of the raw material used. With only two exceptions all the handaxes were made from phthanite, a coarse-grained calcareous variety of chert with a subconchoidal fracture, which occurs in nodules, blocks and large cobbles measuring up to 100 centimetres in length. In contrast, pebble tools/cores and some flake tools were preferentially made from chert, which usually occurs in the form of small spherical cobbles measuring about 5–7 centimetres in diameter, although the fact that one of the two chert handaxes discussed below measures 13 centimetres in length suggests that larger nodules were occasionally available. In the Oriolo terrace unit the percentage of artefacts made from chert ranges between 0–11%, while in the Lower Molino terrace unit the value increases up to a maximum of 20%. More rarely silicified limestone was also used to make flake tools. The

fact that some of the assemblages are made exclusively of phthanite cannot be attributed to sample size: at Cave S.A.F.R.A., for example, all 399 artefacts were made from this raw material.

One of the largest assemblages from the Lower Molino terrace unit comes from the site of Palazzina in the Quaderna valley. The majority of the artefacts are made of phthanite and only 1% of chert. The chert artefacts consist of seven unretouched flakes, one sidescraper, one pebble tool/core and one platform core. The phthanite is of alluvial origin, as can be deduced from the spherical form of the pebbles and the surface abrasion on the cortex, and it is easily found eroding out of the margins of the foothills and in the river bed. Chert is also present in the area in the form of small and medium sized spherical and sub-spherical pebbles (Milliken *et al.* 1996a).

The assemblages from the Upper Molino, San Biagio and Bellaria terrace units are characterised by an increase in the number of retouched tools, and by a Levallois index generally greater than 10. All the handaxes are made from phthanite. The percentage of artefacts made from chert ranges between 2–33%, and silicified limestone was also occasionally used to make flake tools. In contrast with the assemblages from the Oriolo and Lower Molino terrace units, there are no assemblages where phthanite was the only raw material used.

Compared with the assemblage from the lower part of the Molino terrace unit, the assemblage from the Bellaria terrace unit at Palazzina witnesses an increase in the use of chert (12%). There is also an increase in the frequency of retouched flakes, while the frequency of handaxes remains stable. While once again all the handaxes are made of phthanite, in this assemblage 14% of the retouched tools are made of chert, although this raw material was only used to make sidescrapers, while phthanite was also used to make endscrapers, notches and denticulates. Of the Levallois flakes, 6% are made of chert, although no chert Levallois cores were found. The chert cores are mainly unprepared platform cores, accompanied by a very few discoidal cores. Phthanite was used for prepared platform, discoidal, Levallois and unprepared platform reduction techniques (Milliken and Nenzioni 1996).

The site of Podere Due Pozzi is located 2.5 kilometres to the north-west of Palazzina, in the Bellaria terrace unit of the Idice valley. There are two main sources of phthanite in the area: one, 500 metres away, corresponds with the bed of the river Idice; the second is the gravel substrate where the site itself is located. At both localities the nodules have dimensions greater than 20 centimetres in length. Chert is present locally in the form of small and medium sized pebbles, and the sources of this raw material in the area consist of the Lower Pleistocene littoral deposits (the so-called *Sabbie Gialle* or 'Yellow Sands') immediately uphill of the site. The majority of the artefacts are made from phthanite while chert accounts for 18%. Once again phthanite was used exclusively for the manufacture of hand-axes. There is a wide variety of tool types in the assemblage:

chert was used to make points, sidescrapers, notches and denticulates, while phthanite was used to make endscrapers and truncations as well. Phthanite was chosen preferentially for the Levallois and discoidal reduction techniques, while chert was chosen for single platform and double platform core reduction. There is a significantly higher percentage of facetted platforms among the flake tools made of chert compared with those made of phthanite, which would appear to indicate flaking modes which were differentiated according to raw material quality, with an apparently greater investment of time and effort in the preparation of the striking platform on chert cores (Milliken *et al.* 1996b).

In summary, the Acheulian sequence from the alluvial terrace units between Bologna and Imola is characterised by a steady increase through time in the use of chert at the expense of phthanite, and an increase in the percentage of retouched tools. The percentage of handaxes in each terrace unit is extremely variable (Table 17.2). Though there is evidence for the use of a prepared core technique in the assemblages from the Oriolo and Lower Molino terrace units, the Levallois method *sensu stricto* (*sensu* Boëda 1995) does not appear until the Upper Molino terrace unit (late OIS 9).

HANDAXE VARIABILITY

The presence of Acheulian industries in distinct litho-stratigraphic contexts offers a valuable opportunity for exploring aspects of the much debated issue of handaxe variability. Though the sample size is frustratingly small, to the extent that it precludes any tests of statistical significance from being carried out, the fact that there are only 126 handaxes from 211 sites in the study area is in itself an interesting phenomenon. While at first sight this

may seem to suggest that these tools were highly curated, it is important to bear in mind the fact that the area has been the focus of antiquarian collecting since the mid nineteenth century (see above).

The handaxes were studied using the method for morphometric description and analysis devised by Roe (1964, 1968). Other attributes recorded included raw material, blank type (*façonnage* of a nodule or *débitage* of a flake), method of flaking (hard hammer or soft hammer), mean scar count, mean size adjusted scar count (the number of scars divided by maximum length), and mean residual cortex.

Oriolo unit

The handaxes in the Oriolo terrace unit, which were made exclusively by *façonnage*, are of variable form. The high degree of weathering reflects the fact that they were found in secondary contexts in gravel deposits. One handaxe is made of chert, the remainder being of phthanite. The phthanite handaxes range between 10 and 21 centimetres in length, and the majority are pointed (Fig. 17.1). They were shaped using the hard hammer technique, with the removal of wide centripetal flake scars around the edges, often leaving large areas of cortex in the butt area and on one or both faces. The single handaxe made of chert (11.5 centimetres in length) is an ovate, also shaped using the hard hammer technique, but with no residual cortex.

Lower Molino unit

The handaxes in the Lower Molino unit were made predominantly by *façonnage* of phthanite cobbles. The phthanite handaxes range between 9 to 20 centimetres in length, and were shaped using the hard hammer technique

Terrace	Site	Assemblage size	Handaxes %	Retouched flake tools %
Bellaria	Bellaria	402	0.25	4
	Ca' San Carlo	2044	0.04	14
	Collegio di Spagna	124	0.80	17
	Due Pozzi	4764	0.08	6
	Palazzina	955	1.15	10
	Palazzone-Ca' Roma	226	3.00	24
	Scornetta	965	0.72	15
	Pescatore Piccolo	1418	0.00	8
San Biagio	Pasotta	376	4.20	22
	Poggio Domini	142	3.50	23
	Riniera	123	0.80	20
	Tombazza	129	3.10	18
Upper Molino	Camponi	217	3.20	17
Lower Molino	Cave dall'Olio	494	3.03	5
	Cave S.A.F.R.A.	399	0.25	3
	Fornace di San Lazzaro	1759	0.05	4
	Palazzina	636	0.78	4
Oriolo	Torrente d'Idice	137	2.91	3

Table 17.2. Percentages of handaxes and retouched flake tools in assemblages numbering more than 100 artefacts

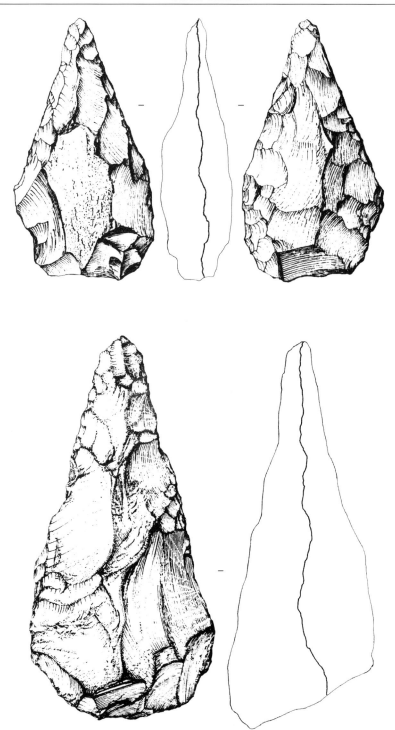

Fig. 17.1. Handaxes from the Oriolo terrace unit: Podere Castello and Torrente d'Idice (1/2 natural size)

with the removal of wide centripetal flake scars around the edges often leaving large areas of cortex in the butt area and on one or both the faces (Fig. 17.2). The majority are pointed. The ovate handaxes were preferentially made on large flakes. The single handaxe made from chert (13 centimetres in length) is an ovate, with residual cortex in the butt area. It was made by *façonnage* and shaped using the hard hammer technique.

Upper Molino Unit

The handaxes in the Upper Molino were made exclusively of phthanite, and predominantly by *façonnage*. The size of the handaxes varies considerably, ranging between 7.5 to 23 centimetres in length. After initial shaping by means of hard hammer retouch, many of the handaxes were then finely shaped using soft hammer retouch to remove thinning flakes (Figs. 17.3–17.4). Traces of residual cortex are found on one or both faces and, more rarely, in the butt area. The majority of the handaxes are pointed; there is only only one ovate, which was made on a large flake and shaped using soft hammer retouch.

San Biagio Unit

The handaxes in the San Biagio unit were also made exclusively of phthanite, and predominantly by *façonnage*. They range between 7.5 and 19 centimetres in length, and the majority are pointed. Ovate forms were made by either *façonnage* or *débitage*, while pointed forms were only rarely made by *débitage* (Figs. 17.5–17.6). After initial shaping by means of hard hammer retouch, some of the handaxes were then finely shaped using soft hammer retouch. Traces of residual cortex are found on one or both faces and, more rarely, in the butt area.

Bellaria Unit

The handaxes in the Bellaria unit were made exclusively of phthanite and predominantly by *façonnage*. They range

between 9 and 20 centimetres in length, and the majority are pointed. Ovates were made by either *façonnage* or *débitage*, while pointed forms were only rarely made by *débitage* (Figs. 17.7–17.8). After initial shaping by means of hard hammer retouch, some of the handaxes were then finely shaped using soft hammer retouch. Traces of residual cortex are found on one or both faces and, more rarely, in the butt area.

Table 17.3 presents a selection of descriptive statistics for the handaxes. The following observations may be made:

(1) The majority of the handaxes in each terrace unit are pointed, although ovate types are always present, to a greater or lesser degree. There has recently been renewed interest in the significance of these two planforms, which in Britain Roe (1981) attributed to distinct cultural traditions. Ashton and McNabb (1994) implicitly questioned the validity of such a distinction, by pointing out that the division between the two forms is arbitrary and that there is continuum in between. Roe's division between the planforms is based purely on the ratio of the distance from the widest point to the butt over length; handaxes with ratios below 0.35 are pointed, while those between 0.35 and 0.65 are ovate (Roe

	Oriolo	Lower Molino	Upper Molino	San Biagio	Bellaria
Sample size	12	31	24	26	33
Pointed (%)	83	74	96	58	64
Ovate (%)	17	26	4	42	36
Façonnage (%)	100	81	83	77	73
Débitage (%)	0	19	17	23	27
Completely worked (%)	42	19	46	65	52
Completely worked butt (%)	67	48	71	81	55
Mean cortex (%)	23	22	5	3.5	4
Mean scar count	45.33	48.80	71.91	61.15	67.66
Mean size adjusted scar count	2.97	3.76	5.38	5.35	5.81
Mean length (L)	15.25	13.47	13.89	11.85	11.97
Mean width (B)	8.27	8.15	7.50	6.83	6.67
Mean thickness (Th)	5.18	4.58	4.43	3.39	3.54
Mean elongation (B/L)	0.55	0.62	0.55	0.59	0.56
Mean refinement (Th/B)	0.61	0.56	0.59	0.50	0.54
Mean tip thickness/butt thickness (T1/T2)	0.67	0.65	0.48	0.58	0.58
Standard deviation of length	3.31	3.08	3.34	2.65	2.55
Standard deviation of width	1.56	1.48	1.51	1.36	1.60
Standard deviation of thickness	1.83	1.53	1.33	0.78	1.06
Standard deviation of B/L mean	0.06	0.12	0.07	0.09	0.11
Standard deviation of Th/B mean	0.12	0.14	0.11	0.12	0.12
Standard deviation of T1/T2 mean	0.18	0.15	0.14	0.15	0.14

Table 17.3. Descriptive statistics of the handaxes

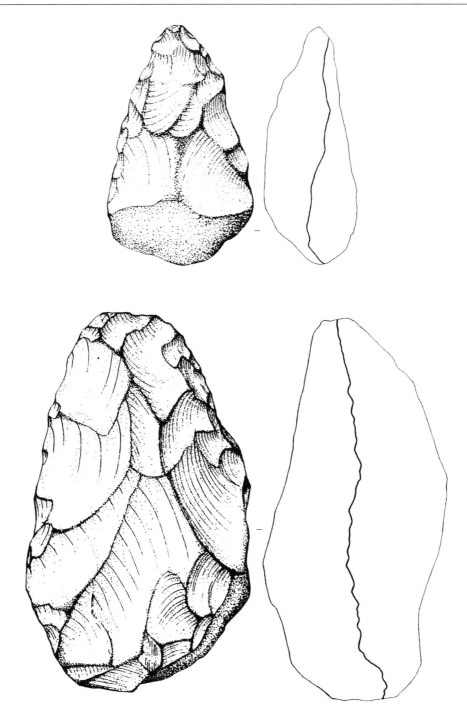

Fig. 17.2. Handaxes from the Lower Molino terrace unit: Cave dall'Olio (1/2 natural size)

1964, 1968). In a recent study White (1998) found that the southern British ovate handaxes are characterised by higher flake scar counts, less cortex, higher levels of refinement, more lenticular profiles and more fully worked butts than pointed handaxes. He also found a convincing correlation with raw material size: ovate handaxes were preferentially produced where raw materials were large enough to permit intensive reduction sequences, while the more moderately reduced pointed forms were manufactured on smaller and narrower blanks which therefore imposed restrictions on the location and extent of reduction (White 1998). Similar conclusions have also been reached by McPherron (1995, 2000), who sees ovate and pointed handaxes as representing different points on the reduction continuum, with ovate handaxes being more heavily reduced than pointed ones. The analysis of the handaxes from Emilia-Romagna, however, revealed that here ovate handaxes do not necessarily have a higher size adjusted scar count and/or less cortex than pointed handaxes (Table 17.4). This would appear to be because many of them were made on large

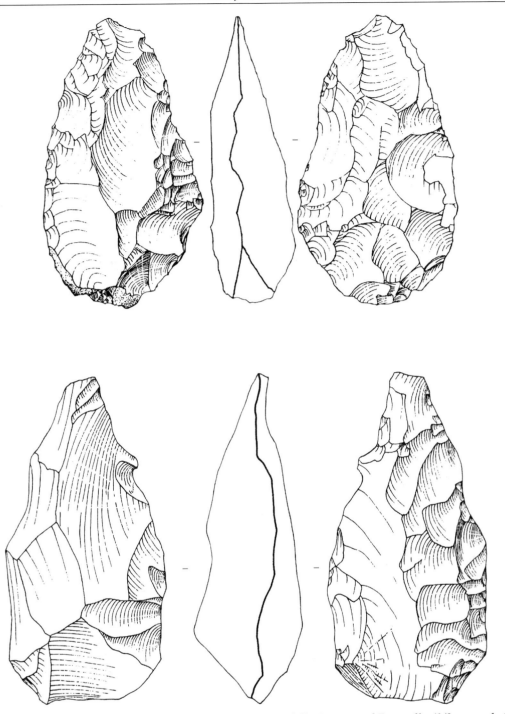

Fig. 17.3. Handaxes from the Upper Molino terrace unit: Ca' delle Donne and Peverella (1/2 natural size)

flake blanks rather than nodules (in other words by *débitage* rather than by *façonnage*), which therefore required less reduction to achieve an all round cutting edge. I shall return to this point later. Neither are the ovates necessarily more lenticular in profile (which would be indicated by higher tip thickness/butt thickness ratios). On the other hand, in agreement with White's results, the ovate handaxes in each terrace unit are consistently more refined than the pointed ones (which is indicated by lower thickness/breadth ratios) and have more fully worked butts.

In the literature, opinions differ about the relative merits of the two handaxe forms from a functional and ergonomic point of view. While White suggests that pointed forms represent the least-effort approach to handaxe manufacture, he argues that ovate forms presented hominids with a greater amount of usable cutting edge and a more efficient use-mode than most pointed forms of the same dimensions. Therefore, assuming a universal function, ovates were more efficient than pointed handaxes (White 1998, 22). Similarly, Ashton and McNabb (1994) argue that the ideal form of a handaxe is an ovate, since this form maximises the length of the cutting edge. In contrast, Jones (1994) has argued that elongated shapes provide a better ratio of cutting edge to weight than do broader, more rounded shapes. Regardless of their differences of opinion, all these studies implicitly assume that a particular shape is the desired end-product of the reduction sequence. However McPherron's suggestion, that ovate forms are produced by default as a result of continued resharpening, challenges this assumption. He argues that handaxes start out large, elongated, pointed and relatively thick, and through reduction become smaller, broader, more rounded and thinner (McPherron 2000, 662). However, with the exception of those from the Lower Molino terrace unit, the relative size attributes of the ovate and pointed handaxes in the assemblages from Emilia-Romagna do not support this model.

(2) The majority of the handaxes in all terrace units were made by *façonnage* rather than by *débitage*. Considering the assemblages as a whole, equal numbers of ovates were made by *débitage* and *façonnage*, while the majority of the pointed handaxes (91%) were made by *façonnage*. A comparison between selected attributes of the handaxes made by *débitage* with those made by *façonnage* reveals that in all terrace units the former have a consistently lower size adjusted flake scar count and less cortex (Table 17.5). That this is the case should come as no surprise, since the ventral face of the flake would have needed very little refinement and would obviously have been cortex-free. Therefore the use of *débitage* may be explained by the fact that this technique, as opposed to *façonnage*, represented the least-effort approach which would have been adopted whenever possible, since less refinement was needed to achieve an all round cutting edge. Since the handaxes produced by *débitage* were only minimally shaped, their size and shape give an indication of the original size and shape of the flakes on which they

	Oriolo	Lower Molino	Upper Molino	San Biagio	Bellaria
More completely worked butts	√	√	√	√	√
Less cortex	√	√			
Higher size adjusted flake scar count	√	√			√
More refined	√	√	√	√	√
More lenticular profiles		√		√	√
Shorter	√	√			√
Broader	√		√	√	
Thinner		√		√	√

Table 17.4. Selected attributes of the ovates compared with the pointed forms

	Lower Molino	Upper Molino	San Biagio	Bellaria
More completely worked butts	√	√	√	√
Less cortex	√	√	√	√
Higher size adjusted flake scar count				
More refined	√			√
More lenticular profiles	√		√	√
Shorter	√			√
Broader		√		
Thinner	√			√

Table 17.5. Selected attributes of the handaxes made by débitage compared with those made by façonnage

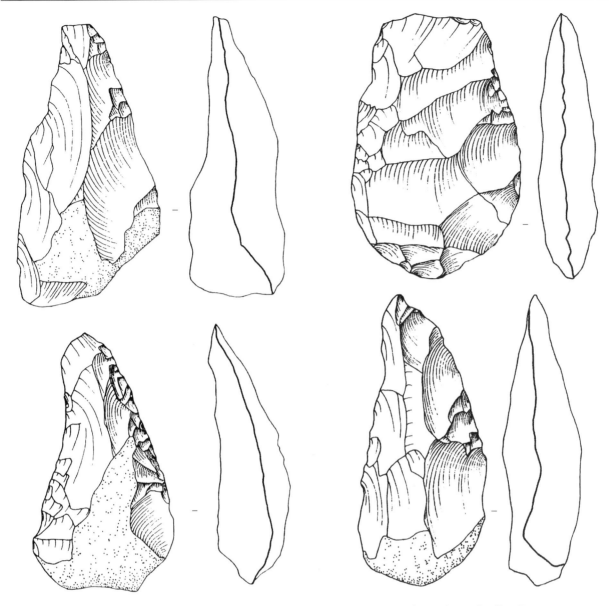

Fig. 17.4. Handaxes from the Upper Molino terrace unit: Peverella (1/2 natural size)

Fig. 17.5. Handaxes from the San Biagio terrace unit: Tombazza (1/2 natural size)

were made. Two-thirds of these had an oval form, which explains the correlation between *débitage* and ovates, while only one-third had a pointed form. The lack of correlation between the size attributes of the handaxes produced by *débitage* (Table 17.5) suggests that it was not the size of the raw material unit that dictated when such a technical choice was possible, but more likely its morphology.

(3) There is a significant difference between the amount of mean cortex on handaxes from the Oriolo and Lower Molino terrace units, and those from the younger terrace units. The marked decrease in mean cortex in the three younger assemblages may be related to the fact that there is a gradual temporal increase in mean size adjusted scar count, which suggests that the handaxes were more intensively reduced.

(4) There is a gradual temporal decrease in the size of the handaxes, reflected in decreasing values for mean length, mean width and mean thickness. However, the relative relationships between these three variables remain fairly constant. This is demonstrated by the mean elongation and mean refinement indices, which are similar for each terrace unit. In other words, it appears that the dimensional relationships of the different size-related variables (length, width, thickness) are held constant regardless of decreasing size. This means that allometry, or size-related variability, which has been found to be a major factor in handaxe variation in some case studies (e.g. Crompton and Gowlett 1993; Gowlett and Crompton 1994), does not seem to apply here. One could go further to suggest that the relationship between these three variables seems to have

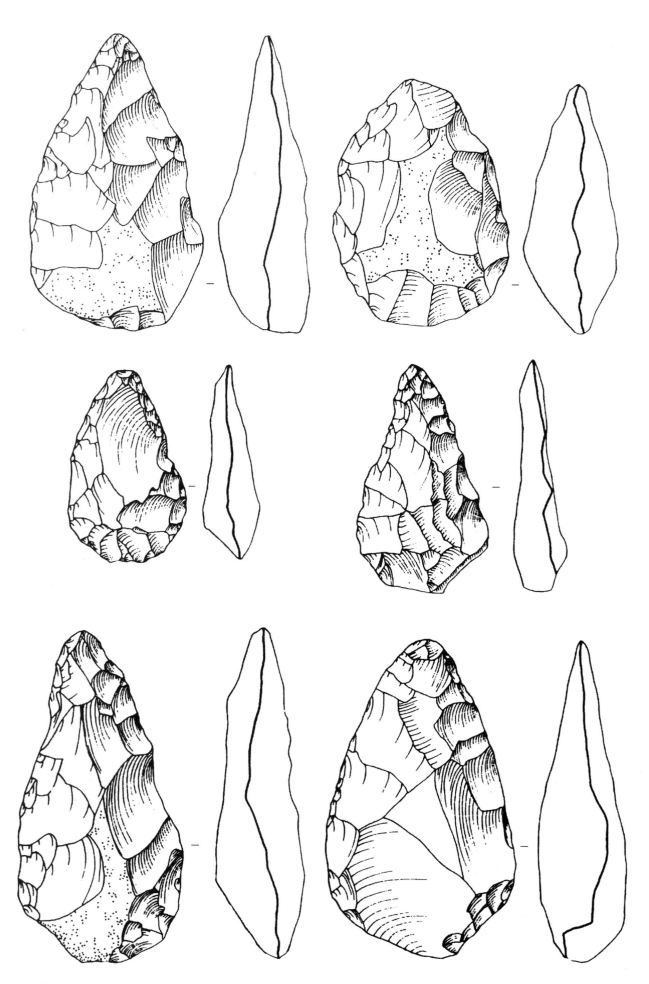

Fig. 17.6. Handaxes from the San Biagio terrace unit: Villa Resta, Pasotta and Marascelle (2/3 natural size)

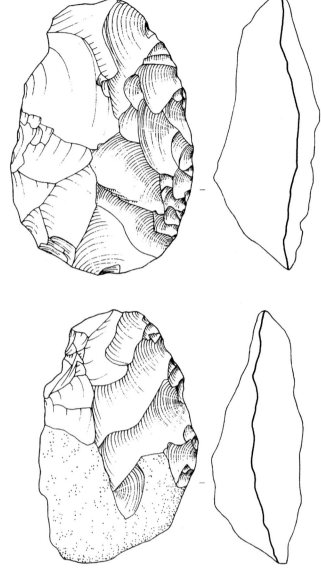

Fig. 17.7. Handaxes from the Bellaria terrace unit: Palazzina (1/2 natural size)

handaxe was made on, and therefore judge the extent to which the hominids were constrained in their technical choices. Consequently, the reconstruction of the two reduction sequences used in the manufacture of handaxes in Acheulian Emilia-Romagna should be regarded as hypothetical:

1. The most frequently used reduction sequence involved cobbles or nodules which were reduced bifacially. This resulted in the creation of predominantly pointed forms, often with cortical butts and residual cortex on one or both faces.

2. When possible a large flake was struck off a cobble or nodule, and this was subsequently thinned, predominantly on the dorsal face and around the butt, to produce a handaxe which was normally ovate but sometimes pointed in planform, depending on the morphology of the struck flake. In most cases the concentration of retouch around the butt of the handaxe would appear to have been aimed at producing a more lenticular profile, by reducing the thickness of the flake around the bulb of percussion.

These two reduction sequences remained essentially unchanged over the duration of the Middle Pleistocene. The only clear temporal changes through the sequence are a reduction in size, an increase in mean size adjusted scar count and a reduction in mean residual cortex, all of which indicate increased reduction of the blanks, and which coincide with the introduction of the soft hammer technique for the removal of thinning flakes. In the absence of refitting evidence it is impossible to say whether this reduction in size was intentional, or simply the result of handaxes being more intensively reworked and resharpened prior to being abandoned.

CONCLUSIONS

Though chronological trends were noted in the Acheulian sequence from the study area, with an increase in the percentage of retouched tools, and variability in the raw materials from which they were produced and in the methods by which they were made, in contrast the handaxes show considerable stasis and continuity. In this study I have adopted what Isaac (1986) called a 'step-wise approach' to explaining variability, whereby one begins with the most basic level of explanation and then proceeds step by step in a process of accounting for and eliminating sources of variability within and between assemblages. In this way it has been possible to combine lower level explanations of raw material variability, reduction intensity and technological constraints, with higher levels of explanation such as mental templates. The results of this study suggest that raw material morphology may have been largely responsible for the different proportions of handaxes made by *débitage* and *façonnage*, which in turn seems to have exerted some influence on the relative proportions of ovate and pointed

been standardised in the minds of the makers, which might suggest that we can indeed speak of enduring shape-specific *mental templates* (*sensu* Gowlett 1984), rather than a generalised *mental construct* of a bifacial functional tool with a basic level of symmetry and sharp durable edges (*sensu* Ashton and McNabb 1994).

(5) There is a noticeable change from the exclusive use of hard hammer technique in the Oriolo and Lower Molino terrace units, to the combined use of hard hammer for shaping and soft hammer for thinning in the Upper Molino, San Biagio and Bellaria terrace units.

Even when large areas of cortex are preserved in the butt area and on both faces, in the absence of refitting evidence it is extremely rare to be able to reconstruct accurately the original size and shape of the nodule or cobble that a

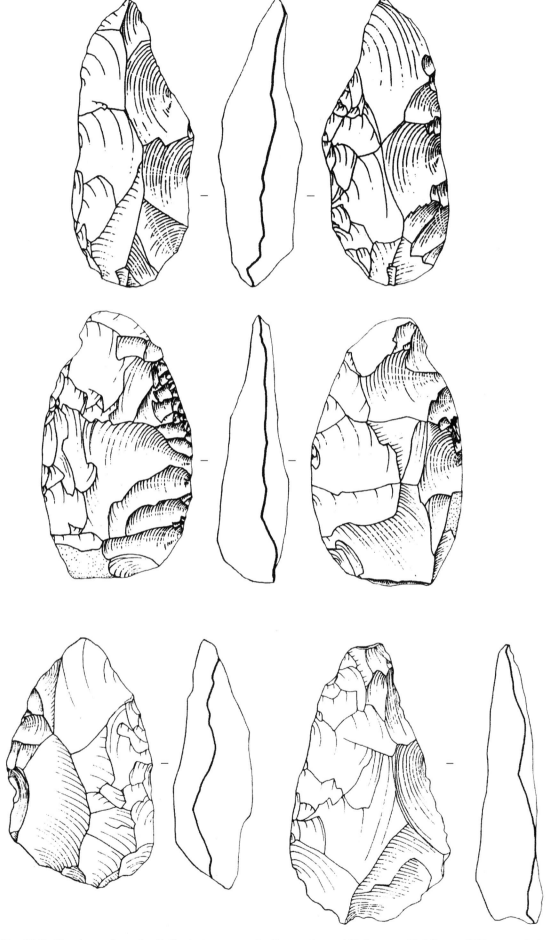

Fig. 17.8. Handaxes from the Bellaria terrace unit: Scornetta and Palazzone Ca' Roma (2/3 natural size)

types. However, regardless of the planform of the artefact, or the reduction sequence by which it was made, the relatively constant dimensional relationships between handaxe length, width and thickness suggest that the relationship between these three variables was standardised in the minds of the makers.

ACKNOWLEDGEMENTS

This research was funded by the *Istituto per i Beni Artistici e Naturali della Regione Emilia-Romagna*. I would like to thank Gabriele Nenzioni and Fiamma Lenzi of the Museum at San Lazzaro, Bologna, for giving me permission to study these assemblages. The illustrations are by Davide Mengoli.

REFERENCES

Ashton, N.M. and McNabb, J. 1994. Bifaces in perspective. In N.M. Ashton and A. David (eds.) *Stories in Stone*, 182–191. Lithics Studies Society Occasional Paper 4, London.

Boëda, E. 1995. Levallois: a volumetric construction, methods, a technique. In H.L. Dibble and O. Bar-Yosef (eds.) *The Definition and Interpretation of Levallois Technology*, 41–68. Prehistory Press, Madison.

Bridgland, D.R. 1994. Dating of Lower Palaeolithic industries within the framework of the lower Thames terrace sequence. In N.M. Ashton and A. David (eds.) *Stories in Stone*, 28–40. Lithics Studies Society Occasional Paper 4, London.

Bridgland, D.R. 1998. The Pleistocene history and early human occupation of the River Thames Valley. In N.M Ashton, F. Healy and P. Pettitt (eds.) *Stone Age Archaeology: Essays in Honour of John Wymer*, 29–37. Lithics Studies Society Occasional Paper 6, Oxbow Monograph 102. Oxbow Books, Oxford.

Capellini, G. 1870. Armi ed utensili di pietra del Bolognese. *Memorie dell'Accademia dell'Istituto delle Scienze di Bologna* 2 (9), 1–16.

Crompton, R.H. and Gowlett, J.A.J. 1993. Allometry and multidimensional form in Acheulean bifaces from Kilombe, Kenya. *Journal of Human Evolution* 25, 175–199.

Davidson, I. and Noble, W. 1993. Tools and language in human evolution. In K. Gibson and T. Ingold (eds.) *Tools, Language and Cognition in Human Evolution*, 363–388. Cambridge University Press, Cambridge.

Fantini, L. 1954. Il Paleolitico nel Bolognese. *Bologna* 40 (12), 15–18.

Fantini, L. 1955. Nuovi ritrovamenti paleolitici nell'Imolese. *Studi Romagnoli* 6, 63–72.

Fantini, L. 1956. Giacimenti paleolitici nel bolognese. *Strenna Storica Bolognese* 7, 45–68.

Farabegoli, E. 1996. The Palaeolithic sites between Bologna and Imola related to the geomorphological and palaeogeographical evolution of the environment. In F. Lenzi and G. Nenzioni (eds.) *Lettere di Pietra. I Depositi Pleistocenici: Sedimenti, Industrie e Faune del Margine Appenninico Bolognese*, xix–xxxvii. Editrice Compositori, Bologna.

Farabegoli, E. and Onorevoli, G. 1996. The Emilia-Romagna Apenninic margin during the Quaternary: stratigraphy and events. In F. Lenzi and G. Nenzioni (eds.) *Lettere di Pietra. I Depositi Pleistocenici: Sedimenti, Industrie e Faune del Margine Appen-*

ninico Bolognese, xxxix–lxv. Editrice Compositori, Bologna.

Gamble, C. 1998. Handaxes and Palaeolithic individuals. In N. Ashton, F. Healy and P. Pettitt (eds.) *Stone Age Archaeology: Essays in Honour of John Wymer*, 105–109. Lithics Studies Society Occasional Paper 6, Oxbow Monograph 102. Oxbow Books, Oxford.

Gilead, D. 1970. Handaxe industries in Israel and the Near East. *World Archaeology* 2, 1–11.

Gowlett, J.A.J. 1984. Mental abilities of early man: a look at some hard evidence. In R. Foley (ed.) *Hominid Evolution and Community Ecology*, 167–192. Academic Press, London.

Gowlett, J.A.J. and Crompton, R.H. 1994. Kariandusi: Acheulean morphology and the question of allometry. *African Archaeological Review* 12, 3–42.

Isaac, G. 1986. Foundation stones: early artefacts as indicators of activities and abilities. In G.N. Bailey and P. Callow (eds.) *Stone Age Prehistory: Studies in Memory of Charles McBurney*, 221–241. Cambridge University Press, Cambridge.

Jones, P.R. 1994. Results of experimental work in relation to the stone industries of Olduvai Gorge. In M.D. Leakey and D.A. Roe (eds.) *Olduvai Gorge Volume 5: Excavations in Beds III, IV and the Masek Beds, 1968–1971*, 254–298. Cambridge University Press, Cambridge.

Kohn, M. and Mithen, S. 1999. Handaxes: products of sexual selection? *Antiquity* 73, 518–526.

Lenzi, F. and Nenzioni, G. (eds.) 1996. *Lettere di Pietra. I Depositi Pleistocenici: Sedimenti, Industrie e Faune del Margine Appenninico Bolognese*. Editrice Compositori, Bologna.

McPherron, S.P. 1995. A re-examination of the British biface data. *Lithics* 16, 47–63.

McPherron, S.P. 2000. Handaxes and the mental capabilities of early hominids. *Journal of Archaeological Science* 27, 655–663.

Milliken, S. and Nenzioni, G. 1996. Palazzina. In F. Lenzi and G. Nenzioni (eds.) *Lettere di Pietra. I Depositi Pleistocenici: Sedimenti, Industrie e Faune del Margine Appenninico Bolognese*, 606–621. Editrice Compositori, Bologna.

Milliken, S., Lenzi, F. and Nenzioni, G. 1996a. Palazzina. In F. Lenzi and G. Nenzioni (ed.) *Lettere di Pietra. I Depositi Pleistocenici: Sedimenti, Industrie e Faune del Margine Appenninico Bolognese*, 273–289. Editrice Compositori, Bologna.

Milliken, S., Malisardi, S. and Nenzioni, G. 1996b. Due Pozzi. In F. Lenzi and G. Nenzioni (eds.) *Lettere di Pietra. I Depositi Pleistocenici: Sedimenti, Industrie e Faune del Margine Appenninico Bolognese*, 480–516. Editrice Compositori, Bologna.

Roe, D.A. 1964. The British Lower and Middle Palaeolithic: some problems, methods of study and preliminary results. *Proceedings of the Prehistoric Society* 30, 245–267.

Roe, D.A. 1968. British Lower and Middle Palaeolithic handaxe groups. *Proceedings of the Prehistoric Society* 34, 1–82.

Roe, D.A. 1981. *The Lower and Middle Palaeolithic Periods in Britain*. Routledge and Kegan Paul, London.

Saragusti, I., Sharon, I., Katzenelson, O. and Avnir, D. 1998. Quantitative analysis of symmetry of artefacts: Lower Palaeolithic handaxes. *Journal of Archaeological Science* 25, 817–825.

Scarabelli, G. 1850. Intorno alle armi di pietra dura che sono state raccolte nell'Imolese. *Nuovi Annali di Scienze Naturali di Bologna* 3 (2), 258–266.

Scarabelli, G. 1890. Sulle pietre lavorate a grandi schegge del Quaternario presso Imola. *Bullettino di Paletnologia Italiana* 16, 157–166.

White, M.J. 1998. On the significance of Acheulean biface variability in southern Britain. *Proceedings of the Prehistoric Society* 64, 15–44.

Wynn, T. and Tierson, F. 1990. Regional comparison of the shapes of later Acheulean handaxes. *American Anthropologist* 92, 73–84.

18. Palaeoliths in a lost pre-Anglian landscape

John Wymer

ABSTRACT

This paper discusses a number of find-spots around Feltwell, Norfolk, which are associated with terrace deposits of the Bytham River. The proposed chronology of the river terraces suggests that the Palaeolithic artefacts may be of pre-Anglian date. This has profound implications for the earliest occupation of Britain and north-west Europe.

INTRODUCTION

When Derek Roe published his monumental book on the *The Lower and Middle Palaeolithic Periods in Britain* in 1981, he could make few positive statements concerning the chronology of many of the sites, especially the earlier ones. In many cases he noted the various possible interpretations. He speculated on the possible Cromerian age, *sensu lato*, of deposits and artefacts at sites such as Kent's Cavern and Westbury-sub-Mendip, and carefully noted the geological evidence recorded at sites such as High Lodge and Warren Hill before cautiously citing their interpretation as Wolstonian, as widely accepted at the time. Indeed, if he were to produce a second edition, it would not be a question of removing errors but, in many instances, converting his suggestions and possibilities into what can or cannot now be accepted as facts. This paper is a contribution to this process of conversion using the cluster of associated localities around Feltwell in East Anglia (Wymer 1985) to stress the growing evidence for a much earlier occupation of Britain than was realised in 1981, as well as our much greater understanding of the enormous changes in the topography of that time.

THE FELTWELL LOCALITIES

Feltwell, Norfolk, lies about 7 km north-west of Brandon (Fig. 18.1). Fluvial gravels and sands exposed in the Frimstone Pit belong to the so-called Bytham River which, prior to the Anglian Stage glaciation, flowed from the Midlands westward to near Downham Market, and veered sharply southward at Shouldham Thorpe towards Feltwell. The ice sheet totally blocked the whole of this drainage system and obliterated it forever. This Bytham River had not been recognised prior to Roe's 1981 volume, although his 1968 Gazetteer lists numerous handaxes from another site in the same parish some 8 km away but at the level of the present fens, and about nineteen handaxes in another closer site and at the same level as Feltwell, at Hockwold (Roe 1968, 231, 233). Other sites considered to belong to this lost river system are further south at Lakenheath, Eriswell, Brandon (Gravel Hill), Warren Hill and Icklingham (Rampart Field), and have all produced palaeoliths, Warren Hill being one of the most prolific sites for palaeoliths in Britain (Wymer 1999).

The Frimstone pit was a working pit until 1999, when most of the old workings became buried under a landfill site. During its commercial activity over several decades it does not seem to have produced any Palaeolithic artefacts until the late 1980s, when Mr Eric Secker and his sons, of Feltwell, began to find handaxes on the reject heaps from the screening plant. The Seckers have been avid flint collectors for many years. They keep careful records and report their findings to the Norwich Castle Museum, where Dr P.A. Robins takes details and makes 1:1 drawings of them, hence on to the Sites and Monuments Records for the

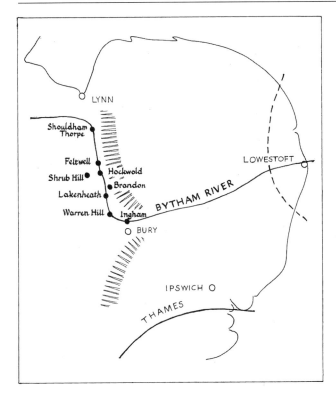

Fig. 18.1. Simplified map of the Bytham River and Thames prior to their obliteration or diversion respectively by the ice sheet of the Anglian Stage glaciation. The hachures represent the Chalk escarpment which in this area was virtually removed by the same ice sheet. Its presence before the Anglian Stage explains the southward swing of the Bytham River at Shouldham Thorpe, and it is suggested that it resumed its eastward course through an existing ancient 'wind gap'. Sites mentioned in the text are shown as closed spots. The dashed line west of Lowestoft is regarded as the probable coastline of the Lower Pleistocene (after Clayton 2000 and Rose et al. 1999b).

Plate 18.1. Upper part of section cut in Frimstone Pit, Feltwell, in April 1999. Note the white solifluction lens of chalk and stones. This contained four flakes, all slightly rolled with edge damage. It is suggested that this was solifluction from the Chalk slopes on the side of the valley prior to the removal of most of the Chalk escarpment by the Anglian ice sheet. Above the top of the section is chalky disturbed ground and Oxford Clay dumped in advance of the use of the pit as a landfill site. Three metres of undisturbed sediments were exposed above rubbly chalk at the base. The present land surface at the top of the dumped Oxford Clay is at about the same height as the general level of the Till Plain in this area.

County. He has also kept me informed of all their discoveries, as has Mr R.J. MacRae who, more recently, has recovered material from the reject heaps. A brief report on the findings has been given by MacRae (1999). The palaeoliths include ovate and pointed forms, both of elegant or crude workmanship, cores and flakes. A few of the handaxes are made from quartzite pebbles. At least fifty handaxes are known from the site. A selection is shown in Fig. 18.2.

In April 1999 gravel working ceased and the last exposures of the deposits were about to be covered by Oxford Clay before being used as a further landfill site. The opportunity was taken to cut a test section at the north end of the pit. This was done by the writer, in conjunction with Dr Simon Lewis, Dr Jim Rose and Dr David Bridgland, and Mr R.J. MacRae. The section (Plate 18.1) was eminently successful as five flint flakes were found *in situ* during the course of the excavation, four in a Chalky solifluction layer and one at the base of chalky

sandy gravel and cross-bedded sands on top of rubbly chalk bedrock. There can be little doubt that in view of these *in situ* flakes, the artefacts found on the reject heaps came from these deposits of the Bytham River.

THE BYTHAM RIVER

There is a lengthy literature on the subject of the Bytham River and disagreement, especially as to when or if the river joined the ancestral Thames at Ingham, near Bury St Edmunds (see especially Lewis *et al.* 1999; Rose *et al.* 1999a, 1999b). Other sites yielding palaeoliths from Bytham

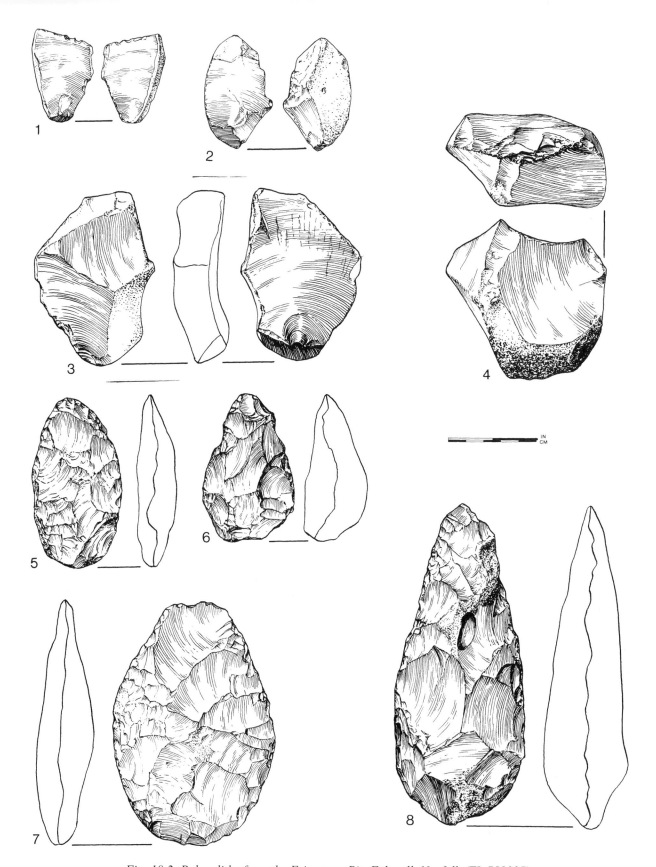

Fig. 18.2. Palaeoliths from the Frimstone Pit, Feltwell, Norfolk (TL 758927)

No. 1. Primary flake with plain striking platform and clear cone of percussion and bulbar scar. One negative removal on dorsal side. Thin cortex remains on both edges. Slightly rolled with edge damage. Found in situ, *immediately above Chalk Breccia at base of section. Also at this level, a very rolled flake from a quartzite pebble, possibly a natural removal. No. 2. Thick, mainly cortical flake with pronounced cone of percussion, slightly rolled but with considerable edge damage. Slightly stained and patinated. Some later flaking on dorsal side is patinated white. Found* in situ *in lens of soliflucted chalk fragments and stones between fluvial sand and gravel, in upper part of section as shown in Plate 18.1. Three other flakes were also found in the same lens, all slightly rolled and patinated, with edge damage.*

The following artefacts were all found at various times on the gravel company's reject heaps: No. 3. Large primary flake from alternately flaked nodule. Rolled, stained and patinated, with edge damage (found by R.J. MacRae). No. 4. Alternately flaked core. Very rolled, stained and patinated (found by R.J. MacRae). No. 5. Elegant small ovate handaxe. Sharp condition, patinated white (found by J. Wymer).

No. 6. Small, crude pointed handaxe, made by use of hard hammer. Rolled and stained (found by J. Wymer). No. 7. Large, elegant ovate handaxe sharpened by tranchet flake. Skilfully fashioned by soft-hammer flaking. Sharp, patinated white with faint staining (found by J. Lord). No. 8. Large, thick-butted pointed handaxe. Made for the most part if not entirely by hard-hammer technique. Slightly rolled with mottled staining and patination (found by R.J. MacRae).

Sands and Gravels on the east side of the Wash have been mentioned above, but only at Waverley Wood in Warwickshire (Shotton and Wymer 1989) on the west side.

Coming from the Midlands it is not surprising that there is a high content of quartzose rocks in the Bytham Sands and Gravels, and the proportions of such to other rocks measured by lithological analysis can determine its identity. Stone counts of the Feltwell section made by Dr Simon Lewis equate the proportions with those of the Bytham Sands and Gravels. Study of these Bytham Sands and Gravels from exposures in commercial quarries clearly denotes its eastward flow from Warwickshire across to Lincolnshire, where at Witham on the Hill the river is truncated by the vast embayment of the Wash. It is a stimulating geological experience to stand at the top of the Hill and look across the fens towards King's Lynn and Downham Market on a clear day and see the distant rise of Norfolk some 56 km away, then drive to Shouldham Thorpe south of King's Lynn and see the same quartzose gravel exposed in the parish pit. It is awesome to look across that gap and consider what has been eroded away into what is now the North Sea, since the Bytham River flowed at about 30 m OD. Similarly, on the edge of the Frimstone Pit, the surrounding surface is not that of a floodplain in a valley, which it must have been once, but the flat Till Plain left by the recession of the Anglian ice sheet some 400,000 years ago.

It is generally accepted that the Anglian Stage equates with Oxygen Isotope Stage 12 of the deep-sea core sequence and time-scale. At various sites in the Midlands and East Anglia the Bytham Sands and Gravels are covered by glacial till. At Feltwell the deposits are on rubbly Chalk. It is clear that they pre-date Stage 12 for several reasons. Most markedly is the fact that the great embayment of the Wash and fens could not have existed when the Bytham River flowed across to Feltwell. The Anglian Glaciation is thought to have scoured out this embayment, pushing its sediments from the west on to much of East Anglia. Clayton (2000) has made a profound study of the 'landscape changes brought about by the Anglian glaciation', particularly by quantifying the mass of material removed by the ice sheet from the west side of the chalk escarpment in relation to the mass of till on the other. There is enough coincidence to demonstrate that the Anglian ice was responsible for it. The possible age of the Bytham Sands and Gravels at Feltwell is critical, as obviously the palaeoliths contained in them are as old as the date of their deposition. They could be older, but not younger. However, this is discussed later. What concerns this note from an archaeological angle is the fact that they unequivocally denote a human presence, but just what sort of landscape surrounded them?

THE BYTHAM LANDSCAPE

It can be seen in Plate 18.1 that there is a white, sloping lens of chalky sediment in the upper part of the section.

This is a solifluction deposit that has sludged down some nearby chalky slope, but there are now no chalky slopes above it. Yet, there must have been when the river was actively flowing at this level. The river was flowing north–south along the edge of the Chalk escarpment, as Clayton has shown. The escarpment must have been there, probably as impressive as the Chiltern escarpment is today. It was the reason for the Bytham River making its change of course at Shouldham Thorpe. There would have been a relatively steep slope on the east side of the river, rising to whatever height remained prior to the Anglian Stage. At this level of about 30 m OD, the river would not have cut down to the Lower Cretaceous and Jurassic Clays of the present Fenland. It is reasonable to visualise an outcropping to the west of sandy Lower Cretaceous beds, and to judge by the dip slope of the solid geology, the nearest point to inhospitable wetlands of Kimmeridge Clay could not have been closer than about 10 km. Flint was probably available in plenty on the slopes of the escarpment in the upper part of the Lower Chalk, or along the gravelly banks of the river. Such a landscape would seem very suitable for Palaeolithic hunter-gatherers, although we know nothing of the climate they were living in or the contemporary vegetation. Presumably it was during some part of an interglacial period and there could have been a considerable time interval between the manufacture and use of flint tools on the riversides and the advent of glacial conditions, which would have been the most likely time for major erosion of the valley sides and inclusion of palaeoliths into reworked sediments.

South of Brandon the river changed its course to flow eastwards through a Chalk gap. The most likely explanation for this is that a gap already existed (a so-called wind gap), being the relic of some earlier vanished drainage pattern. This, however, would have meant easy access of communication towards the estuary of the Bytham River and the coast, then seemingly somewhat inland of the present one (Fig. 18.1). This could have given access to the south across land which existed in what is now the southern North Sea, and thus into north-west Europe. Possibly this was a more accessible route than the Thames estuary of the time, as suggested by Rose (1995). Certainly, there is more evidence of pre-Anglian occupation in East Anglia than there is along the ancestral Thames. As yet, nothing Palaeolithic has been found in the Kesgrave Sands and Gravels of this pre-Anglian Thames.

CHRONOLOGY AND TYPOLOGY

Another, more geological and chronometric matter, is that just because the level of the Bytham River as shown by the sands and gravels it deposited lies at the level of the Anglian Till Plain, it is not necessarily of an age immediately preceding the onset of the Anglian Stage. It could be very much older. Different levels have been observed of the Bytham Sands and Gravels and, in fact, Feltwell and Leet

Hill (nearer its former estuary) have been referred to as Terrace 2 (Rose *et al.* 1999a). That terraces must have existed along this river seems certain: Dr Simon Lewis has identified four levels which represent terraces of the Bytham River (Lewis pers. comm.), but with only very scattered remnants of them preserved from Warwickshire to Norfolk, interpretation is limited. However, if a terrace system is visualised akin to such systems which are preserved along major rivers such as the Thames (Bridgland 1994), Trent and Ouse dating from after the Anglian Stage, then something similar must have existed prior to the Anglian along the Bytham River. The pattern is of flights of terraces representing erosion and aggradation, linked to terrestrial uplift and glacial–interglacial cycles, with decreasing age from top to bottom, i.e. the earliest terraces are the highest. Feltwell may not have been the highest. Higher ones may have been stripped off by the Anglian ice, but neither was it necessarily the youngest. There is a rich Palaeolithic site, still in the parish of Feltwell, only about 8 km away but at a much lower level at 1 m OD. This has always been a great puzzle, as it is not far from Lakenheath and Eriswell with palaeoliths in Bytham Sands and Gravels at about the same height as Feltwell. If Shrub Hill should be a low terrace of the Bytham River, it could be explained as a much more recent terrace to Feltwell but still pre-Anglian. The typology of the palaeoliths would, in the past, have disputed such a conclusion, but there is now ample evidence to show that a repertoire of similar forms can occur throughout the Lower Palaeolithic for about a million years, if one includes Africa. There is nothing to indicate any consistent change in typology until what may be termed the Middle Palaeolithic, with the use of Levallois technique and Mousterian tool-kits. None of such is known from Shrub Hill, let alone Feltwell. On the analogy that some 300,000 years are considered to exist between the highest post-Late Anglian terrace of the Thames and the present Flood Plain Terrace, some similar order of time could exist in this hypothetical Bytham River terrace sequence. This would have profound implications for the earliest occupation of Britain and, indeed, of north-west Europe as that would have been the only way to get here. By definition, if Feltwell is of pre-Anglian age, then it must be of the Cromerian *sensu lato* or earlier. Only in Norfolk and Suffolk, along the coast, are there rich exposures of these Early Middle and Lower Pleistocene deposits. This classic area has and is receiving much attention in view of recent extensive coastal erosion, exposing cliff sections that have not been seen since the nineteenth century. The basic background is already there, with the meticulous and detailed publication of the lithostratigraphy, sedimentary history, biostratigraphy and vegetational history of cliff and foreshore sections and boreholes between Weybourne and Southwold by West (1980). Sadly, nowhere is there a long, unbroken, stratigraphical succession. As usual with Quaternary events, there are only parts of such in different localities, which can sometimes be correlated, sometimes not. Preece and Parfitt (2000) have made an intense study of the mollusca

from many localities in these Cromerian and earlier formations and find it difficult not to conclude that six interglacial periods may be represented, though they are hesitant to confirm it. Whatever the number, if these are interglacials and not just warm periods, then glaciations are implied. This is a further puzzle, for the Oxygen Isotope chronology indicates four other cold periods (glaciations?) prior to the paleomagnetic reversal of the Brunhes-Matuyama boundary, and others before that. In fact OIS 16 looks more severe than OIS 12. Yet, the identified glacial deposits between Sheringham and Lowestoft are all regarded as of the Anglian Stage. Was this really the only time that ice covered East Anglia during the Pleistocene? I doubt it, and recent work by the British Geological Survey supports a sequence of three separate glaciations rather than one (Hamblin *et al.* 2000). Already there is some possible evidence that the occupation of Britain will be pushed back well before the Anglian Stage in East Anglia. We already have Boxgrove and Westbury-sub-Mendip elsewhere. A small flint flake was found in the Pastonian 'Rootlet Bed' at Pakefield during the Quaternary Research Association's Easter excursion in 2000, but as with the proverbial confrontation of one swallow and the summer, one mint flake can hardly uphold the earliest occupation of north-west Europe. The dating of another site is not yet unequivocal. I shall emulate Roe's scientific caution and wait until it is not a matter of 'it could be', but 'it is'.

ACKNOWLEDGMENTS

Thanks go to my Quaternary geological colleagues as mentioned in the text, and to the patient sifters of the gravel reject heaps. Without them this short note would not have been possible. Most of all, however, to Derek Roe himself, who has been a source of encouragement since I first met him, tempered in a most courteous manner with advice and criticism.

REFERENCES

Bridgland, D.R. 1994. *Quaternary of the Thames.* Chapman and Hall, London.

Clayton, K. 2000. The landform changes brought about by the Anglian glaciation. In S.G. Lewis, C.A. Whiteman and R.C. Preece (eds.) *The Quaternary of Norfolk and Suffolk: Field Guide*, 55–60. Quaternary Research Association, London.

Hamblin, R., Moorlock, B. and Rose, J. 2000. A new glacial stratigraphy for Eastern England. *Quaternary Newsletter* 92, 35–43.

Lewis, S.G., Rose, J. and Davies, H. 1999. Pre-Anglian fluvial and Anglian glaciogenic sediments, Knettishall, Suffolk, England. *Proceedings of the Geologists' Association* 110, 17–32.

MacRae, R.J. 1999. New Lower Palaeolithic finds in Norfolk. *Lithics* 20, 3–9.

Preece, R.C. and Parfitt, S.A. 2000. The Cromer Forest-bed Formation: new thoughts on an old problem. In S.G. Lewis, C.A. Whiteman and R.C. Preece (eds.) *The Quaternary of*

Norfolk and Suffolk: Field Guide, 1–27. Quaternary Research Association, London.

Roe, D.A. 1968. *A Gazetteer of British Lower and Middle Palaeolithic Sites*. Council for British Archaeology Research Report 8, London.

Roe, D.A. 1981. *The Lower and Middle Palaeolithic Periods in Britain*. Routledge and Kegan Paul, London.

Rose, J. 1995. Britain 'colonised via Bytham River'. *British Archaeology* 5, 5.

Rose, J., Lee, J.A., Candy, I. and Lewis, S.G. 1999a. Early and Middle Pleistocene river systems in eastern England: evidence from Leet Hill, southern Norfolk. *Journal of Quaternary Science* 14, 347–360.

Rose, J., Whiteman, C.A., Allen, P. and Kemp, R.A. 1999b. The Kesgrave Sands and Gravels: 'pre-glacial' Quaternary deposits of the River Thames in East Anglia and the Thames Valley. *Proceedings of the Geologists' Association* 110, 93–116.

Shotton, F.W. and Wymer, J.J. 1989. Handaxes of andesitic-tuff from beneath the standard Wolstonian succession in Warwickshire. *Lithics* 10, 1–6.

West, R.G. 1980. *The Pre-glacial Pleistocene of the Norfolk and Suffolk Coasts.* Cambridge University Press, Cambridge.

Wymer, J.J. 1985. *Palaeolithic Sites of East Anglia.* Geo Books, Norwich.

Wymer, J.J. 1999. *The Lower Palaeolithic Occupation of Britain.* Trust for Wessex Archaeology and English Heritage, Salisbury.

19. New Lower Palaeolithic finds from the Upper Thames

Terry Hardaker

ABSTRACT

The recovery of over four hundred stone tools, two-thirds of them of non-flint material, from the Upper Thames gravels between 1989 and 2000 has allowed a reappraisal of the significance of quartzite as a raw material during the Lower Palaeolithic in this region. The quartzites are linked with the tongue of quartzite-bearing fluviatile gravels that demarcate the course of the Evenlode river in the Lower to Middle Pleistocene period. They provided a local source for blanks as an alternative to flint, which had to be imported at least 18 km, but this alternative was not taken up by all communities. The implications of sourcing and transporting flint from afar are examined. For the first time quartzite artefacts have been found on a high-level terrace away from a river bed, raising questions of date and occupation patterns. The juxtaposition of fine and poor workmanship, in both flint and quartzite, prompts speculation that finely made handaxes may have had symbolic rather than workaday significance. Finds of implements at Cassington Pit suggest two converging routes of flow for the Devensian gravels, and clustering of quartzite artefacts on the gravel floor is discussed. The paper attempts to maximise the information that can be extracted from derived deposits.

INTRODUCTION

The Lower Palaeolithic material from the Upper Thames, housed in the Donald Baden-Powell Quaternary Research Centre in Oxford under Derek Roe's custodianship, is of such magnitude that one might be forgiven for assuming that little more needed to be collected. It includes some of Britain's finest Acheulian handaxes from the Wolvercote Channel site, as well as abundant finds from Berinsfield and significant numbers from Wallingford, Abingdon, Stanton Harcourt and Iffley. However, the scarcity of primary context finds from the Lower Palaeolithic in Britain makes it important that all localities such as gravel pits should be thoroughly investigated and recorded, even if they yield only derived material. Such investigations were begun in the Upper Thames by R.J. MacRae in the 1970s and, with Derek Roe's encouragement, they culminated in the publication of *Non-Flint Stone Tools and the Palaeolithic Occupation of Britain* edited by MacRae &

Moloney (1988). This volume marked a turning point in our view of the Lower Palaeolithic of the Upper Thames. At the time of its publication, a total of 882 artefacts had been recorded from this region, of which 687 were flint and 175 quartzite. As prolific amounts of gravel have continued to be extracted from the Upper Thames throughout the 1990s, continuation of the search has been imperative and new finds are providing evidence to change previous perceptions.

Until the early 1970s, the acquisition of artefacts in the Upper Thames region had been selective in favour of flint handaxes. The Oxford collections contained almost none of the many other types of artefact such as choppers, cores, flakes and hammerstones made from quartzite as well as flint, which had been overlooked in the nineteenth and early twentieth century gravel diggings. MacRae's recognition of these less obvious artefacts, many in quartzite, prompted the publication of *Non-Flint Stone Tools and the Palaeolithic Occupation of Britain*, and this in turn heralded the way for others, including the present author and Jeffrey Wallis, to join in the search. As a result, the count of artefacts has dramatically increased, with quartzites in the period 1989–2000 comprising 66.4% of total finds as opposed to 14.6% for all finds previous to 1989 (Table 19.1).

This paper describes the different Upper Thames sites that have yielded artefacts in the period 1989–2000, and examines whether the increased proportion of quartzites offers any new evidence on the Lower Palaeolithic presence in this area. The relationship between finds of flint and quartzite artefacts and the proximity or otherwise of these finds to the parent sources of these rocks is discussed. The range of river terraces from which artefacts have come now extends from the Freeland Formation of the Northern Drift, with a date of Stage 13(?), through the Hanborough Terrace (probably Stage 10), the Stanton Harcourt Channel and adjacent Gravel (Stages 7 and 6), and the Floodplain Gravel (Stages 5 and 4). Most sites in the Upper Thames have yielded material in a derived context, although some finds, such as the Wolvercote and Gravelly Guy assemblages, had not moved far from their point of manufacture, and others, from the Stanton Harcourt Channel and the Northern Drift at Freeland, may be close to primary context. The distribution of finds in the Upper Thames is shown in Fig. 19.1, which also shows the distribution of the main parent raw material sources, flint from the chalk and quartzite from the Northern Drift. The archaeological sites are discussed in chronological order, starting with the oldest.

STRATIGRAPHIC CONTEXT OF THE NORTHERN DRIFT

The Northern Drift is the highest and oldest of the fluvial terrace sequences in the Upper Thames, representing more than one outwash event but none later than the Cromerian, or possibly early Anglian. Previous work on these deposits has been summarised by Bridgland (1994). Also known as the Plateau Drift, the Northern Drift comprises a wide variety of deposits from coarse pebble beds to fine silts and clays, which are termed, in increasing age order, the Freeland, Combe, Wilcote, Ramsden Heath and Waterman's Lodge Deposits (Hey 1986). Apparently lying between the Freeland and Combe deposits was the Sugworth Channel near Abingdon, an interglacial deposit with a profile of flora and fauna suggesting that the (pre-Sugworth) Drift is Cromerian and pre-Cromerian rather than Anglian as had previously been assumed (Shotton *et al*. 1980). Hey also pointed to a fluvial origin for the Drift. Previously Arkell (1947, 196) had suggested it was the deposit of an ice lobe.

The present distribution of the Drift is highly fragmented, as would be expected for a surface deposit that has survived more than a million years of warm–cold climatic fluctuation. It lies almost exclusively on the tops of the plateau-like terrain that represents the dip slope of the Cotswolds. Little of the Drift has migrated downslope, but it is occasionally seen in the form of a few quartzite pebbles, on the upper slopes of small valleys originating on the plateau. The fact that there is so little downslope movement of this material indicates that since the last wholesale erosional event at

Site	Quartzite	Flint	Andesite	Total	% Quartzite
Total Upper Thames finds before 1989	101	587	0	688	14.6
Finds from 1989 to December 2000					
Sutton Courtenay	89	84	1	174	51.1
Abingdon Sewage Works	10	3	0	13	76.9
Abingdon Drayton	3	6	1	10	30.0
Abingdon Tythe Farm	2	1	0	3	66.6
Abingdon Thrupp	4	7	1	12	25.0
Abingdon Culham Hill	0	2	0	2	50.0
Abingdon Lodge Hill	1	0	0	1	100.0
Radley Home Farm	15	3	0	18	83.3
Radley Lower	1	0	0	1	100.0
Yarnton West	91	1	1	93	97.8
Yarnton East	0	7	0	7	0.0
Hardwick	21	1	0	22	95.5
Gill Mill	38	0	0	38	100.0
Freeland Surface	13	0	0	13	100.0
Stanton Harcourt Channel	3	20	0	23	86.9
Stanton Harcourt Other	0	2	0	2	0.0
Latton	0	6	0	6	0.0
Totals 1989-December 2000	291	143	4	438	66.4
Grand Totals	392	730	4	1126	34.8

Table 19.1. Total artefact finds in the Upper Thames

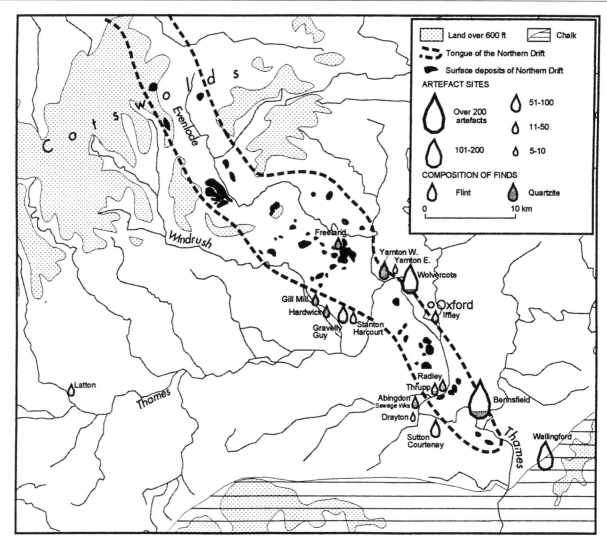

Fig. 19.1. Distribution of Upper Thames artefact finds in relation to raw material sources.

the end of the Devensian cold period about 13 kyr, such surface drift as remained has barely moved. This observation fits with the increasing recognition that, while geomorphological change is continuous at a low energy level, really large changes often take place quickly when, for example, a landscape is vulnerable through absence of vegetation, or when a catastrophic event occurs, such as a natural dam breaking. Both examples have played their part in shaping the present landscape of the Upper Thames.

The remnants of the Northern Drift form a tongue deposited by the waterborne deposit that flowed from the north, over the Cotswold escarpment, and roughly down the course of the present Evenlode valley into the Thames basin just south of Abingdon (Fig. 19.1). The present Evenlode valley had of course not been cut; the Drift represents a proto-Evenlode at a higher level, and from the variable stratigraphy of the Drift it is probable that this river flowed for a prolonged period, suggested by Maddy to date back 1.8 myr (Maddy 1997).

The Northern Drift is of immense importance to Lower Palaeolithic archaeology in this region, since virtually all non-flint, mostly quartzite, artefacts found in the Upper Thames are fashioned on pebbles originating from it. There is no other local source of quartzite material, except a few scattered high level gravels containing both quartzite and flint lying between Faringdon and Malmesbury (Briggs 1988). The discontinuous nature of the present surface deposits of Drift indicates that most of it has been washed away, and every subsequent terrace has its share of quartzite pebbles derived from the Drift, ranging from pieces the size of a walnut to rounded boulders larger than an ostrich egg. Thus, at every period of the Lower Palaeolithic, there has theoretically been quartzite material available in the vicinity of the tongue and downstream of it, which people could find for tool making.

The quartzite pebbles contained in the Northern Drift may be traced to various pre-Jurassic rocks in the Midlands, most notably the Bunter beds of Triassic age. They vary in hardness, a few being soft and almost crumbly, but the vast majority are extremely hard and difficult to work. Geologically they are classified as metaquartzite and orthoquartzite, a distinction difficult to see unless the pebbles are broken. The majority of the quartzites chosen for tool manufacture are orthoquartzite.

Westwards towards the higher reaches of the Upper Thames, the terraces are seen to contain progressively less quartzite material, but because Northern Drift quartzite seems to have been redeposited in all subsequent terraces close to the parent source, it is impossible to date artefacts made from it *per se*. Only the terrace from which the tools come can provide a *terminus ante quem* for dating.

ARTEFACTS FROM THE NORTHERN DRIFT

Until 1999, no quartzite artefacts of Lower Palaeolithic age had been recorded from the surface deposits of the Northern Drift. This is rather surprising, since the Drift comprises the greatest surface exposure of quartzite material anywhere in the region, which we can reasonably assume has been lying on the surface during all of the human occupations in the last half million years. In many parts of East and South Africa, Lower Palaeolithic artefacts are frequently seen on the surface; the present author has personally seen numerous examples in West Turkana and the Transvaal. I began looking for stone tools on the Northern Drift surface in 1994, but although percussive scars were common on quartzite pebbles, nothing could with certainty be ascribed to the work of Man. Colleagues

were sceptical; the assumed early date of the Drift would seem to rule out a human presence.

However, when a freshly ploughed field in the parish of Freeland was seen to contain a high concentration of larger pebbles, a renewed search was undertaken. In a few hours, thirteen items which could be claimed as artefacts were recovered (Table 19.2). All came from a concentrated area about 150 metres in diameter, which belongs to the Freeland Formation of the Drift, at an elevation of 350 feet (105 metres) (Fig. 19.2).

The date of the Freeland Formation, which is the latest of the Drift deposits, is suggested as Stage 11 or 12 (Sumbler 1995), Stage 12, Anglian, or 13, Cromerian (Bridgland 1994), or Stage 16 (approximately 650 kyr) if Maddy's model is correct (Maddy 1997, 543). The discovery of artefacts on such an old terrace could make this site one of the earliest in Britain. However, the finds raise more questions than they answer. There are uncertainties as to whether the pieces are artefacts rather than products of nature, and about their age. Furthermore, it is not clear whether the pieces were *in situ* in a primary context or derived from a source yet to be established. The following discussion addresses some of these uncertainties.

The pieces have been shown to Dr Derek Roe, Dr John Wymer, R.J. MacRae, Ray Inskeep and Dr Norah Moloney. All agreed that at least three of them were of human manufacture (Fig. 19.3), and that the others now listed were either probable or possible. A number of items in addition to the thirteen, which were initially regarded as possibles, have been rejected as a result of these consultations.

Description	Size (mm)	Condition	Removals	% Cortex	Comment
Artefacts					
Bifacial handaxe	135×95×68	slightly rolled	c. 18	50	Coarse workmanship but fine finishing at tip
Flake	65×96×19	slightly rolled	2 dorsal	20	Prominent bulb and cone and two previous dorsal removals
Split pebble core	66×79×36	slightly rolled	3	30	Naturally split pebble with three removals
Probable artefacts					
Unifacial handaxe	120×85×50	moderately rolled	2 or 3	70	Acheulian shape but removals with shallow bulbs
Flake	119×95×41	well rolled	–	50	Classic cortical flake with butt and bulb
Core	80×115×75	slightly rolled	5	60	Four removals in a row, all with radial scars, one opposite
Core on flake	97×115×47	sharp	3	30	Flake with butt and bulb and two other removals
Unifacial chopper	135×103×80	very rolled	3	75	Classic chopper
Possible artefacts					
Flake	115×130×64	slightly rolled	–	60	Large radial scar from percussive blow
Core?	76×100×33	slightly rolled	2	80	Both removals with strong scars – unfinished piece?
Debitage	95×104×30	sharp	5	50	All facets one side suggests human work
Bifacial chopper	135×112×81	well rolled	2 or 3	90	Alternate flaking on naturally split pebble
Core/chopper	110×85×51	sharp	2	90	Too sharp?

Table 19.2. Freeland surface artefacts

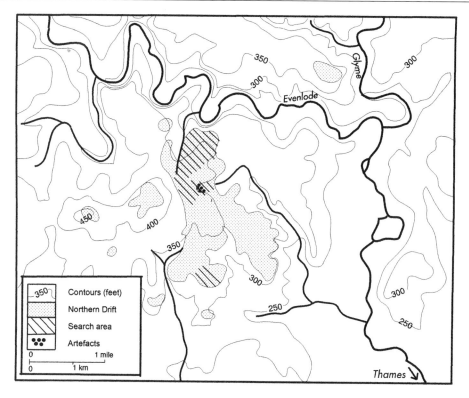

Fig. 19.2. Distribution of surface artefacts from the Northern Drift at Freeland.

The classification of the Freeland artefacts into certain, probable and possible categories requires explanation. Distinguishing artefacts from naturally struck stones is difficult at this site. The Drift deposits show a high incidence of naturally fractured stones, whether by recent plough action or ancient abrasion and percussion, which could superficially resemble Palaeolithic work. However, the likelihood of the probable and possible items being genuine is enhanced when viewed in the overall context of six years of field walking on the Drift: in no other area were there any items which could even gain possible status as Palaeolithic artefacts.

In assessing the artefacts, the criteria laid down by Saville (1988) have been taken as a guideline. Saville examined the Waite collection of surface quartzites from near Nuneaton, and only accepted pieces as artefacts if they showed some rolling and had two or more removals or a definite platform and bulb. It has sometimes been contended that quartzite surface artefacts may be of Mesolithic or even Neolithic date. For example, some of the Langdale handaxe roughouts of the Neolithic period resemble Lower Palaeolithic material. However, all who have seen the Drift artefacts agree that they have no such affinities.

Regarding the date of manufacture of the artefacts, there are three possibilities. They could have been made from earlier Drift material which has since been worked into the Freeland formation, they could be contemporary with the Freeland Formation, or they could have been made at any time later when this deposit was accessible on the land surface. Absence of artefacts from the older Drift formations corroborates other lack of evidence for the presence of man in Britain prior to the Cromerian, thus making the first option unlikely. If the plateau deposits of the Northern Drift as a whole had been used as a source for stone tools, we might expect to find tools scattered all over the Drift. Their restriction to this small area therefore perhaps hints at contemporaneity with the Freeland Formation, when it was fresh and not covered with vegetation. The variation in wear on the thirteen artefacts, from sharp to very rolled, might seem to contradict this, although the displacement of a few metres between artefacts, one in the bed of a stream and another on the bank, could produce marked differences in rolling on artefacts made at the same time.

The question of whether this cluster of artefacts represents an *in situ* event is not yet answerable: there are too many unresolved factors. The clustering of large pebbles at this site is unmistakable, and would seem to be the work of natural forces. The presence of a flake (Fig. 19.3c) hints at the possibility of knapping on site. As the most recent of the Northern Drift deposits, the Freeland Formation is likely to be the least disturbed by subsequent fluvial action at this elevation. However, 500,000 years or more is a long time for artefacts to be lying on the surface, and some movement cannot be ruled out, as documented by the rolling on some artefacts. Indeed, we do not know whether the deposits now seen on the surface have at some time in the past been buried by other material which has since been washed away.

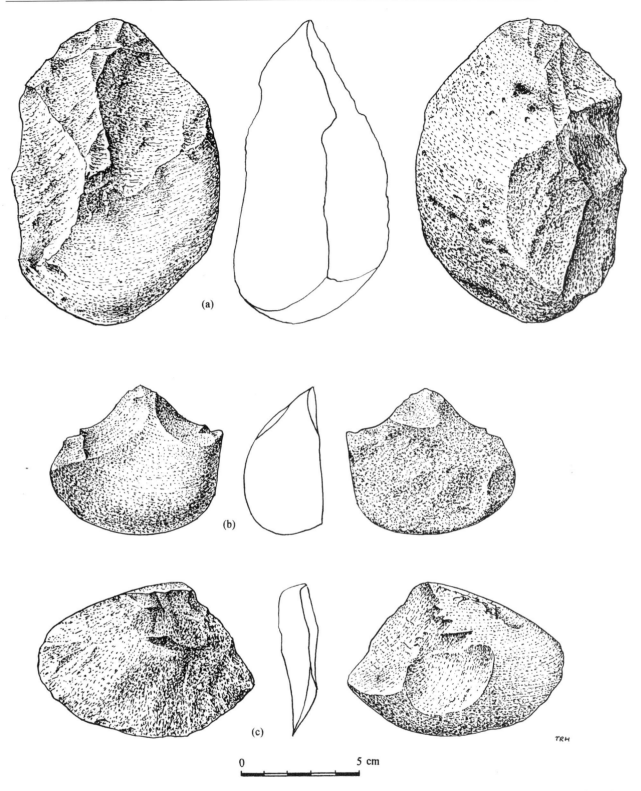

Fig. 19.3. Quartzite artefacts from the Northern Drift including handaxe (a); split pebble core (b) and flake (c).

There are certain elements of uniformity in the thirteen items recovered which may have a bearing on their contemporaneity. They are all made of non-flint material and all share a low level of technical skill. The erratic forms show that some stones were perhaps being tested but not made into finished implements, or that they were partially exploited cores.

Freeland is not the only place where surface finds of Palaeolithic material have been made from the Upper Thames. Jeffrey Wallis, working in the Abingdon area, has recovered six artefacts (four of them handaxes) from ploughed fields, although all have been isolated finds, probably reworked (pers. comm.). The nearest parallel to the Freeland artefacts is the site at Bramcote Hill in Warwickshire assembled by Waite (Saville 1988), where seventeen quartzite implements in four adjacent fields were found. Shotton (1988, 89) indicated that all of these were from a Wolstonian gravel lying on the surface and that they had been transported in the gravels from their original place of manufacture. The discovery of the surface finds at Freeland is an exciting development which will hopefully be expanded when ploughing allows further searching.

ARTEFACTS FROM STANTON HARCOURT (STAGE 6 AND 7 GRAVELS)

The complex of gravel pits in the region of Stanton Harcourt, near the junction of the Windrush with the Thames, have been under extraction since the 1930s. The artefacts from this area come from two different contexts: those recovered by MacRae from the base of the Stage 6 gravels in the pit know as Gravelly Guy, and others from the excavations less than a kilometre to the east of this pit at Stanton Harcourt (Stage 7) by Dr Katherine Scott and Christine Buckingham (Fig. 19.6). The forty-nine flint and nineteen quartzite artefacts (Figs. 19.4 and 19.11a–c and Fig. 19.5, respectively) from Gravelly Guy were collected as gravel extraction progressed between 1983 and 1994. The flint implements include both classic Acheulian and more roughly made handaxes (MacRae 1988). The twenty flint and three quartzite artefacts from Stanton Harcourt include handaxes, cores and flakes (Buckingham *et al.* 1996; Scott and Buckingham this volume). The Stanton Harcourt Channel represents part of a fossil course of the Thames underlying the cold Stage 6 gravels.

Although recovered from the lower levels of the Stage 6 gravels, the artefacts from Gravelly Guy are unlikely to represent a human presence during so cold a period. They must date to an earlier, warmer period within the Stage 7 bracket, although whether they are exactly contemporary with the artefacts recovered from the Stage 7 channel excavations (Scott and Buckingham this volume) is difficult to prove. Unfortunately, the ancient land surface which was recognised beneath the Stage 6 gravels at Gravelly Guy was never fully investigated, but there is some evidence

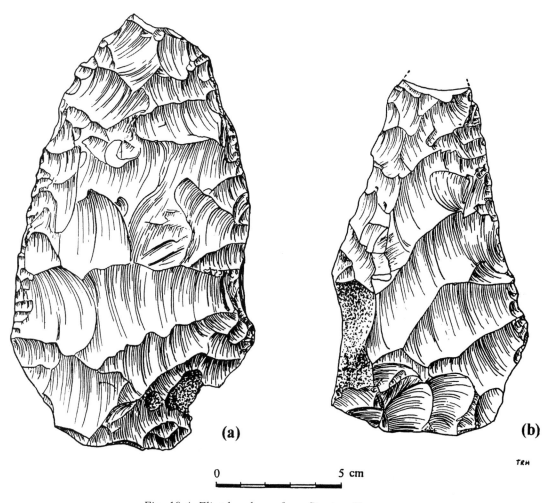

(a)   (b)

0 ┤━━━━━━━━┤ 5 cm

Fig. 19.4. Flint handaxes from Stanton Harcourt.

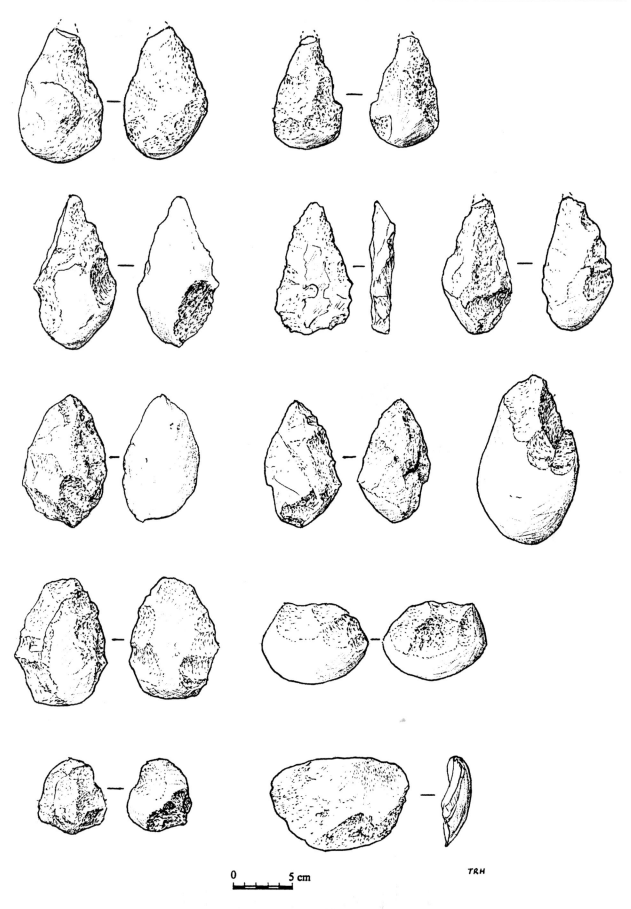

0 ⊢⊣⊢⊣⊢⊣ 5 cm

TRH

Fig. 19.5. Sketches of quartzite artefacts from Stanton Harcourt.

that the artefacts lay close to the place where they were used: the majority of implements were contained in an area of around 200 square metres, and 'three flint handaxes, almost fresh and much alike in size and technology, turned up in the same small section' (MacRae 1988, 130).

THE DEVENSIAN GRAVEL PITS OF THE UPPER THAMES

Each pit and its finds are described one by one, followed by a general discussion on all the finds.

Hardwick and Gill Mill Pits

These two pits lie close to one another in the floodplain of the River Windrush 5–6 km short of its confluence with the Thames (Fig. 19.1). Both have been visited regularly since the mid 1980s, at first by MacRae and, since 1989, also by the present author. At Hardwick, the Windrush becomes a braided river comprising three roughly parallel streams; the gravel pit is located in the floodplain between these streams. The quarried sections vary from three to four metres in depth and comprise mainly flat bedded fine to medium gravels with a predominance of limestone and about 10% quartzite. From 1987 to 2000, visits have been made roughly once every two months. Twenty-two artefacts have been recovered, of which only one is of flint. At Hardwick the proportion of flakes (eight examples) is unusually high, and six of these were found in the period 1987 to 1989. Apart from this, finds have been fairly evenly spaced in time.

At Gill Mill thirty-eight artefacts, all of quartzite, have been recovered from the gravels which are located a little upstream from Hardwick, not between the braided streams but on the east bank of the Windrush. In contrast to the steady, but thin, flow of artefacts from Hardwick, Gill Mill yielded only three items up to 1990, then none at all until May 1997. The remainder have formed a significant cluster from then to March 2000, with a peak of nine items in January 2000. This cluster has coincided with an area of excavation generally within 200 metres of the main channel of the Windrush.

Pits in the Abingdon area

The finds from the Devensian pits in the Abingdon area including Sutton Courtenay and Radley, have been mainly accumulated by Jeffrey Wallis and are summarised in Table 19.1. They will be published by him more fully at a later date. These finds closely parallel those of the present author's in the predominance of quartzite items.

Yarnton-Cassington Pit

A commercial gravel extraction plant known as Cassington Pit was opened by ARC one kilometre south of the village of Yarnton in 1989, and extraction has continued to the present day. This is the pit at which the author has spent most time in the last eleven years and will therefore be covered in some detail. So far eight flint and ninety-two quartzite pieces, along with one of andesite, have been found from this pit from June 1989 to December 2000 (Table 19.3).

The gravels lie close to the present course of the Thames (Fig. 19.7) and belong to the Floodplain (Northmoor) Terrace, with a date commencing at Stage 5a, or possibly 5c, from about 100 kyr (Maddy *et al.* 1998, 227–229).

	Hardwick		Gill Mill		Cassington	
	Flint	Quartzite	Flint	Quartzite	Flint	Quartzite
Bifacial handaxe	1	6	0	5	4	7
Unifacial handaxe	0	1	0	1	0	0
Handaxe roughout	0	0	0	1	1	0
Cleaver	0	0	0	1	1	0
Bifacial chopper	0	0	0	1	0	7
Copper-core	0	2	0	5	0	15
Unifacial chopper	0	0	0	4	0	12
Core	0	2	0	7	0	34
Flake	0	8	0	2	1	5
Retouched flake	0	0	0	2	1	0
Split pebble core	0	1	0	5	0	11
Core/hammerstone	0	0	0	2	0	0
Hammerstone	0	0	0	1	0	1
Chopper/hammerstone	0	1	0	0	0	0
Debitage	0	0	0	1	0	0
Totals	1	21	0	38	8	92

Table 19.3. Artefacts from Hardwick, Gill Mill and Cassington, 1989–2000

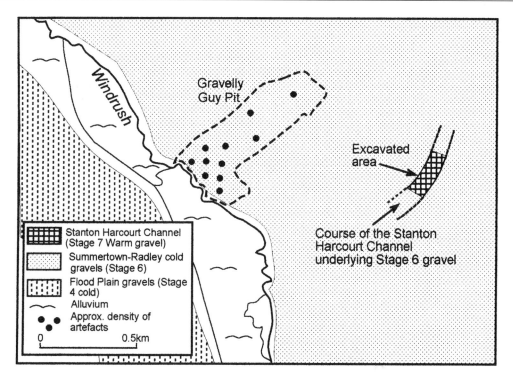

Fig. 19.6. Stanton Harcourt.

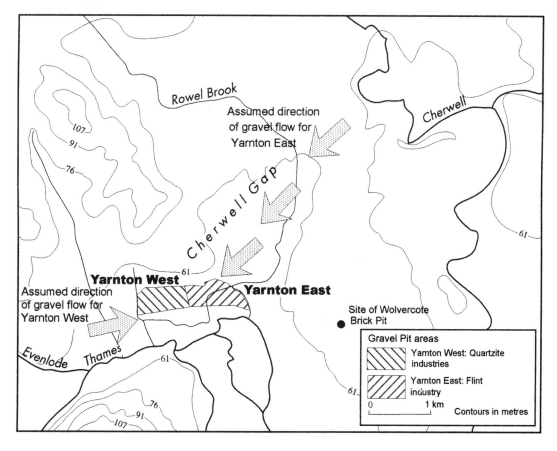

Fig. 19.7. Cassington gravel pit.

The present surface of the floodplain at this point is about 59 m OD, and the gravels reach a maximum depth of 4 m. Within the same pit at 62 m OD lies a remnant of the Second Terrace, classed on the BGS map as undifferentiated Summertown-Radley Terrace. The detailed stratigraphy of the floodplain gravel has been fully described, mainly from observations in the east end of the pit, by Maddy *et al.* (1998) who recognised five facies in the gravels. In terms of the archaeology, the two basal beds A and B may be significant, comprising a layer of coarse gravel (A) closely associated with discontinuous pockets of channel fills (B), the latter containing remains of vegetation and animal bones.

Artefacts from the Yarnton-Cassington Pit

It is believed that the search at the Cassington pit begun by MacRae and continued by the present author over eleven years, represents the most detailed Palaeolithic investigation of a Devensian floodplain terrace anywhere in Britain. Hopefully, it dispels the idea that derived material is of little interest. The main factors of importance here are:

• the distinct division between flint implements from the east of the pit and quartzites from the west, its significance to the availability of raw materials for artefact manufacture, and the implication that this division has on the geological separation of the Devensian gravel into Cherwell-driven and Thames-driven members;

• a strong indication that flint found in local gravels was used in conjunction with flint imported from afar;

• the recognition of clusters and voids in the spatial distribution of the artefacts;

• the prominence of a simple quartzite flake-and-core industry with few handaxes; and

• the absence of Mousterian or later artefacts from the gravels.

These points are discussed below and descriptions of key artefacts are highlighted in the course of the discussion.

The division between flint and quartzite implements

For the first four years after the pit opened, only flint artefacts were found, and these were scarce, averaging one or two a year. In December 1994, a superb quartzite handaxe was picked up by the writer on the floor of the pit (Fig.

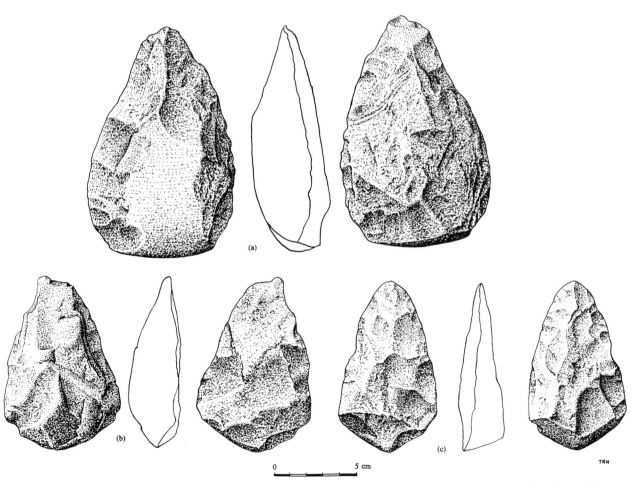

Fig. 19.8. Non-flint handaxes from Cassington made from plano-convex quartzite (a and b) and andesite (c).

19.8a), and for the next seven years only quartzite artefacts were found, with the single exception of a broken tip of an Acheulian flint handaxe in 1997. As the search for artefacts followed the progress of gravel extraction from east to west, an approximate geographic distribution map of finds was built up. A remarkable spatial separation of the flint from the quartzite implements became apparent. An examination of the local topography (Fig. 19.7) shows the present course of the Cherwell (a tributary of the Thames) flowing from the north and joining it 8 km further downstream from Yarnton. However, a broad channel, now occupied by the tiny Rowel Brook, cuts across from the Cherwell to the Thames 7 km upstream from the present confluence in the vicinity of Yarnton village. As may be seen from the BGS 1:50,000 map, this channel once represented the course of the Cherwell which drained into the Thames close to the eastern end of the present Cassington pit. All but one of the flint artefacts were found in this end of the pit and the quartzites have been found to the west of this. The presence of flint artefacts at the east end of the pit lends weight to the theory that the gravel here has come from a different direction from the quartzite-bearing gravels, confirming that the Rowel Brook is the former course of the Cherwell in the Devensian. However, the archaeological interpretation to be put on this observation is not so clear cut. MacRae (pers. comm.) has drawn attention to the possibility that the separation of flint and quartzite could simply be the result of a time difference, the flint being transported in gravels of later (or earlier?) date than the quartzites. This is a complex subject, raising the question not only of the relative age of the two different floodplain gravels, but also the variable age of their constituents. Thus two gravels deposited at the same time may contain artefacts derived from other gravels of different ages. The Devensian gravels are the final resting place of water worn materials shaped during previous glacial periods. There is little way of telling which stones have come from which climatic event. There is, however, some indication that the flint artefacts from the east end of the pit were manufactured at a place where there was no local access to quartzite (Fig. 19.1). If the home of this flint using community had been close to a major source of quartzite material, we might expect to see a mixture of flint and quartzite implements as seen in the nearby Wolvercote or Stanton Harcourt assemblages, but the Cassington flint implements are not mixed with quartzite. This suggests they originated some distance northwards up the Cherwell valley, away from the Drift, and have since been transported towards their present position near the confluence with the Thames. It is noteworthy that these flint implements were not clustered but spread widely: seven implements in five years of gravel excavation.

Local versus imported flint

Amongst the gravels of Cassington Pit, especially towards the east end, nodules of natural, unworked flint occur. Seldom larger than a cricket ball, and almost always frost-cracked, so that they shatter when dropped, these nodules are of two types: some reveal a light brownish interior of unevenly constituted material while others, generally having a smooth cortex the colour of milk chocolate, have a black interior. Two of the flint artefacts from the east end of the pit retain the same milk chocolate cortex and black interior of the local nodules. They are also small enough to have been fashioned on these nodules. Another item is an unfinished roughout from this material (Fig. 19.9c).

This is the clearest evidence we are likely to find that local flint nodules contained within the gravels were being exploited for artefact manufacture (cf. Fig. 19.11c, from Stanton Harcourt). At the time they were knapped, these two nodules were unaffected by frost cracking. However, implements that are demonstrably not made on these local nodules are also present in the Cassington assemblage, in particular the massive cleaver (Fig. 19.9a, MacRae 1993–94) and the moderate sized handaxe (Fig. 19.9b). Their cortex is quite different, and they are far too large. Assuming this flint assemblage belongs to a single industry, we see that to supplement the flint from local river gravels it was preferred to import other flint from afar, rather than turn to the quartzite which must have been present in the Upper Thames valley. This situation is the exact opposite to that in the western part of Cassington Pit, where quartzite was apparently the exclusive choice of material for implements.

Clusters and voids

The distribution of artefacts in Cassington has been uneven. From 1994 the pit was visited on a weekly basis and the time spent collecting was recorded. This averaged five hours per month. Table 19.4 shows the monthly totals of artefacts found. Significant clustering occurred between August 1997 to January 1998 and December 1998 to August 2000. A similar situation has been noted above for Gill Mill Pit, where the distribution has been even more erratic, and MacRae has noted similar patterns (MacRae 1988, 129).

Although there is no reason to rule out the occurrence of stray artefacts from the body of Devensian gravels, there is good reason to believe that most come from the coarse gravels that lie directly upon the Oxford Clay bedrock. These reasons are (1) that the artefacts are of a range of sizes commensurate with the large stones that are only found in quantity towards the base of the gravel (only occasional medium size stones are seen throughout the gravel in the many sections exposed by extraction), (2) that a considerable number of artefacts have been recovered direct from the pit floor, that is to say they are a part of the remnant of basal gravels not scooped up by the digger; (3) that some of the artefacts show adherence of Oxford Clay betraying their original resting place partly embedded in the Oxford Clay bedrock; and (4) that the concentrations of finds of artefacts from the reject heaps seem to coincide with the appearance of the coarse basal gravels in the pit.

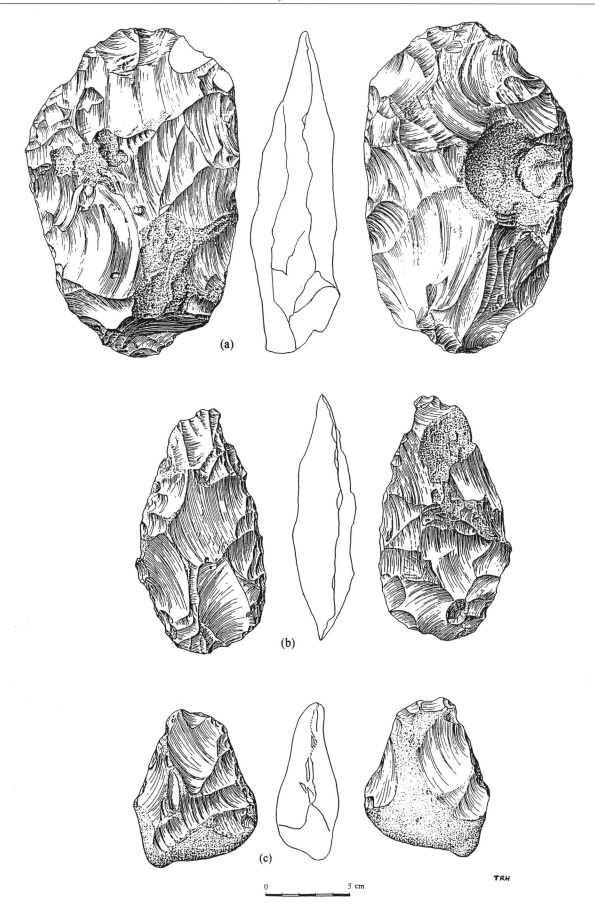

Fig. 19.9. Flint artefacts from Cassington: cleaver (a); plano-convex handaxe (b); handaxe roughout (c).

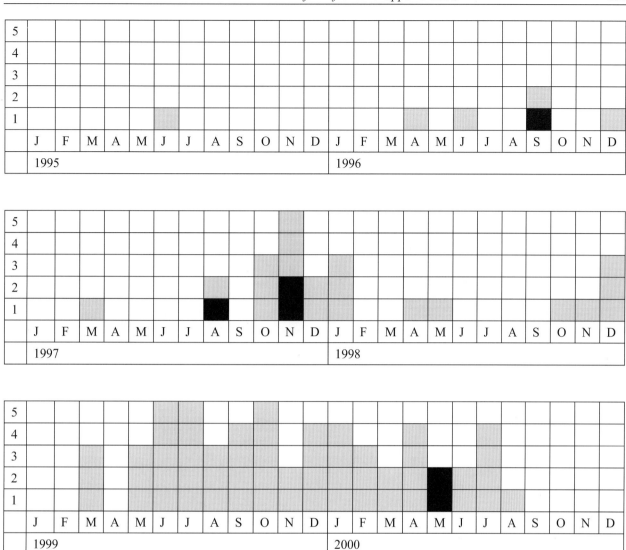

Handaxe Other artefact

Table 19.4. Number of finds per month 1995–2000 at Cassington Pit.

It has been assumed that all the artefacts in the Devensian gravels are in a derived context. There are no signs of *in situ* working, such as dense scatters or refits, and most of the artefacts are rolled. Obviously, any artefacts contained in the Devensian gravels will have been transported with these gravels from wherever they came; they certainly do not represent a human presence during the Devensian. Although Maddy *et al.* (1998) did not find any evidence that the coarse gravels they noted at the base of the sequence were pre-Devensian, it has to be asked whether there existed a pre-Devensian lag deposit on the surface of the Oxford Clay floor prior to Stage 5e and, if so, whether the clusters of artefacts belong to it (D. Bridgland pers. comm.). The possibility of similar lag deposits at Stanton Harcourt and Berinsfield was first mentioned by Roe (MacRae 1987, 9). It is also observed

that the coarse basal gravels in all these cases sometimes lie not upon true Oxford Clay but on a brown-grey weathered clay, occasionally containing black lenses rich in vegetational remains.

A SIMPLE FLAKE-AND-CHOPPER INDUSTRY?

A look at the artefacts from these two clusters (Table 19.5) shows assemblages with a heavy bias towards a simple flake and chopper industry. The three non-flint handaxes (one is made on a flake [not illustrated], one is a fine andesite handaxe, and the third a small plano-convex type, see Fig. 19.8 b–c) do not share a family likeness with the other artefacts. They are small and more delicately made, especially the andesite one which is an exquisite piece of

	1997–1998	1999–2000
Handaxe	1	2
Bifacial chopper	0	5
Unifacial chopper	2	3
Chopper-core	1	7
Core	5	24
Split pebble core	3	8
Flake	2	2
Hammerstone	0	1
Totals	14	52

Table 19.5. Artefact clusters from Cassington

work. The cores and choppers are mostly of crude style and frequently made on large pebbles (Fig. 19.10e, f and j). This raises the question of whether the handaxes are actually strays from the body of the gravel, or in some other way not part of an industry which otherwise has a uniformity in its simplicity and limited range of artefact types. If this is the case, the dominant assemblage at Cassington West is a non-handaxe quartzite industry of a kind unparalleled outside the Upper Thames. It is perhaps significant that the two handaxes from the 1998–2000 cluster appeared within seven days of each other. The question must, however, remain open, because the derived nature of the Upper Thames artefacts and the absence of *in situ* contexts deprives us of absolute proof of contemporaneity. Another possible explanation of the presence of these rare handaxes is discussed in the conclusions below.

The absence of Mousterian or later material

In gravels of Devensian age, any contemporary artefacts would be from Mousterian or Upper Palaeolithic industries. Apart from one doubtful flake, there have been no finds of this material at all from Cassington. If they were there, eleven years of searching would have revealed them. Throughout the whole of the Upper Thames there have been few finds relating to these periods, except for a handful of *bout coupé* handaxes from the western Upper Thames and a scatter of solitary finds of Upper Palaeolithic material. It seems to confirm the growing belief that Britain was unoccupied for the larger part of the Ipswichian until perhaps some time later in the Devensian (Wymer 1999, 33–34). Maddy *et al.* (1998) suggest that the Cassington deposits were laid down from Stages 5c/a to 2, but mostly before the end of Stage 4 (c. 73 kyr). Clearly, no human occupation is indicated in this area during this time.

DISCUSSION

Recovery of artefacts from the Upper Thames from the 1980s onwards has provided a markedly different picture from that pertaining before. Although there were probably plenty of quartzite artefacts in the Upper Thames gravels excavated in the past, they went largely unrecognised until MacRae's pioneering work. At last we now have a more balanced perspective.

The whole assemblage of Upper Thames material has to be set in the context of its geographic position in relation to the prevailing movement of peoples in the Palaeolithic. It is hardly likely that people migrated from the north southwards, except perhaps when in retreat in the face of deteriorating climate. The Upper Thames would normally be populated by people coming from a generally southerly direction, and thus they would in all probability have crossed flint-bearing rocks in their passage. Consequently they, or their ancestors, would have had a familiarity with flint, which would facilitate the tradition of flint importation to the region. When the flint implements from the Waite collection in the Coventry area, and other isolated finds from the Midlands, are also taken into account, it is clear that the practice of collecting flint from far away may have been a widespread activity when Lower Palaeolithic peoples occupied territories beyond the natural flint zone.

Gravel pits are usually located in river valleys, so the vast majority of our artefacts come from river valleys. Gibbard (1994, 166) has proposed that such concentrations may actually reflect a human preference for living near rivers, to avoid dense forest, to access blanks for stone tools, or to seek concentrations of animals. The Freeland artefacts tell us that in the Upper Thames this was not always the case.

The finds from the Upper Thames described in this paper suggest a preference for local material over flint, which had not been so apparent before. It is probable that three kinds of industry are represented: flint only (as at Cassington East, Wallingford, or Latton), flint and non-flint mixed (as at Gravelly Guy, Stanton Harcourt Channel, or Sutton Courtenay) and non-flint only (as at Freeland, Gill Mill, or Cassington West). It is particularly interesting that the flint finds are predominantly of handaxes with few flakes, cores, or choppers, whereas the non-flint finds are the opposite, with few handaxes and an overwhelming number of other types.

It should come as no surprise that in areas further from the Northern Drift, flint predominates in the assemblages. Thus at Latton, further upstream, or at Ewelme, close to the Chiltern flint, the finds contain only flint. More interesting are the pits that have yielded a mix of flint and quartzite, of which the Gravelly Guy Pit at Stanton Harcourt is representative. There is no significant difference in wear between flint and quartzite items in this assemblage, and if, as seems probable from the 'family likenesses' noted by MacRae, these artefacts are substantially the work of a single community, they were using both flint and quartzite in their toolkit. Since this area contains little local flint of knappable quality, it is clear that most of the flint was imported (Fig. 19.11a and c). The nearest natural flint is some 18 km to the south, which is the minimum distance the material would have had to be carried. As with the other pits where flint is recorded at some distance from its natural source, the implications for the level of social organisation in the community are profound. Knowledge of a distant source and the route to reach it, ability to organise a search party, with the level of communication which that implies, and ability to transport rocks, probably ready-knapped and possibly curated, are but some of the preconditions which must have been in place. Mellars (1996, 386) has pointed out that even in the Middle Palaeolithic, cases of fully worked tools being carried long distances to areas where lithic raw materials are lacking are scarce. Clearly, flint was the preferred material at Gravelly Guy, but it was evidently insufficient for their needs and was supplemented by local quartzite which was more difficult to fashion but much more easy to obtain. Although the quality of knapping is variable, the best shows skilled soft hammer work with a good command over shape. The overall impression is of a versatile community with a range of at least 18 km and possessing a more thorough knowledge of the local terrain than would be possible with mere transient occupation.

One entirely new factor to emerge from the Upper Thames since 1989 is the presence of assemblages devoid of any flint at all, notably at Freeland (13 items), Cassington West (92 items) and Gill Mill (38 items). The explanation for lack of flint would seem to be simple: in the Thames valley from the lower Windrush to Abingdon we have an unusual, if not unique, situation, in that quartzite pebbles suitable for artefact manufacture were abundant in the river beds or outwash gravels in Palaeolithic time. This provided an on-the-spot source for implements, thus making the need to import flint unnecessary. However, only some communities responded in this way; others used a mixture of both materials.

Another new factor is confirmation of the existence of the split pebble core, discussed by MacRae (1988, 134), and Wallis (1988, 155–157). These comprise naturally split quartzite pebbles where the platform so created has been exploited for removal of flakes. So far fourteen have been recovered, eight from Cassington, four from Gill Mill, one from Freeland and one from Hardwick (Fig. 19.10a–d).

Some of the quartzite artefacts are massive, the heaviest weighing over 1.5 kilos. Most at this size are oval pebbles exploited for the removal of a few large flakes, but some choppers are seen (Fig. 19.10j). To achieve a removal from such a large pebble requires a very heavy blow from a large hammerstone. The author has tried on pebbles half this weight and failed to make any impact. In these examples, we have clear evidence of the extreme robustness of their makers, boldness of ambition and, probably, the size of their hands.

The Upper Thames finds may have relevance to a question that repeatedly arises in Palaeolithic studies: why the Acheulian shape of handaxe, in Africa and elsewhere, persists for over a million years. This is especially curious, as the bilateral symmetry so painstakingly achieved on

many Acheulian items would seem (to us) hardly worth the effort for the marginal practical advantage over a non-symmetrical cutting tool. Artefact size and shape may well be influenced by the raw material available. Thus flint will knap easily and so allows handaxes to be made, but quartzite is hard to work and so usually permits only cruder implements. However, that does not explain the care lavished on symmetry, as seen in some handaxes, both of quartzite and flint, from the Upper Thames.

Here, fine Acheulian quartzite handaxes are found alongside cruder tools at Cassington (compare, for example, Figs. 19.8 and 19.10). Hardwick, Gill Mill, Gravelly Guy and some of the pits near Abingdon have a similar mix of quality both in flint and quartzite, using both hard and soft hammer techniques (Fig. 19.11). It would be difficult to imagine people occasionally rousing themselves from a mundane routine to produce exceptional pieces of work, unless there was some special motive. Some recent studies have raised the concepts of inequality and power in remote prehistory (Boone 1992, 301–337; Dobres and Robb 2000, 8 *inter alia*), and it is possible that the Upper Thames assemblages offer evidence for this. The juxtaposition of fine and poor workmanship may be understood if a community was making quickly-produced, 'fit for purpose' tools for its daily needs, but also required symbolic items from time to time. The most skilled craftsmen in the community may have made the finely-finished, symmetrical handaxes, such as the magnificent large demi-ficron (Fig. 19.11a), for these occasions.

CONCLUSION

This paper has described artefacts from surface drift as old as half a million years, and others perhaps deposited after 80 kyr. Whereas the deposits from the older terraces have a *terminus ante quem* to assist in their dating, the Devensian material is more problematic. If there was an absence of human occupation in Britain for the larger part of the Ipswichian until perhaps some time after 73 kyr (see above), the Lower Palaeolithic artefacts which found their final resting place in Devensian gravels (or even in a pre-Devensian lag deposit), must have been made at least 100,000 years before. Any conclusions based on the distribution patterns (clusters) of such artefacts must be tentative, because of the huge lapse of time between manufacture and final deposition.

Unfortunately, the archaeologist has little control over where investigation of gravels can be conducted. Fig. 19.1 shows the limitations of the study: large tracts of the Upper Thames and the Cherwell remain uncharted, and only the zone adjacent to the Northern Drift has had adequate sampling. Thus the question of whether the absence of local material for artefact manufacture restricted the wider geographic range of early humans can barely be addressed, although the imported flint tools suggest it did not. The other side of this coin is clearer: people were certainly

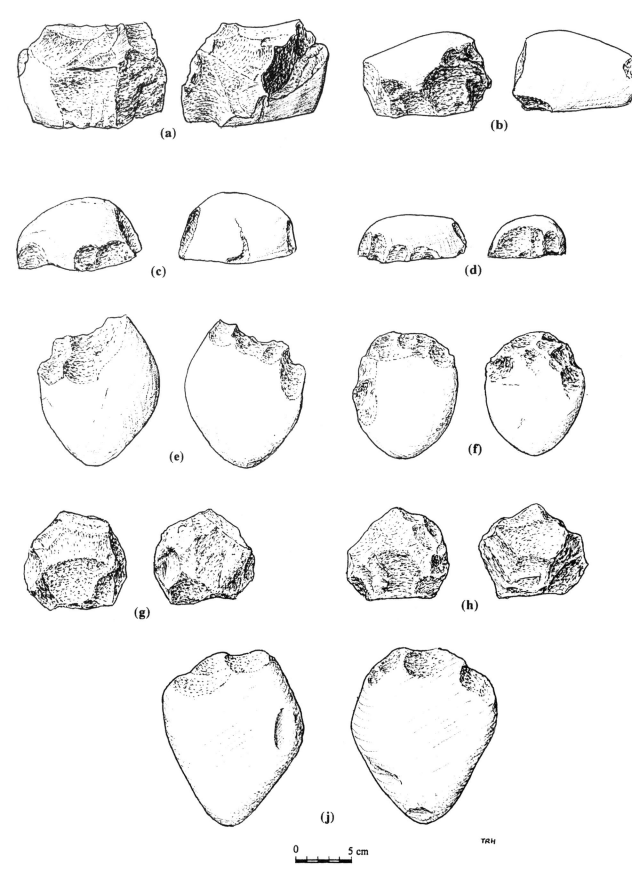

Fig. 19.10. Sketches of quartzite artefacts from Cassington: split pebble cores shown with natural split of pebbles face down (a–d); choppers (e, f); cores (g, h); massive chopper (j).

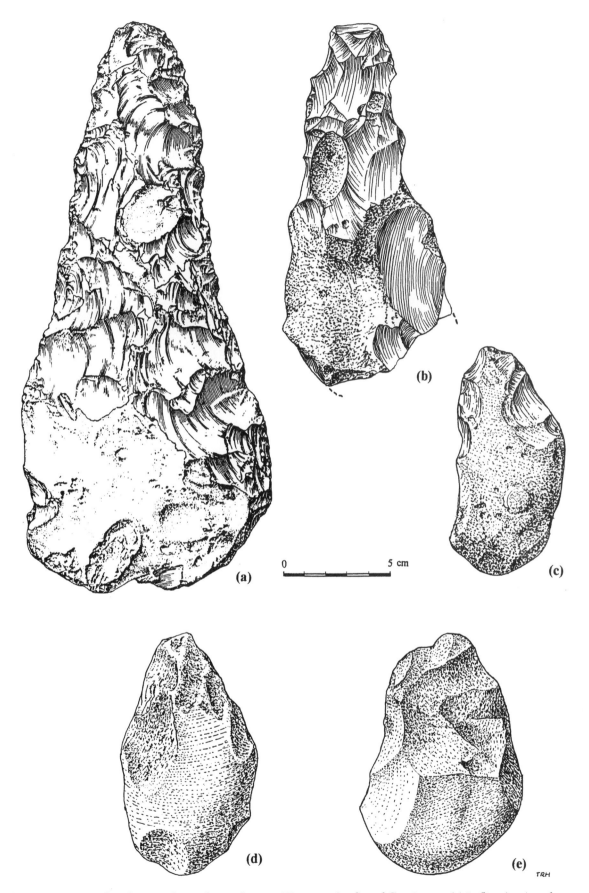

Fig. 19.11. Variation in handaxe workmanship at Stanton Harcourt (a–d) and Cassington (e) in flint (a–c) and quartzite (d–e).

present where source material was available, whether flint or quartzite.

In an ideal world every gravel pit would have its local archaeologist monitoring extraction on a regular basis. However, sadly, the number of people with the right combination of experience, enthusiasm and free time is insufficient to achieve this. As a result, data on the Palaeolithic are being irretrievably lost each day throughout southern Britain, as gravel pits are worked without any archaeological attendance. If this paper helps to enhance the interest in this lacuna and raise the profile of the humble gravel pit, the credit must go to R.J. MacRae for beginning the whole crusade and to Derek Roe for his unfailing support over more than twenty-five years.

ACKNOWLEDGEMENTS

My thanks to Jill Cook and Sarah Milliken for inviting me to write this paper. For their kind advice and guidance I thank David Bridgland, Ray Inskeep, Darrel Maddy, Norah Moloney, and John Wymer. I am grateful to Jeffrey Wallis for allowing me to use his list of the quartzite artefacts found in the Abingdon area and for permission to use his drawing of the Stanton Harcourt demi-ficron (Fig. 19.11a). Special thanks to Bob Turner and Guy Pharon at the ARC (now Hanson) pit at Cassington, Bob Bacon at the Smiths Gill Mill Pit and Darrel Mears at Hardwick Pit, for allowing me access over many years. Simon Lewis has most kindly offered valuable comments on the Northern Drift and the Cassington gravels. As mentioned above, Derek Roe's helpful guidance is deeply woven into this paper. Most of all I am indebted to R.J. MacRae whose enthusiasm inspired this work, and whose careful checking of the manuscript has saved me from many pitfalls, both literary and scholarly.

REFERENCES

Arkell, W.J. 1947. *The Geology of Oxford*. Clarendon Press, Oxford.

Boone, J.L. 1992. Competition, conflict and development of social hierarchies. In E.A. Smith and B. Winterhalder (eds.) *Evolutionary Ecology and Human Behaviour*, 301–337. Aldine de Grutyer, New York.

Bridgland, D.R. 1994. *Quaternary of the Thames*. Chapman and Hall, London

Briggs, D.J. 1988. The environmental background to human occupation in the Upper Thames Valley during the Quaternary period. In R.J. MacRae and N. Moloney (eds.) *Non-Flint Stone Tools and the Palaeolithic Occupation of Britain*, 167–186. British Archaeological Reports British Series 189, Oxford.

Buckingham, C.M., Roe, D.A. and Scott, K. 1996. A preliminary report on the Stanton Harcourt Channel deposits (Oxfordshire, England). *Journal of Quaternary Science* 11, 397–415.

Dobres, M.A. and Robb, J. (eds.) 2000. *Agency in Archaeology*. Routledge, London.

Gibbard, P.L. 1994. *Pleistocene History of the Lower Thames Valley*. Cambridge University Press, Cambridge.

Hey, R.W. 1986. A re-examination of the Northern Drift of Oxfordshire. *Proceedings of the Geologists' Association* 97, 291–302.

MacRae, R.J. 1987. Tool manufacture in quartzitic and similar rocks in the British Palaeolithic. *Lithics* 7, 7–12.

MacRae, R.J. 1988. The Palaeolithic of the Upper Thames and its quartzite implements. In R.J. MacRae and N. Moloney (eds.) *Non-Flint Stone Tools and the Palaeolithic Occupation of Britain*, 123–154. British Archaeological Reports British Series 189, Oxford.

MacRae, R.J. 1993–94. The case of the migrating cleaver. *Lithics* 14–15, 21–23.

MacRae, R.J. and Moloney, N. (eds.) 1988. *Non-Flint Stone Tools and the Palaeolithic Occupation of Britain*. British Archaeological Reports British Series 189, Oxford.

Maddy, D. 1997. Uplift-driven valley incision and river terrace formation in Southern Britain. *Journal of Quaternary Science* 12, 539–545.

Maddy, D., Lewis, S.G., Scaife, R., Bowen, D.Q., Coope, G.R., Green, C.P., Hardaker, T., Keen, D.H., Rees-Jones, J., Parfitt, S. and Scott, K. 1998. The Upper Pleistocene deposits at Cassington, near Oxford. *Journal of Quaternary Science* 13, 227–229.

Mellars, P. 1996. *The Neanderthal Legacy: An Archaeological Perspective from Western Europe*. Princeton University Press, New Jersey.

Saville, A. 1988. The Waite collection of Palaeolithic artefacts from the Nuneaton area of Warwickshire. In R.J. MacRae and N. Moloney (eds.) *Non-Flint Stone Tools and the Palaeolithic Occupation of Britain*, 67–88. British Archaeological Reports British Series 189, Oxford.

Shotton, F.W. 1988. The Wolstonian geology of Warwickshire in relation to the Lower Palaeolithic surface finds in North Warwickshire. In R.J. MacRae and N. Moloney (eds.) *Non-Flint Stone Tools and the Palaeolithic Occupation of Britain*, 89–94. British Archaeological Reports British Series 189, Oxford.

Shotton, F.W., Goudie, A.S., Briggs, D. and Osmaston, H.A. 1980. Cromerian Interglacial deposits at Sugworth near Oxford. *Philosophical Transactions of the Royal Society of London* B 289, 55–86.

Sumbler, M.G. 1995. The terraces of the rivers Thame and Thames and their bearing on the chronology of glaciation in central and eastern England. *Proceedings of the Geologists' Association* 106, 93–106.

Wallis, J. 1988. Natural damage in quartzite pebbles. In R.J. MacRae and N. Moloney (eds.) *Non-Flint Stone Tools and the Palaeolithic Occupation of Britain*, 155–157. British Archaeological Reports British Series 189, Oxford.

Wymer, J.J. 1999. *The Lower Palaeolithic Occupation of Britain*. Trust for Wessex Archaeology and English Heritage, Salisbury.

20. One step beyond. Flint shortage above the Goring Gap: the example of Wolvercote

Nick Ashton

ABSTRACT

Wolvercote is one of the few sites with a sizable assemblage of flint bifaces from an area in which usable flint raw material is locally scarce, and as such it holds a rare position in the British Lower Palaeolithic. The evidence for secondary retouch on many of these bifaces, which in some cases has led to the creation of plano-convex cross-sections, suggests that they had been resharpened as an economising measure. In contrast, the bifaces made from locally abundant quartzite are characterised by significantly lower incidences of secondary retouch and plano-convexity. These results lend further weight to the suggestion that variation in biface form can best be explained by non-cultural factors, such as raw material availability.

INTRODUCTION

In 1981 Derek Roe wrote of the 'bewildering variety rather than an orderly and predictable pattern of variation' in British Lower Palaeolithic assemblages (1981, 270). This assessment was primarily based on his unparalleled metrical analysis of 38 biface assemblages (Roe 1968a). His hopes for the future were mixed. Some of the apparent confusion he attributed to 'the lack of clear dating for so many British sites', a problem that could perhaps be solved (Roe 1981, 270). But tempering this, a clear pattern of continuity was not to be expected; with people 'arriving from different sources and staying for a while ... there was no permanent local population to absorb each new incursion and provide continuity. Rather, the story is one of stops and starts' (Roe 1981, 269–270). Fundamentally, though, the variation was due to the traditions and styles of different peoples.

Twenty years later we do have the benefit of a longer chronology and more refined means of dating, but perhaps with little surprise, the variation in biface assemblages remains difficult to interpret. As a result of these apparent difficulties, it has become increasingly popular over the last ten years to seek non-cultural explanations for the variation in biface assemblages and biface form. One model that has been put forward is that biface variation is due to differences in the degree of resharpening, with pointed bifaces being the initial form and ovates being created through progressive resharpening (McPherron 1994, 1995). A variety of metrical analyses were used (based on Roe's data) to show that pointed bifaces retained more cortex, were more elongated and had fewer flake scars, leading to the conclusion that they were an early stage in the reduction to resharpening process. Ashton and White (in press) have provided a critique of this model. They argue that although the analyses show less reduction on pointed bifaces, it does not necessarily indicate resharpening. Equally, at the individual site level, the model would appear to fail, where at Boxgrove, for example, complete knapping sequences and stages can be recognised, from ovate-shaped roughouts to final discarded ovates, but without the intermediate pointed forms (Austin *et al.* 1999).

An alternative model has been invoked for biface variation, arguing that raw material shape was a major determinant of eventual biface shape (Ashton and McNabb 1994; Ashton and White in press; White 1995, 1996,

1998a). It is suggested that ovate bifaces were the preferred form, produced where raw material would allow, but other forms were conditioned by the shape of the original nodule, pointed forms tending to be produced on thick, elongated nodules. This model was given greater credence through the demonstration of the close correlation between biface form and raw material source, with ovate dominated assemblages being closest to fresh Chalk flint, and point dominated assemblages being reliant on gravel flint (White 1998a, 26).

Although this interpretation may explain an important part of the variation in biface form, there are some bifaces and some assemblages that defy logical explanation in this way. Twisted ovates, for example, appear to be limited to OIS 11, are largely from Britain, and have yet to be explained through function (White 1998b). They may truly represent a distinctive style or tradition. Equally, satisfactory explanations for over-large bifaces, such as that from Furze Platt, are lacking, other than the models of the role that bifaces might play in sexual selection, suggested by Kohn and Mithen (1999). One assemblage that also stands out is that of Wolvercote. This site was the sole occupier of Roe's Group III of British biface assemblages, as the bifaces displayed quite different characteristics, being pointed in form and having plano-convex cross-sections (1968a, 78). These attributes he compared to both German and French Micoquian industries (1981, 123). As Roe has continuously encouraged the study and interpretation of this assemblage over the last thirty years, it seems appropriate here to re-examine this site in the light of the models above.

WOLVERCOTE

The site at Wolvercote lies just to the north of Oxford and was discovered in a brick-pit towards the end of the nineteenth century (Bell 1894, 1904). Sandford (1924, 1926) studied the geology in greatest detail, describing Oxford Clay at the base, overlain by fluvial gravel (Wolvercote Gravel), into which a channel was cut. This channel contained a calcareous gravel, including artefacts, followed by sands, peat and clays, the whole sequence being overlain by later solifluction. The pit was closed in the 1930s, and although attempts have been made to relocate sections through the channel, these have met with mixed success (Bridgland and Harding 1986; Briggs *et al.* 1985; Tyldesley 1986).

The dating of the Wolvercote sequence remains controversial. Many workers have accepted the long-held interpretation that the apparently high flint content in the Wolvercote Gravel (compared to higher terrace gravels) was due to input from, and therefore contemporary to, glacial sediments in the Midlands, in particular the Midlands Chalky Boulder Clay (Briggs 1988; Sandford 1932; Shotton 1953, 1983; Tomlinson 1929). These sediments were originally interpreted as Wolstonian in age (Shotton 1983), but have now been interpreted as Anglian (correlated with OIS 12) (Bowen *et al.* 1986; Rose 1987; Sumbler 1983). According to this interpretation the Wolvercote Channel would therefore date to OIS 11 (Briggs 1988). This argued increase of flint in the gravel compared to the earlier and higher Hanborough Terrace Gravel has been disputed by Maddy *et al.* (1991) who point out that there is no clear increase in flint in the Wolvercote Gravel relative to other foreign lithologies. They also state that recent lithological analysis suggests that the flint is not derived from the Midlands Chalky Boulder Clay, but instead from the much older Northern Drift.

Bridgland considers that the Wolvercote sequence represents a cold–warm–cold aggradation that can be correlated to the Lynch Hill Gravel of the Middle Thames (1994, 63–64). This would suggest that the Wolvercote Gravel dates to late OIS 10, and that the channel sequence and the associated artefacts date to the following warm phase, OIS 9. Any correlation, however, between the Upper and Middle Thames has been argued to be tentative, given the absence of terrace deposits around the Goring Gap (Maddy *et al.* 1991). Perhaps the strongest argument is that the gravel from the earlier and higher Hanborough terrace contains a Hoxnian (OIS 11) fauna (Bridgland 1994, 63), and on this basis an OIS 9 date for the channel would seem most likely.

In total 185 artefacts are listed as coming from the Wolvercote Channel of which 75 are bifaces (Roe 1968b, 253). They have been argued to be in generally fresh condition which suggests that they constitute a primary context assemblage (Tyldesley 1986, 84). Their morphology, which is predominantly pointed and often plano-convex, led Evans to describe them as 'shoe-shaped' (1896, 593) and later Sandford as 'slipper-shaped' (1926, 132). Sandford attributed them to an Upper Acheul-Micoque (1932, 9), after similar looking bifaces from the site of La Micoque, particularly level N (Dordogne, France). Wymer referred them to 'a highly refined Acheulian industry' (1968, 90). Roe (1981, 123), following Sandford, also found continental parallels, again suggesting comparisons with La Micoque, but also Bockstein III levels of the Bockstein sites near Ulm and Klausennische near Lekheim, both in Germany. Certainly all three sites have produced pointed bifaces with a plano-convex cross-section.

The latest analysis of the assemblage by Tyldesley (1986) has provided a much more detailed picture. She emphasised that only eight of the bifaces examined were of a classic Wolvercote style, although many others did share some of these features. A specific manufacturing technique was recognised that might be due to functional or stylistic reasons, perhaps even representing the work of one individual. Although similar bifaces could be found in other British assemblages, none showed this consistency in technique. Comparisons with sites from Germany and France showed some similarities in biface form, but differences in assemblage composition. She did, however, conclude that 'the name "Western Micoquian" would seem appropriate for the British and French group' (Tyldesley 1986, 173).

RECENT STUDY

The assemblage has been re-examined with particular reference to the raw material and reduction models discussed above. The study includes sixty bifaces, which are all the complete bifaces listed in the catalogue of Tyldesley (1986) with the exception of those regarded as of uncertain origin. The general characteristics of the assemblage are discussed below.

Of the sixty bifaces, fifty are made from flint, and ten from quartzite. The source of the quartzite is probably from the Wolvercote Gravel, which includes both pebbles and 'boulders' of reasonable quality and size (Sandford 1924, 136). However, the source of the flint has been the subject of some debate. The Wolvercote Gravel does contain flint, but the clasts have been argued to be too small for biface production (Briggs *et al.* 1985, 10; Roe 1981, 118). Recent lithological analysis by Maddy *et al.* (1991) has also noted that this flint is decayed and weathered and is in a similar condition to that contained within the Northern Drift, remnants of which lie within 5 km of the site. Fresher flint from the Midlands Chalky Boulder Clay appears to be entirely absent. MacRae (1988) has suggested the Wallingford Fan Gravels as a source, although that flint is also of poor quality (White 1998a, 44) and lies 25 km to the south-east. The source favoured by most authors is that from the Chalk of the Chilterns, lying over 20 km to the south (Bridgland 1994, 62; Briggs *et al.* 1985, 11). However, analysis of the cortex on the Wolvercote bifaces by White suggests that over 90% are made on gravel flint (1998a, 27) and he argues for a more local gravel source (1998a, 44). The important point is that raw material, whether local or otherwise, was probably in short supply in the immediate vicinity of Wolvercote, and is likely to have had some effect on the character of the industry.

The quartzite bifaces are often made on split pebbles, but the blank form of those made from flint varies. Where determinable, twenty-two bifaces have been made on nodules, whereas seven have been made on large flakes. The use of flakes as a blank form has been argued to be one of the reasons for plano-convexity. This may have contributed to the prevalence of this type of morphology, but does not appear to be the sole reason.

The plano-convex cross-section has been argued to be one of the main unifying features of the assemblage, though as Tyldesley pointed out, comparatively few bifaces actually show this feature (1986, 184). Of the flint bifaces, twenty have a distinct plano-convex cross-section, compared to ten where this feature is slightly apparent (often on the tip), and twenty where it is absent (Fig. 20.1). On the twenty bifaces where this feature is distinct, it has usually been caused by secondary flaking, where all the final flaking has

been concentrated on one face. On examination of all the bifaces, this technique of selective flaking is in fact a far greater unifying feature than the plano-convex cross-section. Of the fifty bifaces, thirty-two seem to have been flaked in this way (Fig. 20.1b). This suggests that the plano-convex cross-section is an accidental by-product of a technique, rather than a desired end form. What is also apparent, is that this final selective flaking on one face is characterised by small removals, often resembling retouch. This retouching is also present on ten of the other bifaces that have not been flaked selectively (Fig. 20.1; Table 20.1). In other words, forty-two flint bifaces bear secondary retouch, usually on one face, which has sometimes resulted in plano-convexity.

Plano-convexity is less of a feature on the quartzite bifaces (Table 20.1), but where it is present it appears to have been caused by the minimal flaking and the form of the split pebbles used as blanks. The type of secondary retouch found on the flint bifaces is rare.

The other feature that has been argued to unify the assemblage is the pointed plan-form. There is little doubt that the majority of the flint bifaces bear this morphology, although fifteen ovate forms also occur. The pointed plan-form has been created in many cases through increased fine flaking or retouch at the tip. Flaking of this type is much less prevalent around the basal half of the biface, where on thirteen examples the butt is entirely cortical. However, of the quartzite bifaces, only 50% are pointed in form, the remainder being ovates.

Some authors have described the Wolvercote bifaces as large (e.g. Bridgland 1994, 62). This observation is certainly true of the nine flint pieces over 150 mm, the largest being 244 mm, but does not entirely reflect the remainder of the assemblage. Of the other forty-one flint bifaces, twenty-four are under 120 mm, the smallest being 73 mm, and the overall average 121 mm. The quartzite bifaces vary between 146 and 79 mm, with an average of 106 mm.

Another term often used to describe the bifaces is 'refined' (Roe 1968a, 73; Wymer 1968, 90). This seems to be partly based on the increased flaking around the

	Flint bifaces	Quartzite bifaces
% of pointed forms (Roe's definition)	70	50
% with pointed tip	68	40
Plano-convexity		
% marked	40	30
% slight	20	20
% absent	40	50
% with 'retouch' on one face	64	20
% with 'retouch' on both faces	20	0
Total bifaces	50	10

Table 20.1. Comparison of technological features of flint and quartzite bifaces from Wolvercote.

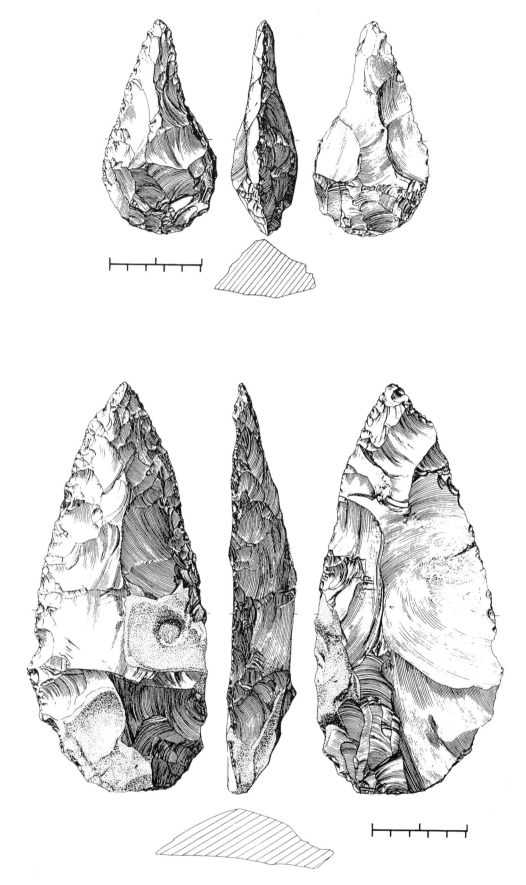

Fig. 20.1. Bifaces from the Wolvercote Channel, illustrated by C.O. Waterhouse and reproduced with permission of the Pitt Rivers Museum.

tips, but also on Roe's measure of relative thickness (thickness/breadth) (1968a, 24). It is of interest that using this measure the quartzite bifaces are generally more refined than those made of flint.

INTERPRETATION

The raw material model, as outlined above, has been put forward strongly for Wolvercote by White (1998a, 31). Although a source for raw material cannot be identified, from the evidence of the worn cortex he argues that most of the bifaces are made on gravel flint, often with the selection of either flake blanks, flat tablets or thin, flat-sided nodules. As argued above, therefore, the plano-convexity is a by-product of the technology, which itself was determined by the raw material. The choice of this raw material form, he suggests, might have been an economising measure in an area scarce in flint. He develops the argument with the further suggestion that the assemblage might divide into two, with the majority being an expediently produced local element, and the larger classic bifaces being imported.

These arguments undoubtedly have some merit, although there are two elements that perhaps require further explanation. First, if flatter nodules, flint tablets and large flakes are being selected as biface blanks, then it would be expected that at least some of these would be produced as ovates, as according to the raw material model they would be the preferred form. This does not appear to be the case. Second, the arguments do not account for the characteristic retouching, particularly towards the tips, that is rather different from bifaces from other assemblages in Britain.

These problems can be addressed and the model taken further through the examination of the role that resharpening might play. It is argued above that at most sites, the impact of resharpening was probably of minor importance in determining biface form, due in part to the ready availability of flint at most other sites. At Wolvercote flint raw material, whether local or otherwise, was arguably scarce, leading to economising measures and perhaps resharpening. The effects of resharpening would be twofold: firstly, a reduction in the size of the bifaces; and secondly, an increase in flaking around the resharpened areas. Furthermore, if the raw material arguments are accepted and at least some of the bifaces were brought from some distance, then the initial forms would be expected to be ovate in shape. To avoid minaturisation, any resharpening would be expected to be concentrated at one end, and have the effect of producing more elongated, pointed forms. This, it should be noted, is the opposite of the prediction made by McPherron (1994).

The first of these predictions cannot be assessed, as the initial size of the bifaces is unknown. The second prediction, however, is possibly met by the increased flaking and retouch towards the tips. Equally, the third prediction would appear to be met, but this is based on the assumption that the raw material model is correct.

So far these arguments do little to counter the alternative cultural models, where precisely the characteristics of pointed forms and plano-convex cross-sections, created by increased flaking around the tip, are argued to be the desired end product. However, one possible approach is to make a direct comparison between the flint and quartzite bifaces. If a specific planform was desired, then it might be expected to be imposed on flint and quartzite bifaces alike.

Given the dangers of using a small sample, the ten quartzite bifaces do seem to show some differences in form from those made of flint. Five of them classify as ovates, they are on average smaller, they are comparatively less thick and although some of them display a plano-convex cross-section, this is not produced through the retouch-type flaking. Raw material has clearly played a key role in the form of these pieces, with the frequent use of split pebbles making the production of plano-convex bifaces almost inevitable. Raw material also accounts for their smaller size. The absence of retouch around the tips suggests that there was little resharpening. It seems likely that these bifaces were produced expediently from very local raw material, in a variety of forms, including ovates, and quickly discarded. In contrast, the flint bifaces were produced on scarcer, more valued raw material, and were perhaps resharpened to produce the characteristic pointed form, the plano-convex cross-section being a by-product of initial blank type. Their greater relative thickness could also be a result of resharpening, through the reduction in width.

Proponents of the cultural interpretation might well argue that if different values were placed on different raw material types, then the imposition of design might also vary. This is a valid point and cannot be ignored. But if the design of these pieces is so important, can it be traced in other industries in Britain and western and central Europe? This question was thoroughly examined by Tyldesley (1986). Her conclusions were that several other assemblages in Britain, such as Whitlingham (Norfolk), Hitchin (Hertfordshire) and Warsash (Hampshire), did contain occasional bifaces that resemble those from Wolvercote, but none of the assemblages formed a close parallel. Red Barnes has been more recently analysed and identified as a site with plano-convex bifaces (Wenban-Smith *et al.* 2000), although it should be noted that of the nineteen bifaces or parts of bifaces that were identified, only two complete bifaces and two biface tips bore this feature. One of the bifaces is certainly reminiscent of those from Wolvercote and the tips hint at a similar technology, but such comparisons should be treated with caution given the small database.

Previous comparisons of Wolvercote with assemblages from western and central Europe have focused on similarities to the Micoquian (Roe 1981, 123; Wymer 1982, 145). Unfortunately the term has been used very loosely over the last forty years and covers a diverse range of industries stretching from La Micoque itself in south-west France to Romania (cf. Bosinski 1967; Gabori 1976; Patte

1971). The supposed unifying feature is the Micoquian handaxe, which according to Bordes is a pointed form with a finely-worked tip, often concave sides and a globular butt (1961, 57). Although some of the bifaces from La Micoque (Dordogne, France) conform to this description, most of them lack the thick butt, and only rarely have concave edges. However, according to Patte an important distinguishing feature of the bifaces from La Micoque is '*les retouches du second temps, les plus fines en général, étaient portées sur un tranchant et sur une face puis sur l'autre tranchant sur l'autre face*' (1971, 384). In other words, secondary retouch, on one face and then the other. This, at times, certainly resulted in plano-convexity. A feature that is also present on some of the Micoque bifaces is an asymmetry in planform, perhaps created by the secondary retouch. Both these attributes are also found on bifaces in assemblages described as Micoquian across western and central Europe (e.g. Vinneuf and Verrières-le-Buisson, northern France; Bocksteinloch and Bocksteinschmiede, Klausennische, Germany; Kulna Cave, Czech Republic), and it is perhaps these features that provide more of a unifying umbrella for the industries, rather than Micoquian bifaces (as defined by Bordes) *per se.*

The Wolvercote bifaces undoubtedly share some of the features found on the bifaces in these industries, but only rarely the asymmetry in plan-form. However, the biggest stumbling block to any cultural interpretation that links Wolvercote to these sites is the dating. The dating of La Micoque is unclear; whereas the site was previously dated to the earlier part of the last glaciation (Laville 1975), recent work on the geology suggests that the upper part of the sequence including bed N should be attributed to OIS 10 (Turq 1999). ESR determinations indicate an OIS 8 date (Schwarcz and Grün 1988), while the fauna suggests a date at least earlier than OIS 6 (Delpech *et al.* 1995). However, the dating of sites described as Micoquian across western and central Europe tend to be later, with, for example, Vinneuf and Verrières-le-Buisson, Bocksteinloch and Bocksteinschmiede III and Kulna Cave all being attributed to the beginning of the last glaciation (later OIS 5) (J.-M. Gouédo pers. comm.; Roebroeks *et al.* 1992; Svoboda 1999). Although the arguments are strong for linking these later sites together, the inclusion of Wolvercote and probably La Micoque as part of a Micoquian tradition seems problematic given their dispersal in space and time.

How, then, do we interpret this apparent unifying feature of secondary retouch, resulting in varying degrees of plano-convexity and in some cases asymmetry? One model that has been put forward by Boëda *et al.* (1990) and Gouédo (pers. comm.) is that Middle Palaeolithic bifaces should be understood through two distinct concepts. The first is the volumetric shape of the piece which encompasses the prehensile qualities of the tool. The second involves the specific functional edges of the tool. They argue that in some Middle Palaeolithic industries, specifically the Micoquian, bifaces had become the support for other tools. As such, they are argued to contain different functional areas on different edges of the same piece, and are the subject of resharpening. This flexibility in function has also been noted by Turq (2000, 207–211; pers. comm.) on bifaces from Combe Grenal (bed 59), La Rochette and Le Moustier (Dordogne, France) where tools such as scrapers and notches are imposed on bifaces, or bifaces are converted into cores.

If these interpretations are correct, then it would seem that the mental concepts behind biface manufacture change slightly in the Middle Palaeolithic. In the Lower Palaeolithic, at least in Britain, it has been argued that biface manufacture is guided by a *mental construct* which provides parameters, or rules of conduct, within which production proceeds (Ashton and McNabb 1994; Ashton and White in press). These can be summarised as bifacial flaking, the production of a sharp, durable cutting edge, the imposition of symmetry, and the maintenance of good prehensile qualities. Function seems to have been largely limited to butchery (Austin *et al.* 1999; Isaac 1986; Jones 1980; Keeley 1980; Mitchell 1995; Toth 1985; Villa 1990). The two concepts of volumetric shape and functional edge are very much united within the piece.

In contrast, the concept of the biface in some Middle Palaeolithic industries, particularly the Micoquian, seems to have changed, with more flexibility in function, leading sometimes to more frequent modification and resharpening, which itself often led to an asymmetry in form. In essence, the dual concepts of volumetric shape and function are more distinct and combined in a variety of different ways. Such interpretations may well explain the form of the bifaces in some later Middle Palaeolithic assemblages.

How, then, might this explain the Wolvercote bifaces? The assemblage from Wolvercote is arguably earlier and is probably best interpreted as Lower Palaeolithic. The one feature that it may share with some later Middle Palaeolithic bifaces is that of resharpening. In the case of Wolvercote this feature is interpreted as being due to shortages in raw material, whereas for the Middle Palaeolithic it is argued to be caused by their increased diversity in function, which entailed a greater degree of modification and resharpening. If this is the case then bifaces from Wolvercote bear only a superficial resemblance to those from Micoquian industries of a later date.

CONCLUSION

Wolvercote holds a rare position in the British Lower Palaeolithic, as being one of the few sites with a sizable assemblage of flint bifaces where usable flint raw material is locally scarce. The expected effect of economising through resharpening appears to be borne out by the evidence of secondary retouch on many of the bifaces, which in some cases has led to the plano-convex cross-section. Although similar features occur on bifaces in many of the much later Micoquian assemblages from northern France and central Germany, this is more likely to be by chance rather than design. This interpretation may well explain the majority of the bifaces from Wolvercote, but there still remain the four bifaces that are over 20 cm in length. If economising was so important, why were these pieces not reduced further in size? This remains an enigma, and is a good reminder that functional explanations rarely provide all the answers, and that individual human behaviour on occasion upset what can otherwise be quite striking patterns of the more automated human responses to resources, landscape and use. Perhaps part of this sentiment was being expressed when Derek Roe, referring to Wolvercote, wrote of the 'strikingly individual character of the industry' (1981, 118). Whatever interpretation is favoured, most researchers would agree that the Wolvercote assemblage 'is genuinely of far more than local interest' (Roe 1994, 13).

ACKNOWLEDGEMENTS

I thank Alison Roberts at the Ashmolean Museum, Philip Powell at the University Museum of Natural History, and Vicky Winton at the Donald Baden-Powell Quaternary Research Centre for access to the Wolvercote Collections, and Roger Jacobi, Simon Lewis and Mark White for commenting on earlier drafts of this paper.

REFERENCES

Ashton, N.M. and McNabb, J. 1994. Bifaces in perspective. In N.M. Ashton and A. David (eds.) *Stories in Stone*, 182–191. Lithic Studies Society Occasional Paper 4, London.

Ashton, N.M. and White, M. in press. Bifaces and raw materials: flexible flaking in the British Early Palaeolithic. In H. Dibble and M. Soressi (eds.) *From 'Coups de Poing' to Clovis: Multiple Approaches to Biface Variability*. University of Pennsylvania Press, Philadelphia.

Austin, L.A., Bergman, C.A., Roberts, M.B. and Wilhelmsen, K.H. 1999. Archaeology of the excavated areas. In M.B. Roberts and S.A. Parfitt (eds.) *Boxgrove: A Middle Pleistocene Hominid Site at Eartham Quarry, Boxgrove, West Sussex*, 313–378. English Heritage, London.

Bell, A.M. 1894. Palaeolithic remains at Wolvercote, Oxfordshire, I and II. *Antiquary* 30, 148–152, 192–198.

Bell, A.M. 1904. Implementiferous sections at Wolvercote (Oxfordshire). *Quarterly Journal of the Geological Society of London* 60, 120–132.

Boëda, E., Geneste, J.-M. and Meignen, L. 1990. Identification de chaînes opératoires lithiques du Paléolithique ancien et moyen. *Paléo* 2, 43–80.

Bordes, F. 1961. *Typologie du Paléolithique Ancien et Moyen*. Delmas, Bordeaux.

Bosinski, G. 1967. *Die Mittelpaläolithischen Funde im Westlichen Mitteleuropa*. Böhlau Verlag, Köln.

Bowen, D.Q., Rose, J., McCabe, A.M. and Sutherland, D.G. 1986. Correlation of Quaternary glaciations in England, Ireland, Scotland and Wales. *Quaternary Science Reviews* 5, 299–341.

Bridgland, D.R. 1994. *Quaternary of the Thames*. Chapman and Hall, London.

Bridgland, D.R. and Harding, P. 1986. An attempt to locate the 'Wolvercote Channel' in the railway cutting adjacent to Wol-

vercote Brick Pit. *Quaternary Newsletter* 48, 12–16.

Briggs, D.J. 1988. The evironmental background to human occupation in the Upper Thames Valley during the Quaternary period. In R.J. MacRae and N. Moloney (eds.) *Non-Flint Tools and the Palaeolithic Occupation of Britain*, 167–185. British Archaeological Reports British Series 189, Oxford.

Briggs, D.J., Coope, G.R. and Gilbertson, D.D. 1985. *The Chronology and Environmental Framework of Early Man in the Upper Thames Valley: A New Model*. British Archaeological Reports British Series 137, Oxford.

Delpech, F., Geneste, J.-M., Rigaud, J.-Ph. and Texier, J.-P. 1995. Les industries antérieures à la dernière glaciation en Aquitaine septentrionale: chronologie, paléoenvironnements, technologie, typologie et économie de subsistance. *Paléo* supplement 1, Actes du Colloque de Miiskolc, 133–163.

Evans, J. 1896. *Ancient Stone Implements of Great Britain* (second edition). Longmans, Green and Co., London

Gabori, M. 1976. *Les Civilisations du Paléolithique Moyen entre les Alpes et l'Oural*. Akadémiai Kiadó, Budapest.

Isaac, G.Ll. 1986. Foundation stones: early artefacts as indicators of activities and abilities. In P. Callow and G. Bailey (eds.) *Stone Age Prehistory: Studies in Memory of Charles McBurney*, 221–241. Cambridge, Cambridge University Press.

Jones, P.R. 1980. Experimental butchery with modern stone tools and its relevance for Palaeolithic archaeology. *World Archaeology* 12, 153–165.

Keeley, L.H. 1980. *Experimental Determination of Stone Tool Uses: A Microwear Analysis*. University of Chicago Press, Chicago.

Kohn, M. and Mithen, S. 1999. Handaxes: products of sexual selection? *Antiquity* 73, 518–526.

Laville, H. 1975. *Climatologie et Chronologie du Paléolithique en Perigord: Etude Sédimentologique de Dépôts en Grottes et sous Abris*. Université de Provence, Laboratoire de Paléontologie Humaine et de Préhistoire. Etudes Quarternaires 4, Marseille.

MacRae, R.J. 1988. Belt, shoulder bag or basket? An inquiry into handaxe transport and flint sources. *Lithics* 10, 2–8.

Maddy, D., Lewis, S.G. and Green, C.P. 1991. A review of the stratigraphic significance of the Wolvercote Terrace of the Upper Thames Valley. *Proceedings of the Geologists' Association* 102, 217–225.

McPherron, S.P. 1994. *A Reduction Model for Variability in Acheulian Biface Morphology*. Unpublished PhD dissertation, University of Pennsylvania.

McPherron, S.P. 1995. A re-examination of the British biface data. *Lithics* 16, 47–63.

Mitchell, J. 1995. Studying biface butchery at Boxgrove: roe deer butchery with replica handaxes. *Lithics* 16, 64–69.

Patte, E. 1971. L'industrie de La Micoque. *L'Anthropologie* 75, 369–396.

Roe, D.A. 1968a. British Lower and Middle Palaeolithic handaxe groups. *Proceedings of the Prehistoric Society* 34, 1–82.

Roe, D.A. 1968b. *A Gazetteer of British Lower and Middle Palaeolithic Sites*. Council for British Archaeology Research Report 8, London.

Roe, D.A. 1981. *The Lower and Middle Palaeolithic Periods in Britain*. Routledge and Kegan Paul, London.

Roe, D.A. 1994. The Palaeolithic archaeology of the Oxford region. *Oxoniensia* 59, 1–15.

Roebroeks, W., Conard, N.J. and van Kolfschoten, T. 1992. Dense forests, cold steppes, and the Palaeolithic settlement of northern Europe. *Current Anthropology* 33, 551–586.

Rose, J. 1987. Status of the Wolstonian Glaciation in the British Quaternary. *Quaternary Newsletter* 53, 1–9.

Sandford, K.S. 1924. The river gravels of the Oxford district. *Quarterly Journal of the Geological Society of London* 80, 113–179.

Sandford, K.S. 1926. Pleistocene deposits. In J. Pringle (ed.) *The Geology of the Country around Oxford*, 104–172. Memoir of the Geological Survey of Great Britain. HMSO, London.

Sandford, K.S. 1932. Some recent contributions to the Pleistocene succession in England. *Geological Magazine* 69, 1–18.

Schwarcz, H.P. and Grün, R. 1988. ESR dating of level 2/3 at La Micoque (Dordogne), France: excavations of Debénath and Rigaud. *Geoarchaeology* 3, 293–296.

Shotton, F.W. 1953. The Pleistocene deposits of the area between Coventry, Rugby and Leamington, and their bearing on the topographic development of the Midlands. *Philosophical Transactions of the Royal Society of London* B 237, 209–260.

Shotton, F.W. 1983. The Wolstonian Stage of the British Pleistocene in and around its type area of the English Midlands. *Quaternary Science Reviews* 2, 261–280.

Sumbler, M.G. 1983. A new look at the type Wolstonian glacial deposits of central England. *Proceedings of the Geologists' Association* 94, 23–31.

Svoboda, J. 1999. Environment and Middle Palaeolithic adaptations in eastern central Europe. In W. Roebroeks and C. Gamble (eds.) *The Middle Palaeolithic Occupation of Europe*, 81–92. University of Leiden Press, Leiden.

Tomlinson, M.E. 1929. The drifts of the Stour-Evenlode watershed and their extension into the valleys of the Warwickshire Stour and Upper Evenlode. *Proceedings of the Birmingham Natural History and Philosophical Society* 15, 157–195.

Toth, N. 1985. The Oldowan reassessed: a close look at early stone artefacts. *Journal of Archaeological Science* 12, 101–120.

Turq, A. 1999. Reflections on the Middle Palaeolithic of the Aquitaine Basin. In W. Roebroeks and C. Gamble (eds.) *The Middle Palaeolithic Occupation of Europe*, 107–120. University of Leiden Press, Leiden.

Turq, A. 2000. *Paléolithique Inférieur et Moyen entre Dordogne et Lot*. Paléo supplement 2.

Tyldesley, J.A. 1986. *The Wolvercote Channel Assemblage: A Comparative Study*. British Archaeological Reports British Series 153, Oxford.

Villa, P. 1990. Torralba and Aridos: elephant exploitation in Middle Pleistocene Spain. *Journal of Human Evolution* 19, 299–309.

Wenban-Smith, F.F., Gamble, C.S. and ApSimon, A.M. 2000. The Lower Palaeolithic Site at Red Barnes, Portchester, Hampshire: bifacial technology, raw material quality, and the organisation of archaic behaviour. *Proceedings of the Prehistoric Society* 66, 209–255.

White, M.J. 1995. Raw materials and biface variability in southern Britain: a preliminary examination. *Lithics* 15, 1–20.

White, M.J. 1996. *Biface Variability and Human Behaviour: A Study from South-Eastern England*. Unpublished PhD thesis, University of Cambridge.

White, M.J. 1998a. On the significance of Acheulean biface variability in southern Britain. *Proceedings of the Prehistoric Society* 64, 15–44.

White, M.J. 1998b. Twisted ovate bifaces in the British Lower Palaeolithic: some observations and implications. In N.M. Ashton, F. Healy and P. Pettitt (eds.) *Stone Age Archaeology: Essays in Honour of John Wymer*, 98–104. Lithic Studies Society Occasional Paper 6, Oxbow Monograph 102. Oxbow Books, Oxford.

Wymer, J.J. 1968. *Lower Palaeolithic Archaeology in Britain as Represented by the Thames Valley*. John Baker, London.

Wymer, J.J. 1982. *The Palaeolithic Age*. Croom Helm, London.

21. A river runs through it: a decade of research at Stanton Harcourt

Katherine Scott and Christine M. Buckingham

ABSTRACT

Ten years ago we began our investigation of the late Middle Pleistocene Channel deposits at Stanton Harcourt in Oxfordshire. It is primarily a palaeontological and geological site. Nonetheless, somewhat unexpectedly, among the mammoths and elephants, shells, logs and other debris of the ancient river, we found twenty-seven artefacts. In this tribute to Professor Derek Roe, whose interest in the Thames and its tributaries ranges from professional to piscatorial, we offer an alternative view on artefacts which, in the purest archaeological terms, might be considered 'derived'.

INTRODUCTION

In the many publications which reflect his principal research interests since he produced his *Gazetteer of British Lower and Middle Palaeolithic Sites* in 1968, Derek Roe has described and sought to explain the character of the earlier Palaeolithic industries of Britain. These he has periodically reassessed according to the extended timescale of recent years and in the light of the increasing amount of data provided by Quaternary specialists that suggest an ever more complex Pleistocene climatic sequence. An understanding of the British Palaeolithic is still largely a matter of interpreting various lithic assemblages, the majority of which are concentrated in southern Britain. From an archaeological point of view this is a difficult, even frustrating, area. Earlier Palaeolithic sites are relatively scarce for a number of reasons. Artefact distribution maps (Roe 1994; Wessex Archaeology 1996) suggest that the Upper Thames region lay at the extreme north-western edge of possible human expansion. Advancing ice sheets curtailed movement northwards during cold stages, and partial or complete isolation from the Continental mainland occurred during interglacial periods. However, the thousands of earlier Palaeolithic artefacts

known in Britain attest to the fact that, at times, it was a place where early colonisers were happy to be. We might imagine that they arrived in the Upper Thames Valley by following the River Thames upstream and we must assume that they had the necessary skills to adapt and survive the local conditions. The best known of their tools is the flint handaxe although, once past the flint rich Chiltern Hills, it is clear that they also had to use local materials such as quartzite. We cannot know why so many such carefully crafted artefacts as the handaxes, evidently still useful, were abandoned at various points on the landscape but indeed they were.

LOCALITIES AND CONTEXTS IN THE UPPER THAMES

The documented isolated finds from the Upper Thames region number several hundred (MacRae 1982, 1990, 1991). Wessex Archaeology (1993) records sixty-three locations in the Upper Thames Valley alone. If it were possible also to include the private and undocumented collections, it is probable that the real number of sites and artefacts is many times greater. Handaxes far out-number other tool types, but this may reflect a collecting bias. Most of the collections were made in gravel pits, frequently from the reject heaps, where it is likely that the handaxes, always much prized by collectors, were also more easily noticed than smaller or less aesthetically pleasing tools.

Reviewing these handaxe collections, Roe (1996) posed two principal questions that might direct an archaeologist's research: How did they get where they are found? What can we learn about past human behaviour? He had pre-viously stated that 'the need for new well-preserved sites in primary context remains crucial to our understanding of the British earlier Palaeolithic' (Roe 1986). At that time Boxgrove was in the early stages of excavation and has since exceeded anything in Britain with its uniquely outstanding mint condition handaxes, refitting flakes, and abundant faunal remains (Roberts and Parfitt 1999). Certainly, there is nothing remotely comparable in the Upper Thames. The further north we look, the less likely such an occurrence will be. Upstream of the Goring Gap, Roe (1994) states that 'too often all that survives is a portion of the stone artefacts, probably in secondary context. There is a limit to what one can learn from such discoveries'.

We take a more optimistic view of the Upper Thames and its palaeoliths. We argue that there are different degrees of *in situ* where artefacts are concerned, and that there is something to be learned from each type of situation. There is a perception among archaeologists

that material which is not *in situ* is of limited value unless it occurs on an ancient land surface with virtually un-disturbed evidence of human activities such as tool manu-facture or butchery. At the other end of the spectrum are the artefacts in ancient river beds that have tumbled downstream through successive seasons, decades or mil-lennia. In between these extremes is a category of tools that we would argue to be *almost* where they were discar-ded. In the case of these, we believe that their value may be enhanced if one takes into account their geological context, their state of preservation, and any associated finds.

Over the years, we have developed an interest in this 'in between' category. If we leave aside the many single artefact finds from the Upper Thames for which we have little or no contextual data, we might consider five locations with assemblages which range in size from about two dozen to more than two hundred artefacts. These collections are all from the Summertown-Radley Terrace Formation and come from Gravelly Guy, Smiths Pit and Dix Pit near Stanton Harcourt, Cornish's Pit at Iffley, and Queensford Farm and Mount Farm at Berinsfield (Fig. 21.1). In a recent study by Lee (2000), all are described as typically Lower Palaeolithic of mid Acheulian tradition. Lee divides these five sites into two groups on the grounds that their different surface patination suggests different post-depositional histories. By his criteria, Iffley and Berinsfield fall into one group and Gravelly Guy, Smiths Pit and Dix Pit into the other. As our fieldwork was at Dix Pit, we propose to discuss the second group.

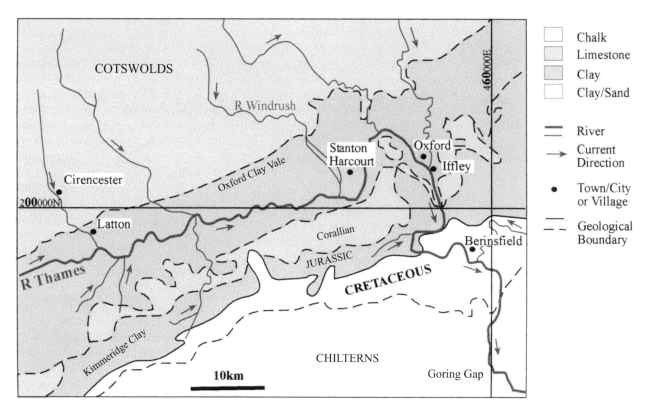

Fig. 21.1. Simplified geological map of the Upper Thames Valley

GRAVELLY GUY AND SMITHS PIT

Gravelly Guy and Smiths Pit, near Stanton Harcourt, were adjoining gravel quarries regularly patrolled by R.J. MacRae whose dedication and observation ensured that, despite the difficulties of retrieving material during active gravel extraction, ninety-nine artefacts were recovered (MacRae 1982, 1990, 1991). The most abundant tool type from these quarries is the pointed handaxe, but there are also chopping tools, ovate handaxes, cordate handaxes, and cleavers. The raw material is primarily flint, the source of which is believed to be in the Chiltern Hills area, but other materials were used on occasion (MacRae and Moloney 1988). In close proximity to the above-mentioned quarries was a third, known as Dix Pit, the site of our own excavations of the Stanton Harcourt Channel (Buckingham *et al.* 1996; Scott and Buckingham 1997). Twenty-seven artefacts were recovered here, including eleven handaxes (nine flint, one quartzite and one other), two choppers, eight flakes of which three are handaxe trimming flakes, and a flint core showing Levallois preparation. According to Lee (*ibid.*), the artefacts from Gravelly Guy, Smiths Pit and Stanton Harcourt are so similar typologically and in the degree and colour of their patination as to suggest that the tools from all three sites were made within a short space of time. At the start of our fieldwork, the Gravelly Guy/Smiths Pit artefacts already constituted an important collection but no artefacts were known from the Channel. The age and origin of the Gravelly Guy material was in dispute. MacRae (1990) suggested that, although they came from the base of the 'cold gravels' (either Devensian or Wolstonian), they might have been discarded during interstadial periods during the deposition of these gravels. Another possibility he offered was that they originated from some earlier landscape.

We would not presume to comment on these three assemblages from an archaeologist's point of view, but we believe that consideration of their context and condition sheds light on their origin and their spatial and temporal relationship. It is important to note here that MacRae (pers. comm.) found all the artefacts (unless they were from the quarry's reject heaps) at the very base of the quarried gravel or on the floor of the pit at the junction with the Oxford Clay. He never observed them higher up in the gravel sections. This is also true for most of the other recorded Lower Palaeolithic finds from the Upper Thames. MacRae also noted that the majority was in good, that is to say little damaged, condition. In which case, we ask how likely is it that the artefacts actually date to the gravel in which they were found?

In the Upper Thames Valley the main gravel deposits of the Summertown-Radley Formation are believed to have accumulated under the extremely cold climatic conditions of Oxygen Isotope Stage 6. If one believes that the artefacts date to the period when these gravels were being deposited then, by inference, the people who made and discarded them were in Britain during these very cold conditions, probably the coldest in the last half million years. It has been said that human occupation was more likely during the cold stages than during interglacials, as the forested landscape of the latter would not have been a favourable habitat (Currant 1986; Gamble 1987). If we consider the Gravelly Guy and Smiths Pit artefacts in the light of our excavations of the Channel, we suggest that the reverse was true: that the artefacts were discarded by people during the previous interglacial (Oxygen Isotope Stage 7) and that this landscape was subsequently buried by gravel deposited under the cold, even arctic, conditions of Oxygen Isotope Stage 6. Moreover, we suggest that the condition of most of the artefacts indicates that their burial and preservation took place soon after discard and that they did not lie about exposed to the elements. In support of these suggestions, we consider three lines of evidence: the stratigraphic context of the artefacts, their condition and especially the degree to which they are patinated and, finally, the associated faunal remains.

Stratigraphy

The main commercial gravel deposit to the west and south-west of Stanton Harcourt village, which underlay the Summertown-Radley Terrace surface, was originally known as the Linch Hill gravel. To avoid confusion with a similarly named deposit in the Lower Thames area, it is now known as the Stanton Harcourt Gravel Member of the Summertown-Radley Formation. Opinions differ regarding the age of this gravel. Seddon and Holyoak (1985) propose a Devensian age, whereas Briggs *et al.* (1985) and Bridgland (1994) attribute the deposit to OIS 6.

Sections exposed in the excavation trenches at Dix Pit (Buckingham *et al.* 1996) illustrated that the Stanton Harcourt gravel is definitely stratigraphically higher and therefore younger than the Stanton Harcourt Channel, which we attribute to OIS 7. Therefore the stone tools from Gravelly Guy must be younger than those in the Channel, or they are from a common source but have somehow become incorporated in a younger deposit. We believe the latter to have been the case. Current directions measured by Bryant (1983) suggest that the Stanton Harcourt Gravel at Gravelly Guy was deposited by the river Windrush flowing NW to SE across the site. As the artefacts at Gravelly Guy occur about 1 kilometre north-west (i.e. upstream) of Dix Pit, they could not therefore be derived directly from the Channel deposits. Our fieldwork leads us to suggest that the main river channel never flowed north-west in the direction of the Gravelly Guy Pit. Bearing in mind that the courses of the rivers evidently shifted progressively southwards during the Pleistocene (Sandford 1926), we conjecture that the river Windrush flowing across this area during OIS 7, joined the river Thames in the Dix Pit area, to the south-west of the Channel excavations (Fig. 21.2). Artefacts could have been discarded in the river and quickly buried, or flood events might have provided a mechanism for swiftly burying any

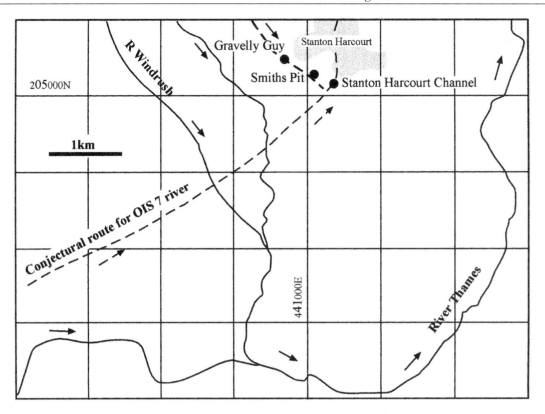

Fig. 21.2. The Stanton Harcourt area

stone tool lying on the current land surface. All three sites would have been in the flood plain area of the ancient Thames and its tributaries during Oxygen Isotope Stage 7. As for the influence of the river Windrush, it is likely that this river became more dominant during the subsequent cold stage. In arctic conditions, without the binding effect of vegetation, there would have been greater potential for incision and erosion of any earlier sediments in its valley. The resulting vast amount of cold-climate gravel, now commercially exploited, destroyed or buried the Earlier Palaeolithic landscape.

Artefact condition and patination

There is no appreciable difference in the degree of erosion of the artefacts between the three sites. Although some show evidence of water erosion and none could claim to be 'mint', the fresh condition of the majority of the Gravelly Guy and Smiths Pit artefacts suggests that they have not been moved far from the place where they were discarded. In the case of the Stanton Harcourt Channel, there is no evidence of any old land surface that pre-dates the Channel, nor is there evidence of any earlier sediment body from which the artefacts could have been derived, without considerable transport within a fluvial environment. The topography at this location in the Oxford Clay Vale is low, and there is no evidence of any head deposits, which one would expect if solifluction or other debris

flow had brought the artefacts to this vicinity. All the sediments in the Dix Pit Complex are fluvial and where the basal contact has been observed, there is a sharp, erosive boundary with undisturbed Oxford Clay.

As regards patination, the crucial questions are when and how the patination occurred. Did it occur during the interglacial or considerably later, on a periglacial land surface? Typically, the white patination that is common on the Gravelly Guy/Smiths Pit handaxes and on some of the Channel ones, is where the flint has become white and opaque almost to the core. Lee (2000) suggested that deep patination was due to exposure on an ancient land surface as an effect of rainwater (a weak carbonic acid). However, we note that the patination is even on both sides of the tools, which suggests that it is probably the result of some chemical reaction when the tools were buried within the sediment, rather than due to exposure on the surface. A few of the Gravelly Guy handaxes show evidence of exfoliation and a difference in the patination colour on either side. This could be the result of sub-aerial exposure before burial but, equally, could have occurred after the quarrying activities, when the artefacts were exposed on the pit floor before recovery. Not one of the excavated artefacts from the Channel showed these features.

The Channel tools showed more variability in the degree of patination. The artefacts that were found in sediments that showed the least oxidation did not have the deep white patination. Handaxe no. 3 (Buckingham *et al.* 1996, fig. 8), which most closely resembles those from Gravelly Guy, was found just above a red, iron rich horizon in a clast-supported gravel associated with rotted limestone pebbles. This implies that some chemical weathering had occurred. This horizon was just below calcareous sand and gravel from the overlying Stanton Harcourt Gravel. Iron-stained or cemented horizons were common throughout the Channel sediments at Dix Pit but, almost always, they were where a permeable bed overlay a less permeable one, and had probably been the result of oxidation by percolating groundwater. Iron cementation was enhanced wherever there was organic matter, such as wood or bone. There was little iron staining or cementation in any bed with a high silt or clay component. Bones and wood within these beds were also better preserved and the flint artefacts were less patinated. Another handaxe was interesting in that it was found at the junction of a yellowish-brown oxidised gravel above a grey silt bed and, when first uncovered, it had the distinct two-tone colour of the two deposits. With exposure to the air since excavation, this colour difference has disappeared. Also, this particular tool did not have the white patination.

As the patination of the artefacts from the three sites is comparable, this suggests that the chemistry of the sediment in which they were buried was also similar. We conclude that it is likely that patination occurred *after* the artefacts were buried within the ancient river or within the sediments of its adjacent flood plain. One thing is certain: once patinated, the tools become brittle. Edge damage, exposing the white core, would have occurred if they were transported or reworked by successive events. We suggest that, in order to preserve the flaking detail that most of these artefacts have, they would have had to remain buried fairly close to their point of discard.

The faunal evidence

We have reported elsewhere that the fauna and flora from the Stanton Harcourt Channel indicate an interglacial climate (during OIS 7) with temperatures not dissimilar to those of today (Buckingham *et al.* 1996; Scott 1998). Herds of mammoths, elephants, bison and horses roamed open grassland. Forests nearby offered shelter and wood. Thus the combination of a temperate climate with abundant meat, various seeds and nuts, and the resources provided by the forest and the river, offered an ideal environment for people.

Let us then consider the evidence for human occupation of the area following this warm period. The gravel that buries the Channel, the Stanton Harcourt Gravel, we equate with OIS 6 following Briggs *et al.* (1985) and Bridgland (1994). It is characterised by intra-formational ice wedge casts indicative of severe cold (Seddon and Holyoak 1985). This gravel, some 6–8 metres deep across the entire valley, is virtually devoid of any organic remains except occasionally in the lowermost deposits. One might reasonably suppose that the proximity of ice sheets, perhaps extending

as far south as Coventry, and successive deluges of water-borne gravel under bitter climatic conditions, made the Upper Thames Valley uninhabitable for most of OIS 6.

DATING AND INTERPRETATION

How, then, should we interpret the Gravelly Guy handaxes at the base of the OIS 6 (Stanton Harcourt) gravels? When MacRae collected these artefacts, he also collected from the same deposits a number of mammoth teeth and bones, which he interpreted as indicative of a cold climate. However, closer examination by us of this fauna revealed them to belong to two species: an early form of *Mammuthus primigenius* (the small 'Ilford' mammoth) and straight-tusked elephant *Palaeoloxodon antiquus*. The elephant is known only from interglacial deposits and the small mammoth is a characteristic member of OIS 7 faunal assemblages. Both occur in the Stanton Harcourt Channel deposits, the mammoth being the most common of all the herbivores represented. We suggest that their presence with the handaxes at Gravelly Guy and Smiths Pit indicates that the fauna and artefacts are contemporary, and predate the OIS 6 gravel in which they were buried. We conclude that they belong to an earlier landscape, probably the same landscape in which the Stanton Harcourt Channel and its tributary, the Windrush, flowed. Further up the Thames at Latton (Fig. 21.1), we have recently excavated a similar deposit: handaxes comparable to those at Stanton Harcourt in deposits with 'Ilford' mammoth and biological evidence for a mild climate, buried by gravel of periglacial origin (Scott and Buckingham in press).

In our view, the makers of the abundant and quite beautiful tools from the Stanton Harcourt area and very likely those from Iffley, Berinsfield and beyond as well, enjoyed a mild climate surrounded by large game, extensive grassland and stands of forest. We have suggested that for most of Stage 6, the Upper Thames Valley was uninhabitable. This was probably true for the whole of Britain south of the Stage 6 glacial advance. It is interesting to look at the faunal evidence for this time. Do the assemblages attributed to OIS 6 necessarily reflect the climate and environment of the deposits in which they were found?

In her study of the British Middle Pleistocene vertebrate faunas, Shreve (1997) allocates seven faunal assemblages to OIS 6 on the grounds that they occurred stratigraphically between deposits attributed to OIS 7 and OIS 5e. None of the sites has abundant fauna and none has any stone artefacts. Where there are contextual data, the bones are reported to occur in deposits laid down in periglacial conditions from which Shreve deduces that the animals lived in a severe periglacial climate. We suggest an alternative scenario such as we have proposed for the Gravelly Guy artefacts: that the animals represented lived in one environment but were buried by another.

Of the seven sites discussed by Shreve (*ibid.*), consisting of three caves, three gravel pits and a raised beach deposit, only two of the caves, Bacon Hole and Minchin Hole, were systematically excavated. The vertebrate fauna from both caves was overwhelmingly dominated by small mammals: the northern vole *Microtus oeconomus* and an unidentified vole. Eight bones of horse, three of fox and one unidentified bovine complete the combined vertebrate list for the two caves. The third cave assemblage, Clevedon, is also dominated by northern vole, and has horse, red fox, brown bear and wolf. All the above species are known from a wide range of Pleistocene deposits, but none is particularly associated with conditions of extreme cold (Burton 1979; Stuart 1982). The northern vole and the horse indicate open vegetation conditions and, at Bacon Hole and Clevedon Cave, there is a molluscan fauna indicative of a cool climate with sparse vegetation. It seems that predators such as owls or any of the carnivores represented were occupying these caves during cool episodes of OIS 6 rather than during the climatic extremes.

The remaining four sites used by Shreve (*ibid.*) are the three gravel pits at Marsworth, Stanton Harcourt and Balderton, and the raised beach deposit at Black Rock near Brighton. The faunal remains were collected rather than excavated and no artefacts were found. If we exclude the faunas from Stanton Harcourt and Balderton which have contextual problems, the two remaining assemblages are from Marsworth and Black Rock. At both sites the most common species is a small horse which also occurs at Bacon Hole and Clevedon Cave. Both sites have a few remains of mammoth of an evolved type and, at Black Rock, there are also four woolly rhinoceros bones. While neither the mammoth nor woolly rhino are characteristic of interglacial deposits they, together with the horse, indicate the presence of abundant grassland which would not have been available in conditions of extensive permafrost. The Black Rock fauna is within periglacial Coombe Rock sediment deposited during OIS 6. Interpreting the Marsworth fauna Shreve (*ibid.*) states that 'the fossiliferous chalky muds and solifluction deposits at Marsworth are clearly the product of deposition under cold-climate conditions, as attested to by the presence of periglacial phenomena, such as ice wedge casts. A severe periglacial climate is inferred'. We suggest that solifluction could have occurred and ice-wedge casts formed *after* the incorporation of the bones in the sediments. On balance, we suggest that the molluscs and vertebrates from these sites might be interpreted to reflect the situation throughout southern Britain during Stage 6: short intervals of climatic amelioration with open terrain and a cool climate during an otherwise uninhabitable period.

CONCLUSION

In defence of the Lower Palaeolithic of the Upper Thames, we hope we have illustrated that supportive fieldwork, in what appears to be an unpromising 'cultural' landscape, holds the key to a better understanding of the past. If it is possible to demonstrate whether or not the artefacts might have been part of the deposit in which they were found, it should be possible to include any accompanying environmental data to describe the kind of environment to which early people adapted. It is often expected that if early people were making stone tools in the vicinity, there should be a large amount of debitage. At all the sites near Stanton Harcourt there is a lack of such material. However, this should not be used to imply that there was less hominid activity here. In this area, where good quality flint is scarce, it is likely that ready-made flint tools were brought in. The occasional trimming flakes, such as those found in the Stanton Harcourt Channel, are exactly what would be expected, with people occasionally finding it necessary to make a new sharp edge on a prized handaxe. The opportunistic use of local raw materials, such as quartzite and chert, is also exactly what would be predicted. One might easily disregard artefacts from Upper Thames sites because they are in gravel. We agree that they are far from being in 'mint' condition but, because of their context, they enable us to describe in some detail the landscape, the climate and the resources of their makers.

ACKNOWLEDGEMENTS

From the outset, Professor Derek Roe encouraged us in our venture and welcomed us to make the Donald Baden-Powell Quaternary Research Centre our base. He supported countless grant applications, devoted his exceptional editorial talents to our various drafts, and never failed to show interest or sympathy in our successes and disasters. Above all, he provided an environment for many thought-provoking discussions on the wider issues of multidisciplinary research.

REFERENCES

Bridgland, D.R. 1994. *Quaternary of the Thames.* Chapman and Hall, London.

Briggs, D.J., Coope, G.R. and Gilbertson, D.D. 1985. *The Chronology and Environmental Framework of Early Man in the Upper Thames Basin: A New Model.* British Archaeological Reports British Series 137, Oxford.

Bryant, J.D. 1983. Facies sequences associated with some braided river deposits of late Pleistocene age from Southern Britain. *International Association of Sedimentologists, Special Publications* 6, 267–275.

Buckingham, C.M., Roe, D.A. and Scott, K. 1996. A preliminary report on the Stanton Harcourt Channel Deposits (Oxfordshire, England): geological context, vertebrate remains and palaeolithic stone artefacts. *Journal of Quaternary Science* 11, 397–415.

Burton, R. 1979. *Carnivores of Europe.* Batsford, London.

Currant, A.P. 1986. Man and the Quaternary interglacial faunas of Britain. In S.N. Collcutt (ed.) *The Palaeolithic of Britain and its Nearest Neighbours: Recent Trends*, 50–52. University of Sheffield, Sheffield.

Gamble, C.S. 1987. Man the shoveler: alternative models for Middle

Pleistocene colonization and occupation in northern latitudes. In O. Soffer (ed.) *The Pleistocene Old World*, 81–98. Plenum Press, New York.

Lee, H.W. 2000. *A Study of Lower Palaeolithic Stone Artefacts from Selected Sites in the Upper and Middle Thames Valley, with Particular Reference to the R.J. MacRae Collection.* Unpublished DPhil thesis, University of Oxford.

MacRae, R.J. 1982. Palaeolithic artefacts from Berinsfield, Oxfordshire. *Oxoniensia* 47, 1–11.

MacRae, R.J. 1990. New finds and old problems in the Lower Palaeolithic of the Upper Thames Valley. *Lithics* 11, 3–15.

MacRae, R.J. 1991. New Lower Palaeolithic finds from gravel pits in central southern England. *Lithics* 12, 12–20.

MacRae, R.J. and Moloney, N. (eds.) 1988. *Non-Flint Stone Tools and the Palaeolithic Occupation of Britain.* British Archaeological Reports British Series 189, Oxford.

Roberts, M.B. and Parfitt, S. (eds.) 1999. *Boxgrove: A Middle Pleistocene Hominid Site at Eartham Quarry, Boxgrove, West Sussex.* English Heritage, London.

Roe, D.A. 1968. *A Gazetteer of British Lower and Middle Palaeolithic Sites.* Council for British Archaeology Research Report 8. London.

Roe, D.A. 1981. *The Lower and Middle Palaeolithic Periods in Britain.* Routledge and Kegan Paul, London.

Roe, D.A. 1986. Introduction: progress in the British Palaeolithic. In S.N. Collcutt (ed.) *The Palaeolithic of Britain and its Nearest Neighbours: Recent Trends*, 1–2. University of Sheffield, Sheffield.

Roe, D.A. 1994. The Palaeolithic archaeology of the Oxford Region. *Oxoniensia* 59, 1–15.

Roe, D.A. 1996. Artefact distributions and the British Palaeolithic. In C. Gamble and A.J. Lawson (eds.) *The English Palaeolithic Reviewed*, 1–6. Trust for Wessex Archaeology, Salisbury.

Sandford, K.S. 1926. The river gravels of the Oxford District.

Quaternary Journal of the Geological Society of London 80, 113–179.

Scott, K. 1998. Southern rivers. In N. Ashton, F. Healy and P. Pettitt (eds.) *Stone Age Archaeology: Essays in Honour of John Wymer*, 110–113. Lithics Studies Society Occasional Paper 6, Oxbow Monograph 102. Oxbow Books, Oxford.

Scott, K. and Buckingham, C.M. 1997. Quaternary fluvial deposits and palaeontology at Stanton Harcourt, Oxfordshire. In S.G. Lewis and D. Maddy (eds.) *The Quaternary of the South Midlands and the Welsh Marches: Field Guide*, 115–126. Quaternary Research Association, London.

Scott, K. and Buckingham, C.M. in press. Preliminary report on the excavation of Late Middle Pleistocene deposits at Latton, near Cirencester, Gloucestershire. *Quaternary Newsletter* 94.

Seddon, M.B. and Holyoak, D.T. 1985. Evidence of sustained regional permafrost during deposition of fossiliferous Late Pleistocene river sediments at Stanton Harcourt (Oxfordshire, England). *Proceedings of the Geologists' Association* 96, 53–71.

Shreve, D.C. 1997. *Mammalian Biostratigraphy of the Later Middle Pleistocene in Britain.* Unpublished PhD thesis, University of London.

Stuart, A.J. 1982. *Pleistocene Vertebrates in the British Isles.* Longman, London.

Wessex Archaeology 1993. *The Southern Rivers Palaeolithic Project, Report No. 2. 1992–1993: The South-West and South of the Thames.* Trust for Wessex Archaeology, Salisbury.

Wessex Archaeology 1996. *The English Rivers Palaeolithic Project. Report No. 1. 1994–1995: The Thames Valley and the Warwickshire Avon.* Trust for Wessex Archaeology, Salisbury.

Wymer, J.J. 1986. Overview: recent trends in British Palaeolithic studies. In S.N. Collcutt (ed.) *The Palaeolithic of Britain and its Nearest Neighbours: Recent Trends*, 103–106. University of Sheffield, Sheffield.

22. Recent investigations at Dickett's Field, Yarnhams Farm, Holybourne, Hants.

Julie E. Scott-Jackson and Vicky Winton

ABSTRACT

This paper briefly addresses the problems and opportunities associated with Dickett's Field, a Lower and Middle Palaeolithic high-level find-site on deposits mapped as Clay-with-flints. In addition to describing the results of recent, and not so recent, field investigations, the paper corrects the varying designations of this site, which have led to data distortion, confusion and incorrect cataloguing of the site itself and the finds associated with it. For many years Palaeolithic artefacts have been collected as surface-finds in Dickett's Field. In order to better understand the integrity and context of these artefacts, the PADMAC Unit (Unit for the study of Palaeolithic artefacts and associated deposits mapped as Clay-with-flints, University of Oxford) is using Dickett's Field as a test-site for the development and testing of specialist techniques and methodologies. Preliminary results are included here in appreciation of the support offered to the work by Derek Roe.

INTRODUCTION

Among Derek Roe's many scholarly publications there are two books, *A Gazetteer of British Lower and Middle Palaeolithic Sites* (1968) and *The Lower and Middle Palaeolithic Periods in Britain* (1981) which have, in particular, become essential to every British Palaeolithic archaeological researcher. Many of the sites and artefacts recorded in these volumes and the supporting card index kept in Oxford have remained relatively obscure. One such site is Dickett's Field, Yarnhams Farm, Holybourne, near Alton, Hampshire (Fig. 22.1). The following description of recent discoveries at this site is offered here as a small contribution to the British Palaeolithic archaeological record in tribute to Professor Roe.

DICKETT'S FIELD: THE TRUE IDENTITY

A key component in the discovery and recording of a great majority of Palaeolithic artefacts was, and is, the contribution of experienced and knowledgeable amateurs. One such group of dedicated individuals, who scoured the North Hampshire Downs over many years, particularly from the early part of 1920 to around 1950, in their search of all manner of archaeological remains, consisted of Mr W.G. Willis FSA, Messrs. J.R. Ellaway, H. Rainbow, and occasionally Mr (later Dr) O.G.S. Crawford (Crawford *et al.* 1922; Ellaway and Willis 1934 *inter alia*). The museum in Basingstoke was later named after Willis.

In his (1947) paper entitled *Hampshire palaeoliths and the Clay-with-flints*, Willis records their findings of Palaeolithic artefacts in Dickett's Field thus:

'… on visiting the 730 O.D area above Holybourne the unusual experience was enjoyed of having decided to go and find Palaeoliths at a given spot and finding them! On the first visit, two implements and a good flake were picked up on the open field, one of the implements being a long pointed ovate of yellow-buff colour, while the other and the flake were of the typical

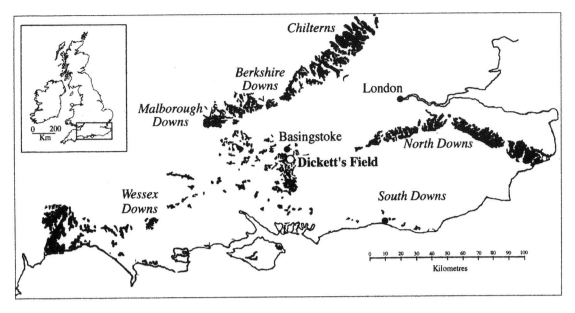

Fig. 22.1. Map showing Dickett's Field in relation to the generalized distribution of deposits mapped as Clay-with-flints.

red-brown surface. The area about 40–50 yds [*sic*] across has since received intensive and continuous examination (until war transport difficulties stopped it) and every visit has resulted in the acquisition of at least one implement, besides flakes. Finds include ovates and pointed ovates, some of a clear orange yellow, others of the old granular patina, several small specimens, ovates and pointed, being less than 2 inches in length. Altogether some 60 and [to?] 70 implements have been secured from this compact area.

The importance of this site rests on two factors, the limited area on which the relatively abundant implements and flakes occur and the high ground on which it is situated. The range of hills runs parallel to the River Wey, sloping steeply down to Holybourne and Froyle in the Wey Valley and forming the watershed between the Wey and the lower ground to the north. The concentration of material strongly suggests a working site, and the high altitude makes it difficult to suppose that it could be brought from any higher ground' (*ibid.*, 255).

The finders also add:

'It is to be noted that these high-level palaeoliths are much more deeply patinated than the usual implements found in the lower gravels which have obviously come from a higher source'(*ibid.*, 255).

Several of the handaxes collected by Willis *et al.* from this site are on display at the Alton and Basingstoke museums, while the other artefacts are now held by HCMS (Hampshire County Museum Services) at Chilcomb House, Winchester, and by the PADMAC Unit (Unit for the study of Palaeolithic

artefacts and associated deposits mapped as Clay-with-flints, University of Oxford). Roe (1981) notes the condition of the assemblage:

'At first sight the artefacts look somewhat abraded and even water-worn, but this is not the case: their surfaces have merely been altered, and the ridges worn down, by weathering presumably during long exposure on the surface or just below it' (*ibid.*, 183–184).

A similar view is also held by John Wymer (pers. comm.).

In 1989, while compiling the *Gazetteer of Palaeolithic Find-spots on the North Hampshire Downs* (Scott-Jackson 1991) a visit was made to Dickett's Field. Information derived from this research was subsequently incorporated into *The Southern Rivers Palaeolithic Project* (Wessex Archaeology 1993, 50–51). Here the estimated position of the find-site was given as SU 721435 (E) and it was listed under its generally accepted name which at that time was Holybourne Down, Froyle. However, as a direct result of the 1998 and 1999 investigations, this find-site reference must be corrected to avoid ambiguity as follows: Dickett's Field, Yarnhams Farm, Holybourne, near Alton, Hampshire.

The find-site is centred at SU 725438 (A) in Dickett's Field, east of Dickett's Plantation; a reference point noted by G.W. Willis. This field is on the plateau, which is situated at the highest point of 225 m (740 feet) OD in this part of Hampshire. This is the same site as that which Willis (1947) records as Yarnhams Farm. Dickett's Field is and was farmed by Yarnhams Farm and is about 1.5 kilometres (1 mile) from the farm itself, and 2 kilometres (1.5 miles) west of the village of Lower Froyle with Upper Froyle about the same distance to the north. The nearest town is Holybourne, approximately 3 kilometres (2.5 miles) away, situated low down in the Wey valley near the larger town of Alton. The county parish is Froyle in the district of East Hampshire.

Prior to the present investigation, this high-level find-site in Dickett's Field has been variously referred to as: 'Yarnhams Farm'; 'Yarnhams'; 'Froyle'; 'Holybourne' or 'Holybourne Down'. These names are both incorrect and confusing, not least because Holybourne and Holybourne Down are separate areas and sites. Holybourne, as previously noted, is a town in a low-level area in the Wey valley on the outskirts of the larger town of Alton whereas Holybourne Down, approximately 0.5 km (0.25 miles) from Dickett's Field, is a south-east facing, long 'tongue' shaped sloping hillside which runs right down to the town of Holybourne. It has an OD range of around 197 m to 110 m. At its highest part, it is still lower than the Dickett's Field plateau which lies at 225 m (740 feet) OD.

Although Roe alludes to an apparent confusion between find-site names and artefacts in his card index, the full extent of this confusion has only now come to light. In his gazetteer (Roe 1968, 98–99) entries are listed as 'Yarnhams, Froyle' and 'Holybourne Down, Holybourne' with twenty four handaxes and about fifty flakes being assigned to 'Holybourne Down, Holybourne'. (Note: in a publishing error (*op. cit.* 153, fig. 5.14 no.28), Holybourne, is missing from the list of sites). The confusing nature of this entry is now fully apparent, as the only artefacts to come from Holybourne Down *per se* are a few later prehistoric artefacts.

Further problems have now arisen as the Dickett's Field find-site and artefacts have been variously referenced simply as 'Holybourne' (Roe 1981; Tyldesley 1987, 54) and Holybourne Down (White 1998). Data distortions have also found their way into Sites and Monuments Records. *The Southern Rivers Palaeolithic Project* (Wessex Archaeology 1993, 50–51) also now needs updating, as there are six entries for 'Holybourne Down' of which two are prefixed by 'Alton' and four by Froyle. (Note: A=accurate; E= estimated). The two entries prefixed by Alton are correct as they do indeed relate to artefacts which were actually found in Holybourne and Holybourne Down. They are: Alton, SU 734415 (A) Holybourne and Alton, SU 734418 (A) Holybourne Down. However, two of the four entries prefixed by Froyle are somewhat misleading. The original and amended references are as follows in Table 22.1.

The omission of any future reference to 'Holybourne Down' in this paper about Dickett's Field will, it is hoped, eventually eliminate the data distortions and confusions discussed above.

TOPOGRAPHY AND GEOLOGY

Dickett's Field is situated on a high Chalk Downland plateau, which is capped with deposits mapped as Clay-with-flints. The blanket term Clay-with-flints has been used by many people, including map makers, to include all the different components that make up these superficial deposits, that is to say Clay-with-flints *sensu stricto* and Clay-with-flints *sensu lato*, which can, for example, include Plateau Drift and Brickearths. It is not a homogeneous deposit. It varies greatly from one place to another and is generally made up of a number of different deposits and sedimentological layers formed by a variety of processes. The use of the term 'mapped as Clay-with-flints' as a general term is therefore more accurate and preferable to simply 'Clay-with-flints'.

Petrographic studies of the various deposits mapped as Clay-with-flints have shown that they are derived mainly from a thin remnant of a variety of basal Palaeogene (early Tertiary) sediments with the flints ultimately coming from the Chalk. These Sub-Palaeogene deposits, which formed in the sea and which overlie the Cretaceous Chalk, have undergone a number of changes over geological time. Tectonic activity lifted and folded the Chalk, isolating the deposits on what are now the Chalk Downlands. The superficial deposits were then reworked during the Eocene period. However, during the Pleistocene, the Downlands capped with deposits mapped as Clay-with-flints lay beyond the ice-sheets and above the meltwater throughout the Anglian and subsequent glacial maxima, thereby escaping the devastating effects of direct glacial processes. As such, deposits mapped as Clay-with-flints have been subjected to only restricted change since the late Cromerian at least 500,000 years ago.

THE ENIGMA OF HAMPSHIRE

The readily available supply of flint suitable for knapping, both from the eroding Chalk Downland hill-sides

Original reference	Correct designation
Froyle, SU 724426 (A) Holybourne Down	Alton, SU 724426 (A) Brockham Hill
Froyle, SU 724432 (A) Holybourne Down	Alton, SU 724432 (A) Brockham Hill
Froyle, SU 721435 (E) Holybourne Down, edge of Clay-with-flints	Alton, SU 725438 (A) Dickett's Field, Yarnhams Farm, Holybourne, Clay-with-flints

Table 22.1. Amendments correcting find-site designations in the Alton area.

and in certain areas (reflecting the great variability of the deposits mapped as Clay-with-flints) from the actual Clay-with-flints deposits, appears to have provided Palaeolithic people with many opportunities for the manufacture, as well as the use of, stone tools. Discrete groups of waste flakes and debitage from stone tool manufacture have often been discovered located together within a single high-level field. Whether such finds represent single period artefact groups, or a palimpset of occupations of various ages brought together by ploughing or natural processes, is rarely known as there is a general lack of appropriate research. The greatest number of Lower and Middle Palaeolithic artefacts collected over the past 100 years or so, on the highest levels in areas mapped as Clay-with-flints in southern England, have been surface finds. Occasionally artefacts have been recovered from below the topsoil, actually 'embedded' within the underlying deposits mapped as Clay-with-flints when the topsoil was removed. Embedded finds are particularly important, as they may be indicative of *in situ* sites.

To date, there are 98 entries for Hampshire in the *Gazetteer of Lower and Middle Palaeolithic Artefacts from Deposits Mapped as Clay-with-Flints on the Chalk Downlands of Southern England* (Scott-Jackson 1999). Large areas of Hampshire are mapped as Clay-with-flints. Yet, in spite of the depth and breadth of knowledge of Willis *et al.* and their well organised, close monitoring over many years of specific fields which had yielded a great many Lower and Middle Palaeolithic artefacts as surface finds from discrete areas, they make no certain reference in their Hampshire reports to Palaeolithic artefacts being recovered from deposits below the topsoil. Perhaps the postholes or the plough did not, at that time, penetrate the sub-soil. If this was indeed so, then artefacts embedded within the underlying deposits would not have been found.

The only documented report of possibly embedded Palaeolithic artefacts in these deposits are two flakes, which are reported to have been recovered from a hole dug for a pylon stay but which, unfortunately, cannot now be traced. A more recent problem not necessarily unique to high-level sites on deposits mapped as Clay-with-flints, is that of embedded artefacts brought to the surface by modern deep ploughing being relegated to the category of surface finds. The ploughing depth and the accurate position of discovery are therefore omitted from the archaeological record.

The fact that so many well documented Lower and Middle Palaeolithic surface finds have been found in what appear to be discrete assemblages on the highest levels in areas mapped as Clay-with-flints in Hampshire, suggests that *in situ* Palaeolithic sites remain to be discovered on these hilltops and plateaux. One such find-site is Dickett's Field, Yarnhams Farm, Holybourne, near Alton, Hampshire.

DICKETT'S FIELD AS A TEST-SITE

Dickett's Field encapsulates a wide range of archaeological and geological possibilities and problems. It is, therefore, a perfect area of investigation for the PADMAC Unit as the main objective of its research is to understand and establish the context of the Lower and Middle Palaeolithic artefacts on high-level sites on deposits mapped as Clay-with-flints through the testing of models and methodologies developed by PADMAC.

Dickett's Field, referred to here as Field 1, is a large field on a large plateau. The field is surrounded by hedges or thin strips of woodland, one such woodland being 'Dickett's Plantation'. A number of pits and hollows are to be found within the woods, which are readily identified as old chalk pits. The track of a Roman road runs between Fields 1 and 4 but there is little evidence of it in Field 1. During August 1998, a basic survey of part of Dickett's Field was undertaken by the Unit and the first of the fieldwalking programmes initiated. The initial research revealed a number of features and occurrences associated with this high-level plateau. Almost immediately, several deeply patinated waste flakes of a dark ocherous colour were found. It then became apparent that these flakes and other naturally fractured flints of a similar colour were coming from specific areas of the field. Furthermore, this material was confined to one half of the field: that which contains wide basin-like depressions that have all the characteristics of solution features. The presence of Lower and Middle Palaeolithic artefacts as surface finds in the same half of the field as what appeared to be solution features was intriguing. A unifying feature of *in situ* Palaeolithic sites on deposits mapped as Clay-with-flints is the presence of solution features, which are formed as the calcium carbonate in the Chalk goes into solution (see Scott-Jackson 2000). The deposits mapped as Clay-with-flints are effectively retained in these basin-like hollows or pipes in the underlying Chalk. Over geological time, as the solution features deepen, there is a slow vertical lowering of the deposits but without substantial lateral transport. Any Palaeolithic assemblage manufactured in the solution hollow itself or on its edge, would be retained and covered by windblown material or waterlain deposits removed from the sides of the hollow, or brought in by soil creep or solifluction.

One line of research which we have been pursuing looks at the possibility of identifying solution features from aerial photographs to provide an additional tool in the quest for *in situ* high-level Palaeolithic sites in areas mapped as Clay-with-flints. In the course of these investigations, we came across references to an area of the plateau on which Dickett's Field is situated, being used as a dummy airfield during World War Two to deflect the Luftwaffe's attention away from the airfield at Lasham. Lights and cables are reported to have been laid on the plateau but it was not specified exactly where. Aerial photographs taken by the

RAF in 1947 were revealing: there was absolutely no sign of the airfield in Dickett's Field, a fact confirmed by Mike Anderton, an expert in aerial photography and military installations. Instead, in the far end of the field, apparent only in the 1947 photographs, was the ploughed-out outline of an Iron Age hillfort. Significantly, the remains of this hillfort were not seen by Willis and his contemporary workers.

Further research revealed that, in 1978, a small-scale reconnaissance excavation had been undertaken by the Alton Archaeological Committee to determine the nature of the enclosure and to date it as part of 'a continuing programme of research into the development of the nucleation of the settlement pattern around Alton' (Millet 1981, 49). Their report notes the omission of the hillfort from the standard texts or distribution maps. This they suggest 'was due presumably to the lack of dating evidence and the fact that ploughing had now reduced it to virtual invisibility on the ground' (*ibid.*). However, they also record that the hillfort is shown on the 1962 Ordnance Survey map of southern England, where it is called Dickett's Plantation. Clearly, this high-level plateau has held a continuous key position in the social landscape.

By October 1999, the PADMAC Unit had completed: the basic survey of Dickett's Field (Field 1) including the area of the ploughed-out Iron Age hillfort, Field 2 and the slope of Field 3; a second programme of fieldwalking, which confirmed the distribution pattern of the Palaeolithic material in Fields 1, 2 and 3; and a geophysical survey of what appeared to be two large solution features.

The 1999 geophysical surveys

Dickett's Field is an excellent place to test geophysical exploration theories and practices as the surveys here are complicated by the presence on the perimeter of the field of an electrical sub-station, communication masts and pylons and the possible presence of buried wire and cables. Such installations can produce an effect known as 'backscatter', which may distort the readings.

The aims of the geophysical (tomographical) survey of the site were to: locate the Chalk, and map its shape covering the outline of the solution feature(s); determine the quality of the Chalk by assessing the presence or absence of shattered material; determine the depth of the overburden, that is to say the deposits mapped as Clay-with-flints and the thickness of the topsoil; and, most importantly, to identify any disturbed stratigraphy, whether recent or ancient, within the solution features. Many sophisticated methods of geophysical exploration are totally unsuitable for investigating the sedimentology and geology of high-level sites. To date, the only really suitable method is the Resistivity (direct current) sounding method. This is a slow process but gives the accuracy and details required. Electromagnetic ground conductive mapping has limited value and is only of some use if employed in conjunction with the Resistivity sounding method. The

Geophysical survey was undertaken by Reynolds Geo-Science Ltd. using Resistivity Imaging (electrical imaging survey, alternatively known as resistivity tomography) and Ground Conductivity (Electro-magnetic) Mapping. The resulting data were interpreted by Dr J. Reynolds, an expert in the identification of disturbed stratigraphy and the investigation of solution features.

Following the prescribed methodology for the sampling of deposits on high-level Palaeolithic sites on deposits mapped as Clay-with-flints (see Scott-Jackson 2000), samples were carefully collected at specific points in conjunction with the basic survey, to provide *inter alia* information on the nature and distribution of the deposits mapped as Clay-with-flints. This information could then be linked to the geophysical survey.

THE DICKETT'S FIELD PALAEOLITHIC ARTEFACTS

In his assessment of the Willis *et al.* surface finds Roe (1981, 154) included the Dickett's Field handaxes in his Group VI along with those from Round Green, Barnfield Pit Swanscombe (Upper Loam) and Caversham Ancient Channel. He also records that out of the twenty-four handaxes and about fifty flakes, there were sixteen handaxes having a tranchet finish, three twisted handaxes, none with twisted tips (*ibid.,* 163) and, as previously noted, that these artefacts were of a distinctive colour and condition.

The majority of the Palaeolithic surface finds recovered during the 1998, 1999 and 2000 field surveys by the PADMAC Unit are the classic, highly ocherous and very weathered artefacts, characteristic of the type found earlier by Willis *et al.*. Amongst these artefacts there are two fragments of bifaces and a nearly complete (Roe pers. comm.) small biface (49 mm long), which were recovered along with biface thinning flakes. A core, exhibiting rudimentary Levallois technique (confirmed by Roe), was also found. This is the second of such artefacts to come from Dickett's Field. The flake scar patterns and the position of the cortex on a number of the flakes suggest that they too could be related to a coarse Levallois technique based on the reduction of quite poor quality small flint or cherty nodules.

Palaeolithic surface-finds from Dickett's Field vary in condition from very weathered to quite sharp. The differing conditions and the apparent continual replenishment of Palaeolithic artefacts in this constantly monitored field has both worrying and exciting implications. The significant number of Palaeolithic artefacts which continued to be brought to the surface may be the result of the plough just moving the artefacts around in the deep top soil or plough action cutting into the underlying subsoil at a yet unrecorded natural stratigraphic high in this area, possibly the edge of another solution feature(s). It would appear from our investigations that both things are indeed happening. At a survey point in the west of Dickett's Field, towards the north-eastern edge of the hillfort, in an area which had previously yielded only ocherous patinated and weathered artefacts, an interesting discovery was made. Six Palaeolithic flakes, all slightly weathered and all of a similar pale yellow patination, were found in a close concentration, within a square metre.

Such an assemblage poses the question of what significance, if any, there is in these distinctive artefacts being found so close together. It could be argued that the close proximity of these flakes is no more than a matter of a chance occurrence directly associated with the activities of Iron Age hillfort builders, who, as they constructed the hillfort, moved large clods of earth around, one of which contained the Palaeolithic flakes. Chance would then see that these flakes remained together for thousands of years, despite being removed from their original context, incorporated in the hillfort ramparts, and later when the hillfort was subsequently ploughed-out, they were still found together. Alternatively, these distinctive light coloured Palaeolithic artefacts are indicative of an *in situ* Palaeolithic site now in the course of destruction as the plough cuts into the subsoil!

Interestingly, if the Iron Age hillfort builders had disturbed a level containing Palaeolithic material during ditch digging and rampart building, and if the earth thrown up to construct the ramparts contained Palaeolithic artefacts, then these artefacts may conceivably have undergone a different form of weathering from those artefacts lying prone on the surface of the field. This is pure speculation of course, but such a process may account for both the classic extreme degrees of weathering and dark chocolate coloured patination seen on so many Palaeolithic artefacts and clasts from Dickett's Field.

WOC 3219 – the bout coupé shaped handaxe

Collected by Willis *et al.* and now stuck on a board in a sealed case at the Curtis Museum, Alton, is a single handaxe described as a *bout coupé* Mousterian handaxe around 70,000–30,000 years old (Shackley 1973, 550). This handaxe is unpatinated but has iron staining and is slightly weathered. The most striking thing about it, however, is that it is utterly unlike any of the other Palaeolithic handaxes from Dickett's Field, in its shape, colour or condition. Although Roe (1981, 257) acknowledges this artefact as a small *bout coupé*, he also noted that 'in condition it is quite different from the other Holybourne Palaeolithic artefacts, being unworn and showing only a little white patination and intermittent iron staining'.

In all respects therefore, it is identical, both in its unpatinated condition, colour and degree of weathering, to the later prehistoric artefacts we have found both in Dickett's Field and the surrounding fields. Furthermore, the colour and condition of this artefact correspond well to the uniformity seen in the difference between Palaeolithic and later prehistoric high-level finds from deposits mapped as Clay-with-flints. In southern England, isolated finds of the shaped handaxes described as *bout coupé* (cut-end), vary

a great deal in shape (Cook and Jacobi 1998, 135; Coulson 1986; Tyldesley 1987). These cordiform or sub-triangular handaxes could, in many cases, realistically be described either as pointed handaxes retouched to a more rounded shape or, conversely, ovate handaxes retouched to a more pointed shape.

We are not at all confident that this surface find from Dickett's Field is a Middle Palaeolithic Mousterian *bout coupé* handaxe. It may equally well be a core, core tool, or roughout from a later period of prehistory. Of course, we could be wrong and it may be that we do indeed have an unpatinated handaxe, perhaps thrown up by the Iron Age builders during the construction of the hillfort.

QUESTIONS AND ANSWERS

The 1998 and 1999 investigations in Dickett's Field by the PADMAC Unit generated a number of questions concerning the recent use of Dickett's Field, its geology, geomorphology and archaeology. By the end of October 1999, fieldwork and research had provided a number of answers.

The true location of the dummy airfield was identified as Field 2, known locally as 27-Acre Common, not Dickett's Field, Field 1. Over the years disturbance had occurred as farm workers removed cables from the edge of Dickett's Field and wire and cable from 27-Acre Common. The geophysical survey results identified two major solution features. These depressions, with diameters of 20 m and 10 m respectively, contain sub-depressions. The maximum depth is around 4 m, with three distinct layers being clearly identified across the whole of the area of investigation: a clay-rich topsoil; a layer of Clay-with-flints *sensu stricto* and a Chalk sub-stratum. Also identified was a fourth layer of what appears to be Shattered Chalk existing between the Clay-with-flints and the Chalk bedrock. Most importantly there is no evidence of disturbance of the deposits within the solution features. The geophysical survey also confirmed the diagnostic value of aerial photographs in the search for high-level sites on deposits mapped as Clay-with-flints, as the features identified in the photographs of Dickett's Field were proved to be solution hollows.

Finally, there is no evidence either in the literature or in the field to suggest that the Alton Archaeological Committee's excavations of the Iron Age hillfort encroached into the area where the Palaeolithic artefacts were reported found. No Palaeolithic artefacts were found during their excavation and the only stone tools discovered were a scatter of Mesolithic flints which appear to have been in a derived context (Millett 1981, 50).

Further investigations are required before the actual nature of deposits mapped as Clay-with-flints in Dickett's Field can be determined and the question of whether unpatinated and/or light coloured patinated Palaeolithic artefacts are to be found embedded in the sub-surface deposits can be answered. Unfortunately, the basic problem of the Dickett's Field site reference remains, since although the data distortions have been eliminated, confusion still exists in the published literature.

DICKETT'S FIELD: THE FIRST EXCAVATION

During the summer of 2000, the PADMAC Unit conducted the first of the excavations planned for this site. A trench 3 metres by 1 metre and an auger pit 75 cm by 75 cm were excavated on the southern edge of one of the large basin-like solution features identified by the 1999 geophysical survey (Fig. 22.2). To facilitate direct correlation between the geophysical data and the results of the 2000 excavation, the trench and auger pit were precisely aligned along the resistivity survey transects using an EDM (electronic measuring device). The following is a preliminary account of our findings.

Geology and stratigraphy

In the areas excavated, the depth of the loamy topsoil varied from between 33–35 cm due to the irregular interface between the topsoil and the underlying deposits. The topsoil contained many angular clasts, predominantly ancient and modern shattered flints, ocherous sub-rounded clasts and a few Tertiary pebbles. At 5–10 cm (spits 1 and 2) from the base of the topsoil there was a 'flinty layer' of blue, blue/grey, blue/white, beige/white and yellow/white patinated and fractured/frost shattered, possibly *in situ* clasts. These angular to sub-angular clasts in a compacted clayey/silty/sandy matrix had a clast ratio of 60–65% and were different from those in the topsoil, exhibiting a great deal less variation, and being generally lighter in colour. Although ocherous sub-rounded clasts were relatively abundant in the topsoil, less than 5% were found below the topsoil in the clayey/silty/sandy, yellow/beige, brick earth type deposit. Tertiary pebbles were also conspicuous

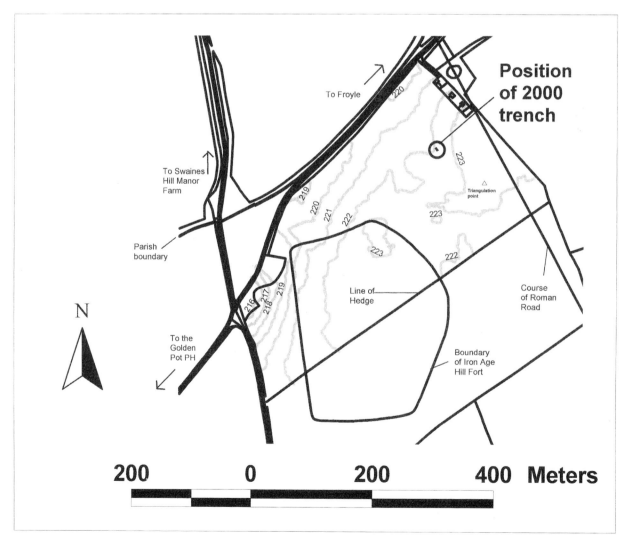

Fig. 22.2. Position of the trench excavated in Dickett's Field in 2000.

by their absence. The shattered flints, which formed this intractable flinty layer, were distributed evenly across the areas of excavation to a depth of around 25 cm (spits 3, 4 and 5). When this irregular shattered flint layer was removed, the underlying deposit (from spits 6–9, depth range of 30–45 cm) was found to be a silty/clayey matrix containing a variety of clasts, similar to that found in the topsoil. Spit 6 was characterised by a silty-clay deposit containing many flints, spit 7 was distinguished by silty pockets and fewer flints, and pockets of sandy-clay were seen in spit 8. Across the excavated areas, Clay-with-flints *sensu stricto* was located at a depth of between 50–60 cm (spits 10–12) from the base of the topsoil. This deposit was distinctive, being very much redder in colour (Munsell colour: 10YR 4/4 or 4/6), with far higher clay content than the other overlying deposits and, unlike the overlying deposits, it contained many small Tertiary pebbles. The stratigraphy can be summarised as follows:

> Topsoil with silty layer at base
> Shattered flint layer
> Flint nodules in silty/clayey matrix
> Clay-with-flints *sensu stricto*

The flinty layer is therefore, 'sandwiched' between two occurrences of silty/clayey deposits, all of which lie immediately above the Clay-with-flints *sensu stricto*.

Excavated artefacts

All the artefacts found in the excavated areas were small flakes exhibiting a range of patination varying from unpatinated to ocherous. The depositional status of the artefacts should become clearer when the sampled clast orientation data have been processed and the particle size analyses completed. More work is also required before we can confidently assign these flakes to any particular archaeological period.

The artefacts were predominately recovered from a depth of 5–10 cm (spits 1 and 2) and from a depth of 30–35 cm (spits 6 and 7). Several white patinated flakes were found in Square B (spit 7). At a depth of approximately 54 cm (spit 10/11) in the Clay-with-flint *sensu stricto*, several unpatinated flakes were found. Samples of charcoal and burnt flint collected at various spits may, possibly, provide environmental information and age estimates.

EXISTING PROBLEMS
AND FUTURE INVESTIGATIONS

When the clast orientation data have been processed and the particle size analyses completed, we will better understand the geomorphology of the 'flinty layer' in relation to its position within the solution feature. At this stage of investigations it would seem that slope processes of some description are implicated. What is not clear from either the investigations of Osborne White (1909) or our own

work during 1998, 1999 and 2000, is the extent of this flinty layer. Is it a localised feature or does it exist in other areas on the plateau? We also need to know if the flinty layer, which has the appearance of being shattered *in situ*, is in any way associated with the ploughed-out walls of the Iron Age hillfort. Clearly, if there are *in situ* Palaeolithic sites in the solution features on the Dickett's Field plateau they are well and truly sealed in. A full detailed report of this excavation is planned for a later date.

Dickett's Field does indeed present a challenge. The opportunities and problems facing the PADMAC Unit are the sheer size of the site, the presence of many large solution hollows, the distribution pattern of the Palaeolithic surface finds and the problem of access to a site which is weather dependent and restricted to a few weeks in late summer at the end of harvesting and before winter planting.

ACKNOWLEDGEMENTS

We would like to offer our gratitude to Professor Roe for his academic leadership, his personal support, his sense of humour and for his encouragement of the continuing quest for a greater understanding of prehistory.

REFERENCES

Cook, J. and Jacobi, R. 1998. Discoidal core technology in the Palaeolithic at Oldbury, Kent. In N. Ashton, F. Healy and P. Pettitt (eds.) *Stone Age Archaeology: Essays in Honour of John Wymer*, 124–136. Lithic Studies Society Occasional Paper 6, Oxbow Monographs 102. Oxbow Books, Oxford.

Coulson, S.D. 1986. The *bout coupé* handaxe as a typological mistake. In S.N. Collcutt (ed.) *The Palaeolithic of Britain and its Nearest Neighbours: Recent Trends*, 53–54. University of Sheffield, Sheffield.

Crawford, O.G.S., Ellaway. J.R. and Willis, G.W. 1922. The antiquity of Man in Hampshire. *Proceedings of the Hampshire Field Club* 9, 173–188.

Ellaway, J.R. and Willis, G.W. 1934. Field Notes – Basingstoke District. *Proceedings of the Hampshire Field Club* 12, 87–88, 309–310.

Millet, M. 1981. An Iron Age univallate hillfort on Holybourne Down, near Alton. *Proceedings of the Hampshire Field Club and Archaeological Society* 37, 49–53.

Osborne White, H.J. 1909. *The Geology of the Country around Basingstoke*. Memoirs of the Geological Survey, Explanation of Sheet 284. HMSO, London.

Roe, D.A 1968. *A Gazetteer of British Lower and Middle Palaeolithic Sites*. Council for British Archaeology Research Report 8, London.

Roe, D.A. 1981. *The Lower and Middle Palaeolithic Periods in Britain*. Routledge and Kegan Paul, London.

Scott-Jackson, J.E. 1991. *Gazetteer of Palaeolithic Find-spots on the North Hampshire Downs*. Unpublished study.

Scott-Jackson, J.E. 1999. *A Gazetteer of Lower and Middle Palaeolithic Artefacts from Deposits Mapped as Clay-with-flints on the Chalk Downlands of Southern England*. Unpublished study.

Scott-Jackson, J.E. 2000. *Lower and Middle Palaeolithic Artefacts from Deposits Mapped as Clay-with-Flints: A New Synthesis with Significant Implications for the Earliest Occupation of Britain.* Oxbow Books, Oxford.

Shackley, M.L. 1973. A contextual study of the Mousterian industry from Great Pan Farm, Newport, Isle of Wight. *Proceedings of the Isle of White Natural History and Archaeological Society* 6, 542–554.

Tyldesley, J.A. 1987. *The Bout Coupé Handaxe: A Typological Problem.* British Archaeological Reports British Series 170, Oxford.

Wessex Archaeology 1993. *The Southern Rivers Palaeolithic Project, Report No. 2. 1992–1993: The South-West and South of the Thames.* Trust for Wessex Archaeology, Salisbury.

White, M.J. 1998. On the significance of Acheulean biface variability in southern Britain, *Proceedings of the Prehistoric Society* 64, 15–44.

Willis, G.W. 1947. Hampshire palaeoliths and the Clay-with-flints. *Proceedings of the Hampshire Field Club and Archaeological Society* 16, 253–256.

23. The *Sackung* Hypothesis: a challenge for Palaeolithic prospection

Simon Collcutt

ABSTRACT

Accelerated surface erosion during the Pleistocene, especially during colder stages with significant mass-movement and fluvial incision, repeatedly produced remodelling of the landscape as a whole. Such remodelling caused significant lateral unloading of hill-forms which, in turn, would tend to respond through deep-seated structural deformation, involving general subsidence of higher terrain coupled with bulging of valley floors. Whilst deeper phenomena can be grouped under the heading of 'rock-creep' (plastic deformation and microfaulting/thrusting), nearer-vertical structures (mostly normal faults and fault-sets) developed high on slopes and at hilltops, producing a variety of relatively superficial subsidence forms (gulls, troughs, basins, micrograben), grouped here under the heading of '*Sackung*-related' phenomena, a German term, denoting 'sagging', previously defined during studies of unloading in hard-rock contexts. The hypothesis set out in the present paper is: first, that such *Sackung*-related phenomena will inevitably have occurred within most softer geological basements (including Chalk), and will thus be present, for instance, over a very large proportion of England; second, that such phenomena will have served to capture Pleistocene surface sediments, together with any included Palaeolithic and palaeontological assemblages, commonly in more or less unmixed context and sometimes (given larger-scale structures) in strictly primary context; and third, that once captured, the relevant contexts would tend to be preserved from subsequent erosion by the same *Sackung*-related mechanisms (continued gentle subsidence, with erosion at least balanced by local, neotectonically induced sedimentation). Past Pleistocene research has tended to ignore structural readjustment and to concentrate upon low-level, 'normal' depositional sequences in valleys, where primary archaeological contexts are difficult to locate and often deeply buried. Under the *Sackung* Hypothesis, it is expected, albeit counter-intuitively on the face of it, that accessible primary contexts, at least for Devensian times and probably significantly earlier in many regions, will be common and relatively easy to predict, at or near local topographic high points.

INTRODUCTION

Looking at open-air Pleistocene contexts around Britain, only two categories have long-term relevance. First, there are the subsiding structural basins in which thick sedimentary sequences have accumulated. These occur mainly in submarine settings. They are basins controlled by deep seated and persistent tectonic systems. There is a reasonable chance that such sequences may survive to become part of the enduring geological record. Second, there is the rest, broadly the 'land'. Here, epeirogenic tilting effects complicate the matter, and landblocks may also be subject to extremely slow tectonic subsidence trends. Nevertheless, as a reasonable generalisation in the medium-term, much of the terrestrial British Isles is in a regime of isostatic uplift, responding both to pulses of denudation and to deglaciation rebound; within river valleys, the fluctuating process of gradient evolution also contributes to the development of stacked landscape segments. At a gross scale, on much of the land 'older' is 'higher', as compared with the reverse (normal stratigraphic) trend in the subsiding structural basins. There is little chance that most terrestrial Pleistocene sequences will survive to become part of the enduring geological record.

Be this as it may, as researchers in the present, we do not waste effort in regretting deposits which in practice are beyond our reach, nor are we greatly concerned that most deposits which we can indeed study are unlikely still to be extant twenty million years from now. However, too parochial a perspective could lead us to concentrate exclusively on models in which geological basement and large-scale geomorphology are taken as an effectively static substrate upon which interesting Pleistocene terrestrial deposits are overlaid as a 'superficial patchwork' by the function of primary deposition-erosion systems. Such models lack the important dimension of dynamic geological structure, the fact that the substrate may show deep activity which can significantly affect the survival-potential of Pleistocene deposits, at specific sites and over surprisingly short timescales. The ground does move, and in archaeologically significant ways.

SURVIVAL POTENTIAL

Consider the proposition that archaeological sites will be available for present-day study if:

1) Palaeolithic activity leaving physical traces potentially capable of being recovered now occurred in the first place (in terms of formal taphonomy, the biotic, thanatic and perthotaxic stages);

2) the physical traces have become stabilised reasonably quickly by incorporation into deposits with minimal disturbance (the syntaphic stage);

3) the resulting deposits have managed to survive intact (the peritaphic and apotaphic stages), avoiding all or most later disturbance (a marked anataxic stage); and

4) we have methods of predicting promising locations and of accessing such locations (the sullegic and trephic stages).

Condition 1 includes the issue of original Palaeolithic site location strategies which archaeologists studying later periods might call 'land use'. We will leave this aside for the moment.

More immediately interesting are conditions 2 and 3, involving details of sedimentation and deposit survival, details which can be subsumed under the general label of *sediment-trapping*. If we look at classic Palaeolithic sites, we find that the majority fall into a small set of broad-brush sediment-trap types with subdivisions/combinations depending on scale of interest: basins, or multi-sided concave-up traps such as lake basins; troughs, or two-sided concave-up traps such as channels and dry valleys; shoulders, or one-sided concave-lateral/oblique traps such as marine cliffs and riverine bluffs; re-entrants, or multi-lateral and often roofed traps; and flats such as plains and terrace segments. Geomorphological contexts that are, apparently, concave-down (hilltops) or markedly sloping (hillsides) are, of course, rare among the known better quality Palaeolithic sites. Indeed, such settings do not spring readily to mind as likely sediment-traps in the first place, nor, on the face of it, does it appear probable that any deposits which do form will persist over long periods, continual relocation and mixing being more plausible.

Condition 4 depends on our understanding, as well as on any difficulties of scale and access. We know that Pleistocene deposits, especially those containing significant archaeological and palaeontological assemblages, are often highly discontinuous in space and may only represent one point in time. Thus, we work backwards through the taphonomic process, taking our Palaeolithic sites where we know, or at least hope, we can find them. Paradoxically, this often leads us to the remains of relatively high but well organised energy systems with chronologically informative morphologies, such as river terrace suites (cf. Wessex Archaeology 1992, 1993, 1994, 1996a, 1996b, 1997), even though we understand that only the tiniest proportion of what actually does survive represents depositional environments of sufficiently low energy to have allowed the preservation of *in situ* primary context archaeological sites. Furthermore, most of these systems are 'wide' and 'deep' and we are usually reduced to the role of passive observers, waiting for someone else to come along and dig a large enough hole in a likely location. Given the methods and speed at which large holes are dug nowadays, we have even less access. Consequently, significant Palaeolithic sites now come to light in Britain at a rate of little better than one a decade. Although we may put a brave face on this situation (Wenban-Smith 1994), it is actually an indictment of our prospection techniques.

DOWN-SITES

Most classic Palaeolithic sites can be termed *Down-Sites*. A *Down-Site* is, quite literally, a site which is *down*, that is, one which, due to gravity, is on the receiving end of the sedimentary system, one where accretion dominates over erosion. Such sites tend to form at low regional altitude and, even today, we still look for them at relatively low levels. Thus, we study terrace suites, knowing that even the highest terrace once lay at, or close to, the local baseline; even after successive fluvial incisions, the surviving terrace remnants provided flats, and the intermediate risers/bluffs provided shoulders, at which local sedimentary regimes could produce more *Down-Sites*. When considering the formation of typical *Down-Sites*, we think in terms of *anterior morphology* and, when considering the survival of such sites, we think in terms of the *persistence of (fossil) anterior morphology*. Most geomorphological changes post-dating site formation will be damaging, destroying large numbers, probably the great majority, of *Down-Sites*, even if some changes might be useful, in as much as they might favour sediment accretion, leading to deeper, safer burial, or, by downcutting, might isolate a terrain from more active, that is to say erosive, regimes. However, we would not commonly think of *posterior morphology* as being the key to site survival, perhaps in the absence of a major sediment-trap pre-dating the archaeological event. Note that the terms 'anterior' and 'posterior' which refer to time relative to an archaeological event, are used here in order to avoid confusion with the established terms of 'antecedent' and 'subsequent' in drainage system dynamics, which have different meanings.

The above analysis seems reasonable, indeed, rather mundane, although the general implication is dissatisfying. *Down-Sites*, by definition, do not include hilltops and significant slopes but common sense tells us that such zones which comprised the greater part of the available surface, even in many 'lowland' parts of the country, must have been involved in the varied ways in which Palaeolithic people used complex landscapes. Indeed, in particular for the Lower Palaeolithic, there is indirect proof of such broader landscape use in the artefacts found, sometimes in large numbers, in mass movement mantles and in river gravels: the secondary and tertiary contexts towards the end of the local sedimentary conveyor belt which have been subject to multiple disturbances and diachronous mixing. The problem is the considerable effectiveness of cool climate and periglacial slope-stripping, together with the ability of contemporary rivers to evacuate the debris. We know this, both directly from observation of the resulting deposits and indirectly from our refusal to be deceived by the abundance of Holocene colluvia, there being an extreme rarity of warm climate colluvia surviving from earlier periods (cf. Kirby 1987). As noted above, we are based upon the vulnerable 'land', and the ultimate sediment-sinks, the currently submarine basins, are not accessible to us.

UP-SITES

To extend our prospecting away from the *Down-Site* localities which have dominated our thinking for over a century, we must consider the proposition that there could be plausible mechanisms which might allow survival of another type of geological context: the *Up-Site*. Here the situation is not necessarily subject to obviously favourable (tending towards concave-up) anterior morphology. It is not in a dominantly accretive context, lying at higher local altitudes and is, perhaps, even surprisingly dependent for survival upon posterior morphological development. There are already known examples of hilltop sites but a few examples are not much good beyond their intrinsic interest, if their survival turns out to be incredibly capricious, merely the result of idiosyncratic local factors unlikely to be repeated on any useful scale. However, if *Up-Sites* occur due to commonly acting mechanisms, then we may have a significant prospection tool.

THE *SACKUNG* HYPOTHESIS

Zischinsky (1969) began a paper in rock mechanics with the following simple statement:

> '*Wenn man aus einem belasteten Körper oder konkret aus einer unter Eigengewicht stehenden Masse einem Teil entfernt, so muß die Umgebung sich auf die neue Verteilung der Kräfte einstellen* [When a part is removed from a loaded rock or concrete body subject to gravitational stress, a new distribution of forces necessarily comes into play in the remaining material]' (*ibid.*, 30).

He went on to describe natural examples in the Tyrol where slopes in hard rock had been oversteepened by glaciation and periglacial processes following deglaciation, giving rise to readjustment by down-slope movement of enormous coherent masses of rock on the valley flanks. He defined the term *Sackung* ('sagging') to cover the process whereby deep-seated rock creep produces a ridgetop (or near-ridgetop) 'trench', roughly parallel with the ridge-line, behind the apex of a major rock slab which has settled gradually into the adjacent valley. The term has become current in English, particularly in the Americas (cf. McCalpin and Irvine 1995), to refer to the resulting trench and the sediments which are commonly captured within the evolving form; it is also commonly used in both American and Italian texts in connection with terrains destabilised yet further by recent earthquake activity. This term has been borrowed in the phrase '*Sackung* Hypothesis' of the title of the present paper for two reasons. First, it is relatively unfamiliar and so provides a succinct label with little risk of confusion with other phenomena. Second, the classic forms are in relatively bare, hard rock, showing clearly the surface expression of the mechanics involved: Zischinsky explained the holistic process, whereas related component phenomena in other regions can often be observed only in part, due to difficulties in perceiving scale and to masking of the crucial evidence in softer rocks, sediments and slope mantles. At first sight, the glaciated Tyrol seems an unlikely model for understanding Pleistocene deposits in lowland Britain but, in fact, phenomena which conform with the basic mechanical pattern are common in this country. Under the *Sackung* Hypothesis, we are looking for evidence of relatively deep-seated movements, variously termed in the literature as 'gravity spreading', 'gravity tectonics', 'non-diastrophic adjustment' or 'topographic adjustment', caused by the rapid lateral unloading which we know to have occurred during periglacial slope erosion and fluvial incision. These movements would have favoured the development of posterior sediment traps, 'trenches' of some sort, possibly containing archaeological *Up-Sites*, at or towards the top of slopes (Fig. 23.1).

UP-SITE FORMATION

Cambering is one element of a set of interrelated phenomena affecting significant landscape tracts at a wide range of

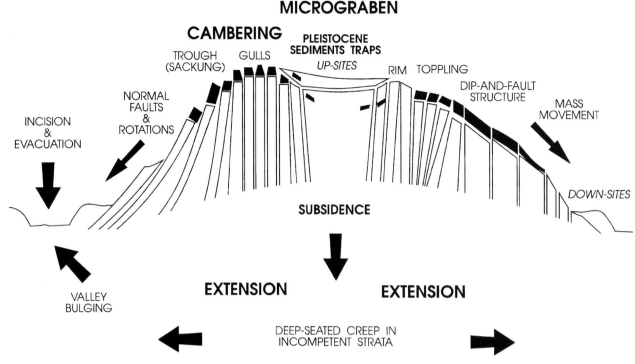

Fig. 23.1. The Sackung *Hypothesis*

both geographical and temporal scales. For example, in Britain, cambering is associated with almost every formation of Carboniferous or later age containing or overlying argillaceous beds. Cambering in itself is the down-bending of a competent rock stratum, underlain by a less competent stratum which is forced to distort laterally towards an adjacent void (valley). In the British context, Ballantyne and Harris (1994), noting the dominant duration of cold stages and the fact that periglacial slope denudation is likely to be an order of magnitude faster than under temperate conditions, conclude that it is most likely that the large-scale cambering phenomena observed all across the country actually developed over successive episodes of Pleistocene periglaciation (*ibid.*, 139 and comprehensive bibliography).

Cambering is usually associated with other phenomena (for discussion of the wider system see Hutchinson 1991; Parks 1991). As it bends, the upper surface of the competent stratum is subjected to severe tension and stress-perpendicular (usually cross-surface-slope) fractures, known as *gulls*, result. Ground-ice may also play a part in gull-widening. The loss of lateral support due to the presence of flanking valleys may also cause much deeper fractures to occur, producing either regular, high-angle normal faulting (extensional downthrow of blocks in the valleyward direction) or rotational slips (clockwise rotation of blocks towards a valley to the left), both forms often in step-like suites, the exact form(s) in a given case being dependent upon a variety of factors (primarily the physical properties,

both absolute and relative, of the strata involved, and speed of lateral recession and vertical incision of the valley). Other structural effects such as block-toppling, localised reverse faulting, dip-and-fault structure or low-angle thrust-faulting may sometimes occur in cases where the interaction of surface morphology and stratum geometry is favourable. At the deepest level, the incompetent strata may actually creep (deform) sideways and then upwards, causing valley-floor bulging, an effect probably accelerated during periods when permafrost is degrading from the bottom up. Given the capacity of flood-stage periglacial rivers, the excess bulge is continually eroded. Consequently, general valley-side unloading is also a result of deep delivery of sediment to the thalweg, and not just near-surface conveyance.

Gulls developed during cambering may progressively capture overlying weathering mantle and other soft deposits; indeed, gulls are rarely obvious at the surface, since they are usually draped by these materials. However, cross-slope 'troughs', 'gullies' and even true anti-slope scarps may sometimes still be apparent, the most commonly reported examples being in Jurassic strata, which are widespread at outcrops in lowland Britain and which show particularly conducive soft/hard alternations in much of the geological sequence (cf. Briggs and Courtney 1972, Gloucestershire; Whittaker 1972, Worcestershire; Horswill and Horton 1976, Rutland). In a few observed cases, there has been significant slippage of valleyward blocks (i.e. true fault movement, not simply gull-widening), such that 'sags' and 'troughs' approach the classic form of Sackungen (cf. Chandler *et al*. 1976, Somerset; also, the large, partially sediment-filled gulls and sags in the Permian Magnesian Limestone escarpment exposed at the western end of Creswell Crags gorge, of interest especially on the more stable north-western, Derbyshire, side). The gull-capture mechanism obviously requires the contrast between harder rock and soft overlying deposits. Fractures in unconsolidated sediment themselves may involve block displacement but the opening 'fissures', needed to trap surface material, cannot develop; the incompetent sediment simply distorts, by plastic deformation and/or microfaulting, to prevent formation of significant sub-surface voids.

However, we must not miss the breadth of the archaeologically relevant point here. By definition, ancient hard rocks cannot themselves contain archaeology, but any younger Pleistocene deposits can. We do not need hard 'containers' (gulls), simply the 'sagging' of sediments perhaps already containing archaeological material (*dynamic posterior morphology*). The general mechanical regime (stress pattern) is the same for any substrate composition, whatever the balance between rigid or bulk-plastic responses in any given case. Laterally continuous ancient strata show an approximation to a simple vertical increase of compressive stress with depth. Once a valley is incised into the formerly continuous sequence, there must be lateral unloading and the stress pattern, whatever the local detail but always involving tensional stresses, deviates from the vertical, working towards trying to fill the valley void again.

Most researchers to date have adopted the 'valley', effectively the unilateral 'half-valley', as their frame of reference. There are chapters in geomorphological texts entitled 'Slope Processes' but one never encounters a chapter on 'Hilltop Processes'. We now need to pan our frame of reference sideways, as it were. As a single-plane simplification, a true topographical hill is a 'bilateral' form, standing in an 'interfluve' position between two valleys. If the hill is unloaded from both directions, suites of fracture forms develop on both slopes and, if there is reasonable balance between opposing forces, the entire hill-core may be placed under tension, encouraged by gravitation spreading at depth whether or not there is actual faulting below the flanks. Under these circumstances, and especially given hill-core geology dominated by unconsolidated sediment or softer rocks, downward-converging normal faults may develop and the central block, the actual hilltop, may sink. The stress patterns involved (pressures down and out on the flanks) are mechanically identical to the pattern developed by upward pressure at the centre coupled with lateral extension of the crown. The latter case occurs during tectonic up-doming, as well as in a few other situations, such as plutonic or diapiric intrusion, and the large-scale result is a rift valley. More regionalised doming gives smaller forms such as the Rhine Valley *Graben* (Ger. 'ditch'). It is convenient to refer to any local situation with a central foundered block, whether produced by down-flank or up-centre stress, as a *micrograben*; indeed, the same geometrical form may result, on a smaller or tiny scale, in frost-wedge cast material or the fill of solution pipes, as lateral support is withdrawn during further activity. In theory, a circular hill could develop a central conical foundered plug but, in practice, the stresses are never so finely balanced and even approximately circular hillforms are more likely to have elongate micrograben oriented roughly parallel to the maximum diameter of the hill or to the axes of the flanking thalwegs, tapering at the ends, or even in a closed lenticular form, when seen in plan. Because of departures from an ideal symmetrical geometry, longer ridgeforms will tend to have suites of lenticular micrograben or more irregular 'chains' of potential or actual depressions near their summits. Just as with gulls, it is not always the case, depending upon the fluctuating balance between surface erosion and local deposition and the foundering of the central block, that a functional micrograben system will show surface expression at any given time, including the point of formation of a hilltop archaeological site and the point of observation in the present. Indeed, common experience tells us that we do not ordinarily see 'rift valleys' in our hilltops today. Also, even if there is some surface depression at a time of interest, the micrograben borders in softer substrates will not usually stand as individual 'clifflets' (equivalent to anti-slope scarps lower on the flanks) but will appear simply as local *reverse-slope rims*, underlain not by one but by many parallel faults in relatively broad belts. The micrograben is not often one block but, rather, a complex set, approximating to a 'cone-in-cone' structure.

The implications of micrograben formation for hilltop archaeological sites seem promising. The characteristics closely resemble the specification for an *Up-Site*. The effect is not dependent upon obviously favourable anterior morphology, although, if a micrograben system is already active at the time of archaeological activity and there does happen to be a surface depression at the hilltop, the localised concave-up context will obviously help. Nevertheless, any reduction at the time of the archaeological event and/or shortly afterwards in out-facing surface slopes at the hilltop must increase chances of survival. Hilltops, by definition lying at higher local altitude, are not dominantly accretive contexts but, rather, are extremely sediment poor, aeolian input being the only plausible mechanism by which significant sediment could be added to the system as a whole. Nevertheless, the micrograben mechanism slows or prevents loss by erosion and it may 're-use' sediment from the hill itself, a process equivalent to tectonic sedimentation in larger scale systems, so that no new input is required to ensure burial of archaeological material. Finally, the action of the micrograben mechanism after the archaeological event ought to be capable, in some cases, of keeping pace albeit not necessarily in a steady manner, with the severe periglacial erosion expected on the outer hillsides. This dynamic posterior morphology could maintain an archaeological site just below the surface, despite continual lowering through time of the overall hill profile. Such an *Up-Site* will not often constitute a perfect primary context, especially if there is only shallow burial for much of the time, leaving the archaeology constantly or repeatedly within reach of ground-ice and bioturbation effects. Nevertheless, because the system will be relatively large-scale by comparison with, say, a single gull, and subsidence will be gradual, a significant underlying void never developing, there is a good chance that at least blocks of the original site will be 'sampled' by faulting or downwarping, without too much distortion and certainly without mass-mixing, leaving traces of spatial organisation and even of intrinsically fragile features such as hearths.

The theory behind the overall *Sackung* Hypothesis is compelling in itself but, if this is indeed such a commonly acting set of mechanisms, it should be possible to point to plausible archaeological examples, even if, to date, our frame of reference has been largely tied to the valley.

THE EARLY UPPER PALAEOLITHIC SITE OF BEEDINGS, WEST SUSSEX

The remarkable Early Upper Palaeolithic lithic assemblage from the Beedings, Pulborough, West Sussex, provides an excellent example of a significant archaeological assemblage caught in what was probably a relatively small-scale trap or traps. The site lay at about 90 m OD above the scarp of a ridge capped by sandstone of the Lower Greensand Hythe Beds. Jacobi (1986), with considerable insight, has collated and interpreted the information available about the find context. The flint artefacts were recovered in 1900 from the sandy fill of gulls, trending parallel to the strike of cambered strata. As Jacobi (*ibid.*) has pointed out, gulls are commonly widened under periglacial conditions, causing the subduction of overlying sediments and, in this case, the capture of Palaeolithic artefacts. The undamaged condition of the material, the coherent typology and technology, and the presence of conjoinable pieces, led Jacobi to rely upon the quality of the capture mechanism and to interpret the assemblage in terms of likely site function. Jacobi also mentioned nineteenth century finds of Devensian faunal material from features certainly or probably developed on gulls such as Ightham Fissure, Kent. In his conclusion (*ibid.*, 67), Jacobi noted: 'The reported find context is important in highlighting an unexpected taphonomic situation within which evidence for an open-air find-spot of pre-last-glacial-maximum age could become preserved'.

Moving to larger scale phenomena, indisputable proof that the micrograben mechanism has been involved in a particular case will rarely be easy, principally because there will not be simple and continuous bounding faults. However, the site of Glaston, Rutland, where the present author developed his concept on the topic, provides at least an extremely suggestive example.

THE EARLY UPPER PALAEOLITHIC SITE OF GLASTON, RUTLAND

The Pleistocene material at Glaston is composed primarily of the remains of hyaena denning activity. This is currently the only demonstrable case of true open-air denning in Britain but there is also a modest Early Upper Palaeolithic presence at the site. Whilst much analysis remains to be done, the initial impression is that significant zones show near primary context, that is to say original spatial organisation. The site lies at about 122 m OD, towards the southern 'rim' (see below) of a broad ridge, with a stream to the south (tributary to the River Welland and locally flowing at 65 m OD) and a stream to the north (tributary to the River Chater and locally flowing at 75 m OD). The east–west trending interfluve at this point is some 2500 m wide at the base between the streams and some 750 m wide across the hilltop. The basement Jurassic geology is mapped as Grantham Formation (formerly, Lower Estuarine Series), with a capping of Collyweston Facies continuous across the hilltop. No Quaternary or other drift deposits are mapped anywhere in the vicinity above the deposits in the flanking valleys. The BGS have shown a 'notional' normal fault, with valleyward downthrow, on each of the southern and northern flanks of the hill.

The actual disposition on the ground is significantly different in detail from the generalised mapping. First, the carbonate rich sandstone of the Collyweston Facies is a discontinuous stratum surviving only as thin, isolated or clustered 'rafts', only a few metres across at most. The ridgetop morphology, somewhat obscured by a modern sandpit, comprises slightly raised southern and northern rims, with an intervening broad and relatively flat depressed area (the vertical interval between rim crests and depression base at the modern surface is estimated to be no more than 2 m); all geological observers are agreed that an underlying micrograben system appears to be indicated (facilitated by additional normal faults on the outer hillsides). The Pleistocene site lies on the 'inner' (northern to north-western) slope of the southern rim, at a depth of about a metre below the surface, a calculation complicated by Medieval activity in the excavated zone. Once allowance has been made for later illuviation, the sediment containing the palaeontological and archaeological remains appears to have been almost exclusively derived from the fine sands of the Grantham Formation substrate which contains some muddy units, thus requiring further study to ascertain whether the slightly 'dirty' sands of the Pleistocene context have received subsidiary aeolian input. The Pleistocene context also contains a small proportion of dispersed ironstone and a little flint, fine grit, as well as clasts of the Collyweston sandstone. Setting aside the variously sized burrows, much of the structure of the Pleistocene context is composed of 'compartments' defined by boundary phenomena in a continuum between pure plastic deformation, often involving injection from the muddy zones in the Jurassic, and pure faulting. There are some high, thin and roughly horizontal survivals of Pleistocene sediment just below the Medieval activity and Holocene bioturbate zone, but survivals at least 75 cm deeper occur in downthrown 'compartments'. There are at least two separate, superimposed, generations of compartmentalisation, each with laterally discontinuous examples of minor ice-wedge casts. These are usually linked at triple-junctions, as opposed to quadruple 'crossroads' junctions, and with true cast material, as opposed to injected material from below, rarely wider than 10 cm at the top or penetrating downwards over about 75 cm which plug the tops of deep faults. Although the effects of ground-ice are clear, they do not obviously include significant cryoturbation, and there are absolutely no signs of significant lateral mass movement such as gelifluction. However, with rare minor/localised exceptions, all faults of all generations show a markedly extensional regime towards the floor of the depression, towards the centre-line of the ridge. The most laterally continuous faults are oriented broadly south-west to north-east, parallel to the local inner rim slope, and they are normal, showing a consistent down-stepping, to a degree significantly in excess of the recent surface slope. Faults perpendicular to this dominant axis are less laterally continuous, are variously normal or reverse (locally) but, when well exposed, commonly show rotational shear at the fault planes, that is to say, the blocks dominantly step down towards the central depression but they 'juggle about' a little as they do so. A few compartments also show local normal faults dipping to the south-east, such that they combine with the dominant faults to form extremely small-scale micrograben in their own right. Whilst a few of the observed faults showed incipient curvature at depth in the vertical plane, concave to the north-west, none of the faults with significant surface extent of, say, over a metre laterally, could be observed to terminate downwards. Although the excavations were necessarily shallow, usually about 1 m but never deeper than 1.5 m, the faults are passing down, well below obvious Pleistocene ground-ice phenomena, into the completely undisturbed micro-bedded Jurassic basement. None of these observations absolutely proves the presence of a major micrograben in the ridgetop broadly north of the known Pleistocene site but they are all entirely consistent with, and are most parsimoniously explained by, such a hypothesis.

Glaston therefore looks like a good *Up-Site*. It seems likely that the micrograben system would already have been operative possibly long before the palaeontological and archaeological activity. Thereafter, morphological readjustment kept the site on the inner rim, away from the erosive environment on the outer hillslope. No great influx of sediment was needed, the Pleistocene context comprising dominantly reworked, strictly local Jurassic sediment. Whilst the site remained within reach of subsequent ground-ice effects, these were not markedly disruptive because the forces could be largely absorbed within the continuously extensional structural context. The downthrow of individual compartments took material beyond the reach of any near-surface erosion and of the worst of Holocene bioturbation and more recent human activity.

Glaston also has other characteristics which have favoured the Pleistocene remains. The remnants of Collyweston sandstone, lying as blocks which must have been apparent at the surface, were attractive to both hyaenas and humans, giving this particular point on the hilltop a specific 'identity' or 'sense of place', as well as the potential for a little shelter, and as a source of carbonate gradually released to the proximal sediments, without which there would have been no bone preservation. Similarly, the well sorted Jurassic fine sand provided an excellent matrix for faulting, a ready and mobile surface material in wash or wind in which objects could be buried, and a degree of retardation of ice-segregation; a silty context would probably have shown much greater cryoturbation disturbance. These characteristics are not idiosyncratic, peculiar to the exact location/geology/history of the Glaston site. The Collyweston Facies is a well lithified stratum, overlying the Grantham Formation which is not. As the sandstone cap was incised and reduced by erosion, presumably during earlier parts of the Pleistocene, cambering would have begun at the developing valley sides; when the sandstone became thin enough, gulls and faults would have penetrated right through the stratum, breaking it up into individual blocks and eventually allowing the micrograben mechanism to come into full play. Furthermore, once the sandstone was isolated into blocks, its continued removal by erosion would have been hampered; instead of erosion concentrated near surfaces by rock impermeability, percolation into the unconsolidated sands now exposed would have slowed water-dependent surface erosion. The Glaston disposition, with only thin and fragmented cap-rock, therefore represents a near-equilibrium situation, which one would expect to persist over significant lengths of time.

However, in order to generalise a Glaston-like model, we still need carbonate-rich rock above unconsolidated (preferably not too silty, and free-draining) sediment, best disposed in near-horizontal beds (so as not to complicate the stress geometry). The particular Glaston Jurassic stratigraphic interval, or reasonably close equivalent in the early Middle Jurassic, is mapped at, or close to, outcrops in hilly terrain not only across Rutland but also from Banbury, through Northampton, west of Peterborough, east of Grantham and Lincoln, and northwards to the Humber, a distance of over 200 kilometres in a strip over 15 kilometres wide in the central section; there are even mechanically similar dispositions as far as Dorset and Yorkshire/Cleveland. Furthermore, the markedly cyclic Jurassic as a whole in England has many other intervals with carbonate rock above sandy sediment. Indeed, whilst thinner carbonate strata and thus the potential for Pleistocene bone preservation are not always available, hard–soft alternation is also common in most post-Jurassic strata in this country. Only slightly less conducive conditions might also pertain with clayey/colloidal sediment units with or without caprock, even with the Anglian tills from which many Midland hills are formed. Indeed Cooper (1997 and pers. comm.) has already reported a terminal Upper Palaeolithic Long Blade site at Launde (on the Leicestershire/Rutland border, only nine kilometres west of Glaston), on till capping a ridgetop at 190 m OD between the Chater to the north and the Eye Brook to the south, a position from which even such a late site may have benefited if there are local sagging structures. The BGS have mapped a persistent normal fault striking along the northern slope of the Eye Brook valley a kilometre south-west of the archaeological site. The present author (Collcutt 1992), in describing the geological setting of the Later Upper Palaeolithic site on Hengistbury Head, Dorset, assumed that the relevant 'perched depression' with its lowest observed surface point at 11 m OD, was an idiosyncratic erosional form developed through superficially melted permafrost. It now seems much more likely, subject to future testing in the field, that this feature is, or is a part of, a micrograben, with Pleistocene sands above Eocene silts and clays, formed above the confluence of major river valleys: the Avon/Stour rivers and the 'Solent'. The presumed Middle Palaeolithic *bout coupé* biface found on the foreshore below the modern coastal cliff which is encroaching on the headland might also be noted as having a source in this context. The geological prerequisites for micrograben sites are extremely common.

The upper limit on the scale of micrograben-like features is not yet clear. A single depression, at least two kilometres across, has been indirectly but very plausibly demonstrated to be due to the 'sagging' mechanism by Brunsden *et al.* (1996; see also the useful comparative bibliography), taking up much of the centre of the Isle of Portland, Dorset. The later Jurassic geology comprises Purbeck and Portland Limestones and Portland Sands above Kimmeridge Clay. Most of the boundaries of the Isle show suites of landslip features with broadly normal faulting leading to rotational slips, tumbles and mudslides. Behind the landslips, there is a raised rim to around 100 m OD and the central depression, probably floored by isolated blocks of limestone foundered into incompetent strata below, separated by gulls and other linear features, drops, at its modern surface, by as much a 10 metres. Whilst the lateral unloading by landslipping and deep creep is still very active due to marine erosion, as it would already have been in the Ipswichian, Brunsden *et al.* suggest that the process would also have occurred during extreme periglacial conditions at least as early as the Devensian. There are Tertiary faunas known from Portland, as well as Quaternary material from gulls and even some fissures or structural 'caves' (cf. Stopes *et al.* 1953). There is copious Mesolithic material from various points within the depression (Palmer 1977) and a few possible Later Upper Palaeolithic pieces from Verne Ditch (Campbell 1977; Palmer 1967).

LOWER PALAEOLITHIC SITES

Another widespread geological unit in England, one which is not very 'hard' and which has been demonstrably subject to Pleistocene cambering in many locations, is the Chalk. An Oxford colleague, Julie Scott-Jackson, has been doggedly championing the importance of Palaeolithic material found in Clay-with-flints (*sensu lato*) on the Chalk for many years (Scott-Jackson 2000; Scott-Jackson and Winton this volume), often in the face of considerable professional scepticism, initially shared by the present author. The main issue has been whether artefacts in these 'drifts', on hilltops and in other high-level situations, might be in near-primary context or, at least, in stratigraphic intervals of discrete secondary context, or are always just a jumble, as in normal slope mantles.

Scott-Jackson's previous field work had centred on the site of Wood Hill, Kingsdown, in Kent, a small ridge rising to 65 m OD, with flanking coombes below 40 m OD. In fact, Wood Hill is probably one of the most difficult sites which could have been studied, primarily because the 'drift' in question is extremely stony, consisting of natural flint. Nevertheless, Scott-Jackson managed to demonstrate two, plausibly discrete, Lower Palaeolithic artefact assemblages in superposition, each comprising a reasonably full range of material from all stages of the knapping sequence suggesting lack of strong differential sorting by natural agencies, including fine debris and even a couple of conjoins which are sequential, technological conjoins, not simple breaks. The contention that these are near-primary context assemblages probably affected significantly only by creep is supported by different, but internally consistent, fabrics (axes-orientation sets) in the two artefact groups and by consistent 'banding' of sediment characteristics suggesting a true depositional stratigraphy, albeit in a body in which it is practically impossible to see stratigraphic boundaries in the field. The present author remains a little sceptical over the validity of two thermoluminescence dates obtained from burnt flint, one from each assemblage, but the determinations are at least consistent with the order and temporal separation of the assemblages suggested by the other data. In order to examine the geometry of the deposit, resistivity tomography, supported by augering, was conducted in the vicinity of the artefact finds, with the result that an irregular 'basin' in the underlying Chalk was demonstrated, over a distance of about 35 m, in the order of 10 m wide, and with a maximum filled vertical extent of about 2 m. Scott-Jackson envisaged a progressive solution mechanism, allowing the gradual downwarping of archaeological levels and thus their superposition and survival. She noted the view of Goudie (1993) that the most important distributional control of solution features on the Chalk is the disposition of Tertiary and Quaternary cover sediments, which tend to acidify groundwater as it passes downwards. In passing, one may mention the fact that there is still considerable disagreement amongst professionals concerning rates of limestone solution, one faction championing increase under warmer climate (due to biogenic CO_2 partial pore pressure) and the other, increase under colder climate (due to primary CO_2 solubility).

Subsidence caused by solution of Chalk bedrock would therefore seem to be a different type of posterior dynamic morphology, capable of preserving *Up-Sites*. However, looking further at solutional forms on Chalk, it appears to the present author that larger features and wider scale geometries of groups of smaller features must have some relationship to structural factors of whatever age, that is to say joints and ancient faults, as well as more recent structures caused by cambering, lateral normal faulting beneath hillslopes or even the micrograben mechanism. Most deeper solution pipes in Chalk are only a few metres across, and well-documented reports of larger scale dolines are rare when compared with those on hard limestones. Although the survey at Wood Hill could only be carried out over a small area, the elongation-axis of the 'basin', roughly east to west, may be of interest. The gross topographical trend (ridge/coombe lines) in the area is roughly south-west to north-east, and the few faults mapped by the BGS lie on a similar trend, if perhaps a little more anti-clockwise in places. The geometry of any structural control is therefore unclear in this case, although Scott-Jackson (2000) did comment in an introductory section of her text, that solutional forms may be 'developed at joint inter-sections' (*ibid.*, 10). Reading through Scott-Jackson's compilation of known Palaeolithic sites on Chalk, there are many instances in which the local topography appears highly suggestive of structural control, perhaps the best example (*ibid.*, 32) being Round Green, Bedfordshire, with a well defined basin lying at the hilltop at 160 m OD, precisely in the centre of the angle of an interfluve above a major valley confluence; the suspected micrograben probably extends further than the 80 by 110 m phenomenon actually recorded. White (1997), in discussing several classic Chiltern sites, including Round Green, has taken for granted the proposition that such sites occur within dolines, although no unequivocal, primary evidence of such an origin, nor of the accompanying 'ponding' hypothesis, is known to the present author. Whilst White's reinterpretation of the probable geometry of these sites as 'basin-form' appears highly plausible, more attention should be given to the overall geomorphological/structural setting and to the indications of postdepositional adjustment (subsidence) of the deposits. The present author therefore feels that the *Sackung* Hypothesis also has significance for medium-hardness lithologies, such as Chalk, although a considerable effort involving observation of fault displacement, shear zones and/or clay extrusion, and even micropalaeontology (cf. Griffiths *et al.* 1995) will be needed to prove the point in individual cases, especially since local evidence will indeed have been overprinted by solutional effects in most instances. Completing the range right up to the hardest rocks brings us back to the classic Sackungen and to hilltop and high plateau subsidence basins (cf. references in Brunsden *et al.* 1996). There might even

be a possibility that certain features on granite, such as so-called 'cryoplanation benches', might sometimes have a dynamic structural input.

THE *SACKUNG* HYPOTHESIS: A CHALLENGE

The *Sackung* Hypothesis is so economical because of the recognition that the destructive and protective aspects of periglacial processes will commonly have gone hand-in-hand. The faster a valley is incised by rapid cold-climate incision, responding to low marine base levels and high peak discharge from meltwater, the slopes stripped by periglacial mass movement, and any clayey substrate deformed by gravity spreading and valley bulging, the more dynamic the evolving stress pattern. Thus, the very mass movement which threatens an existing archaeological *Up-Site* also unloads the hillside, possibly allowing fractures (gulls, Sackungen, micrograben and other basins/troughs) which may help the site survive, at least in part and with less than extreme disturbance. The stress patterns, and thus the potential for shear along fractures, persist over relatively long geological periods; as a reasonable generalisation, all coupled aspects of the system tend to accelerate during cold periods and slow during warmer periods, except when high interglacial sea-level takes on the unloading role at eroding coastal cliffs. This climatic dependency is also likely to favour survival of colder-period archaeology and palaeontology in *Up-Sites*, an interesting contrast to, and compliment of, *Down-Sites* which are biased by their modes of formation towards warmer periods. The wide lithological range of operation of sagging mechanisms has been demonstrated, corresponding to a wide geographical range (including the greater part of England within the UK alone). Because of differing process speeds and equilibria, it seems plausible to suggest that Devensian Middle and Upper Palaeolithic sites will more commonly be found in association with relatively soft geologies, whereas older Lower Palaeolithic sites may have had a better chance to survive on harder geologies. Indeed, the currently known distribution of high-level sites on Chalk, with many Lower Palaeolithic, a few Middle Palaeolithic and hardly any Upper Palaeolithic occurrences, would fit expectations of slower subsidence activity whether by solution alone or combined with structural dynamics. The disadvantages of relatively shallow burial turbation effects must be weighed against the decided advantage of ease of prospection. In any case, it may prove possible, with larger subsidence features, to follow archaeological material progressively downwards into deeper burial contexts. Palaeoenvironmental data at *Up-Sites* will be of variable quality; soft 'acid' organics will survive only in the most favoured sites as a result of special local factors but bone, and even mollusca, should survive with increasing matrix carbonate content. On a cautionary note, the *Sackung* Hypothesis also implies that care must be taken in correlating highly dissected or restricted-outcrop occurrences of ancient 'terraces' and other assumed planation surfaces, since the relative altitude of all such features may not be stable.

Having discussed the geological background, we can even speculate more freely upon the site location strategies of the original occupants. The advantages of *Down-Sites* such as proximity to water and woody materials have commonly been stressed, with little mention of the disadvantages such as dampness, biting insects, danger from hunting carnivores and even larger herbivores, and unexpected flooding. *Up-Sites* will often have been much safer for smaller camps and may have been reasonably comfortable, especially if there was a little shelter from caprock remnants or an existing fault-rim. However, the most important thing in a cold, open environment, where prey, competitors, predators and collaborators could move very quickly, would have been information: a good line of sight and long range audibility would often have been much more important than the ground tracks needed in woodland. The hyaenas and birds of prey of Glaston did not need humans to teach them this lesson in survival.

The *Sackung* Hypothesis has great potential but a considerable amount of work is now needed to move from a qualitative towards a quantitative basis; the geomorphological and structural processes must be analysed closely in a wide range of real cases, to allow accurate definition of distribution, scales and rates of relevant sagging phenomena. The links with 'traditional' morpho-sedimentological units such as terrace suites should also be examined wherever possible, and there is scope for revitalising the whole 'denudation chronology' approach to Pleistocene landscapes which, quite rightly due to a lack of insightful, truly three-dimensional models and to over-reliance upon the simplistic 'planation' concept, fell into disuse in the 1960s. In the meantime, a purely empirical approach may be adopted: we can simply start looking for sites in generally likely high-level situations, a point which archaeological resource managers and contractors, working within the Town and Country Planning system, should take to heart in the design of evaluations. During recent discussions, colleagues have already mentioned a surprisingly large number of 'unexplained' Palaeolithic high-ground occurrences not detailed here for reasons of space alone, but which could well be relevant. The present author would like to throw out a challenge to archaeologists, vertebrate palaeontologists and physical geographers alike by predicting that, in years to come, significant and accessible *Up-Sites* will be found to outnumber recorded *Down-Sites* by at least an order of magnitude, probably in most stages of the Palaeolithic.

ACKNOWLEDGEMENTS

The wholly unexpected Pleistocene context at Glaston Manor Farm was excavated with the forbearance of the then landowner, Captain Boyle, in 2000, by University of Leicester Archaeological Services, under the site direction of John Thomas, supported by Lynden Cooper and Richard Buckley. The excavation was a rescue operation primarily funded by English Heritage with Jon Humble as monitor, following a developer-funded excavation of mostly Medieval remains monitored by Anne Graf for the LPA. Additional support and sponsorship has been provided by Andy Currant (The Natural History Museum) and by Jill Cook and Roger Jacobi (The British Museum). The present author, aided by Christine Buckingham (Oxford University) and with useful site discussions of the Jurassic geology with Clive Jones (retired, formerly BGS), Roy Clements (Leicester University) and other visiting colleagues, is responsible for the physical sedimentology. I would thank the team for the opportunity of collaboration at this thought-provoking site and for agreement that I might publish this early comment; the reader should watch out for the full publication in the near future.

REFERENCES

Ballantyne, C.K. and Harris, C. 1994. *The Periglaciation of Great Britain.* Cambridge University Press, Cambridge.

Briggs, D.J. and Courtney, F.M. 1972. Ridge-and-trough topography in the north Cotswolds. *Proceedings of the Cotswold Naturalists and Field Club* 37, 74–103.

Brunsden, D., Coombe, K., Goudie, A.S. and Parker, A.G. 1996. The structural geomorphology of the Isle of Portland, southern England. *Proceedings of the Geologists' Association* 107, 209–230.

Campbell, J.B. 1977. *The Upper Palaeolithic of Britain: A Study of Man and Culture in the Late Ice Age.* Clarendon Press, Oxford.

Chandler, R.J., Kellaway, G.A., Skempton, A.W. and Wyatt, R.J. 1976. Valley slope sections near Bath, Somerset. *Philosophical Transactions of the Royal Society* A 283, 527–556.

Collcutt, S.N. 1992. Physical setting and geology. In R.N.E. Barton (ed.) *Hengistbury Head, Dorset. Volume 2: The Later Upper Palaeolithic and Early Mesolithic Sites*, 23–44. Oxford University Committee for Archaeology Monograph 34, Oxford.

Cooper, L. 1997. Launde (SK 80 03) – Archaeology in Leicestershire and Rutland 1996. *Transactions of the Leicestershire Archaeological and Historical Society* 71, 91–92.

Goudie, A.S. 1993. *The Landforms of England and Wales.* Blackwell, Oxford.

Griffiths, J.S., Brunsden, D., Lee, E.M. and Jones, D. 1995. Geomorphological investigation for the Channel Tunnel and Portal. *Geographical Journal* 161, 257–284.

Horswill, P. and Horton, A. 1976. Cambering and valley bulging in the Gwash Valley at Empingham, Rutland. *Philosophical Transactions of the Royal Society* A 282, 427–451.

Hutchinson, J.N. 1991. Periglacial and slope processes. In A. Forster, M.G. Culshaw, J.C. Cripps, J.A. Little and C.F. Moon (eds.) *Quaternary Engineering Geology*, 283–331. Geological Society Engineering Geology Special Publication 7, London.

Jacobi, R.M. 1986. The contents of Dr. Harley's show case. In S.N. Collcutt (ed.) *The Palaeolithic of Britain and Its Nearest Neighbours: Recent Trends*, 62–68. University of Sheffield, Sheffield.

Kirby, M.J. 1987. General models of long-term slope evolution through mass movement. In M.G. Anderson and K.S. Richards (eds.) *Slope Stability*, 359–380. John Wiley and Sons, Chichester.

McCalpin, J.P. and Irvine, J.R. 1995. Sackungen at Aspen Highlands Ski Area, Pitkin County, Colorado. *Environmental and Engineering Geoscience* 1, 277–290.

Palmer. S. 1967. Upper Palaeolithic artefacts from Portland. *Proceedings of the Dorset Natural History and Archaeological Society* 89, 117–119.

Palmer, S. 1977. *Mesolithic Cultures in Britain.* Dolphin Press, Dorset.

Parks, C.D. 1991. A review of the possible mechanisms of cambering and valley bulging. In A. Forster, M.G. Culshaw, J.C. Cripps, J.A. Little and C.F. Moon (eds.) *Quaternary Engineering Geology,* 373–380. Geological Society Engineering Geology Special Publication 7, London.

Scott-Jackson, J.E. 2000. *Lower and Middle Palaeolithic Artefacts from Deposits Mapped as Clay-with-Flints: A New Synthesis with Significant Implications for the Earliest Occupation of Britain.* Oxbow Books, Oxford.

Stopes, M.C., Oakley, K.P. and Wells, L.H. 1953. A discovery of human skulls, with stone artefacts and animal bones, in a fissure at Portland. *Proceedings of the Dorset Natural History and Archaeological Society* 74, 39.

Wenban-Smith, F. 1994. Managing the Palaeolithic heritage: looking backwards, looking forwards. In N.M. Ashton and A. David (eds.) *Stories in Stone,* 104–111. Lithic Studies Society Occasional Paper 4, London.

Wessex Archaeology 1992. *The Southern Rivers Palaeolithic Project. Report No. 1. 1991–1992: The Upper Thames Valley, the Kennet Valley and the Solent Drainage System.* The Trust for Wessex Archaeology, Salisbury.

Wessex Archaeology 1993. *The Southern Rivers Palaeolithic Project. Report No. 2. 1992–1993: The South-West and South of the Thames.* The Trust for Wessex Archaeology, Salisbury.

Wessex Archaeology 1994. *The Southern Rivers Palaeolithic Project. Report No. 3. 1993–1994: The Sussex Raised Beaches.* The Trust for Wessex Archaeology, Salisbury.

Wessex Archaeology 1996a. *The English Rivers Palaeolithic Project. Report No. 1. 1994–1995: The Thames Valley and the Warwickshire Avon.* Trust for Wessex Archaeology, Salisbury.

Wessex Archaeology 1996b. *The English Rivers Palaeolithic Project. Report No. 2. 1995–1996: The Great Ouse Drainage and the Yorkshire and Lincolnshire Wolds.* Trust for Wessex Archaeology, Salisbury.

Wessex Archaeology 1997. *The English Rivers Palaeolithic Project. Report No. 3. 1996–1997: East Anglian Rivers and the Trent Drainage.* Trust for Wessex Archaeology, Salisbury.

White, M.J. 1997. The earlier Palaeolithic occupation of the Chilterns (southern England): re-assessing the sites of Worthington G. Smith. *Antiquity* 71, 912–931.

Whittaker, A. 1972. Geology of Bredon Hill, Worcestershire. *Bulletin of the Geological Survey of Great Britain* 41, 1–30.

Zischinsky, U. 1969. Über Sackungen. *Rock Mechanics* 1 (for 1968), 30–52.

24. A Lyngby point from Mildenhall, Suffolk, and its implications for the British Late Upper Palaeolithic

Alison J. Roberts and R. Nick E. Barton

ABSTRACT

The identification of a tanged point from Mildenhall as being a Lyngby point raises issues concerning human activity in Britain during the Late Glacial interstadial. The large tanged point industries of the European Upper Palaeolithic are reviewed, as is the interpretation of these points. The typological determination, which is the main focus of the paper, also introduces the question of the possibility of Bromme activity in Britain during this period. The need for further research is highlighted.

'*If firm stratigraphic evidence or other means of relative dating for the various deposits which contain the [Palaeolithic] industries cannot be obtained, then there will be a strong temptation or even a positive need to date the artefacts by their appearance and by comparison with similar looking industries elsewhere whose age is known*' (Roe 1981, 11).

This paper is offered in the spirit of the above statement by Derek Roe.

INTRODUCTION

The tanged point is a well-known tool type in the lithic inventories of the European Upper Palaeolithic. Large examples, 55 mm or more in length, have been recorded in a number of assemblages across northern Europe, where they are referred to under a variety of different cultural terms. For example in the early Gravettian (c. 28,500 BP) they are known as Font Robert points, in the Final Magdalenian (c. 13,500–12,000 BP) as Teyjat points and in the Brommian (c. 12,000–10,800 BP) as Bromme or Lyngby points. Close to the end of the Late Glacial period (10,000

BP) there is a tendency towards a diminution in size and smaller examples (<55 mm) of tanged points characterise the Ahrensburgian, Swiderian, Hensbacka, Mazovian, Fosna and assemblages of related type.

Despite the apparently clear chronological and geographical separation that exists between each of the main groupings (Gravettian, Final Magdalenian and Brommian), there remains a lack of consistency in the way the points have been described and in the criteria used to differentiate them. The tanged flint point described and discussed in this paper is of a type known as a Lyngby or Bromme point. It comes from the area of Mildenhall, Suffolk, in East Anglia and is part of the vast collection of flint artefacts which was bequeathed to the British Museum by Dr William Allen Sturge in 1919. The find is housed today in the collection of the Quaternary Section of the Department of Prehistory and Early Europe at The British Museum. There is no individual accession number for the artefact.

The description of this retouched tool highlights the presence of a point type whose nearest typological analogue in Europe can be found in southern Scandinavia, and therefore raises intriguing questions about if, or how, it might be related to the Brommian.

THE MILDENHALL POINT

The Mildenhall tanged point (Fig. 24.1) is mottled reddish-brown in colour and measures 88.9 mm × 30.1 mm × 10.6 mm, and weighs 22.1 grams. It is made on a blade support with the tang situated at the proximal end. The tang is formed by direct abrupt retouch and tapers slightly towards the base. It occupies well over a third of the total length of the implement. The point at the distal end is slightly offset to the long axis of the tool. It is formed by an oblique truncation made by direct abrupt to semi-abrupt retouch. The blade support on which the tool is made appears to have been detached from a single platform core. Despite a fairly prominent bulb, still partly preserved at the proximal end, the blade is straight in profile and evidently required little extra modification except for the truncation at the tip. The prominence of the bulb and the straightness of profile imply that the blade was hard hammer struck.

The tool is in fresh condition, except for relatively minor nicking damage visible on the ventral and dorsal surfaces of the lateral margins, which is likely to be of modern origin. The tool has a reddish-brown patina which varies across the surface. This is most noticeable in a small negative scar on the ventral surface near the pointed tip. The fresh, lightly patinated appearance of the scar suggests it was probably the result of post-depositional breakage of more recent age.

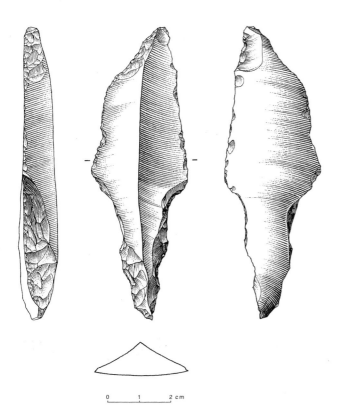

Fig. 24.1. The Mildenhall point

HISTORY OF THE FIND

No precise provenance exists for the tanged point. The only firm information is provided by an attached printed paper label marked 'Mildenhall (F)', indicating that it was from the Mildenhall area and had originally been from the Simeon Fenton collection. Simeon Fenton was a well-known collector of local flint implements who lived at Mildenhall, and Sturge had purchased a large part of his collection on the advice of Fenton's son, Samuel, when it was sold at auction by Sotheby's in 1900 after the older Fenton's death (Sturge 1911, 44–45). As Sturge himself recorded after discovering the presence of Upper Palaeolithic type material in the collection: 'Unfortunately Mr. Simeon Fenton, who probably attached no great importance to them, had not labelled them in any way. All we know is that everything in his collection came from within a few miles of Mildenhall, and these flakes were certainly from that district in North-West Suffolk. They varied so much in patina that it was practically certain that it was not one great find, but that they had come from various parts of the district and at various times' (Sturge 1912, 220). Letters from Samuel Fenton to Dr Sturge, now curated at the British Museum, show that the younger Fenton had tried to find provenances for some of the material in his father's collection for Dr Sturge. Unfortunately, he was unable to do so because of 'gaps' in the information contained in his father's notebooks caused by Fenton's brother 'destroying what had come to him' (Fenton to Sturge, 16 September 1900). There seems to be little possibility that an exact provenance for the point will ever be determined.

Nevertheless, the distinctive mottled reddish-brown colour of the tanged point may provide an important clue concerning the original provenance of the find. Mildenhall is located roughly at the border between the Fens to the west and the Breckland to the east (Scarfe 1972, fig. 1). In the Sturge collection there are numbers of artefacts from findspots on the dry, sandier Breckland soils near Mildenhall. These are generally characterised by a whitish surface patina (for example, the material from Wangford Warren, where Sturge found what he described as a 'Magdalenian Floor' in a clearing where two feet of sand had been removed from the surface for building purposes: 1912, 226–227). On the other hand, artefacts from the acid soils of the Fen edge from locations such as Eriswell, Burnt Fen and Beck Row often display the more reddish-brown patination similar to that of the tanged point. This observation would seem to provide circumstantial evidence for an original context for the point from deposits bordering the Fen close to Mildenhall. It should also be noted that Samuel Fenton wrote to Sturge in 1899, saying that he had found a flint artefact with 'a deep red lustrous appearance' during a cycling trip around the region, and asking Sturge if he had 'some theory about that deep red color [sic]'. Fenton continued, 'I have often noticed these red flints on the Suffolk sands ...' (Fenton to Sturge, 7 November 1899). The 'sands' that Fenton mentions could hint at the additional possibility of a find location on the West Suffolk Sands, to the south of Mildenhall.

Unfortunately the tool's distinctive character seems to have gone unnoticed and it is not mentioned or figured specifically either by Sturge in his paper describing Upper Palaeolithic material from East Anglia in his collection (1912), or in the published catalogue of the Sturge collection (Smith 1931). Until now the find has only received oblique mention in the literature. Initially, it was listed as a late Upper Palaeolithic tanged point in the Gazetteer of Upper Palaeolithic sites in England and Wales (Bonsall 1977), although with the provenance of 'Mildenhall Fen'. More recently, Roger Jacobi has included the point on his map of possible Font Robert point findspots in Britain, but with no further detail (1980, 1990).

The Sturge collection contains several other pieces from Mildenhall which were also originally from the Fenton collection, and which are in the same condition as the tanged piece. These include over twenty blades, many hard hammer struck, six or seven end-scrapers and a dihedral burin made on a large blade. There is no evidence to link these pieces with the tanged point, and the point must be considered in isolation from the other artefacts.

EUROPEAN UPPER PALAEOLITHIC POINT TYPES AS POTENTIAL PARALLELS FOR THE MILDENHALL FIND

As stated above, large tanged points are recurrent components in three of the major north-west European Upper Palaeolithic assemblages. In order to make a case for assigning the Mildenhall find to one of these types, it is essential first to review briefly each of the point types in turn.

Font Robert point

This point type is described by Djindjian *et al.* (1999, 182), where it is attributed to the earliest phase of the Western European Gravettian. In south-west France it is still considered a *'fossile-directeur'* of Perigordian Va (Demars and Laurent 1989, 136). The points were originally described by Bardon *et al.* (1908, 10), as *'lames dont la moitié inferieure fortement rabattue sur les deux bords a été transformée en pédoncule. L'autre extremité, au contraire restée large et aplatie, se termine en pointe dont le contour est celui d'un arc brisé d'ogive plus ou moins ouvert'* (blades the lower half of which have been modified to form a tang by marked backing of both edges. By contrast, the other end is left broad and flat, terminating in a point the form of which is a more or less open ogival arc). The type was subsequently redefined by de Sonneville-Bordes and Perrot (1956, 547) as a *'pointe à long pédonculé axial nettement dégagé par retouches abruptes ou semi-abruptes, à tête sublosangique parfois triangulaire parfois arrondie, à retouches souvent envahissantes*

parfois de type solutréen, plus rarement bifaciales et, dans ce cas, intèressant surtout l'extrémité distale' (point with a long axial tang deliberately formed by abrupt or semi-abrupt retouch and an almost rhomboidal, triangular or rounded tip, often modified by invasive, Solutrean type retouch or, more rarely, by bifacial retouch concentrated, in this case, at the distal end). In addition, eight major sub-types of the points are distinguished at the site of Abri de la Ferrassie in south-west France on the basis of the shape of the tang and the type of retouch (Delporte and Tuffreau 1972–73).

Font Robert points have a widespread geographic distribution in western Europe ranging from the Upper Danube and Thuringia in the east, northwards as far as Britain and the Paris Basin, and as far south as the Dordogne and Corrèze regions (Djindjian *et al.* 1999). Despite their extensive distribution, there are as yet few reliably associated radiocarbon dates for this phase. The earliest known examples, at least in north-west Europe, would appear to date to the Maisières interstadial. A direct date of $27,965 \pm 260$ BP (GrN-5523) has been obtained on the interstadial palaeosol at Maisières-Canal, Belgium, which underlies the archaeological horizon with Font Robert points (Haesarts and de Heinzelin 1979, fig. 19). Elsewhere, at Abri de la Ferrassie, Dordogne, the phase has recently been dated to $27,900 \pm 770$ BP (OxA-402) (Djindjian *et al.* 1999, 44). Of the eight potential findspots in Britain so far identified by Jacobi (1990, fig. 5), most derive from older excavations and the dating evidence is generally poor. At Pin Hole, Creswell, a complete Font Robert point was recorded amongst a collection of Upper Palaeolithic blades near the base of the Upper Cave Earth, and stratigraphically above Mousterian artefacts in the Lower Cave Earth (Jacobi pers. comm.). Recent re-excavation of Paviland Cave has been disappointing in terms of recovering more *in situ* Early Upper Palaeolithic material (Aldhouse-Green 2000), although examination of the earlier collections by Swainston (2000, 107–108) has reinforced the typological similarities between the British finds and those of Maisières-Canal.

The Mildenhall point was originally included in Jacobi's list of eight Font Robert point findspots from Britain, although with no accompanying description or discussion (1980, 25–27, fig. 2.3; 1990, 283–285, fig. 5). Typologically, we do not see any obvious similarities between the Mildenhall point and those of Font Robert type. The stems of the latter are generally narrower and much more accentuated, whilst in profile view the tanged ends themselves may show a slight curvature (R.N.E. Barton pers. observ.). Furthermore, many Font Robert points exhibit an invasive retouch developed on the ventral or dorsal surfaces near the pointed end (Demars and Laurent 1989, 136–137), which is clearly lacking in the Mildenhall example. Jacobi has also recently indicated to the authors that he no longer necessarily considers the point to be of Font Robert type (pers. comm.).

Teyjat point

Tanged points of this kind were first identified as components of the Final Magdalenian by early French prehistorians (Breuil 1912; Capitan *et al.* 1908). The term 'Teyjat point' was only adopted much later by de Sonneville Bordes and Perrot (1956) who described it as a '*pointe à pédonculé axial relativement court par rapport à la longeur totale de la pièce, plus ou moins nettement dégagé par retouches abruptes souvent alternes, à tête généralement en forme de triangle allongé dont les côtés ne portent habituellement de retouches qu'à la pointe*' (point with a relatively short, axial tang in relation to the overall length of the piece. The tang is formed by more or less definite, abrupt, often alternate retouch. The shape of the top is generally an elongated triangle, the edges of which are not usually retouched except at the tip) (*ibid.*, 547). Heinzelin proposed a close relationship between the Teyjat point, also referred to as the '*pointe à soie Magdalénienne*', and the Lyngby point, especially in the appearance of the '*pédoncle court et large obtenu par retouches abruptes éventuellement alternes, dessinant des crans. Pointe peu ou même non-retouchée*' (broad, short tang produced by abrupt, occasionally alternate retouch up to the shoulders. Point more or less unretouched) (Heinzelin 1962, 36). This view was not shared by Bohmers (1960, 36), who saw the Teyjat point as being generally smaller and less robust than the Lyngby examples.

The distribution of sites with Teyjat points is geographically restricted to south-west France, with outlying examples appearing as far north as the Loire Valley (Demars and Laurent 1989, 146). The northernmost occurrence is at the site of Le Bois-Ragot, Vienne (Chollet *et al.* 1979, 1999), where a Final Magdalenian level with Teyjat points (5b) is recorded between an Azilian level (4b) and a lower Final Magdalenian level (6) lacking in points. Level 5b has a single radiocarbon determination on charcoal of 11,030± 140 BP (Gif-2537), which some commentators have questioned as too young (published discussion in Chollet *et al.* 1979). On the basis of dates from various Late Magdalenian sites, other authors would also prefer an earlier dating of this phase to 13–12,500 BP (Djindjian *et al.* 1999, 262). Despite these reservations, it should be noted that in level 5b at Le Bois-Ragot there is an appreciable increase in the presence of forested elements amongst the recorded microfauna (*Clethrionomys glareolus*, bank vole; *Apodemus sylvaticus*, wood mouse), which would be consistent with an Allerød age and therefore in agreement with the published radiocarbon date for this layer (*ibid.*, table 3).

From a typological viewpoint we would accept that there is a potential size overlap between Teyjat points and Lyngby points, but we would also concur with Bohmers' observation that they fall into recognisably distinctive types. One major distinguishing feature seems to be in the production of the tang. In the French examples, the stemmed end is produced by a variety of methods including indirect or alternate retouch, as well as by direct retouch. In Lyngby points direct retouch is the only method used and this is also seen on the Mildenhall example. The lack of apparent standardisation in the Teyjat points may reflect absolute differences in the thickness of the tangs and be dependent on a range of variables from raw material quality to the choice of blank, but equally, such features may be deliberate embellishments added for stylistic purposes (Wiessner 1983). To date, we know of no convincing examples of Teyjat points from Britain.

Lyngby/Bromme point

The site of Nørre Lyngby, north Jutland, gave its name to this tool type after the discovery of an isolated large tanged flint point eroding out of the cliff-line (Jessen and Nordmann 1915). The same location also gives its name to another Late Glacial tool form, the shaped reindeer antler 'Lynbgy axe' found there in 1889 (Müller 1896). Near the tanged point were recovered remains of Late Glacial floral species, including dwarf birch (*Betula nana*) and arctic willow (*Salix polaris*), and the analysis of pollen samples later identified the deposits as being of Younger Dryas stadial age (Iversen 1942). Following similar discoveries of large tanged points at the site of Bromme near Søro (Zealand), these artefacts also became more commonly known as Bromme points (Mathiassen 1946). Although the greatest distribution of sites with Lyngby or Bromme points lies in Denmark and South Sweden, identical types are known from much of the Great European Plain at least as far east as the Upper Dnieper and Sozh basins of Byelorussia (Zaliznyak 1999).

Lyngby points have been described by various authors (Becker 1971; Fischer 1985; Johansen 2000; Madsen 1996; Mathiassen 1946). They are typically made on blades and may range in total length from about 34 to 110 mm (Barton 1986), although examples of up to 150 mm long are also known (Johansen 2000, 208). Despite the great variation in size, they are all characterised by a tang at the proximal end of the blank which typically makes up about one-third of the total length of the implement. The tang is usually broad, parallel-sided and defined by direct abrupt retouch, often leaving a remnant of the bulb intact. The straight profile of the blades and the bulbar features indicate preferential use of the hard hammer percussion technique (Johansen 2000, 208). The tip end is sometimes modified by direct abrupt retouch to increase the symmetry of the point.

Based on palaeoenvironmental indicators and radiocarbon dating, the Scandinavian assemblages with Lyngby points are believed to be mainly of late Allerød and Younger Dryas age. At the Nørre Lyngby type-site the associated floral components indicate a Younger Dryas age, while more typically Allerød conditions are shown by the presence of birch and pine at Bromme (area IX) (Iversen 1942), and by birch, juniper and willow at Trollesgave (Fischer and Mortensen 1977). Moreover, faunal associations at both of these sites reveal the presence of species normally associated with birch woodland, such as elk and beaver. The latter is actually present at Bromme, while at Trollesgave it was inferred from gnawed birch branches. Beaver and roe deer are amongst the faunal remains recorded at the Swedish site of Segebro (Salomonsson 1964), although the roe deer may be a later intrusion (L. Johansen pers. comm.). Elk is present also at Langå (B. Madsen pers. comm.; Johansen 2000). Of the few published radiometric determinations, two charcoal dates exist for Trollesgave of 11,070±120 BP (K-2641) and 11,100±160 BP (K-2509) (Fischer 1996). A further date of 10,810±120 BP (OxA-3614) has been recorded from the nearby location of Fensmark, but here the exact relationship between the charcoal and artefacts, which lie in soliflucted deposits, remains uncertain (Fischer 1996).

Based on typological and technological considerations we would identify the Mildenhall point as being of Lyngby type.

Other Late Glacial tanged points

Various other points are not considered in this review, either because they fit more closely the definition of shouldered points, such as the Havelte point (Bohmers and Wouters 1956), or because of their small and sometimes microlithic form, as in the case of Swidry points (Krukowski 1920), Fosna points (Freundt 1948), Hensbacka points (Fredsjö 1953) and Ahrensburgian points (Rust 1943). The latter are less than 55 mm in length, and usually considerably smaller, with the tang often at the distal, rather than the proximal, end of the blade (Fischer 1991). They are also characterised by a straight and generally very narrow retouched stem (Taute 1968). However, as has been noted above, examples of large tanged points have occasionally been recorded in association with the diminutive Ahrensburgian forms, as for example at Stellmoor (cf. Taute 1968, fig. 83). Late prehistoric tanged points, which are generally quite distinct from Upper Palaeolithic examples, have also been excluded.

INTERPRETATION AND FUNCTION OF TANGED POINTS

The function of large tanged points has been much discussed, particularly in relation to Lyngby points. An early suggestion that they were inserts in reindeer antler clubs (Rust 1943) was dismissed in favour of their function as spearheads (Becker 1971; Mathiassen 1946). Since then relatively little attention has been focused on this aspect of study, with the result that scholars have accepted implicitly that most large points, including Font Robert and Teyjat forms, were too large for arrowheads (but see Clark 1975, 83–84) and therefore, by default, were spearheads.

Two studies appeared during the 1980s that challenged these assumptions. The first concerned Font Robert points from the site of Maisières-Canal, Belgium (Otte and Caspar 1987). These authors questioned the assumption that the points were employed solely as projectile points. They drew attention to the general absence of damage on the pointed ends of Font Robert points, as might have been expected if they had been used as projectile tips and had impacted on hard materials. Subsequent experiments, accompanied by microwear analyses, revealed that the tools were capable of use either hafted or unhafted, and were probably employed in a variety of ways that included sawing, cutting, scraping and engraving, with only the lighter versions being used as hunting weapons (Otte and Caspar 1987, 73).

The other empirically based study was initiated to explore the possibility that the larger tanged points served as arrowheads rather than spearpoints (Fischer et al. 1984). The experiments revealed that Lyngby points made surprisingly good arrowheads with a high precision of accuracy guaranteed over distances of at least 20 m (Fischer et al. 1984). Our own observations would endorse the view that Lyngby points were employed as disposable projectile heads. A measured sample of 50 tanged points from the site of Bromme showed only a small variation in mean tang lengths (22±6 mm) and widths (11±3 mm), which is wholly consistent with their use as replaceable elements in ready-made hafts, and explains their highly standardised shape and form (Barton 1986).

CONCLUDING REMARKS

On the basis of the preceding discussion we would argue that the Mildenhall tool displays closest similarities with the Scandinavian Lyngby points. The occurrence of this point type in a British context would also fit well with our current understanding of the geographic distribution of Lyngby tanged points which have been recorded across much of the Great European Plain from Scandinavia as far east as Byelorussia. The exposed North Sea basin and the adjacent low lying lands of East Anglia would have facilitated a westward expansion of hunting communities employing this type of technology.

A more difficult question to contemplate at the moment is whether the Mildenhall discovery could be part of a so far unrecognised Bromme component in the British Late Glacial record. Certainly, on current evidence, there are a number of other locations where possible Lyngby points have been recovered (Jacobi 1980, fig. 2.13) but, with one exception, they are all isolated finds and are lacking in reliable stratigraphic or dating information. It is also interesting to note that the distribution of the Late Glacial large tanged points is restricted to open-air sites. Despite claims to the contrary (Campbell 1977, 118), none of these forms is yet known from a cave or rockshelter.

In order to fully confirm a Bromme presence we would require evidence of some of the other special hallmarks of the Scandinavian technology, such as the use of hard hammer percussive technique, large and thick pointed blades, and typical single platform pyramidal cores with a high angle between the platform and the core-front of 80–90° (Johansen 2000, 208). While the soft hammer technique and the presence of other core types are known in the Bromme, these rarely, if ever, occur in the absence of the other characteristics. In Britain, apart from one potential example of an excavated assemblage with hard hammer struck blades at Deer Park Farm, Dorset (Green *et al.* 1998), such a technology does not appear to be widely represented in native Late Glacial contexts. It is worth keeping in mind, however, that apparently hard hammer struck flakes and blades were reported in possible association with a tanged point from Stone Point, Walton-on-the-Naze, Essex (Jacobi 1981; Warren *et al.* 1936), as well as the examples from the Mildenhall area, mentioned above.

Currently, the only large assemblage with Lyngby-type points is that of Hengistbury Head, Dorset (Mace 1959). Here, the excavated collection contains a variety of retouched tools dominated by backed bladelets but including shouldered forms and occasional large tanged points. The blade technology reflects a predominantly soft hammer mode of percussion (Barton 1992, table 4.5). Dating of burnt flint artefacts by thermoluminescence has provided an average age for the site of 12,500±1150 years (OxTL-707a) (Barton and Huxtable 1983). If the lithic assemblage is genuinely homogeneous, as implied by the refitting evidence, and is not a palimpsest of different occupations, then it may suggest that some form of cultural and geographical overlap occurred between Federmesser groups and the more northerly Lyngby culture, as has been proposed elsewhere (Taute 1968). Equally, it appears likely to us that the spread of woodland documented in the Allerød interstadial provided ideal conditions for the development of bow hunting technology, and this might provide a better explanation for the almost contemporary appearance of large tanged points in *various* parts of Europe in the Late Glacial. Thus, their occurrence in the Final Magdalenian and the Bromme could be seen in terms of independent parallel developments.

The recent hypothesis that the distribution of Bromme sites in southern Scandinavia and Germany reflects reindeer hunting patterns along migration routes (Petersen and Johansen 1996) raises further intriguing possibilities concerning the interpretation of the presence of a Lyngby point in East Anglia. Reindeer are generally regarded as an exceedingly rare component of the British native Late Glacial interstadial fauna (Currant 1991; Jacobi 1997). Indeed, it has been suggested that if tundra species of reindeer occurred at all in Britain during the second half of the Interstadial (Allerød equivalent), then they would have been confined to the northern parts of the country (Barton and Dumont 2000). If Lyngby points were components of a reindeer hunter's tool kit, then perhaps the rarity of the point form in Britain is predictable.

Going further into the realms of speculation, it could be suggested that Brommian hunters occasionally followed an east–west reindeer migration route into eastern Britain, although we believe this is inherently unlikely because it does not fit the model of Petersen and Johansen (1996, 87) and no Bromme points have yet been reported further south of Denmark, in the Netherlands (D. Stapert pers. comm.). Alternatively, on the basis of the recent reconstruction of the Late Glacial landscape of eastern Britain and the exposed North Sea basin, it is possible to recognise a north–south route along the valley of the river Ouse, which ran north from more or less its present position in East Anglia, to a point roughly level with the Scottish border (Coles 1998). Just like any tunnel system in northern Germany, this valley or a parallel north–south example may have served as a conduit for migrating herds of reindeer. Had Brommian hunters followed such a migration route along the Ouse, they would have passed by the area of modern-day Mildenhall. The find may therefore represent evidence of a short-term occupation site, or simply a hunting loss.

All of this may seem a long way from the typological description of a large tanged point that was found in the vicinity of Mildenhall over 100 years ago. The identification of it as a Lyngby point, a type rarely found in Britain but quite common elsewhere in Northern Europe during the second part of the Late Glacial interstadial, raises interesting questions about the interpretation of the piece and reasons for its occurrence. The presence of this typologically distinctive Late Glacial tanged point in East Anglia highlights the need for new research in this area, to look for further open-air sites of Bromme or other Late Upper Palaeolithic types.

ACKNOWLEDGEMENTS

We would like to thank Phil Dean for the illustration of the point. We are also grateful to Dick Stapert, Lykke Johansen, Jean-Pierre Fagnart, Martin Street and Roger Jacobi for discussions concerning the tanged point industries of northern Europe. The initial identification of the point, examination of the Mildenhall collection, and the archival work was conducted while Alison Roberts was employed at The British Museum.

REFERENCES

Aldhouse-Green, S. (ed.) 2000. *Paviland Cave and the 'Red Lady': A Definitive Report*. Western Academic and Specialist Press Ltd., Bristol.

Bardon, L., Bouyssonie, A. and Bouyssonie, J. 1908. Stations préhistoriques du Château Bassaler, près Brive (Corrèze). I. La grotte de la Font-Robert. *Extrait de la Bulletin de la Société Scientifique, Historique et Archéologique de la Corrèze* 19.

Barton, R.N.E. 1986. *A Study of Selected British and European Flint Assemblages of Late Devensian and Early Flandrian Age*. Unpublished DPhil thesis, University of Oxford.

Barton, R.N.E. (ed.) 1992. *Hengistbury Head, Dorset. Volume 2: The Late Upper Palaeolithic and Early Mesolithic sites*.

Oxford University Committee for Archaeology Monograph 34, Oxford.

Barton, N. and Dumont, S. 2000. Recolonisation and settlement of Britain at the end of the Last Glaciation. In B. Valentin, P. Bodu and M. Christensen (eds.) *L'Europe Centrale et Septentrionale au Tardiglaciaire: Confrontation des Modèles Régionaux de Peuplement*, 151–162. Memoires du Musée de Préhistoire d'Ile-de-France 7. APRAIF, Nemours.

Barton, N. and Huxtable, J. 1983. New dates for Upper Palaleolithic and Mesolithic occupations at Hengistbury Head, Dorset. *Antiquity* 57, 133–135.

Becker, C.J. 1971. Late Palaeolithic finds from Denmark. *Proceedings of the Prehistoric Society* 37, 131–139.

Bohmers, A. 1960. Statistiques et graphiques dans l'étude des industries lithiques préhistoriques. V. Considérations générales au sujet du Hambourgian, du Tjongérien, du Magdalénien et de l'Azilien. *Palaeohistoria* 8, 15–38.

Bohmers, A. and Wouters, A.Q. 1956. Statistics and graphs in the study of flint assemblages. *Palaeohistoria* 5, 27–38.

Bonsall, C.J. 1977. Gazetteer of Upper Palaeolithic sites in England and Wales. In J.J. Wymer (ed.) *Gazetteer of Mesolithic Sites in England and Wales*, 417–432. Council for British Archaeology Research Report 20, London.

Breuil, H. 1912. Les subdivisions du Paléolithique supérieur et leur signification. *Comptes Rendus du 14ᵉ Congrès International d'Anthropologie et d'Archéologie Préhistorique, Genève*, 165–238.

Campbell, J.C. 1977. *The Upper Palaeolithic of Britain: A Study of Man and Culture in the Late Ice Age*. Clarendon Press, Oxford.

Capitan, L., Breuil, H., Bourrinet, P. and Peyrony, D. 1908. La Grotte de la Mairie à Teyjat (Dordogne). Fouilles d'un gisement magdalénien. *Revue de l'Ecole d'Anthropologie de Paris* 18, 153–173, 198–218.

Chollet, A., Boutin, P., Debénath, A., Delpech, F. and Marquet, J.-C. 1979. La grotte du Bois-Ragot à Gouex (Vienne). Industries, géologie, paléontologie. In D. de Sonneville-Bordes (ed.) *La Fin des Temps Glaciaires en Europe*, 365–378. CNRS, Paris.

Chollet, A., Fouéré, P., Hantaï, A. and Le Licon, G. 1999. L'évolution des choix techniques et économiques entre le Magdalénien supérieur et l'Azilien: l'exemple de la Grotte de Bois-Ragot (Vienne, France). In A. Thévenin (ed.) *L'Europe des Derniers Chasseurs*, 275–285. CTHS, Paris.

Clark, G. 1975. *The Earlier Stone Age Settlement of Scandinavia*. Cambridge University Press, Cambridge.

Coles, B.J. 1998. Doggerland: a speculative survey. *Proceedings of the Prehistoric Society* 64, 45–81.

Currant, A.P. 1991. A Late Glacial Interstadial mammal fauna from Gough's Cave, Somerset, England. In N. Barton, A.J. Roberts and D.A. Roe (eds.) *The Late Glacial in North-West Europe: Human Adaptation and Environmental Change at the End of the Pleistocene*, 48–50. Council for British Archaeology Research Report 77, London.

Delporte, H. and Tuffreau, A. 1972–73. Les industries du Périgordien supérieur de la Ferrassie. *Quartär* 23–24, 93–123.

Demars, P.Y. and Laurent, P. 1989. *Types d'Outils Lithiques du Paléolithique Supérieur en Europe*. CNRS, Paris.

Djindjian, F., Koslowski, J. and Otte, M. 1999. *Le Paléolithique Supérieur en Europe*. Armand Colin, Paris.

Fischer, A. 1985. Late Palaeolithic finds. In K. Kristiansen (ed.) *Archaeological Formation Processes: The Representativity of Archaeological Remains from Danish Prehistory*, 81–88. National Museum, Copenhagen.

Fischer, A. 1991. Pioneers in deglaciated landscapes: the expansion and adaptation of Late Palaeolithic societies in southern Scandinavia. In N. Barton, A.J. Roberts and D.A. Roe (eds.) *The Late Glacial in North-West Europe: Human Adaptation and Environ-*

mental Change at the End of the Pleistocene, 100–122. Council for British Archaeology Research Report 77, London.

Fischer, A. 1996. At the border of human habitat. The Late Palaeolithic and Early Mesolithic in Scandinavia. In L. Larsson (ed.) *The Earliest Settlement of Scandinavia and its Relationship with Neighbouring Areas*, 157–176. Acta Archaeologica Lundensia 24. Almquist and Wiksell International, Stockholm.

Fischer, A. and Mortensen, B.N. 1977. *Trollesgave-bopladsen: Et Eksemple på Anvendeise af EDB inden for Arkaeologien*. Nationalmuseets Arbejdsmark, Copenhagen.

Fischer, A., Hansen, P.V. and Rasmussen, P. 1984. Macro and microwear traces on lithic projectile points: experimental results and prehistoric examples. *Journal of Danish Archaeology* 3, 19–46.

Fredsjö, A. 1953. *Studier i Västveriges Äldre Stenålder*. Arkeologiska Museet, Göteborg.

Freundt, E.A. 1948. Komsa, Fosna, Sandarna. Problems of the Scandinavian Mesolithicum. *Acta Archeologica* 19, 1–68.

Green, M., Barton, R.N.E., Debenham, N. and French, C.A.I. 1998. A new Lateglacial open-air site at Deer Park Farm, Wimborne St Giles, Dorset. *Proceedings of the Dorset Natural History and Archaeological Society* 120, 85–100.

Haesarts, P. and de Heinzelin, J. 1979. *Le Site Paléolithique de Maisières-Canal*. Dissertationes Archaeologicae Gandenses 19. De Tempel, Brugge.

Heinzelin de Braucourt, J. de, 1962. *Manuel de Typologie des Industries Lithiques*. Institut Royale des Sciences Naturelles, Bruxelles.

Iversen, J. 1942. *En pollenanalytisk Tidsfæstelse af Ferskvandslagene ved Nørre Lyngby*. Meddelser fra Dansk Geologisk Forening 10, Copehagen.

Jacobi, R.M. 1980. The Upper Palaeolithic of Britain with special reference to Wales. In J.A. Taylor (ed.) *Culture and Environment in Prehistoric Wales: Selected Essays*, 15–99. British Archaeological Reports British Series 76, Oxford.

Jacobi, R.M. 1981. The Late-glacial settlement of Essex. In D. Buckley (ed.) *The Archaeology of Essex to A.D. 1500*, 12–13. Council for British Archaeology Research Report 34, London.

Jacobi, R.M. 1990. Leaf-points and the British Early Upper Palaeolithic. In J.K. Kozlowski (ed.) *Feuilles de Pierre*, 271–289. ERAUL, Liège.

Jacobi, R.M. 1997. The 'Creswellian' in Britain. In J.-P. Fagnart and A. Thévenin (eds.) *Le Tardiglaciaire en Europe du Nord-Ouest*, 497–505. CTHS, Paris.

Jessen, A. and Nordmann, V. 1915. *Ferskvandslagene ved Nørre Lyngby*. Danmarks Geologiske Undersøgelse, Raekeke.

Johansen, L. 2000. The Late Palaeolithic in Denmark. In B. Valentin, P. Bodu and M. Christensen (eds.) *L'Europe Centrale et Septentrionale au Tardiglaciaire: Confrontation des Modèles Régionaux de Peuplement*, 197–216. Memoires du Musée de Préhistoire d'Ile-de-France 7. APRAIF, Nemours.

Krukowski, S. 1920. Swidry Wielkie I Gorki (pow. Warszawski). *Wiadomo ci Archeologiszne* 5, 164–166.

Mace, A. 1959. An Upper Palaeolithic open site at Hengistbury Head, Christchurch, Hants. *Proceedings of the Prehistoric Society* 25, 233–259.

Madsen, B. 1996. The Late Palaeolithic cultures of southern Scandinavia: tools, traditions and technology. In L. Larsson (ed.) *The Earliest Settlement of Scandinavia and its Relationship with Neighbouring Areas*, 61–74. Acta Archaeologica Lundensia 24. Almquist and Wiksell International, Stockholm.

Mathiassen, T. 1946. En senglacial boplads ved Bromme. *Aarbøger for Nordisk Old Kyndighed og Historie* 1946, 121–231.

Müller, S. 1896. Nye Stenalders Former. *Aarbøger for Nordisk Old Kyndighed og Historie* 1896, 303–419.

Otte, M. and Caspar, J.-P. 1987. Les pointes de la Font Robert: outils emmanchés? In D. Stordeur (ed.) *La Main et l'Outil:*

Manches et Emmanchements Préhistoriques, 65–74. Collections des Travaux de la Maison de l'Orient 15, Lyons.

Petersen, P.V. and Johansen, L. 1996. Tracking Late Glacial reindeer hunters in eastern Denmark. In L. Larsson (ed.) *The Earliest Settlement of Scandinavia and its Relationship with Neighbouring Areas*, 75–88. Acta Archaeologica Lundensia 24. Almquist and Wiksell International, Stockholm

Roe, D.A. 1981. *The Lower and Middle Palaeolithic Periods in Britain*. Routledge and Kegan Paul, London.

Rust, A. 1943. *Die Alt- und Mittelsteinzeitlichen Funde von Stellmoor*. Karl Wachholz, Neumünster.

Salomonsson, B. 1964. Découverte d'une habitation Tardiglaciaire à Segebro, Scanie, Suède. *Acta Archaeologica* 35 (2–4), 1–28.

Scarfe, N. 1972. *The Suffolk Landscape*. Hodder and Stoughton, London.

Smith, R.A. 1931. *The Sturge Collection: An Illustrated Selection of Flints from Britain Bequeathed in 1919 by William Allen Sturge*. British Museum, London.

Sonneville-Bordes, D. de and Perrot, J. 1956. Lexique typologique du Paléolithique supérieur. Outillage lithique. V) Outillage à bord abattu, VI) Pièces tronquées, VII) Lames retouchés, VIII) Pièces varies, IX) Outillage lamellaire. Pointe azilienne. *Bulletin de la Société Préhistorique Française* 53, 547–559.

Sturge, W.A. 1911. The Chronology of the Stone Age. *Proceedings of the Prehistoric Society of East Anglia* 1, 43–105.

Sturge, W.A. 1912. Implements of the Later Palaeolithic 'Cave' Periods in East Anglia. *Proceedings of the Prehistoric Society of East Anglia* 1, 210–232.

Swainston, S. 2000. The lithic artefacts from Paviland. In S. Aldhouse-Green (ed.) *Paviland Cave and the 'Red Lady': A Definitive Report*, 95–113. Western Academic and Specialist Press Ltd., Bristol.

Taute, W. 1968. *Die Stielspitzen-Gruppen im Nördlichen Mitteleuropa: Ein Beitrag zur Kenntnis der späten Alsteinzeit*. Böhlau Verlag, Köln.

Warren, S.H., Piggott, S., Clark, J.G.D., Burkitt, M.C., Godwin, H. and Godwin, M.E. 1936. Archaeology of the submerged land surface of the Essex coast. *Proceedings of the Prehistoric Society* 2, 178–210.

Wiessner, P. 1983. Style and social information in Kalahari San projectile points. *American Antiquity* 48, 253–276.

Zaliznyak, L.L. 1999. Tanged point cultures in the western part of Eastern Europe. In S.K. Kozlowski, J. Gurba and L.L. Zaliznyak (eds.) *Tanged Point Cultures in Europe*, 202–218. Maria Curie-Sklodowska University Press, Lublin.

25. Out of Abbeville:
Sir John Evans, Palaeolithic patriach and handaxe pioneer

Mark J. White

ABSTRACT

Sir John Evans' contribution to Palaeolithic archaeology lay not only in helping to establish the antiquity of humanity, but also in his treatment of the lithic evidence, particularly handaxes. He touched on issues such as the meaning of variability in handaxe shape, the significance of raw materials, artefact function, chronological variation and reduction strategies, which are still of interest. His work therefore remains fresh and modern in its outlook, and his observations laid some of the foundations upon which others have built.

INTRODUCTION

John Evans is best known for his role in establishing the antiquity of humanity and, thereby, helping to kick-start the discipline of Palaeolithic archaeology. His heavy tomes (Evans 1872, 1897) and dense papers (Evans 1860, 1862) are read mostly as historical documents relating to the debate which established the greater length of human antiquity, or as surveys containing valuable eye-witness details of the earliest discoveries, many now lost or inaccessible. Few realise that in the thirteen years between 1859 and 1872, in amongst his vast descriptive tracts, Evans also made some of the most perceptive and clear-sighted observations regarding Palaeolithic stone tools of the Victorian or any other age. This paper examines through modern eyes some of the observations contained in these books and papers. It suggests that when drawn together, Evans' work on early Palaeolithic stone tools, especially handaxes, has a remarkably modern, analytical feel, and despite its different vocabulary, anticipates several major research agendas of the present day.

ABBEVILLE AND AMIENS

One hardly need repeat the tale of how Evans, in the company of the geologist Joseph Prestwich, visited Boucher de Perthes in Abbeville in the late Spring of 1859; how both men were convinced by the claims that human artefacts and extinct mammals occurred together in the Pleistocene gravel deposits of the Somme; and how they subsequently presented a joint paper on 26 May 1859 to a distinguished audience at the Royal Society, cogently detailing their observations and conclusions (Joan Evans 1943, 103; Grayson 1983). It is true that neither Prestwich nor Evans could claim the original discoveries as their own, nor to have been the first to champion Boucher de Perthes (Rigollot 1855), but nevertheless their timing and reputations were impeccable.

Earlier claims for a long human chronology such as those suggested by Frere (1800) for the handaxes from Hoxne, Suffolk, by MacEnery (Vivien 1856) for Kent's Cavern, Devon, and by Schmerling (1833–34) for Engis in Belgium were generally ignored, argued away or dismissed (Grayson 1983; Van Riper 1993). Despite showing Herculean tenacity over some 20 years, Boucher de Perthes' work (Boucher de Perthes 1847, 1857) was similarly disregarded. The world may not have been ready for his conclusions but Boucher de Perthes did not help his own cause by adhering to theories of catastrophism, offering wild interpretations and unnecessarily including many dubious pieces within his collections of genuine artefacts. By 1859, however, developments in the natural sciences and a growing receptivity to the possibility of a great human antiquity provided Prestwich and Evans with a scientific establishment in Britain that was finally ready to listen (Grayson 1983; Van Riper 1993). Their high standing in the scientific world, especially that of Joseph Prestwich, undoubtedly gave their word the stamp of authority, but it was their careful empirical validation using the evidence from the Somme Valley and the re-discovered site at Hoxne that ultimately overcame the doubters. The rest of the world soon followed. By 1860 Edmond Hébert, Professor of Geology at the Sorbonne, declared human antiquity a dead issue (Grayson 1983, 193).

Abbeville was arguably Evans' defining moment. By being the first British antiquarian of any note to seriously champion the evidence for human antiquity he, along with his colleagues Prestwich, Flower, Lyell, Falconer and Lubbock, made an enormous contribution to prehistory and the wider sciences and practically invented the new discipline of Palaeolithic archaeology. They forced Victorian society to re-evaluate not only the history of the World, but humanity's place within it. In the process they made the application of Darwinian evolution to the human species a tenable proposition (Joan Evans 1943).

However, one might be excused for thinking that Evans was simply the right person, in the right place, at the right time, and that his actual original contribution was quite unremarkable. This view would be wrong. Evans was only thirty-five years old when he visited Abbeville and his later career, which spanned some forty-nine years, was as diverse as it was long. For Palaeolithic archaeology his major contribution lay not only in helping establish the discipline, but also in his later treatment of the lithic evidence, particularly handaxes.

ANCIENT STONE IMPLEMENTS OF THE RIVER DRIFT

Evans' expressed objective in studying the past was 'from the examination of ancient remains, [to] recall into an ideal existence days long since passed away, to trace the conditions of a previous state of things and, as it were, to re-people the earth with its former inhabitants' (1860, 280). Unlike many of his peers, such as Lyell (1863), Lubbock (1865) and Dawkins (1874), whose researches emphasised the geological, ethnographical or palaeontological side of human antiquity, Evans remained far more concerned with the evidence provided by stone artefacts, which he attempted to use as a direct analytical means for understanding how humans had made and used stone implements and what this might tell us about them. While his earliest concerns revolved around the anthropogenic nature of stone implements and their occurrence together with the remains of ancient extinct animals, these ventures ultimately led him to a more detailed consideration of methods of manufacture, the character and causes of variability, function and activity facies (Evans 1860, 1862, 1872).

This is far from the kind of archaeology that many today would associate with Victorian antiquarianism.

His first statement on the nature of Palaeolithic stone tools (Evans 1860) divided the available material into three categories: flakes, to which he later added trimmed flakes, pointed implements (handaxes) and oval or almond shaped implements (handaxes), with a cutting edge all round. For the remainder of his life he saw little reason to alter this basic classificatory system, and seems to have been suspicious of more complex typologies. Indeed, when discussing his handaxe categories, he noted that there was 'so much variety among them that the classes ... may be said to blend or run one into the other' (Evans 1860, 288). This suggests to me that rather than attempting to pigeon-hole the wide range of handaxe shapes into arbitrary types, Evans identified a continuum of variation between two extreme end forms.

Like most typologies, that of Evans contained a functional element, although on function in general he was fairly pessimistic, vague and even contradictory. He found base speculation a useless enterprise. He shied away from notions that the myriad forms of handaxe were deliberately created to serve different functions, like modern tools, but did entertain the possibility that the major classes of pointed and ovate implements might have had different purposes. He initially suggested that pointed handaxes were hafted as spear-points (Evans 1860, 289), but later rejected this, preferring the possibility that they were hand-held devices for piercing, digging and boring (Evans 1872, 565), whereas ovates had been used for scraping and cutting. However, the continuum of variation he detected between the two classes led him to question even this (*ibid.*, 567). Evans found little value in Prestwich's suggestion that handaxes had been used for cutting holes in ice, asking why they should then be found in India. He further wondered how one went about choosing between the more plausible suggestions. As analogy, experiment and macroscopic use-wear could provide no concrete solutions, Evans eventually adopted Lubbock's (1865) position that one might just as well ask for what purposes they could *not* have been employed, perhaps tacitly suggesting they were multi-purpose tools. The task was fruitless (Evans 1897).

Elsewhere Evans is more positive about the potential causes of handaxe variability. There are hints that he believed some degree of variability reflected localised, inherited knapping practices or mental templates (1872, 564, 574). He attributed much to other factors, however, particularly the knapping process and the nature of the raw materials:

> 'variations in [handaxe] form are, no doubt, mainly due to the nature of the material' (1862, 78)
> 'the character of [the roughly shaped implements] was no doubt in some measure determined by the shape of the original fragment of flint from which they were fashioned' (1872, 508)
> 'In some instances it is very remarkable how little

the original shape of the flint has been altered in order to convert it into one of these points' (1862, 77)

'[There] are some characteristic types, to attain which would seem to have been the aim ... though they were not always successful, and an innumerable variety of intermediate types has been the result' (1872, 564)

'The[se] implements ... are possibly mere accidental varieties of the oval or ovate form ... many of which must, no doubt, have resulted from the manner in which the flint happened to break during the process of manufacture' (1872, 567)

For me this creates an impression of hominids engaged in a reflexive mutual relationship with their environment, the actions of the individual guided by their socially acquired knowledge and skills but mitigated by the nature of the flint available. For Evans (1872), it showed intelligence and skill, particularly in the way hominids responded to knapping events as they unfolded, and the initial choice of nodule. This was especially clear on pointed handaxes with unworked butts, which he suggested were made from 'suitably rounded pebbles' (Evans 1862), and the plano-convex pieces whose form and mode of manufacture were influenced by the flake blanks from which they were frequently produced. Evans also pointed out that although most British handaxes were made on flint, this had not all been obtained directly from the Chalk. Some had come from secondary sources and by careful examination of their original surfaces (cortex) the proximate origin of the flint could be identified (1862, 64).

The establishment of a chronology for the stone age was one of the key issues of the Victorian era, and Evans insisted on a division between the drift implements and surface implements from early on in his work. For these divisions, Lubbock (1865) would later provide the modern terminology, Palaeolithic and Neolithic, respectively. Evans was more cautious about uncritically using Lartet's faunal sequence for the Palaeolithic, with its cave bear, mammoth, reindeer and bison 'ages'. Lubbock (1865), who essentially supported the scheme, had questioned the age of the cave bear, pointing out that its presence/absence was largely dictated by the presence of habitable caves. Evans was more sweeping in his criticism, thinking it likely that local variation and short-term shifts in human food preferences could produce different faunal assemblages in different caves. He encouraged further research to determine how far human agency might actually have shaped the character of the large mammalian fauna in a region. He was equally sceptical of de Mortillet's (1869, 1872) framework, which proposed several chronological subdivisions of the Palaeolithic based on type fossils. Although Evans accepted it in principle, especially when combined with faunal evidence, he found the proposed sequence and some of the selected type-sites unsatisfactory (Evans 1872, 1897). He seems particularly troubled by the division between Chellean/Acheulean and the Mousterian (1897, 528), which some suggest may have left him

a little blinkered and unyielding on these and related questions (Cook and Jacobi 1998).

Although he firmly expressed his belief that some of the contrasts reflected chronological variation, as caves often contained distinctive implements belonging to much later phases of the Palaeolithic, in terms of the earlier material he saw chronology as just one of several possible explanations. Different activity facies and taphonomy were forwarded as other particularly significant factors (1872, 427; 1897, 475). To Evans, the cave sites 'undoubtedly' represented camps with greater opportunity for the 'reception' of varied tools for varied tasks, but the fact that they contained a greater proportion of small tools might equally relate to the higher chances of preservation and recovery in such contexts. The paucity of larger implements (handaxes) in the caves but their dominance in the drift deposits, on the other hand, was suggested to stem from these implements having been mainly used for 'out of doors' activities. He urged antiquaries to compare assemblages from different contexts to establish the true range of this variation.

Interests in geological processes and site formation proved valuable in other areas. In 1865, Mr Sheriff Fitch had suggested that large hollows in gravels of the Little Ouse River near Thetford had been excavated by recent colonies of subterranean dwellers, bringing into question the antiquity of the contained implements. By studying the geological context and formation process, Evans was able to refute these claims and demonstrate that the hollows had been formed by solution of the underlying Chalk. This was achieved at no small personal risk; Evans, Flower and Fitch had just finished inspecting the interior of one hollow when it collapsed, bringing down tons of gravel (Evans 1865).

Like his contemporaries, Evans illustrated his work with ethnographic examples, although rather than seeking direct analogues for specific practices or individual artefacts, his interests lay more in general process. He was especially keen to use ethnographic and modern methods of lithic manufacture to further his understanding of Palaeolithic stone tool manufacture. He researched and described a large number of stone-working techniques and studied first-hand the Brandon knappers, detailing their manufacturing techniques and carefully refitted blades back onto a gun-flint core in order to understand better the process of manufacture (Fig. 25.1). Evans was also a keen experimental archaeologist. He taught himself to knap using only 'authentic' stone and antler hammers (Joan Evans 1943), a skill that did much to inform his research (Fig. 25.2). He disdained forgers who used only metal hammers (Evans 1872), although Flint Jack, the famous English forger, was more complimentary, regarding Evans as one equally skilled as himself (Joan Evans 1943). This knowledge of manufacturing techniques, the tell-tale signs of a metal hammer and a careful eye for artefact condition, also made him acutely aware of possible forgeries. Following the infamous Moulin Quignon hoax of 1863, Eduard Lartet declared

Fig. 25.1. Conjoining gun-flint core used by John Evans to examine stone tool manufacture (Evans 1872).

Fig. 25.2. An experimental handaxe made by Sir John Evans using 'authentic' tools (courtesy of the Ashmolean Museum, Oxford).

Fig. 25.3. A Palaeolithic Patriarch: John Evans, probably c. 1880s (courtesy of the Ashmolean Museum, Oxford).

simply being waste products (Evans 1872, 24). His early proposal that some flakes were arrowheads was recanted in later writings, although he did regard some as being suitable for hafting as spear tips (Evans 1860, 1872). He also divided flakes up into different types that broadly reflected their position in the reduction sequence (Evans 1897, 642) and highlighted what might be termed a 'principle of limited possibilities' (cf. Rolland 1981) whereby the technological simplicity of basic core reduction would automatically produce similarities between flakes and cores from different periods and different cultures (Evans 1860, 289). His geological knowledge caused him to be cautious regarding the authenticity of trimmed (retouched) flakes (scrapers) found in the drift and he solidly rejected claims for Tertiary eoliths, even though he firmly believed that traces of human presence would eventually be extended back beyond the Pleistocene. Echoing Darwin, he did not think that this evidence would be found in Europe.

POLYMATH

Palaeolithic archaeology was neither Evans' only interest nor his main occupation. At sixteen, he was appointed as a junior at his uncle's paper mill and for the remainder of his working life was kept busy running several paper mills

Evans the 'inspector general of forgeries' in France and Britain (Joan Evans 1943; Evans 1863).

The data available were heavily biased towards hand-axes, but Evans' work led him to value debitage and to recognise its analytical importance. In this he was unusual. He regarded unretouched flakes as efficient cutting tools that formed the primary goal of core reduction, with cores in Hertfordshire and the north of England, fitting his personal studies into a hectic work schedule (Joan Evans 1943). His entry into business also meant he missed out on the privileged Oxbridge education enjoyed by his siblings.

His early interests lay in fossil hunting and coins. He wrote extensively on numismatics, between 1850 and 1872 publishing some forty-seven papers in the Numismatic Chronicle, which he also helped to edit (Joan Evans 1943). During this time, he produced a seminal paper on the typology of British coinage, suggesting that minted coins had existed in Britain prior to Caesar's invasion and that these were derived from a Greek model (Evans 1850). In addition to his books on prehistoric stone tools (Evans 1872, 1897) he produced an authoritative volume on ancient bronze implements (Evans 1881). He was the first person to describe the braincase, jaws and teeth of *Archaeopteryx* (Evans 1865), setting himself up against the powerful palaeontologist Professor Richard Owen. He was also interested in climate change, and offered an ingenious model invoking crustal movements and shifts in the earth's axis as a major causal factor (Evans 1866). An expert on hydrodynamics and water rights (Evans 1876, 1878), a skill developed initially through his battles over the Metropolitan Water Company's usurping of the waters of the River Gade which flowed past his Mill in Hertfordshire, he acted as advisor in several legal battles. Indeed, he had first met Joseph Prestwich, a wine importer by trade, when the two men had found themselves on opposite sides of a water rights case at Kingston Assizes. He was, in addition, a local magistrate and a member of many learned societies and committees. To later prehistorians he is perhaps most famous for being Arthur Evans' father.

TIME AND CHANCE

Evans work was founded on pragmatism and inductive empiricism, his statements based on careful personal observation and well founded interpretation. He worked with a minimum of received wisdom or historical baggage concerning his subject matter, and although he often relied on the endeavours, opinions and advice of his friends and colleagues (Cook 1997; Evans 1872), they were all novices in a new trade. Fundamentally, he and his colleagues were inventing the Palaeolithic as they went along, according to their own skills and interests. This makes it all the more remarkable just how far Evans' work seems to anticipate the concerns of current lithic studies. On early Palaeolithic artefacts, he made statements on important current issues, such as the meaning of inter and intra-assemblage variability, in both overall composition and handaxe shape, which he tried to explain through raw materials, activity facies, artefact function, chronological variation and reduction strategies. Experimental archaeology and site formation studies also came within his sphere of interest. Obviously, pioneering workers will lay foundations, but

my point is this: this really is not the type of archaeology that many routinely associate with Victorian antiquaries. Indeed, in the popular perception they were just collectors who spent most of their time organising their treasures in chronological order according to shape and sophistication. Not only this, but Evans' observations on many of these aspects were remarkably perspicacious and robust.

Evans was a powerful synthesist, and his national and regional surveys helped to lay the foundations for later and even more ambitious projects such as that undertaken by Roe (1968b). His simple binary division of handaxes, into points and ovates, still serves as a valuable heuristic tool and remarkably similar questions are still being asked about it. In his work on handaxes, Roe (1968a) devised a morphometrical scheme around these two types, as well as a graphic means of highlighting the variation in between, while my own work has attempted to explain this variation in terms of raw materials (White 1998). Evans was making similar observations over 130 years earlier. Several workers today also share Evans' suspicions of complex typological schema and favour the continuum of variation in handaxe morphology above rigid types (Ashton and McNabb 1994; Dibble 1989; White 1998). Few would trace this idea to Evans. Many today also feel the same exasperation shown by Evans when it comes to function, although Roe and his students have done more than anybody to resolve this question with pioneering advances in microwear (Keeley 1980; Mitchell 1997 *inter alia*).

Evans' emphasis on experimental studies finds modern parallels in the work of Toth (1985) and Jones (1981). His recognition of refitting as a potentially rich source of archaeological information was quickly realised in the work of Spurrell (1880) and Worthington Smith (1894), and today forms a standard but nonetheless essential tool in understanding Palaeolithic technology, site formation processes and small-scale human behavioural variability (Loecker 1994; Roberts and Parfitt 1999; Roebroeks *et al.* 1997; Villa 1982 *inter alia*). With his bold statements regarding the nature and function of cores and flakes he unwittingly opened a debate that carries behavioural, cultural and cognitive implications which is still far from resolved (Ashton *et al.* 1992; Breuil 1932; Leakey 1971; Toth 1985; Warren 1922 *inter alia*). The facies argument for the contrasts between the drift and cave implements similarly anticipated major hypotheses designed to explain phenomena such as the Clactonian (Oakley 1961) and, most famously, Mousterian variability (Binford and Binford 1966). Finally, but not exhaustively, his comments regarding the principle of limited possibilities which acts to suppress differences in basic stone working, has recently risen to the fore in relation to the Mousterian (Rolland 1981) and the relationship between the Clactonian and Acheulian (White 2000).

Many of the issues discussed by Evans did not become major concerns for Palaeolithic archaeology until well into the twentieth century. By that time they had become disassociated from Evans and the Victorian era. A different agenda was set that not only pushed Palaeolithic research off in a new direction, but which has totally shaped our impression of the late twentieth century. The question of antiquity was quickly followed by the question of succession: how had humanity evolved, physically and culturally? In 1861, Lartet devised a biostratigraphical sequence to divide the Pleistocene into four ages. This was followed in 1869 by G. de Mortillet's first attempt at an archaeological seriation, proposing the still familiar sequence of Acheulean, Mousterian, Aurignacian, Solutrean and Magdelenian: universal epochs in humanity's immutable progress. De Mortillet revised this model several times during his career; it eventually became so powerful that in the second edition of *Ancient Stone Implements of Great Britain,* Evans, the doubter, practically laments that as everybody else seemed to be using it, he might just as well do the same (1897, 483). Later still de Mortillet's basic framework would be transformed to incorporate notions of culture-history, embracing ideas of parallel cultural evolution and regional variation, as workers such as Breuil (1932) struggled to come to terms with increasing complexity, using index fossils to link stone tool assemblages together in patterns of cultural relatedness, acculturation and replacement. Only with the advent of processualism would the more analytical approach to stone tools become a routine part of a major research paradigm, although Bordes in the 1950s and Roe in the 1960s had already made strides in this direction.

Evans was arguably neither the first nor the only British or European worker to take an interest in using stone tools in this manner; contemporary and later nineteenth century workers, as well as some even earlier workers, discussed similar topics to some degree. Moreover, Evans was not precociously forging a 'proto-processualism' but simply using direct observation on new materials to reach original conclusions. He never presented his ideas as well-honed hypotheses or critical research agendas, but typically for the time hid his insights amongst dense and largely descriptive prose. We must be careful not to read into these texts things that the original authors never dreamed of, but this does not mean that we should not bother to critically re-read them. Regardless of any caveats, Evans' work was stunning in its breadth and scope, it remains fresh and modern in its outlook, his observations were sensible, robust and durable, and his theoretical ponderings grounded. He clearly laid foundations upon which others could build.

John Evans changed his family motto to 'I desire to deserve', a poignant illustration of an unassuming man who felt humbled by his own discoveries. He was, quite clearly, 'one of a coterie of men who had created sciences out of their own observations and had made in biology, anthropology, palaeontology and archaeology not only new forms of knowledge, but also new ways of thinking about the world and its history' (Joan Evans 1943, 108). He was lauded by his peers, becoming something of a patriarch for the 'geological archaeology' of the late 1800s (Van Riper

1993), but history has been strangely neglectful. I am sure that Derek Roe would be the first to agree that hidden among the works of Evans and many other early prehistorians are unrealised gems. We ignore them at our peril. Time and chance are capricious mistresses.

REFERENCES

Ashton, N.M. and McNabb, J. 1994. Bifaces in perspective. In N.M. Ashton and A. David (eds.) *Stories in Stones,* 182–191. Lithic Studies Society Occasional Paper 4, London.

Ashton, N.M., McNabb, J. and Parfitt, S. 1992. Choppers and the Clactonian: a reinvestigation. *Proceedings of the Prehistoric Society* 58, 21–28.

Binford, L.R. and Binford, S. 1966. A preliminary analysis of functional variability in the Mousterian of Levallois facies. *American Anthropologist* 68, 238–295.

Boucher de Perthes, J. 1847. *Antiquités Celtiques et Antédiluviennes: Mémoire sur l'Industrie Primitive et des Arts à leur Origine.* Tome I. Treuttel et Würtz, Paris.

Boucher de Perthes, J. 1857. *Antiquités Celtiques et Antédiluviennes: Mémoire sur l'Industrie Primitive ou des Arts à leur Origine.* Tome II. Treuttel et Würtz, Paris.

Breuil, H. 1932. Les industries à éclats du paléolithique ancien, I. Le Clactonien. *Préhistoire* 1, 125–190.

Cook, J. 1997. A curator's curator: Franks and the Stone Age Collections. In M. Caygill and J. Cherry (eds.) *A.W. Franks: Nineteenth Century Collecting and the British Museum,* 115–129. British Museum Press, London.

Cook, J. and Jacobi, R. 1998. Discoidal core technology in the Palaeolithic at Oldbury, Kent. In N. Ashton, F. Healy and P. Pettitt (eds.) *Stone Age Archaeology: Esssays in Honour of John Wymer,* 124–136. Lithics Studies Society Occasional Paper 6, Oxbow Monograph 102. Oxbow Books, Oxford.

Dawkins, W.B. 1874. *Cave Hunting: Researches on the Evidence of Caves Respecting the Early Inhabitants of Europe.* Macmillan, London.

Dibble, H. 1989. The implications of stone tool types for the presence of language during the Lower and Middle Palaeolithic. In P.A. Mellars and C. Stringer (eds.) *The Human Revolution: Behavioural and Biological Perspectives on the Origins of Modern Humans,* 415–433. Edinburgh University Press, Edinburgh.

Evans, Joan. 1943. *Time and Chance: The Story of Arthur Evans and his Forebears.* Longmans, Green and Co., London.

Evans, J. 1850. On the date of British coins. *The Numismatic Chronicle* 12, 127–137.

Evans, J. 1860. On the occurrence of flint implements in undisturbed beds of gravel, sand and clay. *Archaeologia* 38, 280–307.

Evans, J. 1862. Account of some further discoveries of flint implements in the drift of the Continent and England. *Archaeologia* 39, 57–84.

Evans, J. 1863. The human remains at Abbeville. *Athenaeum* 42, 19–20.

Evans, J. 1865. On portions of a cranium and a jaw in the slab containing the fossil remains of the *Archaeopteryx. Natural History Review,* 415–421.

Evans, J. 1866. On a possible geological cause of changes in the position of the axis of the Earth's crust. *Proceedings of the Royal Society* 15, 46–54.

Evans, J. 1872. *Ancient Stone Implements, Weapons and Ornaments of Great Britain.* Longmans, Green and Co., London.

Evans, J. 1876. On the percolation of rainfall on absorbent soils. *Proceedings of the Institute of Civil Engineering* 45, 203–216.

Evans, J. 1878. The Hertfordshire Bourne. *Transactions of the Watford Natural History Society* 1, 137–140.

248

Mark J. White

Evans, J. 1881. *The Ancient Bronze Implements, Weapons and Ornaments of Great Britain and Ireland.* Longmans, Green and Co., London.

Evans, J. 1897. *Ancient Stone Implements, Weapons and Ornaments of Great Britain* (second edition). Longmans, Green and Co., London.

Frere, J. 1800. Account of flint weapons discovered at Hoxne in Suffolk. *Archaeologia* 13, 204–205.

Grayson, D.K. 1983. *The Establishment of Human Antiquity.* Academic Press, London.

Jones, P. 1981. Experimental implement manufacture and use: a case study from Olduvai Gorge, Tanzania. In J.Z. Young (ed.) *The Emergence of Man*, 189–195. Philosophical Transactions of the Royal Society of London 292, London.

Keeley, L.H. 1980. *Experimental Determination of Stone Tool Uses: A Microwear Analysis.* University of Chicago Press, Chicago.

Leakey, M.D. 1971. *Olduvai Gorge: Excavations in Beds I and II, 1960–1963.* Cambridge University Press, Cambridge.

Loecker, D. de, 1994. On the refitting analysis of Site K: a Middle Palaeolithic findspot at Maastricht-Belvédère (The Netherlands). *Ethnographisch-Archäologishe Zeitschrift* 35, 107–117.

Lubbock, J. 1865. *Pre-historic Times.* Frederick Norgate, London.

Lyell, C. 1863. *Geological Evidences of the Antiquity of Man.* Murray, London.

Mitchell, J.C. 1997. *Functional Analysis of British Lower Palaeolithic Handaxes: A Study Utilising Optical Microscopy, Computer Aided Image Analysis and Experimental Archaeology.* Unpublished DPhil thesis, University of Oxford.

Mortillet, G. de, 1869. Essai d'une classification des cavernes et des stations sous abris. *Comptes Rendus de l'Académie des Sciences de Paris* 68, 553–555.

Mortillet, G. de, 1872. Classification des diverses périodes de l'Age de la Pierre. *Comptes Rendus du Congrés International d'Anthropologie et d'Archéologie Préhistorique, sixième session, Bruxelles*, 432–444.

Oakley, K. 1961. *Man the Tool-Maker* (fifth edition). British Museum (Natural History), London.

Rigollot, M.-J. 1855. *Mémoire sur des Instruments en Silex Trouvés à St Acheul, près d'Amiens, et Considérés sous les Rapports Géologiques et Archéologiques.* Duval et Hermant, Amiens.

Roberts, M.B. and Parfitt, S.A. (eds.) 1999. *Boxgrove: A Middle Pleistocene Hominid Site at Eartham Quarry, Boxgrove, West Sussex.* English Heritage, London.

Roe, D.A. 1968a. British Lower and Middle Palaeolithic handaxe groups. *Proceedings of the Prehistoric Society* 34, 1–82.

Roe, D.A. 1968b. *A Gazetteer of British Lower and Middle Palaeolithic Sites.* Council for British Archaeology Research Report 8. London.

Roebroeks, W., Kolen, J., Van Poecke, M. and Van Gijn, A. 1997. Site J: an early Weichselian (Middle Palaeolithic) flint scatter at Maastricht-Belvédère, The Netherlands. *Paléo* 9, 143–172.

Rolland, N. 1981. The interpretation of Middle Palaeolithic variability. *Man* 16, 15–42.

Schmerling, P.-C. 1833–34. *Recherches sur les Ossemens Fossiles Découverts dans les Cavernes de la Province de Liège.* Collardin, Liège.

Smith, W.G. 1894. *Man the Primeval Savage.* Stanford, London.

Spurrell, F.J.C. 1880. On implements and chips from the floor of a Palaeolithic workshop. *Archaeological Journal* 37, 294–299.

Toth, N. 1985. The Oldowan reassessed: a close look at early stone artefacts. *Journal of Archaeological Science* 12, 101–120.

Van Riper, A.B. 1993. *Men Among the Mammoths: Victorian Science and the Discovery of Human Prehistory.* University of Chicago Press, Chicago.

Villa, P. 1982. Conjoinable pieces and site formation processes. *American Antiquity* 47, 276–290.

Vivien, E. 1856. On the earliest traces of human remains at Kent's cavern. *Annual Report of the British Association for the Advancement of Science* 26, 119–123.

Warren, S.H. 1922. The Mesvinian industry of Clacton-on-Sea. *Proceedings of the Prehistoric Society of East Anglia* 3, 597–602.

White, M.J. 1998. On the significance of Acheulean biface variability in Southern Britain. *Proceedings of the Prehistoric Society* 64, 15–45.

White, M.J. 2000. The Clactonian Question: on the interpretation of core and flakes assemblages in the British Isles. *Journal of World Prehistory* 14, 1–64.

26. Old collections – a new resource?
The history of some English Palaeolithic collections in Cardiff

Elizabeth A. Walker

ABSTRACT

The National Museum and Gallery in Cardiff is not an obvious place for researchers interested in studying collections found in England to consult. However, the research collection contains a number of potentially important Lower Palaeolithic artefacts. This paper investigates the reasons why so many artefacts from sites far from the Welsh border are curated in Cardiff, and provides a history and inventory to encourage their use.

BACKGROUND

The few researchers who venture to Cardiff to study the Museum's non-Welsh Palaeolithic collections have mostly been made aware of their existence by Derek Roe's important reference work *A Gazetteer of British Lower and Middle Palaeolithic Sites* published in 1968. Here, mention is made of various collections held in Cardiff, particularly the artefacts from Swanscombe that comprise much of Henry Stopes' large collection made during the late nineteenth century. Roe states in this Gazetteer that he was only able to examine a part of this collection (Roe 1968, v). Unfortunately, little opportunity was afforded to him in his study of the Stopes Collection since, at the time of his visit, the collection was largely inaccessible, being stored in a basement prone to frequent flooding. The then Museum Assistant, George Evans, recalls that it was not unusual for researchers consulting the Stopes Collection to be handed a pair of wellington boots before being sent into this basement store. Access was also impeded by the fact that the collection was stored in heavy wooden crates packed full and stacked one upon the other (G.C. Evans pers. comm. 2001). Despite this inauspicious start to his relations with the National Museum, Roe has been an active supporter of the National Museum, playing a key role as a member of the Archaeology Advisory

Committee 1982–1999 and, more recently, as a member of the Museum's Collections and Education Committee. In these roles he acts as one of a panel of independent experts advising the Museum on its collection acquisition and management policies, fieldwork and research strategies, as well as advising on the storage, display and educational use of the collections. The issues regarding the acquisition of collections being debated today are rather different from those that arose over a hundred years ago when ideas for the formation of a National Museum of Wales were first mooted. The summary that follows reflects some of these changes.

ESTABLISHING AN ACQUISITION POLICY

The National Museum of Wales (now the National Museums and Galleries of Wales) was granted its Royal Charter of Incorporation in 1907. The passing of the Cardiff Corporation Act in 1909 authorised the transfer of the collections held by the Welsh Museum of Natural History, Arts and Antiquities (formerly the Cardiff Municipal Museum, founded in 1868) to the National Museum. Legal transfer of the collections took place on 15 November 1912 at which time space was allocated in the neighbouring

City Hall for temporary exhibitions (Bassett 1982, 182; 1993, 4–5). In this same year the foundation stone of the present Museum building in Cardiff's Civic Centre was laid and the first Director Dr William Evans Hoyle was appointed. Both institutions displayed archaeological artefacts in parallel until the closure of the Cardiff Museum and the transfer of its collections to the National Museum in 1919 (Ward 1920).

The public galleries of the Cardiff Municipal Museum and the National Museum of Wales understandably had a Welsh focus and collections were sought through donation, bequest, purchase and the Museums' own excavations in Wales, as well as funding other researchers' projects in exchange for the finds. With the exception of the large Upper Palaeolithic collection from Paviland Cave, acquired in 1924 by part-funding of the excavations of Professor William J. Sollas of Oxford University (Walker 2000, 270), the two Museums had little in the way of Palaeolithic collections to display in their galleries. This lack of Lower Palaeolithic artefacts is in large part a consequence of the ravages of the glaciation that saw most of Wales covered with ice at the Last Glacial maximum (Green and Walker 1991, 32; Wymer 1999, 181). It was not until the discovery of lithic artefacts along with human and faunal remains at Pontnewydd Cave in 1979 that the National Museum had significant Lower Palaeolithic collections from Wales to display (Green 1984). These collections have been summarised elsewhere by Aldhouse-Green (1998). In the early days of both the Cardiff Museum and the National Museum of Wales, it was therefore necessary to turn attention to obtaining artefacts from sources in England and beyond to fill these gaps.

The early collection policies of museums were concerned with the need to obtain complete series, or typological sets, of artefacts. Indeed, one of the stated aims of the National Museum of Wales' Charter reads:

> 'The object of the Museum shall be mainly and primarily the complete illustration of the geology mineralogy zoology botany ethnography archaeology art history and special industries of Wales … and further the collection preservation and maintenance of all objects and things … whether connected or not with Wales'.

The understanding of these series was dependent on systematic classification, the principles of which were brought into use in archaeology, in part at least, as a result of Pitt Rivers' work. He had studied the technological development of firearms and from this suggested that it might be possible to apply evolutionary processes to material culture as a whole (MacGregor 1997, 16). Pitt Rivers' own museum followed the principle that material culture can reveal human nature and its changes through artefactual development. The artefact types that developed evolved into new types according to Darwinian selection processes (Pearce 1992, 85). Many other museums, including the Cardiff Museum and later the National Museum of Wales, adopted such ideas readily, for if it were logical to display

their natural science collections in this way, why not archaeology as well? These principles were applied to archaeological artefacts in the displays in Cardiff and cases were arranged in such a way that the perceived sequences of development could easily be followed by museum visitors (Plate 26.1; Pitt Rivers 1888, 826). Not all museums, however, adopted this approach. Indeed, Franks and his successors at The British Museum were amongst critics of this practice. Their more conservative approach to display by site protected the collections from such passing academic fashions and helped to maintain the integrity of individual site collections (Cook 1997, 116). In Cardiff, it is undoubtedly unfortunate that the displays adopted this evolutionary trend and that the importance of cross-disciplinary displays or interpretation was largely ignored at this time.

In order to display series of lithic artefacts, museums needed to ensure they had a fully representative collection and would seek out artefacts from a variety of sources and locations to complete their displays. Until the arrival of the modern communication systems we now take for granted, the motor car, television, publications aimed at the non-specialist reader, global travel and the world-wide web, museum curators had a difficult task. The only easy way that most people could learn about their past and other cultures was by visiting their local museum. The Public Libraries and Museums Act of 1850 and subsequent legislation enabled access to museums for everyone and aimed to help people extend their education through visits to museums. When a collection was acquired by a museum, artefact types which were present in large numbers were frequently set aside to offer to other museums. These became known as 'duplicates'. Their exchange ensured that, as far as possible, each museum was able to display a representative series of prehistoric artefacts.

It is worth remembering that during the latter half of the nineteenth century scientific debates about the origin and antiquity of Man engaged the minds of scholars and scientists based, not only in universities, but also in museums. Acquiring lithic artefacts was helpful to museum curators who were forming opinions on these important issues, enabling them to participate in such debates. Museum curators played a doubly important role (and one which continues today) not only by participating in the debate, but also by educating museum visitors through their displayed collections and their interpretation. It is against this background that many acquisition decisions were taken by the fledgling National Museum of Wales.

THE EARLIEST ACQUISITIONS

The first Palaeolithic collection to be acquired from England was offered as a donation by Mr Francis R. Crawshay of Lee-on-the-Solent, Hampshire, in 1896. Crawshay had family links with South Wales, being a descendant of the important industrialists, the Crawshays of Merthyr, who were responsible for establishing Merthyr's iron industry (S. Crawshay pers. comm. 2001). The Cardiff Museum

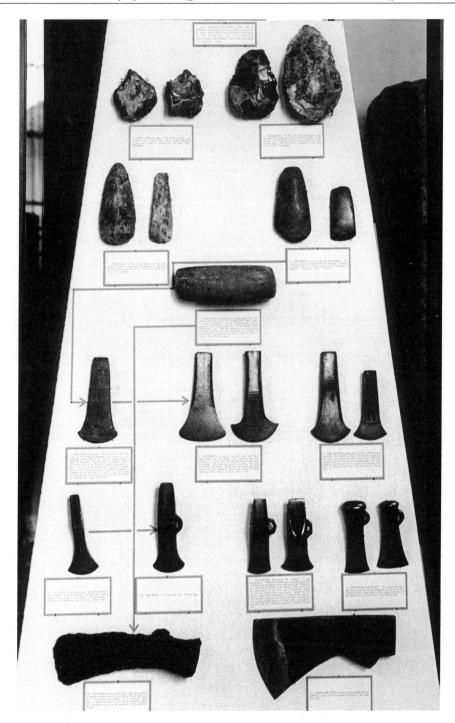

Plate 26.1. 'Archaeology is concerned with the evolution of common objects'. National Museum of Wales display 'The Evolution of the Axe' (c. 1930).

was particularly keen to acquire its first real Palaeolithic artefacts for the collection, for prior to this donation it only held casts, mostly of French Palaeolithic artefacts (Ward 1896, 11). Crawshay had collected these artefacts himself from Hill Head, near Southampton, Hampshire, some years prior to their donation (*ibid.*). Roe (1968, 99) records many finds with a general Hill Head attribution amongst museum collections. The following year Crawshay donated further artefacts from Hill Head to the Cardiff Museum (Table

26.1) and in 1898 donated a rolled biface from Lee-on-the-Solent (Roe 1968, 101; Ward and Ward 1898, 21).

The next acquisitions to be made by the Cardiff Museum were sought out from amongst the duplicates of the Blackmore Museum at Salisbury. These artefacts were selected by the curator Dr H.P. Blackmore, from whom they were purchased. The collection comprises bifaces from Moor Down, Bournemouth, the Test Valley at Romsey, Woodgreen in the Avon Valley, Bemerton,

	Provenance	Bifaces	Cores	Flakes	Flake Tools	Levallois Cores	Levallois Flakes	NMGW acc. no.
Berks.	Maidenhead	7	–	–	–	–	–	01.404
	Reading area	–	–	7	1	–	–	87.38
Bristol	Shirehampton	1	–	–	–	–	–	77.19H
Dorset	Ballast Hole, Broom	1	–	–	–	–	–	Unnumbered
	Broom	4 chert 1 flint	–	–	–	–	–	14.239/2
		15 chert 2 flint	–	–	–	–	–	98.405
	Moor Down, Bournemouth	1	–	–	–	–	–	98.407
Kent	Aylesford	4	1	–	–	–	–	02.3
	Baker's Hole, Northfleet	–	–	–	–	4	25	14.239/1
	Crayford	–	–	2	–	–	1	01.382
	Swanscombe	1	–	–	–	–	–	27.618
Hants.	Dunbridge	1	–	–	–	–	–	14.239/2
	Hill Head	1	–	–	–	–	–	97.2
		–	–	–	1	1	–	97.3
	Lee-on-the-Solent	–	–	4	–	–	–	96.284
		1	–	–	–	–	–	02.144
	Old Shirley	1	–	–	–	–	–	14.239/2
	Romsey	6 flint 1 chert	–	–	–	–	–	98.406
	Woodgreen	3	–	–	–	–	–	98.408
	Tidworth	1	–	–	–	–	–	68.487
Heref.	Welsh Newton	1	–	–	–	–	–	77.7H
Norfolk	Beeston Beach	–	1	–	–	–	–	38.22
	Cromer	–	–	10	5	–	–	38.22
	East Runton	–	–	2	3	–	–	38.22
	West Runton	–	4	3	4	–	–	38.22
Suffolk	Bramford Pit No. 2	–	–	6	1	–	–	38.22
	Bolton and Co.'s Pit, Ipswich	–	–	2	2	–	–	38.22
	Bury St. Edmonds	1	–	–	–	–	–	01.65
	Fornham	1	–	–	–	–	–	01.65
	Fornham (probably)	1	–	–	–	–	–	01.65
	Icklingham	3	–	–	1	–	–	01.65
	Mildenhall	3	–	–	1	–	–	01.65
	Warren Hill	1	–	–	–	–	–	01.65
Wilts.	Bemerton	1	–	–	–	–	–	98.410
	Knowle Farm, Savernake	6	2	–	–	–	–	02.4
		2	–	2	–	–	–	04.175
		–	–	3	–	–	–	14.239/2
		–	–	–	–	1	–	14.304
	Milford Hill	3	–	–	–	–	–	98.409
Unlocated	Thames River Valley	1	–	–	–	–	–	87.91H/1
	Hill Lane	1	–	–	–	–	–	14.239/2
	Horslands surface	1	–	–	–	–	–	01.65
	Inidanbury Hill	–	1	–	–	–	–	14.239/2
Unprov.		5	–	1	–	–	–	14.239/2

Table 26.1. Summary of English Collections held by the National Museums and Galleries of Wales.

Milford Hill near Salisbury and Broom in the Axe Valley, Dorset. All these sites have many bifaces recorded from them, Woodgreen being prolific (Roe 1968, 117; Wymer 1999, 113).

Following the turn of the century a number of acquisitions were made by the Cardiff Museum from sites in England. A collection of Palaeolithic implements originating from sites on the terraces and high gravels of the River Lark at and near Bury St. Edmunds, Suffolk, were purchased from Moyses Hall Museum, Bury St. Edmunds (Table 26.1; Thomas and Ward 1901, 22). The lack of provenance information accompanying them, typical of this time, appears not to have been a concern, for these collections were obtained merely for the types of tools represented rather than their source or context. The next collection to be acquired, however, has rather more in terms of a pedigree for it originates from excavations by Mr F.C.J. Spurrell at Crayford, Kent (Spurrell 1880). The finds, consisting of two flakes and one Levallois flake, are accompanied by a card on which they were originally mounted, which reads 'presented on the occasion of the excursion of the International Geological Congress of 1888' (NMGW archive: original presentation mount). One of the Honorary Curators of Cardiff Museum, Mr T.H. Thomas, donated these to Cardiff Museum in 1901.

An acquisition entry reported in the Cardiff Museum's 1902 Annual Report reads 'Flint implements. Several types, pointed and axe-like, all rudely worked on both faces.

Several have butts formed of the natural surface of the flint. One is conspicuously water rolled. Thames river-gravels, Maidenhead, 1901. Palaeolithic. Purchased' (Thomas and Ward 1902, 18). Roe has attributed these bifaces to Furze Platt, Berkshire (Roe 1968, 10); but the vendor's name and the exact history of these artefacts are unrecorded.

In the 1903 Annual Report, there is a contradictory report on some eoliths (NMGW accession 02.2; Robinson and Ward 1903, 37) as: '15 natural fragments more or less rudely chipped into rude scrapers and other tools (Eolithic or Plateau implements)'. The report records that they were collected by Mr Benjamin Harrison of Ightham, Kent, from the North Downs. All the pieces are marked with catalogue numbers and are likely to have originally been purchased from Harrison as a boxed set (J. Cook pers. comm. 2001). The eoliths were purchased by the Cardiff Museum. Although the vendor's name is not recorded, it is possible that they were purchased from Harrison himself. Alternatively, they may be the eoliths referred to in a letter from Harrison to Edmund J. Jones of Blackwood (NMGW archive; Stanton 1983, 258–259). In 1903 the debate about whether eoliths were created by human or natural forces was hotly in progress and is succinctly summarised by Roe (1981, 27–28). The description given above in the Museum's annual report possibly reflects the author's (probably John Ward, Curator of Cardiff Museum) unwillingness to take sides in the eolith debate.

1902 and 1904 saw donations of bifaces and flakes from Knowle Farm Pit, Savernake, in Wiltshire. These artefacts may originate from investigations at the site undertaken by Dixon in 1901 (Dixon 1904). The 1902 donation was made by Mr William Heward Bell, a Trustee and Librarian of the Wiltshire Archaeological Society who later became its President. Bell had business interests in South Wales, being a colliery owner and director of the Taff Vale Railway and, later, the Great Western Railway (P. Robinson pers. comm. 2001). The Cardiff Museum Annual Report records the second accession as collected by J.E. Pritchard, who was a regular benefactor to both the Wiltshire Archaeological Society and Cardiff Museum (Thomas and Ward 1905, 31; P. Robinson pers. comm. 2001).

THE STOPES COLLECTION

Prior to 1912, the Museum sought to build up a representative collection of Palaeolithic artefacts from sites across southern England, but it was doing so in a somewhat haphazard manner. Most of the collections were acquired largely fortuitously, as was the case in 1912 when the important Stopes Collection was offered for sale to the Museum. This collection had an interesting formation and history, before it eventually found its permanent home in Cardiff.

The collection was brought together by Henry Stopes and by the time of his death in 1902 it was enormous,

filling a house and overflowing into the garden (NMGW archive: letter from Professor W. Boyd Dawkins to Dr Evans Hoyle, 15 February 1912). Indeed, it was one of the largest private collections of lithic artefacts made at the end of the nineteenth century. Henry Stopes F.G.S. (1852–1902) was the son of a prosperous brewer who lived in Colchester, Essex (Plate 26.2). He qualified as an engineer and architect and established a company, Henry Stopes and Co., specialising in building breweries (Kennard 1949, 157). In 1879, he married Charlotte Carmichael, a Shakespearean scholar and early proponent of women's suffrage (Hall 1977, 15–16). It is perhaps as the father of a famous daughter, Dr Marie Stopes, that he has gained his place in history. Dr Marie Stopes, his eldest daughter, was a palaeobotanist and later became well known as an advocate of birth control and eugenics. This has perhaps overshadowed Henry's role in recognising and establishing Swanscombe as a key location to the understanding of British Palaeolithic archaeology. Stopes lived in Hampstead, but it was whilst at his country home, the Mansion House, Swanscombe, that he devoted much of his time to collecting lithic artefacts. Stopes acquired his collection by excavation, by discoveries made by workers in the local gravel pits, by travelling abroad and by purchasing from sale rooms. By the time of his death he had amassed many

Plate 26.2. Henry Stopes 1887.

tens of thousands of specimens ranging from eoliths (which he collected with Benjamin Harrison), Palaeolithic, Mesolithic and Neolithic artefacts and ethnographic items including a fine collection of North American arrowheads. His collection cost the family dearly both through the actual collecting expenses and in the neglect of his business (Hall 1977, 28). Letters in The British Museum's Sturge archive from Charlotte Stopes to Dr W. Allen Sturge, a private collector, indicate the seriousness of these financial problems. Indeed, in one letter written before Stopes' death, Charlotte Stopes suggests that Sturge should write to her husband offering £3000 to buy the collection. He is urged not to mention that she has suggested this course of action to him (Quaternary Section, Prehistory and Early Europe, The British Museum archive: letter from Charlotte C. Stopes to Dr W.A. Sturge, 7 July 1902).

Upon Henry Stopes' death, his widow soon started to seek a buyer for the collection. She initially entreated Sturge to buy it from her in its entirety, but he declined, being only interested in acquiring a selection of the finest artefacts with which to enhance his own already vast collection. Attempts to find a buyer appear to have been difficult. An undated sale notice prepared by Dr Marie Stopes describes the collection as:

'... perhaps the largest private one of its kind in the world, contains sixty to seventy thousand implements brought together by one who was trained in the knowledge of modern tools, and also interested in the psychological question of the evolution of Man. The resulting collection is therefore one essentially suited for students as it includes a number of series showing the evolution of certain types of tool from the rudest efforts of Eolithic (plateau) age, up to the highly finished symmetrical products of the Neolithic period'.

The notice makes it clear that:

'the great value of the collection lies in the long series of specimens, and this cumulative evidence would be destroyed were it to be broken up, consequently every effort will be made to keep it intact'.

The price asked was £5000 and the document is endorsed, amongst others, by Sir John Evans, author of the classic work *The Ancient Stone Implements, Weapons and Ornaments of Great Britain* (1872). It appears that an offer for £5000 was received and accepted from the Field Museum of Natural History, Chicago, but negotiations broke down over who was to pay for the packaging and transportation costs (NMGW archive: letter from A.C. Haddon, Cambridge, to Dr Evans Hoyle, 15 February 1912). No sale had been secured by 1 February 1912 so Dr Marie Stopes wrote to Dr Evans Hoyle asking him to consider purchasing the collection for the National Museum of Wales.

'... it is almost the only thing left to give any clue to my father's greatness of thought and work – all alas unpublished – but also for general ones, because it is a

unique and most valuable scientific collection I want to see the collection being used and not packed away in boxes as it now is. Consequently the other day I was speaking to Dr Woodward about it and asked if the Geol. Dept. Nat. Hist. Mus. wd. not be a good place for it. He says it is forbidden them and even just now they are refusing the gift of some because Bloomsbury won't allow them to have any. I myself don't care to offer our collection to Bloomsbury because they have already so many and so little space the collection wd. be lost and swamped and also because, according to Dr Allan Sturge's will which is well known, they will get also his *huge* collection, ∴ they will not buy any more. Dr Woodward immediately suggested the National Museum of Wales as a suitable place for our collection – and – strange as it may seem, it hadn't presented itself to me!'

Dr Evans Hoyle undertook some investigations into the collection, immediately contacting Professor W. Boyd Dawkins, Dr A. Smith Woodward at the Natural History Museum, A.C. Haddon of Cambridge and Sir C.H. Read at The British Museum. All agreed the collection was important and that the asking price of £1000 was reasonable. They all added their views that the collection contained a vast quantity of material, which could be described as duplicates and used for exchanges with other museums.

Following receipt of these letters of support, Dr Evans Hoyle wrote to Dr Charles Tanfield Vachell, chairman of the Honorary Curators of the Cardiff Museum, commending him to make the necessary arrangements for the purchase of the collection. It appears that in February 1912, just before the formal handing over of the Cardiff Museum collections to the National Museum of Wales in November 1912, the Cardiff Museum was still in a position to purchase items, whereas all the money allocated to the National Museum of Wales was being put into the fund for the building of the new Museum in Cathays Park.

The National Museum of Wales was naturally keen to acquire more artefacts for its new building and exhibitions and saw the opportunity to obtain the Stopes Collection as a *coup* for the Museum. It would put Cardiff on the map of research centres for Palaeolithic collections and, as a result, increase the status of the Museum by drawing respected academics to Cardiff to consult its collections (NMGW archive: letter from Dr Evans Hoyle to Professor W. Boyd Dawkins, 14 February 1912).

The Cardiff Museum was, however, unwilling to make an offer for the purchase of the collection without first seeking its own independent report on it. The person they commissioned to undertake this work was Professor W.J. Sollas of Oxford University. He was instructed to travel to Hampstead to examine the collection where, since 1905, parts of it were exhibited and the rest stored at the Hampstead Library (it appears that between 1902 and 1905 Charlotte Stopes had disposed of a proportion of the least interesting parts of the collection). Professor

Sollas reported back to Dr Vachell commending the collection although stating that it is not

'... in any sense a representative collection, on the contrary it is very one sided. The Palaeolithic implements are chiefly Lower Palaeolithic; of the upper Palaeozoic [*sic*] I could not discover any. The French caves are scarcely, if at all represented and these missing horizons are the most interesting. It is a good representative *British* Collection, and will be therefore only representative in an insular sense. As to duplicates it overflows with them, beyond all reason' (NMGW archive: letter from Professor W.J. Sollas to Dr C.T. Vachell, 6 March 1912).

Meanwhile, Dr Stopes wrote to Dr Evans Hoyle reiterating her position regarding the importance of the collection. She is particularly concerned about 'duplicates' and indeed she is the only person who states that 'duplicates' have a place in a collection.

'Then as regards 'duplicates'. I think Professor Sollas doesn't see the meaning of big series of duplicates (though he did say that there is no such thing as a duplicate in science) for research purposes. But in the special case of this collection you must realise that my father lived a hundred years before his time and that only now some of his contentions are beginning to be accepted and so we must keep the 'duplicates' together – (all stored away in boxes in a cellar if you like) for the next generation' (NMGW archive: letter from Dr Marie Stopes to Dr Evans Hoyle, 4 March 1912).

'Duplicates' within collections were actively sought out by most museums and the importance of keeping a collection together to facilitate research was not commonly recognised at this time. Indeed, the 1907 Royal Charter of the National Museum of Wales made collecting 'duplicates' an objective of the Museum stating it should

'... further the creation and maintenance of duplicates or multiplicate specimens and collections to be lent and used from time to time for the purposes of exhibition or instruction at or in connection with [the University Colleges of Wales] and other educational institutions in Wales'.

It would seem, therefore, that as a scientist, Marie Stopes foresaw the need to keep everything together, rather than selecting a representative sample and disposing of the rest. However, it was not until very much later in the century that we see this practice adopted by museums.

In May 1912, the Cardiff Museum's Treasurer, Alderman Illtyd Thomas, offered Dr Stopes £600 for the collection, which she accepted. It is interesting that half way through the day on which John Ward, Mrs Stopes, her two daughters and men from the removal firm were packaging the collection, Dr Jordan, Director of the Philadelphia Museum, called at Hampstead Library to offer Mrs Stopes £1100 for the collection. Ward observed

in a letter to Dr Evans Hoyle that Dr Jordan seemed disappointed and that, had they not been well advanced with the packaging by the time of his visit, the National Museum would probably not have acquired the collection (NMGW archive: letter from John Ward to Dr Evans Hoyle, 24 May 1912). The National Museum of Wales was now the legal owner of many crates containing the Stopes Collection along with its catalogue. The catalogue is in Dr Marie Stopes' handwriting, and a page at the front of the volume explains how it was compiled. Every piece in the collection can be related back to the catalogue since all the artefacts are labelled in black ink with a number.

Nothing was done with the Stopes Collection until 1918 when Mr Reginald A. Smith of The British Museum wrote requesting to examine it. Smith had previously written to the National Museum of Wales in March 1912 enquiring whether or not the collection had been purchased and expressing his desire to examine it (NMGW archive: letter from Mr R.A. Smith to Dr Evans Hoyle, 30 March 1912). Smith had already commenced excavations at Swanscombe (Smith and Dewey 1913) and was interested in comparing his excavated collection with Stopes', but at this date the purchase was not yet secured. In response to his enquiry in 1918, The National Museum of Wales suggested that rather than just study the collection for his own purposes, he should be commissioned to prepare a report on its contents. This report states how important he considered the Stopes Collection to be, although he noted the absence of accompanying stratigraphic information (Smith 1918, 36). Smith sorted the collection, selected the best artefacts for future exhibition, made sets of type-series for circulating on loan to other Welsh museums, and then repackaged the collection into its wooden crates which he labelled with details of their contents.

On 15 March 1933, a report was presented to the Art and Archaeology Committee of the National Museum of Wales in which it is reported that Dr Nash-Williams, Keeper of Archaeology, had consulted Smith again regarding the future of the collection. The report recommended that it would be possible to sort out seventy-five percent of the remaining collection for disposal. There is no certain record that this actually happened, although George Evans recalls tipping several crates of natural flint into the foundation trenches of the Museum Schools Service store in the late 1970s (G.C. Evans pers. comm. 2001).

The collection remained more or less as Smith had left it in 1918 until the mid 1970s, when building works removed the problems of frequent floods in the stores and it was once again possible to examine the crates. During 1977–1978 Jill Cook, then a research student, worked on the collection and prepared a report (unpublished) about it. John Wymer also spent three days looking through the collection preparing a report about its usefulness to modern research. Wymer's report concluded that the collection was mostly worthy of preservation (NMGW archive: letter from John Wymer to George C. Boon, 31 January 1975).

The Stopes Collection is now temporarily housed in an overflow store within the National Museum and Gallery in Cardiff where it fills two hundred and five of the original wooden crates. The composition of the collection has not been reassessed for this paper but what follows draws on the notes prepared by Jill Cook and John Wymer.

The majority of the collection comprises British Lower Palaeolithic artefacts. (The parts relating to British Mesolithic, Neolithic and all foreign artefacts are omitted from this paper). Much of the collection comes from the Great Pit, Milton Street, Swanscombe. The part of the collection marked with catalogue no. 20 is recorded as 'found *in situ* in the top gravel and Bullhead'. Catalogue no. 21 was 'found by the men ditto' (Plate 26.3). Wymer notes that most of the bifaces are typical of the Middle Gravels, whilst Cook notes that of the 1269 bifaces bearing this number only thirteen have the white patination, abrasion and damage found on material now known to come from the Upper Gravels and none of these are the ovate forms which have been found more recently in this deposit (Cook 1978). She therefore suspects that Stopes was in fact referring to the Middle Gravels at the time when the Upper

Gravel had either been stripped off or was not exposed. The number of bifaces recorded are: 1269 (catalogue no. 20) and 2300 (catalogue no. 21) (Cook 1978). The flakes, flake tools and cores were not studied or recorded in any detail and whilst the presence of a Clactonian type industry is noted, other researchers would make the case for such flake industries being technologically indistinguishable (Conway *et al*. 1996, 239). It is, therefore, possibly best to see this collection as one originating predominantly from the Middle Gravels. But there is the probability that artefacts from other horizons have become incorporated into this collection.

Several entries in Stopes' catalogue refer to Bevan's Pit, Northfleet. The majority (catalogue no. 26) comprise 215 bifaces (Cook 1978), but have no further information associated with them. Catalogue no. 597 is recorded as 'In the brickearth at the foot of Bevan's Pit. These stones were touching the bones and tusks of mammoth'. Also recorded is a Levallois flake (Cook 1978; Roe 1968, 168) and core (Roe 1968, 169; Smith 1918, 36).

Stopes also collected at Ingress Vale Road, Northfleet, from where Cook (1978) recorded seventy-eight bifaces

Plate 26.3. Bifaces from the Great Pit, Milton Street, Swanscombe – 'found by the men'.

as well as flakes and flake tools. Wymer notes that there are a few bifaces resembling those of the Swanscombe Middle Gravels whilst many large flakes, scrapers and other worked flakes not common in these gravels were also present amongst this assemblage. There can thus be little certainty about the exact origin of these implements (Cook 1978).

Other sites represented in the collection are listed in Table 26.2. The Stopes Collection, whilst certainly of mixed use to present-day archaeologists, would undoubtedly merit further study and consultation, for information contained both within the crates and indeed in the catalogue could potentially be of use to future Palaeolithic research. However, the lack of detailed contextual information will undoubtedly prove to be the inherent weakness of this large, yet interesting collection.

From the Museum's perspective the Stopes Collection has justified its acquisition. Its purchase enabled the National Museum to fill in gaps in its early archaeology displays. The selection made by Smith in 1918 for display was shown until later refurbishment of the galleries in the 1960s. The collection has also been used extensively for educational purposes, with some items forming an element of the Museum's school loan service for classroom teaching and some groups of material have been lent to museums around the world. Students from the University of Wales continue to visit and use this collection to learn about aspects of Palaeolithic lithic technology. So despite its minimal curatorial care, it is in fact a very important resource and one it is hoped will continue to be consulted by twenty-first century researchers.

THE LATER ACQUISITIONS

With the new National Museum building in Cardiff underway in 1912, there would soon be ample space in which to display lithic artefacts. So, after acquiring the Stopes Collection, the National Museum continued to look for English Lower Palaeolithic artefacts with which to fill in the gaps in its display. In 1914 Dr Evans Hoyle wrote to Sir Charles Hercules Read, Keeper of British and Medieval Antiquities and Ethnography at The British Museum, asking to receive any items he may have for disposal from a recent bequest made by Richard Jones. The National Museum received seventeen artefacts from this bequest from various provenances including Broom, Dorset, Knowle Farm Pit, Wiltshire and Dunbridge, Hampshire (Table 26.1). Also included in the package were thirty Levallois cores and flakes from excavations by R.A. Smith at Baker's Hole, Northfleet, Kent (Smith 1911). This collection was split between a number of museums, each receiving a representative selection. Little attention appears to have been given to the relationships between individual artifacts, as has been demonstrated by Dr Wenban-Smith who has refitted a failed Levallois flake in the collections of Cheltenham Museum with a struck Levallois core in the

collections of the National Museum (Wenban-Smith 1995, 149).

Following the formal opening of the National Museum a number of private donations of artefacts were received. The donors were presumably made aware of the potential interest in their own artefacts through visiting the new Museum galleries. Unfortunately, few of the donations accepted at this time have contextual information with them. In 1937 W.F. Grimes, Assistant Keeper of Archaeology, approached J. Reid Moir directly to obtain artefacts from the Cromer Forest Beds in East Anglia with which to enhance the Museum collections. Grimes justified his request to spend £5 purchasing sixty-three artefacts from Reid Moir writing,

> 'We have no material of this type, and the series had behind it the authority of the original discoverer of the industries represented' (NMGW archive: memorandum from W.F. Grimes to V.E. Nash-Williams, 15 November 1937).

A heavily rolled and red patinated biface was found at the Meadow Grove housing estate, Shirehampton, Bristol, by George C. Boon. It is believed to be derived from the 100 foot terrace of the River Avon, an area at the northern end of the Clifton Gorge from which a number of bifaces are recorded (Wymer 1999, 184). This biface was donated to the collections of the University of Bristol Spelaeological Society (Clevedon Brown 1957, 43) from whom George Boon, by then Keeper of Archaeology, borrowed it for display in 1977. The National Museum's present gallery displays were being refurbished at this time so a biface from Welsh Newton, a single surface find discovered just over the Welsh border in Herefordshire (Wymer 1999, 181), was also borrowed for exhibition. Both bifaces remain on display today.

CONCLUSION

The National Museums and Galleries of Wales has a large collection of material from England and one which far outnumbers its Palaeolithic collections from Wales. Although this collection is, in large part, poorly provenanced it has a role to play in the Museum as a research tool accessible to those interested in studying the history of specific sites and the finds discovered at them. The collection also has a role as an educational resource used by university and school students. Today, offers of artefacts from England would not be accepted as they do not fall within the scope of the Department of Archaeology and Numismatics' acquisition policy, which focuses solely on acquiring archaeological artefacts with Welsh provenances. The Museum would also not now endorse the splitting up of any excavated collection, thus ensuring it remains in one place to facilitate future research.

It is hoped that this paper, which elaborates on and extends Roe's Gazetteer, will raise awareness of the

Place	Provenance Information	Stopes catalogue nos.
Swanscombe, Kent	Great Pit, Milton Street. Found in the gravel	2, 447, 449, 476, 531
	Great Pit, Milton Street. Found in the top gravel and 'bullhead'	20, 719
	Great Pit, Milton Street. Ditto found by the men	21
	On the top fields adjacent to Great Pit, Milton Street	22
	Milton Street Pit. Found in a swallow hole with animal bones	668
	Milton Street Pits	443
	Craylands Pit, Milton Street	45, 480, 680
	Mansion House	3, 619
	The Mounts	5, 41, 477, 484, 486
	The Wash Pit. Opposite the farm	14
	The Wash Pit. In field between Russell's hop garden and the Wash Pit, New Barn	688
	Higgins Pit. Where the Galley Hill skull was found	17
	Galley Hill	454, 478
	Botany Bay Pit, Galley Hill	34
	Clappernappers Hole	25
	Bevan's Pit.	26, 42, 483
	Bevan's Pit. In the brickearth at bottom of pit	26b, 597, 715
	Bevan's Pit. In old beach cutting approaching the pit	26c
	Bevan's Field and hopgarden	487
	New Barnes Pit in London clay being washed down to brickyard, Bevan's	27
	Bevan's Wash Pit. Opposite Treadwell, New Barn	593, 598
	Barnsley Field Pit	568, 569, 570, 571, 572, 573
	Chamber's Farm	588
	Found on land between Swanscombe and Northfleet, Station	30
	Field leading to Bartholomew's Hill next to Sandy Lane and Hop garden to left of Sandy Lane leading to Grub Wood and the Mounts	31
	Swanscombe Wood. Found during tree planing in the top gravel	29
	Bartholomew's Hill	32, 39
	Strawberry bed near hut Treadwell's Farm	33
	Vicinity. Surface finds	4, 230, 231, 451, 455, 485, 519, 603, 636, 656, 659, 687
Northfleet, Kent	Vicinity	450, 452, 518, 532
	Northfleet Station. On the bank of the South Eastern Railway	18, 534
	Shore	52
	White's no. 5 Pit	24
	White's no. 5 Pit. In the field next to the pit	622
Southfleet, Kent	Southfleet Church. Surface	686
	Treadwell's hopground	19
	Snellings Garden and field	23
	Betsham	35
	Vicinity	50, 482, 594, 595, 599
Greenhithe, Kent	Greenhithe Pit	590
	Globe Pit	758
	Ingress Abbey, Old garden	751
	Beach at low tide	587
	Vicinity	37, 459
Fawkham, Ash, Kent	Dundells Farm	44
	Vicinity	51
Ash, Kent	Vicinity	36, 48, 67, 439, 526, 527, 536, 596, 634, 661, 714
	North of church	528
Galley Hill, Kent	On gravel. Site of new church	38, 654
	Vicinity	60
Springhead, Kent	One Tree Field	28, 47, 101
Higham, Kent	Odgers Street	56
Farningham Road, Kent	Vicinity	62
	Station	618
Ingress Vale, Kent	Ingress Vale Road Close to the railway arch on the opposite side of the valley to Craylands, Northfleet. This sand is white and in places has a great profusion of shells, bones, teeth etc.	65
Ightham, Kent	Vicinity	438, 460, 543
	In the garden of The Old House	530
Rainham, Kent	Vicinity	674, 709, 711
West Ham, London	Victoria Graving Yard, Silvertown	59
Leyton, London	Vicinity	499
	Pit near station	576
Warren Hill, Suffolk	Vicinity	66b, 90, 414, 496, 610
	Three Hills	235
Lakenheath, Suffolk	Vicinity	66c, 457, 756
Shrub Hill, Feltwell, Norfolk	Vicinity	498
Hitchin, Herts.	Ickleford Gravel Pit	548
	Highbury	557
	Foley Pit, Ranson's Brickyard	547, 556
	Vicinity	229, 550
Seaton Junction, Dorset	Vicinity	626
Broom, Dorset	Ballast Hole	86
	Vicinity	624
Axe Valley	Vicinity	248
Axminster, Somerset	Vicinity	625
Chard, Somerset	Vicinity	87, 627

Table 26.2. Principal entries in the Stopes catalogue, excluding Milton Street, Swanscombe.

English Lower Palaeolithic collections in the home of the national archaeological collections of Wales.

ACKNOWLEDGEMENTS

I would like to thank Sarah Milliken and Jill Cook for inviting this paper. Jill Cook has kindly permitted me to quote from her unpublished research and has offered encouragement along the route of preparing this paper. Thanks are due to John Wymer for granting permission to quote from his report on the Stopes Collection, and to The British Museum for permission to quote from letters in their collection. Richard Brewer, Edward Besly and Bryony Coles' comments on early drafts of this paper were very helpful. Special thanks must also go to Derek Roe for his encouragement and support over the past fourteen years.

REFERENCES

Aldhouse-Green, S. 1998. The archaeology of distance: perspectives from the Welsh Palaeolithic. In N. Ashton, F. Healy and P. Pettitt (eds.) *Stone Age Archaeology: Essays in Honour of John Wymer*, 137–145. Lithic Studies Society Occasional Paper 6, Oxbow Monograph 102. Oxbow Books, Oxford.

Bassett, D.A. 1982. The making of a National Museum. *Transactions of the Honourable Society of Cymmrodorion*, 153–185.

Bassett, D.A. 1993. Wales in miniature. *Amgueddfa Autumn 1993*. National Museum of Wales, Cardiff.

Clevedon Brown, J. 1957. Archaeological notes: Palaeolithic and other implements from the Shirehampton district. *University of Bristol Proceedings of the Spelaeological Society 1956–1957*, 43–44.

Conway, B., McNabb, J. and Ashton, N. 1996. *Excavations at Barnfield Pit, Swanscombe, 1968–72*. British Museum Press, British Museum Occasional Paper 94, London.

Cook, J. 1978. Unpublished *Interim report on a study of the Lower Palaeolithic material in the Stopes Collection of the National Museum of Wales, Cardiff.*

Cook, J. 1997. A curator's curator: Franks and the Stone Age Collections. In M. Caygill and J. Cherry (eds.) *A.W. Franks: Nineteenth-Century Collecting and the British Museum*, 115–129. British Museum Press, London.

Dixon, S.B. 1904. On the Palaeolithic flint implements from Knowle, Savernake Forest. *The Wiltshire Archaeological and Natural History Magazine* 33, 139–144.

Green, H.S. 1984. *Pontnewydd Cave: A Lower Palaeolithic Hominid Site in Wales*. National Museum of Wales, Cardiff.

Green, H.S. and Walker, E. 1991. *Ice Age Hunters: Neanderthals and Early Modern Hunters in Wales*. National Museum of Wales, Cardiff.

Hall, R. 1977. *Marie Stopes: A Biography*. André Deutsch, London.

Kennard, A.S. 1949. Henry Stopes. *Proceedings of the Geologists' Association* 60, 157–159.

MacGregor, A. 1997. Collectors, connoisseurs and curation in the Victorian Age. In M. Caygill and J. Cherry (eds.) *A.W. Franks: Nineteenth-Century Collecting and the British Museum*, 6–33. British Museum Press, London.

Pearce, S.M. 1992. *Museums, Objects and Collections*. Leicester University Press, Leicester.

Pitt Rivers, A.H.L.F. 1888. Presidential Address to the Anthropology Section. *Report of the Fifty-Eighth Meeting of the British Association for the Advancement of Science 1888*, 825–835.

Robinson, S. and Ward, J. 1903. *The Welsh Museum of Natural History Arts and Antiquities Report to the Town Council for the Year Ending March 31ˢᵗ 1903*. The Welsh Museum of Natural History Arts and Antiquities, Cardiff.

Roe, D.A. 1968. *A Gazetteer of British Lower and Middle Palaeolithic Sites*. Council for British Archaeology Research Report 8, London.

Roe, D.A. 1981. *The Lower and Middle Palaeolithic Periods in Britain*. Routledge and Kegan Paul, London.

Smith, R.A. 1911. A Palaeolithic industry at Northfleet, Kent. *Archaeologia* 62, 515–532.

Smith, R.A. 1918. Report on an examination of the 'Stopes' Collection of stone implements. In I.J.C. Herbert (First Baron Treowen) and W. Evans Hoyle, *Eleventh Annual Report (1917–18) presented by the Council to the Court of Governor*, 35–37. National Museum of Wales, Cardiff.

Smith, R.A. and Dewey, H. 1913. Stratification at Swanscombe: report on excavations made on behalf of the British Museum and H.M. Geological Survey. *Archaeologia* 64, 177–204.

Spurrell, F.C.J. 1880. On the discovery of the place where Palaeolithic implements were made at Crayford. *The Quarterly Journal of the Geological Society of London* 36, 544–548.

Stanton, Y.C. 1983. Researches and discoveries in Kent: Benjamin Harrison and Henry Stopes. *Archaeologia Cantiana* 99, 257–259.

Thomas, I. and Ward, J. 1901. *The Cardiff Museum and Art Gallery Annual Report to the Town Council November 1ˢᵗ 1899–March 31ˢᵗ 1901*. Cardiff Museum and Art Gallery, Cardiff.

Thomas, I. and Ward, J. 1902. *The Welsh Museum of Natural History Arts and Antiquities Report to the Town Council for the Year ending March 31ˢᵗ 1902*. The Welsh Museum of Natural History Arts and Antiquities, Cardiff.

Thomas, I. and Ward, J. 1905. *The Welsh Museum of Natural History Arts and Antiquities Report to the Mayor and Corporation for the Year ending March 31ˢᵗ 1905*. The Welsh Museum of Natural History Arts and Antiquities, Cardiff.

Walker, E.A. 2000. Paviland Cave: the curatorial and scientific history of the museum collections. In S. Aldhouse-Green (ed.) *Paviland Cave and the 'Red Lady': A Definitive Report*, 265–274. Western Academic Specialist Press Ltd., Bristol.

Ward, C.A.J. and Ward, J. 1898. *The Cardiff Museum and Art Gallery Annual Report to the Town Council for the Year ending October 31ˢᵗ 1898*. Cardiff Museum and Art Gallery, Cardiff.

Ward, J. 1896. Notes on the collections (Year ending October 31ˢᵗ 1896). In T. Rees and J. Ward, *The Cardiff Museum and Art Gallery Annual Report to the Town Council for the year ending October 31ˢᵗ 1896*, 11–25. Cardiff Museum and Art Gallery, Cardiff.

Ward, J. 1920. The history of museums in Cardiff. 1. The museum as a municipal institution. In H.M. Hallett (ed.) *The British Association Cardiff Meeting 1920: Handbook to Cardiff and the Neighbourhood*, 112–119. Cardiff.

Wenban-Smith, F.F. 1995. The Ebbsfleet Valley, Northfleet (Baker's Hole). In D.R. Bridgland, P. Allen and B.A. Haggart (eds.) *The Quaternary of the Lower Reaches of the Thames: Field Guide*, 147–164. Quaternary Research Association, Durham.

Wymer, J.J. 1999. *The Lower Palaeolithic Occupation of Britain*. Trust for Wessex Archaeology and English Heritage, Salisbury.

27. A burnt Mesolithic hunting camp on the Mendips: a preliminary report on structural traces excavated on Lower Pitts Farm, Priddy, Somerset

Joan J. Taylor

ABSTRACT

This paper gives the results of an excavation of a burnt flint scatter found during the Priddy Plateau Project. Two burnt Mesolithic huts were found protected by a natural limestone outcrop from later agricultural activity on the Priddy Plateau between Lower and Upper Pitts farms. The radiocarbon date of 5000±80 BP suggests these are one of the more recent Mesolithic sites, possibly contemporary with the Neolithic activity that built the Sweet Track on the Somerset Levels less than ten miles south-west of the Priddy Plateau.

INTRODUCTION

While I was Curator of Archaeology and History at the Bristol City Museum, I received many enquires about stone artefacts found in the surrounding area. This ultimately resulted in the Priddy Project, and in the excavation of flint concentrations around the Lower Pitts Farm area of the Mendips. This paper offers a preliminary report on a Mesolithic site of unusual interest.

THE PRIDDY PLATEAU PROJECT

Interest in the topographical features of the Mendips by antiquarians such as the Reverend John Skinner began a tradition of research in this area that persists to the present day. Boyd Dawkins, by excavating Hyena Den, Wookey Hole, from 1859–63, inspired interest in the Palaeolithic occupations of the cave systems lying below the plateau. The richness of one particular area in evidence from the Palaeolithic to the Roman period and beyond, both below and above the scarp of the Mendip, inspired the first systematic field survey of about four square kilometres (circa 1000 acres) by the Priddy Plateau Project in the mid-1970s. Amongst other results, this survey revealed a Mesolithic hunting camp, with traces of hut structures destroyed by fire, which was excavated from 1974 to 1977 (Fig. 27.1).

LITHIC RAW MATERIALS ON THE MENDIPS

Numerous well known 'flinters', the most recent of whom is Brian Hack, have contributed many tea chests filled with flints, collected from the Mendip surface, to the local museums (Bristol City Museum, King John's Hunting Lodge in Axbridge, Somerset, and the Wells Museum *inter alia*). All this flint found on the surfaces of the Mendip Plateau actually came from Cretaceous chalk at least forty kilometres (25 miles) away, in the area of Westbury and Tisbury, Wiltshire. In the collections curated by Wells Museum, a large rectangular block of light grey/buff translucent flint with darker flecks, labelled 'Mesolithic core from Slab House' (ST592482, which is north-east of Wells), epitomises much of the flint picked up from the plateau surface. Although a variety of flints and high quality cherts, frequently with traces of cortex on them, as well as a flint nodule in an unrolled but weathered condition, were collected from the surface of Yard Park field, all reflect a post-glacial arrival in the field.

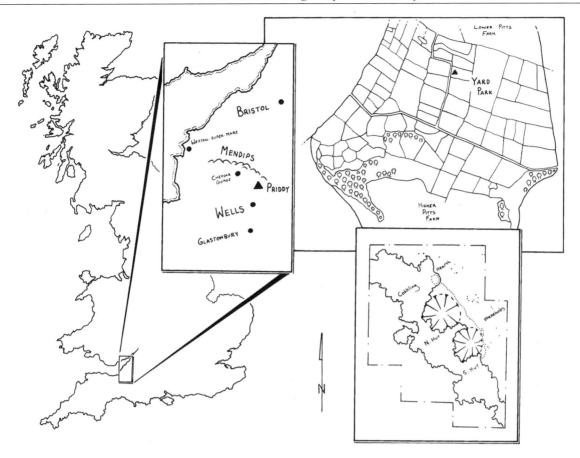

Fig. 27.1. Map showing the location of Yard Park field. The Mesolithic excavation was on the western end of the field to the south of the gate.

Apart from the flint, chert is also found in the Priddy area. It too is introduced. Lumps of local cherts have been found but these are unmodified, being too impure to work (Findley 1965, 14–15), which conforms to our experience. At Tisbury, Wiltshire, however, not only flint, but also Portland Chert beds of high quality with noted 'star agate' characteristics are well recorded (Chatwin 1960, 32). Dr F.S. Wallis believed this was the source of Portland Chert found on the Priddy Plateau, including that from Ebbor Gorge (pers. comm.). Palmer, however, suggests the Ebbor source was towards the Bristol Channel (Palmer 1970, 92), rather than looking towards Westbury, but Professor C. Paul confirms that geologically the beds do not occur further west than the Tisbury scarp (pers. comm.). A range of distinctive grey cherts, some with speckled white inclusions, are represented both in the surface scatters and in the excavation of the Mesolithic hut site at Lower Pitts Farm, Priddy, described below. The source of the imported flint and chert remains to be scientifically identified in the full forthcoming publication of the site, but this does not change the point that the nearest locality from which most, if not all, of the flint could come are the geological beds at Tisbury some forty kilometres (25 miles) away.

GEOLOGY

It appears from our research that geologists have mainly been interested in the Higher and Lower Pitts Farm area because of its complex solid and soil geology. Yard Park lies at 240 meters (about 850 feet) OD and seems to share its soil series more with Higher Pitts Farm than with that of Lower Pitts Farm. At least two different carboniferous limestone formations with different fossil components underlie the soils of Yard Park field. There are also other formations in the area, such as a local dolomitic conglomerate in Ebbor Gorge to the west and Old Red Sandstone at Pen Hill to the east, while in the dry valley along the road running by Lower Pitts Farm into Priddy Green there are deposits of 'head' or alluvium common to old stream beds.

THE PRIDDY PLATEAU PROJECT

The Priddy Plateau Project (Taylor 1976, 1977, 1978, 1979) directed by the author between 1973 and 1980, with generous support from numerous bodies acknowledged at the end of the paper, was the first to make a systematic survey of about four square kilometres (900–1000 acres) of plateau bounded by the primaeval forest of Ebbor Gorge to the west, Rookham Coombe to the east and the Mendip scarp to the south (Fig. 27.1). This plateau has no outstanding topographical features of an archaeological nature, not even residual ghosts of outlines in aerial photographs, yet it still produced some of the heaviest flint concentrations from the prehistoric period. R. Smart, during her postgraduate study linked to the Project, produced maps of the detailed coverage of the survey, which illustrate concentrations found by the Priddy Plateau Project, particularly by Smart herself, even after substantial removal of material from these fields by at least three serious 'flinters', who had collected the previously mentioned tea chests of flints.

The author's attention was attracted to this area by John Loveder, at that time a submariner with the Royal Navy, who brought flint implements into the Bristol City Museum in 1972, on behalf of his mother and the Dyke family, who farmed Lower Pitts, Priddy. Yard Park field had just been ploughed for the first time in many years, and was yielding concentrations of archaeological material which included much burnt flint, calcined bone, and other debris at the western edge of the field (ST538502). General field walking in Yard Park field had produced material of all periods, including Roman Samian ware and black slag, mimicking 'brittle obsidian', from the lead processing at nearby St. Cuthbert's mine, which ceased production just prior to World War I. Earlier mining, similar in pattern to that of individual stannary workings in the Forest of Dean, riddled the area in a search for minerals such as calamine, manganese oxide for the Wedgewood Black Basalt wares (Higher Pitts Farm) and other minerals deposited during the Mendip Hydrothermal Episode, which extends from the Mendips to North Wales, and now is noted for the copper deposits exploited by the Bronze Age copper production mine at the Great Orme, Llandudno, North Wales (Fletcher *et al.* 1993; Jenkins *et al.* 1990; Joel *et al.* 1995, figs. 4–7). The region of Priddy was notably marginal, even after enclosure, and Findley noted that it was all but abandoned between the 4th and 13th Centuries AD and only recently became agricultural (Findley 1965, 54–55). This would explain the ultra-conservative nature of society in this area even in prehistoric times, as the heaths were not good tilling land, and pasturalism probably followed the hunter-gatherers. Enclosure of the agricultural fields was late: it did not occur until the physical construction by Napoleonic prisoners of war of dry stone walls in circa 1810, which fortuitously included windbreaks along the prevailing wind side of many fields that today provide pre-enclosure soil profiles.

THE GEOGRAPHICAL SETTING

Topographically, there are two natural rills or depressions, one leading from the west, that is the Ebbor Gorge

direction, up through Sandpits field onto the plateau and another leading off the plateau to the north down through One Hundred Acres field towards an ancient stream bed. These are overlooked by higher vantage points to either side of them on the top of the plateau. These well-placed higher locations all show Mesolithic flint concentrations around them, as if hunters occupied themselves working flint, while watching for large game to appear, following these natural access routes, probably towards open grassland on the treeless plateau or down to water. During the project, The Nature Conservancy stated that the only primaeval forest to survive in this region of Somerset today was Ebbor Gorge. No doubt it provided good game cover, and particularly good shelter in the winter, in the past as well as now.

The soils of the Priddy Plateau are complex with a high loess content. Findley's soil survey (1965) was of immense use during the Project, as was his observation of the truncated nature of the site during excavation. Much of the soil in Yard Park proved to be as complex as that of Higher Pitts Farm, which had been mapped for the Ordnance Survey soil map, and contained numerous different soil series. Findley (*ibid.*) describes the soils of Yard Park field as part of the Mendip Complex, which means that the depth of soil is variable between his shallow Lulsgate and the deeper Nordrach series of free draining soils. The Nordrach series, however, is present in its full profile in the windbreaks behind the Mesolithic excavation, and Findley himself felt that he had been misled by the truncated nature of the field's ploughed profile (pers. comm.). The Nordrach profile has in its uppermost component loess mixed with brown silt loam, but in ploughed areas, the loess is harder to detect because there is a conscious effort by farmers to mix a little of the sterile reddish brown silty clay with the better top soil each time they plough so as to deepen the soil, thereby causing the sequence to become truncated as the field is levelled. Generally, the soil is stone free until near the boundary of weathering limestone and dark brown clay, when it becomes mixed with friable chunks of limestone and black stains of manganese oxide (Findley 1965, 48–50, 68). Due to the slow build up of soil on the Mendip, the prehistoric sites lie close to the surface.

Dr F.S. Wallis, a noted geological authority on the limestone formations of the Mendip, was also able to offer us observations on the nature of the solid geological outcrops on site. He shared his view that the Mendips were once capped with chalk, and that glaciation had removed this (pers. comm.). This might explain the different nature of the Palaeolithic flints with their very heavily patinated white surface, from that of the later flints on the Mendip surface derived from Wiltshire. Certainly, the material from the Middle Pleistocene site of Westbury-sub-Mendip was, in some instances, reduced to a chalky residue as a result of desilisification. It was in the Westbury-sub-Mendip Quarry, which is nearby, that the author in 1977 observed in the quarry face below this early site, *in situ* blocks of yellow loess, similar in nature to that found much more extensively as a pure loess soil at, for example, Bylany in the Czech Republic. It demonstrated why Findley found such a high loess component in the plateau soil profiles, such as his Nordrach series (Findley 1965). The red Jurassic weathered clay sub-soil that covered most of the excavated Mesolithic area in Yard Park field was previously recorded only from Higher Pitts, and gave scope during our excavation of the Mesolithic site for us to develop a technique of cleanly shaving the surface in half centimeter levels with turf cutters. This revealed sharp contrasts that were immediately detected when we left the oxidized disturbed plough soil and entered the undisturbed sub-soil. We could distinguish features that contained the browner oxidized material in the distinctive red clay, such as stake holes, mole burrows, traces left by tent pegs, and so on, and it would surely have revealed any old tree root systems had they existed. None were seen and, as the presence of the stakes, which were part of the Mesolithic feature, showed clearly, roots too would have been as apparent if they had been present. This confirms that no trees were in the area immediately around the huts. The stake screen erected to the north and north-east side of the huts further suggests that it may have been necessary to camouflage the huts from more distant and higher views. One may assume that tree cover was sparse over this part of the Priddy Plateau, and hence its attractiveness to grazing for larger game.

THE MESOLITHIC HUT EXCAVATION

Time and funding were restricted at the beginning of the excavation period, so careful covering of the site at the end of each excavation, followed by the overlapping of the next season's trench, became the routine throughout the excavations. The main campaign during the drought of 1976 enabled much of the evidence to be consolidated. The technique of shaving with turf cutters provided a clean precise method of excavation that enabled detailed recording at shallow intervals, and enabled the retrieval of all traces of surviving evidence.

It also enabled the detection of the direction and depth of plough movement in recent times, which had truncated the original soil profile now surviving in the windbreak to the west of the field, from whence the prevailing wind blows. The levelling of the field also disguised the former existence of a limestone outcrop which had provided shelter to its east for at least two Mesolithic huts, giving protection from the wind and from visibility. The modern plough, when approaching the vulnerable eastern edge of the site, was lifting to make the turn at the western headland of the field, and the limestone outcrop forced the plough upwards and away from the site as it ran eastwards. Three recent mine pits had also damaged the remains of the northernmost hut. The outcast from the pits caused some confusion as soil and clods of burnt turf had been thrown

by the miners over the *in situ* evidence for the burning of the Mesolithic site, and in most cases the outcast material did not oxidise (Fig. 27.2, indicated next to B).

As mentioned, the soil accumulation on this region of the Mendips is shallow, and some fields away from Lower and Higher Pitts land will never yield surface remains, as the farmers are growing turf for urban lawns. When they roll the turf, much of the accumulated soil goes with it. Shallow ploughing is considered essential for good agricultural yield in this area and, after twenty years, the deep ploughing of a field known erroneously as One Hundred Acres by the son of a lowland farmer from Coxley, near Wells, is still having adverse effects on its fertility. Elevation, too, precludes winter wheat sowing, and oats and barley are the only crops possible off these fields, if they are not left in pasture. Lowland farmers own highland fields in this area for winter grazing of their animals, at times when flooding affects their fields adjacent to or on the Somerset Levels. So, although one may assume that the climate was milder at the end of the Mesolithic, one can still envisage a marginal nature for this region, which would have persisted for the first farming colonies in Somerset, who are well represented on the Levels.

The Mesolithic site (ST538502), therefore, has been physically protected in modern times by its location near the western enclosure wall of the field, by the late enclosure of the area, by the presence of the outcrop and its depression, and by the reluctance of highland farmers to plough deep in case they brought up too much sterile subsoil. It was noticeable that another excavation in 1977 at the eastern end of the same field showed much greater erosion by the plough because it was in a less protected position with deeper depth of soil (Taylor and Smart 1983).

The presence of a staked windbreak with a gap in the middle, mentioned above, to the north and north-east of the site, suggests a need to conceal the huts from view, rather than just wind protection, although wind prevailing from the west might at times swing north, and the screen may have had a dual purpose. Two excellent excavators did not observe signs of burning to the north or east of these lines of stakes, suggesting they were still extant and contained any embers or blowing ash when the huts burnt at the time of the fire (Figs. 27.2 and 27.3). There seems to be a compacted floor over softer loam, noticed on several occasions during excavation in the region of the habitation; this had a mixed colour of brown loam, not pure weathered Jurassic red clay. As Yard Park field faces a higher crest of a 1000 foot ridge on which are situated barrows south-east of the Ashen Hill barrow cemetery, the Mesolithic site would in its day have been exposed to view from the higher opposite ridge across the stream (now dry alongside the modern road) and, at times, to strong winds from the north.

The remains of the two huts left a substantial burnt area. Mike Barbetti, at the time a postdoctoral assistant to Martin Aitken at the Oxford Research Laboratory for Archaeology and the History of Art, took samples of the

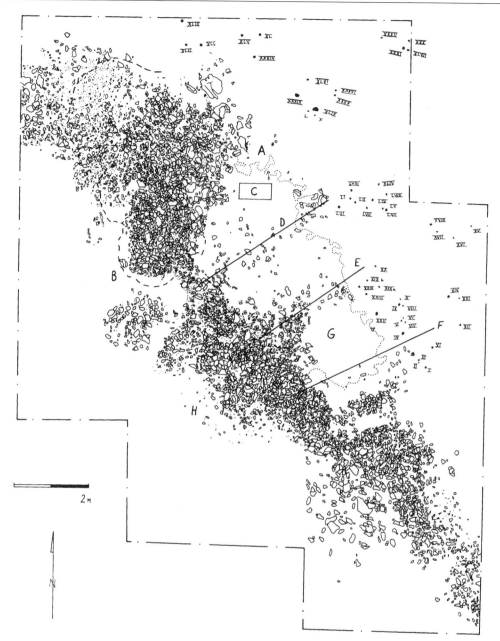

Fig. 27.2. The composite plan of the burnt Mesolithic hut excavation. 'A' indicates the hearth reconstructed in Fig. 27.5 with detail of plan in Fig. 27.6. 'B' is beside the dotted outline of three pits which are the result of modern disturbance encroaching on part of the northern hut. 'C' is the soil plinth left after baulks were removed (see Fig. 27.7 for its section). 'D' is the cross-section of the northern hut (see the middle section in Fig. 27.4). 'E' is the cross-section of the cobbling that runs between the two huts (see the top section of Fig. 27.4). 'F' is the cross-section of the southern hut (see the bottom section of Fig. 27.4). 'G' is within the dotted outline of the burning, which extended north of the soil plinth ('C') and south of the cross-section line ('F') of the southern hut. 'H' lies just behind the stone in situ *over the limestone outcrop, which gives the appearance of cobbling.*

burning for archaeomagnetic readings. He continued to show interest in the project over its duration and suggested that the profile of the burning in section indicated a double turf construction which had burnt with intense ferocity. Experiments in burning double turfs off-site did not replicate the thorough burning of soil and grass found *in*

situ. This suggests that some additional fuel would have been present, probably in the form of supporting saplings covered with a wickerwork frame, which would have supported the inner turfs of the structure and greatly increased the intensity of a fire. The colour profile of the burnt material was red on the outer surface with a black

Fig. 27.3. The reconstruction of the burnt turf huts with windbreaks behind the huts. These windbreaks were still standing when the huts burnt as they contained the fire to the side of the huts; no flecks of burning occur on the opposite side.

interior. This further suggests that the builders felt a need to camouflage the site with the outer turfs. This outer layer, which would have continued growing, would have masked any human odour emanating from the interior which might otherwise have scared game away. The huts do not appear to have interior hearths, but the fire may have made their detection during excavation difficult. A definite hearth certainly occurs outside the huts (Figs. 27.2, 27.5 and 27.6), with possibly some others, suggesting by their location that the huts were primarily for sleeping and shelter. Flints were evidently worked away from the huts, as only a few flint chips from blades and tools, a few utilised blades, scrapers and one or two Mesolithic cores were associated with the immediate site, although 656 fragments of flint were recovered from the whole excavation area, mostly as quite tiny spalls, as well as broken blades. The majority of the local Mesolithic flint working evidence has been recovered from the higher vantage points besides the rill in the Hundred Acre field, as if it was 'make work' done while waiting for game to arrive. A causeway of small cobbled stones was laid between the two huts to keep the area dry and to stop erosion, again suggesting that the entrances faced each other off the cobbling (Figs. 27.2 and 27.3).

In 1973, the first two weeks of excavation, in what was to become a four year campaign, defined oxidized soil from the Mesolithic site and burning *in situ* over an area of 10 by 4.5 meters. The brown occupation level around the burning was covered by small stones which appear to have settled out of the plough soil and are, indeed, indicative of the bottom of plough disturbance. One mole burrow was noted within the burning. Analysis showed that the burnt layer consisted primarily of fine ash with no substantial pieces of charcoal for dating. This confirms the fierce burning. As the burnt area was more than 6 cm thick over a large area, it suggests a collapsed structure. The Groningen radiocarbon laboratory identified charred heather among the samples. Structures burnt in the open landscape are usually so thoroughly burnt that they are reduced to ash without sufficient carbon surviving to obtain good samples for dating, and these were no exception. Luckily, one good sample was obtained, giving a date of 5000±80 BP (GrN-7800), which will be discussed later.

In 1974, another two weeks of excavation, with trenches overlapping those previous by less than 20 cm on two sides, revealed traces of cross-ploughing aligned both with the present dry stone enclosure wall on the west and with the limestone outcrop lying at 60 degrees to that wall. The latter obviously indicates pre-enclosure ploughing. The Mesolithic feature nestled into the limestone outcrop to its east, possibly improving the depth of the 'wind break', and with a cobbled area about 10 cm thick protruding from a large burnt area (Fig. 27.4). Here the burning came into contact with the red Jurassic clay. No colour change occurred but a definite textural change was apparent. There was also a demarcation line between a stone edge and the sterile clay, with a line of stake holes along the edge of the feature (Figs. 27.2 and 27.8). Again the soil in the habitation area under the burning was softer, but showed no colour change. This surface suggests a compacted floor over the old ground surface.

In 1975, five weeks of excavation established continuity with features observed earlier and revealed some new ones, including three small circles of stones near the burning, and one rectangular setting near the edge of the stones, which may have been hearths. The three stone

hearth settings preserved some charcoal under one of the stones which is associated with the floor. The continuous black surface of burning suggests that it remained undisturbed, so these would be Mesolithic in date. A larger hearth labelled A in the plan (Fig. 27.2), may have been the principal cooking hearth as it was surrounded by stakes (Figs. 27.5 and 27.6).

After removing the burning, the feature extended along the natural depression for about 7.5 meters in front of the limestone outcrop, which had probably been altered in shape by the human occupants of the site to contain the width of their circa 3.5 meter wide huts (Fig. 27.2). The burnt hut material had collapsed over a narrow spur of cobbling that protruded at right angles to the outcrop, which had originally been interpreted as cobbled flooring. This divided the underlying depression into two. As the baulks were removed during excavation, a soil plinth was preserved from the bottom of the plough surface downwards, to retain a stratigraphic soil record (Figs. 27.2c and 27.7). From this plinth, a column was removed by the Soil Survey of England and Wales. Although this sampling missed the thick burning, it does contain some of the re-deposited Nordrach series thrown out by more recent

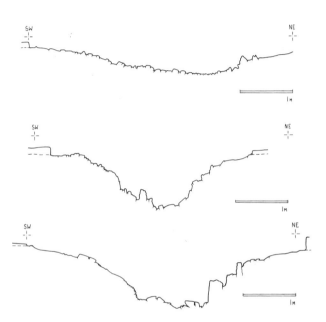

Fig. 27.4. Cross-section of the cobbling between the two huts (top). The cross-section of the northern hut (middle) and of the southern hut (bottom). Note the depth of the floor in both the huts, which is deeper than that of the cobbling.

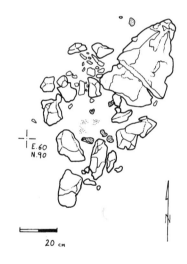

Fig. 27.6. Detailed plan of hearth 'A'.

Fig. 27.5. Artist's reconstruction of hearth 'A'. The largest stone is an in situ *limestone rock which has deflected the plough several times, thereby saving the hearth.*

Fig. 27.7. Section of the soil plinth which was left to give the total stratigraphy of the site.

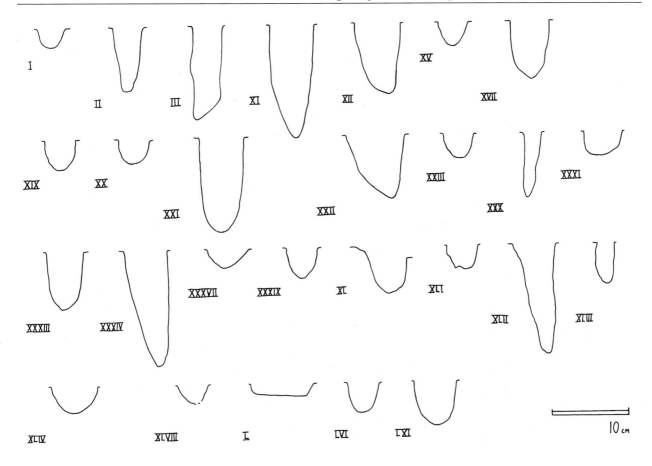

Fig. 27.8. Stake profiles. The numbers by each correspond to the numbers on the general plan in Fig. 27.2.

mining activities. Not far from the plinth, some badly decayed animal teeth, probably of deer, were recovered, but bone does not survive well in this soil, and their condition was much deteriorated.

In 1977, two final months of excavation were spent finishing off the work at the site, determining that two huts were present and that the site had been occupied at least twice, although undulations of the old ground surface caused difficulties in interpretation as the site existed on several different levels; in particular, a hearth on the southeastern edge of the hut area was at a higher level, resulting in it being plough damaged (Figs. 27.2–27.5). The intense burning of the huts, and the higher placement of the hearths on the red Jurassic clay, no doubt led to the destruction of carbon, reducing all to ash, and restricting the availability of samples for dating. It is also possible that other hearths once existed in this area and have been completely destroyed by ploughing.

A hearth (A in Fig. 27.2) with an *in situ* limestone boulder, was protected by this limestone scarred by the plough, as it was on a higher level to that of the depression with the burning, and it appeared to have a small number of stake holes associated with it, perhaps as part of a rudimentary cooking spit similar to that suggested by Higgs (1959, 227) for the stakes he found at Downton, Wiltshire.

However, the majority of the stake settings, including two with stone settings to support the stakes, appear to be associated with the collapsed burnt structure (Figs. 27.2 and 27.8).

Lack of dating samples hampers any attempt to determine the duration of the site's occupation: whether it represents a single occupation, or a site that was occupied repeatedly over a substantial period. We were also unable to interpret the pattern of hearth use: whether one hearth served both huts, or multiple contemporary hearths existed. Of course, plough erosion and mining prospection would have destroyed the evidence of other huts if they existed outside the shelter of the limestone outcrop. It is likely, on the pattern of Morton Farm, Fife, that the people who built the huts would seek some form of natural depression to increase their effectiveness (Coles 1971). The hut areas lacked hearths (Figs. 27.2 and 27.4), and apart from the higher hearth (A) (Figs. 27.2, 27.5 and 27.6), there did not appear to be obvious sequences of re-use such as those demonstrated in T46 at Morton Farm, Fife (Coles 1971, 322–324, fig. 17 and plate XXI, upper).

As stated, by shaving sufficiently moistened stone-free clay in 5 mm levels, all features filled with darker oxidized soil are cleanly bisected. Round stake holes are often indistinguishable from mole holes in cross-section, so they must be vertically sectioned to discern their profile. Profiles of some of the stakes found in the windbreaks and around the huts are illustrated in Fig. 27.8; as they are just the tips or lower portion, one can judge to some extent the degree of plough damage to the site by their considerable erosion on the higher ground around the natural depression containing the huts. Although having variable depths, they are all likely to be contemporary, cut and pointed by tranchet axes and shoved into the soil at irregular depths. S.R. Williams suggests (pers. comm.) that a wicker framework would be required to support the turf walls. The saplings would have to be under one inch in diameter, probably more in the range of half an inch, to bend into an igloo shape.

DATING

Although several samples were sent for dating, many were too small for the radiocarbon techniques available at the time, and two were wrongly combined, so had to be excluded. Consequently, only one date is available: 5000± 80 BP (GrN-7800). Mike Barbetti and the author collected this sample from the area were the archaeomagnetic samples were taken, in an undisturbed area well into the burning in 1974. Using Calib (Pearson *et al.* 1986), this recalibrates with a 98% chance at two standard deviations to within 3978 and 3673 BC, and could possibly be little older, with a 46% chance of being between 3941–3855 BC at one standard deviation. This would overlap on the other two 1 standard deviation dates with the Sweet Track's dendro-chronological date of 3807/6 BC. One standard deviation places this date in the following range: 3941–3855 BC, 3820–3773 BC, or 3756–3704 BC. Although the 5000 BP date is late for the Mesolithic, it is not out of keeping with the Mesolithic lithic evidence from some of the Burtle beds on the Somerset Levels, which could have involved a seasonal interchange with the Neolithic discussed below. Certainly, some of the later flints, in particular the asymmetrical tanged points attributed to the Neolithic, are common to both the Priddy Plateau and the Somerset Levels, suggesting a later interchange of territories. Coles (1989, 19), however, interprets the Mesolithic hunter-gatherers of the Somerset Levels absenting themselves before the arrival of the first farmers. Apparently Yard Park was a hunting camp, not a settlement, which may have been used more than once, but it does not appear to have been used over many seasons.

In the author's experience, under the direction of Professor John Coles, from 1965–71, on the Somerset Levels, and with access to the Mesolithic artefacts collected during that time on the Somerset Levels, and from Morton Farm, Fife, it seems likely, given the close correspondence of the Priddy lithic tool kit to those from the Levels, that a form of transhumance was practised by the hunters, who moved to their spring or, more likely, summer camp on the Mendip, from their winter's fowling and fishing

on the Somerset Levels. Their sources of game probably moved down off the plateau in the autumn and winter to the shelter of the gorges, only to move up again to graze in the late spring or summer.

PARALLELS FOR SHELTERS IN THE MESOLITHIC OF THE BRITISH ISLES

A full review of other relevant British and Irish sites must await the final report on the Priddy site, but some preliminary thoughts can be offered. Although windbreaks in the form of lines or semicircles of stake holes, often around slight depressions, are present on a number of Mesolithic sites dating to both the early and late phases of the Mesolithic, more substantial shelters have only been recognised at Mount Sandel (Woodman 1985), Ferriter's Cove and Simonstown (Woodman *et al.* 1999) all in Ireland. Windbreaks were noted at Morton Farm (Coles 1971, fig. 21, 328, fig. 24, 332, fig. 26, 336) dated to circa 5400 BC, although a long range of dates and a long sequence of hearth re-use suggests recurrent visits over time in this case (Coles 1983). Later Mesolithic arcs of stakes were excavated at Downton, Wiltshire (Higgs 1959), Moynagh Lough, County Meath (Bradley 1999) and at Ballydown, County Antrim (Crothers 1997). The hut structures of Mount Sandel date between 7010 and 6490 BC, the earliest recognised, while those at Ferriter's Cove, on the Dingle Peninsula in County Kerry, are of later Mesolithic date (Woodman *et al.* 1999). At Simonstown, a circular structure of 5–6 metres excavated by E. Kelly was also of a Late Mesolithic date (Woodman *et al.* 1999).

Professor J.G.D. Clark (in Clark and Rankine 1939) suggested that pit dwellings were found at Farnham in Surrey in 1937–38. Although this interpretation has been disputed, it is interesting to note that Clark also suggested that their substantial nature, with earth huts over them, was similar to those of the Thule culture found from the Bering Straits to Greenland, where they were used as a type of winter shelter (*ibid.*, 101). He called attention to the privately published account of Buckley's excavation, sometime before 1924, at Badger Slacks in the Pennines, which sounds closer to the Priddy structures, in that it consisted of burnt stakes and ling, overlying clusters of flint (Clark and Rankine 1939, 104). Clark also suggested that shallow pit dwellings are linked to Tardenosian industries, citing Swinnerton's excavations of Glen Wyllan on the Isle of Man as being associated with an industry of Middle Tardenoisian type (Clark and Rankine 1939, 105).

Whatever the other evidence for Mesolithic structures may be, the burnt turf huts at Yard Park, Lower Pitts Farm, Priddy, give a unique record of two huts sheltered by a natural limestone outcrop, which are not what one would term 'pit dwellings' (Figs. 27.2 and 27.3). They are small, but observations made by Clark suggest that the shelters of this period were for small numbers of people, from three to four persons (in Clark and Rankine 1939, 106–107) and, at 3.5 meters in diameter, these could sleep four people. They would not necessarily be winter dwellings, just protection from strong prevailing winds and well camouflaged by their growing turf. Woodman noted that all the shelters he knew in Ireland had cleaned interiors (Woodman *et al.* 1999, 144). This was also true of the Priddy huts. There was no accumulation of debris either inside or out, but the interior seemed particularly devoid of flint implements apart from one or two thumbnail scrapers, with only small chips off flint blades or spalls from utilised tools.

As was the case at Ferriter's Cove, the Mesolithic people of Priddy may have lived in close proximity to Neolithic agriculturists: some flint implements found in Yard Park but not directly associated with the Mesolithic huts are closely paralleled on the Levels. From this one can postulate a pattern of territorial movement that involved both areas.

CONCLUSION

Although a certain amount of plough damage cut through the Mesolithic site, the western end of the ten acre field was far less damaged and remained higher in its original profile than did the eastern end of the field, because of its rocky, limestone outcrop and the turning area for the modern ploughs. Two huts were present here, sheltered from the western prevailing winds in the natural dip beneath the limestone outcrop, which may have been deepened by the Mesolithic hunters as they constructed their turf covered dwellings. Each hut, about 3.5 meters in diameter, was turfed over completely, using double turfs, presumably obtained from the immediate locality. Heather was growing on some of these turfs, suggesting open moorland. This plant mixture further reinforces the other evidence for heathland or open landscape that would attract grazing animals. It suggests that the use of turf, which would be watered by natural rainfall and continue to grow as the outer skin of the huts, would act as camouflage on the outside while suppressing human smells emanating from the people who slept or sheltered within. The huts had subsequently been destroyed by fire.

As all the detected hearths were outside the hut depression, and beyond the cobbling, it seems likely that the huts were solely for shelter or for sleeping. Working debris on the higher points of the plateau at the head of the rills suggests that all knapping of tools took place off the site. However, six hundred fragments and spalls of flint were retrieved from the immediate location of the huts and beneath the burning. While the hearths seem to have been outside the huts, it is possible that the extensive burning may have obscured evidence of any within. Modern mining exploitation confused the interpretation of the site around the northern hut because the outcast was little oxidized and had relocated some of the burnt material in large chunks.

Findley dismissed the idea that the inhabitants tried to douse the fire with soil, having identified the latter as throw-out from the pit (C in Fig. 27.2), which he confirmed was man-made, not a natural swallet, and he suggested the high loess component of the throw-out was typical of the upper Nordrach sequence (pers. comm.).

It is hoped that a definitive account of the site will be published shortly. A previous draft of the publication was lost in a move of departments at Liverpool University, when the Department of Prehistoric Archaeology became the Institute of Prehistoric Sciences and Archaeology in 1984, so the writing up was seriously disrupted. Reconstruction of the plans through original drawings and site notebooks was only possible with the help of John Swogger, who also reconstructed the huts.

ACKNOWLEDGEMENTS

I wish to thank Sarah Milliken and Jill Cook for inviting me to contribute to this Festschrift for Derek Roe. The support and encouragement from John Swogger who worked under difficult conditions to produce the drawings that make up the Figs. 27.1, while in the midst of a move back to the United States, is greatly appreciated, and to David Dawson, who was in on the inception of the Priddy Plateau Project, and in his current busy life as Director of the Somerset Museum Service, managed to find some of the brief reports I had published during the years of excavation, sometimes in obscure places. The tenants of Lower Pitts Farm, Henry and Bob Dyke, and Audrey Loveder could not have been more helpful over the years, as was Edward Masters, when the Dykes retired. The Edwards family of Higher Pitts Farm were also willing to let us walk their fields. Funding from numerous grants combined to make this project possible, and I would like to thank the Maltwood Fund for its repeated grants, the Society of Antiquaries of London, the Crowther-Beynon fund of the University of Cambridge, the Department of the Environment through CRAAGS, CRAAGS for their occasional loan of their digging team, the University of Bristol, Dr A. Parker for the loan of tents, Bristol City Museum, the field team of Bristol City Museum, and the Universities of Nottingham and Liverpool for the student man-power and grants to conduct excavation. Expert assistance came from Dr F.A. Wallace, Dr Derek Findley, Professor Chris Paul, Dr Mike Barbetti and Dr J.J. Butler, to name but a few, and from colleagues such as Alan Insole, Colin Shell, and my own department at Bristol City Museum: David Dawson, Mike Ponsford and Janet Escritt Warren. Numerous volunteers repeatedly came such as Dr and Mrs. R. Everton, Norman Cook, Chris Salisbury and Dorothy Van Arsdale. Many students showed great promise as future archaeologists, and I would like to single out Rebecca Smart, who unfortunately for me, but probably as a career move correct for her, left before she completed her research degree to join the British Post Office.

REFERENCES

Bradley, J. 1999. Excavations at Moynagh Lough, Co. Meath, 1997–98. *Riocht na Midhe* 10, 1–17.

Chatwin, C.P. 1960. *The Hampshire Basin and Adjoining Areas.* HMSO, London.

Clark, J.G.D. and Rankine, W.F. 1939. Excavations at Farnham, Surrey: the Horsham Culture and the question of Mesolithic dwellings (1937–38). *Proceedings of the Prehistoric Society* 5, 98–107.

Coles, J.M. 1971. The early settlement of Scotland: excavations at Morton, Fife. *Proceedings of the Prehistoric Society* 37, 284–366.

Coles, J.M. 1983. Morton revisited. In A. O'Connor and D.V. Clarke (eds.) *From The Stone Age to the 'Forty Five*, 9–18. Edinburgh University Press, Edinburgh.

Coles, J.M. 1989. Prehistoric settlement in the Somerset Levels. *Somerset Levels Papers* 15, 14–32.

Crothers, N. 1997. Ballydown, Co. Antrim. In I. Bennett (ed.) *Excavations 1996*, 1. Wordwell, Bray.

Findley, D.C. 1965. *The Soils of the Mendip District of Somerset.* Memoirs of the Soil Survey of Great Britain and Wales. Crown Copyright, Harpenden.

Fletcher, C.J.N., Swainbank, I.G. and Colman, T.B. 1993. Metallogenic evolution in Wales: constraints from lead isotope modelling. *Journal of the Geological Society* 150, 77–82.

Higgs, E.S. 1959. The excavation of a Late Mesolithic site at Downton, near Salisbury, Wiltshire. *Proceedings of the Prehistoric Society* 25, 209–232.

Jenkins, D.G., Copestake, P., van Calsteren, P. and McDermott, F. 1990. Correlation of lead isotopes in Lower Jurassic rock of South Wales. *Proceedings of the Geologists' Association* 101, 341–343.

Joel, E.C., Taylor, J.J., Ixer, R.A. and Goodway, M. 1995. Lead isotope analysis and the Great Orme Mine. In A. Sinclair, J. Gowlett and E. Slater (eds.) *Archaeological Science '95*, 123–131. Oxbow Books, Oxford.

Palmer, S. 1970. The Stone Age industries of the Isle of Portland, Dorset, and the utilisation of Portland Chert as artefact material in Southern England. *Proceedings of the Prehistoric Society* 36, 82–115.

Pearson, G.W., Pilcher, J.R., Baille, M.G.L., Corbet, D.M. and Qua, F. 1986. High-precision ^{14}C measurements of Irish oaks to show the natural ^{14}C variations from AD 1840–5210 BC. *Radiocarbon* 28, 911–934.

Taylor, J.J. 1976. Mesolithic site from Yard Park Field, Lower Pitts Farm, Priddy, Somerset, *Bulletin of Bristol Archaeological Research Group* 5 (8), 210–211.

Taylor, J.J. 1977. Lower Pitts Farm, Priddy ST 538502, *Proceedings of the Somersetshire Archaeological and Natural History Society* 121, 109–110.

Taylor, J.J. 1978. Lower Pitts Farm, Priddy ST 538502. *Proceedings of the Somersetshire Archaeological and Natural History Society* 122, 120.

Taylor, J.J. 1979. Priddy Plateau Project. *Proceedings of the Somersetshire Archaeological and Natural History Society* 123, 85.

Taylor, J.J. and Smart, R. 1983. An investigation of surface concentrations: Priddy 1977. *Bristol and Avon Archaeology* 2, 2–11.

Woodman. P. 1985. *Excavations at Mount Sandel, 1973–77.* Northern Ireland Archaeological Monographs 2. HMSO, Belfast.

Woodman, P.C., Anderson, E. and Finlay, N. 1999. *Excavations at Ferriter's Cove, 1983–95: Last Foragers, First Farmers in the Dingle Peninsula.* Wordwell, Bray.

28. Derek Roe, A Bibliography

The following bibliography includes all books and articles produced by Derek Roe as an author, editor, co-author or co-editor. Minor publications of record and description, prefaces and forewords, or invited comments have not been included.

1964

The British Lower and Middle Palaeolithic: some problems, methods of study and preliminary results. *Proceedings of the Prehistoric Society* 30, 245–267.

1968

A Gazetteer of British Lower and Middle Palaeolithic Sites. Council for British Archaeology Research Report 8, London.

British Lower and Middle Palaeolithic handaxe groups. *Proceedings of the Prehistoric Society* 34, 1–82.

1969

An archaeological survey and policy for Wiltshire, part I: Palaeolithic. *Wiltshire Archaeological and Natural History Magazine* 64, 1–18.

1970

Prehistory: An Introduction. Macmillan, London, and University of California Press, Berkeley.

1974

Palaeolithic artefacts from the River Avon terraces near Bristol. *Proceedings of the University of Bristol Spelaeological Society* 13, 319–326.

Holden, E.W. and Roe, D.A. The Ade Collection of flints and a Palaeolithic handaxe from Hassocks. *Sussex Archaeological Collections* 112, 1–8.

1975

Some Hampshire and Dorset Palaeoliths and the question of 'Early Acheulian' in Britain. *Proceedings of the Prehistoric Society* 41, 1–9.

1976

(ed.) *Field Guide to the Oxford Region*. Quaternary Research Association, London.

The Palaeolithic. In P.B. Hammond (ed.) *Physical Anthropology and Archaeology* (second edition), 201–238. Macmillan, New York.

Typology and the trouble with handaxes. In G. de G. Sieveking, I.H. Longworth and K.E. Wilson (eds.) *Problems in Economic and Social Archaeology*, 61–70. Duckworth, London.

The Evolution of the Acheulian in Britain. *U.I.S.P.P. Congress, Nice, France, Colloque X*, 31–45.

The earliest industries in Britain. *U.I.S.P.P. Congress, Nice, France, Colloque VIII*, 76–95.

1978

(with a contribution by John Wymer) *A Survey of the Palaeolithic and Mesolithic Periods in Berkshire*. Berkshire Archaeological Society Occasional Papers 1.

Three Lower Palaeolithic handaxes from Rough Common, Canterbury. *Archaeologia Cantiana* 94, 158–164.

1981

The Lower and Middle Palaeolithic Periods in Britain. Routledge and Kegan Paul, London.

Amateurs and archaeologists: some early contributions to British Palaeolithic studies. In J.D. Evans, B. Cunliffe and C. Renfrew (eds.) *Antiquity and Man*, 214–220. Thames and Hudson, London.

1982

The transition from Lower to Middle Palaeolithic, with particular reference to Britain. In A. Ronen (ed.) *The Transition from Lower to Middle Palaeolithic and the Origin of Modern Man*, 177–191. British Archaeological Reports International Series 151, Oxford.

Roe, D.A., Olsen, J.W., Underwood J.R. and Giegengack, R.F. A handaxe of Libyan desert glass. *Antiquity* 56, 88–92.

1983

(ed.) *Adlun in the Stone Age: The Excavations of D.A.E. Garrod in the Lebanon 1958–1963*. British Archaeological Reports International Series 159, Oxford.

The Lower and Middle Palaeolithic of Britain, with particular reference to the penultimate glaciation. *Studia Praehistorica Belgica* 3, 11–27.

1985

The handaxe makers. In A. Sherratt (ed.) *The Cambridge Encyclopaedia of Archaeology*, 71–78. Cambridge University Press, Cambridge.

Archaeology in York. *The Quarterly Review of Archaeology* 6 (1), 8–10.

Some recent research involving microwear analysis. *The Quarterly Review of Archaeology* 6 (3), 4–6.

1986

(ed.) *Studies in the Upper Palaeolithic of Northwest Europe*. British Archaeological Reports International Series 296, Oxford.

The Palaeolithic period in the Oxford region. In G. Briggs, J. Cook and T. Rowley (eds.) *The Archaeology of the Oxford Region*, 1–17. Oxford University Department for External Studies, Oxford.

1988

The Neopalaeolithic. *The Quarterly Review of Archaeology* 9 (3), 1–3.

The study of non-flint artefacts in the British Palaeolithic: its value and significance. In R.J. MacRae and N. Moloney (eds.) *Non-Flint Stone Tools and the Palaeolithic Occupation of Britain*, 1–9. British Archaeological Reports British Series 189, Oxford.

1989

Advancing the study of early man in East Africa. *The Review of Archaeology* 10 (1), 82–88.

1990

Two archaeological phenomena: B.A.R. and the beginnings of the Upper Palaeolithic. *The Review of Archaeology* 11 (1), 28–35.

1991

Barton, R.N.E., Roberts, A. and Roe, D.A. (eds.) *The Late Glacial in North-West Europe: Human Adaptation and Environmental Change at the End of the Pleistocene*. Council for British Archaeology Research Report 77, London.

1992

Palaeolithic studies: an open letter to Asok K. Ghosh. In P. Bellwood (ed.) *Man and his Culture: A Resurgence*, 105–122. Books and Books, New Delhi.

1993

Landmark sites of the British Palaeolithic. *The Review of Archaeology* 14 (2), 1–9.

1994

Leakey, M.D. and Roe, D.A. (eds.) *Olduvai Gorge Volume 5: Excavation in Beds III, IV and the Masek Beds, 1968–1971*. Cambridge University Press, Cambridge.

A metrical analysis of selected sets of handaxes and cleavers from Olduvai Gorge. In M.D. Leakey and D.A. Roe (eds.) *Olduvai Gorge Volume 5: Excavation in Beds III, IV and the Masek Beds, 1968–1971*, 146–234. Cambridge University Press, Cambridge.

Summary and overview. In M.D. Leakey and D.A. Roe (eds.) *Olduvai Gorge Volume 5: Excavation in Beds III, IV and the Masek Beds, 1968–1971*, 299–309. Cambridge University Press, Cambridge.

The Palaeolithic archaeology of the Oxford region. *Oxoniensia* 49, 1–15.

1995

The Orce Basin (Andalucía, Spain) and the initial Palaeolithic of Europe. *Oxford Journal of Archaeology* 14, 1–12.

Tixier, J., Roe, D., Turq, A., Gibert, J., Martínez, B., Arribas, A., Gibert, L., Gaete, R., Maillo, A. and Iglesias, A. Présence d'industries lithiques dans le Pléistocène inférieur de la région d'Orce (Grenade, Espagne): quel est l'état de la question? *Comptes Rendus de l'Académie des Sciences de Paris* Series 2, 321, 71–78.

Father Thames and the British Pleistocene. *The Review of Archaeology* 16 (1), 9–15.

1996

Artefact distributions and the British Earlier Palaeolithic. In C. Gamble and A.J. Lawson (eds.) *The English Palaeolithic Reviewed*, 1–6. Trust for Wessex Archaeology, Salisbury.

The start of the British Palaeolithic: some old and new thoughts and speculations. *Lithics* 16, 17–26.

Buckingham, C.M., Roe, D.A. and Scott, K. A preliminary report on the Stanton Harcourt channel deposits (Oxfordshire, England): geological context, vertebrate remains and Palaeolithic stone artefacts. *Journal of Quaternary Science* 11, 397–415.

'Acheulean Tradition' and 'Paleolithic: Lower and Middle Paleolithic'. In B.M. Fagan *et al.* (eds.) *Oxford Companion to Archaeology*, 1–2, 552–553. Oxford University Press, New York.

Proctor, C.J., Collcutt, S.N., Currant, A.P., Hawkes, C.J., Roe, D.A. and Smart, P.L. A report on the excavations at Rhinoceros Hole, Wookey. *Proceedings of the University of Bristol Spelaeological Society* 20, 237–262.

1997

Summary and overview. In G.Ll. Isaac and A.B. Isaac (eds.) *Koobi Fora Research Project Volume 5: Plio-Pleistocene Archaeology*, 544–567. Clarendon Press, Oxford.

1998

As represented by the Thames Valley. In N. Ashton, F. Healy and P. Pettitt (eds.) *Stone Age Archaeology: Essays in Honour of John Wymer*, 38–42. Lithic Studies Society Occasional Paper 6, Oxbow Monograph 102. Oxbow Books, Oxford.

1999

The earlier stages of the Palaeolithic in Britain. In J. Gibert, F. Sánchez, L. Gibert and F. Ribot (eds.) *The Hominids and their Environment during the Lower and Middle Pleistocene of Eurasia*, 415–421. Ayuntamiento de Orce, Museo di Prehistoria y Paleontología J. Gibert, Orce.

Gibert, J., Campillo, D., Eisenmann, V., García-Olivares, E., Malgosa, A., Roe, D.A., Walker, M.J., Borja, C., Sánchez, F., Ribot, F., Gibert, Ll., Albadalejo, S., Iglesias, A., Ferrández, C. and Maestro, E. Spanish Late Pliocene and Early Pleistocene hominid, palaeolithic and hominid finds from Orce (Granada) and Cueva Victoria (Murcia). *Human Evolution* 14, 29–46.

2000

Early human migrations: using all the evidence. In D. Lordkipanidze, O. Bar-Yosef and M. Otte (eds.) *Early Humans at the Gates of Europe*, 87–92. ERAUL 92, Liège.

Retrospective review from the archives: D.A. Roe, The Neopalaeolithic (review of Gamble). *The Review of Archaeology* 20 (2), 48–52.

Review Article: The British Lower Palaeolithic: out of the doldrums. *Proceedings of the Prehistoric Society* 66, 397–403.

2001

The Kalambo Falls large cutting tools: a comparative metrical and statistical analysis. In J.D. Clark (ed.) *Kalambo Falls Prehistoric Site, III: The Earlier Cultures: Middle and Earlier Stone Age*, 492–599. Cambridge University Press, Cambridge.

A view of the Kalambo Falls Early and Middle Stone Age assemblages in the context of the Old World Palaeolithic. In J.D. Clark (ed.) *Kalambo Falls Prehistoric Site, III: The Earlier Cultures: Middle and Earlier Stone Age*, 636–647. Cambridge University Press, Cambridge.

Site Index

Abbeville 86, 88, 107, 242–243
Abingdon 180–182, 185–186, 188, 195
Abri de la Ferrassie 236
Acacia 106
Achalkalaki 80, 84
Achenheim 86
Adamgarh 109
Adrar Bous 2, 6, 10, 106
Aïn Hanech 81
Ak-Koshkar 139
Amanzi Springs 2, 4, 21–23, 29, 105
Amar Merdeg 80–81
Ambrona 75, 106, 116
Anagwadi 109
Arba 2, 7, 13
Arce 86
Aridos 106
Ash 258. See also Fawkham
Atapuerca 75, 86–89, 92, 95, 106, 115–117, 154
Atbara 70
Axe valley 252, 258
Axminster 258
Aylesford 252
Azraq 108, 128
Azykh 80, 84, 108, 138

Bacon Hole 212
Badger Slacks 268
Baker's Hole see Northfleet
Balderton 212
Ballydown 268
Ban Don Mun 80, 82
Banshan 80, 83
Barbas 86
Barkly West 2, 7
Barranco León 144–150
Batpak valley 139–142
Beck Row 235
Bečov 86, 107, 116–117
Beedings 228
Beeston Beach 252
Bellaria 161, 163
Belver 106
Bemerton 251–252
Berinsfield 180, 182, 193, 208, 211
Beroun 107
Berzine 108
Biache 117
Bilzingsleben 75
Bir Sahara 2–3
Bizat Ruhama 80–81
Black Rock 212
Blandè 61
Blombos Cave 71
Bockstein 129, 200, 204
Bodo 2–3, 5
Bolton and Co.'s Pit 252
Bondeville 107
Border Cave 116

Bori 80, 82
Bose Basin 25, 80, 83, 135
Bouri 2, 4–6, 11
Boxgrove 75, 86, 88, 92, 178, 199, 208
Bramcote Hill 186
Bramford Pit 252
Brandon 174–175, 177, 244
Broken Hill 2, 4, 154
Bromme 237–238
Broom 252, 257–258
Brusaida 161
Burganes 106
Burnham 86
Burnt Fen 235
Bury St Edmunds 252

Ca' Belvedere I 161
Ca' Belvedere di Monte Poggiolo 86–88
Ca' delle Donne 161, 167
Ca' Fiume 161
Ca' Fontana 161
Ca' Rio 161
Ca' San Carlo 161, 163
Cagny-la-Garenne 107, 115
Caillevat-Beuret 86
Camp de Peyre 86
Camponi 161, 163
Cantalouette 107
Canteen Koppie 29, 37–45
Cape Hangklip 2, 7, 21–24, 29
Casella di Maida 86
Casetta Tomba 161
Cassington 188–197
Castillo 107
Castro dei Volsci 86, 88
Cava Fiorini 161
Cava Valfiore 161
Cave dall'Olio 161, 163, 166
Cave of Hearths 2, 4, 105
Caversham Channel 86
Cave S.A.F.R.A. 161–163
Ceprano 86, 88
Červeny kopec 86
Changpyungri 136
Chard 258
Chaudon 107
Chilhac 86
Chirkinala 108–109
Chongokni 83, 109, 133–136
Clacton 66
Clevedon Cave 212
Collegio di Spagna 161, 163
Colle Marino 86
Collinaia 86
Colombarina di Sopra 161
Combe Grenal 204
Contrada Maddaluso 108
Cornelia 2, 4
Costa del Forgione 86
Côte Bar 86
Crayford 252

Cromer 252
Cueva Negra 156 158
Cueva Victoria 151
Cúllar de Baza 86, 88

Dafuna 67
Dakhla Oasis 2, 5, 16
Dauqara Formation 80–81
Dawatoli 11
Deer Park Farm 239
Dickett's Field 214–221
Dingcun 109
Dix Pit see Stanton Harcourt
Dmanisi 80–81, 84–85, 101, 138, 146, 151
Dolina del Budriolo 161
Donggutuo 80, 83
Doornlaagte 21–23, 29
Douro terraces 86–87
Downton 267–268
Duinefontein 2–3, 29
Dunbridge 252, 257
Dursunlu 80–81

Early Khartoum 70
East Runton 252
East Turkana 97, 146. See also Koobi Fora
El Aculadero 86
Elands Bay Cave 70–71
Elandsfontein 2–4, 21–25, 29
El Espinar 86
El Omari 69
Engis 242
Erg Tihodaïne 106
Eriswell 174, 178, 235
Evron Quarry 80–81, 108, 128

Fabron 86
Farnham 268
Farningham Road 258
Fauresmith 20–23, 25
Fawkham 258
Fayum 70
Feltwell 174–178
Ferriter's Cove 268–269
Florisbad 115
Fondo Vigna 161
Fontanaccio 161
Fontana Liri 86
Fontana Ranuccio 86, 88, 92
Fornace di San Lazzaro 161, 163
Fornham 252
Freeland 181–186, 194–195
Fuentenueva 86–88, 144–149
Furze Platt 200, 253
FxJj12 (Koobi Fora) 70
FxJj20 (Koobi Fora) 97

Gadari 109
Gadeb 2–3, 5–6, 10, 14, 16, 110
Gademotta 7
Galisancho 106
Galley Hill 258

Gerasimovka 86, 88
Gesher Benot Ya'aqov 6, 80–81, 108, 122, 128
Gilf Kebir 2, 4
Gill Mill 181–182, 188, 191, 194–195
Glaston 228–230, 232
Glen Wyllan 268
Godavari river 109
Gongwangling 80, 83
Gravelly Guy see Stanton Harcourt
Greenhithe 258
Greenlands Pit 115
Guadalquivir terraces 86–87, 106
Gudian 109

Haaskraal Pan 29–30, 35
Hangenbieten 86
Hardwick 181–182, 188, 195
Hargulia 11
Haua Fteah 16
Hayonim Cave 115
Hengistbury Head 230, 239
Hexian 154
Higham 258
Highlands Farm 137
High Lodge 75, 86, 174
Hill Head 251–252
Hill Lane 252
Hitchin 203, 258
Hockwold 174–175
Hohdale 107
Horslands 252
Hoxne 3, 25, 75, 242–243
Hungsi valley 109
Huojiadi 80, 83
Hyena Den, Wookey Hole 260

Icklingham 174, 252
Iffley 180, 182, 208, 211
Ightham 228, 258
Il Borghetto 161
Ingress Vale 258
Inidanbury Hill 252
Irrawaddy terraces 80, 82
Isernia La Pineta 75, 86–88, 92
Ishango 70
Isimila 2–3, 106
Ittouchi Matsuba-yama 80, 83

Janda 106
Jaštuch 108
Jebel Irhoud 2, 16
Joubb Jannine 108

Kabwe see Broken Hill
Kalambo Falls 2, 4–5, 7, 12–16, 19, 66, 106
Kamabai 51
Kamitakamori 80, 83, 109
Kamoa 2, 10
Kangra valley 108
Kapthurin 2–6, 115
Kara-Bom 135

Karatau 138
Kariandusi 2–3, 6, 106
Kärlich 86, 88, 107
Kashaf Rud 80, 84
Kathu Pan 2, 4–5, 29
Kent's Cavern 86, 174, 242
Kharga Oasis 2, 4–5, 9, 16, 106, 115
Khonako 80, 84
Kilombe 2, 4, 25
Klasies River Mouth 71
Klausennische 129, 200, 204
Klippaadrif 105
Knowle Farm 86, 252–253, 257
Kochkurgan 139
Koktas 139
Königsaue 129
Konso-Gardula 2, 6
Koobi Fora 70, 97
Korolevo 86, 107, 138
Kudaikol 139
Kudaro 84, 108
Kul'bulak 138
Kul'dara 80, 84, 138
Kulna 129, 204
Kulpori 83, 134
Kumpari 83, 134

La Casaccia 161
La Cava 161
La Cotte de Saint-Brelade 88
Lagar Velho 114–115
Laguna de Medina 106
Lake Langano 7
Lake Ndutu 2, 4
Lakenheath 174–175, 178, 258
Lakhuti 84, 138
Lalitpur 108–109
La Maya 106
La Micoque 75, 129, 200, 203–204
La Nauterie 86
Langå 238
Lantian 138
La Rafette 86, 88
La Rochette 204
Laše-Balta 108
La Selva 107
Latamne 75, 108
Latton 181, 194, 208, 211
Launde 230
Le Bois-Ragot 237
Lee-on-the-Solent 251–252
Lehringen 66
Le Moustier 204
Les Graves 86
Les Pierres 86
Les Vergnes 86
Leyton 258
Lichtenberg 129
Lochard 2, 4
Longgupo 83
Lowasera 70
Lower Pitts Farm, Priddy 260–269

Maastricht-Belvédère 40, 116–117
Ma'ayan Barukh 108, 128
Mae Tha South 80, 82
Maidenhead 252–253
Maiidon Toro 106
Maisières-Canal 236, 238
Maka 11
Malaga 106
Maleret 86

Maliang 80, 83
Manianbougou 61
Manjungou 80, 83
Marascelle 161, 170
Markkleeberg 75, 107
Marsworth 212
Mauer 86
Melka Kunturé 2, 6, 106
Melkhoutboom 69
Merlina 161
Miaohoushan 109
Miesenheim 86
Mildenhall 234–239, 252
Milford Hill 252
Minchin Hole 212
Mizar 139
Modjokerto 80, 138
Molino del Imperador 86
Monfarracinos 86
Montagu Cave 20–24, 29
Montauban 107, 110
Montauto 86
Moor Down 251
Morgah 108
Morton Farm 267–268
Mount Do 109
Mount Sandel 268
Moynagh Lough 268
Mugharet El' Aliya 76
Mumba Cave 2, 15
Münzenberg 107
Muzbel 139, 141–142

Nagaone 83
Nagarjunkonda 108–109
Nakajdimajama 109
Néa Skala 86
Nelson Bay Cave 70–71
Ngebung 80, 82
Nile valley 70
Nok 106
Nørre Lyngby 237
Northfleet 252, 256–258
Nsongezi 2–3, 6, 106

Ogasaka 80, 83, 92
Ola 107
Old Shirley 252
Olduvai Gorge 2, 6, 16, 19, 25, 70, 97–98, 100, 105, 110, 146
Olorgesailie 2–3, 15, 98, 106
Orce *see* Barranco León, Fuente-nueva, Venta Micena

Pabbi Hills 80, 82
Pakefield 178
Palazzina 161–163, 171
Palazzone-Ca' Roma 161, 163, 172
Palmar de Conde 106
Pasotta 161, 163, 170
Passo della Portezza 161
Patpara 109
Patu 109
Paviland Cave 117, 236, 250
Peninj 105–106
Pergole 108
Pescatore Piccolo 161, 163
Peverella 161, 167, 169
Piangipane 161, 163
Pinedo 86, 106
Pingell 106
Pin Hole 236
Pniel 21–23, 29
Podere Castello 161, 164
Podere Due Pozzi 161–163

Poggio Domini 161, 163
Pointe de Saint-Colomban 86
Pointes aux Oies 86
Pont de la Hulauderie 86
Pontnewydd Cave 114, 116–117, 250
Prezletiče 107
Puente Morena 86
Puig d'Esclats 106

Radley 181–182, 188
Rainham 258
Reading 252
Red Barnes 203
Redcliff 2, 4
Reutersruh 107
Riniera 161, 163
Rogbing West 54–55
Romsey 251–252
Rooidam 2–3, 29
Rosaneto 108
Round Green 231

Saccopastore 154
Saint-Acheul 86
Saint-Pierre les Elbeuf 107
Saint-Selve 86
Saint-Thibéry 86
Sambungmachan 80, 82
Sangiran 80
Sangmooryoungri 133–134
San Isidro 106
Sartolejo 106
Schöningen 66, 75, 87
Scornetta 161, 163, 172
Seacow valley 28–35
Seaton Junction 258
Segebro 238
Sel'ungar 108
Sept-Fronts 86
Sesselfelsgrotte 129
Sheikh Muhamad 81
Shirehampton 252, 257
Shoktas 139
Shrub Hill 175, 178, 258
Shuigou 109
Sidi Abderrahman 2, 4–5, 7–8, 81, 106
Sidi Zin 2, 4, 6
Sima de las Palomas 153–158
Simbi 2, 4
Simonstown 268
Singi Talar 109
Sinmakri 136–137
Sitt Markho 81
Smiths Pit *see* Stanton Harcourt
Sodekhara 109
Sokchangri 133–135, 137
Soleihac 86, 88, 92
Somerset Levels 268
Southfleet 258
Springhead 258
Stanton Harcourt 180–182, 186–187, 189, 191, 193–195, 197, 207–212
Starě město 86
Steinheim 154
Stellmoor 238
Sterkfontein 20, 105
STIC Quarry *see* Sidi Abderrahman
Stone Point 239
Stránská skála 86
Sunghir 117
Sutton Courtenay 181–182, 188, 194

Suyanggae 133–135
Svédské šance 86
Swanscombe 115, 249, 252–253, 256–258
Swartkrans 106

Tabalbala 2, 4, 7, 106
Tabun Cave 96, 108, 115, 120–128, 130
Tachengit 2, 4, 7–9
Takamori 80
Talaveira de la Reina 86
Ternifine 2–5, 8–9, 14, 81, 106
Terra Amata 107, 116
Tidworth 252
Tighennif *see* Ternifine
Tombazza 161, 163, 169
Torralba 106
Torrente d'Idice 161, 163–164
Trollesgave 237–238
Trzebnica 86
Twin Rivers 116–117

Uan Afuda 67
'Ubeidiya 80–81, 108, 128
Umm Qatafa 108, 121

Vaal valley 7, 21–22, 29, 41, 105
Vadamadura 109
Valencia 106
Vallonet Cave 86
Venosa-Loreto 86–88, 92
Venosa-Notarchirico 75, 86–88, 92
Venta Micena 144–151
Verdier 86
Vergranne 86
Verne Ditch 230
Verrières-le-Buisson 204
Victoria West 2, 4, 6–7, 10, 37
Vidauban 86
Villa Resta 161, 170
Vinneuf 204
Vishněvka 139, 141
Visogliano 86, 88

Wallingford 180, 182, 194
Wangford Warren 235
Warren Hill 86, 174–175, 252, 258
Warsash 203
Waverly Wood 177
Welsh Newton 252, 257
Westbury-sub-Mendip 86, 88, 174, 178, 262
West Ham 258
West Runton 252
Whitlingham 203
Wolvercote 180–182, 189, 191, 200–205
Wonderwerk 2, 4, 29
Woodgreen 251–252
Wood Hill 230–231

Xiaochangliang 80, 83, 92

Yagala 51
Yarnton 181–182. *See also* Cass-ington
Yengema Cave 47, 50–51, 57, 59–61
Yulchonri 136–137
Yunxian 154

Zhoukoudian 97, 109, 154
Zona 108
Zuttiyeh 154